A WRITER'S WORLDS

Explorations through Reading

Second Edition

A WRITER'S WORLDS

Explorations through Reading

Second Edition

Edited by
Trudy Smoke

Hunter College, City University of New York

St. Martin's Press
New York

This book is dedicated to the memory of my mother
Lucy (1918–1994),
a woman of intellect and great courage

Senior editor: Karen Allanson
Development editor: Clare Payton
Manager, publishing services: Emily Berleth
Editor, publishing services: Doug Bell
Project management: Julie C. Sullivan
Production supervisor: Joe Ford
Art direction and cover design: Sheree Goodman
Text design: Nancy Sugihara and Julie C. Sullivan
Photo research: Ann Barnard
Cover art: Leslie Szabo

Library of Congress Catalog Card Number: 94-65192

Manufactured in the United States of America.

9 8 7 6 5
f e d c b a

For information, write:
St. Martin's Press, Inc.
175 Fifth Avenue
New York, NY 10010

ISBN: 0-312-09564-3

Acknowledgments

PREFACE

A Writer's Worlds: Explorations through Reading is designed to help prepare students for their college writing and reading assignments. The book begins with an extensive explanation of the writing process and offers activities to help students think about their own writing process. The readings are organized into ten thematic units that explore the worlds that shape our thinking and behavior. These worlds are: self-identity, gender, family, intimacy, learning, community, nature, myths, science, and society. Following the units in sequence, students will progress from the inner world of personal perspectives to the outer worlds of more global concerns.

The second edition of *A Writer's Worlds* again contains works by a wide variety of writers, many never before included in an anthology, representing many regions and cultures within the United States and the rest of the world. The fifty-nine selections include writings in psychology, sociology, anthropology, ecology, and geology, as well as literature. These subjects were chosen because of their high interest for entering college students and because familiarity with the styles of writing and vocabulary in these areas will ease the transition to other college reading assignments.

To offer variety for instructors and students alike, each unit contains selections of different types of writing (news articles, short stories, academic writing) on each theme. As students read a unit, they can develop a common vocabulary about a subject, discover the ways writers use different styles depending on their audience and purpose, and reflect on their own development as writers and thinkers as they write the various assignments.

Instructors may prefer to read all the selections in a particular unit or may decide to pick and choose selections throughout the book according to the needs and interests of their students. There are abundant examples of specific types of writing so that instructors can choose to focus on literary selections, academic types of writing, or essays. The reading and writing assignments were chosen to provide students with a solid background in the types of reading and writing that will help them succeed in their academic endeavors.

New to This Edition

Expanded Introduction on the Writing Process: Now *A Writer's Worlds* contains a helpful introduction to the writing process, from inventing to drafting to revising. Included are clear discussions on finding a topic, the elements of good writing, and the features of a good essay. Instructors will find it easy to adapt some of the writing techniques presented here to the essay assignments and revision strategies that accompany each of the reading selections.

Student Writing: Student essays have been added to this edition to show students authentic writing by their peers. The essays will help provide realistic models of the kinds of writing students are asked to do in their courses.

Vocabulary: New vocabulary lists and definitions appear immediately after each reading selection to broaden students' understanding of language as they read. The concise definitions help students place the meaning of words within the context of the essay.

New Selections: Of the fifty-nine selections, forty-five are new to this edition, offering a wider variety of diverse perspectives. Almost half are written by women. Each unit includes one more challenging piece of academic writing, which should help bridge the gap between the composition class and the student's other areas of study.

New Themes: The themes of education and learning, gender, and self-identity are new to the second edition, giving instructors new focus issues for discussion.

Features of *A Writer's Worlds*

The extensive apparatus in *A Writer's Worlds* provides individual instructors with many possibilities for their students to develop an understanding and breadth of thinking and master the basic elements of good writing. Each reading is supported by journal assignments, a headnote, and three sets of questions designed to help students think critically about the selection and the issues it raises. Finally, writing assignments and revision strategies help students craft a more carefully written response to the selections.

Journal Assignments: Each of the fifty-nine selections begins with a journal entry which asks students to explore some of their own ideas about a topic before they read. This activity helps students realize how prior knowledge and experience affect their reading and writing. After the selection, a second journal entry instructs students to examine some aspect of the selection they have just read. Students are encouraged to compare their two journal entries to see how reading, thinking, and writing are intertwined and can change their perceptions.

Biographical Headnotes: Every selection is preceded by headnotes which provide information about the author and help students place both the writer and the writing in context. Additional information about the subject matter is also often given.

A Closer Reading: These questions help students analyze the selections immediately after they've finished reading them. The questions encourage students to read carefully and to grasp the basic content of the material.

Drawing Your Own Conclusions: This second set of questions lend themselves to good class discussion and engage students in thinking about the complex issues raised by the readings.

Thinking about Writing: The final set of questions asks students to reexamine the selection to discover the writer's purpose, intended audience, organization, and other choices a writer makes when creating an essay.

Suggestions for Writing: These include a wide variety of topics for students to write on, and they are designed to cover a broad range of rhetorical possibilities. Students can complete them on their own or as collaborative projects. The essay assignments ask students to focus on the particular themes presented or investigate the different possibilities that each theme brings forth for discussion. In addition, these questions can be used as models for students who want to develop their own essay topics.

Strategies for Revision: Specific strategies for revision follow the essay assignments in order to give the students the chance to reread, rethink, and rewrite their essays. These exercises complement the general revision strategies provided in the Introduction by applying some of them to the different types of writing and essay assignments. The revision strategies have been designed to be used individually, with a partner, or in a small group. Instructors should feel free to choose among the many revision activities throughout the book. If a particular activity works well, it may be used repeatedly. The revision activities are designed to help students view their work as a process and to view their peers and their instructor as collaborators trying to help them create the best expression of their ideas and feelings.

Making Connections: These questions are featured at the end of each unit, asking students to compare the essays in a unit and to link the issues presented to the world at large.

Acknowledgments

The writing of a book involves the ideas, commitment, and encouragement of many people over a long period of time. I have been fortunate to have worked with the very professional staff at St. Martin's Press. I especially want to thank Karen Allanson, Senior Editor at St. Martin's Press, for her knowledgeable assistance and tremendous support throughout this project. I also would like to express my gratitude to Clare Payton, Associate Editor at St. Martin's, for the time, energy, and intelligence she brought to this project. I also thank Doug Bell, Project Editor, Julie Sullivan, Project Manager, and Cheryl Besenjak, Permissions Consultant, for their time and effort.

I would like to thank the following reviewers for their insightful criticism and much appreciated encouragement: Samuel I. Bellman, California State Polytechnic University–Pomona; Paul Beran, North Harris County College; Therese Brychta, Truckee Meadows Community College; Kay Halasek, Ohio State University; Harold N. Hild, Northeastern Illinois University; Raymonda Johnson, Harold Washington College; Robert Johnson, Indiana University of Pennsylvania, Armstrong County Campus; Kate Mangelsdorf, University of Texas–El Paso; Jane Peterson, Dallas County Community College; Ruth Ray, Wayne State University; William Roberts, University of Lowell; Norman Stahl, Northern Illinois University; and Harold Stusnick, George Mason University.

I thank all my hundreds of students who teach me every day and without whose ideas and criticisms this book could not have been written. Above all, I thank Alan Robbins, my husband, for his extraordinary patience and support. His belief in me is what helped me to complete this project and to believe that it was worth doing.

Trudy Smoke

CONTENTS

1

THE WORLD OF THE SELF
Developing an Identity   1

"Nopalitos": The Making of   Helena María
Fiction (memoir)   Viramontes   5

Writing about her past, her family, and her heritage has enabled a
Latina writer to understand her personal identity.

A Bracelet, an Odd Earring,   Ewa Zadrzynska   14
Cracked Teacups

A writer describes how the objects found in a stranger's discarded
trunk help her find her identity in the United States.

First Born (story)   Danjuma Sinue
                                         Modupe   20

Recollecting a childhood incident leads to a deeper understanding
of the importance of names and the way names shape identity.

Growing Up Asian in America   Kesaya E. Noda   31

A Japanese-American woman explains how her family history has
helped to shape her identity in an often racist society.

2

THE WORLD OF THE FAMILY
Making the First Connections   57

3

THE WORLD OF LEARNING
Finding One's Purpose   115

4

THE WORLD OF GENDER
Being Men and Women   179

5

THE WORLD OF INTIMACY
Connecting with Another Person   233

7

THE WORLD OF NATURE
Connecting with the Wilderness   345

A close examination of the relationship between predator and prey
teaches a writer to respect nature's ability to maintain its equilibrium.

8

THE WORLD OF OUR PAST
Learning from Myths and Rites   405

A journalist and writer interviews a leading authority on myth and
folklore about the purpose of myths and how they function in our
society.

Representatives of three different cultures express respect for the
recurring cycles of nature.

A Native American writer tells the story of a death and a ritual
burial, surrounded by the conflicts between traditional culture and
Christianity.

A writer and mythographer describes three Greek myths that tell
the stories of the origins of some well-known flowers.

9

THE WORLD OF SCIENCE
Understanding and Exploring   459

10

THE WORLD IN REFLECTION
Examining Complex Issues   513

Rhetorical Table of Contents

The selections in *A Writer's Worlds* are organized in ten thematic units. This table of contents arranges the nonfiction selections according to the rhetorical strategies they best illustrate. It is meant as a guide and is by no means exhaustive. This is followed by a list of the rest of the selections arranged by genre such as poems, prose fiction, and interviews.

NARRATION

DEFINITION

FICTION

INTERVIEW

INTRODUCTION

Reading and writing are both important tools for learning about ourselves and the world. In *A Writer's Worlds: Explorations through Reading,* you will find a variety of interconnected reading and writing activities intended to expand your knowledge of yourself and the complex issues and problems that face our world today. Reading, thinking, discussing, and writing about these topics will help you grow intellectually and succeed both academically and personally.

A Writer's Worlds is designed to ease your transition into college and at the same time to introduce you to new subjects and fields of study. Arranged in ten thematic units, the reading selections move through the different worlds that shape our thinking and behavior. Many of the readings raise questions about the serious issues we face as adults, questions for which there are no easy answers. You will find yourself reflecting on your own identity, your family history, your life as a man or woman, your cultural heritage, and your interactions in society and in nature.

To guide you through each of these explorations, every unit begins with a set of questions that ask you to evaluate what you already know about the topics to be discussed. Then there are questions included with each reading selection that urge you to think critically about what you have read. You will develop your academic vocabulary by using the vocabulary lists provided. The writing assignments encourage you to reach conclusions about a topic based on your own experiences and ideas, and to notice how writers say things in certain ways according to their particular purpose or audience and how various types of writing (essays, fiction, academic writing) can express the same concern in different ways.

Exploring Reading and Writing

A Writer's Worlds has also been designed to help you make connections between reading and writing. Reading helps us to learn, to gain new ideas, and to understand the way other people think. Every day of our lives we learn something about the world by reading. We read signs, directions, correspondence, newspapers, magazines, and books. Writing is also an important part of the learning process. Writing helps people to communicate, to remember important information, to understand new ideas, and to develop new concepts. Writing can help clarify your own thinking and lead you to review and refine your original ideas.

Reading Exercise

1. During the first week of classes, jot down every single thing you read (at school or home)—a campus map, course assignments, the back of a cereal box, or your favorite magazines. At the end of the week, answer the following:
   - How many times a day did you read something?
   - What kind of reading did you do the most? the least?
   - What kind of reading did you enjoy the most? the least?
   - What did you find out about your reading habits? Is this what you expected?
   - What would you like to change about your reading habits?
2. What is your first memory of reading? How did you learn to read? What did you read? What did you enjoy (or dislike) most about reading? Why?

Writing Exercise

1. Again during the first week of classes, jot down every single thing you write (at school or home)—class notes, this exercise, a shopping list, a reminder, or a letter. At the end of the week, answer the following:
   - How many times a day did you write something?
   - What kind of writing did you do the most? the least?
   - What kind of writing did you enjoy the most? the least?
   - Did you write more often to communicate ideas to others or did you write more often for yourself?

2. What is your first memory of writing? Who taught you? What did you write? What did you enjoy (or dislike) most about writing? Why?

Keeping a Journal

Throughout *A Writer's Worlds* you will find opportunities to do some writing on your own, which may or may not be seen by your instructor. Keeping a journal will give you the place to expand your ideas on a subject without being limited to specific assignments or expectations. The act of writing itself changes our thinking about the world. The series of questions entitled IN YOUR JOURNAL provide plenty of chances to think on paper and to experience the flow of writing.

You will probably want to do this writing in a separate notebook. Check with your instructor for directions on how he or she plans to use the **journal entries** during the semester. Date and label your entries so that you can look through your journal later for paper topics or when you study for an examination. Remember that this journal will not be a personal diary. Record personal events only if they directly relate to your work in this course.

The IN YOUR JOURNAL suggestions appear in two places in the text: immediately before an essay and directly after it. You'll find most require only short written responses but feel free to continue in any direction that interests you. You should by no means feel limited to these questions, and you will find that they serve as a good springboard to further inquiry about a topic.

Reading Journal

You may also want to use your notebook as a reading journal to help you understand and think about what you are reading in this course. To do this, take notes *as* you read a selection. Quote any phrases or sentences that strike you as particularly meaningful. When you're finished reading, consider these questions:

- What new things have I learned from reading this selection?
- How have my perceptions about the subject been challenged?
- Have I changed my mind about the subject? In what way?

Write down your answers in an extra paragraph or two.

Learning the Writing Process

Although most of us write something every day of our lives, it is important to recognize that good writing requires time, commitment, and the willingness to rethink and rewrite what we have written. The effort always pays off: developing new writing skills leads to a better ability to express yourself clearly and powerfully.

All writers approach writing a bit differently, and the act of writing is a unique process for everyone. So too, the writing of an essay is rarely a neat sequence of events from beginning to end. Most writers go back and forth between what they are thinking and what they are writing. As they do, they engage in what has been identified as four basic writing activities: **inventing, drafting, revising,** and **editing.**

INVENTION TECHNIQUES

Writing usually begins by selecting a subject area. A subject is usually too broad to write a short essay on, so the next task is to narrow down your subject to a single **topic,** or single idea, you want to explore. You may already have some knowledge of this topic, you may simply be eager to know more about this topic, or you may have a question about it for which you don't yet have an answer. It should be a topic that interests you since you will be spending a good deal of time on it.

Getting Started

Sometimes it is difficult to come up with a topic, or you have a topic but need help deciding what point you want to make, or you need to gather additional ideas to support your main point. One or all of the following tactics may be helpful in establishing your paper topic.

Reading for Ideas

Reading provides a rich source of ideas. If you don't know where to begin, start by doing one of the following reading activities:

- Reread any of your journal entries relating to this topic. Perhaps even write a new entry summing up the entries you've read.
- Reread any of the selections in this book that you especially liked or found stimulating.
- Skim sections of any of your textbooks relating to the subject you want to write on.

- Read additional sources such as newspapers, magazines, or books for ideas.
- Read over an essay you wrote earlier. Think about how you discovered the topic and successfully narrowed it down. Try to relate your past experience to this one.

Collaborating with a Peer

Because most of us write to communicate with other people, many writers begin their work by bouncing ideas off others—friends, family members, editors, business associates—before they write, as they write, or before they prepare their final drafts. Open up the lines of communication early by sharing your ideas for paper topics with your classmates.

Working with a partner, discuss the "Suggestions for Writing" that interest you most, and together try to come up with ideas for your paper topic:

- Write down the different options that come to mind, especially those that intrigue you and seem to lead to more ideas.
- Once you find an interesting topic, try tossing out additional thoughts and see if your partner reacts favorably.
- Take some quick notes to help you remember the discussion.

Now follow the above steps, focusing on your partner's interests.

Exploring through Brainstorming

Brainstorming is an activity that involves thinking and writing down your ideas about a subject as quickly as they occur to you. It can be a free and relaxing way to develop ideas before beginning to write an essay, and you can brainstorm on your own or with a peer (see above, for example). Try not to judge the ideas as they emerge; the time for being critical comes later. With pen or pencil in hand, do the following for at least ten minutes:

- In your notebook or journal, write down the general topic and/or the writing suggestions from this text or from your instructor.
- Then without stopping to worry, write down whatever comes to mind in relation to these. Write down everything, even if it does not seem relevant to your topic right now.
- List any words or phrases that occur to you about the topic. You do not need to write full sentences, just key words. This will help your pen keep pace with your brain.

- When you've written all you can, go over the reading selection you're working from to spot any ideas you've overlooked. Notice any words, phrases, or similarities in the reading selection to the brainstorming notes you've just written down and make a few notes on these as well.
- Now read through your list. Mark words, phrases, or ideas that seem related. You may find that you have several sets of related ideas, so mark each set differently.
- Choose one set of these related ideas and rewrite them on a separate sheet. When you're done, look back at your original list and add any ideas you may have missed. Put aside the original list now that it is no longer useful.
- Spend a minute writing down any new ideas that occur to you after you've created the new list.

Now you should discover the **theme** for your paper, the common idea that connects every entry on your list. Keep this brainstorming list beside you as you write your first draft. Once you begin writing, you may find that your ideas move in a different but better direction than the one you had anticipated. At that point you may want to brainstorm again within the narrow focus of your paper topic. You will be writing down only those ideas that fit within this topic.

Creating Clusters

Clustering, or mapping as it is sometimes called, involves taking key words or ideas and writing them down according to how they relate to each other, circling them, and drawing lines to connect them. It is a good technique for visual thinkers, especially those who can imagine designs or networks (i.e., computer networking), and it is a little like doing a jigsaw puzzle. Using the diagram on the opposite page as an example, complete the following steps to create a clustered image of ideas for your paper.

- In the middle of a blank piece of paper, write down the **central idea,** or the subject, of your paper. Draw a circle around it.
- Around this circle, write down any words, phrases, or ideas that come to mind on this subject. For each new idea decide whether it relates best to the central idea or to one of the new ideas. Circle each one and draw a line connecting it to the other idea.

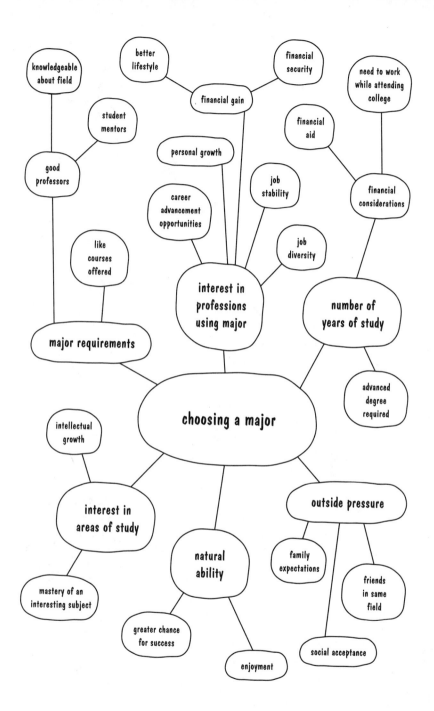

- Think of new ideas that complement the ones you've just completed, write them down, circle them, and draw the connecting lines. Continue to do this until all your ideas appear somewhere on the page.

When you are done, look over your cluster. Identify the groups that have formed. Try to organize the ideas within each group. Take the main idea at the center and organize the outer ideas into supporting ideas. Which supporting idea should be presented first? Second? Next? Last? Then try to organize the groups in the same manner. Take the central topic and organize the groups to follow in a logical and meaningful order. By organizing them in this manner, you can discover the outline for your first draft.

Freewriting

Freewriting is a good technique for experiencing the act of writing, even when you are worried that you have nothing to write. When freewriting, concentrate only on how your thoughts flow through your pen. Remember that freewriting means letting go and just writing, without worrying about being correct, making connections, or even making sense.

Decide on a reasonable time limit, say five or ten minutes, and then write whatever occurs to you. At first you may find yourself writing, "I can't think of anything to write" or "I'm hungry." It does not matter. DO NOT STOP until your time is up. The idea is to pay attention to the act of transferring your thoughts from your mind to paper.

When you're done, read over what you have written. What ideas have you written down that seem interesting? What ideas might be useful in a paper?

You might want to try **focused freewriting** at this point. To do focused freewriting, start off with a word, phrase, or topic as you did with clustering. Look at it for about a minute, then start writing. Keep glancing at it and write whatever comes to mind. Freewriting while focusing on one of these ideas allows you to see if you have enough interest, information, and ideas to write an essay.

Making a Rough Outline

For some writers the next step is to plan the order of their essay. A rough organization of your ideas can help you decide where to begin, what to say first, next, and last.

To create a rough outline of your paper, look at the ideas you have generated from any of the invention techniques. Try to organize your ideas in a way that seems logical to you at this time (it may change later). Your main idea will be most important, of course, so put that first. Then arrange the supporting ideas. Which supporting idea is the most important? Which idea should come first? Second? Next? What idea might you end with and leave your reader thinking about?

Below is a rough outline for ideas generated by the clustering technique on choosing a major:

```
                  Choosing a Major
A. Interest in Area of Study
   1. Intellectual growth
   2. Mastery of an interesting subject

B. Major Requirements
   1. Like courses offered
   2. Good professors
      a. knowledgeable about field
      b. student mentors

C. Professions Using Major
   1. Like potential careers
   2. Career advancement opportunities
   3. Job diversity
   4. Job stability
   5. Personal growth
   6. Financial gain
      a. financial security
      b. better lifesyle

D. Number of Years of Study
   1. Advanced degree required
   2. Financial considerations
      a. financial aid
      b. need to work while attending college

E. Outside Pressure
   1. Family expectations
   2. Friends in same field
   3. Social acceptance
```

F. Natural Ability
   1. Enjoyment
   2. Greater chance for success

DRAFTING TECHNIQUES

At this point in the process you should have a topic for your paper, some supporting ideas, and a tentative plan. You are now ready to write. What you will be writing is a **draft.** Consider the following points as you go:

- Plan a schedule. Give yourself time to write.
- Don't expect yourself to produce a perfect, finished piece right away.
- Do set reasonable goals during the drafting process. Try setting time limits such as writing for one hour before taking a break. Or try page limits such as writing one or two pages before quitting.
- Skip anything that brings you to a halt (you can always come back to it later). Often writers have trouble with the introduction and the opening sentences. If necessary, skip to where you can comfortably begin.
- Feel free to cross out ideas, move them around, and add details as you think of them. Sometimes, marking A,B,C,D, etc . . . next to circled blocks of writing helps you remember what order you are planning for the sentences.
- When you've completed your first draft, go ahead and reward yourself for meeting your goals. Writing is hard work; recognize the effort you have made.

Writing the Introduction

Each essay needs an introduction to help you capture your reader's interest and to state the thesis or main idea of your essay. Many writers also use the opening paragraph to introduce the main points that will be developed later.

There are several ways to write a successful introduction:

- *General statement*—Begin with one strong statement about your subject that opens up the lines of discussion.
- *Anecdote*—Introduce your essay with an anecdote or brief story that relates to the main topic.

- *Question*—Ask a question in the introduction and then answer it in the body of your essay.
- *Quotation*—Start with a quote that relates to your main topic.
- *Definition*—Define a term that will be explored in the essay.

Using a general statement is the most common way to open a formal essay. Begin with the general statement that alerts your readers to the subject and follow it with a stronger sentence that clearly states what you want to say about this topic. This is your **thesis sentence.**

If you are writing a narrative essay or story, you have much more freedom to choose how you want to introduce your paper. Often an anecdote is used for these kinds of writing.

Developing the Body

Follow your organization plan, according to your rough outline. Start a new paragraph every time you present one of your ideas. Make sure you have enough details to support or explain the point you are making in that paragraph.

Concluding Your Essay

In your conclusion, you tie together your ideas with a final statement that makes sure that your readers understand your main point. To be effective:

- Make it positive and strong.
- Make it short.
- Don't simply repeat your ideas. Use what you've said earlier to make a final statement.
- Don't introduce new ideas that you won't go on to explain.
- Use a phrase or detail from your introduction to bring readers full circle.
- When appropriate, try using a humorous comment, a short related anecdote, a short quotation, or a piece of dialogue. These kinds of phrases tend to stick in a reader's mind and help the reader to remember your essay.

REVISION TECHNIQUES

Most writers need to write more than one draft in order to present their ideas clearly and in an interesting style. The first draft is a rough presentation of your ideas that you will refine over time. Some writers prefer to go over their first drafts on their own, others find it helpful to read the drafts with a partner, or in a small group. Throughout the book you will find revising suggestions at the end of each reading selection. Try all these techniques until you find the ones that work best for you.

Read your first draft over, trying to make sure that your meaning is well presented. Make sure that you have provided enough supporting evidence to make your points. Make sure that you have chosen the most effective words and phrases to convey your ideas. Your goal in revising is to create a piece of writing that is as clear and interesting as possible so that your readers will understand and care about the ideas you have presented.

Revision Exercise

Look over some of the writing you did last semester (or last year). Make a list of the changes you made as you wrote your second, even third drafts. Why did you make these changes? Were these changes effective? Watch how you improved your writing with each draft. Use those skills and the following revision checklist as you revise again and again throughout this semester.

Revision Checklist

If possible, put your draft away for a few days before you begin the revising process. (If you need to revise an in-class assignment, put it away for ten or more minutes. Use the time to write in your journal or read.) This delay allows you enough distance from your work to discover things you may have missed before and to more easily recognize weaknesses in your writing. When you are ready, read the draft over yourself (or with a partner) and ask yourself the following questions:

1. Does your **introduction** convince the reader that the topic you have chosen is interesting? What could be changed to engage the reader even more?

2. What is the **main idea** of your essay? Is the main idea directly stated, or is it merely implied? How could it be stated more clearly or concisely?

3. What **specific evidence** or ideas support the main idea? What can you do to make the use of supporting evidence more effective?

4. Which of the **supporting ideas** is the strongest? Which is the weakest? Why? Should the weaker ideas be replaced, or can you improve on the presentation of the ideas and successfully convince your reader of your point?

5. Are any **words or phrases repeated** too often? Using a dictionary and/or thesaurus, can you find new words to help you say exactly what you want to say?

6. Are your ideas connected? What **transitions** or key words connect ideas from sentence to sentence and paragraph to paragraph? Does every transition seem logical? Could you improve the essay by rearranging some of your ideas?

7. Does your **ending** bring together the ideas you have presented? Do you leave the reader with some kind of concluding idea? What specific words and phrases could you use to clarify your final points?

8. What particular ideas in your essay interest you the most? What would make these parts stand out even more?

You will find these questions useful for every kind of writing you do. Come back to this page again and again as you revise throughout the course.

EDITING TECHNIQUES

Few writers are able to edit as they write their drafts, continually correcting grammar, punctuation, and spelling. This requires an ability to concentratte on both the content of the writing and the surface presentation of it. Most writers prefer to draft and revise their work first, waiting until the second or third and final draft to begin focusing on editing concerns.

Everyone has difficulty with some aspect of grammar, punctuation, or spelling; some people have difficulty with commas, others get confused over verb agreement. It is useful to know what common errors you make in your writing, and then watch out for them. Your goal in editing your work is to create a piece of writing that is as correct as possible so that your readers will understand the ideas you have presented.

Editing Exercise

Look over some of the writing you did last semester (or last year). Make a list of the errors you find. Consider discussing your findings with your instructor. Think of ways you can catch these kinds of errors in your current writing. For instance, you might want to read through your whole draft looking only at one trouble spot, such as commas. Then, you might go back and check verb tenses and agreement in every sentence. And so on. . . . To help you strengthen your writing skills throughout the semester, keep the lists you create and the editing methods you have devised alongside the following editorial checklist.

Editing Checklist

The checklist that follows will help you edit your work. Use it after revising your essay (or whenever you want to edit). Pause to pay special attention to any of the following areas that have occurred in your writing before. Paying attention to these details will give your essay a final polish and allow your readers to concentrate on the meaning of your words and not on the words themselves.

1. **Subject and verb agreement:** Check to be sure all verbs agree with their subjects.

2. **Verb tense:** Verb tenses (past, present, future, etc . . .) should be consistent. Make sure there is a reason for each time you change tenses.

3. **Pronoun agreement:** Check to be sure every pronoun agrees with its **antecedent**—the noun to which it refers.

4. **Spelling:** Consult a dictionary whenever you are not sure of the spelling of a word.

5. **Punctuation:** Use proper punctuation in every sentence, such as end punctuation to finish every sentence and commas whenever necessary.

6. **Capitalization:** Every sentence should begin with a capital letter. Check for other words that require capitalization, such as the names of people and places.

7. **Word choice:** Avoid sexist, racist, or other offensive language. If you have used any dialect or slang, consider whether it is appropriate for your intended audience. If not, be ready to change it.

8. **Acknowledge your sources:** Be prepared to acknowledge and give credit to all of the sources you used in preparation for your essay. This includes whenever you quote from another person or source, summarize the content from another source, and paraphrase the ideas expressed in another source.

9. **Presentation:** Turn in a paper that is double-spaced if it is to be typed or neatly handwritten (according to your instructions), with wide margins for your instructor's comments (usually 1″), and each paragraph indented five spaces.

1

THE WORLD OF
THE SELF

Developing an Identity

Each of us is born into the world at large, and each is part of a smaller set of worlds that influences who we are and who we become. As we grow, we develop a personal identity that is affected by our background, our family, our family's culture, and the larger culture around us. As you read through the selections in this unit, think about your own cultural, ethnic, religious, and racial background. How has your background affected the way you perceive the world?

In " 'Nopalitos': The Making of Fiction" by Helena María Viramontes, the author recalls her Latina childhood in East Los Angeles. Viramontes explains how writing about her past, her family, and her heritage has enabled her to find strength through the goodness that has shaped her personal identity.

"A Bracelet, an Odd Earring, Cracked Teacups" by Ewa Zadrzynska, who immigrated to the United States from Poland in 1983, describes how finding an old discarded trunk on the street helps her find a piece of her "old" self. Zadrzynska uses some of the items found in the trunk, things from someone else's life, to re-create her "new" self and find a new life.

"First Born" by Danjuma Sinue Modupe is an autobiographical story about an African American who gains an understanding about the importance of names, the way names shape identity, and the power of renaming oneself. In this story, Modupe recalls a childhood incident that influenced his feelings about himself and his racial identity.

"Growing Up Asian in America" by Kesaya E. Noda tells how race affects the quality of life one experiences in the United States. As a Japanese American, Noda has experienced racism, but she has also found stability through her family and her history.

"Coming Out Now" by James N. Baker is an essay about Daniel Layer, an eighteen-year-old homosexual, who grew up in an unstable family. Part of learning to accept himself involved learning to live with estranged parents who had conflicting views of life.

"Early Adulthood: Roles and Issues" by Grace J. Craig is from Craig's textbook, *Human Development*. Believing that development is a lifelong process, Craig identifies some of the developmental stages of adults from the ages of sixteen to forty-five. She describes a project in which extensive life histories of a large group of adults were collected. The examination of these life histories led to the development of a theory of life stages that describes the ways adults change and reshape their lives over time.

Yvette Montalvo, a student writer, writes about discovering an imaginary trunk. She explains how the contents of the trunk help her to reflect on important moments and people in her own life.

*   *   *

Think about the following questions before reading the selections in this unit:

1. How do you identify yourself? Make a list of four words that describe who you are. You can start your sentence, "My name is _____ and I am _____."

2. Which of the above four words is most important to you for defining who you are? Why?

3. In what ways would your list have been different ten years ago? Why?

IN YOUR JOURNAL

Viramontes describes the process of thinking about family events and writing about them to understand herself and her culture. Make a list of three events that happened in your family life and explain why they were important to you.

"Nopalitos": The Making of Fiction

Helena María Viramontes

Helena María Viramontes teaches at the University of California in Irvine. She has been coordinator of the Los Angeles Latino Writers Association and editor of the *Xhisme Arte* magazine. She published *The Moths and Other Stories,* a collection of short stories, in 1988.

Fiction is my jugular. For me it is a great consolation to know that whatever miserable things happen in my lifetime, goodness will inevitably result because I will write about it. There is strength in this when none is left in the soul.

I was born and raised in the U.S., East L.A., Califas, to be more exact, on First Street not too far from Whittier Blvd., close enough to enable me to see the smoke from the Chicano Moratorium riots. I come from a family of eleven, six sisters and three brothers, but the family always extended its couch or floor to whomever stopped at our house with nowhere else to go. As a result, a variety of people came to live with us. Former boyfriends of my sisters who were thrown or pushed out of their own homes, friends who stayed the night but never left, relatives who crossed the border and stayed until enough was saved. Through all this I remember two things well: first, the late night kitchen meetings where everyone talked and laughed in low voices, played cards, talked of loneliness, plans for the future, of loves lost or won. I heard men cry, drunken stories, women laughing. It was fascinating to listen in the dark, peek into the moments of their lives. For me, it seemed like a dream to wake up at midnight and hear the voices and listen to the soft music, see the light under the door. This was adulthood and I yearned to one day be the one on the other side of that door.

Little did I realize that this is the stuff good fiction is made of: the   3
stories, the fascination of the subject matter, capturing the moments
and fleeing with them like a thief or lover. I began my apprenticeship
without even knowing it.

The other thing I remember is my mother. Her relentless energy.   4
She must have been tired a good part of her life and yet she had to
keep going and going and going. I also remember her total kindness,
the way a sad story made her cry, the way she always found room
somehow in an already-crowded household for those with the sad
stories. The nights she would stay up, a small black and white T.V.
blaring, waiting for the girls to come home. The mornings she would
get up, KWKW Spanish radio low, making the big stack of tortillas
for the morning breakfast.

These two things, love of stories and love of my mother, or all that   5
seemed female in our household, influenced me to such an extent that it
became an unconscious part of me, so unconscious that I didn't realize
it until just moments ago. In fact, the first story that I wrote, titled
"Requiem for the Poor," opened with my mother awaking to make
breakfast. To think: she was the first image in my mind, my heart, my
hand. Naturally.

If my mother was the fiber that held a family together, it was my   6
father who kept snapping it with his oppressive cruelty. With virtually
no education, stressed with the responsibility of supporting such a large
family, he worked as a hod carrier—a carrier of cement in construction.
He drank, and was mean. Impatient, screaming a lot of the time, temper
tantrums, we were often trembling in his presence. If my mother
showed all that is good in being female, my father showed all that is bad
in being male. I'm only now understanding the depth of this conclusion, and am making a serious effort to erase this black and white. See
the good and bad in both sexes. That's the power of imagination,
peeking beyond the fence of your personal reality and seeing the possibilities thereafter.

A basic problem for any writer is time. I lament the lack of time. As I   7
pass my shelves of books, I think, these are books I will never read; or as
my notebooks pile up, spilling over with plots, characters, great and
moving sentences, I think, these are the words that will never find a
story. Ideally, it would be bliss to manipulate the economic conditions
of our lives and thus free our minds, our hands, to write. But there is no
denying that this is a privilege limited to a certain sex, race, and class.

The only bad thing about privilege, Virginia Woolf wrote (I'm paraphrasing from Tillie Olsen) was that not every one could have it.

How does one solve the problem of time? Fortunately, we mujeres   8
are an inventive people. My mother, for example, faced the challenge of
feeding eleven people every evening. Time and time again, I saw her cut
four pork chops, add this and that and this, pour water, and miraculously feed all of us with a tasty guiso. Or the nopales she grew, cleaned,
diced, scrambled with eggs, or meat, or chile, or really mixed with
anything her budget could afford, and we had such a variety of tasty
dishes!

I have never been able to match her nopales, but I have inherited her   9
capacity for invention. I myself invent time by first conjuring up the
voices and spirits of the women living under brutal repressive regimes.
In the light of their reality, my struggles for a few hours of silence seem
like such a petty problem. I am humbled, and no sooner do I think of
their courage than I find my space on the kitchen table, my time long
after midnight and before the start of the children's hectic morning.
Because I want to do justice to their voices. To tell these women, in my
own gentle way, that I will fight for them, that they provide me with my
own source of humanity. That I love them, their children. Once seen in
this perspective, the lack of sleep is more of an inconvenience than a
sacrifice.

What little time we do invent we guard like our children. Interrup-   10
tion is a fact in our lives and is as common as pennies. Solely because we
are women. A man who aspires to write is sanctioned by society. It is an
acceptable and noble endeavor. As for us, writing is seen as a hobby we
do after all our responsibilities are fulfilled. Nay, to write while the baby
is crying is a crime punishable by guilt. Guilt is our Achilles' heel. Thus
the work of the mujer suffers immensely, for the leisure of returning to
her material, to rework it, polish it, is almost impossible. Because
phones will ring, children will cry, or mothers will ask for favors. My
mother, it seemed for a time, believed me to be half-baked for wanting
desperately to write. It was inconceivable to her that I spent mornings
scratching a sharpened pencil against paper. She would stand and look
over my shoulder, try to read a paragraph or two, and seeing that I was
simply wasting my time staring into space, she'd ask me to go get some
tortillas, or could you vacuum the living room, maybe water the plants
outside? After turning her away with a harsh no, guilt would engulf me
like a blob, and although I hated myself for doing it, there I was, once
again, holding a garden hose, watering her roses.

We must come to understand that stifling a woman's imagination is   11
too costly a price to pay for servitude. The world would be void of any
depth or true comprehension if we were not allowed to exercise our
imaginations. We must challenge those beliefs which oppress us within
our family, our culture, in addition to those in the dominant culture.

Family ties are fierce. Especially for mujeres. We are raised to care   12
for. We are raised to stick together, for the family unit is our only source
of safety. Outside our home there lies a dominant culture that is foreign
to us, isolates us, and labels us illegal alien. But what may be seen as a
nurturing, close unit, may also become suffocating, manipulative, and
sadly victimizing. As we slowly examine our own existence in and out of
these cultures, we are breaking stereotypes, reinventing traditions for
our own daughters and sons.

What a courageous task! In the past, we have been labeled as the   13
weaker sex, and it is logical to assume that we are of weaker minds as well.
As women, we have learned to listen, rather than speak, causing us,
historically, to join with others who maintain we have nothing to say.
Only now we are discovering that we do. And those who do not seem
interested in knowing our voices are just plain foolish. To limit their
knowledge of people, places, cultures, and sexes is to live in a narrow,
colorless world. It is not only a tragedy, but just plain silly, for only foolish
people would not be interested in embracing such knowledge.

We can not, nor will we divorce ourselves from our families. But we   14
need a change in their attitudes. If I am to succeed as a writer, I need my
family to respect my time, my words, myself. This goes for my parents,
brothers, sisters, my children, my husband. Respectability is a long and
sometimes nasty struggle. But you'd be surprised at the progress one
can make. Eventually, my mother proved to be very flexible. When I
signed my first honorarium over to her, she discreetly placed it in her
pocket. Later, as I spread my notebooks over the dining room table, she
carried in a streaming cup of coffee, sweetened just the way I like it.

Now for some nopalitos.   15

My tío Rogelio was one of those who stayed for years. I became his   16
consentida, he my best friend, until other interests developed in my life.
He eventually moved and the distance between his house and mine
became so far it took years to get together again. Recently, he visited me
and was astonished to find that I spoke only in English. Straightfor-
ward, as has always been his manner, he asked me: "Why don't you
speak Spanish anymore?"

Good question. What happened? I did as a child, I know only from   17
others' recollection, but what happened? Somewhere along the educational system I lost it, and with it I lost a part of me. Yes, I can
communicate all right now, but to feel that it is my own, to feel comfortable enough to write in it, that's what I am missing. As a result, I will
not be a whole person until I reacquire this part of me. For you see, a
good part of my upbringing was in Spanish. Spanish images, words,
moods that I feel I must explore before they are buried for good.

Of course English is my language too. I'm entitled to it, though it is   18
the one I have learned artificially. But having Spanish stolen from me is
lingual censorship. A repression that reveals to me the power of the
language itself.

Consequently, I do not feel comfortable in either language. In fact, I   19
majored in English and acquired a degree to erase what Lorna Dee
Cervantes calls "my excuse me tongue." However, my English is often
awkward, and clumsy, and it is this awkwardness that I struggle so hard
with. But isn't that what writing is all about? The struggle with the
word for the perfect meaning? Sometimes my mistakes turn out to be
my best writing. Sometimes I think in Spanish and translate. Sometimes
I go through the dictionary and acquaint myself with words I wouldn't
otherwise use in conversation. Sometimes I am thrilled by the language
and play with its implications. And sometimes I hate it, not feeling
comfortable.

And yet, I am amazed when people say one of my greatest strengths   20
is my language. Funny, no? I was also recently informed that my book,
The Moths and Other Stories, will be included as required reading in the
English Department's qualifying exam for the Ph.D. program at University of Texas, Austin.

I still say that if my works were translated into Spanish, they would   21
somehow feel better. More, more, what's the word? At home.

In my case, Faulkner was right; I became a short story writer be-   22
cause I was a failed poet. But when I began to write, I honestly went
into it rather blindly. I never once thought of a potential audience.
Perhaps just starting out, I didn't have the confidence to think that
people would actually be interested in reading it. I wrote what was
natural, personal to me. I showed my work to Chicanas mostly, and
since they related to it, they became supportive and thrilled at what I
was doing. And the more they were thrilled and supportive, the more I
wrote.

By that time, I had discovered the Latin American writers: Borges,   23
García Márquez, Rulfo, Yañez, to name a few. Their exploration with
form and voice was a thrilling experiment in modern fiction, I felt, and
was eager to try my hand at it. It was a rebellion against accepted rules
that, in essence, reflected their politics as well. Like Faulkner, they
sought to see what they could get away with, and, as a result, gave birth
to such a rich texture of literature that it is a sheer celebration to read.

This is where I got my angst for form, technique. But my worldview was   24
obviously a different one because I was a Chicana. Once I discovered the
Black women writers—Walker, Morrison, Brooks, Shange, again to name
a few—womanism as subject matter seemed sanctioned, illuminating,
innovative, honest, the best in recent fiction that I've seen in a long time.

Subject matter and form. They met, became lovers, often quarrelled,   25
but nonetheless, Helena María Viramontes was born.

As Chicanas, we must continue to have the courage to examine our   26
lives. Sometimes, when I see all that goes on around me, I begin to
question the importance of fiction and its value against the face of a
starving child. Yet, we continue to write. Perhaps it is because we have
such a strong belief in the power of the written word. It is a link which
bonds us. Their starvation becomes mine, their death becomes mine.
Our destiny is not embedded in cement. We can determine its destination. Some use the soapbox, others, weapons. I choose to write.

I am genuinely happy to be a part of a growing, nurturing group of   27
writers, radical women of color who are not afraid to explore culture,
politics, humanity, womanism, not afraid to sabotage the stereotypes
with whatever words are necessary to get the job done.

Vocabulary

jugular (1)—two large veins in the neck, symbolically refers to strength and power

Chicano (2)—person of Mexican descent; *Chicana* is a woman of Mexican descent

mujeres (8)—Spanish word for women

Achilles' heel (10)—vulnerable or sensitive spot. Achilles was a Greek warrior in the Trojan War who was killed by Paris with an arrow that struck him in his only vulnerable spot, his heel.

tío (16)—Spanish word for uncle

consentida (16)—Spanish word for favored or spoiled child

IN YOUR JOURNAL

Reread the entry you wrote before reading Viramontes's selection. Choose the one event that made the most impact on you. Write about what this event has taught you about yourself, your family, and your culture.

A Closer Reading

1. What does writing fiction enable Viramontes to do with the "miserable things" that have happened during her lifetime?

2. What personal characteristics does Viramontes's mother have? Why does she admire her mother?

3. Writers often provide background information, creating a context to help readers understand them better. What specific background information does Viramontes provide? What does this background tell her readers about who she is as a person?

4. What events does Viramontes describe that suggest that she was not respected as a writer in her family? What events suggest that this has changed?

Drawing Your Own Conclusions

1. In what ways does Viramontes question the idea that women are the weaker sex? Do you think that there is a weaker sex?

2. Why do some people who are oppressed by society (like Viramontes's father) oppress others when they have the opportunity? What can be done to break this cycle?

3. Viramontes writes about feeling like an "alien" in the dominant culture. What does she mean by the term "dominant culture"? Why does she feel like an alien?

4. Viramontes states that she loses her ability to speak Spanish as an adult. In this essay, she considers her Spanish background and then writes about it to understand her identity. Why does she need to immerse herself in her past to develop her self-identity? What is self-identity to you?

Thinking about Writing

1. Viramontes names many writers in this essay. Identify and focus on each of these writers. As a class project, discuss who each writer is and list at least some of their writing projects. What do these writers have in common? Why did she choose each one?

2. What does Viramontes refer to as "the stuff good fiction is made of"?

3. Viramontes describes her mother not by her physical appearance but by her actions. Reread the essay focusing on the mother's actions. What do we learn about the mother from her actions?

4. Viramontes uses some Spanish words in her writing. Some have been defined in the vocabulary list. Why does she include these words? Why doesn't she define them? In which language does she express herself better?

*   *   *

Suggestions for Writing

1. As you have seen through your own journal entry, one can discover one's self-identity by writing about family stories. This time choose a family story that reveals the power structure in your family—the way people relate to each other, who assumes leadership and who does not, and how the stronger and weaker members fit into the family scenario. Write the story describing what family members said and did. Then explain what you learned about your family and about yourself by writing this story.

2. Part of growing up may involve realizing that the language spoken at home by your family is not acceptable in school. Interview someone for whom this was true and write an essay outlining the events in that person's life and telling how the person resolved the problem. Did he or she give up one language or learn to speak one language at home and one in school? What did the person learn from the experience? How did the experience shape who he or she is?

3. Choose one of the writers to whom Viramontes refers. Using your college library, write a brief biography of that person. At

the end, explain in what ways the person's family and cultural background affected his or her writing.

4. Read one of the stories in Viramontes's book, *The Moths and Other Stories*. Based on this, decide whether you would like to have her book included in a course in your school. Write an essay describing the story you read and explain why you think the book should or should not be taught in a course.

Strategies for Revision

Viramontes has been told that one of her great strengths is her use of language—her careful choice of words to express her ideas.

Reread your draft by yourself or with a classmate, focusing on the language you have chosen. Do your words express your ideas clearly?

Decide which points in your draft are particularly important in defending your main point. Does your language tell your reader that this is an important point? If you read with a classmate, ask your classmate to identify which parts of the essay seem most important.

Change all words that seem repetitive and unclear. Rewrite your important points using direct and powerful language. Then, reread what you have written and revise any parts of your essay that you think could be better.

IN YOUR JOURNAL

In this selection, the author finds something in the street that makes her remember a series of old events and feelings in her past. Before you read this selection, think about a similar experience when you saw something, heard something, or even smelled something that made you think about an important event in your past. Write about your experience.

A Bracelet, an Odd Earring,
Cracked Teacups

Ewa Zadrzynska

Born in Poland, Ewa Zadrzynska left her homeland in 1983 after martial law was declared. She now lives in the East Village section of New York City. After coming to the United States, Zadrzynska wrote *Girl With a Watering Can* (1989). Her essay "A Bracelet, an Odd Earring, Cracked Teacups" appeared in *The New York Times* on June 8, 1988. Zadrzynska writes: "I looked for something I could identify with, something that would make my present more secure. It seemed hopeless." She tells how the discovery of a discarded trunk filled with another family's memories enabled her to recall her own past and to rethink her personal identity.

I came to live in the United States believing I was profoundly pre-   1
pared. I had studied the works of Flannery O'Connor in Polish, and had learned English by reading J. D. Salinger's short stories. I had seen all of Woody Allen's movies, and could sing Duke Ellington's "Take the 'A' Train."

But I found myself living in Washington Heights, at the end of   2
Manhattan. . . . My only connection with the rest of the world was the famous A train. But this train didn't lightly swing like Ellington's. It rocked and rolled like Motley Crüe's heavy metal: slow, noisy and crowded.

How was I to make myself at home on 190th Street and Broadway in   3
the middle of 1983? I looked for something I could identify with, something that would make my present more secure. It seemed hopeless.

Then one day, in 1984, at the corner of Hillside Avenue and Broadway,   4
I saw an old wooden trunk that looked very familiar. Only its location,
next to some garbage cans, indicated that it was meant to be trash. Even
the strange tag—"Destination: America; Address: Unknown"—didn't
change my impression that I had seen this trunk before.

And I had.   5

In Poland, my sister stored her blankets and pillows in exactly the   6
same kind of trunk. She had bought her vintage trunk in a small village
in the vicinity of Wroclaw, within the so-called "post-German" regions.

When I forced the lid of this trunk open, I was not surprised to find   7
yellowing postcards from Breslau—the German name for Wroclaw.

It was an "all-my-life-in-one-package" trunk. It contained a broken sil-   8
ver bracelet, an odd earring with the Star of David carved on it, two teacups,
silk dresses for a very slim young woman and dresses for a more mature,
older woman. There were bundles of letters, papers and photographs.

Once, the trunk had belonged to the Mueller family. The trunk and   9
the Muellers came to the States in 1936. (The tag on the lid was dated
August 1936.) They had probably lived in Wroclaw. At least in Germany they had been well off. One of the photographs was taken in an
expensively furnished living room. They were in their 20's. Full of good
expectations and confidence, they looked straight into the camera.

They were Jewish. (A later photograph, probably taken in the United   10
States, showed the family celebrating Hanukkah.) They spent at least 50
years together. There was a letter written by Mr. Mueller to Mrs. Mueller
in 1976. Hesitantly, I looked at it. As far as my German and shame let me
understand it, Mr. Mueller was in Los Angeles visiting relatives. He was
missing his wife and looking forward to seeing her.

Mr. Mueller probably died not long after. If he were alive, he   11
wouldn't have dumped their personal letters. If he had died recently,
there would have been men's clothing in the trunk.

She, or rather they, like to drink tea. There were two old Meissen   12
teacups with a pink and blue rose pattern. Mrs. Mueller must have been
fond of them. The cups had broken twice. The first accident was mended
with an old-fashioned glue that left brown lines in the cracks; the second
accident occurred much later, when better glues were available.

Only a person who cared about memories would have bothered to   13
apply the glue. Mrs. Mueller cared, but whoever threw away the teacups
judged them in cold blood.

How did she lose only one earring? And why did she keep the odd   14
one? Maybe she believed, as do some Europeans, that things have souls

and suffer when they are thrown away. There was also a bracelet that seemed to have been broken on purpose, deliberately twisted and bent in a few places. When I looked at the pieces, I could picture the infuriated Mrs. Mueller destroying the bracelet with the hope of punishing her husband. Later, when the fury was gone, Mr. Mueller was forgiven and the bracelet, too. It was put back into its Tiffany cotton envelope and stored away. I think Mrs. Mueller meant to fix it someday.

The trunk contained not only Mr. and Mrs. Mueller's past but also some of mine. Two years after getting married, I tore apart a silver necklace I had received from my husband as a wedding gift. I keep a few silver pieces in a little box, and someday I am going to link them together. In Warsaw, I had a similar set of Meissen china cups. I would never throw out an odd earring. I store my correspondence—bound with a blue ribbon—the way Mrs. Mueller did. I even know the Wroclaw street pictured on one of her postcards. 15

I took home the broken bracelet, the earring and two photographs of the Mueller family. The trunk was too heavy to carry. But when I came back with my husband, Janusz, it had been taken away. Only the two china cups still leaned against the trash can, awaiting the sanitation truck. I thought about the Muellers drinking their afternoon tea for 50 years. Over my husband's protests, I took the cups home. 16

Two years later, when we were moving 180 blocks downtown, the cups broke again. I didn't glue them. I had just begun to work full time and to adjust to the American pace. I didn't have time to bother about two old cups. The cups, after all, were someone else's memory. By then I had my own New York past. 17

But I still have the broken bracelet and the nicely framed photo of Mr. and Mrs. Mueller in 1929. Too many times my friends asked, "Are they your grandparents?" so I slipped a picture of my daughter wearing her P.S. 41 sweatshirt into the frame. Zuzana doesn't know that behind her back there is a young couple, full of confidence, staring straight ahead. 18

Vocabulary

profoundly (1)—very or extremely

Hanukkah (10)—an eight-day Jewish celebration commemorating the rededication of the Temple by Judas Maccabaeus in 165 B.C.

Meissen (12)—a famous type of porcelain made in the German city of Meissen

infuriated (14)—very angry

IN YOUR JOURNAL

Make a list of items that, if you discovered them in a trunk, would trigger a certain set of memories of your own life. What are these memories, and how does each item awaken your mind to past events?

A Closer Reading

1. What did Zadrzynska do to prepare herself for life in the United States?
2. What does she find in the trunk? How does she relate these items to her own life?
3. What does she take with her from the trunk? Why? Why does she leave the trunk in the street? Why does she return later?
4. What does she do with the photograph of the Mueller family?

Drawing Your Own Conclusions

1. What does it mean for Zadrzynska to belong to a neighborhood, a city, or a country? For you?
2. Zadrzynska writes that Mrs. Mueller was "a person who cared about memories." What in the selection tells you that Zadrzynska is also such a person?
3. What is more important in Zadrzynska's life—her family or personal possessions? Explain your answer using evidence from the essay.
4. What evidence does Zadryznska use from the trunk to reconstruct the lives of the Mueller family? Could you interpret the evidence in any other way? How much of her interpretation relies on Zadrzynska's need to find her own past?
5. If you were to move into a college dorm, what items would you take with you so you would feel at home and have something with which you could identify?

Thinking about Writing

1. What does the title mean? What is another title that would work equally well?

2. Zadrzynska names some well-known people in the first two paragraphs of her essay. Identify and focus on each of these people. As a class project, discuss them and list some of the accomplishments in their lives. What do these people have in common? Why did she choose each one?

3. What words and phrases does Zadrzynska use to contrast the past and present in her life? In the Mueller family history? In New York? In music?

4. Reread the first three paragraphs and the last two paragraphs. How do these paragraphs relate to each other? How is the essay tied together at the end?

*   *   *

Suggestions for Writing

1. Begin your own story by rewording paragraph 4 as your first paragraph. Use your imagination to describe the contents of the trunk you found, what you did with it, and what it meant to you.

2. In paragraph 1, Zadrzynska describes the books, movies, and music she thought would prepare her for life in the United States. Write an essay in which you choose one writer, one filmmaker, and one song that would prepare a person for life in the United States as we enter the twenty-first century. Explain the reasons for your choices and describe what they will teach a person about life in our world today.

3. Write an essay in which you describe three items that reflect your personality and show what is important to you. These three items should relate to your self-identity. Describe them in detail and explain why they are important to understanding who you are.

4. Imagine that a family is moving to your community from another country. Write a letter of advice telling that family what they need to bring, what they need to learn, and what they should know in order to prepare them for life where you live.

Strategies for Revision

Make a list of the three most important points in your essay. Share your first draft with a classmate and ask that person to make a list of the three points that seem most important to him or her. Compare the lists. Revise what you have written so that your important points are clear and strong.

If you have referred to any people (writer, filmmaker, musician, for example) in your essay, make sure your reader knows who these people are and why you refer to them.

IN YOUR JOURNAL

Make a list of the names that you have been called by at different points in your life. Next to each name, write who called you that name and what the name meant to you. Which name or names do you prefer and why?

First Born

Danjuma Sinue Modupe

Danjuma Sinue Modupe, aka Henry Evans, is a writing instructor at Hunter College in New York City. He has written many stories and essays that have appeared in a variety of publications including *Essence* magazine, the literary journals *Persea* and *Balaam's Ass/Fiction,* the Random House anthology *Amistad III,* and most recently, in 1994, in Viking Press's *Illuminating Tales of the Urban Black Experience.* This autobiographical story recalls events that happened when he was seven years old and that shaped his developing awareness of himself as an African American.

I'm not a person who remembers names. In fact, at a party once, three years into my marriage, to my mortification when making introductions, I blocked my wife's name. My friends have all learned to suffer this frailty and, recently, have taken great pleasure in my having several times forgotten my own name—that is, my reconstructed self, my African name. And yet, a name I haven't heard in over forty years rings in my ears now as sharply and familiarly as the chimes announcing 9:00 P.M. on the opposite, exposed-brick wall. "Missy," I write, putting pen to paper after a writer's block of seven years, and there is a tingle of expectancy. Missy, catalyst to my rebirth! This seems somehow so appropriate, like an African-fabled lesson I grasp at the level of intuition but fear I cannot yet put into words.

My immediate family—my mother, my four-year-old baby brother, and I—had just recently arrived in Harlem, a place I return to frequently now, to attend Black arts and political functions, eat soul food, and buy African clothes. Though our street was One-Hundred-Thirty-Eighth Street, I had spent school-day afternoons at Brownie's, the sitter's, on

One-Hundred-Fortieth Street. My brother and I wound up there on most weekends, too. The Harlem street—the corner fruit stand under whose bright green awning we kids sheltered from the rain, the "nickle-a-pickle" candy store, the row of five-story houses, the stoops upon which we children played—casualties of progress, are now gone. The oasis of a playground, which lay beyond the forbidding two-way traffic of Lenox Avenue, crossed only in the company of some responsible adolescent or adult, remains, dense with renovations and vibrant with colorful community murals. On occasion, Wendel, the super's adolescent son, volunteered to escort us kids—when he was not tinkering with his chemistry set or sneaking around the corner to a Lenox Avenue storefront, where between the spaces of the large, painted symbols on the windows I would peek in to see him among men wearing long white dresses and crocheted little caps and women wearing even longer dresses and white scarfs over their heads. The scene reminded me then of how Grandma Allie had insisted we boys wear "Grannie sack" smocks and had braided our hair until with the help of the menfolks we rebelled with the starting of school. It was one thing to dress those kids like that on the farm, the menfolks said, but another to send them boys like that to school. The men I saw through the storefront window spoke funny words, and always some person up front was yelling angrily at the audience about white and black people. The *I*-talian boys across the street from Brownie's would fight if you called them white, said they were black, a word I was not allowed to use. It was like a cuss word, but Missy used it, freely. She didn't believe those *I*-talian boys, said the black people that looked like them *I*-talian kids didn't have *two* white parents. I sort of sensed this was true.

Missy and I were both seven years old that early summer. But she was two grades ahead of me—one because I had been put back for having come up from the South, and another because she had already been skipped. But I was soon to gain back my grade the following year when I transferred to the all Black school up on Sugar Hill. 3

Missy was "wild," most grown-ups said, and her mother didn't go to church. Instead, she practiced something that had to do with "roots." But I knew, as my uncle said, Grandma Allie "fooled around with them roots," and it seemed like everybody around for miles at one time or another appeared on the horizon walking or poking along in a buggy or spinning up dust clouds in their fast cars as they came down our winding dirt road past the cemetery, the cow pasture, the wooded area of pines, then were announced by a front-yard flurry of black birds in the 4 plum, apple and lotus trees, then finally strolled up onto our porch for the "workings" of them roots. And yet, Grandma Allie went to church *every* Sunday, *and* got the spirit, spoke in tongues.

When Missy showed up on our stoop, Brownie never called us kids   5
inside, as did some mothers, who hung out of their windows and monitored street-life with a sagacity and moral aptitude that rivalled the attention paid to their "dreamed" numbers. "She's just a child, like any other child," Brownie would argue to the women in the building, including my aunt Minnie who, with her husband Bennie and my cousin Marie, lived "temporarily" on the top floor front, three-bedroom apartment with two other families, each saving for a "home." If memory hasn't deceivingly slipped into hindsight, I had already learned, intuited actually, not to notice Missy too much. Sometimes when I had jumped the most stoop steps or won at "skellies" or made my yoyo "sleep" the longest, I would look over and find Missy staring. My skin felt prickly, and yet underneath I glowed.

Skinny, ashy legs, limbs quick with a movement I can describe now as   6
a want of freedom that twirled her short, colorful skirts, and the glimpse of white cotton drawers seen and unseen back then return suddenly, and I pause from the writing, sit up at the desk, sigh, and sip my lukewarm coffee. There is a longing—for some "Missy-quality" apprehended but still not at the level of consciousness. Usually, I'm good at faces, but Missy's features remain a blur. Her hair was plaited in short tight braids, the prominent black eyebrows shiny against a velvety skin almost as black. Nothing memorable about her eyes, only they could narrow and pin you down like a won thumb wrestle. I remember her smell, clean, a scrubbed-child smell. She had this habit of biting down on the corner of her lip and staring off into the distance, and then . . .

The chipped slate steps were hot to the touch every afternoon those   7
last days of school. But on either side of the top step gray marble pillars set in blocks supported a shading, concrete overhang. Between the blocks and the buildings was a balustrade, forming an area we called wells. Cool places not much help in "hide-and-seek," they formed cul-de-sacs. Through the apartment building glass doors, at the end of a long, tiled hall, the older kids hung out in a much cooler place under the stairwell. They smoked cigarettes and allowed us smaller kids in only by invitation.

For whatever reason, the two of us, Missy and I, wound up on the   8
stoop, alone, that afternoon. I sat realizing a prayer had been answered I hadn't even known I'd said.

"Where you from, again," Missy was saying. 9

"I done told you I don't know how many times." 10

"Well, say it, again. I like the way you say it—all sing-song and 11
smooth like."

With anyone else I would have been fighting mad, but Missy really 12
liked my accent. She could imitate it perfectly.

"Nort Calinna," I said, and I remember Missy's flashy infectious 13
smile that made me homesick for the warm starry nights on our back
porch laid out with "pallets" for us kids and all around me late into the
night the eruption giggles and laughter until my sides ached.

Missy and I watched the street life and talked and talked and 14
talked. Then we were slapping and bumping each other, laughing as
the *I*-talian kids across the street, all six of them, stripped to their
underwear and darted in and out of the water spray of the "dump"
truck as it whined and groaned its way down the block. Under our
laughter, though, was a heaviness, an envy and regret which made us
avoid each other's eyes. At one point in the conversation, Missy said
matter-of-factly, as she stretched her forearm out along side of mine,
"You're as black as me."

We had moved from the steps to the secrecy and cool of one of the 15
stoop's wells. I stretched my arm the length of hers, coming into a
startled, queasy recognition.

"Yes," I said. 16

Grown-ups didn't care much about being tattletales. In fact, in those 17
days, if you sneezed on the steps after school, by the time you walked
those few blocks home, your mother would be waiting with a handkerchief.

When the woman had come up on us, unheard and unseen, Missy 18
had me pinned down against her in a headlock, her legs wrapped
around mine to keep me from getting leverage by pushing off the wall.
Before capitulating, I was suffering the indignity and pain as long as I
could. "Give? You give?" she screamed.

"Get up off of that girl," the woman exclaimed. And she was reach- 19
ing for me, jerking me by the arm. Looking up into a yellow-brown face
with a small scattering of cheek moles, I saw a pinched mouth as pink as
my favorite doll's, secreted away and waiting for me in the bureau
drawer of the attic back home in North Carolina. I resisted, frightened
and confused.

"Where's your mother, boy," the woman demanded, shaking me. 20
"And you, you little hussy."

Missy had sat up, and the way she looked into the woman's eyes so   21
questioningly seemed for a moment to make the woman falter. I didn't
want to tell the woman anything, but I didn't want to be spanked in
front of Missy, either.

"You wait right here, you hear me. Don't either of you budge, not   22
one inch!"

Through the glass doors I watched the woman, listened to the click   23
of her high heels fading down the hall until she reached the two doors
past the stairs. The one on the right was Brownie's. When I turned to
Missy, she was gone.

"Too big for your britches, boy," Brownie said.   24
"But I didn't *do* nothing."   25
"Then why you running from me?"   26

In the South, having around always anywhere from two to two dozen   27
cousins of all ages, there was always someone who had done something
to get a switching. I felt I had been getting them all along, too, but
realized I hadn't, hadn't even been slapped. I had always been "sickly,"
and "bright," and like Grandma Allie, "saw things." I was certain to be a
minister, everybody said. But I didn't think Brownie knew all this. Although I was terrified, my running was more a function of just not
knowing how to stand still for a beating. I was on the corner, attracting
attention. God didn't like ugly, and I was surely acting ugly. I felt if I
could just draw this out, the truth would somehow materialize. But there
were all these people standing around now, and Brownie, big and square
and black, and breathing scarily deep, her brow wrinkled, catching the
beads of sweat, was still clutching the cut-off broom handle.

Mr. Lionel, the corner fruit stand man, had actually left his cash   28
register, stood just outside his door. Like my never-seen father, he too
was called a "Geechee." He was between me and any attempt at turning
the corner, and although he had complimented my mother on how
mannerly and well-behaved her southern children were, I was sure he
was out of his store with the express purpose of grabbing me. Terror
swept me again, and I almost sprinted. Instead, I merely shifted from
one foot to the other, clutching myself. I had to go something terrible.
Then, to my amazement, Brownie had turned and was walking away. I
wanted to melt into the ground. After a while, quick stepping, I followed her.

As always, the apartment was surprisingly cool and occupied famil-   29
iarly with gospel music, like back home. Brownie was standing over the

ironing board. Behind her one of the two windows that looked out onto the back yard, from which we children dropped kitchen matches to explode on the concrete, was sucking the thin curtains out onto the fire escape. The Chesterfield hanging from her lips was half ash, but it never dropped to the clothes. The broom handle was nowhere in sight.

"Shut the door, boy, and go on in there and use the bathroom." 30

I stood my ground. 31

"Didn't you hear me, boy!" 32

"I don't have to go," I said softly. 33

"What?" 34

"Said I don't have to go." 35

Brownie looked up, stared at me a moment. 36

"Mr. Big britches," she said, "Well, you're going to stay in those wet 37
pants until your Mama comes."

I closed the door. 38

"And don't go sitting your stinking butt on any of my furniture." 39
She looked down at my pants again. "In the hall?"

I managed a nod. 40

She sighed. 41

I shifted away from the door when she passed, mop in hand. "A big 42
boy like you!" she added.

Mary and Carol-Anne were taking a dance class at the "Y" (they had 43
my brother with them, took him everywhere), so the sounds coming from the rear of the apartment meant that Bill was up. But that didn't matter, at least in terms of my catching it. It did somehow seem to mean that I couldn't watch Bill shave, then comb his hair. Always before he put on his mailman's uniform, he would stand before the bathroom mirror in his BVD's and with each front to back stroke of the comb run a hand over the jet-black straight hair with the waves up front.

I was sitting in the window praying for a breeze when Brownie 44
came in with the mop. She cut me that "Be still!" look, which meant don't go out onto the fire escape, don't go get any books off the self, and don't go bothering Bill, don't go doing *nothing!* When my mother arrived—the woman I was just getting to know, whom I still called by her first name and who still awed me with her fair-skinned and long, straight-haired beauty, Brownie didn't mention a thing about that afternoon. No one ever found out. The next time that I spent the night at Brownie's, when my mother was around the corner at the Savoy (she was always being asked out somewhere, sometimes with us kids), Brownie did something funny—gave me my bath with Carol-Anne.

No one after that had to tell me to leave Missy alone. She sensed   45
my coolness quickly, gradually stopped hanging around on our stoop,
and didn't walk with me and the guys anymore on the way home from
school. Then the week between school letting out and my being sent
south for the summer, Wendel had taken a group of us kids over to the
playground one day. Off in a far corner, a bunch of older girls were
jumping rope. Among them was Missy. It wasn't long before I spied
her coming across the playground. The way she was biting down on
her lip, I thought she was going to give me a good tongue-lashing or
sock me one, and when she didn't, I reached for the hope that she
might even apologize for leaving me to face Brownie alone and we
could maybe be friends again. I knew now that I wanted to be her
friend.

When she reached the monkey bars, she jerked me by the hand so   46
hard that I almost fell, then pulled me over to the back, shading wall of
the recreation center. She let go my hand and it remained for a moment
suspended, filled with the imprint of hers. She was looking at me
queerly, like you look at a stranger, someone you wanted to but wasn't
quite sure you could trust.

"I just wanted you to know," she said. "My name."   47
I stared at her, confused, somehow both relieved and disappointed.   48
"I already know your name," I said.   49
"My real name," she said. "It isn't Missy." Then she said it, and told   50
me what it meant.

I felt somehow betrayed, but felt, too, the revelation sink into   51
place somewhere deep inside me like a "click." Before I could respond,
she had turned and was running back across the playground to her
friends.

I put down my pencil, the fourth from a bunch of freshly sharpened   52
ones with crisp clean erasers taken from a cup on the desk. First drafts I
always do in longhand. I get up to go into the kitchen, just as the
chimes begin to strike for a new day. In the dark hall, the wall display of
African art objects and masks remind me of something, but I lose it as I
step into the white glare of kitchen light. Waiting for the water to boil, I
go to the kitchen window, pull back the left curtain. Lamplight pools on
the glistening wet street below, illumines a sheet of fine, gentle rain.
Before my divorce, before my psychic change, I was in love with the
Upper West Side, particularly its brownstone floor-through apartments, in one of which I now reside. The empty, bright-lighted street

that I now look down upon appears hard, foreign, and alien—softened and rendered hospitable only by the rain. I make a mental note to call my mother and ask for the photograph taken of me and my brother that summer, the one of us sitting on the running board of my uncle's, my namesake's, forty-seven Chevrolet, the summer I returned to find Missy had moved. The story written, I want to see myself, as if to reaffirm something I only half-believe I will recognize in myself in the photograph. The kettle whistles, and I go to the stove and pour the water for the coffee.

Sitting in the study again, I look at the title of the story, "Missy," written in large block print at the top of the yellow legal pad. At the bottom of the pad I begin to doodle. It is not long before I am somewhere distant, just below the line of wakefulness. Suddenly, I am remembering the two outstretched arms, mine perhaps even darker than Missy's. The face that appears before me is Missy's and not Missy's, is a carved, ebony mask. Like a blind man sensing with his fingers, I touch the almond eyes, the nose, the chin, then hear her voice. It sends me back above the line, and I am awake. I sit for a weary moment, trying to remember Missy's face, but it is no use. I rise finally, sighing, ready for bed. I take a few steps toward the light switch by the door, only to return to the desk and pick up the pencil and pad. I put a line through the story's title and write "Mosi," which I recall Missy having told me means first born.

Vocabulary

mortification (1)—shame, extreme embarrassment

catalyst (1)—a person or thing that brings about or hastens a result

sagacity (5)—wisdom

apprehended (6)—known

plaited (6)—braided

balustrade (7)—a railing held up by posts as on a staircase

cul-de-sacs (7)—passages or streets with only one exit; dead ends

Geechee (28)—a person born on the islands off North or South Carolina; a hick

IN YOUR JOURNAL

Think about a childhood playmate who made an impression on you. Write about that person. By what names did you call or refer to that playmate? What did that playmate call you?

A Closer Reading

1. What is Missy's real name? What does it mean? Why is it important to know this for your understanding of this story?

2. What is the meaning of "roots" as it is used in this story? What other meaning does the term "roots" have? How does the other meaning relate to the meaning of the story?

3. What indications do you get from this story that the community felt a responsibility for its children, for disciplining and making sure that children behaved correctly?

4. How does Modupe characterize the relationship between the African-American and the Italian-American people in the neighborhood? What stereotypes have the two groups developed about each other? Why do you think Modupe includes this information in this story?

Drawing Your Own Conclusions

1. Why does Modupe refer to his African name as his "reconstructed self"? Do you know anyone who has changed his or her name? Why? What effect did it have on this person's life?

2. Why do you think Modupe has begun to reflect on his early friendship with Missy/Mosi? How was Missy a "catalyst to his rebirth"?

3. Why does the woman call Missy a "little hussy"? Why doesn't she call the little boy by a similar term? What does this tell us about expectations for boys and girls?

4. Why do some women today decide to change or not to change their names when they get married? What is the significance of changing one's name upon marriage in relation to self-identity?

5. Why is the story in the unit on self-identity? How does the narrator indicate that he has changed his self-identity?

Thinking about Writing

1. Modupe switches time periods from paragraph 1 to paragraph 2. He switches time periods in other parts of the story as well. Find these time switches. What verbs tell you that it is in the past? What verbs tell you it is in the present? What other temporal words or phrases guide the reader? How does he make the transitions?

2. How do the last two words of the story connect to the rest of the story? Where in the story does Modupe reveal the birth order in his family?

3. Modupe tells his readers that he cannot remember Missy's face, but he does describe other aspects of her. What characteristics of this girl does he describe?

4. To what locations does Modupe refer in this story? What words does he use to describe these locations? What do these words reveal about Modupe's feelings for each of the places?

*   *   *

Suggestions for Writing

1. Write an essay about the origin of your name. Explain what your name means traditionally and/or today and why your family chose the name. What nicknames do you have and why? If you were to rename yourself, would you choose to keep your name? If so, why? If not, explain why not, and if possible offer a new name and explain why you chose it.

2. Write an autobiographical story about a childhood friend with whom you have lost contact. Tell about an event that took place with this friend that has influenced who you are today. As Modupe did, begin in the present, tell the story in the past, and return to the present to explain the significance of the story for you.

3. Write a story about a neighbor or distant relative who influenced you in some way. As Modupe did, begin in the present, tell the

story in the past, and return to the present to explain why this story has significance for you.

4. Write a story about an event that took place in a location other than the one in which you now live. Describe the place using language that helps your reader to know how you felt about this place. Again, as Modupe did, begin in the present, tell the story in the past, and return to the present to explain why this story has significance for you.

Strategies for Revision

You have written stories in which you had to use the past and present tenses. Reread what you have written focusing on verbs, descriptions of time, and other phrases that indicate to your reader whether you are writing about the past or the present. Share what you have written with a classmate and make sure that your references to time are clear. Make whatever revisions are necessary for your readers to follow your writing from present to past and back again.

IN YOUR JOURNAL

How do you identify yourself? As a woman or a man? As an Asian American, African American, European American, White, Black? As a Protestant, Jew, Catholic, Buddhist, or Muslim? These are just a few of the categories that people think about when they think about identity. Which groups do you identify with most when you describe yourself? In your journal, write about how you include yourself in particular groups.

Growing Up Asian in America

Kesaya E. Noda

Kesaya E. Noda was born in California and grew up in rural New Hampshire. She learned to speak Japanese after graduating from high school, when she spent two years living and studying in Japan. After she completed college, she spent two years researching and writing *The Yamato Colony,* a history of the California community where her grandparents settled and her parents grew up. Noda now works at Lesley College in Massachusetts. Her essay "Growing Up Asian in America" was published in Beacon Press's 1989 *Making Waves: An Anthology of Writings by and about Asian American Women.* It is about Noda's awareness of the stereotyping of Asians in the United States today and her developing sense of an Asian-American identity.

Sometimes when I was growing up, my identity seemed to hurtle   1
toward me and paste itself right to my face. I felt that way, encountering the stereotypes of my race perpetuated by non-Japanese people (primarily white) who may or may not have had contact with other Japanese in America. "You don't like cheese, do you?" someone would ask. "I know your people don't like cheese." Sometimes questions came making allusions to history. That was another aspect of the identity. Events that had happened quite apart from the me who stood silent in that moment connected my face with an incomprehensible past. "Your parents were in California? Were they in those camps during the war?" And sometimes there were phrases or nicknames: "Lotus Blossom." I was some-

times addressed or referred to as racially Japanese, sometimes as Japanese American, and sometimes as an Asian woman. Confusions and distortions abounded.

How is one to know and define oneself? From the inside—within a   2
context that is self defined, from a grounding in community and a connection with culture and history that are comfortably accepted? Or from the outside—in terms of messages received from the media and people who are often ignorant? Even as an adult I can still see two sides of my face and past. I can see from the inside out, in freedom. And I can see from the outside in, driven by the old voices of childhood and lost in anger and fear.

I Am Racially Japanese

A voice from my childhood says: "You are other. You are less than.   3
You are unalterably alien." This voice has its own history. We have indeed been seen as other and alien since the early years of our arrival in the United States. The very first immigrants were welcomed and sought as laborers to replace the dwindling numbers of Chinese, whose influx had been cut off by the Chinese Exclusion Act of 1882. The Japanese fell natural heir to the same anti-Asian prejudice that had arisen against the Chinese. As soon as they began striking for better wages, they were no longer welcomed.

I can see myself today as a person historically defined by law and   4
custom as being forever alien. Being neither "free white," nor "African," our people in California were deemed "aliens, ineligible for citizenship," no matter how long they intended to stay here. Aliens ineligible for citizenship were prohibited from owning, buying, or leasing land. They did not and could not belong here. The voice in me remembers that I am always a *Japanese* American in the eyes of many. A third-generation German American is an American. A third-generation Japanese American is a Japanese American. Being Japanese means being a danger to the country during the war and knowing how to use chopsticks. I wear this history on my face.

I move to the other side. I see a different light and claim a different   5
context. My race is a line that stretches across ocean and time to link me to the shrine where my grandmother was raised. Two high, white banners lift in the wind at the top of the stone steps leading to the shrine. It is time for the summer festival. Black characters are written against the sky as boldly as the clouds, as lightly as kites, as sharply as the big black

crows I used to see above the fields in New Hampshire. At festival time there is liquor and food, ritual, discipline, and abandonment. There is music and drunkenness and invocation. There is hope. Another season has come. Another season has gone.

I am racially Japanese. I have a certain claim to this crazy place   6 where the prayers intoned by a neighboring Shinto priest (standing in for my grandmother's nephew who is sick) are drowned out by the rehearsals for the pop singing contest in which most of the villagers will compete later that night. The village elders, the priest, and I stand respectfully upon the immaculate, shining wooden floor of the outer shrine, bowing our heads before the hidden powers. During the patchy intervals when I can hear him, I notice the priest has a stutter. His voice flutters up to my ears only occasionally because two men and a woman are singing gustily into a microphone in the compound, testing the sound system. A prerecorded tape of guitars, samisens, and drums accompanies them. Rock music and Shinto prayers. That night, to loud applause and cheers, a young man is given the award for the most *netsuretsu*—passionate, burning—rendition of a song. We roar our approval of the reward. Never mind that his voice had wandered and slid, now slightly above, now slightly below the given line of the melody. Netsuretsu. Netsuretsu.

In the morning, my grandmother's sister kneels at the foot of the   7 stone stairs to offer her morning prayers. She is too crippled to climb the stairs, so each morning she kneels here upon the path. She shuts her eyes for a few seconds, her motions as matter of fact as when she washes rice. I linger longer than she does, so reluctant to leave, savoring the connection I feel with my grandmother in America, the past, and the power that lives and shines in the morning sun.

Our family has served this shrine for generations. The family's need   8 to protect this claim to identity and place outweighs any individual claim to any individual hope. I am Japanese.

I Am a Japanese American

"Weak." I hear the voice from my childhood years. "Passive," I hear.   9 Our parents and grandparents were the ones who were put into those camps. They went without resistance; they offered cooperation as proof of loyalty to America. "Victim," I hear. And, "Silent."

Our parents are painted as hard workers who were socially uncom-   10 fortable and had difficulty expressing even the smallest opinion. Clean, quiet, motivated, and determined to match the American way; that is us, and that is the story of our time here.

"Why did you go into those camps," I raged at my parents, fright- 11
ened by my own inner silence and timidity. "Why didn't you do anything to resist? Why didn't you name it the injustice it was?" Couldn't
our parents even think? Couldn't they? Why were we so passive?

I shift my vision and my stance. I am in California. My uncle is in 12
the midst of the sweet potato harvest. He is pressed, trying to get the
harvesting crews onto the field as quickly as possible, worried about the
flow of equipment and people. His big pickup is pulled off to the side,
motor running, door ajar. I see two tractors in the yard in front of an
old shed; the flat bed harvesting platform on which the workers will
stand has already been brought over from the other field. It's early
morning. The workers stand loosely grouped and at ease, but my uncle
looks as harried and tense as a police officer trying to unsnarl a New
York City traffic jam. Driving toward the shed, I pull my car off the
road to make way for an approaching tractor. The front wheels of the
car sink luxuriously into the soft, white sand by the roadside and the car
slides to a dreamy halt, tail still on the road. I try to move forward. I try
to move back. The front bites contentedly into the sand, the back lifts
itself at a jaunty angle. My uncle sees me and storms down the road,
running. He is shouting before he is even near me.

"What's the matter with you," he screams. "What the hell are you 13
doing?" In his frenzy, he grabs his hat off his head and slashes it through
the air across his knee. He is beside himself. "Don't you know how to
drive in sand? What's the matter with you? You've blocked the whole
roadway. How am I supposed to get my tractors out of here? Can't you
use your head? You've cut off the whole roadway, and we've got to get
out of here."

I stand on the road before him helplessly thinking, "No, I don't 14
know how to drive in sand. I've never driven in sand."

"I'm sorry, uncle," I say, burying a smile beneath a look of sincere 15
apology. I notice my deep amusement and my affection for him with
great curiosity. I am usually devastated by anger. Not this time.

During the several years that follow I learn about the people and the 16
place, and much more about what has happened in this California
village where my parents grew up. The issei, our grandparents, made
this settlement in the desert. Their first crops were eaten by rabbits and
ravaged by insects. The land was so barren that men walking from
house to house sometimes got lost. Women came here too. They bore

children in 114 degree heat, then carried the babies with them into the fields to nurse when they reached the end of each row of grapes or other truck farm crops.

I had had no idea what it meant to buy this kind of land and make it grow green. Or how, when the war came, there was no space at all for the subtlety of being who we were—Japanese Americans. Either/or was the way. I hadn't understood that people were literally afraid for their lives then, that their money had been frozen in banks; that there was a five-mile travel limit; that when the early evening curfew came and they were inside their houses, some of them watched helplessly as people they knew went into their barns to steal their belongings. The police were patrolling the road, interested only in violators of curfew. There was no help for them in the face of thievery. I had not been able to imagine before what it must have felt like to be an American—to know absolutely that one is an American—and yet to have almost everyone else deny it. Not only deny it, but challenge that identity with machine guns and troops of white American soldiers. In those circumstances it was difficult to say, "I'm a Japanese American." "American" had to do. 17

But now I can say that I am a Japanese American. It means I have a place here in this country, too. I have a place here on the East Coast, where our neighbor is so much a part of our family that my mother never passes her house at night without glancing at the lights to see if she is home and safe; where my parents have hauled hundreds of pounds of rocks from fields and arduously planted Christmas trees and blueberries, lilacs, asparagus, and crab apples; where my father still dreams of angling a stream to a new bed so that he can dig a pond in the field and fill it with water and fish. "The neighbors already came for their Christmas tree?" he asks in December. "Did they like it? Did they like it?" 18

I have a place on the West Coast where my relatives still farm, where I heard the stories of feuds and backbiting, and where I saw that people survived and flourished because fundamentally they trusted and relied upon one another. A death in the family is not just a death in a family; it is a death in the community. I saw people help each other with money, materials, labor, attention, and time. I saw men gather once a year, without fail, to clean the grounds of a ninety-year-old woman who had helped the community before, during, and after the war. I saw her remembering them with birthday cards sent to each of their children. 19

I come from a people with a long memory and a distinctive grace. We live our thanks. And we are Americans. Japanese Americans. 20

Vocabulary

hurtle (1)—move quickly with great force

perpetuated (1)—preserved or maintained

allusions (1)—indirect references

abounded (1)—existed in large numbers

samisens (6)—Japanese musical instruments resembling a banjo with three strings

harried (12)—worried or tormented

IN YOUR JOURNAL

Looking at your earlier journal entry in which you listed the groups with which you identified, decide with which of these groups you identify the most. Explain your choice and why it means so much to you. How does belonging to this group affect your identity, the way you see yourself, and the way others see you?

A Closer Reading

1. According to Noda, what is the difference between knowing and defining oneself from the outside and doing so from the inside? Which method does she choose for herself?

2. To what stereotypes about Asians does Noda refer in her essay? What is her opinion of these stereotypes?

3. What historical examples of anti-Asian prejudice does Noda present as evidence in her essay? Why? How do these examples affect Noda today?

4. About which members of her family does Noda choose to write in this essay? What differences do you find in the lives and personalities of these individuals? What similarities do you find?

Drawing Your Own Conclusions

1. Why is it important to Noda that she see herself as a Japanese American and not just an American?

2. According to Noda, why did Japanese Americans submit to being sent to detention camps? How does their response affect her as a young Japanese American woman today?

3. What does Noda mean when she writes, "I can see myself today as a person historically defined by law and custom as being forever alien"?

4. What recent events have shown that anti-Asian prejudice still exists in the United States? Why do incidents of prejudice against different racial, religious, and ethnic groups still take place in our society today? Do you think they will lessen or increase in the future? Explain your answer.

Thinking about Writing

1. What Japanese words does Noda use in her essay? How does she indicate to her readers what these words mean? Why does she include these words?

2. Reread the parts of the essay in which Noda describes being in Japan. What does she feel about this visit? Point out words or phrases that reveal her feelings to you.

3. Which location contributed most to her self-identity? Explain your answer, citing parts of the essay for evidence.
   a. Look at the passages in which Noda describes being in California. How does she feel about this experience? What specific words indicate her feelings to you?
   b. Consider how Noda describes being in New Hampshire. What does she feel about this experience? Choose the specific words that indicate her feelings to you.

4. What is the significance of farming and planting? What do these activities mean symbolically for the future?

*   *   *

Suggestions for Writing

1. Write an essay in which you define what it means to be an American. Include some examples that explain why your definition is appropriate in today's world.

2. Some people believe that it is wrong to use the name "American" for people who are citizens of the United States. They are con-

cerned because people who live in countries such as Canada, Mexico, Peru, and Guatemala are Americans too. What name do you think people who live in the United States should be called? Explain your answer in an essay.

3. Have you ever experienced prejudice? Write an essay in which you describe your experience. How did this experience affect you?

4. Can learning about different cultures help to make people more tolerant of each other? In an essay, answer this question and support your answer with specific incidents and events that you have experienced or read about.

Strategies for Revision

Two of the four essays you have read include *definition* in one form or another. Reread your drafts, making sure that you include details of special characteristics that describe the term or idea clearly. You may want to look at a dictionary for ideas and then paraphrase or rewrite in your own words. When you paraphrase, you do not need to use quotation marks, but you do need to acknowledge or state the source from which you got your ideas.

If you use someone else's exact words, make sure you use quotation marks and acknowledge the title and page number of the source you used.

IN YOUR JOURNAL

Our self-identity includes our sexual identity and our ability to be intimately involved with another person. Write about this aspect of your self-identity in your journal. (This need not be turned in to your instructor.)

Coming Out Now

James N. Baker

James N. Baker wrote this article for a special issue of *Newsweek* written for young people that was published in 1990. In it, Baker describes the lifestyle of Daniel Layer, an eighteen-year-old gay man who is learning the importance of finding role models and planning for future possibilities in the time of the AIDS crisis.

Here's how Daniel Paul Layer Jr., 18, of Castro Valley, Calif., sees himself in 20 years: "I'll have my own business and have made enough money to do what I want . . . I'll have a house in the country . . . I'll have been settled down with somebody for a long time, and have three children: a boy to carry on my family name, a girl to spoil and an 'It'—whatever the third child happens to be. The first two will be mine, but the third could be adopted."

An ordinary enough dream for a teenager—but Daniel Layer is gay. Ten years ago not many gay adolescents would have considered such a dream obtainable. Traditionally, growing up gay has meant years of self-loathing and a sense of isolation from classmates and family. Hesitant to combat the social sentiments that gay is not good, many gay teenagers still repress their homosexuality until adulthood, spending their adolescence pretending to be straight. Meanwhile, other impulses are at work: in an era when teens feel peer pressure to experiment with sex earlier, many are often forced to face the question, "Am I gay or not?" long before they're ready. For those who are gay, the strain often leads to depression. Paul Gibson, a San Francisco social worker who did a study of teen suicide for the U.S. Department of Health and Human Services, believes gays nationwide account for 30 percent of all teen attempts. "The root of the problem," says Gibson, "is a society that stigmatizes homosexuals while failing to recognize that a substantial number of its youth are gay."

On top of that, young gay men must now confront the specter of an   3
early death from AIDS. But ironically the AIDS crisis has also made it easier for some homosexual teenagers: over the last decade Gay America has become more visible, often in a positive light as it took care of its own sick and dying. Gay characters now show up on television and in movies, such as the recent "Longtime Companion," the first feature film about AIDS in the gay community. News reports proliferate about the gay-rights movement, the phenomena of gay surrogate parenting and adoption, and about prominent figures who are homosexual—all of them, from congressmen to local AIDS volunteers, providing high-profile role models and raising the expectations of gay youth. Daniel Layer believes AIDS has made many Americans recognize that a gay subculture exists. "AIDS has gotten the straight world involved in the gay world," he says.

The future looks bright to Daniel, thanks to good counseling and an   4
understanding mother. But getting this far was a struggle. His parents divorced when their only child was 3, and Daniel lived with his mother in Auburn, Wash., where she was studying to be a draftsman. On some weekends he visited Daniel Sr., a diesel mechanic, and after his father remarried, Daniel was joined by a stepbrother and a baby sister. Though Daniel liked having a family, he says his father, once a paratrooper in Vietnam, could be intense. His stepmother was a fundamentalist Christian, and Daniel says that she and his father were strict disciplinarians who didn't hesitate to punish him severely. "When he'd come back it'd take two weeks to put him back together," says Heather, 37, Daniel's mother. In 1981, to get a fresh start, Heather took her son to live in Tulsa, Okla., her hometown.

In sixth grade, Daniel got an early taste of homophobia. He and   5
Heather had just moved back west to Tracy, Calif. "A redneck town," says Daniel. "The kids were all Chicanos and cowboys, very rough." On his first day Daniel wore a brightly colored jacket with a big collar that he thought was hip and would help him fit in. He miscalculated—drastically—and heard himself called "fag" for the first time. "The word meant absolutely nothing to me," he said. "I just knew I'd gone from being a popular kid [in Tulsa] to one of the biggest nerds in school."

Daniel says junior high was a nightmare. Because he didn't conform   6
to the local macho standards of dress and behavior, he was challenged to fistfights daily. Once in biology lab classmates threw frogs that they had

been dissecting at him. Another time, after a water-polo game, a student held him underwater so long that he almost drowned. Daniel grew depressed, got erratic grades and became rebellious. His weight shot up—"I oinked out," he says—and he quarreled constantly with Heather.

At the same time, Daniel says he recognized that the name-calling 7 wasn't entirely off the mark. "Their words hurt a lot worse because I knew they were true," he says. He was beginning to realize he was sexually attracted to boys, and went to the library to find books and magazine articles on homosexuality. He also started seeing a family counselor to make peace at home, and a school counselor with whom he discussed his feelings of homosexuality. The school counselor's response was orthodox; she told him youngsters often go through a homosexual phase and that he could still grow up straight, marry and have a family. Hoping the counselor was right, he dated girls, but says he soon realized he was deceiving himself. Daniel kept his homosexuality from his mother and the family counselor, but his sexual confusion and years of taunting had taken their toll. "The family counselor told me to take him out of there and move to the Bay Area," says Heather, "or I would wind up with a dead son." Daniel never considered suicide, but he believes he might have if he had stayed in Tracy.

During his four high-school years in the suburban Bay Area, Daniel 8 continued the painstaking process of accepting his homosexuality. Students at Castro Valley High School are tolerant of differences—one popular clique, with spiky, tie-dyed hair, would look at home in New York's East Village. Though he never came out publicly at school, he was discreetly involved with another gay student for two years.

What helped most was his improved relationship with his mother. 9 Heather says she always worried about the absence of a male role model; she suspected he might be gay, but says, "He had me fooled with all that talk about wanting children." When, at 15, he finally told her he was homosexual, he says she didn't berate him, but instead tracked down a counseling group for gay teenagers in Berkeley. "She thought I would make friends," says Daniel.

Daniel's development took a critical turn in the summer of 1988. 10 Working as a salesclerk at a shopping mall, he fell in with a suburban network of young gay men who copied the fast-track behavior of San Francisco: a steady round of dance clubs, stylish clothes—and casual sex. Daniel followed the pack, but says he has since pulled away. He wants someone steady in his life, and doesn't think he can find him there. "They see someone for a month and say they have a boyfriend," he says.

In this period, Daniel also learned firsthand about fear of AIDS. He   11
insists that he and his generation practice safe sex as a matter of course. "We grew up with AIDS," Daniel says. "You just use condoms without thinking about it." But as his sexual experience grew, Daniel began to worry that he may have somehow been exposed to the virus. In October 1989 he took the HIV-antibody test—and was negative.

Daniel appears to have adjusted to his homosexuality at an age when   12
many teenagers are just beginning the struggle. "My friends are starting to call me the gay poster child," he says. But he still attends a group-therapy session in San Francisco where gay teens complain of being harassed for their sexuality. "When I say 'Mom, Dad, I can't solve this math equation'," says Peter, a member of Daniel's group, "they answer, 'Well, if you weren't gay . . .' " The group shares its thoughts of suicide, fear of AIDS and anger at being ostracized by classmates. "You miss out on dating," says another group member. "You feel socially retarded."

Adolescence is never easy, but growing up gay has always been   13
trying. For Daniel Layer, the path to self-esteem and sexual maturity dovetails with a quest for stability in his home life. Recently he walked around San Francisco's predominantly gay Castro district, where bar-hopping young men bustle past neighbors on canes, their unearthly pale faces the hallmark of AIDS. But which of all the images of gay life in the Castro struck Daniel most? A couple in their 70s, helping each other down the street, both of them men.

Vocabulary

repress (2)—strictly control

stigmatizes (2)—marks as shameful

specter (3)—a ghost or a strange frightening figure

proliferate (3)—multiply rapidly

homophobia (5)—hatred or fear of homosexuals

berate (9)—scold angrily

ostracized (12)—banished or excluded

IN YOUR JOURNAL

How do you see yourself in twenty years? Think about yourself in relation to your sexual identity and the intimate connections you would like to have with another person. Write about the future that you would like to see for yourself.

A Closer Reading

1. What have been some of the effects of the AIDS crisis on gay people?

2. According to the article, why do gays make up such a large percentage of the teenagers attempting suicide in the United States?

3. When did Daniel Layer realize he was gay? What steps did he take to understand his feelings?

4. Why did Daniel and his mother move to San Francisco? What did they both gain from this move? Why did these positive changes occur?

5. What in society has changed that makes Daniel Layer's dream to have a family more possible today than it was ten years ago?

Drawing Your Own Conclusions

1. How are gays and lesbians treated in your college? How were they treated in your high school? Are there clubs for gays and lesbians? How are they described in the college newspaper?

2. In what public ways have gay men and lesbians attempted to make the non-gay segment of society aware of their lifestyles, their problems, and their successes in recent years?

3. Are young people in the United States forced to deal with sexuality at too early an age? What examples support your point of view?

4. Should colleges take substantial steps to ensure that all students know about safe sex? If so, what information should they provide at the college level? How could they get this information to

students on your campus? If not, state reasons why sex education should not be provided in college.

Thinking about Writing

1. In paragraph 4, the author begins with the following statement: "The future looks bright to Daniel, thanks to good counseling and an understanding mother. But getting this far was a struggle." What evidence does he provide in this paragraph that life was a struggle for Daniel?

2. In paragraph 6, the author states, "Daniel says junior high was a nightmare." What evidence does he provide to support this idea?

3. Reread the article looking at the use of quotation marks. When did the author choose to quote Daniel and for what purposes?

4. What are the names and positions of the authorities to whom Baker refers when he describes some of Daniel's problems? Why would an author want to include statements by authorities in his or her writing?

*   *   *

Suggestions for Writing

1. Write an essay in which you describe a movie, book, or television program in which a gay or lesbian was depicted as either the central or supporting character. Explain why you think the depiction was fair or unfair. In your essay, include a paragraph or two on how this description affected your perception of gays and lesbians.

2. Write an essay in which you analyze how popular media influence the development of sexual identity. Think about advertisements, television programs, films, newspapers, and magazines. What has the role of media been in the development of your sexual identity? What changes, if any, would you like to see made in the way sexuality is portrayed in the media? Explain the reasons for your choices.

3. In some cities, small alternative high schools have been set up for gay students. In an essay explain why you think this is a good or bad idea. Show what you perceive to be the positive or negative effects of such an institution.

4. Presently, many school systems are making decisions about sex education. At what grade should it begin? What types of information should children receive at different ages? Should students study about homosexuality? Is there still a need for sex education in college? What would you include in a program in your school? Write an essay answering these questions about the role schools should play in sex education.

5. Should all people be required to be tested for the HIV virus? What are the implications of the fact that thousands of people have this virus who do not know it now? What are the consequences of knowing this? Write an essay in which you explore these questions.

Collaborative Project

According to this article, the media (television, films, newspapers, and magazines) have affected the public's perception of the gay lifestyle. What examples does this article provide? As a class, discuss the ways in which the media present the gay lifestyle in your community. Review recent local newspaper and magazine articles that describe issues relating to gay men and lesbians. Watch television and listen to the radio, searching for references to gay and lesbian issues. How are they covered? What terms are used to describe people? Think about how this coverage has affected your feelings and perceptions.

Strategies for Revision

Reread your essay focusing on the use of authorities in supporting your ideas. Do you give each person's full name and title? If you refer to the person again, do you refer to the person by her or his last name only? ("Baker states that teens may have to face the question of whether they are gay or not before they are ready to handle the consequences.") Do you quote from this person, or do you directly paraphrase what he or she said? If you quote, use quotation marks. If you paraphrase, make sure your readers know from where your ideas originated. Make sure your readers know why this person's authority adds weight or substance to your point of view.

IN YOUR JOURNAL

In young adulthood, according to the author, "decisions must be made. Problems must be solved. The very ability to respond to change and to adapt successfully to new conditions is a hallmark of maturity." Write about a recent decision that you made and a recent problem that you solved.

Early Adulthood: Roles and Issues

Grace J. Craig

Grace J. Craig teaches at the University of Massachusetts. In 1992, her textbook, *Human Development,* was published in its sixth edition. The book is used by thousands of college students as they learn about the life span of humans from conception to death. The following excerpt from the book deals with the part of life from age sixteen to age forty-five. In it, Craig describes a study conducted by a psychologist, Roger Gould. Using extensive interviews, Gould developed life histories or biographies of a large group of men and women. He wanted to find out about their assumptions, ideas, myths, and world views during different periods in their early adult life.

Development—or at least the potential for development—continues 1
throughout life. Although some theorists argue that there are recognizable developmental stages in adulthood, the developmental process during maturity differs somewhat from the developmental processes that take place during childhood and adolescence. Changes in adult thought, behavior, and personality are less a result of chronological age or specific biological changes and are more a result of personal, social, and cultural events or forces. The social milestones and cultural demands of the young adult disrupt behavior patterns laid down in the teenage years, requiring that new ones be developed. Decisions must be made. Problems must be solved. The very ability to respond to change and to adapt successfully to new conditions is a hallmark of maturity. A positive resolution of contradictions and difficulties is the basis of adult activity (Datan & Ginsberg, 1975). This more gradual structuring and restructuring of social under-

standing and behavior does not fit neatly into a stage development theory. Not all adults progress in the same way or structure their lives in a similar fashion. Nevertheless, there are some commonalities in the developmental processes of adulthood.

Psychologist Roger Gould's (1978) studies of adults included both men and women, although his subjects are by no means representative. Gould and his colleagues examined extensive life histories of a large group of men and women, aged 16 to 60. From these profiles, they extracted world views characteristic of different adult stages. Gould views growth as the process of casting off childish illusions and false assumptions in favor of self-reliance and self-acceptance. . . . he believes that an individual's system of "meaning making" shapes his or her behavior and life decisions.

From ages 16 to 22, according to Gould, the major false assumption to be challenged is: "I'll always belong to my parents and believe in their world." To penetrate and discard this illusion, young adults must start building an adult identity that their parents cannot control or dominate. Young people's sense of self, however, is still fragile at this point, and self-doubt makes them highly sensitive to criticism. Young adults also begin to see their parents as imperfect and fallible people, not the all-powerful, controlling forces they once were.

From 22 to 28, young adults make another false assumption that reflects their continuing doubts about self-sufficiency: "Doing things my parents' way, with will-power and perseverance, will bring results. But if I become too frustrated, confused, or tired, or am simply unable to cope, they will step in and show me the right way." To combat this notion, the young adult must accept full responsibility for his or her life, surrendering the expectation of continuous parental assistance. This involves far more than wresting oneself from a mother's or father's domination; it requires the active, positive construction of an adult life. Aggression is rechanneled toward adult work instead of ancient grievances. Conquering the world on one's own also diverts energy from constant introspection and self-centeredness. Gould found that the predominant thinking mode during this period progresses from flashes of insight to perseverance, discipline, controlled experimentation, and goal orientation.

In Gould's view, from ages 28 to 34 a significant shift occurs toward adult attitudes. The major false assumption during this period is: "Life is simple and controllable. There are no significant coexisting contradictory forces within me." This attitude differs from those in the previous stages in two important respects. First, it indicates a sense of competence and, second, an acknowledgment of limitations. Enough adult consciousness has been achieved to admit inner turmoil without calling strength or integrity into doubt. Talents, strengths, and desires, suppressed during the 20s because they did not fit into the unfolding blueprint of adulthood, may resurface. Gould cites examples of the ambitious young partner in a prestigious law firm who begins to consider public service; also, the suave, carefree bachelor who suddenly realizes that his many relationships with women are not satisfying because of some inadequacy of is own. (This development closely resembles [developmental psychologist] Levinson's prediction about the dream: Those who ignore and suppress it in early adulthood will be haunted later by the unresolved conflict.) Even those who have fulfilled youthful ambition still experience some doubt, confusion, and depression during this period. They may begin to question the very values that helped them to gain independence from their parents.

Growth during this period involves breaking out of the rigid expec-   6
tations of the 20s and embracing the more reasonable attitude: "What I get is directly related to how much effort I'm willing to make." Those in this period of life cease to believe in magic, and they begin to put their faith in disciplined, well-directed work. At the same time, Gould believes, they now begin to cultivate the interests, values, and qualities that will endure and develop through adult life.

The age period of 35 to 45 brings definitive involvement in the   7
adult world as these people become the final authority to those both younger and older than themselves. Their parents no longer have control of them; their children have not yet effectively challenged them. They are, as Gould says, "in the thicket of life." At the same time, they experience a sudden time pressure and fear that they will not accomplish all of their goals. The beginning physical changes of middle age frighten and dismay them; reduced career mobility pens them in. The drive for stability and security, which was paramount in the 30s, is replaced by a need for immediate action and results. There can be no more procrastination. The deaths of their parents and their acute awareness of their own mortality bring them face to face with the unfairness and pain of life. In acknowledging the ugly side of human existence, they let go of their childish needs for safety. They also become free at last to examine and discard the deep sense of their own worthlessness and wickedness, which was left over from childhood. This, Gould believes, represents a full, autonomous adult consciousness.

Theories that emphasize period or "stages" are valuable in under- 8
standing adult development, but they should not be too rigidly interpreted. First, the notion of stages in adulthood tends to obscure the
stability of personality, which is somewhat true throughout adulthood.
Second, these theories pay little attention to the unpredictability of life
(Neugarten, 1979). Third, most subjects of stage theories thus far have
been men, and much of the research has concentrated on the same age
cohorts (individuals born in the late 1920s or 1930s).

References

Datan, N., & Ginsberg, L. (Eds.). (1975). *Life-span developmental psychology.*
New York: Academic Press.

Gould, R. L. (1978). *Transformations, growth, and change in adult life.* New
York: Simon & Schuster.

Levinson, D. J. (1978). *The seasons of a man's life.* New York: Knopf.

Levinson, D. (1986). A conception of adult development. *American Psychologist, 41,* 3–13.

Levinson, D. (1990). *The seasons of a woman's life: Implications for women and
men.* Presented at the 98th convention of the American Psychological
Association, Boston.

Neugarten, B. L. (1979). Time, age and the life cycle. *American Journal of
Psychiatry, 136,* 887–894.

Vocabulary

wresting (4)—pulling or forcing
away

introspection (4)—a looking into
one's own feelings and
thoughts

coexisting (5)—existing or living
together at the same time

turmoil (5)—confusion or com-
motion

suppress (5)—to put down by force

thicket (7)—a thick growth of
small trees or bushes

procrastination (7)—the habitual
putting off of doing something to the future

autonomous (7)—functioning in-
dependently without the control of others

obscure (8)—not clear, not easily
seen

cohorts (8)—a group that has
something in common

IN YOUR JOURNAL

Looking back at your original entry, explain how you made the decision or handled the problem in a way that was different from the way you would have handled similar circumstances at another point in your life.

A Closer Reading

1. What differences are there between the developmental processes that occur during childhood and adolescence and those that occur during early adulthood?

2. What is the major change that is made from ages sixteen to twenty-two, according to Gould?

3. What is the major change that is made from ages twenty-two to twenty-eight, according to Gould?

4. What is the major change that is made from ages twenty-eight to thirty-four, according to Gould?

5. What is the major change that is made from age thirty-five to forty-five, according to Gould?

Drawing Your Own Conclusions

1. How does self-identity change in adulthood? Based on your own observations, identify any aspects of self that do not change throughout life.

2. What are some of the social milestones and cultural demands of young adulthood? How can these affect life behavior patterns?

3. One limitation of the study is that the stages of early adulthood may not be generalizable to all cultures and societies. What differences might there be in different societies and/or cultures? Give examples to explain your answers. What other limitations are there to the Gould study?

4. Reread the Viramontes (see page 5), Modupe (see page 20), Noda (see page 31), and/or Baker (see page 39) selections. Thinking about the issues on which they focus, decide in which life

stage these authors are. If their birthdates are not identified, check biographical sources in your college library to find out this information about them.

Thinking about Writing

1. What is the main idea of this selection? Where in the selection is the main idea stated?

2. Why did Gould use interviews to conduct his study? Judging from the information he discovered, what questions did he ask the people who participated in the study?

3. In presenting Gould's theory, Craig introduced the material and divided the findings of the study into categories. What categories did she use to divide the study? What other way could she have presented this material?

4. To what do the names and dates in parentheses throughout the section refer? Look at the references listed at the end of the selection and match them up with the names cited in the selection. Why is it important to include a date? Why are certain words in italics? To what do the numbers at the end of Levinson and Neugarten citation refer?

*   *   *

Suggestions for Writing

1. Reread your answers to questions 2 through 5 in "A Closer Reading." Using that information as a starting point, write a summary of the Craig selection.

Writing a Summary

Writing a *summary* is a method of processing at a deeper semantic level or a deeper level of meaning since you as a reader and writer are examining a piece of writing very closely. You are then rewriting it in your own words and in that way making it your own.

You are looking for the main ideas and the supporting details to better understand what you have read. Then you are reconstructing or rewriting in your own words just those points. A summary shortens a piece of writing to its main ideas, the supporting details, and any important quotations. The summary is usually written in the same order as the original.

One technique for writing a summary includes the following. First, number the paragraphs in the piece of writing that you are going to summarize; write the numbers in pencil in the margin. Then on a blank piece of paper, write the number one. Next to this write the main point of the paragraph and just list the supporting details or any interesting quotation. Do this for each paragraph. When you finish this, you will have the outline or basic parts of your summary. Then rewrite what you have written in essay form.

When you have finished your summary, look it over and ask yourself the following questions:

- Is the author's main idea clear?
- Is the main point from each paragraph clearly stated?
- Have I included the most important supporting details—facts, observations, and experiences?
- If I read this summary later on, will I understand what the original article was about?

2. Reread the description of the life stage that is appropriate for your age group. Write an essay in which you compare your own experiences with the life stage as described in Gould's findings. What similarities and differences are there? Explain whether the similarities and differences can be explained by the information provided in paragraph 8 of the Craig selection.

3. Write an essay in which you focus on one of the authors in this unit in relation to the life stages described in this selection. Describe the author's background, interests, assumptions, and to what degree he or she corresponds to one of the life stages described in this selection. What did you learn about the author, the life-stage theory, and other factors in writing about this?

4. Interview a person in your class, family, or neighborhood. Ask the person to tell you about his or her life. Take notes as the person talks to you. Read through your notes identifying the person's background interests, and assumptions. Describe the person in your essay and decide to what degree he or she corresponds to one of the life stages described in this selection.

Collaborative Project

As a class, discuss the differences you would expect to find in the life stages of men and women. Make a list of differences you would expect to find.

At what points in life would the following be more important for women than for men, for men than for women? Having independence? Belonging to something? Finding a spouse? Having children? Getting a good job? Finding a place to live? Taking care of children? Taking care of appearance? Write an essay in which you describe some of the differences and explain why they exist.

Strategies for Revision

Because most of the writing you have done thus far has been about people's lives, it is important to focus on:

1. The order in which you present information. Reread your draft looking at:
   a. The ways you indicate past, present, and future.
   b. Temporal words you use to indicate *when* events took place—first, next, then, before, after.
2. The way in which you describe people and events. Reread your draft looking at:
   a. The words you use to describe appearances of people. Make sure you use strong, clear, interesting words that make the person come alive to a reader.
   b. The words you use to indicate *where* an event occurred. Make sure you use varied and interesting words so your reader can picture the event and follow your story.
   c. The words you use to indicate *what* a person said. Make sure that each of the people you describe has a personal voice. They should not all talk exactly the same way.

Yvette Montalvo wrote this essay for her writing class. She was responding to suggestion 1 from the Suggestions for Writing that follow the Zadrzynska section: Begin your own story by rewording paragraph 4 as your first paragraph. Use your imagination to describe the contents of the trunk you found, what you did with it, and what it meant to you.

The Trunk

Yvette Montalvo

As I was on my way home from school, I saw a trunk that looked just like the one I had at home. I stopped and stared at it. I knew I had to open it and find out what was inside. I went up to the trunk and opened it. Inside it had many different things that reminded me of someone close to my heart. 1

The first thing I saw was an old teddy bear that looked just like the one I have had for sixteen years. The trunk also had a chewed cigar that reminded me of my grandmother. When I was little, I watched my grandmother smoke big fat cigars. After she would finish smoking her cigar, she would bite a piece off the end and chew it. 2

The trunk also had a little piece of fur from a strange animal. The fur made me think of my little brother. In order for him to fall asleep, he needs something with a lot of fur on it. My brother likes the way fur feels. It allows him to relax and eventually fall asleep. 3

As I looked further in the trunk, I saw a very old blow dryer. The blow dryer was rusty and dirty. All the control buttons had fallen off. This reminded me of my sister because she is always blowing her hair out. The trunk also had a black skirt in it. The skirt went down below the knees with a split in the back. That automatically made me think of my mother. This is because my mother is always wearing black skirts. She never wears pants because she does not like them. 4

All the way at the bottom of the trunk, I found an old cooking pot. That made me think of my stepfather who makes a living making pots. Inside the pot, I found a bunch of love letters with a friendship bracelet. The bracelet was handmade in black. This made me think of my boy- 5 friend who has written me so many letters. The friendship bracelet was given to him by me when we first started dating.

After looking through the trunk, I realized that the trunk meant a 　6
lot to me. It was my memories, my life, in someone else's trunk. I decided to take the trunk home with me. I had my boyfriend help me carry it to the apartment. I kept the trunk and everything that was inside. I set the trunk right next to my trunk that had the exact same things inside.

Questions to Think About

1. According to this essay, who are the the most important people in Yvette Montalvo's life? What else did you learn about the writer from this essay?

2. Which item in Montalvo's trunk was the most interesting to you? Which item would you like to know more about?

MAKING CONNECTIONS
The World of the Self: *Developing an Identity*

1. Using the selections that you have read in this unit, write an essay explaining how the various authors found their self-identity. You may want to paraphrase or directly quote from some of the articles you have read or develop further some of the writing you have already done in this unit.

2. Using the selections that you have read in this unit, write an essay explaining how the cultural backgrounds of one or more of the various authors influenced their self-identity. Compare your own experiences with culture and self-identity to the author(s) you have chosen.

3. Write an essay in which you examine the ways in which place, the area in which people live has influenced their concept of self. Reread the Viramontes (see page 5), Modupe (see page 20), Noda (see page 31), and Baker (see page 39) selections, focusing on their descriptions of the places where they live now and when they were younger. Explain how these places affected their self-identity.

4. Write an introduction to this unit in which you tell other students which piece of writing is the most interesting, the most informative, the best written. Recommend one piece of writing out of those you have read. Using quotations from the selection, convince a potential reader to choose this particular piece of writing to read.

5. Imagine that Kesaya E. Noda (see page 31) and Helena María Viramontes (see page 5) meet to discuss self-identity. Using dialogue and quotations, write down their conversation after rereading their selections.

6. Go to the reference section of your college library. Ask the librarian for the appropriate biographical listing (*American Authors, Women Writers,* etc.) and read the short biographical entry on one of the authors in this unit. Write an essay in which you tell about the writer and explain which specific elements in the person's background give you insights into this person's writing.

2

THE WORLD OF THE FAMILY

Making the First Connections

Through our families, we learn how to reach out to the world, to make our needs known, to find our way, and to feel the joy of being loved and the pain of being rejected. Each family is unique in relation to particular events and individual people. However, the structure of every family is always a complex web that reveals much of who we are and what we need and want from our lives.

Pearl Rowe's story tells about the love of a mother for her family. In it, a mother who is unable to write in English keeps her nine-year-old daughter up past her bedtime to write a letter that contains a final message for the whole family.

Next, John Edgar Wideman's story, set in a world of racism and inequalities, is about a father and son. The story takes place in several time frames as the narrator tells his tale through the eyes of a child and then of an adult.

"Beginnings" by educator and sociologist Sara Lawrence Lightfoot is an excerpt from Lightfoot's biography of her mother, child psychiatrist Margaret Lawrence. The selection is about their relationship and about the enduring power of family.

The next selection is from Maxine Hong Kingston's second book, *China Men*. Kingston tells the story of the fifteen-year separation of a couple and their individual adjustments to their new life as a couple in the United States. It is a story of growth and change and the endurance of a marriage despite distance and years of separation.

"Myths of Blame: The Family Scapegoat" by Elizabeth Stone shows how family secrets and myths often reveal much about the structure of the family. Stone tells about a successful man who explains his childhood weakness in a very strange way. Stone demonstrates how his story maintains the myth that his sister is the bad one in the family. Stone believes that by telling family stories, people can often free themselves from the tyranny of the past.

In "Families of the Future," Alvin Toffler, a social analyst, explains that the nuclear family is undergoing change and that the varieties in the structures of the modern family are not easily defined. Toffler uses examples from around the world to illustrate the wide range of family structures that exist in our world today.

Student writer Sharon Cassell writes a family story about her father, reflecting on the ways her relationship with him has changed over time.

*　　*　　*

Think about the following questions before reading the selections in this unit:

1. What does your family mean to you? Make a list in order of the five members of your family who are most important to you.

2. If you had written this list ten years ago, what people would you have included?

3. What differences are there between your two lists? Why?

IN YOUR JOURNAL

When we think back to our childhood, there are certain memorable events that stand out. These events made a deep impression on us as young children. Before you read the following story, write about an event that stands out from your childhood.

Cookies at Midnight

Pearl Rowe

The following story by Pearl Rowe was published in the *Los Angeles Times* in 1980 and then in the *Pittsburgh Press* the same year. It is a tender story about a mother who must find a way to communicate her special wishes to her family. It is also an example of fine storytelling, originally presented in a journalistic format.

My mother and I stayed up almost all night once when I was 9. She 1 sat at the kitchen table laboring over a letter that she was writing in Yiddish. (She was unable to write English; even Yiddish was hard for her.)

Like a restless puppy, I circled the kitchen table, sensing that some- 2 thing was wrong. My mother always sent me to bed early on school nights. But not that night.

"Ma, don't you think I should be in bed by now?" I asked, uncom- 3 fortable with the lawless freedom.

"I want you should stay up for a while yet. It wouldn't hurt one 4 night."

My four brothers, sister, and father, all older than I, were properly 5 asleep. I took my rag doll by the arm and swung her around over my head, trying to get some attention. "Dolly's dizzy, Ma."

"Put her head between her legs." 6

"Could I have some cookies?" 7

She answered without looking up. "Take some out of the box, but 8 close it tight, I think I saw a rat in the pantry."

It was unheard of. Cookies at midnight. I threw in some heavy 9 artillery. "They sent Ida home from school today with nits. Teacher said you should wash my hair with kerosene because I sat next to her."

"That's nice."   10

"Maaa!" I started to cry.   11

My mother looked up.   12

"Ma, are you smoking?"   13

"Just for a change. Only for a change."   14

That was some crazy night. My mother was so different from how I   15
had ever seen her before. I decided it would be a good time to sneak in
the important question. At least she wasn't busy plucking dead chickens
or washing laundry on the scrub board. In her preoccupation she
seemed somehow more accessible to me.

"Ma, do some people live forever?"   16

I had reached her. She looked up. "Yes, baby. Special people."   17

"Am I special?"   18

"Absolutely. Positively. You're one of the special people who will   19
live forever."

Boy, was that a relief. I had needed to know that for a long time. I   20
was sure glad to finally get it cleared up. My eyelids grew heavy. The
prospect of living forever had made me even sleepier. I stretched out on
a step and put my doll beneath my head for a pillow. The next thing I
knew, my mother was shaking me awake.

"I finished my letter. Now I want you to do something real nice for   21
me. I want you should write something on the envelope in English."

I was sleepy and cranky. "Maaa, I want to go to bed. And I don't like   22
writing. I only like printing big."

"Then print big."   23

"Can't I go to bed instead? My head's loose on my neck."   24

"Just do this one thing and you can go right upstairs—Okay, baby?"   25
My mother led me over to the table and sat me down on the wooden
kitchen chair and pushed the chair way under the table as far as it would
go. She put the envelope down on the worn oilcloth, right under my
chin.

"I want a red crayon."   26

She rummaged around in a drawer and found one.   27

"But I don't know what to print. You'll have to tell me."   28

"I'll tell you exactly." She dictated silly words. Words I was too   29
sleepy to understand or spell right. I sounded them out like in school,
moving my mouth as I put them down. My head nodded lower and
lower over the paper. When I finished, my mother slid the envelope
from under my limp hand.

"Did you finish, baby? Did you put all the words down? All the 30
words like I told you?"

"Yeah. Now can I go to bed?" 31

She helped me up the stairs to where my sister, Anna, was sleeping. I 32
collapsed into bed beside her. I felt my mother cover and kiss me.
Finally. I was fast asleep before she left the room.

That's all I remember from the night my mother seemed to be under 33
a gypsy spell. The next morning it was no better. I sat in the kitchen
before school, tracing stick men on the steamy windows, noticing that
my mother and father were all dressed up before breakfast, and it wasn't
even a holiday.

My father said to my mother, "We have to go now, Freida. You said 34
you wanted to stop at Mr. Moscowitz's grocery."

Before they went out the back door, my mother turned and looked 35
around the room at all six of us kids, her eyes like the lens of a camera,
taking pictures fast, before clouds blocked the sun. My father was carrying a small suitcase. My mother told me not to forget to wash my socks
for school the next day, and then they were gone.

We all stared at the closed door. Nobody had kissed anybody. No- 36
body had even said goodby. Everything was tangled and different from
ever before, and everybody was just letting it be that way. My big
brother Harry would explain it to me, I thought. He knew everything.
He could even mix chemicals in his laboratory in the attic and make real
crystal out of milk bottles. I asked him where Ma and Pa had gone.

"To the hospital. Ma's having an operation tomorrow." 37

"Like my tonsils?" 38

"Something like that." 39

That night I dreamed that I washed my red socks and something in 40
the red dye in the water scared me and I awoke hugging my doll tight,
with my thumb in my mouth and my forefinger in my ear. It was
Saturday. I didn't need to go to school or wash my socks after all. My
father left for the hospital early, and only Morry and I were in the
kitchen. Harry was in the attic making gold. I was sitting on the floor
playing jacks. Morry was doing his favorite thing—eating. I don't remember about the other kids.

The doorbell rang. It was always exciting when that happened, 41
because our friends usually just walked in. A doorbell meant something
special, like somebody selling encyclopedias or potato peelers. Morry
answered the door. It was a telegram for my father. Morry opened it. I

stood on my toes behind him and read. "Your wife Freida died . . ." The rest got all blurred up. Morry ran upstairs to the attic.

"It's my fault," I thought to myself. I hadn't asked my mother if she   42
was one of the special people who would never die, like me.

That night Mr. Moscowitz came over. He looked at my father: 43
"Your missus told me to give you this if . . ." Mr. Moscowitz covered his face with his hand and I could hear him choking and sobbing. He handed my father a thick letter. My father opened it and laid the envelope on the dining-room table. I read the big letters printed crookedly in red crayon across the front of the envelope. I sounded the awful words out as I read them:

"MY LAST WILL AND TESTIMINT. DO NOT OPIN UNTILL   44
I AM DETH."

Vocabulary

Yiddish (1)—a language spoken by many Jewish people of Eastern European origin that is written with Hebrew letters, and is derived from German, with additional words from Hebrew, Russian, Polish, English, and other languages

pantry (8)—a closet off the kitchen where cooking utensils and canned foods are stored

rummaged (27)—searched by moving things around

IN YOUR JOURNAL

Retell "Cookies at Midnight" in your own words. How did the story make you feel? Would you recommend this story to a friend? Why or why not?

A Closer Reading

1. What happens to the narrator of the story that makes the night in her story different from other nights in her life?

2. What are some indications in the story that the little girl's mother is acting in an unusual manner?

3. Why does the mother keep her little girl up so late?

4. Describe the relationship between the mother and the children. Use evidence in the story to support your point of view.

5. Describe the house and the lifestyle of this family, using evidence from Rowe's story to support your point of view. Think about such things as: Do they have a telephone? A washing machine? Do the children have their own rooms? What else do you notice?

Drawing Your Own Conclusions

1. Why does the mother choose her youngest daughter to stay up late instead of one of her other children?

2. Why does the mother stop and stare at her children before she leaves for the hospital? Why doesn't she stop to kiss her children?

3. Why doesn't the mother tell her children that she is going into the hospital? Do you think that she should have told her children? Why or why not?

4. At the end of the story, how do you feel about the mother? How do you feel about the little girl? What in the story made you feel the way you do?

Thinking about Writing

1. What is the tone of this story, the feeling of the story—warm, funny, sad, sweet, and so on? What words and phrases in the story create this tone?

2. This story is told in the first person (I, me, my) or from the first-person point of view. Rewrite the first paragraph in the third person (he, she, they) and reread it. Which do you prefer? Why do you think Rowe uses the first person?

3. Rowe wrote this story in chronological order, in the order in which the events took place. Find any words or phrases that relate to time. What other selections in this book are written in chronological order?

4. What is the effect of the last paragraph, all in capital letters with misspellings? How did it make you feel as a reader?

5. Why does Rowe entitle the story "Cookies at Midnight"?

*   *   *

Suggestions for Writing

1. Referring to your journal entries for ideas, write a story about an unusual event that took place in your childhood. Use descriptions of people and places to bring your story to life.

2. Write a story in which you describe a meaningful event that occurred in your family. Use dialogue and details to make your writing vital and interesting to read.

3. Think about some of the selections you have read about families in this book and in other places. Write an essay in which you explain some of the insights and understandings that people can gain from reading stories about other people's families. Be sure to include specific examples from your reading.

4. Should parents always be totally honest with their children? Take a position and write an essay supporting your point of view with observations and experience.

5. Write a letter attempting to convince a television producer that "Cookies at Midnight" should be made into a drama for television. In this letter you will have to tell about the story, make suggestions about the time period in which it should be shown, and make suggestions for the actors and actresses you think would be effective in the main roles.

Strategies for Revision

The following revision strategy takes place in two steps. First you'll work alone, and then you'll work with a classmate.

Begin by rereading your writing with a colored pencil or pen in your hand. With the pencil or pen, do the following:

- Circle any words that you would like to replace or rethink.
- Circle any sentences that you think are weak or repetitive.
- Practice changing the sound of what you have written by turning one sentence around so that the beginning of the sentence is now the end portion.

- Put a check mark next to any sentences that you are considering moving or in the places where you would like to add something else.

Then share these possible changes with a classmate. Discuss whether the classmate agrees with you that the changes would make your writing smoother and clearer. Then reverse the process and do the same for your classmate. Using the ideas from your discussion, revise your writing. When you are satisfied with it, share it with someone who has never before read your writing.

IN YOUR JOURNAL

When we look back at our life, special memories, both good and bad, stand out. The following story is about one of those memories, and it is also about the relationship of a son and his father.

Before you read this story, write about a childhood relationship with your father or with any other influential adult.

Across the Wide Missouri

John Edgar Wideman

Born in Washington, D.C., John Edgar Wideman presently teaches English at the University of Massachusetts at Amherst. He has written several books including *Hiding Place* (1981), *Sent for You Yesterday* (1983), *The Lynchers* (1986), and *Philadelphia Fire* (1991); a memoir, *Brothers and Keepers* (1984); and many short stories, including the collection entitled *Damballah* (1981), from which the following short story is excerpted. Wideman has won many prizes for his writing, among them the PEN/Faulkner Prize for Fiction in 1984. This story is about the bits and pieces that make up a young man's memories, and the powerful impact his father has had on his life.

I say to myself, *Where is he?* I stare at all the black faces. They won't   1
stay still. Bobbing and bowing into the white faces or gliding toward the far swinging doors, the closely cropped heads poised and impenetrable above mandarin collars. Toomer called the white faces petals of dusk and I think now of the waiters insinuating themselves like birds into clusters of petals, dipping silently, silently depositing pollen or whatever makes flowers grow and white people be nice to black people. And tips bloom. I am seeing it in slow motion now, the courtship, the petals, the starched white coats elegant as sails plying the red sea. In my story it is noise and a blur of images. Dark faces never still long enough to be my father.

"Hey, Eddie, look who's here."   2

There is a white cloth on the table that nearly hangs to the floor. My   3
knees are lost beneath it, it's heavy as a blanket, but Oscar has another

white cloth draped over his arm and unfurls it so it pops like a flag or a shoeshine rag and spreads it on top of the other so the table is covered twice. When Oscar sat me down, two cups and saucers were on the table. He went to get my father and told me he'd be right back and fix me up and wasn't I getting big and looked just like my daddy. He had scraped a few crumbs from the edge of the table into his hand and grinned across the miles of white cloth at me and the cups and saucers. While he was gone I had nudged the saucer to see if it was as heavy as it looked. Under the edge closest to me were three dimes. Two shiny ones and one yellow as a bad tooth. I pushed some more and found other coins, two fat quarters neither new nor worn. So there I was at that huge table and all that money in front of me but too scared to touch it so I slid the ten-pound cup and saucer back over the coins and tried to figure out what to do. Knew I better not touch the table cloth. Knew I couldn't help spotting it or smudging it if my hand actually touched the whiteness. So I tried to shove the money with the base of the saucer, work it over to the end of the table so it'd drop in my hand, but I couldn't see what I was doing and the cup rattled and I could just see that little bit of coffee in the bottom come jumping up out the cup and me worried that whoever had forgotten the quarters and dimes would remember and surely come back for them then what would I say would I lie and they'd know a little nigger at a big snow white table like this had to be lying, what else I'm gonna do but lie and everybody in the place know the thief had to be me and I was thinking and worrying and wondering what my father would do if all those people came after me and by that time I just went on and snatched that money and catch me if you can.

"Look who's here, Eddie." And under my breath I said shut up Mr. Oscar Parker, keep quiet man you must want everybody in here listening to those coins rattling in my pocket. Rattling loud as a rattlesnake and about to bite my leg through my new pants. Go on about your business, man. Look who ain't here. Ain't nobody here so why don't you go on away. [4]

Then my father picked up the saucers and balled up the old top cloth in one hand, his long fingers gobbling it and tucking it under his arm. Oscar popped the new one like a shoeshine rag and spread it down over the table. Laid it down quiet and soft as new snow. [5]

"Busboy'll git you a place setting. Eddie, you want one?" [6]

"No, I'll just sit with him." [7]

"Sure looks like his daddy." [8]

"Guess he ought to."   9

"Guess he better."   10

I don't remember what I ate. I don't recall anything my father said   11
to me. When I wrote this before there was dialogue. A lot of conversation broken by stage directions and the intrusions of restaurant business
and restaurant noise. Father and son in an island in the midst of a red-
carpeted chaos of white people and black waiters and the city lurking in
the wings to swallow them both when they take the elevator to the
ground floor and pass through Kaufman's green glass revolving doors.
But it didn't happen that way. We did talk. As much as we ever did.
Both of us awkward and constrained as we still are when we try to talk. I
forget all the words. Words were unimportant because what counted
was his presence, talking or silent didn't matter. Point was he was with
me and would stay with me the whole afternoon. One thing he must
have asked me about was the movies. I believe I knew what was playing
at every theater downtown and knew the address of every one and could
have reeled off for him the names of the stars and what the ads said
about each one. The images are not clear but I can still see the way the
movie page was laid out. I had it all memorized but when he asked me I
didn't recite what I knew, didn't even state a preference because I didn't
care. Going with him was what mattered. Going together, wherever,
was enough. So I waited for him at the table. Wondering what I had
eaten, running my tongue around in my mouth to see if I could get a
clue. Because the food had been served and I had wolfed it down but he
was all I tasted. His presence my feast.

He came back without the white coat. He brought a newspaper   12
with him and read to himself a minute then read me bits and pieces of
what I knew was there. Him reading changed it all. He knew things I
had never even guessed at when I read the movie page the night before.
Why one show was jive, why another would be a waste of money, how
long it would take to walk to some, how others were too far away. I
wanted to tell him it didn't matter, that one was just as good as another,
but I didn't open my mouth till I heard in his voice the one he wanted
to see.

He is six foot tall. His skin is deep brown with Indian red in it. My   13
mother has a strip of pictures taken in a five and dime, taken probably
by the machine that was still in Murphy's 5 & 10 when Murphy's was
still on Homewood Avenue when I was little. Or maybe in one of the
booths at Kennywood Amusement Park which are still there. They are
teenagers in the picture, grinning at the automatic camera they've fed a

quarter. Mom looks pale, washed out, all the color stolen from her face by the popping flashbulbs. His face in the black and white snapshots is darker than it really is. Black as Sambo if you want to get him mad you can say that. Black as Little Black Sambo. Four black-as-coal spots on the strip. But if you look closely you see how handsome he was then. Smiling his way through four successive poses. Each time a little closer to my mother's face, tilting her way and probably busy with his hands off camera because by picture three that solemn grandmother look is breaking up and by the final shot she too is grinning. You see his big, heavy-lidded, long-lashed, theatrical eyes. You see the teeth flashing in his wide mouth and the consciousness, lacking all self-consciousness and vanity, of how good he looks. Black, or rather purple now that the photos have faded, but if you get past the lie of the color he is clearly one of those *brown-eyed, handsome men* people like Chuck Berry sing about and other people lynch.

"Here's a good one. Meant to look at the paper before now, but we   14 been real busy. Wanted to be sure there was a good one but it's alright, got a Western at the Stanley and it's just down a couple blocks past Gimbels. Clark Gable's in it. *Across the Wide Missouri*."

The song goes something like this: *A white man loved an Indian*   15 *Maiden* and la de da-/-la de da. And: *A-way, you've gone away . . . Across the wide Mis-sour-i*. Or at least those words are in it, I think. I think I don't know the words on purpose. For the same reason I don't have it on a record. Maybe fifteen or twenty times in the thirty years since I saw the movie I've heard the song or pieces of the song again. Each time I want to cry. Or do cry silently to myself. A flood of tears the iron color of the wide Missouri I remember from the movie. *A-way, we're gone a-way . . . Across the wide Missouri*. It's enough to have it in pieces. It's enough to have heard it once and then never again all the way through but just in fragments. Like a spring which never comes. But you see a few flowers burst open. And a black cloud move down a grassy slope. A robin. Long, fine legs in a pair of shorts. The sun hot on your face if you lie down out of the wind. The fits and starts and rhythms and phrases from the spring-not-coming which is the source of all springs that do come.

The last time I heard the song my son called it *Shenandoah*. Maybe   16 that's what it should be called. Again I don't know. It's something a very strong instinct has told me to leave alone. To take what comes but don't try to make anything more out of it than is there. In the fragments. The bits and pieces.

Vocabulary

mandarin (1)—close-fitting, stand-up collar that has a small opening in the front

Toomer (1)—Jean Toomer (1894–1967); African-American author who wrote poems and short stories about black people in the South. Toomer is best known for *Cane*, a novelette he wrote in 1923.

dusk (1)—early evening

Chuck Berry (13)—a rock 'n' roll singer who was most popular in the 1960s and 1970s

Clark Gable (14)—a movie star who was most popular in the 1940s and 1950s. Gable is best known for playing the role of Rhett Butler in *Gone With the Wind*.

IN YOUR JOURNAL

Wideman tells a story that is rich in descriptive details. Write about the boy's relationship with his father. What did it mean to the boy? How does this relationship compare with your own relationships with adults as you were growing up?

A Closer Reading

1. Where did you think the first paragraph was taking place? What descriptive words support your answer?

2. Does the boy visit his father at the restaurant very often? What evidence from the story supports your answer?

3. When the father and son sit down at the table, how does the son feel? Why doesn't the boy remember what he has eaten?

4. Throughout the story, Wideman describes the father. List all the words that describe the way the father looked.

5. What does the boy think of the restaurant? Are there black customers in this restaurant? Using this information, decide when you think this story took place.

Drawing Your Own Conclusions

1. What does this story tell us about relations between blacks and whites? What does it tell us about the boy's self-esteem as a

young black man? Use examples from the story to support your answers. Why do you think Wideman presents this point of view of race relations?

2. Why do you think the boy takes the money? How does he feel about doing this?

3. Wideman describes his conversation with his father as "awkward and constrained as we still are when we try to talk." Why do you think they feel this way when they talk?

4. What effect does Wideman's description of his parents as teenagers have on you? Have you ever seen pictures of your parents as young people? How do those pictures make you feel?

5. The title of this story is "Across the Wide Missouri." On one level, the title is appropriate because it is a song from the movie of the same title that the two go to see. Why is it also a good metaphor or symbol for the relationship of the boy and his father?

Thinking about Writing

1. Wideman uses the figure of speech called a *simile*. A simile is a comparison of unlike things that uses the word *like* or *as*. One example from this story is his reference in the first paragraph to "the waiters insinuating themselves *like* birds into clusters of petals, dipping silently, silently depositing pollen or whatever makes flowers grow. . . ." What other examples of similes can you find in this story?

2. In paragraph 3, Wideman describes the table in the restaurant. List all the descriptive words he uses to make that table real. Look for words that describe how the table looks, sounds, and weighs, its size, and so forth.

3. Why do you think Wideman describes the father but never describes the boy except to say that he looks like he is his father's son? Why might a writer do this in a story? Do you prefer that writers describe their subjects, or should they leave this to their readers' imaginations?

4. In this story Wideman moves through several time periods. Reread the story noticing when the narrator (the teller of the story) is an adult and when a child. How do you know when the time changes? Are there differences in the writing as the narrator

becomes an adult? Reread the Modupe story on page 20. How does Modupe signal time changes?

5. Wideman writes this story using the "stream of consciousness" technique, in which a narrator reveals his or her thoughts and feelings in a continuous series of impressions or remembrances. In what ways did you read this story differently from a story written in a more traditional narrative form? Why might a writer use this technique?

*   *   *

Suggestions for Writing

1. Write an essay describing your father, your mother, or any other influential adult from your childhood. Tell a story that illustrates his or her personality and how this person affected your life.

2. A song triggers the narrator's memory in this story. Some researchers believe much of the information in our memory is in verbal or sound form. Write an essay describing an experience in which a song or piece of music was important. Explain why this incident is meaningful to you.

3. One task that writers are often asked to do is to *compare and contrast*. To compare, the writer looks for similarities; to contrast, the writer looks for differences. Then the writer has to decide how to organize these similarities and differences for their particular subject matter. Some writers list all the similarities in one section and all the differences in another. Some writers prefer to focus on their subjects separately, rather than directly comparing individual characteristics.

   For example, if you were writing about fathers and mothers, you could put all their similarities in one section of your essay and all their differences in another. Or you could include everything about fathers in one section and everything about mothers in another. You could also alternate from one to the other. Wideman does this in the following way:

   > They are teenagers in the picture, grinning at the automatic camera they've fed a quarter. Mom looks pale, washed out, all the color stolen from her face by the popping flashbulbs. His face in the black and white snapshots is darker than it really is.

If you were writing about your parents and wanted to contrast and compare their cooking styles, you might alternate within a paragraph or even a sentence. "My father made the best apple pie I ever tasted, but my mother always told us that she taught him how to make it."

Write an essay comparing and contrasting the personalities of your two parents or any other two adults who were influential in your childhood. In what ways are you like either or both of them?

4. Write an essay comparing and contrasting yourself as a teenager with your parents as teenagers. Is it easier being a teenager now? Why or why not?

Strategies for Revision

If you have written an essay in which you compare and contrast, reread your writing, asking yourself the following questions:

- Is there an organizing pattern to help my reader follow my ideas in this piece of writing?
- Are there enough examples of similarities? Where are they located?
- Are there enough examples of differences? Where are they located?
- What do I want my reader to feel after reading this piece of writing? What changes can I make that will make it easier for my reader to follow my ideas?

Using your responses to these questions, revise what you have written. If you have chosen another type of writing, use the questions from another revision strategy in this book.

IN YOUR JOURNAL

The author of the following selection writes, "For most of my life, I was regarded as my father's daughter. My likeness to my father, in appearance, temperament, and style, was always contrasted with my sister, who was seen as my mother's mirror image." Before you read this selection, think about your parents, natural or adopted. Are you more similar to one or the other? When you think about this parent, do you identify yourself with him or her? Do you wish you were more like him of her, or less. Is it a positive identification for you, or a negative one? Write about the role this person plays in your life.

Beginnings

Sara Lawrence Lightfoot

Sara Lawrence Lightfoot was born in Nashville, Tennessee. She is Professor of Education at Harvard University and the author of several books, including *Worlds Apart: Relationships Between Families and Schools* (1978) and *The Good High School: Portraits of Character and Culture* (1983). She was awarded a 1984 MacArthur Prize, a prestigious award that bestows upon its recipients enough money to work for five years on any project that interests them. Lightfoot used this time to write *Balm in Gilead: Journey of a Healer* (1988), a biography of her mother that is excerpted below. Dr. Margaret Morgan Lawrence is a child psychiatrist, one of ten women and the only black in her graduating class at Columbia Medical School.

Even as a young child, I knew both the passion and the reverence   1
my mother brought to her work. At the dinner table, while protecting the privacy and anonymity of her patients, she would reenact the dramas of the clinic, providing enough detail for us to get caught up in the story. I would hear tightness and anger in her voice when children and their families got hopelessly wrapped up in bureaucratic red tape, or when a colleague, out of fear or ignorance, acted unprofessionally. Sometimes I would feel waves of jealousy and abandonment when my mother would go off to help a child in trouble, leaving her three "real" children behind. A Saturday family adventure would be shattered, a

cooking project stopped in the middle, the pansies half-planted. I always screamed loudly as she walked out the door, her cape streaming, her gait purposeful. When she returned to us, leaving the clinical emergencies safely out of our view, we would confront her with "how we felt" about her leaving, and she would carefully and candidly explain her devotion to her work *and* her mother-love for us. Didn't we know that the latter was deeper, that it would last "forever"?

From time to time, I remember my mother saying, without sentimentality, "I love my work," a statement I puzzled over as a child. It made me imagine a day at the office full of pleasure and sunshine. Since the home scene, with all its love and laughter, had its inevitable crises and struggles, I occasionally worried whether my mother liked going to work more than staying home. Many years later, I understood everything she meant by that brief affirmation. Her work—with its frustrations and imperfections—offered endless challenges and a few victories, offered her the chance to use her wisdom and skills, and offered her the "privilege" of healing others. Now that I am middle-aged, and "loving my work" as well, I know even more clearly how much my mother gained fulfillment from balancing work and family. And I also understand some of the high costs of this balance, and of her struggle with many unyielding institutions to live out these deep, dual commitments.

This realization was just one of the ways in which my feelings and attitudes toward my mother were transformed as I grew older. For most of my life, I was regarded as my father's daughter. My likeness to my father, in appearance, temperament, and style, was always contrasted with my sister, who was seen as my mother's mirror image. "You're just like your dad," people would say after giving me just one hard look. "Paula is the spit and image of your mom." For those people who insisted upon attaching labels to children, Chuck, my brother, was perceived as the embodiment of both parents. "He is the combination of Margaret and Charles. . . . You can see his mother's eyes, his father's nose, his mother's quiet, his father's posture. . . ." I remember feeling that my brother's combined label gave him more room, a more generous repertoire of ways to be, while staying "in character."

Mostly I enjoyed the parallels people drew between me and my father. I knew they saw him as handsome, vigorous, and intelligent, and I longed to inherit those fine qualities. But there was a part of me that yearned to be like my mother. People described her as serene, beautiful, and wise—like a clear, still pond. I thought that in being outgoing and energetic like my father, I was missing the mystery, the softness, the feminine *grace*, of my mother. Over the years, the perceived similarities were underscored, exaggerated, and I would alternately welcome and resist them. When, in my mid-twenties, I chose my vocation and my husband, my father joked: "Now I know Sara is thoroughly identified with me. She became a sociologist and she married a psychiatrist."

But by then the likeness was largely family myth. Over the years,   5
without anyone noticing, changes began to take place, until one day I was met by a total stranger on the streets of New York who recognized me because of my mother. From way at the other end of a long block, she watched me striding toward her, *my* cape billowing out behind. As we came closer, she stopped me with a smile and a look that said, "I know you from somewhere." She searched her mind while I waited, feeling no familiarity but believing in hers. After a few moments, her brow relaxed. "You must be Margaret's daughter. You look *just* like her!" . . .

By the time I was in my mid-thirties, with two children of my own,   6
the identification with my mother was complete. Now I became a baker of "Maggie Bread," the hearty whole wheat variety, with my own embellishment of raisins. Now I wore colorful shawls like my mother always did, draped for warmth and drama. Now I plaited my daughter's brown braids and could feel the sensations of my mother's soothing hands on my head as I laid mine on my daughter's. Now I tried to put the pieces of my own too-busy life together, racing home to place bright napkins and candles on the dinner table, to create the appearance that I had been there all day. Now I heard my children's harsh complaints or watched their silent resignation when I flew off to distant places to deliver speeches, attend meetings—to do my version of the teaching/healing legacy. Now I could feel so keenly the mothering I was replaying, while being aware that the father in me had not disappeared.

This slow discovery of identification with my mother became in-   7
triguing to me. I recognized the ways I incorporated her style and her values, sometimes unknowingly, sometimes on purpose. I began to think of writing her story. If I could learn about her origins, her childhood, her dreams, her fears, I might have greater insight into my own life. If I could move beyond family myths—so static and idealized—to trace the actual events of my mother's life, I might uncover the historical patterns that give shape to my own.

My interest in telling my mother's story, however, was charged by   8
more than my emerging identification with her. I wanted to explore

beyond the myth of Margaret Lawrence. All families have elaborate tales that stand as models of courage, wisdom, strength, or loyalty for their members. The tales are told and retold in long embroidered versions or in family shorthand. Everyone is comforted by their familiarity, the promised punch line, but no one would claim that these tales are the whole story. Bigger than life, they have turned into legends, morality plays. For as long as I can remember, my mother had been an idealized figure in our community, put on a pedestal, spoken of with awe and envy. Parents of my friends, neighbors, teachers, shopkeepers in town, would speak about my mother's serenity and quiet intelligence, about the way her very presence seemed to ease their pain. Sometimes their veneration made me wonder.

I remember the day my mother and I went to the Corsette Shop on Main Street to buy my first brassiere. I was twelve and "ample," as my father would say diplomatically. I had been walking around self-consciously for months, enduring my bobbing breasts as a horrible humiliation, and had begged my mother to let me get a bra. She had quietly, but stubbornly, resisted. My mother had never worn a bra, had refused to use the one thrust upon her at age fourteen, and seemed to regard them as nothing but sham and artifice. After weeks of my lobbying, she reluctantly gave in. I think she wanted me to avoid the abuse of my peers, several of whom had sported bras since the fourth grade. The two of us made a special trip to town to search for the most natural, least pointed kind. The Corsette Shop ladies greeted my mother with fanfare, oozing delight out of every pore. "Dr. Lawrence, we are so *thrilled* to see you!" The chatter continued while the ladies passed selections through the green curtains of the dressing room and I fumbled with snaps and straps and "cups." Occasionally one of them would come in unannounced to inspect the fit. During one of those unwelcome intrusions (my mother had gone out briefly to put a nickel in the parking meter), I remember waiting for the inevitable refrain—"Your mother is the loveliest woman I've ever met . . . she's as good as gold." I could be anywhere, even here in this underwear shop, under these embarrassing conditions, and I'd be treated to this familiar litany.

The worshipful praise always seemed genuine, but even as a child I recognized that it came at some cost. People did not always like the image that they had created of Margaret Lawrence. It made them feel inadequate or graceless in contrast. For some, the image of her goodness led to resentment. "How does your mother do it all?" asked the mother of one of my fellow Girl Scouts. "And she always looks so good." Each word of praise bore an edge of cynicism, and I could hear both, having learned early to catch these double-edged inflections.

The world's image of my mother never squared with mine. Yes, I   11
knew she was different, even special, an achiever. I knew of no other mother who seemed to put so many pieces together; whose work seemed to require so much passion, who managed all her competing commitments. But rather than the serenity the world perceived, I saw my mother on the move, beads of sweat above her upper lip, her fingernails filled with paint and clay, brow furrowed, muscles sore and eyelids drooping by day's end. When I bothered to look, I saw a grown-up life that was hard and demanding, that left no time for frivolity. What others saw as peacefulness, I saw as my mother's chief survival strategy—complete concentration. I am sure that the dissonance between the idealized perceptions of Margaret and a daughter's nonheroic view must also have fueled my interest in exploring her life. I mistrusted the legend that seemed in its grandeur to diminish me.

Years later, having written other books that tried to get beyond   12
surface and stereotypes, I felt the impulse to look at my mother's life more deeply, to tell of her grace against odds, of the pain that accompanied achievement, the loss of laughter that came with single-minded pursuits. Not only would the story focus on her triumphs, it would also show how her life was filled with very ordinary twists and turns, with moments of traumatic defeat . . . and slow, purposeful recovery. I wanted to explore the family silences, the breaks in family stories that emerge because people have simply forgotten, because memories have faded with time, because images have had to be repressed in order to move on with life, because people have chosen to hide a piece of the truth of their own peace of mind. In tracing my mother's development, I wanted to undo the caricatures that never wholly fit my view of her. I was particularly fascinated by the way she had transformed hardship into strength, and loneliness into sensitivity and introspection.

The project seemed less daunting than it might have because I ex-   13
pected my mother to be able to tell her story well. As an only child with a ruminative temperament, Margaret had watched the family drama and recorded everything within. She turned the images over in her mind, trying to make sense of the mysteries and silences. In her mid-thirties, when Margaret experienced "the couch" for the first time, she was amazed at how her well-developed introspective capacities translated so easily into the psychoanalytic process, how once she decided to "put it

out there" it all came so naturally. Free association was much like the uninhibited, wandering fantasies she had enjoyed as a child, like the unspoken questions and observations she silently harbored as an adolescent and young adult. It was not hard for her to dig into her past, to revisit old haunts, and enjoy the fuzzy, refracted quality of early images that she calls "screen memories."

Seventy years later, Margaret can draw a detailed plan of the church 14 and rectory at Widewater, Virginia, a remote, tiny cross-in-the-road that no one can find on a map. She can feel her father's large hand holding hers as they take the slop to the pigs. She has been well practiced in exploring these early experiences, and her belief in their power is deep. As she said in her talk to her fellow analysts, her own childhood stories, their pain and their resonance, are central to her therapeutic work with children and their families. She uses that self-knowledge to gain access to her patients' lives and histories.

For my mother, our collaboration is a psychological and spiritual 15 journey. The journey back through time feels like a tunnel, dark, mysterious, and finally luminous.

Vocabulary

reverence (1)—deep respect and honor; veneration

anonymity (1)—the state of not being named or identified

gait (1)—way of walking

vocation (4)—career

plaited (6)—braided

static (7)—inactive; remaining the same

veneration (8)—deep respect and awe; reverence

litany (9)—repetitive prayer or story in which the same phrases are repeated

frivolity (11)—silliness

daunting (13)—intimidating; discouraging

ruminative (13)—meditative; thoughtful

luminous (15)—shining; bright

IN YOUR JOURNAL

Write down all the details you can remember from the Lightfoot selection. What do you think you will remember about this piece several months from now?

A Closer Reading

1. What conflict do you think the children felt when they heard their mother say that she loved her work? How did Margaret Lawrence try to resolve this?

2. What did Margaret Lawrence get from her work that made it worthwhile for her to struggle to keep the balance between home and work?

3. In what ways was the public Margaret Lawrence different from the private Margaret Lawrence?

4. How does Margaret Lawrence's memory help her in her family therapy practice?

5. In what ways has Lightfoot's lifestyle matured into one similar to that of her mother? In what ways do you think they are different?

Drawing Your Own Conclusions

1. Why do you think that Lightfoot decided to write her mother's biography? What do you think Sara Lawrence Lightfoot might have gained from doing this biography project? What do you think Margaret Lawrence gained from it?

2. What does the anecdote about the Corsette Shop tell us about Margaret Lawrence? What does it tell us about Lightfoot?

3. Lightfoot writes, "I saw as my mother's chief survival strategy— complete concentration." How could "complete concentration" help someone to survive a difficult time?

4. Lightfoot writes that although people admired her mother, "for some the image of her goodness led to resentment." How do you explain this statement?

Thinking about Writing

1. Paragraph 1 begins with the line, "Even as a young child, I knew both the passion and the reverence my mother brought to her work." How does Lightfoot support this in the paragraph that follows? What examples does she use; are they sufficient?

2. Reread the selection, noticing when dialogue is used. Why do you think Lightfoot uses dialogue in those particular instances? Does the dialogue add to or detract from the rest of the writing?

3. How do you think Lightfoot found out about her mother, and in what ways do you see this as a collaborative project? If you were to do a similar project with a relative, what steps would you take to organize the project?

4. Based on this excerpt, how do you expect Lightfoot has organized her book *Balm in Gilead*? Are you interested enough in the story to read the rest of the book? Why or why not?

* * *

Suggestions for Writing

1. Write an essay in which you compare yourself to one of your parents. (You may want to refer to your journal for ideas.) In the essay, think about appearance, personality, values, desires, abilities, and the like. (See pages 74–75 for suggestions for comparing and contrasting.)

2. With another member of the class, compose a series of questions for you each to use in interviewing a member of your family or family friend. This interview will give you the information on which to base a biographical essay about this person.

   After you have completed your questions, interview the person, and write an essay telling about that person's life. You may want to include some dialogue and anecdotes in order to help your reader hear and know the person you are describing.

3. In paragraph 8 Lightfoot states:

   > All families have elaborate tales that stand as models of courage, wisdom, strength, or loyalty for their members. The tales are told and retold in long embroidered versions or in family shorthand.

Everyone is comforted by their familiarity, the promised punch line, but no one would claim that these tales are the whole story.

Write an essay in which you relate one of the family tales you heard as you were growing up. Then analyze why the tale continues to be retold in your family.

4. "The world's image of my mother," Lightfoot notes, "never squared with mine." Write an essay in which you describe how the public image of someone you know or have heard of is different from the private image as you know it.

Strategies for Revision

Lightfoot wrote about events in her mother's life in order to understand her mother and herself better. When you read the drafts you have written, think about her selection.

Share your draft with three other class members. In a group, take turns reading your essays aloud to one another. Read as slowly and carefully as you can. Do not write or read while another person is reading. Listen closely, concentrating on the meaning of the essay.

After each person reads, answer the following questions, thinking about the Lightfoot article:

- What stories does Lightfoot tell about her mother? How do they reveal her personality and values? Do your stories reveal the personality and values of the person(s) you are describing?
- What does Lightfoot reveal about the appearance of the people in her writing? How do her descriptions bring these people to life? Do your people seem real? If not, what do you need to include to make them seem alive?
- Which events do you remember from the Lightfoot selection? Why? Do any events stand out from your draft? If not, how can they be made stronger and more memorable?

When each person has finished reading and you have discussed all the drafts, reread your own draft. Decide which changes you should make to improve your writing. Write your revision and share it with your classmates.

IN YOUR JOURNAL

Ed leaves China and his wife and family to come to make a life in the United States. After he has begun to establish himself, he wants his wife to join him. But he worries about how she will be able to live in this new country. He decides that he will "not end his American life but show her how to live one."

Before you read this selection, write down what one needs to know to live an American life.

The Father from China

Maxine Hong Kingston

Maxine Hong Kingston was born in Stockton, California. Her parents were immigrants from China. She lived for seventeen years in Hawaii but now lives in Oakland, California, with her family. Kingston's most recent book, *Tripmaster Monkey: His Fake Book* (1989), is her first novel. Her first book, *The Woman Warrior: Memories of a Girlhood Among Ghosts* (1976), won The National Book Critics Award for best work of nonfiction. "The Father from China" is excerpted from her second book, *China Men* (1980). The husband, Ed, leaves his wife and children in China to settle in America and make a life for them. During the fifteen years of separation, the children die and Ed's wife tries to prepare for American life. Ed opens a laundromat and becomes Americanized. This story tells about the couple's reunion.

Ed's wife wrote often and sometimes sent lichee, which she had   1
picked from the three trees that Ed's father had planted and the twenty trees that Ed's brother had planted. When would he return to plant lichee trees?

Then she wrote that their two children had died. What should she   2
do? "I think you ought to come back right now," she said.

He did much worrying, and hit upon a plan. He would not end his   3
American life but show her how to live one. "Here's what you have to do if I'm to bring you to America," he wrote, though there was a law against her. "I will bring you to America on one condition, and that is,

you get a Western education. I'll send you money, which you must only spend on school, not on food or clothes or jewelry or relatives. Leave the village. Go to Hong Kong or Canton and enroll in a Western scientific school. A science school. Get a degree. Send it to me as evidence you are educated, and I'll send you a ship ticket. And don't go to a school for classical literature. Go to a scientific school run by white people. And when you get your degree, I'll send for you to come here to the United States." He would figure out later how to accomplish that.

When next she wrote, she had enrolled in medical school; she was   4
writing him from there. As years passed and sometimes she became discouraged with how long her education was taking and how difficult the work, he wrote encouragement: "If you don't get that degree, I'll not send for you. We will never see each other again." He did not want an ignorant villager for his American wife.

So much time went by, he saved another two hundred dollars,   5
which he spent on a gray suit and a Countess Mara tie.

At last she mailed him her diploma. He spent another few years   6
saving passage money, and fifteen years after they had last seen one another, he sent for her. Applying for her, he risked having his citizenship again scrutinized. She would enter legally and gracefully, no question of asking a lady to ride the sea in a box or to swim to an unwatched shore.

At dinner one evening, he announced to his partners, "I've sent for   7
my wife, who will be here in January." There were so surprised that they stopped their eating rice.

"How did you save enough money?" Worldster asked.   8

"I guess you'll be moving to your own apartment," said Roosevelt.   9

"Why do you want to do that?" asked Woodrow.   10

After writing letters for fifteen years, Ed and his wife ended their   11
correspondence. They were near each other, she on Ellis Island, where there was no mail, and he on Manhattan. When he saw her on the ferry, she was standing surrounded by bundles and bags, no child tugging her coat and no baby in her arms. He recognized her, though she was older. Her hair was slicked against her head with a bun in back, a proper married-lady hairdo. In spite of the law against her, she was landing, her papers in order. Her immigration verified the strength of his citizenship.

"Here you are," he said. "You've come."   12

"You look like a foreigner," she said. "I can barely recognize you."   13

"Was it a rough journey?" he asked.   14

"It was terrible," she exclaimed. "The Japanese were right behind   15
me. When I tried to board the ship from Canton to Hong Kong, the

man acted as if my papers were wrong and asked for a seventy-five-dollar bribe. So I ran to another gangplank and found out seventy-five dollars wasn't policy at all; this man wanted a hundred dollars. I had to run back to the first entrance. Then I paid another hundred to get off the ship. It was the last ship out of Canton before the Japanese took the harbor. And I was so seasick, I vomited the whole way across the Atlantic. And what a questioning I got on the Island. They asked me what year you had cut your queue, and a workman shook his head, hawked and spat. It was a signal. So I said, 'I don't know.' On my way to be locked up again, I said to that workman, 'That was a delicious bun you gave me. Thank you. I hope you bring me another if you have more.' Get it? It was a code I made up, meaning, 'Thank you for giving me the right answer. Please give me more help.' Oh, I was so scared. If it weren't for him I might not be here."

"Don't worry any more," said Ed. "That's over now. Don't worry any more." Her big eyes had lines around them. "That's all over now," he said. 16

"I had to build roads," she said. "Since your father is too crazy to work, and you were away, I had to pay the labor tax for two men. Your father followed me and wept on the road when I left." 17

"Never mind now," he said. "That's all over now." 18

They rode the subway to the room he had rented in preparation for her coming. He taught her the name of the subway stop for the laundry. "Easu Bu-odd-way Su-ta-son," she repeated. "That's good," he said. "Remember that and you can't get lost." 19

She unpacked jars of seeds. "But we aren't farmers any more," he said. "I'll plant in tin cans and put them here on the fire escape," she said. "You'll see how many vegetables we can grow in cans." 20

She showed him a piece of cloth. "Do you recognize this?" she asked. "The Japanese were right behind me, and I had time to take just one keepsake—the trimming on the bed canopy." She had ripped it off and shoved it in her purse. She unfolded it. "This is the only thing we have left from China," she said. "The heirloom." A red phoenix and a red dragon played across the strip of linen; the Chinese words down one end and English words across the top said, "Good morning." She had cross-stitched it herself. 21

"You could write English even then," he teased her, "and getting ready to come here." "I didn't know what it said," she demurred, "I only copied it from a needlework book." 22

He took her shopping and bought her a black crepe dress with a   23
bodice of white lace ruffles and buttons of rhinestone and silver. "You
look very pretty," he told her. They bought a black coat with a fur collar
and a little black-eyed animal head over her shoulder, high heels, silk
stockings, black kid gloves, and a picture hat with a wide, wide brim
and silk fluttery ribbon. They strolled in their finery along Fifth Avenue.
"I washed all these windows," he told her. "When I first came here, I
borrowed a squeegee and rags and a bucket, and walked up and down
this street. I went inside each store and asked if they wanted the windows washed. The white foreigners aren't so hard to get along with;
they nod to mean Yes and shake their heads to mean No, the same as
anybody." New York glittered and shined with glass. He had liked
pulling the water off the panes and leaving brief rainbows. While working, he had looked over the displays of all the wonderful clothes to own
and wear. He had made the money to pool for starting the laundry. "In
the spring," he promised her, "we'll buy you white cotton gloves."

"On the first day of autumn," he told her, "New Yorkers stomp on   24
one another's straw hats. I wear my gray felt one as soon as summer's
over. I save the straw for spring. I'm not extravagant. You ought to put
your earrings in the safe deposit box at the bank. Pierced ears look a
little primitive in this country." He also told her to buy makeup at a
drugstore. "American people don't like oily faces. So you ought to use
some powder. It's the custom. Also buy some rouge. These foreigners
dislike yellow skin."

She also bought a long black rat of hair to roll her own hair over for   25
an upswept hairdo. At a beauty parlor, she had her wavy hair cut and
curled tighter with a marcel. She washed, ironed, and wrapped her silk
pants and dresses and never wore them again.

He took her to see the Statue of Liberty. They climbed the ladder,   26
she in high heels, up the arm to the torch, then the stairs to the crown.
"Now we're inside her chin. This part must be the nose." From the
windows of the crown, he showed her his city.

They also went to the top of the Empire State Building, took the   27
second elevator to the very top, the top of the world. Ed loved the way
he could look up at the uncluttered sky. They put money in the telescopes and looked for the laundry and their apartment. "So I have been
on the tallest building in the world," she said. "I have seen everything.
Wonderful. Wonderful. Amazing. Amazing."

"Yes," he said. "Everything's possible on the Gold Mountain. I've   28
danced with blondes." "No, really?" she said. "You didn't. You're

making that up, aren't you? You danced with demonesses? I don't believe it."

Her favorite place to go was the free aquarium, "the fish house," 29 where all manner of creatures swam. Walking between the lighted tanks, she asked, "When do you think we'll go back to China? Do you think we'll go back to China?" "Shh," he said. "Shh." The electric eels glowed in their dark tank, and the talking fish made noises. "There are bigger fish in China," she said.

They went to the movies and saw *Young Tom Edison* with Mickey 30 Rooney. They both liked the scene where the mother took Eh-Da-Son into the barn, but only pretended to thrash him; she faked the slaps and crying and scolding to fool the strict father, the father "the severe parent," according to Confucius, and the mother "the kind parent." ("My bones, my flesh, father and mother," said Tu Fu.) After the movie, Ed explained to his wife that this cunning, resourceful, successful inventor, Edison, was who he had named himself after. "I see," she said. "Eh-Da-Son. Son as in *sage* or *immortal* or *saint.*"

They also saw a movie where a big man bridged two mountain 31 peaks with his prone body. He held on to one cliff of a chasm with his fingers and the other with his toes. Hundreds of little people walked across on him.

The four partners no longer had to race to get out of doing the 32 dishes. Ed's wife shopped and cooked. She bought a tiered food carrier, filled each pot with a different accompaniment to rice, and carried it and a pot of soup hot through the subway to the laundry. The first day she did this, she got off at the wrong stop in the underground city. She went from white ghost to white ghost shouting over the trains, which sounded like the Japanese bombing, "Easu Bu-odd-way Su-ta-son?" And a conductor said, "Of course. East Broadway Station. Go that way."

"He understood me," she proudly told the men. "I can speak En- 33 glish very well." She set the table with her homemade meal so they didn't get to buy restaurant take-out food any more. And they did not race but had manners. "Tell me how you started this laundry," she said. Woodrow described their Grand Opening. "Our friends sent stands of flowers tied in wide red ribbons, on which your husband wrote good words in gold ink. We exploded firecrackers out on the sidewalk, right out there on Mott Street. And then the customers came." "Working for ourselves, we can close whenever we please and go do as we like," Ed said.

The partners did not tell her that they hardly ever celebrated holidays. 34
They had learned that holidays do not appear with the seasons; the
country does not turn festive just because a rubric day appears on the
calendar. The cooking women, the shopping and slicing and kneading
and chopping women brought the holidays. The men let holidays pass. If
they did not go to the bother of keeping it, a holiday was another free day.
It was that free a country. They could neglect attending the big public
celebrations such as those at the benevolent associations and New Year's
eve at Times Square, and no one minded. Neglecting the planting and
harvest days made no difference in New York. No neighbors looked
askance. And there were no godly repercussions. They had no graves to
decorate for the memorial days of Clarity and Brightness. They did arrange cotton snow, reindeer, a stable scene, and a Santa Claus in the
laundry window at Christmas. "We don't want them to break our window or not bring their laundry," Ed explained. His wife brought back the
holidays. She made the holidays appear again.

Vocabulary

lichee (1)—a Chinese evergreen
   tree that produces a sweet
   fruit with a papery outer shell
scrutinized (6)—looked over very
   carefully
queue (15)—a single braid worn
   hanging from the back of the
   head
demonesses (28)—female devils
Mickey Rooney (30)—movie star

who began his career as a
child in the 1930s and is still
performing in movies and on
television
Confucius (30)—Chinese philosopher and teacher (551?–
   479? B.C.)
rubric (34)—an established rule
repercussions (34)—effects of an
   action

IN YOUR JOURNAL

Write everything you can remember about how this immigrant couple tried to make a successful life in an American city. In your family or
neighborhood, are there any people who remind you of Ed and his
wife?

A Closer Reading

1. What indications are there in the story that tell you whether or not Ed and his friends' business is successful?

2. Why does the husband change his Chinese name to Ed? Who does he name himself after and why?

3. Why does one partner change his name to Woodrow and another to Roosevelt? What do you think these names mean to them?

4. Why does the wife bring jars of seeds with her? How does Ed feel about her doing this?

5. What does Ed's wife do that changes his and his partner's lives?

Drawing Your Own Conclusions

1. Why do you think that Ed and his friends decide to open a laundry? What other businesses might people who have limited knowledge of English and American customs begin?

2. Why did Ed wait fifteen years to send for his wife? Do you think she wants to come to America? After she arrives, what in the story tells you how she feels about staying in America?

3. Why doesn't Kingston give Ed's wife her own name? What does this tell us about Ed's attitude toward women? What else in the story indicates Ed's attitude toward his wife and toward women?

4. Why does the wife put away her silk clothes but not throw them away? Do you think she would do this if she came to America at this time in history? What other articles does she bring with her from China? Why does she bring these? In Ewa Zadrzynska's essay (see page 14), what objects bring back her memories of Poland? How is her story similar to that of Ed's wife?

5. Why does the wife in this story go to medical school? How does this compare with the reason Margaret Lawrence goes to medical school in "Beginnings" (see page 76)? Why do you think the wife begins to work in the laundry and does not begin a medical practice in the United States?

Thinking about Writing

1. What do you think Kingston wants the reader to feel about Ed? Use examples from the story to explain your answer.

2. What do you think Kingston wants the reader to feel about Ed's wife? Use examples from the story to explain your answer.

3. What in the story made you think that Kingston wrote this for an American audience or a Chinese audience? Be specific in your answer.

4. Reread the story focusing on the items Ed values and the places he takes his wife. What do these tell you about Kingston's view of American society?

*   *   *

Suggestions for Writing

1. Interview a member of your family, a classmate, or a neighbor who came to the United States from another country. Some questions to include in your interview are: What was your first impression of the United States? Was the United States different from what you expected it to be? How have you changed since you moved to this country? Do you still feel homesick when you think about your country? Have you ever returned to your country for a visit? How have things changed in your country? Write your findings in essay form.

2. Imagine that you meet a family who has just moved to your city from another country. Write a letter to this family giving them advice about your city.

3. Many immigrants to this country say that it is easier to settle in a city than to move to the countryside. On the basis of your reading of Kingston's story and your own observations, write an essay in which you take a position about this issue.

4. The American dream of success and happiness can still come true if one works hard enough. Write an essay in which you persuade your reader that this statement is accurate. Use your readings, experiences, and observations to support your point of view.

Collaborative Project

Contact your local library or chamber of commerce to find out about immigration in your area. You should get information about the number of immigrants who move to your area each year, their countries of origin, and any special services your community provides for them. As a class, write about immigration in your area.

Strategies for Revision

Before you start to revise your draft, reread the Kingston story, focusing on the way she describes people and places, the way she includes small details that make a person unique, and the way she chooses which events to focus on over the fifteen-year period of this story. Write in your journal about the way she does these things.

Then reread your draft focusing on the same areas in writing:

- What words do you use to describe people? How effective are you at making each one unique?
- What words do you use to describe places? How effective are you at making it possible for your reader to see the place through your eyes?
- Where did you include small details that tell about people and events? How effective are you at revealing someone's personality through small details?
- Which events does your draft focus on? Is this the best way to get your point across?

Decide what changes you should make to improve your draft. Write your revision and share it with a classmate.

IN YOUR JOURNAL

A family story may not always be true or accurate, but it always serves a function in the family. Write a family story and explain who tells the story, when, to whom, and what the story means to you.

Myths of Blame: The Family Scapegoat

Elizabeth Stone

Elizabeth Stone is an associate professor of English and media studies at Fordham University's College at Lincoln Center in New York City. The following selection is taken from her 1988 book, *Black Sheep and Kissing Cousins: How Our Family Stories Shape Us.* The selection tells a family story about a "bad" child and analyzes the reasons why families tell such stories to each other and the role such stories play in maintaining the relationships in the family.

Peter Mott is a successful nuclear physicist at a large West Coast   1
university. He is an attractive man, with a full head of curly blond hair, bright, amused blue eyes, and the lean build of a born athlete. In fact, up until he was a teenager, his dream was to become a professional tennis player. He had the talent and the speed, too. But the dream came to an abrupt end when Peter Mott came down with polio. In time, he recovered well enough to get around, but not well enough ever to play tennis again. Especially when he's tired, he walks with a discernible limp.

Now in his early fifties, he's had time to make peace with his condi-   2
tion, but he still remembers—and still tells—the story that circulated in his family about how he contracted polio in the first place. "When I got polio, it was in the mid-1940s, ten years before the first polio vaccine began to be used. My mother always said that the reason I got polio was because we had gone to visit my sister at college, and while we were there, we drank water that was no good."

Peter Mott is an entertaining raconteur, and I had been sitting in his   3
kitchen, having brunch, looking through old photographs and listening to his stories rather passively, willing enough for the moment to do nothing more than enjoy them. But when he got to the part about the

water being "no good," I became more alert. It seemed an extremely odd locution for a scientist to be using about contaminated water. Maybe the child who had first heard that story would use that phrase, but not the scientist talking to me now. Besides, the whole story didn't add up. How could the Motts have known that Peter contracted polio from drinking water, much less pointed a finger at a particular faucet?

A rash of questions occurred to me, and I asked them. Had anyone else in the Mott family come down with polio as a result? Had any of the dozens of young women in his sister's dormitory become ill? Had his sister's university ever tested the water to find out whether it was contaminated or not? To all these questions, Peter Mott's answer was no.   4

The story turned out to be not just implausible but one with a covert agenda, comprehended implicitly by the Motts but, without a gloss, incomprehensible to anyone else. And the agenda focused on Peter's sister, Blanche. In every family, say family theorists, individual members have their assigned roles, which they may be well cast for or not. What determines the assigning of roles is not so much who the players really are, but who the family as a whole needs them to be. In the Mott family, Peter was understood to be "the golden boy" while Blanche, as Peter put it, was "dirt."   5

These are the sorts of destructive convictions for which family therapists reserve the term "family myths." The first to elaborate on the notion was psychiatrist Antonio Ferreira, who defined "family myths" as "beliefs shared by all family members, concerning each other and their mutual position in the family life." He asserted that these beliefs "go unchallenged by everyone involved in spite of the reality distortions which they may conspicuously imply. It should be noted that although the family myth is part of the family image, it often differs from the 'front' or social facade that the family as a group attempts to present to outsiders. Instead the family myth is very much a part of the way the family appears to its members, that is, a part of *the inner image* of the group, an image to which all family members contribute and, apparently, strive to preserve. In terms of the family inner image, the family myth refers to the identified roles of its members."   6

Ferreira further characterized the family myth by suggesting that family members may not subscribe to it absolutely. "The individual family member may know, and often does, that much of that image is false and represents no more than a sort of official party line. But such knowledge, when [and if] it exists, is kept so private and concealed that the individual will actually fight against its public revelation, and, by   7 refusing to acknowledge its existence, will do his utmost to keep the family myth intact. For the family myth 'explains' the behavior of the individuals in the family while it hides its motives. . . ."

But why should a family hold on to a belief regardless of its truth? 8
The answer lies in the usefulness of the belief to the individual members. Such beliefs, in whatever way, make other family members feel better about themselves; they allow the family to work, and in doing so, they preserve what Ferreira calls family "homeostasis" or equilibrium.

This is the case even if one member has to bear a socially stigmatized 9
role as a result—as the "bad" one, the "sickly" one, or the mentally ill one. Given this approach, those who do therapy with families make the assumption that the "sick" one is the symptom bearer, the scapegoat, for the entire family. Cure the family and the "sick" one will get better. But this is not so easy to accomplish because all the family members—with the possible exception of the scapegoat—get something as a result of their unconscious conspiracy.

Now, in the Mott family, the central myth was that Blanche was the 10
bad one, the sick one, and the story about how Peter came down with polio was one of many stories used to justify the myth and to keep Blanche tethered to her place in the psychic desert. As the Motts understood that story during the years when Blanche and Peter were growing up, it meant that Peter's polio was Blanche's fault.

Blanche's place in the family was not of course enviable and never 11
had been, and Blanche did not escape the unhappy consequences of her role. If enough people think someone is incompetent or insane or stupid or sickly or bad, that someone may eventually oblige, even if he or she wasn't to begin with.

This is a truth about how families work that Hollywood and movie 12
audiences have long since recognized. In that old film classic *Gaslight* (1944), Ingrid Bergman, as the young wife, is told so often by her husband and maid that she is losing her sanity that eventually she begins to. Similarly, in *Now, Voyager* (1942) and *Separate Tables* (1958), each "spinster" daughter is, at least initially, frail, homely, and invalided because each has dutifully subscribed to her mother's "myth" about her. In each case, it is a myth the mother generates because of her own need to have a companion who won't leave home.

As for the real-life Blanche Mott, she was even more vulnerable than 13
the afflicted young women onscreen. "When my sister was fourteen or fifteen," says Peter, "she had a nervous breakdown. She had shock therapy and saw a psychiatrist and tried to take her own life."

But how had Blanche come to occupy her unenviable role as both 14
"the sick one" and "the bad one"? And how did Peter emerge as the
family's "golden boy"? The answer, or at least part of it, lies with Peter
Mott's mother, Helen; with events in Helen's life at about the time
Blanche was born, as well as earlier; and with the way those events
determined, apparently unconsciously, her vision and expectations of
each of her two children. This perspective, which comes from Peter
Mott, was one he arrived at after several years of analysis.

In the years just before Blanche was born, says Peter, their mother 15
had endured too much tragedy. "My mother's father, whom she always
saw as a comforter, had died," says Peter. "Then her two sisters died—
one of scarlet fever and the other of spilling boiling water on herself.
Then my grandmother, my mother's mother, died of a heart attack. My
mother was pregnant with my sister at this time, and so they named my
sister Blanche, which had been my grandmother's name. In fact my
grandmother's maiden name was Kane, and they named my sister
Blanche Kane Mott."

The conclusion Peter draws from all this now is that at the 16
time of the younger Blanche's birth, Helen Mott was emotionally
devastated and totally depleted; she was not in any psychological
condition to welcome or rejoice over her first child's birth. "My
mother was in terrible shape," says Peter. "She was hospitalized—she
had a nervous breakdown—and there was a nursemaid to take care
of my sister."

The additional twist was that Peter Mott's mother had apparently 17
miscalculated what she would feel about naming her daughter after her
mother, however much she had liked, or wanted to like, the idea of so
honoring her mother. Helen Mott had had a difficult, even stormy
relationship with her own mother and now, having a little girl with the
same name as her mother's, she seemed unable to keep the two separate
in her mind. It was as if once Helen Mott lost her own mother, she took
all the feelings she had had about her and transferred them, part and
parcel, to her little daughter.

"My mother could never bring herself to use the name Blanche 18
with my sister, so she called her Missy. It was just too much, the death
was too much and the daughter was too much. Perhaps my sister was
just too much of a reminder. But anyhow, my sister was the one in the
family who could do nothing right. As a consequence, she was raised
as if she were dirt, or incompetent, or terrible. Growing up, I didn't
consciously recognize how my sister was being devalued, but one of

the most extraordinary aspects of all this family stuff is that for most of my adult life, I dealt with my sister as my mother had dealt with her. As for me," says Peter Mott somewhat ruefully, "I was 'The Golden Boy.' The doctor told my mother to have another child to make her well. I was that child, and I could do no wrong." Perhaps, too, Peter was the replacement for his mother's dead "comfort," her father.

There's nothing in Peter Mott's explanation to explain his father's   19
investment in having Blanche as "the sick one." According to Peter, his father was fairly involved with his own parents, both of whom lived with the Motts. Maybe he was therefore too distant to intercede in the *folie à trois* developing right under his nose. But as for Peter's mother, despite her own fragility, she could redefine herself as healthy once she had a fragile daughter. For Peter, having a disabled sister certainly made it less likely that there would be any encroachment on his role as the "golden" child.

I have gone rather far afield here and made so many incursions into   20
the Motts' prior history—told to Peter as family stories, along the way—to show how any one family story derives its meaning not only from daily family life but from the family's entire jigsaw puzzle of stories. The meaning of any single family story will therefore appear as inevitable, from narrative context alone, to the family members who know the story and tell it.

Relatively few such stories came my way, perhaps because I didn't   21
always recognize them for what they were, but also because family members implicitly recognized their subversive nature and, out of continuing family loyalty, kept them to themselves. Perhaps Peter Mott could afford to tell the story because the event it referred to had happened forty years earlier, both his parents were dead, he was deeply ensconced in his own family of a wife and four nearly grown children, and maybe he was looking for a way to expiate his guilt for whatever part he had played in his sister's long-ago torment.

Could Peter Mott have recognized the implausibility of this family   22
story decades ago? Many family therapists would say probably not. Such stories, as Ferreira points out, serve the family as defense mechanisms serve the individual. "The myth, like the defense, protects the [family] against the threat of disintegration and chaos. . . . Thus, to maintain oneself within a given myth, a certain amount of insight-lessness is necessary." But to outsiders, the family myths that serve to keep a family's specious convictions in place are recognizable by the

same two elements that appeared in Peter Mott's myth—implausible logic and blame.

Vocabulary

raconteur (3)—a skilled story-teller

locution (3)—a particular word, phrase, or expression

rash (4)—large number of examples in a short period of time

covert (5)—secret or hidden

implicitly (5)—in a suggested or implied way

homeostasis (8)—an internal stability

stigmatized (9)—marked in some way as disgraceful

tethered (10)—tied to one place in some way

psychic (10)—of the mind; beyond the physical world

depleted (16)—used up

intercede (19)—to interfere, to mediate

folie à trois (19)—a condition in which three closely associated people who may be mentally ill, share the same false belief or opinion

encroachment (19)—intrusion; trespassing

subversive (21)—trying to overthrow or destroy an established belief

ensconced (21)—placed or settled comfortably or securely

expiate (21)—to make amends or pay the penalty for something

implausibility (22)—state of being not believable or untrue

specious (22)—seeming to be good or correct when it is not

IN YOUR JOURNAL

Look at the family story you wrote about in your earlier journal entry. Who is the good person in your story? Who is the bad person? Who is the sweet one? Who is the mean one? Who seems smart? Who seems foolish? What does this story telll you about your own family?

A Closer Reading

1. What words does Mott use that alert Stone to the importance of his story in understanding his family? Why does he use these words to tell her his story?

2. What is the "covert agenda" and the "unconscious conspiracy" behind the Mott family story? Who is the good one in the story? Who is the bad one? How does that correspond to the pattern of family life Mott describes?

3. What are the purposes of family myths, according to psychiatrist Antonio Ferreira? What are the functions of family myths according to Lightfoot (see page 79)?

4. How does Mott feel about his sister? What evidence of this do you get from the selection? What evidence is presented to show that Mott's feelings about his family change as a result of discussing the story with Stone?

Drawing Your Own Conclusions

1. Why does Mott's mother resent his sister so much? Why does Mott also resent his sister?

2. Of what significance is it that Blanche is named after her grandmother? Have you ever known anyone who was named after a family member? Did this create any problems for the person? By what name did the family call this person?

3. Reread the Modupe story on page 20. Compare the significance of names in both selections. The young girl in each story is usually called "Missy." Why are some children called names such as "Missy," "Junior," "Buddy," and "Sis" instead of their real names?

4. Why is it important to examine family myths? How can a person use writing about such family myths to understand his or her family better?

Thinking about Writing

1. What is the significance of the title of this selection? What is a scapegoat?

2. Which paragraphs in the selection tell the Mott story? Which paragraphs analyze the meaning of the family myth? What differences do you find in the writing style used in each?

3. Why does Stone include the series of questions in paragraph 4? What is their significance in understanding the story of Peter and Missy?

4. What words in this selection are enclosed in quotation marks? Why has the author used quotation marks in each case?

*   *   *

Suggestions for Writing

1. Why do some parents prefer one child over another? What can the unliked child(ren) do in these circumstances? Write an essay in which you describe the problem of having a favorite child and treating that child differently. Explain what a parent can do to avoid having family favorites.

2. Stone writes, "If enough people think someone is incompetent or insane or stupid or sickly or bad, that someone may eventually oblige, even if he or she wasn't to begin with." Is it also true that if someone thinks another person is capable, mentally well, intelligent, healthy, or good, that the person can change for the better? Write an essay in which you take a position about this. Support your point of view by referring to your observations, experiences, and readings.

3. Write an essay in which you describe the family structure of one of the families you have read about so far in this book. What role do the members of the family play? How are these roles reinforced by family behavior? Include any evidence from the reading that supports your point of view.

4. Examine a family in which you know several of the members well. Or examine a family you have read about or seen in a film or on television. Decide if there is a "good" person, a "bad" person, a "selfish" person, a "greedy" person, a "sickly" person, a "rich" person, a "smart" person, a "sweet" person, a "mean" person, and a "victim." (You may think of other categories as well.) Decide how these people were assigned the particular roles in the family. In your essay, describe the family, the roles the people play, and how these roles maintain the family structure.

Strategies for Revision

If you have written a persuasive essay in which you were trying to convince your reader of your point of view, answer the following questions as you reread your draft.

- What is my point of view?
- Where do I state my point of view in the draft? (Double underline this and notice where it occurs in your essay.)
- What pieces of evidence support my point of view? (Underline them in your draft and make sure the examples are clear and well described.)
- Is the evidence organized in a way that is easy to follow? (Notice which piece of evidence comes first, second, etc. Why are they in that order? Change the order and see if this improves the organization of your essay.)
- What is the strongest sentence in the essay? Where is is located? Should it be moved to make a more effective point?

IN YOUR JOURNAL

In today's world, the family unit is going through a change. Families may be husband, wife, and their children; single parents with children; two divorced spouses and their children; and lovers and their children. These changes in the family unit have important effects on our society.

Before you read this selection, write down what you think it means to be a family. Take into consideration the many different types of families today.

Families of the Future

Alvin Toffler

Alvin Toffler is a well-known social critic and educator whose book *Future Shock* (1970) was a best-seller. Toffler also wrote *The Adaptive Corporation* (1984) and *Powershift: Knowledge, Wealth & Violence at the Edge of the 21st Century* (1991). The following excerpt is from his book *The Third Wave* (1980), which describes the major changes in society as coming in three great waves. The first coincides with the agricultural revolution, the second with the Industrial Revolution, and the third with recent scientific and technological advances. The Third Wave, starting from about 1955, when white-collar workers began to outnumber blue-collar workers, is the age of the computer, commercial jet travel, and the birth control pill. This is our time period and this is our future. This excerpt deals with the Third Wave's impact on the family.

The coming of the Third Wave, of course, does not mean the end of the nuclear family any more than the coming of the Second Wave meant the end of the extended family. It means, rather, that the nuclear family can no longer serve as the ideal model for society. 1

The little-appreciated fact is that, at least in the United States where the Third Wave is most advanced, most people *already* live outside the classical nuclear family form. 2

If we define the nuclear family as a working husband, a housekeeping wife, and two children, and ask how many Americans actually still live in this type of family, the answer is astonishing: 7 percent of the 3 total United States population. Ninety-three percent of the population do not fit this ideal Second Wave model any longer.

Even if we broaden our definition to include families in which   4
both spouses work or in which there are fewer or more than two children, we find the vast majority—as many as two thirds to three quarters of the population—living *outside* the nuclear situation. Moreover, all the evidence suggests that nuclear households (however we choose to define them) are still shrinking in number as other family forms rapidly multiply.

To begin with, we are witnessing a population explosion of "solos"—   5
people who live alone, outside a family altogether. Between 1970 and 1978 the number of persons aged fourteen to thirty-four who lived alone nearly tripled in the United States—rising from 1.5 million to 4.3 million. Today, a fifth of all households in the United States consists of a person living solo. Many deliberately choose it, at least for a time. Says a legislative aide to a Seattle councilwoman, "I would consider marriage if the right person came along, but I would not give up my career for it." In the meantime she lives alone. She is part of a large class of young adults who are leaving home earlier but marrying later, thus creating what census specialist Arthur Norton says is a "transitional living phase" that is "becoming an acceptable part of one's life cycle."

Looking at an older slice of the population, we find a large number   6
of formerly married people, often "between marriages," living on their own and, in many cases, decidedly liking it. The growth of such groups has created a flourishing "singles" culture and a much publicized proliferation of bars, ski lodges, travel tours, and other services or products designed for the independent individual. Simultaneously, the real estate industry has come up with "singles only" condominia, and has begun to respond to a need for smaller apartments and suburban homes with fewer bedrooms. Almost a fifth of all home buyers in the United States today are single.

We are also experiencing a headlong growth in the number of people living together without bothering about legal formalities. This   7
group has more than doubled in the past decade, according to United States authorities. The practice has become so common that the United States Department of Housing and Urban Development has overthrown tradition and changed its rules to permit such couples to occupy public housing. The courts, meanwhile, from Connecticut to California, are wrestling with the legal and property complications that spring up when such couples "divorce." Etiquette columnists write about

which names to use in addressing partners, and "couple counseling" has sprouted as a new professional service alongside marriage counseling.

Another significant change has been the growth in the number of those consciously choosing what is coming to be known as a "child-free" life-style. According to James Ramey, senior research associate at the Center for Policy Research, we are seeing a massive shift from "child-centered" to "adult-centered" homes. At the turn of the century there were few singles in society, and relatively few parents lived very long after their youngest child left the home. Thus most households were, in fact, child-centered. By contrast, as early as 1970 in the United States only one in three adults lived in a home with children under eighteen.

Today organizations are springing up to promote the child-free life, and a reluctance to have children is spreading in many industrial nations. In 1960 only 20 percent of "ever-married" American women under age thirty were child-free. By 1975 this had shot up to 32 percent—a 60 percent jump in fifteen years. A vocal organization, the National Alliance for Optional Parenthood, has arisen to protect the rights of the childless and to combat pronatalist propaganda.

A similar organization, the National Association for the Childless, has sprouted in Britain, and many couples across Europe are also deliberately choosing to remain childless. In Bonn, West Germany, for exaple, Theo and Agnes Rohl, both in their mid-thirties, he a city official, she a secretary, say, "We don't think we'll have children. . . ." The Rohls are modestly affluent. They own a small house. They manage a vacation trip to California or Southern France now and then. Children would drastically alter their way of life. "We're used to our life-style the way it is," they say, "and we like being independent." Nor is this reluctance to bear children a sign of capitalist decadence. It is present in the Soviet Union, too, where many young Russian couples echo the sentiments of the Rohls and explicitly reject parenthood—a fact that worries Soviet officialdom in view of the still-high birth rates among several non-Russian national minorities.

Turning now to those *with* children, the breakdown of the nuclear family is even more sharply evidenced in the spectacular increase in single-parent families. So many divorces, breakups, and separations have occurred in recent years—mainly in nuclear families—that today a staggering one-in-seven American children is raised by a single parent, and the number is even higher—one in four—in urban areas.

The increase in such households has brought a growing recognition that, despite severe problems, a one-parent household can, under certain circumstances, be better for the child than a nuclear household continually torn by bitter strife. Newspapers and organizations now serve single parents and are heightening their group consciousness and political clout.

Nor, once again, is the phenomenon purely American. In Britain   13 today nearly one family in ten is headed by a single parent—nearly a sixth of them headed by men—and one-parent households form what *New Society* magazine calls "the fastest growing group in poverty." A London-based organization, the National Council for One-Parent Families, has sprung up to champion their cause.

In Germany, a housing association in Cologne has constructed a   14 special block of apartments for such families and provided them with day-time child care so the parents can work. And in Scandinavia a network of special welfare rights has grown up to support these families. The Swedes, for example, give one-parent households first crack at nursery and day-care facilities. In both Norway and Sweden, in fact, it is sometimes possible for a single-parent family to enjoy a higher standard of living than that of the typical nuclear family.

A challenging new form of family has arisen in the meantime that   15 reflects the high rate of remarriage after divorce. In *Future Shock* I identified this as the "aggregate family," in the which two divorced couples with children remarry, bringing the children of both marriages (and the adults as well) into a new, expanded family form. It is now estimated that 25 percent of American children are, or will soon be, members of such family units. According to Davidyne Mayleas, such units, with their "poly-parents," may be the mainstream family form of tomorrow. "We're into economic polygamy," says Mayleas—meaning that the two merged family units typically transfer money back and forth in the form of child support or other payments. The spread of this family form, she reports, has been accompanied by a rising incidence of sexual relations between parents and nonblood-related children.

The technologically advanced nations today are honeycombed with a   16 bewildering array of family forms: Homosexual marriages, communes, groups of elderly people banding together to share expenses (and sometimes sex), and many other forms coexist as never before. There are contract marriages, serial marriages, family clusters, and a variety of intimate networks with or without shared sex, as well as families in which mother and father live and work in two different cities.

Even these family forms barely hint at the even richer variety bub-   17 bling under the surface. When three psychiatrists—Kellam, Ensminger, and Turner—attempted to map the "variations of families" found in a single poor black neighborhood in Chicago, they identified "no less than 86 different combinations of adults," including numerous forms of "mother-grandmother" families, "mother-aunt" families, "mother-step-father" families, and "mother-other" families.

Faced with this veritable maze of kinship arrangements, even fairly 18 orthodox scholars have come around to the once radical view that we are moving out of the age of the nuclear family and into a new society marked by diversity in family life. In the words of sociologist Jessie Bernard, "The most characteristic aspect of marriage in the future will be precisely the array of options available to different people who want different things from their relationships with one another."

The frequently asked question, "What is the future of the family?" 19 usually implies that as the Second Wave nuclear family loses its dominance some other form will replace it. A more likely outcome is that during Third Wave civilization no single form will dominate the family mix for any long period. Instead we will see a high variety of family structures. Rather than masses of people living in uniform family arrangements, we shall see people moving through this system, tracing personalized or "customized" trajectories during the course of their lives.

Again, this does not mean the total elimination or "death" of the 20 nuclear family. It merely means that from now on the nuclear family will be only one of the many socially accepted and approved forms. As the Third Wave sweeps in, the family system is becoming de-massified right along with the production system and the information system in society.

Vocabulary

condominia (6)—plural of "condominium"; apartments that are owned by the tenants who share joint ownership of the building and grounds

pronatalist (9)—advocate for childbirth

affluent (10)—rich; well-to-do

strife (12)—fighting; arguing

aggregate (15)—total; a group gathered together and counted as one unit

kinship (18)—family relationship

array (18)—orderly grouping or arrangement

trajectories (19)—curved paths of something thrown into space

IN YOUR JOURNAL

What type of family do you live in? What to you is the ideal family situation? Why do you feel this way?

A Closer Reading

1. According to this selection, how is today's family different from the family Toffler described as typical in the Second Wave? Is there a typical family today?

2. Toffler describes the Third Wave as the age of the computer, commercial jet travel, and the birth control pill. How have these three inventions affected family structure and/or family life?

3. What does Toffler mean by the term "aggregate family"? What does his term "economic polygamy" mean? How does this idea connect with the aggregate family?

4. What does Toffler expect to be the future of the family unit?

Drawing Your Own Conclusions

1. Do your observations of the world coincide with Toffler's? Do you notice fewer nuclear families and more people living in other family situations? With your class, discuss how prevalent the nuclear family is in the area where you live. List and discuss some of the types of family structures you have observed.

2. What specific social, economic, health, and employment factors have influenced the development of the types of family units that exist today? How have recent laws altered the influence of any of these factors? How have recent events in your community altered the influence of any of these factors? What changes would you like to see made that would improve any of these existing conditions?

3. What happens to older members of the family in your community? Where do they live? With whom do they spend their holidays? Do they have close ties to their families?

4. According to Toffler, in what situations do people choose to live alone? Has there been, or do you think there will be, a period in your own life when you would prefer to live alone? Explain.

Thinking about Writing

1. What words or concepts does Toffler define in this selection? Which of these does he define by using statistics? Which by using examples? Which by quoting from knowledgeable people? Which way of defining a point is clearest for you?

2. What examples does Toffler provide to persuade his readers that the changes he is describing are international? Does he provide enough examples to convince you?

3. How does Toffler indicate that he is referring to an established fact, or that is his information is from research? How does he indicate that some of the ideas contained in the selection are not his own?

4. Reread the introductory paragraph and the concluding paragraph of this selection. How do these two connect? What has Toffler been trying to prove thoughout this article? How does he state this in each place? How do the statements differ?

* * *

Suggestions for Writing

1. Write a one-page summary of "Families of the Future." What are the main points? What words are defined? What research is cited? (See page 51 for ideas about writing a summary.)

2. Write an essay in which you define the two basic family types—extended and nuclear. Then after defining these, give specific examples of family types from your observations and experiences. Finally, explain which family type you prefer for your own life and why.

3. With the help of older members of your family, construct a family tree in which you trace your grandparents, their parents, aunts, uncles, cousins, and so forth as far back as you are able. Write an essay explaining what you found out about your family by doing this activity. Do you know anything about your family that you did not know before you did it? Did your family ever live in the "extended" family pattern? Are members now an "extended" family, a "nuclear" family, or one of the other forms which Toffler describes?

4. Write an essay in which you explain what our society should do to assist single teenage parents in raising their children. Make specific suggestions and explain why you think these will improve the situation for the parents and for their children.

5. Toffler notes, "Despite severe problems, a one-parent household can, under certain circumstances, be better for the child than a nuclear household continually torn by bitter strife." However, recent research suggests that the effects of divorce are far-reaching. Some adults interviewed on this subject state that their parents' divorce was the most important event of their childhood. Write an essay in which you take a position for or against the following statement: Unhappily married people with children should get divorced because of the effects on their children. Use your observations, experiences, and readings to support your point of view.

Strategies for Revision

If you have written a summary of this selection, review the description of summary writing and the questions that you can ask yourself on pages 51–53. Decide if your summary needs more information. Share summaries with another student in your class. Compare notes as to how you decided what to include and what to omit. What similarities and differences do you find in your two summaries? How do you account for these?

Sharon Cassell wrote an essay in response to suggestion 1 from the Suggestions for Writing that follow the John Edgar Wideman story: Write an essay describing your father, your mother, or any other influential adult from your childhood. Tell a story that illustrates his or her personality and how this person affected your life.

Tearing Down Walls to Build Bridges

Sharon Cassell

As I quickly surveyed the hospital waiting room, I saw him. His legs 1 were crossed with his elbows resting on a small magazine table. His hand, rough and scarred from years of hard work as a part-time mechanic, supported his head. I noticed how the once beautiful auburn hair had now turned to mostly silver gray. His tinted wire framed glasses hid his deep set, dark brown eyes and made it hard for me to see how he was really feeling.

"Hello, Dad," I said. "Have you received a report on Mom yet?"   2

Looking up he gave me a tight smile and replied, "Hi Sherri. Not 3 yet," he replied. "It will probably be an hour or so before we hear anything. Would you like some coffee?"

I realized something as I sat in the suspense filled room with the 4 others: all of my life I had spent looking for ways to please my father, and for the first time I felt he really needed me and wanted me to be with him. As we sat there my mind began to wander to earlier days when our relationship was stressed and distant.

My father has always been a stern man. His deepset eyes often made 5 him appear harsher than he intended to be. As a child I felt his quiet, intense nature was an indication that he disapproved of me. Years of working nights at an automotive factory and repairing cars at home during the day afforded him little sleep and too much work; consequently, his stern nature was intensified. He often spoke harshly, therefore, I learned to fear him. Even so, I looked for ways to please him so that our relationship could be peaceful. However, I still felt a gap between us that I wanted to close, but I felt that I had no bridge with which to do so. I needed and wanted his approval in my life.

When I was sixteen years old I had worked all summer for a dress that I 6 wanted. I remember getting dressed that beautiful morning feeling particularly nice with my long, straight brown hair behaving in an unusually cooperative manner. My dark summer tan had now turned to a golden brown and my new white and blue dress was everything that I hoped it would be. I walked down the hall into the living room where my father was.

He stopped me; placed both hands on my shoulders, looked into my 7
eyes and said, "Sherri, you don't scrub up half bad. You're a good kid, just too bad there's no demand for good kids these days." He patted me twice on the back and went on his way.

I realized in his own way he was trying to tell me he was proud of 8
me but was unable to do so. It was not very long, however, until my father's approval once again had escaped me. As I became older and began to date he distanced himself from me in a manner that I knew was his definite disapproval. He seldom spoke to me unless it was to relate to me his disgust for my short skirts, sassy mouth or new boyfriend. In return I stopped trying to seek his approval.

The day I was married he looked like a defeated man. His eyes were 9
weary and empty. His shoulders were stooped as if he were much older than his youthful 42 years. The only words he spoke that day were when the minister asked, "Who gives this woman?"

He replied, "Her mother and I." 10

The joy of my wedding day was mixed with sorrow as I realized I 11
may never know or understand this man I call father.

It was not until years later after my dad had a serious illness that the 12
wall between us began to come down, and a bridge began to be built. While visiting home one Sunday afternoon Dad began to talk about his life and death experience and what he felt it had taught him. He looked at me as he had many years before only this time he was weary and solemn.

He began to speak softly with tears in his eyes: something very rare 13
for him. "Sherri, I want you to know that I love you. I know we have not always agreed on everything and sometimes we have hurt each other, and I need you to know that I am sorry." He began to speak more quickly as if he thought the words might leave him before he would get them all said. "I have always had a great deal of trouble telling anyone how I feel, but I need for you to know that I am proud of you, and proud of the person that you have become. Please don't ever believe differently. I do love you and have always wanted the best for you."

A heavy silence filled the room; I was unable to speak. There was a 14
tightness in my throat and stomach; my eyes began to burn. After a prolonged silence, I finally found my voice.

"Dad, I have always wanted to be loved and accepted by you. I can't 15 ever remember you telling me that you loved me or were proud of me until just now. Why has it taken you so long?" He thought for a moment; searching for the right words to explain himself. As he spoke his voice was quiet but deliberate.

"I have never allowed myself to confide in anyone except your mom. I have never felt I needed anyone else. I didn't want to depend on anyone: I was wrong. It is going to be very hard for me to change." Dad continued to talk about our old problems and new directions, and how each of us would work on learning to understand the other. I don't remember how the visit ended, but from that day on there was a change in how Dad and I began to relate to each other. We began to tell each other about things that were happening in our lives, and once Dad called just to see if I had made it to work safely on a bad snowy morning.   16

My thoughts were interrupted as a recovery room nurse approached us with a progress report: it was good. Mom had come through the surgery very well and we could see her soon. I saw my Dad's body immediately relax, and a twinkle return to his eyes. As we walked down the long corridor to Mom's room, Dad began to tell me about a fishing experience he had as a child. Dad seldom told me stories from his childhood so I always felt privileged to hear one. I was glad he chose this time to share it with me. Both of us were laughing as we walked into Mom's room; the wall was down: the bricks had been used to complete the bridge. I felt accepted, loved and needed.   17

Questions to Think About

1. Cassell does not identify the subject of her essay in the first paragraph. Do you think this is effective or not in making the reader want to read more?

2. What words and phrases does Cassell use to make the transition from the present to the past?

3. Do Cassell's examples convince you that her father was hard to please? Do they convince you that she was always trying to please him?

4. How does she resolve her conflict in the last paragraph?

5. What does the title of this essay mean? What reference does Cassell make to the title in the body of the essay?

MAKING CONNECTIONS

The World of the Family: *Making the First Connections*

1. Why are our families so important in our lives regardless of our age? Write an essay answering this question. You may want to paraphrase or directly quote from some of the selections you have read or some of the writing you have done in this unit.

2. If you could choose to be born into one of the families described in the various selections in this unit, which family would you choose? Write an essay in which you explain the factors that you took into consideration as you made your choice. Why would you like to be a member of this family?

3. Write an essay in which you compare the lifestyles of the mothers in the Lightfoot story (see page 76) and the Rowe story (see page 61). What similarities and what differences do you find in the lives of these two women? Before you begin to write, reread each selection and note how the two women live and interact with their children.

4. Write an essay in which you choose one piece of writing from this unit that caused an emotional reaction: It may have angered you, made you sad, or made you happy. Explain the effect of this piece of writing, and tell why it had that effect.

5. Write an essay in which you choose one piece of writing that made you think about the family in a new way. Explain what you learned from the piece of writing and how it affected you.

6. Using the definitions presented in Alvin Toffler's selection (see page 103), analyze the structure of the families described in two of the other selections from this unit.

3

THE WORLD OF LEARNING

Finding One's Purpose

Learning is a lifelong endeavor. We begin to learn about the world from the moment we are born. When we first enter school, we begin to find our way in the world by using the knowledge and skills we are acquiring. Many of us begin to find our direction in life during this time. For others, finding a direction takes time and tremendous personal effort. In this unit, we will look at the experiences of learners as they try to understand themselves and what it means to learn.

In the first selection in this unit, "Intelligence: A Revolutionary View" by Daniel Goleman, Paul Kaufman, and Michael Ray, we begin by looking at intelligence: what it is, and how it it should be assessed. Until recently, most intelligence tests focused on skills that could be demonstrated by reading, writing, and computing. Now that trend is changing as we begin to realize that intelligence has more aspects than we knew. This article presents the theory of the seven aspects of intelligence and suggests ways these aspects can be recognized, assessed, and developed.

In our next section, Malcolm X explains the role that literacy had in transforming his life. His dedication to reading and learning new words led him to try to immerse himself in the dictionary. In this selection from his autobiography, we can feel the excitement and pleasure he receives from improving his writing and reading skills.

Personal motivation goes only so far in learning if there is little encouragement and support. K. C. Cole examines some of the difficulties women have experienced as they try to develop a career in physics, traditionally a male field that has been unfriendly and sometimes even hostile to women.

James Thurber takes a humorous look at education in his description of an encounter with an insensitive botany professor. In "University Days," Thurber describes a college that focuses so much on its athletic teams that it may be shortchanging those students who are less physically able.

In "Outsider in a Silent World," Lou Ann Walker focuses on her own life and experiences with the hearing impaired as the child of two deaf parents. She learns much about herself and the insensitivity of the hearing world through observing her parents in their interactions with other people.

Mark Shone also increases his understanding by looking closely at and writing about his experiences as a first-year teacher in an urban school setting. Students rarely realize the problems teachers face every day. In his diary, Shone looks at everyday life in a crowded classroom and analyzes his triumphs and his failures.

Sheila Renee Shallenberger, a student writer, describes the problems she faced in returning to college and in learning to write. Despite high motivation, Shallenberger still faces many frustrations and difficulties; finally, she finds satisfaction in her progress.

* * *

Think about the following questions before reading the selections in this unit:

1. What subject(s) have always been easiest for you to learn? Why?

2. What subject(s) have always been the hardest for you to learn? Why? What can you do to help yourself to do better?

3. What do you want to learn most from college? Why?

Intelligence: A Revolutionary View
  Daniel Goleman, Paul Kaufman, and Michael
  Ray

Learning Words
  Malcolm X

Women and Physics
  K. C. Cole

University Days
  James Thurber

Outsider in a Silent World
  Lou Ann Walker

The Diary of a First-Year Teacher
  Mark Shone

Returning to College
  Sheila Renee Shallenberger

IN YOUR JOURNAL

Write about an experience in your life in which you felt creative. What did you do that gave you that feeling?

Intelligence: A Revolutionary View

Daniel Goleman, Paul Kaufman, and Michael Ray

This article is excerpted from *The Creative Spirit* (1993), which was written as a companion to the public television series of the same name. Daniel Goleman is a psychologist who writes about behavioral sciences for the *New York Times*. He is the former senior editor for *Psychology Today* and has taught psychology at Harvard University. Goleman has writttten seven books about subjects related to psychology.

Paul Kaufman is the creator, writer, and senior producer of *The Creative Spirit* television series. He has been a researcher on creativity at Harvard University and on interpretation of information at Stanford University.

Michael Ray holds the McCoy-Banc chair of Creativity and Innovation at Stanford University's School of Business. He has coauthored three books on business and creativity.

When parents are supportive of their children's creativity, they will   1
discover what psychologists are now confirming: most children have a natural talent, a flair for a particular activity.

A widespread but questionable view of creativity is that it is a singu-   2
lar capacity for originality applicable to whatever people do—a capacity that can be tested and quantified. That view of creativity is increasingly being challenged. Researchers now question whether one can do justice to a child's creativity with a paper-and-pencil test, which offers up a "creativity quotient" much like the score on an IQ test.

For example, one of the most common tests for creativity used in   3
schools asks, "How many uses can you think of?" for objects like a junked car or some other everyday item. The test is scored for how many answers a child gives, for how unusual the responses are, and how many details are given for each. Giving a long list of highly original, intricately described ways the object can be used yields a high score on "creativity."

But many educators and psychologists, such as Howard Gard- 4
ner, are skeptical of such measures of creativity. Instead of relying
on a single test of creativity, Gardner argues that we should see
how children respond to a wide variety of material that draws on
varying areas of ability, including music, dance, and interpersonal
relationships.

That approach avoids assessing creativity through a test that really 5
relies on language ability. In this sense, the direct-assessment approach
is an "intelligence-fair" way to assess creativity—it doesn't evaluate
one kind of creativity in ways that actually demand completely different abilities.

Even with simple objects parents have around the house or can pick 6
up at the store, they can get a sense of where a child's interests and
abilities lie. By letting a child explore a range of activities, passions and
budding talents are more likely to emerge.

The Seven Intelligences

An essential part of the definition of creativity is that it is not only 7
original and useful, but it occurs in a specific domain. This view high-
lights the importance of recognizing the areas in which a child's particular bent or talent falls.

For Gardner, a fruitful way to think about this is in terms of the many 8
kinds of "intelligences." One's intelligence provides the basis for creativity; a child will go on to be most creative in the fields where she has the
greatest strengths. Gardner identifies seven primary intelligences:

Language

Linguistic intelligence is the gift of poets and lyricists, writers and 9
orators—those who love language in any form, from James Joyce and
Vladimir Nabokov to the masters of rap. One way to assess language
skills in small children is by having them make up stories. A parent can
do this by using homemade game boards, dolls, toy figurines, and
small household objects to create an imaginary setting. This setting
can be then populated by characters such as kings, queens, and bears
and feature mysterious places such as caves and swamps. The parent
can pose a question to the child: how does the bear entice the king
into the dark, remote cave? The child then invents a story about how
this comes about.

Not all children can or want to finish a story. When they do, Gard- 10
ner observes whether they do it imaginatively, whether they play with
sounds or create figures of speech, or just rely on humdrum combinations of words and routine scripts. "Some children who are not attracted by these imaginative stories turn out to be quite effective
reporters—they are likely to use their linguistic intelligence to give
accurate accounts in words of what they observe. Maybe they will work
for their local newspaper someday," Gardner says.

Math and Logic

This type of intelligence is exhibited by scientists, mathematicians, 11
and others whose life is governed by reasoning. It has been particularly valued in the West, since the time of Socrates, and is even more
venerated in the computer age. Most standard intelligence tests emphasize logic, the gift of such philosophers and scientists as Descartes and
Newton.

According to Gardner, one way to ascertain this talent is by 12
giving children a chance to test simple hypotheses. Gardner, for example, shows children that if you pour two different-colored sub-
stances together, they produce a third color. He then observes
whether they explore further on their own—for example, whether
they try to produce other color combinations and to figure out how
they have been achieved. That is a clue that they are inclined toward
logical thinking.

When it comes to numerical ability, the question is whether a child 13
has an intuitive knack for numbers. Posing questions like "What's 2 plus
3?" misses the point. But some board games are good tests of the child's
feeling for numbers.

"In our research, we use a board game in which the child has to beat 14
you getting from the head to the tail of the dinosaur," says Gardner.
"The game includes strategy, where the child can not only play his own
dice, but set yours any way he wants to. If a young child is able to set
the dice so that, consistently, you lose and he wins, he is exhibiting both
logical and mathematical skills."

Music

By and large, youngsters who are gifted in musical intelligence are 15
attracted to the world of sound, try to produce appealing combinations
of sound on their own, or ask repeatedly for the opportunity to play an

instrument. In a prodigy like Mozart, this ability flowers early and spectacularly, most professional musicians recall gravitating toward their craft in early childhood.

Kids' exposure to music at home is often limited to what comes   16
over the radio or TV. Gardner advocates giving children the chance to explore sounds and create their own kinds of melodies. For example, there is a special set of bells, originally developed by education pioneer Maria Montessori. Says Gardner, "Playing with the bells lets kids explore the world of sound, to recognize what sounds like what: what's higher, lower, the same or different. What's scary and what's exciting. And then to see if they can actually create some little songs on their own."

Spatial Reasoning

Spatial reasoning is the knack for grasping how things orient in   17
space. It involves the ability to appreciate visual-spatial relations—both those right in front of you, in the manner of a sculptor, and those covering a wider range, as does a pilot flying an airplane.

One of the earliest signs of this ability is skill in building things with   18
blocks. Another is being able to imagine what something looks like from different sides—an ability that makes it easier to assemble and take apart mechanical devices. Being able to find your way around is another spatial talent.

It is not unusual to find a child who is doing poorly at scholastics   19
but excels in working with mechanical objects. If you give such children an alarm clock or some other mechanical device, they will analyze it, figure out how to take it apart, and then put it back together again.

Having a strong spatial intelligence does not predict whether a   20
person will be a scientist or an artist, says Gardner. But it does offer a strong clue as to the *kind* of scientist or artist someone might be.

Einstein had immense spatial skills. It was these skills that allowed   21
him to use a "thought experiment," in which he imagined himself riding on a beam of light, to achieve a crucial insight in his theory of relativity. Leonardo da Vinci was also gifted with great spatial intelligence. Not only was he a spectacular painter, but his anatomical studies and the machines he devised—including tanks and flying machines—all display a strong spatial sense. Da Vinci also wrote poetry and songs, but nobody, Gardner points out, sings his songs.

Movement

It may at first seem odd to consider the body as the locus of a form   22
of intelligence. After all, Western tradition upholds a distinction between the mind and the body. But Gardner believes that the capacity to
use your whole body, or parts of your body (like your hand), to solve
problems or to fashion a product is as intellectually challenging an
activity as figuring out cause-and-effect relations.

Basketball great Michael Jordan and the late dancer Martha Gra-   23
ham share a genius for movement, or *bodily kinesthetic* intelligence.
Surgeons and craftspeople of all kinds rely on this ability to use the
entire body, or parts of the body, to make something or solve a
problem.

Most children begin to show their abilities in movement by using   24
their body to solve problems—orchestrating winning plays in sandlot
football, making up new routines for cheerleading, or whittling in
wood. It is those children who continue to reason with their body, and
to use their bodies in innovative ways, who end up as successful athletes, dancers, actors, or potters.

Interpersonal Intelligence

Just as we tend to divide the body from the mind, we tend to   25
associate intelligence with knowledge of the world of ideas rather than
with knowledge of the world of persons. In fact, however, the ability to
understand other people—what motivates them, how to work effectively with them, how to lead or follow or care for them—is crucial for
surviving and thriving in any human environment.

"Traditional tests of intelligence ignore this knowledge of other   26
persons, perhaps because the academics who designed these tests tended
to be solitary thinkers," says Gardner. "But if intelligence tests had been
invented by politicians or businesspeople, this form of intelligence
would head the list."

He adds, "Even in some very young children, a special sensitivity   27
to others is evident. They are the ones who observe other children
with great care or who are able to influence others to behave in
ways that are desirable to them." And in the natural course of a
child's day, this intelligence shows itself in how well the child gets
along with peers and adults. In the course of playing, making music,
or telling stories, many children give clues to this ability. One sign is

being a natural leader—the one who leads the way in deciding what a group of kids will do next, or who smooths things over and settles disputes.

Interpersonal intelligence includes understanding other people—   28
knowing what motivates them, what they are feeling, and how to get along with them. A child gifted in this area might show an unusual ability to empathize with another child who had fallen and hurt herself, or failed a test. In adulthood, it's the core of talent in fields like sales, politics, therapy, and teaching.

This kind of creative gift can spark vast social movements. Gandhi,   29
the great Indian statesman, developed a strategy of nonviolent, passive resistance that drove the British out of India. It has been the strength and inspiration ever since of heroes like Martin Luther King, Jr., and the Chinese students in Tiananmen Sqaure.

Intrapersonal Intelligence

*Intra*personal intelligence is knowing oneself. A person with a   30
high degree of intrapersonal intelligence knows his strengths and weaknesses, desires and fears, and can act on that knowledge in adaptive ways.

This intelligence shows itself in such things as having a decisive sense   31
of preferences, or in self-discipline and the ability to persevere in the face of frustrations. Even young children display some self-knowledge.

Unlike other forms of intelligence, self-knowledge is likely to   32
deepen throughout life. Encouraging children to be introspective—for example, to keep and reread diaries or journals—and to get to know people who are themselves contemplative or "wise," are all ways to enhance intrapersonal intelligence.

One of the great geniuses in this domain was Sigmund Freud. For   33
decades he psychoanalyzed himself, paying special attention to his dreams and their meaning. And through a combination of his patients' free associations and his own self-analysis, Freud discovered truths about the inner life of people in general, such as the importance of early relationships with parents for relations later in life. In developing psychoanalysis, Freud came up with a method that can help people develop a stronger intrapersonal sense—a path to greater self-knowledge.

"This intelligence is often invisible," Gardner says. "It comes down   34
to knowing yourself very, very well, and using that self-knowledge productively."

Vocabulary

quantified (2)—measured; expressed in numbers

quotient (2)—the result when one number is divided by another

domain (7)—field or area of activity

lyricists (9)—the writers of the words in a song. (Look throughout the article to find names for other kinds of workers or people engaged in creative endeavors.)

hypotheses (12)—tentatively accepted but as yet unproved theories or ideas

scholastics (19)—schoolwork

locus (22)—a mathematical term that refers to a system of points or lines that meets a certain condition

kinesthetic (23)—having to do with a sense of position, movement, or tension in the body perceived through nerve endings

peers (27)—persons of the same rank or ability

empathize (28)—share deeply in the emotions or feelings of others

---

IN YOUR JOURNAL

Decide which name for a type of intelligence describes yours the best. Explain your choice. Choose the ones that you feel describe you the least. Explain.

A Closer Reading

1. What specific activities indicate a child's ability with language? What behaviors or toys develop this type of intelligence?

2. What specific activities indicate a child's ability with math and logic? What behaviors or toys develop this type of intelligence?

3. What specific activities indicate a child's ability with music? What behaviors or toys develop this type of intelligence?

4. What specific activities indicate a child's ability with spatial reasoning? What behaviors or toys develop this type of intelligence?

5. What specific activities indicate a child's ability with movement or bodily kinesthetic intelligence? What behaviors or toys develop this type of intelligence?

6. What specific activities indicate a child's ability to understand or communicate with other people, to have interpersonal intelligence? What behaviors or toys develop this type of intelligence?

7. What specific activities indicate a child's ability in self-awareness, of having intrapersonal intelligence? What behaviors or toys develop this type of intelligence?

Drawing Your Own Conclusions

1. How can knowing your own strengths in intelligence help you in choosing courses to take in college? In choosing a career for your future? Think about people you know and the way they have been able to express their individual abilities through their work.

2. What should parents do to become more aware of their children's abilities? What can they do to help each of their children develop all their different abilities?

3. What can schools do to become more aware of children's abilities? What can teachers do to help each child develop all the different abilities, when present-day classrooms are overcrowded and schools lack funding?

Thinking about Writing

1. Each separate intelligence is classified in a category and described through the use of examples, descriptions, definitions, and suggestions. Reread each of the categories, paying attention to the order in which these four things are presented. Are they presented in the same order in each category? What differences and what similarities do you find?

2. Howard Gardner is a developmental psychologist at Harvard University. Many of the ideas presented in this selection about multiple intelligence are taken from his writing. Do the authors refer to Gardner? How? With quotations or paraphrases?

How do the authors acknowledge Gardner as a source to their readers?

3. What other people do the authors refer to in this article? Why do the writers refer to them in this article? What professions are referred to in the article?

4. Reread the Craig selection on page 46. Compare the way categories are presented in the Goleman et al. selection and in the Craig selection. Which of the following are used in each article: examples, descriptions, definitions, and comparisons? Explain your answer using specific examples from each selection.

* * *

Suggestions for Writing

1. Look at the journal entry you wrote after reading this selection in which you identified the one area in which you feel you have the most intelligence. Explain your choice, citing particular experiences you have had. Tell your readers whether you were ever tested in or given a chance to express this aspect of your intelligence in school. If so, in what ways? If not, what helped you develop this aspect of your intelligence?

2. Write an essay in which you describe an activity that you engage in regularly and in which you can express yourself creatively. Explain the activity, where you do it, the steps you take, and describe the "product" of your creativity.

3. Write an essay in which you describe and classify the different types of tests that you have taken in school, in other words, true/false, essay, and so on. Explain which type of test you think best indicates whether or not a student has learned a subject. Give examples from your own experiences and your observation of others to support your point of view.

4. Write an essay in which you describe and classify different types of students and/or learners, in other words, disciplined, lazy, and so forth. Explain in which category you best fit as a learner. Give examples from your own experiences and your observations of others to support your point of view.

Collaborative Project

Most intelligence tests today test only the areas of language and math and logic. According to this article, to understand the variety of abilities that people possess, we may need to look at other types of intelligence too.

With a partner, choose one of the other intelligences described in this article and create a test that would indicate a person's intelligence in that area. Be specific about the tasks you would want the person to do and the materials necessary for your test. Together, decide what behaviors would indicate that a person has little, moderate, or strong intelligence in the area you are testing. After you complete this project, write about your experience discussing, creating, and shaping the test you created. What did you learn about creating a test from the process of working together?

Most researchers pilot their tests on people to see which aspects are effective and which need rethinking. Pilot your tests on members of the class, your friends, or family members. Write a summary of the testing. What did you learn about your test? What changes do you need to make so that your test will be more effective?

Strategies for Revision

Revise your draft using a different aspect of intelligence from the ones you usually use. For example, if you usually work alone, use your interpersonal abilities to work with another classmate. Read your essay aloud to another student and listen to that student's essay in return, in order to understand what the other person is trying to communicate.

Listen carefully to each other. Then, discuss each essay, focusing on how well you can understand it and on how well it communicates its author's message. Together, locate any places where the essay has problems and as partners, negotiate ways to improve the essay. Write your next draft and share it with the same person.

If you usually discuss your first draft with a classmate, use your intrapersonal abilities to work alone. Reread the Goleman et al. selection and then reread your own writing. Concentrate on developing self-awareness and the ability to be critical and constructive to make your writing more effective.

IN YOUR JOURNAL

Write about Malcolm X. When did he live? Who is he and what do you know about him and his life? How did he die?

Learning Words

Malcolm X

Malcolm Little (1925–1965) developed an interest in the Black Muslim religion when he was in prison. He became a disciple of Elijah Muhammad, the founder of the religion, and changed his name to Malcolm X. At this time, he turned to Islam and to books to change his life. When he was released from prison, Malcolm X became a minister in the Nation of Islam and a spokesperson for African Americans. In 1964, he converted to the orthodox Muslim religion and adopted the Muslim name El Hajj Malik El-Shabazz. He was assassinated in 1965. The selection below is excerpted from *The Autobiography of Malcolm X* (1965), which Malcolm X wrote with Alex Haley. In 1992, Spike Lee wrote and directed *Malcolm X,* a film about Malcolm X's life and death.

It was because of my letters that I happened to stumble upon starting to acquire some kind of a homemade education. 1

I became increasingly frustrated at not being able to express what I 2 wanted to convey in letters that I wrote, especially those to Mr. Elijah Muhammad. In the street, I had been the most articulate hustler out there—I had commanded attention when I said something. But now, trying to write simple English, I not only wasn't articulate, I wasn't even functional. How would I sound writing in slang, the way I would *say* it, something such as, "Look, daddy, let me pull your coat about a cat, Elijah Muhammad—"

Many who today hear me somewhere in person, or on television, or 3 those who read something I've said, will think I went to school far beyond the eighth grade. This impression is due entirely to my prison studies.

It had really begun back in the Charlestown Prison, when Bimbi 4 first made me feel envy of his stock of knowledge. Bimbi had always taken charge of any conversations he was in, and I had tried to emulate him. But every book I picked up had few sentences which didn't contain anywhere from one to nearly all of the words that might as well have been in Chinese. When I just skipped those words, of course, I really ended up with little idea of what the book said. So I had come to the Norfolk Prison Colony still going through only book-reading motions. Pretty soon, I would have quit even these motions, unless I had received the motivation that I did.

I saw that the best thing I could do was get hold of a dictionary—to   5
study, to learn some words. I was lucky enough to reason also that I should try to improve my penmanship. It was sad. I couldn't even write in a straight line. It was both ideas together that moved me to request a dictionary along with some tablets and pencils from the Norfolk Prison Colony school.

I spent two days just riffling uncertainly through the dictionary's   6
pages. I'd never realized so many words existed! I didn't know *which* words I needed to learn. Finally, just to start some kind of action, I began copying.

In my slow, painstaking, ragged handwriting, I copied into my   7
tablet everything printed on that first page, down to the punctuation marks.

I believe it took me a day. Then, aloud, I read back, to myself,   8
everything I'd written on the tablet. Over and over, aloud, to myself, I read my own handwriting.

I woke up the next morning, thinking about those words—   9
immensely proud to realize that not only had I written so much at one time, but I'd written words that I never knew were in the world. Moreover, with a little effort, I also could remember what many of these words meant. I reviewed the words whose meanings I didn't remember. Funny thing, from the dictionary first page right now, that "aardvark" springs to my mind. The dictionary had a picture of it, a long-tailed, long-eared, burrowing African mammal, which lives off termites caught by sticking out its tongue as an anteater does for ants.

I was so fascinated that I went on—I copied the dictionary's next   10
page. And the same experience came when I studied that. With every succeeding page, I also learned of people and places and events from history. Actually the dictionary is like a miniature encyclopedia. Finally the dictionary's A section had filled a whole tablet—and I went on into the B's. That was the way I started copying what eventually became the entire dictionary. It went a lot faster after so much practice helped me to

pick up handwriting speed. Between what I wrote in my tablet, and writing letters, during the rest of my time in prison I would guess I wrote a million words.

I suppose it was inevitable that as my word-base broadened, I could for the first time pick up a book and read and now begin to understand what the book was saying. Anyone who has read a great deal can imagine the new world that opened. Let me tell you something: from then until I left that prison, in every free moment I had, if I was not reading in the library, I was reading on my bunk. You couldn't have gotten me out of books with a wedge. Between Mr. Muhammad's teachings, my correspondence, my visitors, . . . and my reading of books, months passed without even thinking about being imprisoned. In fact, up to then, I never had been so truly free in my life.

11

Vocabulary

Elijah Muhammad (2)—African-American clergyman (1897–1975) who was the leader of the Black Muslims from 1935 to 1975

Bimbi (4)—a fellow inmate whose intelligence and breadth of knowledge impressed Malcolm X

riffling (6)—leafing quickly through a book

IN YOUR JOURNAL

Think about the dictionary and how you use it when you read or write. Then, in your journal write about the following: When did you learn to use the dictionary? Who taught you? When do you use it now? What problems do you have finding words or learning meanings?

A Closer Reading

1. What problems in communicating to others did Malcolm X discover when he was in prison? Why was he able to survive outside of prison despite these problems?

2. What is the effect of Malcolm X's revealing his limited schooling in paragraph 3?

3. What did he do to make the dictionary a tool of learning for him? What else did he do to become a more skilled reader and writer?

4. What does Malcolm X mean when he writes: "I never had been so truly free in my life" about the time he was in prison?

Drawing Your Own Conclusions

1. What are some of the differences between trying to communicate verbally and in writing? What skills help people to communicate clearly in their writing?

2. What personal qualities can you identify about Malcolm X after reading this excerpt from his autobiography?

3. What role does motivation play in Malcolm X's learning process? How do you motivate yourself to study and to learn?

4. Reread the seven types of intelligence listed in the Goleman et al. selection on page 119. Based on what you have read about Malcolm X, what type of intelligence does he display in this piece? Where does his natural ability lie? Explain your answer.

Thinking about Writing

1. What is the purpose of the quotation in paragraph 2? What does it illustrate both about Malcolm X's speech before he went to prison and about the nature of slang? How would you say the same thing in street talk today?

2. What is the main point of this selection? Does Malcolm X state the main point? If so, where?

3. Some writers use words as symbols or metaphors for their ideas. Malcolm X refers to the "aardvark" in paragraph 9. What characteristics does this creature have? What could "aardvark" symbolize to Malcolm X? What connection does he want us to make?

4. What words and phrases does Malcolm X use to refer to the struggle he went through to accomplish his goals? For example,

he describes his "slow, painstaking, ragged hand." What other words and phrases describe his struggle?

5. Malcolm X uses a step-by-step method to explain how he became a proficient reader and writer. What steps does he identify? How does he order these steps?

*   *   *

Suggestions for Writing

1. Write an essay about someone who changed his or her life after having initial problems in school. Describe the person, the problems, and the way the person changed. Explain what motivated the person to change.

2. Write an essay in which you identify five books that have been important in your life. Name the books, tell something about them, and explain why they are important to you.

3. Describe a situation in which you taught yourself to do something. Explain, step-by-step, the process you used to teach yourself. What did you learn about yourself through the experience?

4. Should prisons provide inmates with books, writing materials, and other tools for learning? Why or why not? Write an essay in which you explain your answer, relying on your reading, personal experiences, or observations of others.

Collaborative Project

With a partner or two, make a list of slang expressions that are used today. Write down what you think they mean. Interview people older than yourselves—family members, neighbors, or friends—about the meaning and use of the expressions you know and record their answers. Ask the older people to list and define slang expressions that were used when they were your age and write down their responses.

Together with your partner(s), write an essay in which you discuss the similarities and the differences between popular slang expressions used today and those used in the past.

Strategies for Revision

Reread your first draft and mark five words that you would like to change in your essay. Look up these words in the dictionary and find synonyms that reflect your ideas more closely. Discuss your word choices with a classmate. Change as many of these words as seem appropriate to you both.

Reread what you have written, making sure that the sentences in which you have changed words are clear and don't need any other changes.

IN YOUR JOURNAL

What abilities enable a person to succeed in math and science? What aspects of math and science interest you? Which do not? Why do you think more men than women major in math and science in college?

Women and Physics

K. C. Cole

K. C. Cole's articles on science and on women's issues have appeared in various periodicals. She is a former editor of *Saturday Review* and *Newsday*. Her essays have been published in several collections, including *Between the Lines* and *Sympathetic Vibrations: Reflections on Physics as a Way of Life* (1984). In this article, Cole focuses on why there are so few women physicists. She describes an atmosphere that is unfriendly to women and in which they may be made "to feel unnecessary and out of place."

I know few other women who do what I do. What I do is write 1
about science, mainly physics. And to do that, I spend a lot of time reading about science, talking to scientists and struggling to understand physics. In fact, most of the women (and men) I know think me quite queer for actually liking physics. "How can you write about that stuff?" they ask, always somewhat askance. "I could never understand that in a million years." Or more simply, "I hate science."

I didn't realize what an odd creature a woman interested in physics 2
was until a few years ago when a science magazine sent me to Johns Hopkins University in Baltimore for a conference on an electrical phenomenon known as the Hall effect. We sat in a huge lecture hall and listened as physicists talked about things engineers didn't understand, and engineers talked about things physicists didn't understand. What *I* didn't understand was why, out of several hundred young students of physics and engineering in the room, less than a handful were women.

Some time later, I found myself at the California Institute of Tech- 3
nology reporting on the search for the origins of the universe. I interviewed physicist after physicist, man after man. I asked one young administrator why none of the physicists were women. And he an-

swered: "I don't know, but I suppose it must be something innate. My 7-year-old daughter doesn't seem to be much interested in science."

It was with that experience fresh in my mind that I attended a   4
conference in Cambridge, Massachusetts, on science literacy, or rather the worrisome lack of it in this country today. We three women—a science teacher, a young chemist and myself—sat surrounded by a company of august men. The chemist, I think, first tentatively raised the issue of science illiteracy in women. It seemed like an obvious point. After all, everyone had agreed over and over again that scientific knowledge these days was a key factor in economic power. But as soon as she made the point, it became clear that we women had committed a grievous social error. Our genders were suddenly showing; we had interrupted the serious talk with a subject unforgivably silly.

For the first time, I stopped being puzzled about why there weren't   5
any women in science and began to be angry. Because if science is a search for answers to fundamental questions then it hardly seems frivolous to find out why women are excluded. Never mind the economic consequences.

A lot of the reasons why women are excluded are spelled out by the   6
Massachusetts Institute of Technology experimental physicist Vera Kistiakowsky in a recent article in *Physics Today* called "Women in Physics: Unnecessary, Injurious and Out of Place?" The title was taken from a 19th-century essay written in opposition to the appointment of a female mathematician to a professorship at the University of Stockholm. "As decidedly as two and two make four," a woman in mathematics is a "monstrosity," concluded the writer of the essay.

Dr. Kistiakowsky went on to discuss the factors that make women in   7
science today, if not monstrosities, at least oddities. Contrary to much popular opinion, one of these is *not* an innate difference in the scientific ability of boys and girls. But early conditioning does play a stubborn and subtle role. A recent Nova program, "The Pinks and the Blues," documented how girls and boys are treated differently from birth—the boys always encouraged in more physical kinds of play, more active explorations of their environments. Sheila Tobias, in her book, *Math Anxiety,* showed how the games boys play help them to develop an intuitive understanding of speed, motion and mass. The main sorting out of the girls from the boys in science seems to happen in junior high school. As a friend who teaches in a science museum said, "By the time we get to electricity, the boys already have had some experience with it. But it's unfamiliar to the girls." Science books draw on boys' experi-

ences. "The examples are all about throwing a baseball at such and such a speed," said my stepdaughter, who barely escaped being a science drop-out.

The most obvious reason there are not many more women in science is that women are discriminated against as a class, in promotions, salaries and hirings, a conclusion reached by a recent analysis by the National Academy of Sciences. 8

Finally, said Dr. Kistiakowsky, women are simply made to feel out of place in science. Her conclusion was supported by a Ford Foundation study by Lynn H. Fox on the problems of women in mathematics. When students were asked to choose among six reasons accounting for girls' lack of interest in math, the girls rated this statement second: "Men do not want girls in the mathematical occupations." 9

A friend of mine remembers winning a Bronx-wide mathematics competition in the second grade. Her friends—both boys and girls—warned her that she shouldn't be good at math: "You'll never find a boy who likes you." My friend continued nevertheless to excel in math and science, won many awards during her years at the Bronx High School of Science, and then earned a full scholarship to Harvard. After one year of Harvard science, she decided to major in English. 10

When I asked her why, she mentioned what she called the "macho mores" of science. "It would have been O.K. if I'd had someone to talk to," she said. "But the rules of comportment were such that you never admitted you didn't understand. I later realized that even the boys didn't get everything clearly right away. You had to stick with it until it had time to sink in. But for the boys, there was a payoff in suffering through the hard times, and a kind of punishment—a shame—if they didn't. For the girls it was O.K. not to get it, and the only payoff for sticking it out was that you'd be considered a freak." 11

Science is undeniably hard. Often, it can seem quite boring. It is unfortunately too often presented as laws to be memorized instead of mysteries to be explored. It is too often kept a secret that science, like art, takes a well-developed esthetic sense. Women aren't the only ones who say, "I hate science." That's why everyone who goes into science needs a little help from friends. For the past ten years, I have been getting more than a little help from a friend who is a physicist. But my stepdaughter—who earned the highest grades ever recorded in her California high school on the math Scholastic Aptitude Test—flunked calculus in her first year at Harvard. When my friend the 12 physicist heard about it, he said, "Harvard should be ashamed of itself."

What he meant was that she needed that little extra encouragement   13
that makes all the difference. Instead, she got that little extra discourage-
ment that makes all the difference. "In the first place, all the math
teachers are men," she explained. "In the second place, when I met a
boy I liked and told him I was taking chemistry, he immediately said:
'Oh, you're one of these science types.' In the third place, it's just a kind
of social thing. The math clubs are full of boys and you don't feel
comfortable joining."

In other words, she was made to feel unnecessary, and out of   14
place.

A few months ago, I accompanied a male colleague from the science   15
museum where I sometimes work to a lunch of the history of science
faculty at the University of California. I was the only woman there, and
my presence for the most part was obviously and rudely ignored. I was
so surprised and hurt by this that I made an extra effort to speak
knowledgeably and well. At the end of the lunch, one of the professors
turned to me in all seriousness and said: "Well, K. C., what do the
women think of Carl Sagan?" I replied that I had no idea what "the
women" thought about anything. But now I know what I should have
said: I should have told him that his comment was unnecessary, injurious and out of place.

Vocabulary

askance (1)—with disapproval
innate (3)—inborn
august (4)—worthy of respect
and awe because of age and
dignity

grievous (4)—causing suffering
mores (11)—behaviors and customs that are considered critical to a particular society
comportment (11)—behavior

IN YOUR JOURNAL

How does Cole explain the fact that so few women are in physics today? Do your observations support her conclusions? What other reasons might there be?

A Closer Reading

1. What does Cole tell her readers about the people who attend most scientific conferences? Why does she include this information in the essay?

2. In paragraph 4, Cole states that the chemist had spoken about "a subject unforgivably silly." What is the subject? Why would some people perceive it as "frivolous"?

3. What examples does Cole provide to support her idea that women are discriminated against in science?

4. What historical reference does Cole make in this essay? How does this reference support her point of view?

Drawing Your Own Conclusions

1. How might the fact that families give their sons chemistry or erector sets, telescopes and microscopes, math and logic puzzles, while they give their daughters dolls, cooking toys, and sewing and dress-up kits, influence their career choices? What expectations do families seem to have for their children when they give presents such as these? What materials could develop math and science abilities in both boys and girls?

2. What games do boys play in your neighborhood? What games do girls play? Do any of these games explore scientific ability? If so, in what ways?

3. What differences do you observe in the types of games that each sex plays? According to paragraph 7, these games influence children's behaviors and abilities. Reread the paragraph and compare your observations with the author's.

4. What can toy companies and children's book publishers do to encourage girls to consider science and math careers? Why might these companies resist the idea of change?

5. How are scientists and mathematicians portrayed on television and in the movies? What evidence have you seen that television and moviemakers have tried to make science and math more appealing to both women and men? If you have observed changes, why do you think they have happened? If not, why not?

Thinking about Writing

1. What might be some of the reasons that Cole refers to herself as K. C. Cole and not by her full name? What other writers do you know who are referred to only by their initials? What writers have changed their names to disguise their sex?

2. What purpose does Cole's first sentence, "I know few other women who do what I do," serve? Did it make you want to read the rest of the essay? Why or why not? How would you improve the first sentence to make the essay more interesting to you?

3. In paragraph 6, Cole refers to an article entitled "Women in Physics: Unnecessary, Injurious, and Out of Place?". How does she use this as evidence to support her argument? Where in the essay does she refer to this title again? How does she connect the phrase with her essay as a whole?

4. Cole identifies with the academic context. To which specific academic institutions does she refer in this piece? What do you know about these institutions? Why does Cole think colleges must change before other institutions in society change?

5. Cole uses a number of techniques to present her ideas. Where in the essay does Cole write to persuade, to illustrate, to explain a concept, to tell a story, to compare and contrast, and to analyze? Answer this question by referring to specific passages in the essay. Which of these techniques is the main one used in the essay? What in the essay helped you answer this question?

*   *   *

Suggestions for Writing

1. Write about an experience in which you were successful in a math or science course in any level of school. Describe your experience in detail. Explain whether males and females were treated differently in your class. What made the experience successful for you?

2. Write about an experience in which you were not successful in a math or science course. Describe your experience in detail. Explain whether males and females were treated differently in your class. What made the experience unsuccessful for you? What specific events might have changed your experience?

3. Why do the majority of women today work in teaching, nursing, social work, and clerical jobs? Why is it that 90 percent of the workers in the more highly paid occupations of engineering, computers, or technical areas are men? Explain in an essay what factors seem to be involved: social or economic reasons, genetic factors, or a combination of these? Give examples based on your reading, observations, and experience to support your point of view.

4. Why is "scientific knowledge these days . . . a key factor in economic power"? Explain your answer in an essay. Give examples based on your reading, your observations, or your own experiences.

5. Should colleges provide extra encouragement and support for women who are taking science and math courses? If so, describe the specific methods or types of encouragement and support that would be effective. In either case, explain your point of view in an essay giving examples from your reading, observations, or experiences.

Strategies for Revision

Working with two or three other students, go over the writing you have just done. Make enough copies of your draft to give to each member of your group, and have the others do the same.

Form a small circle and have each person take a turn reading aloud what she or he has written. As the writer reads, the members of the group should read along and make notes in the margin in pencil. These notes will include some of the following considerations:

- What does the author's introduction lead the reader to believe the theme of the writing will be? Does this prove to be true throughout the essay?
- Does the introduction engage you and make you want to read more?
- Is the author's point of view about science clear from the beginning?
- Are there sufficient supporting details or examples to convince a reader of the writer's point of view?
- Is there any place in the draft where you got confused or lost? If so, how can this be improved?
- How does the draft end? Is the conclusion effective?

After reading each piece, discuss the draft, talking about these questions. Bring up any other questions you have as well. Each writer should have a turn reading and having his or her work discussed.

Next, revise your writing, considering your group's discussion and including any new ideas of your own. Share your revision with the same group.

IN YOUR JOURNAL

Write about an incident, past or present, in which you were unable to communicate your questions or problems to a teacher at school.

University Days

James Thurber

James Thurber (1894–1961) was born in Columbus, Ohio. He is known for the humorous writing and illustrations of his many books, essays, and plays, including *The Thurber Carnival* (1945), *Fables For Our Time* (1940) and *Thurber Country* (1953). He often wrote about individuals trying to cope with problems in a confusing and complex world. For example, "The Secret Life of Walter Mitty," one of his best-known short stories, is about a man who deals with his daily problems by resorting to fantasy, a solution that he finds leads him to often hilarious trouble. The following excerpt comes from his book of autobiographical sketches, *My Life and Hard Times* (1933). Thurber suffered from vision problems most of his life, and this story is a humorous reflection on the insensitivity of his botany professor.

I passed all the other courses that I took at my University, but I   1 could never pass botany. This was because all botany students had to spend several hours a week in a laboratory looking through a microscope at plant cells, and I could never see through a microscope. I never once saw a cell through a microscope. This used to enrage my instructor. He would wander around the laboratory pleased with the progress all the students were making in drawing the involved and, so I am told, interesting structure of flower cells, until he came to me. I would just be standing there. "I can't see anything," I would say. He would begin patiently enough, explaining how anybody can see through a microscope, but he would always end up in a fury, claiming that I could *too* see through a microscope but just pretended that I couldn't. "It takes away from the beauty of flowers anyway," I used to tell him. "We are not concerned with beauty in this course," he would say. "We are concerned solely with what I may call the *mechanics* of flars." "Well," I'd say, "I can't see anything." "Try it just once again," he'd say, and I would put my eye to the microscope and see nothing at all, except now and again a nebulous milky substance—a phenomenon of maladjustment. You were supposed to see a vivid, restless clockwork of sharply defined plant cells. "I see what looks like a lot of milk," I would tell him. This, he claimed, was the result of my not having adjusted the microscope properly, so he would readjust it for me, or rather, for himself. And I would look again and see milk.

I finally took a deferred pass, as they call it, and waited a year and 2 tried again. (You had to pass one of the biological sciences or you couldn't graduate.) The professor had come back from vacation brown as a berry, bright-eyed, and eager to explain cell-structure again to his classes. "Well," he said to me, cheerily, when we met in the first laboratory hour of the semester, "we're going to see cells this time, aren't we?" "Yes, sir," I said. Students to right of me and to left of me and in front of me were seeing cells; what's more, they were quietly drawing pictures of them in their notebooks. Of course, I didn't see anything.

"We'll try it," the professor said to me, grimly, "with every adjust- 3 ment of the microscope known to man. As God is my witness, I'll arrange this glass so that you see cells through it or I'll give up teaching. In twenty-two years of botany, I—" He cut off abruptly for he was beginning to quiver all over, like Lionel Barrymore, and he genuinely wished to hold onto his temper; his scenes with me had taken a great deal out of him.

So we tried it with every adjustment of the microscope known to 4 man. With only one of them did I see anything but blackness or the familiar lacteal opacity, and that time I saw, to my pleasure and amazement, a variegated constellation of flecks, specks, and dots. These I hastily drew. The instructor, noting my activity, came back from an adjoining desk, a smile on his lips and his eyebrows high in hope. He looked at my cell drawing. "What's that?" he demanded, with a hint of a squeal in his voice. "That's what I saw," I said. "You didn't, you didn't, you *did*n't!" he screamed, losing control of his temper instantly, and he bent over and squinted into the microscope. His head snapped up. "That's your eye!" he shouted. "You've fixed the lens so that it reflects! You've drawn your eye!"

Another course that I didn't like, but somehow managed to pass, 5 was economics. I went to that class straight from the botany class, which didn't help me any in understanding either subject. I used to get them mixed up. But not as mixed up as another student in my economics class who came there direct from a physics laboratory. He was a tackle on the football team, named Bolenciecwcz. At that time Ohio State University had one of the best football teams in the country, and Bolenciecwcz was one of its outstanding stars. In order to be eligible to play it was necessary for him to keep up in his studies, a very difficult matter, for while he was not dumber than an ox he was not any smarter. Most of his professors were lenient and helped him along. None gave him more hints, in answering questions, or asked him simpler ones than the economics professor, a thin, timid man named Bassum. One day when we were on the subject of transportation and distribution, it came Bolenciecwcz's turn to answer a question. "Name one means of transportation," the professor said to him. No light came into the big tackle's eyes. "Just any means of transportation," said the professor. Bolenciecwcz sat staring at him. "That is," pursued the professor, "any medium, agency, or method of going from one place to another." Bolenciecwcz had the look of a man who is being led into a trap. "You may choose among steam, horse-drawn, or electrically propelled vehicles," said the instructor. "I might suggest the one which we commonly take in making long journeys across land." There was a profound silence in which everybody stirred uneasily, including Bolenciecwcz and Mr. Bassum. Mr. Bassum abruptly broke this silence in an amazing manner. "Choo-choo-choo," he said, in a low voice, and turned instantly scarlet. He glanced appealingly around the room. All of us, of course, shared Mr. Bassum's desire that Bolenciecwcz should stay abreast of the class in economics, for the Illinois game, one of the hardest and most important of the season, was only a week off. "Toot, toot, too-tooooooot!" some student with a deep voice moaned, and we all looked encouragingly at Bolenciecwcz. Somebody else gave a fine imitation of a locomotive letting off steam. Mr. Bassum himself rounded off the little show. "Ding, dong, ding, dong," he said, hopefully. Bolenciecwcz was staring at the floor now, trying to think, his great brow furrowed, his huge hands rubbing together, his face red.

"How did you come to college this year, Mr. Bolenciecwcz?" asked   6
the professor. "*Chuff*a chuffa, *chuff*a chuffa."

"M'father sent me," said the football player.   7

"What on?" asked Bassum.   8

"I git an 'lowance," said the tackle, in a low, husky voice, obviously   9
embarrassed.

"No, no," said Bassum. "Name a means of transportation. What did   10
you *ride* here on?"

"Train," said Bolenciecwcz.   11

"Quite right," said the professor. "Now, Mr. Nugent, will you tell us—" 12

If I went through anguish in botany and economics—for different   13
reasons—gymnasium work was even worse. I don't even like to think
about it. They wouldn't let you play games or join in the exercises with
your glasses on and I couldn't see with mine off. I bumped into professors, horizontal bars, agricultural students, and swinging iron rings. Not
being able to see, I could take it but I couldn't dish it out. Also, in order to
pass gymnasium (and you had to pass it to graduate) you had to learn to
swim if you didn't know how. I didn't like the swimming pool, I didn't like
swimming, and I didn't like the swimming instructor, and after all these
years I still don't. I never swam but I passed my gym work anyway, by having another student give my gymnasium number (978) and swim across
the pool in my place. He was a quiet, amiable blonde youth, number 473,
and he would have seen through a microscope for me if we could have got
away with it, but we couldn't get away with it. Another thing I didn't like
about gymnasium work was that they made you strip the day you regis-
tered. It is impossible for me to be happy when I am stripped and being
asked a lot of questions. Still, I did better than a lanky agricultural student
who was cross-examined just before I was. They asked each student what
college he was in—that is, whether Arts, Engineering, Commerce, or
Agriculture. "What college are you in?" the instructor snapped at the
youth in front of me. "Ohio State University," he said promptly.

It wasn't that agricultural student but it was another a whole lot like   14
him who decided to take up journalism, possibly on the ground that
when farming went to hell he could fall back on newspaper work. He
didn't realize, of course, that that would be very much like falling back
full-length on a kit of carpenter's tools. Haskins didn't seem cut out for
journalism, being too embarrassed to talk to anybody and unable to use a
typewriter, but the editor of the college paper assigned him to the cow
barns, the sheep house, the horse pavilion, and the animal husbandry
department generally. This was a genuinely big "beat," for it took up five
times as much ground and got ten times as great a legislative appropria-
tion as the College of Liberal Arts. The agricultural student knew animals, but nevertheless his stories were dull and colorlessly written. He
took all afternoon on each of them, on account of having to hunt for each
letter on the typewriter. Once in a while he had to ask somebody to help
him hunt. "C" and "L," in particular, were hard letters for him to find.
His editor finally got pretty much annoyed at the farmer-journalist because his pieces were so uninteresting. "See here, Haskins," he snapped at

him one day, "Why is it we never have anything hot from you on the horse pavilion? Here we have two hundred head of horses on this campus—more than any other university in the Western Conference except Purdue—and yet you never get any real low down on them. Now shoot over to the horse barns and dig up something lively." Haskins shambled out and came back in about an hour; he said he had something. "Well, start it off snappily," said the editor. "Something people will read." Haskins set to work and in a couple of hours brought a sheet of typewritten paper to the desk; it was a two-hundred-word story about some disease that had broken out among the horses. Its opening sentence was simple but arresting. It said: "Who has noticed the sores on the tops of the horses in the animal husbandry building?"

Ohio State was a land grant university and therefore two years of military drill was compulsory. We drilled with old Springfield rifles and studied the tactics of the Civil War even though the World War was going on at the time. At 11 o'clock each morning thousands of freshmen and sophomores used to deploy over the campus, moodily creeping up on the old chemistry building. It was good training for the kind of warfare that was waged at Shiloh but it had no connection with what was going on in Europe. Some people used to think there was German money behind it, but they didn't dare say so or they would have been thrown in jail as German spies. It was a period of muddy thought and marked, I believe, the decline of higher education in the Middle West. 15

As a soldier I was never any good at all. Most of the cadets were glumly indifferent soldiers, but I was no good at all. Once General Littlefield, who was commandant of the cadet corps, popped up in front of me during regimental drill and snapped, "You are the main trouble with this university!" I think he meant that my type was the main trouble with the university but he may have meant me individually. I was mediocre at drill, certainly—that is, until my senior year. By that time I had drilled longer than anybody else in the Western Conference, having failed at military at the end of each preceding year so that I had to do it all over again. I was the only senior still in uniform. The uniform which, when new, had made me look like an interurban railway conductor, now that it had become faded and too tight made me look like Bert Williams in his bellboy act. This had a definitely bad effect on my morale. Even so, I had become by sheer practise little short of wonderful at squad manoeuvres. 16

One day General Littlefield picked our company out of the whole regiment and tried to get it mixed up by putting it through one movement 17 after another as fast as we could execute them: squads right, squads left, squads on right into line, squads right about, squads left front into line, etc. In about three minutes one hundred and nine men were marching in one direction and I was marching away from them at an angle of forty degrees, all alone. "Company, halt!" shouted General Littlefield, "That man is the only man who has it right!" I was made a corporal for my achievement.

The next day General Littlefield summoned me to his office. He was   18 swatting flies when I went in. I was silent and he was silent too, for a long time. I don't think he remembered me or why he had sent for me, but he didn't want to admit it. He swatted some more flies, keeping his eyes on them narrowly before he let go with the swatter. "Button up your coat!" he snapped. Looking back on it now I can see that he meant me although he was looking at a fly, but I just stood there. Another fly came to rest on a paper in front of the general and began rubbing its hind legs together. The general lifted the swatter cautiously. I moved restlessly and the fly flew away. "You startled him!" barked General Littlefield, looking at me severely. I said I was sorry. "That won't help the situation!" snapped the general, with cold military logic. I didn't see what I could do except offer to chase some more flies toward his desk, but I didn't say anything. He stared out the window at the faraway figures of co-eds crossing the campus toward the library. Finally, he told me I could go. So I went. He either didn't know which cadet I was or else he forgot what he wanted to see me about. It may have been that he wished to apologize for having called me the main trouble with the university; or maybe he had decided to compliment me on my brilliant drilling of the day before and then at the last minute decided not to. I don't know. I don't think about it much any more.

Vocabulary

enrage (1)—cause to become very angry

nebulous (1)—unclear; indefinite

Lionel Barrymore (3)—American theater and film actor (1878–1954)

lacteal (4)—milky-looking

opacity (4)—state of not letting light go through; dullness or darkness

variegated (4)—marked with spots and streaks; uneven in appearance

animal husbandry (14)—management and care of animals

IN YOUR JOURNAL

A cartoonist creates humor by exaggerating parts of a face, body, or situation to make it funnier than reality. Writers do this too. What elements of the story does Thurber exaggerate to create humor?

A Closer Reading

1. What evidence does Thurber present to illustrate that he has vision problems? How do Thurber's vision problems particularly affect his experiences in botany class? What does Thurber learn about himself, his classmates, and his teacher from this experience?

2. Why does the economics professor work so hard to help Bolenciecwcz to answer the question? What does Thurber learn about the teacher, his classmates, and the system from this experience?

3. How does Thurber solve his problem with gym class?

4. Why is Thurber still doing regimental drills in his senior year at the college? What does Thurber's encounter with General Littlefield teach him about the college and its values?

Drawing Your Own Conclusions

1. What is Thurber's attitude toward the teachers in his college? Support your answer with passages from the story.

2. What is Thurber's attitude toward the other students in his college? Support your answer with passages from the story.

3. If Thurber were in college today, what changes would he find in the way his physical disability is treated?

4. Is the sentence that Haskins wrote: "Who has noticed the sores on the tops of the horses in the animal husbandry building?" an effective beginning for a newspaper article? If you were his teacher, what changes would you suggest he make? Why?

5. What attitude toward college does Thurber reflect in this story? How did his experiences contribute toward his attitude?

Thinking about Writing

1. How does Thurber personalize each of his characters and make him unique? What do we learn about people from this story?

2. Thurber wrote this story more than sixty years ago. Humor is very difficult to write, because what is funny in one context or to one person may not be funny in another. Reread the story and choose any moments in the story that were funny or that you think Thurber thought were funny. Looking at them again, answer the following questions:

   Which parts of the descriptions are funny?
   Which specific words are funny?
   What aspects of the people described are funny?
   Were the sequence of events described as funny?
   Is there any part of the story that may have been funny in the past but that does not seem funny to you today?
   What has changed in our world that makes this not funny today?

*   *   *

Suggestions for Writing

1. Describe one of your college classes in detail. In your essay, write about your teacher, some of the students, the material covered, and the physical setting for the class. Include at least one specific incident from your class (reread the Thurber selection for ideas for characterizing individuals) that illustrates how the teacher and students work together.

2. Write an essay in which you compare two teachers from your college. Explain in what ways they are similar and in what ways they are different. Think about the way they present material, interact with students, respond to the students' work, and seem to feel about the subjects they teach.

3. Write an essay in which you list and explain the four most important characteristics of a successful student. Define the characteristics, give examples, and explain why these characteristics are important.

4. Should colleges require all students to take physical education? Write an essay in which you take a position on this question,

supporting your point of view with your readings, observations of others, and your personal experiences.

Strategies for Revision

Reread the draft you have written and rewrite it trying to make it humorous, or consider developing your journal entry further. Keep in mind your teacher, and the students and friends who will read your essay. What is funny about your school or your school experiences? After you have written your second draft, share them both with a classmate. Discuss the changes you made to create an amusing essay.

IN YOUR JOURNAL

Before you read the following selection, write about any experience you have had with a person who is deaf or hearing impaired.

Outsider in a Silent World

Lou Ann Walker

Lou Ann Walker was born in Indiana to deaf parents. She has been a staff writer for *Cosmopolitan, New York,* and *Esquire* magazines and has written *Amy, the Story of a Deaf Child* (1985) for young readers. The following article appeared in the *New York Times* on August 31, 1986, and was later published as part of her book *A Loss for Words: The Story of Deafness in a Family* (1986). Walker writes about her parents' struggle to function in the world of the hearing. She also explains that, as deep as their relationship is, she will always be an outsider to their world of silence.

When I was born, the obstetrician looked at my mother and traced   1
the hourglass figure of a woman. It was his way of telling her she had
had a baby girl. The doctor then walked over and clapped his hands
near my head to see if I would respond. He went back to my mother
and, smiling, pointed to his ears and nodded. Everyone in the delivery
room was relieved I was a "normal" baby.

Dad passed out cigars to the men at work and cradled his arms to let   2
them know his wife had given birth. He pulled out the small white
notepad he always carried and wrote "girl."

I was their first child. It was 1952, in Blackford County, Ind.   3

Before I was born, Mom and Dad paid $65—more than a week's sal-   4
ary—for a baby cry box, designed to alert deaf parents when their children cry. They placed the dark-brown plastic box, shaped like a radio, next
to my crib and wired it to a lamp by their bed. As I cried, the box transmitted an impulse to the bulb, which flashed on until I paused for breath.

My parents worried about how I would learn spoken language. So   5
when I was barely 2 years old, they bought a television set (one of the
first in Montpelier): a hulking affair with a tiny screen. Sitting in my
small green rocking chair, I would watch that screen for hours on end,

developing what was, for Indiana, a strange, accentless speech. Now and then, I would rush off to sign to Mom or Dad what I had heard about the outside world, about the outbreak of polio, or who had won the baseball game.

I acted as interpreter and guide for my parents the entire time I was   6
growing up. I was an adult before I was a child. I was painfully shy for myself, squirming away when the attention was focused on me, but when I was acting for my mother and father I was fine. I made their doctors' appointments. I interpreted when my mother went to the doctor and told him where it hurt and when he told her what medicine to take. I told the shoe repairman what was wrong with a shoe. When we received a call, I was usually the one to relay to Mom and Dad that a friend had died. This was my life. I didn't know any other.

It has taken me most of my adult life to figure out my own place in   7
the world. We were outsiders, my two younger sisters, my parents and I. It was as if we were clinging together for safety. But while there were unbreakable bonds between us, there was also an unbridgeable chasm. For despite my parents' spirit and their ability to get along, their world is the deaf—it is something separate, something I am intimate with yet can never really know.

In a family in which there is deafness, guilt is a constant undercurrent.   8
Thousands of times during my mother's life when she misinterpreted what someone said, she watched the other person, particularly my father, grow impatient or become angry because she seemed so slow. She had learned early on that it was easier, not only for herself but for everyone else as well, if she simply smiled and nodded. My own grandparents—none of whom had a hearing impairment—constantly exhorted me to "be good"; they themselves felt guilty for not doing more for their children and hoped somehow I would make up for things. But that phrase—I heard it a thousand times as I was growing up: Be good. Be good. Even now I hear it rasping through my head like a handsaw, pushing and pulling, through a plank. How could I ever be good enough?

My mother became deaf at the age of 13 months, when she had a   9
relapse of spinal meningitis. Doris Jean was a wiry, precocious child who had already learned to say "Mamma" when the illness struck. She was up and walking and talking again after her first bout, and the doctor in Greencastle, Ind., decided she was so improved she didn't need to have the complete series of injections. She lost her hearing during the second high fever. It was years before she said anything again, and for the rest of her life few people would understand her when she did talk.

On an aberrantly cold March day in Montpelier, when my father   10
was 2 months old, his mother swaddled him in blankets and took him in
her arms to her brother's burial in Odd Fellows Cemetery. He had died
of pneumonia. My father, Gale, developed what they used to call the
grippe. The fever burned out his auditory nerves, leaving him deaf
before he was 3 months old.

Two chance happenings. Accidents. My father's parents spent the rest   11
of their days in self-recrimination. My father's eldest brother—the first-
born—was a blue baby and probably lost his hearing during childbirth.
Soon after he found out that his first child was deaf, my father's father
became a volatile and self-righteous preacher. When my father, too, lost
his hearing, my paternal grandmother passed much of my father's infancy
grieving, then threw herself into the temperance movement.

My mother's parents, on the other hand, seemed bewildered by her   12
deafness. Grandpa Wells started out as a farmer and ended up a foreman
in a saw-manufacturing plant. I don't think I ever heard him use the
word "deaf" all the time I was growing up. Instead, Grandpa looked to
Grandma to take care of things. He felt she was the "smart" one. When
her daughter was young, Grandma would read books about the deaf
and blind Helen Keller and fret about how she could teach her own
little girl. In old pictures, Grandma had the beauty and mystery of a
silent-film star; but in later photos, both she and my grandfather had
grown self-conscious and the lines of their mouths drew tight.

I must have been about 4 the time Grandma Wells and I were   13
cuddled up in her bed. Grandma had her arm around me and the new
ballerina doll I had just received for Christmas. Grandma started humming, her humming floating into a lullaby: "Sleep, my child and peace
attend thee, / all through the night. / Guardian angels God will send
thee, / all through the night. / Soft the waking hours are creeping, / hill
and dale in slumber steeping. . . ."

Mom and Dad picked me up from Grandma's the next day. That   14
night as Mom tucked me into bed, I asked her to sing me a lullaby, even
though I knew she couldn't.

These days, going back home to visit, I usually find myself sitting in   15
my parents' blue-carpeted living room, listening. I can hear the squeak
of the furnace, the blower over the stove my mother forgot to turn off,
the high-pitched electronic squeal of two table lamps, the overly loud,
slightly irregular ticking of their kitchen clock.

Growing up in our house was anything but quiet. It sometimes felt   16
as if we were living in some kind of amusement park—lights flashing on

and off the way they do around a carousel. Whenever the doorbell rang, a light in our central hall and another in the kitchen flashed on, and a loud buzzer went off for me and my sisters. (The man who had installed our special doorbell was deaf himself, and thus had not known how discordant the sound was.)

When the phone rang, lamps in the living room and in an upstairs 17 bedroom went on and off. If the call was for my parents, we would hear a foreign bleep-bleep, which meant we had to hook up the TTY, a teletype-telephone device with a coupler for the receiver that translated the bleeps into typed-out messages. If Kay or Jan or I answered the phone in the hallway, we would race back to the family room, where the three-foot-high teletype stood. Ours was an early model (newer ones are portable, with electronic read-outs), and whenever a call was going over the machine, the house had all the clatter of a newsroom. My parents even had a pulsing-light alarm clock, which they often silenced by pulling pillows over their heads.

Those weren't the only tricks we had. If my father was in the garage 18 at his workbench, my mother would get his attention by switching the overhead bulb on and off several times in rapid succession. If my mother was reading the newspaper in the living room and he was sitting in his easy chair and wanted to talk with her, he would stamp his foot lightly on the floor until she looked up from her paper, at which time he would wave his hand so she would know who was "calling" her.

Although my parents communicated solely in sign, even that lan- 19 guage isn't completely silent. Signing is vivid, the hands often brushing against a shirt or thumping a chest. If my parents were having an argument—easy to spot because of the velocity of their gestures—my sisters and I would hear hands smacking hands. They could talk, but their words were unintelligible to anyone but my sisters and me.

My mother has a voice that is as soft and cooing as a mourning dove's. 20 She would scold us roundly for coming home late, but her voice never carried. When she called for us in the backyard, my name came out "Looeen." "Kay Sue" and "Jan Lee"—names specifically chosen for ease of pronounciation—turned into unearthly "Kehzoo" and "Zhanli." Often, if we were in another room, my father would come to get us, yet if he did call, the timbre of his voice, slightly higher pitched than Mom's, reminded me of one note played over and over again on a harpsichord.

There are two million deaf people in the United States; a quarter 21 million of them, such as my parents, probably lost their hearing before age 2. About 1 out of every 13 people have some degree of hearing impairment. On the face of it, deafness seems to be a simple affliction. If you can't hear, people assume you can make up for it by writing notes, that you can pass your spare time reading books, that you can converse by talking and reading lips. But things are never that simple.

Until they are about the age of 2, babies are tape recorders, taking in   22
everything that is being said around them. The brain uses these record-ings as the basis of language. If for any reason a baby is deprived of those years of acquiring language, he can never make up the loss. For those who become completely deaf during infancy, using the basics of English becomes a task as difficult as building a house without benefit of drawings or experience in carpentry. Writing a grammatically correct sentence is a struggle. Reading a book is a Herculean effort; even reading a newspaper can be arduous.

Nor is lip reading the panacea hearing people would like to believe.   23
"Bed," "bid," "bud" and "bad" all look identical on the lips, because vowels are formed in the back of the mouth. The best lip readers in the world actually "read" only about a third of what is said; the rest is contextual piecing together of ideas and expected constructions. The average deaf person understands far less.

Children of deaf parents rarely run away from home. Instead, they   24
hide. It's one of those odd phenomena. You don't have to go out the door, because your parents can't hear you rustling or giggling. Besides, you feel too strong a sense of responsibility to leave. Something might happen. You might be needed. Still, for a few minutes you have to get away from that awesome adult role. My sister Jan found a nook under my parents' bed. I curled up in the spot behind the back seat of our red Volkswagen Beetle.

I'm not sure when I decided Mom and Dad were spies. At one point   25
or another, most children think they are adopted. I never saw it that way. At about the age of 8 I was convinced Mom and Dad had been sent to check up on me. They were pretending not to hear so that they would know everything I was saying and denounce me for it.

The tests I devised were simple but fairly ingenious. One of my   26
ploys was to go into another room and scream "Mom! Help!" Nothing. Then I would drop a book on the floor and hold my breath. Still nothing. I would throw myself with a thud on the carpet. Nobody came to check.

Other times I would sit on the floor in the living room and watch   27
them while they read the paper. I wanted to see if they would make a mistake. I would sit for long periods watching the back of my mother's

newspaper. When she brought the two sides together to turn the page, she would catch me staring at her.

"What's the matter?" she signed, her forehead wrinkled.   28

"Nothing."   29

"Why are you looking at me?"   30

(The one thing that completely unhinged her was someone staring   31
at her—at home, in a restaurant, anywhere.)

"Oh, sorry, Mom. I was just thinking," I signed, index finger cir-   32
cling my brow.

She would go back to her newspaper and peer around the corner a   33
couple of times, not able to figure out what I was up to.

One night before I went to bed, I fixed the phone cord just so. The   34
next morning it was in exactly the place I had left it. And the next. And
the next.

A few years later, while vacationing in New York, Mom and Dad   35
and I were at the beach. The sun was setting and the sky was a fiery red
purple. Mom and I stood, arms linked, watching the waves.

"What does it sound like?" Mom signed.   36

I wrinkled my forehead and held out my hand, palm up, hand   37
searching, to show I was thinking of an answer. Then I made a little
gurgling sound with my lips. Mom looked at my lips thoughtfully, then
turned back to watch the waves hitting the rocks and made her own lips
gurgle.

A minute later, Dad came over. He had been watching some fishermen.   38

"What does it sound like?" he signed, pointing to the ocean.   39

Mom grinned and signed that she had just asked me the same ques-   40
tion. Then she made the little lip movement for him. The three of us
stood and watched the waves and the sunset. I tried to imagine the
scene without the sound and, suddenly, everything before my eyes
turned black and white, like a silent movie.

A little while later we got on a ferryboat. As we leaned over the rails   41
watching the cars being loaded and the dock hands at work, Mom
grabbed my arm excitedly.

"Music!" she signed, and she moved to the beat.   42

"No, Mom! It's the engine," and I slapped a fist into my palm in   43
time with the pistons.

"I think music," and she did a little dance.   44

Mom and Dad drove me out to Harvard the fall I transferred there.   45
I had just spent two years at Ball State University, in Muncie, Ind., with
some vague idea that I wanted to be a teacher of the deaf. When the

program turned out to be less than I expected, and when I didn't feel I was getting enough challenge in my other classes, I applied to four Eastern colleges and was accepted.

As I looked up at the backs of my parents' heads, I sank low   46
in the car's rear seat. Filling out the application, I had made prominent mention of the fact that my parents were deaf. The entrance essay, which was supposed to be about me, was actually about them. Many applicants use a father's or grandfather's degree to get into the family alma mater, but neither of my parents had set foot in a college. The irony that I was shamelessly using my deaf parents to get into Harvard was not lost on me. I knew that though I would willingly and openly tell people my parents were deaf and would briefly answer questions, I would refuse to elaborate further. It was all too complicated.

Through most of the 16-hour trip to Cambridge, I brooded over a   47
freshman reading list—the kind given to high-school seniors that includes all the books they should have read by the time they matriculate. I had read very little of what was on that list.

I sat in the back seat, worrying that I would have nothing to discuss   48
in the dining hall. And every once in a while I would look up to watch my parents' conversation.

When the highway was deserted, Dad could shift his eyes from the   49
road to Mom's hands. When traffic got heavy, he had to watch the road, and then his glances were shorter. If he wanted to pass a car, he would hold up an index finger at Mom, signaling her to suspend the conversation for a moment. It was always easier for the driver to do the talking, although that meant his signs were shortened and somewhat less graceful. He would use the steering wheel as a base, the way he normally used his left hand; his right hand did all the moving.

Curled up in the seat, I noticed there was a lull in the conversation.   50
Dad was a confident driver, but Mom was smoking more than usual.

"Something happened? That gas station?" Mom signed to me.   51
"No, nothing," I lied.   52
"Are you sure?"   53
"Yes, everything is fine."   54
Dad and I had gone in to pay and get directions. The man behind   55
the counter had looked up, seen me signing and muttered, "Huh, I didn't think mutes were allowed to have driver's licenses." Long ago I had gotten used to hearing comments like this, but I never could get used to the way they made me churn inside.

Mom was studying me. Having relied on her visual powers all her 56
life, she knew when I was hiding something. "Are you afraid of going
so far away from home? Why don't you stay in Indiana?"

"Mom, no! Cut it out." 57

She turned and faced front again. Dad hadn't seen what either of us 58
said, but he had caught the speed and force of my signs from the
rearview mirror, and he could feel the tension coming from behind him.
Mom had struck several nerves in me. Not only was I stepping into
foreign territory (I hadn't been able to afford to visit any of the schools
to which I had applied), but back home in Indiana, none of my relatives
or friends had been enthusiastic about my going East. To Hoosiers,
Harvard meant highbrow and snooty.

When whe saw the first sign for Boston on the turnpike, Mom 59
tapped Dad's arm rapidly. Soon we were crossing a bridge over the
Charles River. Another sign said, "Cambridge."

Dad pointed to the sign and turned to look at me. In the corner of 60
his eye was the beginning of a tear.

"I never thought my daughter would go to Harvard," he signed. 61
"I'm so proud." To sign "proud," he started with his thumbs at waist
level and drew them up his chest, sitting a little straighter as his chest
welled up. Dad would have been content no matter what college or job
I chose, but this was a dream he—a linotype operator at a newspaper—
never had. Mom, who was then a film librarian, felt the same way; no
one in her family had ever gone to college.

The strain of all those miles was suddenly washed away. I smiled 62
and leaned over to kiss his cheek. Mom patted my hand and then my
face. She was unaware of the long hum of affection coming from her
throat.

The dormitory to which I was assigned was pathetic—a cinderblock 63
room with upended tables and chairs. There was litter in the hallway,
the bathrooms were filthy and the kitchen had an unidentifiable smell.
My dreams of wood-paneled, leather-armchair splendor were not coming true.

"Your room at Ball State was cleaner," Mom said, the sign for 64
"clean" being one palm drawn neatly over the other. I glared at her.

It seemed that only the overstudious "nerds"—whom Harvard 65
termed "wonks"—had also arrived this early. All the glamour that
might still be attached to Harvard disappeared when a peculiar-
looking character with mechanical pencils in his pocket, frizzy hair
and enormous, twitchy eyes, came into my room. He jumped as I

began translating what he was saying into sign for Mom. I felt several worlds collide.

As soon as the last box was moved into the room, I told Mom and Dad they could go to their hotel. I said I needed to plunge into Harvard life. But if I had been honest with myself, I would have known that I was as embarrassed at having them meet the wonk as I was at having the wonk and the rest of Harvard meet my deaf parents. 66

A couple of hours later, my parents and I had an early dinner together and then we said our goodbyes. They were leaving early the next morning for the drive back to Indianapolis. Standing on the sidewalk outside the restaurant, I was in a hurry to get on with things. We hugged and kissed. Mom reached over to smooth the hair from my face. 67

"Promise you'll write often," she signed. 68

"I always do, Mom." 69

Back in the dorm, I unpacked. My roommate had also arrived. Laura was the first person I had ever met from California. A junior with long, wavy dark hair, she was beautiful, long-legged and sinewy. She didn't look at all like my image of the studious 'Cliffie. 70

We talked for a couple of minutes and, except for throwing a sheet over the top of her bed, she didn't bother to arrange any of her things. Instead, she went off to talk to the guy with the pencils. 71

Laura came back. "Howard told me your parents are deaf and dumb. He said he saw you using sign language. That's pretty neat." 72

I cringed. I didn't want to sound priggish, correcting her for saying "dumb." "Um, well, I don't know if I would exactly call it that." 73

At 9:15, Laura announced she was going to bed and took off all her clothes. Throwing them across the room onto a dusty chair she had carried up from the basement, she dived under the sheet to rest on top of the bare mattress. 74

I had never seen anyone sleep nude in my life. There was something in the nimbleness of her movement after she had taken her clothes off that told me there were a number of things I was going to learn at Harvard that I hadn't foreseen. 75

I put on my nightgown, dressing with my back to Laura, carefully pulling the gown to my ankles before reaching under to remove my skirt. I crawled into my crisp bed—made by my mother—and we talked for a few minutes more. Suddenly, Laura directed a foot at the light switch. 76

In the dark, I felt more forlorn than ever. I waited until I thought   77
she was asleep, got up, put my clothes back on and walked outside. I
didn't know where I was going. I headed toward what looked to be
the busiest street and discovered Massachusetts Avenue. Mom and
Dad had told me that was where the Holiday Inn was situated. I
wandered up and down the sidewalk and found myself in front of
their hotel.

I made my way to their room on the third floor and, as I raised my   78
knuckles, it dawned on me that knocking would do no good. I knew
they were awake; I could hear the television. I took a notebook paper
out of my purse and bent down to shove it underneath the door,
working it in and out. There was no response. I tried crumpling up a
small piece of paper to throw into the room, but I couldn't get it
between the jamb and the door. I pounded on the gray metal, thinking
they might feel the vibration. I must have stood there for 20 minutes,
hoping Dad might come out to get ice from down the hall or perhaps
go to the car to retrieve a bag. But he didn't.

Vocabulary

chasm (7)—a break or gap

rasping (8)—grating; irritating

precocious (9)—developed or intelligent beyond what is normally expected for one's age

aberrantly (10)—unusually; un-
seasonably

auditory (10)—hearing

self-recrimination (11)—blame of
oneself

volatile (11)—unstable; explosive

velocity (19)—speed

panacea (23)—cure for all problems

'Cliffie (70)—student from Rad-
cliffe, which was the women's
college of Harvard University

forlorn (77)—miserable and sad

IN YOUR JOURNAL

What did you learn from the article that surprised you? Write about
anything new you now know about the world of the deaf or hearing
impaired that you did not know before.

A Closer Reading

1. What is some of the body language or signals used by deaf people that Walker describes in this article?

2. Describe in what ways Walker's parents' home is specially designed to meet the needs of nonhearing people.

3. Walker states that even though her "parents communicated solely in signs, even that language isn't completely silent." What examples can you cite in the text that support this?

4. Give specific examples to support Walker's allegation that lip reading is "not the panacea hearing people would like to believe."

5. Describe how Walker's parents communicate while driving.

Drawing Your Own Conclusions

1. What responsibilities did Walker have while growing up that most young children do not have? How do you think this affected her? Use the text to support your answer.

2. Why is it true as Walker states that "children of deaf parents rarely run away from home"? Based on your experiences and observations, is this true for children with parents who have other special needs as well?

3. Why do you think that Walker began to think that her parents were only pretending to be deaf? She connects this with the fact that many children at one time or another think they are adopted. How are these ideas related in the text and in your understanding of them?

4. Walker states that she has contradictory feelings about her parents' situation. What evidence of these feelings can you find in the text?

5. Read the Goleman et al. selection on page 119. What aspects of intelligence has Walker developed? How do Walker's intellectual strengths help her make a career decision?

Thinking about Writing

1. As the child of hearing-impaired parents, Walker has a unique point of view. What does she reveal in this article that a social worker visiting the family would not observe?

2. Using the text for evidence, cite passages that show what Walker assumes her readers know about the hearing impaired. How do you think she believes people feel about the hearing impaired? Compare the way Walker discusses stereotypes with the way other authors discuss stereotypes in other selections in this book. See, for example, Cole on page 135, Noda on page 31, and Wideman on page 68.

3. What do you think Walker wants the reader to think about her and her parents at the end of the article? Does she succeed?

4. What was the one anecdote or story that you will remember most from this story? Why do you think this one will remain with you?

* * *

Suggestions for Writing

1. Interview an administrator in your college to find out what special devices are available in your school for students with special needs—for example, students with visual handicaps, students in wheelchairs, or students who are unable to hear in lecture classes. Present a written report of your findings to your classmates.

2. If after finding the information in question 1, you discover that your college is not doing enough for students with special needs, write a letter to the college newspaper describing your findings and making suggestions for improvement.

3. Should people who are hearing impaired be allowed to drive? Take a position, and defend it in an essay based on your experiences and observations.

4. Some people believe that nonhearing people should be taught to speak as well as to sign. Many others think that the ability to sign enables them to communicate effectively. Write an essay in which you take a position on this issue, and support your point of view with your experiences, readings, and observations.

5. Recently students at Gallaudet College, a college for the hearing impaired, rejected a hearing college president. They said they wanted a nonhearing president who had experienced their world. Many educators disagreed with the students and claimed that a

sensitive educated person, whether hearing or nonhearing, could understand the needs of these students. Write an essay in which you agree or disagree with the students.

Collaborative Project

Your college is considering admitting five nonhearing freshmen next semester. As a small group, write a paper making suggestions to the college about what can be done to meet the particular needs of the hearing impaired. What specific problems do you think these students might have? Do you think there are any devices the school should purchase to make available to these students? What can you do as students in the college to make the transition to college easier for hearing-impaired students?

Strategies for Revision

Walker writes about the types of nonverbal communication that occur in her family. Keeping in mind the idea of nonverbal communication, work with a partner and write responses to each other's drafts. Read your partner's drafts and write down your responses to the following questions:

- In which parts of the draft does the writer clearly describe any problems that exist for hearing-impaired or other disabled students? Which sentence or phrase do you think is especially effective? Or especially weak?
- What solutions to these problems does the writer present? What makes them clear or confusing?
- What examples can you find that the writer includes details that help a reader relate to senses other than hearing—sight and touch, for example? Are these vividly described?
- In what ways does the writer show sensitivity to the difficulties and strengths of people with disabilities of any sort? If not, what changes should be made in the essay to do this?

Read the responses your classmate has written to your essay. Make any changes that you think will make your revised essay stronger and more effective. Share this revision with your classmate.

IN YOUR JOURNAL

Write in your journal for fifteen minutes every day this week, focusing on your experiences in school, with teachers, and students, in and out of the classroom, and with your coursework.

The Diary of a First-Year Teacher

Mark Shone

Mark Shone wrote this diary about his first year of teaching in a public school in Brooklyn, New York, in 1993. The following selection appeared in the education section of the *New York Times* on Sunday, August 1, 1993. It describes Shone's sixth-grade students and his experiences with them over a three-month period from March through June 1993. During this time, he meets with successes and failures, as he gets to know his students and himself in the role of teacher.

March 23, Public School 29, Brooklyn, N.Y., Sixth Grade: We 1 had assembly today. It was a musical version of the early life of Helen Keller, and there was a simultaneous sign-language translation on the side. Alonzo, a charming but volatile boy, watched the sign language intently and moved his hands in an attempt to mimic and learn. I watched in silent admiration of his desire to know something new. In a few minutes, however, his concentration turned to frustration and he began mumbling and cursing to himself and thrashing to and fro in his seat. I leaned forward to whisper to him and ask what was wrong. He responded angrily, "I don't know how to do this!" I explained that nobody could learn sign language that fast and that I'd help him get started when we returned to the classroom. I wondered how many children are labeled behavior problems when it is really just a frustration with their capacities failing to keep up with their ambitions.

March 31: Had to raise my voice to regain attention during math. 2 Yet even as I want my students to respond to me, I don't want them to think I am criticizing anything but their current behavior. It disturbs me that Evita is so easily cowed. She occasionally talks incessantly in class, and when I admonish her, she assumes an extremely submissive role. She doesn't apologize; in fact, she says nothing and conveys no message with her face, but instead, with downcast eyes and immobile features, slowly does what I ask. Except for her actions there is no clue that she either hears me or is listening. It disturbs me to see a child so submissive.

April 5: Just assigned everyone to take 15 minutes to write down thoughts on any subject at all. It's been 12 minutes—and no one has talked or been disruptive yet. I'm impressed. It wasn't like this at the start of the year. 　3

April 14: Alonzo came into school with a beautiful diorama of Theseus and the Minotaur. It almost looks as if he tried to imitate Picasso's *Guernica,* although he is unaware of the similarities. He is a talented artist. I understand he was one of the most difficult students last year, and I can see how he misbehaves and how his behavior can be disruptive. But he really likes to achieve and be skillful and admired as an athlete and artist and student, and he is blossoming. He's still very vocal about his likes and dislikes, but has learned to be more diligent in his work, and he's learning to behave like a gentleman even in adversity. I hope he doesn't lose his momentum in junior high. 　4

April 16: Just took down all my materials on ancient Greece, including the Homeric ideal that hung dead center above the blackboard, "Mens sana in corpore sano," for six weeks. Not one student was curious or brave enough to ask me what it meant. Disappointing. 　5

April 19: We began ancient Rome and the topic of Christianity came up. I asked if the Romans were a monotheistic or polytheistic society. Nearly everyone's hand shot up to answer. They'd complained when I made them memorize 75 Greek roots like mono-, poly-, and theo-. I smile and wonder how many realize what they've accomplished. 　6

April 20: I'm annoyed by the constant flow of interruptions we are subject to during lessons. Someone feels compelled to use the intercom at least five times a day, and although sometimes it is important, frequently I feel it is not. Visitors to the classroom are also frequent, at least four or five each day, and many times more. Lessons depend upon timing, and these interruptions break the tenuous thread of concentration these children have. 　7

April 21: Dale is clearly very angry, and this is detrimental to the   8
class as well as to his own ability to learn. I reminded him to write in his
journal today, and he grumbled. I not only asked him to stop reading
his book, but closed it and took it away. He huffed. Then I asked him to
take his feet off the chair next to him, and again he frowned. I didn't yell
or get angry; just explained that what I was requesting was appropriate
student behavior. Although he resisted at first, he now is writing diligently and silently.

No confrontation. Mission accomplished.   9

April 26: Timing again. It's a big factor in classroom success. Right   10
now the children are writing diaries from the point of view of one of the
secondary characters in a story we just read. They'll stay focused for
another 10 to 15 minutes—then we'll have to move on.

April 28: When Tanya writes she likes to invent funny scenes that   11
could have happened but aren't specifically mentioned in the book she
was supposed to be describing. I think her sense of humor is a little silly
and infantile, but it seems to me I have to encourage her creativity, and I
do.

April 30: Lerner has sparks of brilliance and great comprehension.   12
But he is too easily distracted. Most of his trouble arises from his
limited English language capabilities. He is struggling and he gets frustrated easily. With him, I have to praise his ideas and correct his speech
and writing skills separately.

May 11: O.R.P.A.L. (the Office of Recruitment, Personnel Assess-   13
ment and Licensing in the New York City public school system) sent me
a form letter informing me that there is a problem that prevents the
renewal of my certificate after this first year of teaching. They provided
a phone number and requested me to contact them immediately. As is
typical of this bureaucracy-gone-awry, the phone number listed is always busy. I've called at 8 A.M., midmorning, lunchtime, midafternoon
and closing time (5 P.M. on the nose). Always busy. After a week of this,
to comply with their "immediate, urgent request" I go to the office at
65 Court Street. This is easy for me, but what about people who don't
work in the vicinity?

I'm sitting in the office now, waiting for them to "diagnose" my   14
problem. Drab offices. Bored, angry, impatient faces of people sitting

and waiting. But this day isn't bad, compared with others. It's not that crowded; the air-conditioner is working, and no one has had a shouting match. I sit and listen to one articulate gentleman explain that he's filled out all the necessary forms and has no idea why his license renewal has been denied. The answer is that O.R.P.A.L. has no idea either. Only Albany can clarify this, and he should call Albany. But the phones are always busy, he explains. "Then you'll have to wait for them to send you something in the mail." Then why did O.R.P.A.L. tell him to contact them? "Because we needed to figure out what your problem was." Oh, he says. Thanks.

May 13: Complaints on the part of teachers fall into two large categories: (1) how bothersome-meddlesome-overbearing-out-of-touch the principal, assistant principal and district office are; and (2) how unruly the students can be. I like the principal and respect her skills. Think she generally hires teachers with a good teaching philosophy and can remove herself from the day-to-day aspects of teaching. I suspect that this is what most intelligent principals try to do, but it is more easily suggested than accomplished. It's especially difficult to get rid of those tenured teachers who aren't skilled or cooperative. It intrigues me just as much to hear incessant bellyaching about the students. Kids aren't evil—just growing up and testing boundaries.   15

May 14: I used to dismiss the human aspect of teaching, especially the bit about being responsible for the healthy psychological development of students, but now I see my job as a teacher largely as that of a role model. I model not just behavior, but an academic stance toward learning. I must be on from the time I see the first child in the morning until the time I leave the school. I need to let children see me behave and react as I would want them to behave and react.   16

May 25: Today I made a little girl cry. I was trying to get the students to brainstorm about some of the effects of the Crusades. I was able to lead them to give me short answers, like "spices," "clothing" and "gold and jewels," but could not get them to explain their answers. I was already sensationalizing my descriptions to hold their attention and had asked several times politely for their participation, but the undercurrent of discussion and murmuring was on the rise. The breaking point came when Ruth, whom I'd warned against excessive conversation, called out the name of a classmate, obviously intending to ask her   17 something. I looked at Ruth, and she knew that she was wrong not only for talking, but also for talking too loudly. But her shrug of an apology struck me a little too flip, and I zeroed in to make an example of her for the rest of the class.

In quiet, forceful tones I pried from her the intended question. She 18 wanted to know her friend's birthday. Then I shamed her by sardonically pointing out all the benefits we had just derived as a class thanks to her. I capped this bit of sarcasm by writing in the friend's birthday at the tip of our history time line, just past Elizabeth I. The rest of the class struggled to stifle their laughter. I ended this verbal thrashing with a direct threat: One more extraneous noise or action by the end of the lesson and she'd be kept from the park picnic on Friday. I resumed the lesson with an attentive and intelligently participative class. Ruth lay her head down and wept silently.

I hate doing what I did. This method seems to get results in ways 19 other methods don't or can't. I don't do it often, but when I do I am pensive and irritable for hours afterward. Do seasoned teachers do this? Although I can rationalize that at least I don't scream the way I hear some teachers do, I wonder if any of it is necessary. I've looked for other ways. I'm still looking.

May 27: It's a little after 5, and I am still in my classroom. When I 20 hear outsiders complain, jokingly or seriously, about teachers' short working hours or excessive vacation, I smile, amused at their assumptions and ignorance. Yes, it's true that we get July and August off, but many teachers use the time to acquire useful knowledge for their classroom teaching. Yes, it is true that the minimal day-to-day requirements is only 6 hours and 20 minutes, but many teachers put in more than that, before or after school or at home. On the other hand, I have encountered more than a handful who only put in the minimum who are nowhere to be seen before 8:40 or after 3, and I can't figure out how they do their research, or preparation or classroom decoration. I suspect they do very little. Anyway, I'd better finish up soon, otherwise I'll "get in trouble" for working too late.

June 1: I've read a lot about the shabby, decrepit conditions that 21 some teachers work in. Why have I been so lucky?

June 4: Thought of a metaphor. Don't think I've heard it before. A 22 student is a river—in an identifiable course, but not unchangeable, seemingly stationary and predictable, but always in motion and some-times surprising and uncontrollable. We seek to guide its motion and uses, but part of its beauty is its own strength and character. If we try too hard to make it useful and bulkhead all its banks and dam its flow, we turn a thing of individual beauty and power into a public tool devoid of personality. We have to be careful.

June 7: Still don't really understand the don't-smile-until-Thanks-   23 giving rule, even though a good number of teachers have given me this advice. Suppose there are some advantages for the first few months in terms of classroom order to being viewed as a stern, humorless disciplinar-ian, but I haven't been able to muster the energy necessary to affect that pose for six hours at a stretch.

June 11: The kids seem to appreciate that I talk to them a great   24 deal about hypocrisy and contradictions, especially when it involves interaction with adults. They are free to question the status quo, espe-cially as it relates to them. I believe a recognition of ambiguity is the first step on the way to problem-solving. It asks students to engage in higher-level learning about a problem pertinent to them. I try to sneak these same techniques into more abstract questions in social studies or science.

June 21: Can't help but think how my students have changed   25 since September. Some have matured noticeably, and are thoughtful, helpful, polite and good-humored people. Some are more capable students, and have made noticeable progress in their abilities to en-gage themselves as academic beings. A few really don't seem much different at all. Can say with honesty, though, that each one is a thoroughly enjoyable individual.

I tell them this often, but can never tell if they believe me or   26 if they think I'm saying it to be nice. I keep saying it anyway. These students are children on the verge of adulthood, and I let them know what acceptable behavior is, but understand that sometimes they can really be goofy and harshly egocentric and foul-mouthed. Like adults.

I am openly thrilled about their progress and with the way the year   27 has turned out. And am secretly worried about what they'll face in the years ahead.

Vocabulary

thrashing (1)—moving or tossing about violently

cowed (2)—intimidated; frightened into submission

submissive (2)—having a tendency to give in without resistance

adversity (4)—misfortune; trouble

tenuous (7)—slight; flimsy

detrimental (8)—harmful

comply (13)—to obey

articulate (14)—able to express oneself clearly and easily

pried (18)—extracted with difficulty

decrepit (21)—broken down or worn out with age

devoid (22)—empty; completely without

status quo (24)—the existing state of affairs at a given time

---

IN YOUR JOURNAL

At the end of the week, read what you have written in your journal. Reflect on the week as a whole. What moments stand out? What did you learn this week? In what way(s) are you different from the way you were last week?

A Closer Reading

1. What incidents in the diary suggest that Shone cares about the individual needs of his students?

2. What incidents in the diary indicate that Shone is sometimes frustrated by the children in his class?

3. What aspects of teaching, other than the children, frustrate Shone?

4. What techniques does Shone use to gain his students' attention?

Drawing Your Own Conclusions

1. Shone states that his students feel frustrated when their capacities fail to keep up with their ambitions. What does this mean? What examples does he include in his diary? How does this relate to the Goleman et al. selection on page 119?

2. Why is Shone disappointed that his students do not ask about the meaning of "Mens sana in corpore sano"? Why did he display this sign in his class? Do you know what it means? If not, find out. Why might this phrase be important to Shone? Why might it be important to you?

3. Reread the Goleman et al. selection, focusing on the different aspects of intelligence. What specific techniques does Shone use that recognize the different aspects of intelligence in his students? Cite examples from the diary.

4. What technique does Shone use with his class to help them increase their vocabulary? How does this compare with the way that Malcolm X (see page 129) increased his vocabulary? What role does motivation play in the learning taking place in Shone's class? What does he do to try to motivate his students?

Thinking about Writing

1. What in this selection tells you that Shone revised and edited his diary before it was published?

2. What other books or stories have you read that were in diary form? What writing features do you notice when you read a diary?

3. How does Shone explain the metaphor in paragraph 20? In what other ways is a student like a river?

4. Shone uses several rhetorical (writing) techniques for presenting his ideas. Reread the selection, looking for sections in which he tells a story (or anecdote) about an incident that happened in class.

5. Find sections in the diary in which Shone presents his philosophy or overview of teaching and the children. Make a list of the philosophical ideas he presents. Which anecdotes support his philosophy? Show how Shone changes and shapes his philosophy as he learns and grows.

*   *   *

Suggestions for Writing

1. Drawing on question 4, analyze Shone's teaching techniques, his successes and failures. How successful is he according to his own standards? Does he recognize all his strengths; do you see oth-

ers? In what areas does he feel he needs improvement? Do you see other areas in which he could improve? If you directly quote from Shone's diary, remember to use quotation marks.

2. Reread the Shone selection and choose one of the children he describes. Write about the characteristics that the child shows in the classroom. Describe the specific techniques you would use to motivate that child. Explain why you selected the particular child and why you think your techniques would help the child become a more successful student.

3. Describe a frustrating experience that you have had in college recently—for example, registration, buying books, interacting with a teacher or another student, or a difficult assignment. Explain how you dealt with your frustration and make suggestions for improving the situation.

4. "I used to dismiss the human aspect of teaching, . . . but now I see my job as a teacher largely as that of a role model. I model not just behavior, but an academic stance toward learning." Write an essay in which you describe someone who has been a role model for you. Tell about the time or times when you learned something important from this person. What are the personal characteristics of this role model? How did this person teach you: directly or indirectly, through language or actions or both?

Strategies for Revision

As Mark Shone's diary illustrates, we learn through experience, through trying and succeeding as well as trying and failing. We learn through redoing earlier work and making it better.

Think about this as you revise. First, read your first draft, concentrating on descriptive words and phrases. In Shone's diary, for example, he describes Dale using these words: very angry, grumbled, huffed, frowned, resisted, diligently, silently. These words create a mood and tell the readers about the student and the incident. In your draft, make sure you include enough information to evoke a mood.

Second, think about the overall idea that you want your writing to convey. Write this down in one sentence of fewer than twenty-five words on a separate piece of paper. Share it with a classmate. Read your draft together. Concentrate on the ways in which you do or do not communicate your ideas effectively. Revise.

Sheila Renee Shallenberger wrote an essay in response to suggestion 1 in the Suggestions for Writing following the Malcolm X selection: Write an essay about someone who changed his or her life after having initial problems in school. Describe the person, the problem, and the way the person changed. Explain what motivated the person to change.

Returning to College

Sheila Renee Shallenberger

Deciding to come back to college was one of the most difficult decisions of my life. I reported to my first college writing class scared, confused, and convinced that writing was of no interest to me. As I listened to the instructor prepare us for the course I realized—contrary to my first thoughts—that this was not going to be a boring class. An abundance of time would be needed to produce any quality writing. Since spare time was already scarce to me, I knew this was going to be tough.   1

I recall the surprise I felt as I received a somewhat positive response to my first piece of writing. I also remember thinking "this may be easier than I expected!" But, contrary to this thought, each piece of writing seemed harder to organize.   2

I would sit at the table, paper in front of me, pen in my hand, dictionary and thesaurus on one side of me, and a stack of paper on the other. I wondered where the words would come from to fill the paper. I recall the writings of other students in my class. Writing seemed to come naturally for some. They knew just the right words to use and when to use them. Their sentences seemed to be composed perfectly to relay the information interestingly and entertainingly to their readers. Imagination and creativity seemed to flow from them!   3

I pull my thoughts back to the work at hand racking my brain for words to fill the still empty paper. Just a minute ago I had the perfect thought racing through my mind, but as I attempt to write no words will come. Well, not ones above grade school grammar anyway. I tell myself to relax. Picking up the thesaurus I scold myself for not being more imaginative. I skim over the reading in the textbook again. Turning my attention back to the paper, I think out loud, "Why do I have to take this writing class anyway? I'm not going to become a professional writer!" After surviving many hours of frustration, headaches, and   4 much wasted paper, I am ready to proofread what I have written. I look for ways to improve my paper. Finally, I give up and decide to go with what I have.

As I look back through my work, I notice that the length of my writings remain constant. The context of my sentences seem satisfactory and my spelling errors are minimal. I expected punctuation to be easy for me. As I look through my work though, I realize I refrain from using anything needing complicated punctuation. My punctuation errors seem to grow as I concentrate more on the context of my writing. I find myself experimenting with more punctuation; however, I am not yet confident enough to use it in my writing material. 5

As I come to the conclusion of this jumble of words I have written, I admit I am still not an avid writer. Writing is a challenge that I may never conquer; however, I am becoming more interested. I have started to write on a more personal level. While writing does seem a talent for some, I am still striving to achieve personal satisfaction. 6

Questions to Think About

1. Where in the essay does Shallenberger state her problem?

2. What examples does she provide to illustrate her problem?

3. What steps does Shallenberger identify that correspond with the writing process as you know it?

4. What did you learn about Shallenberger from reading this essay? What advice would you give her to help her feel more comfortable about her writing?

MAKING CONNECTIONS

The World of Learning: *Finding One's Purpose*

1. Using the selections that you have read in this unit, write an essay explaining the role learning played in the lives of the various authors. You may want to paraphrase or directly quote from some of the articles you have read or develop further some of the writing you have already done in this unit.

2. Imagine that you had to design a three-credit required course for entering freshmen in your college that could include only three of the following:

   negotiation skills
   study skills
   developing tolerance
   learning how to use source materials for college research
   learning about new technologies
   developing self-awareness

   Write an essay in which you state your choices and explain why you have chosen them, referring to selections you have read in this unit.

3. Imagine that Mark Shone (see page 165) met with Daniel Goleman, Paul Kaufman, and Michael Ray (see page 119) to discuss intelligence and ways he could tap into the differing abilities of his sixth graders. Outline this brainstorming session and write five suggestions that they might come up with together.

4. Imagine that Cole (see page 135), Thurber (see page 143), and Walker (see page 152) met to discuss how stereotyping has affected the lives of women and disabled people. Create a discussion they could have had and write it down in dialogue form. Keep in mind their differing points of view and backgrounds. What conclusion do you think they might come to as a group?

5. Reread the headnotes for each of the writers in this unit. Write an essay in which you explain similarities and differences in their lives and backgrounds. What factors do you think contributed to

their becoming writers? What role has writing played in their lives?

6. Write an introduction to this unit in which you recommend to other students one piece of writing in this unit. Why is this piece of writing is best? Is it the most interesting, the most informative, or the best written? Using quotations from the selection, convince your reader to choose this particular piece to read.

4

THE WORLD
OF GENDER

Being Men and Women

Asoon as we are born, the first words said about us are: "It's a boy" or "It's a girl." We soon find that there are expectations, possibilities, and limitations relating to our sex and gender. Nearing the twenty-first century, we are seriously examining sex differences and gender expectations and the roles they have played in preventing people from exploring a wider range of possibilities to develop and express themselves.

Anthropologists look at the ways people live together, and they often give us insights into familiar and unfamiliar lifestyles. Journalist Kathleen McAuliffe interviews anthropologist Helen Fisher and discovers how in some ways our modern world is moving backward toward the kinds of roles that men and women had on the grasslands of Africa millions of years ago.

John Byrne Barry explores a new role for men, at least in our society, and that is the role of father as caregiver. When his first child is born, Barry decides he wants to be as actively involved in the baby's life as his wife is. In "Daddytrack," he explains some of the adjustments both husband and wife had to make so this could be possible.

In "Sex Differences, Real and Imagined," researchers Carol Tavris and Carole Wade look closely at the differences between men and women. Their research makes them question many of our assumptions about what men and women can or cannot do.

Bob Hoerburger's essay "Gotta Dance" describes his ambivalent feelings toward telling others about his dancing. For a while, he even tries to deny it to himself, but ultimately, Hoerburger decides that he must dance and he must let others know about the pleasures of performance dancing for men as well as for women.

In "Lake Stephen," Charles Baxter tells a story about power relations between the sexes in his tale of a young couple on vacation. When the woman decides she knows what to do to persuade her boyfriend to agree to marriage, she uses some unusual tactics that take him by surprise.

Continuing the theme of power relations, education writer Edward B. Fiske focuses on the college classroom. In this essay, he reveals some of the dynamics between men and women, teachers and students. The essay may surprise and encourage you to observe your own college, and perhaps even make some changes there.

Student writer Lisa L. Smith also responds to the theme of power relations as she questions gender discrimination. Smith thinks that the ultimate blame for gender discrimination lies not with either women or

180

with men alone, but in our society as a whole. To change, we must be willing to question old behaviors and attitudes.

*   *   *

Think about the following questions before reading the selections in this unit:

1. What are the four best aspects of being the sex you are?
2. What are the four worst aspects of being the sex you are?
3. What changes would you like to make in the ways your sex is perceived? Why?

IN YOUR JOURNAL

Men and women are moving closer to equality than ever before. Before you read this selection, think about this statement and write about whether you agree with it and about what it means in your life.

A Primitive Prescription for Equality

Kathleen McAuliffe

Kathleen McAuliffe is one of the senior editors for *U.S. News & World Report*. As part of the magazine's August 8, 1988, special issue on "Men vs. Women," McAuliffe interviewed Helen Fisher, an anthropologist at the American Museum of Natural History, to find out about male/female relationships from an anthropological perspective. McAuliffe reports on this conversation in "A Primitive Prescription for Equality." Fisher told McAuliffe that she believes our relationships are moving "back to the future" in that our society is making a transition from a predominantly agricultural to a technological society that is patterned more closely on the hunter-gatherer society.

Men and women are moving toward the kind of roles they had on 　1 the grasslands of Africa millions of years ago. But this "backward" trend is a step forward, toward equality between the sexes.

The rise of economically autonomous women is a new phenomenon 　2 that is in reality very old. For more than 99 percent of human evolution, we existed as hunters and gatherers, and women in those cultures enjoyed enormous clout because they probably brought back 60 to 80 percent of the food. At least that's the case in most contemporary hunting-gathering communities, such as the !Kung bushmen of Africa, whose lifestyle is thought to mirror that of earliest Homo sapiens.

The recent trend toward divorce and remarriage is another example 　3 of a throwback to earlier times. The constant making and breaking of marital ties is a hallmark of hunting-gathering societies. The trend only seems novel to us because we are just now emerging from an agricultural tradition—a male-dominated culture that, while recent, lasted for a flash in the night on the time scale of human evolution. A peculiarity of the farming lifestyle is that men and women functioned as an isolated, economically dependent unit. Marriage was "till death do us part" for the simple reason that neither partner could pick up half the property and march off to town.

But when men and women left farms for jobs and came back with money—movable, divisible property—we slipped right back into deeply ingrained behavior patterns that evolved long ago. Money makes it easy to walk out on a bad relationship. A man is going to think a lot harder about leaving a woman who picks his vegetables than leaving a woman who is the vice president of Citibank, because she can fend for herself and vice versa. Indeed, around the globe, wherever women are economically powerful, divorce rates are high. You see it in the !Kung, and you see it in the United States: Between 1960 and 1980, when the number of women in the work force doubled, the divorce rate doubled, too.   4

That figure seems bleak until we recall that the vast majority of couples who split up remarry—and that's as true in hunting-gathering communities as in postindustrial America. This suggests that the so-called new extended family may actually have evolved millenia ago. If so, perhaps our tendency to equate divorce with failure has made us blind to the advantages of the extended family: Children grow up with more adult role models and a larger network of relatives, increasing their range of power and influence within society.   5

The trend toward smaller families may not be as modern as we think, either. Although women gatherers had four or five children, only two typically survived childhood—the number found in the average American family today. Even our style of rearing children is starting to parallel hunting-gathering communities, in which girls and boys are permitted to play together from a young age, and consequently experiment at sex earlier and engage in trial marriages. Clearly we've moved away from the agricultural custom of arranged marriages and cloistering girls to preserve their virginity.   6

Moreover, the home is no longer the "place of production," as it was in farm days. We don't make our own soap, grow our own vegetables and slaughter our chicken for the dinner table. Instead, we hunt and gather in the grocery store and return to our "home base" to consume the food that we have collected. No wonder we are so in love with fast foods. It probably harks back to an eating strategy our primate relatives adopted over 50 million years ago.   7

There's no mistaking the trend: Humans are once again on the move. Husband and wife are no longer bound to a single plot of land   8 for their livelihood. Women are back in production as well as reproduction. As we head back to the future, there's every reason to believe the sexes will enjoy the kind of equality that is a function of our birthright. By equality, I mean a more equitable division of power—not that our roles will converge. Alike men and women have never been and never will be. Very simply, we *think* differently, which is again tied to our long hunting-gathering heritage.

For 2 million years, women carried around children and have been   9
the nurturers. That's probably why tests show they are both more verbal and more attuned to nonverbal cues. Men, on the other hand, tend to have superior mathematical and visual-spatial skills because they roamed long distances from the campsite, had to scheme ways to trap prey and then had to find their way back.

That specialization is reflected in genuine gender differences in the   10
brain today. Nature not only intended men and women to put their bodies together; we're meant to put our heads together as well.

That's what's so thrilling about what's happening now. All those   11
male and female skills are beginning to work together again. At long last, society is moving in a direction that should be highly compatible with our ancient human spirit.

Vocabulary

autonomous (2)—having self-government, independence

clout (2)—power or influence

hallmark (3)—mark or symbol of authenticity

ingrained (4)—established; firmly fixed

fend (4)—to get along without help

millennia (5)—plural form of millennium; a thousand-year period of time

equate (5)—to make equal or equivalent

cloistering (6)—secluding or confining in a protected place such as a cloister

equitable (8)—fair or just

converge (8)—to come together at a point

IN YOUR JOURNAL

What is the difference between equality and "a more equitable division of power" between men and women? Write in your journal about what this means for you in our society today.

A Closer Reading

1. What evidence does McAuliffe provide to support the idea that for most of history women have been "economically autonomous"?

2. How does she use the comparison of the hunter-gatherer and agricultural lifestyles to explain the recent rise in divorces in our society?

3. In what ways are we as we move into the twenty-first century similar to the hunter-gatherer societies? In what ways are we changing from an agricultural society?

4. According to the article, divorce and remarriage have created a new form of the extended family. What are some of the advantages of the extended family? What are some of the disadvantages?

Drawing Your Own Conclusions

1. In paragraphs 9 and 10, McAuliffe presents differences between men and women. Do these differences correspond in any way to the ones mentioned in the Fiske article on page 223? Are the characteristics mentioned in these two selections inborn or learned, the famous "nature or nurture" debate? Explain your answer and what it means for men and women.

2. Why do you think the agricultural tradition is so male-dominated? Do the films you have seen, the books you have read, or your own experiences with farm life support this point of view?

3. If today's society is becoming more equal, and there is a "more equitable division of power," how will this affect the treatment of children and old people? What changes can you predict?

4. How does the article indicate that the movement toward equality is a positive one? Can you think of any societies or religious

groups by whom this movement would be viewed negatively? Explain their position as you understand it.

5. How would Alvin Toffler (see page 103) describe or define the types of families that are created from the constant making and breaking of marital ties referred to in this article?

Thinking about Writing

1. According to your dictionary, what does the word "primitive" mean? Is it used appropriately in the title of this article? Or does it stereotype a society of people known as hunter-gatherers?

2. In paragraph 1, McAuliffe puts the word "backward" in quotation marks. How does this change the meaning or intention of this word in this paragraph?

3. This article is based on an interview by a journalist, Kathleen McAuliffe, of an anthropologist, Helen Fisher. Whose ideas are being presented in the article? How could the writer have made this clearer?

4. Does McAuliffe give examples to convince you of Fisher's argument? What is her strongest example? What is her weakest example?

*   *   *

Suggestions for Writing

1. It is stated in paragraph 4 in McAuliffe's article: "Whenever women are economically powerful, divorce rates are high." Write an essay in which you explain why this statement might be accurate. Use examples from your own experience, your observations, and your readings.

2. Paragraph 8 states, "Alike men and women have never been and never will be." Write an essay in which you agree or disagree with this statement, and support your point of view with examples from your readings, experiences, and observations.

3. Write an essay comparing the hunting-gathering society to the agricultural society. (You may want to read Shostak's selection on page 258 for ideas.) As you write your essay, keep in mind the different roles men and women play in these types of societies.

4. Do men and women benefit equally from equality? Before you answer this question, think about the mother and father in the Viramontes essay on page 5, the father in the John Edgar Wideman story on page 68, the wife and husband in Maxine Hong Kingston's story on page 85, and the father and mother in Sara Lawrence Lightfoot's selection on page 76. Think about your own experiences as well. Then, write an essay in which you explore this question, using these readings and your own experiences and observations.

5. Describe ways in which the large extended family can or cannot provide richer child-rearing experiences than the smaller nuclear family. (You may want to reread Alvin Toffler's selection on page 103, Pearl Rowe's story on page 61, or Lou Ann Walker's article on page 152 for ideas.) Use your experiences, observations, and readings for supporting details.

Strategies for Revision

When you have completed your first draft, put it away for at least one day so you can get some distance from your writing. When you read it again, look at your essay with a critical eye, thinking about the following ideas:

- McAuliffe presents the ideas of anthropologist Helen Fisher. How does McAuliffe identify Fisher as a source of information?
- Is it clear when your ideas are your own original ideas and when they come from other sources?
- How do you identify the source of your ideas when you refer to other writers and thinkers?
- When does McAuliffe use direct quotations? How did you decide when to use direct quotations and when to paraphrase other thinkers?
- Where does McAuliffe present the main idea that holds her article together? Where do you put yours?
- Does your draft communicate the ideas as clearly as possible? If not, what can you change to improve it?
- After you have thought about these questions in relation to your own writing, revise your essay. Share your revision with another classmate.

IN YOUR JOURNAL

Write down what you think are the essential qualities a person should
have when bringing up a child. Explain why these qualities are important.

Daddytrack

John Byrne Barry

John Byrne Barry wrote this article for the Spring 1989 issue of
Mothering magazine. It was reprinted in the May/June 1993 issue of
Utne magazine. Barry addresses the problems of balancing father-
hood and a career and explains how he and his wife found one
solution to the "absent father" problem.

It is not news that fathering has changed over the past generation or 1
two, that today's father is more involved in child care than his father was.
But although the involved and nurturing father is becoming more visible
and acceptable, he is still generally regarded as a helper in the world of child
care and housekeeping. He pitches in. He helps *when he wants to*. Fathers are
volunteer providers; mothers are the staff. The household with two "staff
parents" is still rare, especially when it requires father to cut back on work.

TV commercials show fathers in business suits ducking out of con- 2
ferences to attend their children's school plays, but we do not see them
ducking out of work for the plain-old-vanilla caretaking of their
children—the "quantity time" stuff. Support for fathers' involvement in
the day-to-day labor of raising children is growing in the work world
with the speed of a glacier. Whereas employers may not allow a mother
to work part time, they do understand her reason for wanting to. A man
who wants to work part time in order to care for his children is looked
on with suspicion, or, at best, amusement.

Laurie and I decided to share child care before we were married, 3
well before our son Sean was born. Neither of us wanted to stop
working, nor did we want to miss out on this exciting period of newborn growth by being the full-time bringer-home-of-bacon.

In the months before our son was born, we both went to our 4
employers and negotiated a reduction in working hours. We were able
to juggle our time so one of us could always be the primary caregiver.

Our employers were supportive, allowing us the flexibility to work at home and not balking at our patchwork schedules. After Sean was born, I worked long hours two days a week while Laurie stayed home with him. On Tuesdays, I was home on the range. On Wednesdays and Fridays we each worked half a day and spent the other half with Sean.

We managed this arrangement for 17 months and then suffered a   5
temporary setback. A restructuring at my workplace and a promotion I never asked for sent me across the bay to San Francisco . . . full time. Despite an impassioned speech about why I should maintain a flexible schedule, I found myself being a commuter dad, away from home 11 hours a day, five days a week.

The changes in my work schedule provoked changes in Sean. He   6
began to cling more to his mother. And on the one evening a week that I soloed, he would wander through the house baaing "Mama" like a lost sheep and stay awake until she returned home around 10.

After four months of full-time work and a lot of grumbling—I   7
found a flexible, 80-percent-time job. Although our situation is tighter and less flexible than it was originally, we have recovered our sense of balance. My relationship with Sean has improved dramatically.

We've been lucky, yes, but the determining factor in our success has   8
been *asking for* and *looking for* suitable work arrangements. Although part-time professional work, job sharing, and working-at-home situations are still scarce, they have nevertheless entered the vocabulary. According to proponents of alternative work arrangements, such as San Francisco–based New Ways to Work, the most successful route to a flexible situation is to create it yourself, and our experiences attest to that. For now, this is more easily accomplished by workers who have already established the trust and respect of their employers.

Our new arrangement is working well for the entire family. Sean is   9
a good-natured, energetic, outgoing, secure child who laughs more than he cries. Laurie loves the balance of playing with him in the mornings and then working in the afternoons. I also enjoy balancing the intellectual demands of work with the emotional demands of parenting. And the quantity of time we have together frees Sean and I from always having an agenda: We hang out, take aimless walks, play on the swings, eat ice cream, or sit on the corner and watch cars and trucks go by.

Although Laurie and I continue to strive toward equality in our   10
parenting, we realize that it has never been *truly* equal—partly because Laurie logs more hours with Sean, but mostly because of the strong

biological attachment between mother and child. Among couples who are committed to true equality in child care, mothers sometimes opt to nurse for just a few months or not at all. For us, the importance of breast-feeding took precedence over any ideological commitment. In the early months, when Sean nursed a lot, our division of duties was weighted toward me doing most of the household stuff and Laurie doing most of the baby stuff. As Sean grew older and began to nurse less, we adjusted our division of labor. We seem to be mirroring what physician Kyle Pruett calls the Jack Sprat theory of parenting: Our contributions are not similar, but rather complementary.

One way we keep current is by having "business meetings" on Friday   11
evenings after Sean has gone to bed. This gives us an opportunity to check how we are doing with our responsibilities as well as to synchronize calendars, schedule child care, balance the checking accounts, and so on.

All is not milk and honey, of course. Quantity time with Sean trans-   12
lates into a shortage of time for his parents—for romance, for play, for sleep, and for keeping house. We've also made sacrifices—we're renting a house instead of buying one. Career advancement is on idle. And although I know in my heart that nurturing a strong family is more important than owning a house or having a fat paycheck, it's tough to ignore all the people cruising by me on the fast track.

Actually, the career pressure has been of less concern than the lack of   13
peers making similar choices. One of the questioning voices in my head has nagged, "If it's so right, how come more fathers aren't doing it?" I have often felt isolated as a father, a daddy lost in mommyland, especially on weekdays when I find myself in a gym or on a playground filled with babies and their mothers.

When I was a child, no boy ever said he wanted to grow up to   14
be a father. Perhaps when Sean and other boys of his generation start thinking about what they want to be, some will decide to be fathers. And perhaps, when they ask their employers for a reduced schedule in order to care for their children, they will be met with a knowing smile.

Vocabulary

ducking out (2)—slang expression that means moving out quickly

negotiate (4)—to bargain or discuss in order to reach an agreement

balking (4)—refusing to move or act

soloed (6)—did something alone

scarce (8)—not common; not plentiful

attest (8)—to declare to be true

strive (10)—to try very hard

synchronize (11)—to arrange so things happen at the same time

---

IN YOUR JOURNAL

Reread the characteristics that you described in your journal entry before reading this selection. Do the parents in this article have any of those characteristics? Which ones seem most apparent in the way that they live with their child? Which ones did you not see reflected in their parenting methods? Why might they agree with you that certain qualities are essential? Why might they not utilize all the qualities?

A Closer Reading

1. What changes did Laurie and John Barry make in their lifestyles after Sean was born? What problems did they face?

2. What is Laurie's relationship with Sean? How much time does she spend with him?

3. What is Sean's relationship with Laurie? How much time does he spend with her?

4. What concerns does the author have about Sean's being brought up only by his mother? How do his experiences when he is a full-time worker validate his concerns?

5. Why does Barry feel that any sacrifices he has made in his professional life are worth it for the time he has to spend with Sean?

6. What is the difference between "quality" and "quantity" time in child care? Give examples of each, both from the article and from your own observations.

Drawing Your Own Conclusions

1. Why are men who want to stay home to raise their children looked upon with suspicion? Why are women who want to go out to work when their children are young looked upon with

suspicion? What expectations does our society have for parents in relation to their children?

2. According to Barry, very few men have made the decision that he has made. Why do you think this is so?

3. Are there any types of jobs in which the flexibility that John and Laurie need would not be possible? If so, which jobs? What would people in those types of jobs need to do to ensure that both mother and father can spend time with their children?

4. What types of jobs fit the description of "part-time professional work," "job sharing," and "working-at-home" situations?

Thinking about Writing

1. What examples does Barry provide to support the idea that fathering has changed over the past generation or two?

2. Reread the first three paragraphs of the selection. What changes are there between the two introductory paragraphs and the third paragraph? What specific words or ideas does Barry use to connect his personal story with issues he introduces in the very beginning?

3. What examples does Barry provide to support this statement: "Laurie and I decided to share child care before we were married, well before our son Sean was born"?

4. What specific support does Barry provide for this statement: "Our new arrangement is working well for the entire family"? Do the examples he gives convince you? If not, what would you like Barry to include?

*   *   *

Suggestions for Writing

1. Write an essay in which you describe the child-raising experiences of someone you know. In preparation for this essay, interview a classmate, a neighbor, or a family member. Find out who feeds and bathes, who plays with and disciplines the child or children in the family. Find out what work arrangements the parent or parents have made to support themselves and their children's needs. Describe the child-raising arrangement in detail.

2. Write an essay in which you describe your own experiences as a child. Who took care of you when you were a child? Who fed, bathed, played with, and disciplined you? How did the adults in your family get the money necessary to support themselves and their children's needs? Describe the child-raising arrangement in detail.

3. Do you agree with John Barry that it is important for fathers to become involved in the day-to-day care of their children? Or can you think of other ways for a father to develop a meaningful relationship with his children? Write an essay in which you respond to one of these questions by taking a point of view and then supporting it with your own experiences, your observations, and your readings.

4. Write an essay in which you analyze a television program in which a family (adults and children) is depicted. Describe the family. How do the family members interact with each other? Who makes the decisions? Who cooks? Who cleans? Who listens to the children's troubles? Is one member of the family more loving than another? Why is this so? After you have described the family in detail, decide how this family meets or does not meet your criteria for an effective, healthy family. Explain.

Strategies for Revision

This selection was about sharing the responsibilities of parenting, so it seems appropriate that you share the revising process with a classmate. Together, read your first draft, focusing on the following questions:

- Have you included enough descriptive details about the families in your essay? Did you identify the adult(s)—mother, father, grandparent, boyfriend, and so on? Did you include enough statistics such as the number of children, their ages, and sexes?

- Does your essay express your point of view on how families should operate ideally? Are there sufficient and convincing examples to support the point of view?

- Will the essay make your reader think about your subject in a new or different way?

- Now go through this entire process with your classmate's draft. Revise both of your papers, using the conclusions you have reached and share each other's final drafts again for feedback.

IN YOUR JOURNAL

All people have personal characteristics; for example, they may be curious, caring, independent, dependable, responsible, risk-takers, or stubborn. Make a list of any other characteristics you have encountered in people you know.

Some people think that certain characteristics occur more in one sex than in the other. Make a list of three characteristics that you have observed in many women. Then make a list of three characteristics that you have observed in many men. In your journal, write about why these particular characteristics have been developed and nurtured in each.

Sex Differences, Real and Imagined

Carol Tavris and Carole Wade

Carol Tavris has published widely on the subject of differences between the sexes in many magazines, including *Psychology Today, Mademoiselle,* and *Redbook.* Carol Wade teaches at the San Diego Mesa College. Both are interested in sex differences, our society's perceptions of them, and the ways these perceptions affect our lives. Their book from which this article was taken, *The Longest War: Sex Differences in Perspective* (2nd edition, 1984) has enjoyed a wide popularity and is frequently used as a college textbook.

In August Strindberg's play *The Father,* a man says to a woman, "If it's true we are descended from the ape, it must have been from two different species. There is no likeness between us, is there?" Some women agree. Writer Arianna Stassinopoulos (1973) argued that it's "futile to attempt to fit women into a masculine pattern of attitudes, skills and abilities and disastrous to force them to suppress their specifically female characteristics and abilities by keeping up the pretense that there are no differences between the sexes." Even Antoinette Brown Blackwell, a nineteenth-century feminist—whose sister-in-law Elizabeth was the first woman to earn an M.D. degree—wrote that although the sexes are equal, they are different: "Women's thoughts are impelled by their feelings. Hence the sharp-sightedness, the direct instincts, the quick perceptions; hence also their warmer prejudices and more unbalanced judgments."

Are men and women really so unalike? Are the sexes separated by a   2
wide gender gap in abilities and personality? Or was Gloria Steinem
(1972) closer to the truth when she asserted that males and females
share a common humanity with only "minor differences . . . that apply
largely to the act of reproduction"? Everyone can agree that there are
sex *stereotypes;* if only there were as much agreement on how accurately
those stereotypes reflect reality.

But there is not. In an area as controversial as this, personal beliefs can   3
easily affect research results. In the nineteenth century biased assumptions caused scientists to flip-flop in a suspicious manner when they were
looking for sex differences in the brain. Scientists nowadays are more
enlightened about how their expectations can influence their experiments, but it is still difficult to run objective studies. Some years ago
Robert Rosenthal and his colleagues demonstrated in a dramatic way
how belief can become reality. They asked some student-experimenters
to train rats to run a maze. Half of the experimenters believed their rats
had been specially bred to learn maze-running rapidly, while the other
half thought the rats had been bred for dullness. Although there was no
real genetic difference between the two groups of rodents, the supposedly bright rats did, in fact, learn faster. If an experimenter's expectations
can influence rats, Rosenthal concluded, they surely can influence human
beings, and this he demonstrated in many other studies (Rosenthal 1966,
1968).

The manner in which an experimenter produces a self-fulfilling   4
prophecy is usually nonverbal and, like the abominable snowman, hard
to track down. For example, Rosenthal observed that male experimenters gave instructions to the men and women in their studies very differently. Only 12 percent of the researchers smiled at the men, but 70
percent smiled at the women. "It may be a heartening finding to know
that chivalry is not dead," noted Rosenthal (1968), "but as far as methodology is concerned it is a disconcerting finding." It's easy to imagine
how an experimenter's facial expression might affect his results. For
instance, if his smile made people feel friendly and rewarded and his
study happened to concern people's need for affiliation (their desire to
be with others), he might find a sex difference that he himself had
unwittingly caused.

Another methodological problem arises in students that rely on self-   5
reports. Suppose you believe that males are more independent than

females, and you want to prove it. If you merely ask people how independent or dependent they are, your interviewees may slant their answers toward what they believe is socially desirable: A man may try to sound more self-reliant than he feels; a woman, less so. Or your interviewees may have distorted perceptions of themselves that have little to do with the way they behave in daily life. One solution is to question a second party. Many child psychologists use this method; they ask teachers and parents to describe the children in their care. Here again, though, you risk collecting biases instead of objective observations.

Another approach is for the researcher personally to observe the   6
behavior of children or adults in a natural setting, such as home or school. This method allows you to deal with actual behavior, but you still have the problem of your own implicit assumptions. As a psychologist interested in assertiveness, how would you distinguish "passive" behavior from that which is merely "easygoing"? How would you distinguish submissiveness, which is the opposite of assertiveness, from cooperation, which is not? The danger is that you might label the same bit of behavior differently when a female did it than when a male did. (You know: he is "good at details," she is "picky"; he's a "go-getter," she's "pushy"; he's a "demanding" boss, she's a "bitchy" one.) The tendency to label a male's traits as positive and a female's as negative explains why so many people are sensitive about sex differences and their implications for male supremacy.

In addition to assigning different labels to the same act, an observer   7
may simply fail to notice certain kinds of behavior. Someone who claims that housewives are passive and submissive may be overlooking many situations in which housewives are active. (Caring for children and organizing and maintaining a home require considerable assertiveness and initiative.) Similarly, if someone tells you that men tend to be unemotional and insensitive, it may be because she or he has ignored situations that allow men to be expressive.

As if all this were not bad enough, there is another obstacle that im-   8
pedes the pursuit of scientific truth. Studies that identify sex differences are much more likely to be published in professional journals than those that do not. Nonfindings don't have much drama and, besides, scientific convention dictates that it is impossible to prove that a difference between groups does *not* exist. All a researcher can say is that there is no evidence a difference does exist, which is pretty dull compared to proclaiming: "Eureka! Men do X and women do Y." For that reason, studies identifying even small sex differences often have exaggerated clout.

There have been some attempts to review the vast scientific litera-   9
ture on sex differences and to come up with some reliable generalizations. The reviewers have tended to give more weight to studies that
find differences than to those that don't, and they have tended to accept
results uncritically. A good example is a 1968 monograph, "Sex Differences in Mental and Behavioral Traits," by Josef E. Garai and Amram
Scheinfeld. The authors cited 474 studies but did not explain how they
had selected them, nor did they discuss the quality of the procedures
used in the studies. Most of their conclusions conformed to popular
stereotypes. For example, they found that females have greater social
needs than males and that males are superior to females in abstract
reasoning and conceptualizing—which, the authors believed, helps explain "the outstanding achievements of men in science, philosophy, and
the construction of theories."

In 1974, Eleanor Maccoby and Carol Jacklin, two Stanford psycholo-   10
gists, published *The Psychology of Sex Differences,* which quickly became a
classic text. In preparing their book, Maccoby and Jacklin carefully examined a larger body of research than any of their predecessors—over 2,000
articles and books, most of them published after 1966. Unlike other
reviewers, they made a special effort to locate and include studies that
might have found differences but did not. They even reanalyzed data
when they thought it was necessary. So that readers could follow their
analysis, they included a 233-page annotated bibliography and eighty-
three summary tables. Maccoby and Jacklin concluded that many common assumptions about sex differences, including some that Garai and
Scheinfeld maintained were proven, were completely unfounded; they
were simple myths posing as facts. But they also found that males and
females do differ in some interesting ways.

The Maccoby and Jacklin review is not without some serious weak-   11
nesses. Although the authors discussed methodological problems at
length, when it came to evaluating hypotheses their approach was to
tally all the studies pro or con, usually without counting the better
research more heavily. Often they reached conclusions mainly on the
basis of studies with young children, a serious error because some sex
differences do not emerge clearly until adolescence and some are out-
grown in adulthood.

In an incisive critique, psychologist Jeanne Block (1976) reana-   12
lyzed some of Maccoby and Jacklin's data and included some studies
they omitted from their tables. She concluded: "The long, arduous,

complicated evaluation undertaken by [Maccoby and Jacklin] in their efforts to impose organization upon a sprawling, unruly body of data is vulnerable to error and reasonable argument at every step along the way." So Maccoby and Jacklin's book, although far and away the most complete and thoughtful summary to date, is not the final word on sex differences.

In the following sections we will review research findings most relevant to the issue of sex roles and status differences (see summary, Table 1). Our discussion draws on Maccoby and Jacklin's information (1974), but we also question some of their conclusions and bring in more recent studies. As you read, keep two things in mind. First, when we speak of differences we mean group differences, or average differences. To say that one sex outdoes the other on some test does not mean that all members of that sex do better than all members of the opposite sex. Men and women overlap in abilities and personality traits, as they overlap in physical attributes. Men on the average are taller than women, but some women are taller than most men. Second, in this chapter we confine ourselves mainly to describing research findings on sex differences in the United States, which must not be taken to imply universality. Nor does the existence of a sex difference (say, in aggressiveness) prove that biology is more important than learning. *The existence of a sex difference tells us nothing about its origins.*

Works Cited

Block, Jeanne H. Debatable conclusions about sex differences. *Contemporary Psychology,* 1976, 21, 517–522.

Garai, Josef E., and Scheinfeld, Amram. Sex differences in mental and behavioral traits. *Genetic Psychology Monographs,* 1968, 77, 169–299.

Maccoby, Eleanor Emmons, and Jacklin, Carol Nagy. *The psychology of sex differences.* Stanford, Calif.: Stanford University Press, 1974.

Rosenthal, Robert. *Experimenter effects in behavioral research.* New York: Appleton-Century-Crofts, 1966.

Rosenthal, Robert. Self-fulfilling prophecy. *Psychology Today,* September 1968, 2 (4), 44–51.

Stassinopoulos, Adrianna. The natural woman. In *The female woman,* 1973. Quoted in Elaine Partnow (ed.), *The quotable woman 1800-on.* Garden City, N.Y.: Anchor/Doubleday, 1978.

Steinem, Gloria. Sisterhood, *Ms.,* Spring 1972, 46–49.

Table 1. Sex Differences and Similarities

Physical Attributes

Strength	Males taller, heavier, more muscular.
Health	Females less vulnerable to illness and disease, live longer.
Activity level	Some evidence that preschool boys more active during play in same-sex groups; sex differences for school-age children are qualitative, not quantitative.
Manual dexterity	Women excel when speed is important; findings hard to interpret.

Abilities

General intelligence	No difference on most tests.
Verbal ability	Some evidence that females acquire language slightly earlier; males more often diagnosed as having reading problems; females excel on various verbal tests after age ten or eleven.*
Quantitative ability	Males excel on tests of mathematical reasoning from the start of adolescence.*
Spatial-visual ability	Males excel starting in tenth grade, but not on all tests or in all studies.*
Creativity	Females excel on verbal creativity tests, but otherwise no difference.
Cognitive style	Males excel on spatial-visual disembedding tests starting at adolescence, but no general differences in cognitive style.

Personality Characteristics

Sociability	No consistent findings on infant's responsiveness to social cues; school-age boys play in larger groups; women fantasize more about affiliation themes, but there is no evidence that one sex wants or needs friends more.
Empathy	Conflicting evidence; probably depends on situation and sex of participants in an interaction.
Emotionality	Self-reports and observations conflict; no convincing evidence that females feel more emotional; but they may express certain emotions more freely.
Dependence	Conflicting findings; dependence appears not to be a unitary concept or stable trait.

Susceptibility to influence	Preschool girls more obedient to parents; boys may be more susceptible to peer pressure; no overall difference in adult susceptibility to persuasion across different settings in laboratory studies.
Self-esteem and confidence	No self-reported differences in self-esteem, but males more confident about task performance; males more likely to take credit for success, less likely to blame selves for failure.
Nurturance	No overall differences in altruism; girls more helpful and responsive to infants, small children; some evidence that fathers as responsive to newborns as mothers are, but issue of maternal versus paternal behavior remains open.
Aggressiveness	Males more aggressive from preschool age on; men more violent, more likely to be aggressive in public, more likely to be physically aggressive in situations not involving anger.
Values and Moral Perceptions	
	Some controversial evidence that males and females approach choice and conflict somewhat differently. Males seem more likely to emphasize abstract standards of justice, fairness, balancing of individual rights. Females seem more likely to emphasize the ethics of care, human attachments, balancing of conflicting responsibilities.

*Differences statistically reliable but quite small.

Vocabulary

futile (1)—worthless; sure to fail

hence (1)—therefore

biased (3)—prejudiced; unfairly influenced

chivalry (4)—medieval system of knighthood that called for courage, honor, and readiness to help those in need

affiliation (4)—connection with an organization

impedes (8)—hinders or prevents progress

hypotheses (11)—tentatively accepted but as yet unproved theories or ideas

incisive (12)—sharp; keen

peer (chart)—person of the same age

altruism (chart)—unselfish concern for the welfare of others

IN YOUR JOURNAL

Look at the characteristics you identified in your journal before you read the Tavris and Wade article. How do these characteristics correspond to those you have read about in the article? What did you learn about sex differences from reading this article? Would you revise your lists? If so, how?

A Closer Reading

1. In paragraph 1, Antoinette Brown Blackwell is quoted as having stated that although the sexes are equal, they are different. Do Tavris and Wade support this view? How does this attitude correspond to the ideas McAuliffe presented in her article on page 183? What examples do the writers give to support their points of view?

2. What examples do the authors provide to support the idea that biased assumptions can affect research results? According to this idea, what is a "self-fulfilling prophecy"?

3. In paragraphs 4, 5, and 6, Tavris and Wade describe different types of research used to determine sex differences. What are they? How can each lead to problems?

4. According to the chart at the end, what differences seem to exist between men and women? In what ways are the two sexes similar?

5. Compare the findings in the chart to characteristics of men and women as described in another selection you read in this book.

Drawing Your Own Conclusions

1. Do you respond differently if someone gives you directions for a test or interviews you for a questionnaire in a friendly way than if someone does the same thing in a serious way? Have you ever had an experience in which someone's attitude affected the way you performed on a test?

2. Presuming that males are taller, heavier, and more muscular, explain the finding that females are less vulnerable to disease and more likely to live longer.

3. How do you explain the finding that females seem to acquire language earlier than males and that males have more reading difficulties than females? How do you explain the finding that males, starting in early adolescence, do better on mathematical reasoning and begin to excel in mathematics? In what ways might the development of these abilities be nurtured in all children? Why? In what ways might these abilities affect people's career choices?

4. What information from the McAuliffe article on page 183 explains why men are more aggressive and violent from preschool age on? What does the fact that they aren't more aggressive and violent from birth on suggest to you?

5. Why is it so important to our society, and indeed to all societies, that there be real physical, intellectual, emotional, and behavioral differences between the sexes?

Thinking about Writing

1. In paragraph 1, Tavris and Wade quote from three sources. Who are the sources? What are their professions? Why do they add credibility to Tavris and Wade's point of view that there is a confusion in the findings about sex differences?

2. What do the dates after the researchers' names, for example, Arianna Stassinopoulos (1973) in paragraph 1, indicate? How can the references at the end of the article help you find the original sources?

3. What question in paragraph 2 is answered by the first sentence in paragraph 3?

4. Paragraph 8 begins: "As if all this were not bad enough . . ." What does "all this" refer back to? How did you know?

5. What does Tavris and Wade's conversational tone in statements such as "As if all this were not bad enough" say about their assumptions about their audience? Where do they assume your sympathies lie?

*   *   *

Suggestions for Writing

1. Traits and characteristics found in males are often labeled in positive ways, while the same traits or characteristics found in women frequently are labeled in a negative way. A strong male boss might be called "demanding," while a strong female boss might be called "domineering." An unmarried man is a "bachelor," while an unmarried woman is an "old maid" or a "spinster." Create a list of examples that reflect all types of sexual differences: physical, intellectual, emotional, and behavioral. Write an essay in which you explain how some of these perceptions might have developed and how much they affect our understanding of both sexes.

2. Looking at the chart on page 199 of the Tavris and Wade article, choose three of the differences and write an essay in which you tell why you think these differences are inborn (natural) or learned (nurtured in us or as part of the environment). Explain the reasons for your choices.

3. Should male and female children be raised differently? Should they be exposed to different values? Different expectations? Different discipline? Should they be given different toys? A different education? Write an essay explaining your answers to these questions, giving examples from your experiences and reading.

4. Should all colleges require that men take a women's studies course and that women take a men's studies course? Take a position on this issue and support your point of view, basing it on your personal experiences, your observations, and your readings.

Collaborative Project

Write down a question or questions that you would like to ask the males and females in your class, your family, or your community. For example, do men and women act differently in class? Do they ask the same kinds of questions? Do they ask questions differently?

Make copies and distribute them to the members of your class (or to another group). Each person should write "male" or "female" in the upper right-hand corner of the paper and then should answer the questions. Read the answers; as a class, collate them. That is, divide the papers according to sex, then count the number of men who answered in a particular way, then the number of women who gave the same answer. Go to another question and do the same thing until you have gone through all your questions. Discuss what the answers tell you about the group you have studied.

Write an essay in which you explain what you learned by doing this project. In your essay, describe your process for choosing your question(s), the responses you received, and what the responses did or did not tell you about males and females. What problems did you find with your research? What changes would you make in your questions if you were to do it again?

Strategies for Revision

As a class, decide what is meant by the term "sexist" language. Discuss techniques for avoiding sexist language.

Read your first draft, asking yourself the following questions:

- Did I use sexist language? What changes can I make to eliminate such language from this essay?
- Did I make clear when I was writing about men and when about women without stereotyping people? What changes can I make to avoid stereotyping?
- What did I learn from writing this essay?
- What steps did I take in organizing my material?
- Does the order of my ideas make sense? (Try moving your ideas around to find out if your essay can be made more effective.)

IN YOUR JOURNAL

Write about an experience you had performing in front of other people. What did you perform? How did it go? How did you feel about the experience of displaying yourself in front of others?

Gotta Dance!

Bob Hoerburger

Bob Hoerburger is an editor of the *New York Times Magazine*. His essay appeared in the magazine on July 18, 1993. The essay describes an experience in which Hoerburger questions his own acceptance of taboos on activities not acceptable for men. When Hoerburger realizes how much he enjoys dancing, he has to convince himself to accept the pleasure he gets from dancing and performing in order to pursue this new activity in his life.

I walked into the confessional a repentant sinner and walked out a   1
dancer. The priest who heard my sins half-jokingly suggested that for
my penance I join the church's production of *West Side Story*, which he
was directing. I was 27 at the time and hadn't performed on a stage
since fourth grade, but I figured at the very least I could help out with
the lights.

Instead, I ended up with the featured role of Riff, the leader of the   2
Jets, mostly because of a lucky break (as in the ankle of the actor
originally cast), and the usual dearth of male bodies in community-
theater productions. After months of rehearsal, I was comfortable
enough with the dialogue and the singing, but the dancing—and *West
Side Story* is *mostly* dancing—petrified me. Right up to opening night, I
was never sure which foot I would land on.

My anxiety was born of some taboo I had long ago internalized   3
about dancing not being masculine. The typical after-school and after-
supper pastimes for boys in my suburban neighborhood were baseball
and football. Forget that dancing can actually develop the timing and
coordination needed to play second base, or that dancers have phy-
siques that gym rats only dream about. Any parent signing his or her
son up for dance class instead of (or even in addition to) Little League

was practically subject to child-abuse charges—because invariably that boy would be subject to the cruel taunts of his peers.

This unspoken prohibition was especially painful because secretly I   4
loved to dance. Sports were O.K., but there were many nights when I would forgo the pickup game of baseball on the street, throw on some Motown and whirl around my room for a few hours. But always behind closed doors. Now here I was about to make a public spectacle of myself, and in *West Side Story* no less.

Most of the other men in the cast expressed similar anxiety, but we   5
got a reprieve in that the choreography de-emphasized the more balletic turns in favor of macho posturing and finger-snapping and the climbing of fences. When the steps did get a little more complicated, I took the choreographer's advice to "show a lot of attitude" and chalked the rest up to the power of prayer. And I vowed to get better.

But childhood taboos die hard. It took me a year and a half to summon   6
the courage to enroll in a dance class in Manhattan. As I signed my name for a year's worth of lessons, a lifetime of aversion—my own and my friends'—to dancing in public flashed through my head. I thought of line-backers in high school who took and gave poundings on the football field but sweated through the box step at the prom. And I knew firefighters and fleet-footed detectives who had been in shootouts who cowered at the sight of a wood floor with a strobe light above it. Even after John Tra-volta gyrated through *Saturday Night Fever,* tough guys still didn't dance.

I had been assured that there would be other men in the class, but   7
when I arrived for the first one I was surrounded by leggy women in tights and tutus. The only other man was the instructor, Jeff, a former Broadway dancer who had been in *A Chorus Line* early in its run. He wore makeup and several earrings. Would I have felt more comfortable if he looked like Cal Ripken? Probably, but then I didn't have time to dwell on it, because I was immediately barraged with not only new steps but a new language ("plié," "relevé," "jazz third") and lessons in attire. ("This is not aerobics," Jeff would say, casting gentle aspersions at my jock wear—sneakers and sweats, which I clung to as the last bas-tions of my maleness.)

I tried to hide in the back lines, but in dance studios even the   8
support beams have mirrors. I heard my name a lot in those first weeks: "Keep your shoulders down." "Other hand." "Watch your head." Yet every time I was tempted to quit, I also heard Jeff's words of encourage-ment: "If you get only 25 percent of the routine, I'll be happy" or "Just showing up is the victory."

Eventually the routines seemed less tyrannical, and I started to relax.   9
I even compromised my attire—retaining my Nike T-shirt but trading
the sweats and sneakers for black satin jazz pants and jazz shoes. ("Now
those," Jeff said, "have style.") And the benefits of the class were
instantaneous—walking to my train after each session, I felt a kind of
honorable exhaustion, having coaxed into consciousness muscles I
hadn't even known existed. It was the same sense of physical satisfaction
that I'd felt hitting a bases-clearing double or finishing a half-marathon.

My lessons were interrupted when the next show came along: *Man*   10
of La Mancha, which required me to age 30 years but hardly afforded
me an opportunity to show off my new steps. When the show finished
its run, I returned to the studio, only to find Jeff out sick and the class
being taught by a drill-sergeant substitute. She demanded that each
dancer cross the floor individually while she exhorted, "Kick that leg
higher—and now *sell* it." Under Jeff's kid-gloves tutelage, I had imagined myself as Fred Astaire, but now, under this magnifying glass, I
turned back into Fred Flintstone—stumbling, clumsy, self-conscious, as
if all the inhibitions I had been whittling away suddenly gathered themselves back into an intractable whole. On my third or fourth solo flight
across the floor I kept going into the locker room, up the stairs and out
the door.

Jeff's absence turned out to be permanent—his illness was forcing   11
him to retire—and the studio closed soon after that, a victim of the
economy's own failing health. Then I got word of a cast call for a local
production of *South Pacific,* a show whose feats are primarily vocal, at
least for the men. Reluctantly, I auditioned and made the male chorus.
It looked as if my dancing days would be indefinitely deferred.

The men did have one big number—"There Is Nothin' Like A   12
Dame"—which basically involved animated marching. Posture and expression were key, and, because Jeff had emphasized these in class, I had
no trouble picking up the routine. The choreographer even singled me
out to demonstrate a couple of steps, and the other men—most of
whom had never danced on stage before and were wearing the same
long faces I did during *West Side Story*—were saying things like "Obviously you've done this before." Now I was being celebrated for something that most of my life I had feared would bring me ridicule.

After much fine-tuning and many weeks of rehearsal, the other men   13
came around, and by the time the show opened there was a buzz about
"There Is Nothin' Like a Dame." The women in the show had three times
as many dance numbers and their steps were much fancier. But the nov-

elty appeal of "men who can move" ran high, and when we successfully executed a kickline at the end of the song we brought down the house.

At moments like that, and the many since I've had dancing in public and private, I remember that trip to the confession booth, and realize that dance has in fact become a kind of physical and psychic redemption. But it isn't penance anymore. 14

Vocabulary

penance (1)—a voluntary act of self-punishment to show regret or sorrow for a sin or wrongdoing

dearth (2)—a scarcity or lack of something

taunts (3)—ridicules or makes fun of

reprieve (5)—postponement of a punishment

aversion (6)—intense dislike

bastions (7)—strong or fortified places

IN YOUR JOURNAL

Have you ever wanted to try an activity but were told that it was not proper for people of your sex? Explain in your journal. Do you think attitudes about these taboos are beginning to change?

A Closer Reading

1. What actions does Hoerburger take to become a dancer?
2. What taboo had Hoerburger accepted about dancing?
3. According to Hoerburger, who finds sports acceptable but dancing unacceptable for men?
4. What similarities does Hoerburger discover between dancing and playing sports?

Drawing Your Own Conclusions

1. In paragraph 6, what types of men does Hoerburger describe? Why does he want his readers to see him as one of these "tough" men?

2. From what stereotypes of male dancers does Hoerburger want to disassociate himself? Why? Are there any stereotypes you yourself believed without question before you read this article? Now, how do you feel?

3. What characteristics does Jeff have as a dancing teacher that help Hoerburger to improve? What characteristics does the new teacher have that make him drop out of dance class?

4. What kind of dancing do boys do in your neighborhood? What kind of dancing do girls do? What differences do you observe in the types of dancing that each sex does? At what age do boys and girls begin to dance together?

Thinking about Writing

1. Reread paragraphs 1 and 14. What ideas, words, and phrases connect the introduction and conclusion?

2. What specific words relate to dance in the essay? If they are not defined, how did you find out what they mean? How do they enhance the piece?

3. What plays and movies does Hoerburger mention in the essay? Why does he include this information? If you do not know any of these plays or movies, talk to members of your class to find out what type of dancing is featured in each of them.

4. What is the main point of this essay? What examples support Hoerburger's main idea?

*   *   *

Suggestions for Writing

1. What role does dance or music play in your life? Write an essay in which you describe your feelings about dancing, singing, playing a musical instrument, or just listening to music. Explain to your readers the role that dance or music plays in your life.

2. Reread the Cole essay on page 135. Write an essay in which you compare the stereotyping felt by women in science with that felt by men in the performing arts. What similarities are there? What differences? Is it easier for men or for women to succeed in their respective areas?

3. Hoerburger seems concerned that other men and women will think he is homosexual because he likes to dance. Why do some people think their sexuality will be determined by the kind of work they do? In an essay, provide some examples of jobs that are associated with particular sexes and particular sexual orientations. How has job stereotyping affected your choice of major at school or in the career path you're pursuing or in the type of leisure activities you enjoy?

4. In what ways do you feel limited by the expectations of your family, friends, neighbors, or society in general? In an essay, explain your feelings and the ways that you cope with them. Be specific and include the steps you have taken to overcome the limitations.

Strategies for Revision

Reread your draft, asking yourself the following questions. Write your answers on a separate piece of paper to which you will refer as you revise:

- What is the main idea that holds the entire piece of writing together?
- What are the supporting details—facts, observations, and experiences—that support your main idea? Have you used them wisely for emphasis?
- If you wrote about dancing or music, are the details specific—can a reader see, hear, smell, or feel the specifics you experience the way we can through Hoerburger's words?
- Are the descriptive words evocative, special, and well chosen as they are in Hoerburger's piece?

Using your answers to these questions, rewrite what you have written, trying to make it even more interesting and clear. Share your revision with a classmate.

IN YOUR JOURNAL

Has a friend, lover, or family member ever done anything that completely surprised you? Write about that experience in your journal.

Lake Stephen

Charles Baxter

Charles Baxter lives in Michigan and teaches at the University of Michigan at Ann Arbor. He is the author of three short story collections, a novel, and book of poetry. "Lake Stephen" was first published in the *Chicago Tribune Magazine* in 1989 and was included in Baxter's 1990 short story collection, *A Relative Stranger*. It appeared again in 1991 in the book *The Sound of Writing*, a collection of short stories that had been read on National Public Radio. The story is about a young couple on a vacation and the way the woman convinces the man to marry her.

The second week of their vacation, the young man got up early to   1
make pancakes. When his girlfriend smelled breakfast being made, she reached down to the floor and put on her nightgown. She went out to the living room in her bare feet.

"Good morning," she said. "I thought we were going to sleep late."   2

"Want some pancakes?" he asked, flipping them over in the skillet.   3
"They're not great, but they do have a sort of lumberjack appeal. They taste like trees and brush."

"Doesn't this place have an exhaust fan?" she asked. "It's smoky in   4
here."

The young man looked around. "I don't see one."   5

"Why did you get up? I thought we were going to laze around in   6
bed together."

"I was restless."   7

"But it's vacation," she said. "It's our first vacation together. And   8
here we are, surrounded by trees, in the Deer Park Resort. What is there to be restless about?"

"I'm not used to this," he said.   9

"Used to what?"   10

"This." He spread his hand to indicate the cabin's small living   11
room, the door to the bedroom, the pine trees outside the picture
window, and the lake, visible a few hundred feet away. "It's too much
of something."

"It's too beautiful," she suggested.   12

"No." He walked over to the dining room table and dropped three   13
pancakes on a plate. "There aren't any distractions. I'm used to distractions. I'm used to . . . I don't know. Craziness."

"Well, *I'm* a distraction," she said. She leaned back to let him see her   14
in her nightgown. "I can be crazy."

"Yes," he said. "You're wonderful. That's been proved."   15

She nodded.   16

"But it all feels cooped up somehow," he said. "Even when we go   17
canoeing or go for hikes or go swimming, it feels cooped up."

"I don't understand," she said. "How can it be cooped up when   18
you're outside doing things?"

He looked at her for a moment. He seemed to be searching her face   19
for some element there that was bothering him.

"I don't know," he said finally. "I think we have to get out more. Do   20
things."

"Do what things? We've *been* doing things."   21

"What day is it?" he asked.   22

"Sunday."   23

"Well, if it's Sunday, we could go to church." He sat down with her   24
after dishing out two pancakes on his own plate. He reached over for
the can of maple syrup.

She laughed nervously. "Go to church? We don't go to church.   25
We've never gone to church. We aren't Christians or anything. I don't
think there's even a church around here."

"*I* saw one," he said. "About ten miles down the road, in that little   26
crossroads village, where the grocery is, and that gas station."

"You're serious," she said. "You're really serious about this."   27

"Well, why not?" He smiled in her direction and laughed. "I mean,   28
they don't keep strangers out, do they? Of course not. They *want*
strangers to come in. It's a kind of show. It might be interesting. You
could pretend you were an anthropologist."

"I've never been to a church," she said. "Except for weddings and   29
funerals. My parents weren't religious."

"Same here," he said.   30

"They'll look at us," she said. She began eating his pancakes.   31

"That's all right," he said. "We'll look back at them."   32

The church was just inside the village of Wilford and stood next to a   33
small shaded hill and a cemetery. It was a plain white wooden structure
with a sign outside giving its name and its pastor, the Rev. Cedric
Banks. Sunday worship service was scheduled to be at ten o'clock. The
young man and woman drove on the dirt roads close to the church,
wasting time, until five minutes before ten, when they parked their car
behind a line of other cars and went inside. A few members of the small
congregation, mostly middle-aged couples, turned and looked at them
with what seemed to be friendly curiosity. The church smelled of white
pine and cedar. Trying to stay inconspicuous, the two young people sat
in the back pew.

"I think this is wrong," she said. "This is supposed to be serious. It's   34
not supposed to be entertainment."

"Do they kneel in this church?" he asked. He was whispering.   35

"How should I know?" She was looking up at the vaulted ceiling, the   36
support beams, and the one stained-glass window at the back of the altar.

At the start of the service, a woman in a purple robe sat down at an   37
electric organ at the front of the church and began the opening chords
for a hymn. The congregation stood and began singing. Their voices
were weak, except for one woman with a high, shrill soprano, and
although the young woman strained to hear, she couldn't make out the
words clearly. Her boyfriend was looking for the hymn in the hymnal
but had still not found it by the time the music ended. When she next
looked up, she saw the pastor standing in front of the altar. He had a
hard-country face, she thought, a wide head and a crew cut, but somewhat tired eyes, like a boxer between rounds.

"He looks like a logger or something," the young man whispered.   38
"Or maybe a plumber. He doesn't look very spiritual."

"How does spiritual look?" she asked, whispering back.   39

"Different," he said. "Like someone on television."   40

"Shh," she said. "Pay attention."   41

The minister began a series of prayers. Because of the reverberation   42
in the church and his tendency to mumble, many of his prayers were
incomprehensible to the two young people sitting in the back row. But
when the young woman looked over at her boyfriend, she saw an oddly
intense expression on his face.

"Do you *like* this?" she asked.   43

"Shh," he said. "You're just supposed to take it all in."   44

After several more minutes the pastor walked slowly to the right-   45
hand side of the church, mounted a few steps, and stood behind a
lectern. After a brief invocation, he began by quoting from the book of
Jonah. He continued to mumble, so that his sentences went in and out
of focus, but the expression on his face was earnest and direct. The
subject of his sermon seemed to be surprises. The minister said that
Jonah was repeatedly surprised by the persistence of God. Nothing that
happened on earth was a surprise to the Almighty, he said, but then he
said something that the young woman simply couldn't hear. At times he
held his finger up as if to make a point. Once or twice he pounded his
fist lightly on the lectern. We should contribute to the surprise of
creation, the pastor said, by exercising charity, which is always outside
the chain of inevitability.

"This doesn't make any sense," the young woman said in a whisper   46
to her boyfriend. "It's all mixed up."

"He knows everyone here," the young man whispered back. "He   47
doesn't have to explain everything to them."

"Maybe he's been drinking."   48

"No," the young man said. "He just mumbles."   49

When the service was over, the pastor stepped down the aisle and   50
stood at the doorway to shake hands with the members of the congregation as they left. When the two young people approached him, the
minister raised his eyebrows at them and smiled. Close up, he looked
bulky and slightly overweight, like a man who had once played football
and now drank a few beers in the evening to relax.

"I don't know you two," he said, holding out his hand toward them.   51
"Welcome. Are you passing through?" His breath smelled of cigarettes,
and the young woman found herself both pleased and slightly shocked
by this.

"I *think* we're just passing through," the young man said.   52

"You think so?" the minister asked. "You're not sure?"   53

"We like it here," the young man went on. "We'd like to settle down   54
somewhere around here, raise a family. It's such beautiful country."

"Yes, it is," the minister said, glancing down at their ring fingers.   55
The young woman knew that she would look guilty and silly if she tried
to hide the fact that she wore no wedding ring, so she looked back at the
minister with a blank smile, her hand resting easily on her hip. "Well,"
the minister said at last, "enjoy yourselves while you're here."

Back in the car, headed in no particular direction, the young man   56
said, "Well, what did you think of that?"

"It was all right," she said. "But why did you say we were going to   57
settle down and raise a family here? That's kind of a weird fantasy. We
don't live here. And we aren't married."

"Oh I know," he said. "I just think about it. I play with it." He   58
waited. She knew these pauses were awkward for him and she didn't try
to interrupt. "But he was saying that surprises were good things, so I
decided to surprise him and to surprise you. It was stupid, I admit it.
But I agreed with him. I like surprises. I love it when things are unexpected. I *love* it."

"I don't," she said. "I don't like it much."   59

"I know that," he said suddenly, and the way he said it, over-   60
enunciated so that the effort was like underlining the words, made her
sit up straight. She waited inside the air pocket of silence for a moment,
then put her hand on her boyfriend's thigh. She rested it there lightly. It
wasn't for love or for sensuality's sake; it was to calm him.

"The trouble is," he began. Then he stopped. They both looked   61
out through the front windshield at the pine trees on each side of the
road and the occasional farm; the soil was mostly clay and rock up
here, and the farming was poor. There were FOR SALE signs everywhere, on the front yards and nailed to the trees. "The trouble is," he
started again, "that you anticipate every one of my moves. You anticipate everything I do. When we talk or make love or I cook or watch
you or talk about the future or what I'm reading, you anticipate all of
it. You nod and I can tell how predictable I'm already getting. That's
why I feel cooped up. It gets to me. It's like I'm living out a script
someone's written. Only thing is, you've already gotten the script and
I haven't. You know everything I'm going to do. I look into the future
and you still know everything I'm going to do, for years and years,
and it doesn't matter if we're married or not. You know everything
that I'm going to do."

"I don't understand," she said. In fact, she did understand, but she   62
thought the rest of their vacation would go better if she pretended that
she didn't.

"It's like basketball," the young man said. He laughed, a quick   63
intake of breath, but his face became serious again quickly. "You take
Kareem Abdul-Jabbar. You watch him some night. The man is a genius.
You know why?" The young woman shook her head. "The reason
Jabbar is a genius is that you can't anticipate his moves. It's not speed.
Speed's important in basketball but it's not the most important thing.
The most important thing is to do the move, the logical move, so

unexpectedly and gracefully that your opponent is faked out and can't guard against it."

"Basketball isn't the world," she said. "It's not about relationships." 64

"Oh, yes, it is," he said. "It's a relationship between individuals on 65
two different teams. And the more you can't be anticipated, the more effective you are." He turned off the road onto a smaller dirt road that the young woman hadn't seen, and the car took some hard bounces as they proceeded through a cluster of thick trees.

"Where does this go?" she asked. "Where are we?" 66

The young man smiled. "I saw a sign for a lake back there," he said. 67
"Faked you out, didn't I?"

"Yes," she said. "You certainly did." 68

"Never thought I'd take you to a lake, did you?" he asked. 69

"Nope," she said. "You got me this time." 70

The road came out in a clearing for public access. The young man 71
stopped the car and got out, walking down to the shoreline to look into the water and then across the lake to the other side. In the distance they could see one broken-down cabin, its roof fallen in. The water was very clear; they could both see minnows swimming in schools in the shallow water.

"I wonder what the name of this lake is," he said. 72

"*We* can name it," she said. "Let's name it after you. Let's call it Lake 73
Stephen."

"Okay," he said. "Now that it's mine, what do I do with it?" 74

"You don't do anything with it." 75

"Yes, you do," he said. "You have to do something with it, if it's 76
named after you." All at once he straightened up. "I'll surprise you," he said.

"How?" 77

"If I told you," he said, "it wouldn't be a surprise." 78

At exactly that moment, she knew he was going to take all his 79
clothes off and go swimming. She knew that he was going to take off his shirt first, button by button, and hang it on the end of a tree branch, and he did; that he was going to unbuckle his belt, then slip off his shoes and socks, put the socks inside the shoes and put the shoes together neatly at the base of the tree, and he did that too; then he would lower his trousers and fold them at the knee and put the folded trousers over the shoes and socks; and then she knew, quite a bit in advance of his actually doing it, that he would grin at her, a happy smile breaking across his pleasant bearded face, and, with a yelp, lower his

underwear and turn around and dash into the water, shouting as he went and making half-articulate exclamations like a man running into battle. He wanted to be dangerous and unpredictable, and so, watching him, she did her best to look amazed at what he was doing.

He swam back and forth in the water, splashing and barking like a   80
happy seal. She watched the water passing over his pale skin. The rest of the year, he worked indoors at a desk, and he didn't believe in getting sun, so his body was visible underwater even when he dove down, it was that white. She watched him swimming parallel to the shoreline and was pleasantly lost in his physical form, which she liked. As bodies went, his was attractive; he swam regularly and worked out. But the final effect was of frailty. Men, when you got their clothes off, looked rather simple and frail, even the strong ones. The strength was all on the outside. This was no secret, and it became more apparent as they aged.

"Come on in," he shouted. "It's great!"   81

"I don't know," she said, looking around. "Maybe there are people   82
here."

"It's okay," he said. "It's my lake and my beach, and what I say goes.   83
I'm the law here."

"Well, you sure have surprised me," she said. Then, once again, she   84
knew that he would try to scare her and pretend to drown. She knew, before he actually did it, that he would dive down and hold his breath; that he would stay underwater for as long as he could; and that he even might try to inhale some water so that he could choke a little, not much, but just enough to give her a scare. This was just like men, to try to scare you by being dangerous and vulnerable at the same time. She took off her shoes and socks and waded out into the water, soaking her dress as she went. She waited for Stephen to come up, out of the water. She waited for what she thought was a long time. She couldn't see any bubbles; she knew he was holding his breath down there, like a boy among the minnows. He would be curled up, his feet brushing against the sandy bottom. And now he would be feeling as if his lungs were about to explode, and she went further out into the water, so that it came up to her knees.

Then he rose to the surface, coughing and choking. She waded out   85
to where he was and took his hand. "Stephen," she cried, "are you all right?"

He smiled. "Did I frighten you?" he asked. "Good." He spat some   86
water out of his mouth.

"Damn it," she said, pretending to be indignant, "don't do that 87
again."

Another large grin broke across his face. "You should come in," he 88
said. "Come on, Jan. Come in. Take your clothes off."

"I don't want to," she said. 89

And then, suddenly, both of them knee deep in water, he put his 90
bare arms around her, and she gasped. It wasn't his body. They were
lovers, and she was used to that. It was that his skin was ice cold; for a
moment, it didn't feel like his, or like living flesh, but something else. It
was puckered with goose bumps and felt clammy, as if it had come from
some other world into this one, and when he put his lips to her, she
flinched.

"What's the matter?" he asked. 91

She could feel his wet hand soaking through the back of her blouse. 92
He was soaking her down in small stages. Looking at him, at the water
dripping off his beard and down his chest, she thought he looked a bit
like a minor god or a monster, she couldn't decide which.

"Come in," he said, reaching for her. 93

She paused and looked at the future. She knew that he would not go 94
on loving her if she didn't take her clothes off now; he would not,
someday, propose to her; and they would not get married and have
children. Unless she broke the rules now, he would not follow the rules
later. He wanted her to be wild; all right, she would be wild. She
grinned at him. She did a little shimmy, then unbuttoned her blouse and
tossed it on the sand. She unhooked her bra, thinking, He'll still talk
about this when we're old. He'll cherish this because it's our first secret.
She threw her bra toward shore, then took off the rest of her clothes and
dropped them on the sand. Then, knowing how beautiful she was, how
physically breathtaking in sunlight, she walked toward him into the
water, her back straight and her hips swaying, and, reaching him,
pressed herself against him.

"You're something," he said. "I never thought you'd actually do 95
that."

She was about to say, I know, but stopped herself. 96

"I take it all back," he said, his fingers playing with her hair. "I take it 97
all, all, all back. I never expected this. You're crazy. I love you. It's
wonderful."

"Are you all talk," she asked, holding hands, almost pulling him, "or 98
are we going to swim? Come on."

They dove into the water together. 99

Vocabulary

distractions (13)—things that divert one's attention and draw the mind in a new direction

inconspicuous (33)—hard to see; attracting little attention

reverberation (42)—repercussion; response to actions

inevitability (45)—certainty of not being avoided or evaded

overenunciated (60)—pronounced words exaggeratedly clearly and distinctly

frailty (80)—weakness

vulnerable (84)—open to criticism or attack

IN YOUR JOURNAL

Surprise is one of the themes of this story. Write about the various surprises that take place in the story. What do they tell about the characters?

A Closer Reading

1. What is Stephen afraid of? Is this particular fear more common to males or to females? Why?

2. What can we infer about the two main characters? How old do they seem to be? Do they have a long-term relationship? Are they in love? Have they been married to other people before?

3. What does the scene at the church with the pastor tell you about the two main characters? What does each of them seem to want from their relationship?

4. Why does Stephen feel "cooped up"? What insight does Jan have about Stephen's personality? How does her final act affect Stephen? What does it suggest for the future of their relationship?

Drawing Your Own Conclusions

1. What is the significance of the story's taking place on vacation? What do people do on vacation that they usually do not do in ordinary life?

2. At one point Stephen says, "I'm used to distractions. I'm used to . . . I don't know. Craziness." What does he really mean by

this statement? How does his description of basketball and Kareem Abdul-Jabbar fit with your interpretation of his feelings?

3. In the middle of the story, Baxter describes this facet of Jan: " 'I don't understand,' she said. In fact, she did understand, but she thought the rest of their vacation would go better if she pretended she didn't." What does this tell us about Jan's personality? How does her act at the end of the story also reflect this aspect of her character?

4. What does the story suggest about male and female relationships?

5. Why does Jan name the lake Lake Stephen? Why does Baxter make this the title of the story?

Thinking about Writing

1. Baxter does not tell his readers the characters' names until late in the story. How does this affect you as a reader? Would you have liked more description of the characters? Did you picture them in your mind as you read the story?

2. Where in the story, and in relation to the characters, does Baxter use the word "surprise"? What synonyms or events in the story relate to surprise?

3. What other words does Baxter use to express Stephen's feeling of being "cooped up"? What other words or events relate to feelings about predictability and of discontent?

4. What does the concluding paragraph suggest about the future of Jan and Stephen's relationship? How does Baxter do this? What words or phrases signal to you the future outcome?

* * *

Suggestions for Writing

1. Describe an experience in which you discovered a surprising character trait of a close friend or family member. What did you learn from this experience?

2. In an essay, describe the characteristics that are most important to you in an intimate companion. Explain why these characteristics mean so much to you.

3. Should people be completely honest with their intimate partners? Take a position on this issue and support it with your
   experiences, your readings, or your observations of others.

4. Write a story about a relationship in which there is a problem
   that the characters resolve in an interesting and unusual way.

Strategies for Revision

When you read your draft for your essay, think about the following
questions:

- If you wrote about a surprising characteristic, what information
  did you provide about the person before you introduced the
  surprise? What words and phrases did you use to contrast the
  surprising characteristic with the normal behavior of the person?

- If you described characteristics that are important to you in an
  intimate partner, is each characteristic distinctive? Do you give
  examples of them? Do you explain why they are important to
  you?

- How did you decide in what order to present your ideas? Is there
  any other order that would work better?

IN YOUR JOURNAL

According to many recent studies, men and women often have different educational experiences in college.

Before you read this selection, reflect on this by writing in your journal about any of your experiences or observations that reveal how males and females are treated in school in either similar or different ways.

Gender Issues in the College Classroom

Edward B. Fiske

Edward B. Fiske wrote this article for the *New York Times* in 1990. Fiske often writes about educational issues. This article was also included in Paula Rothenberg's 1992 book, *Race, Class and Gender in the United States*. It raises some important questions about how gender affects the way students are educated in our society. Fiske suggests that men and women are not always treated in the same ways in college classrooms.

Do men get more for their money than women do when they slap   1
down $50,000 to $100,000 for a college education? Based on her analysis of thousands of hours of college teaching, Catherine G. Krupnick says the answer is a resounding yes.

Detailed observations of thousands of hours of videotapes of college   2
classrooms show that faculty members consistently take male students and their contributions more seriously than females and their ideas. Moreover, they permit males to dominate discussions far out of proportion to their numbers.

"College catalogues should carry warnings. The value you receive   3
will depend on your sex," she suggested.

Ms. Krupnick's conclusions are bad news for Wheaton College.   4
Until two years ago, it was an all-female institution selling itself as a place where women could flex their intellectual and leadership muscles before moving out into male-dominated work places.

Now Wheaton has bowed to economic necessity, become coeduca-   5
tional and taken up the challenge of providing what Alice F. Emerson,

president of the college, calls "gender-balanced" education. To do so, they have turned to Ms. Krupnick, a researcher at the Harvard Graduate School of Education, for help.

Ms. Krupnick's findings are among the latest in a steady stream of   6
research over the last two decades showing that while they may be sitting side by side, male and female undergraduates have substantially different educational experiences.

In a survey of the literature on the subject for the Association of   7
American Colleges, Roberta Hall argued that women face a "chilly climate" in most college classrooms. Professors are more likely to re-member men's names, call on them in class and listen attentively to their answers. By contrast, they feel freer to interrupt women and ask them "lower order" questions.

For example, an English professor might ask a woman for the year   8
when Wordsworth wrote the first version of "the Prelude," but turn to a male student to ask, "What are the thematic differences between the 1805 and 1850 versions?"

A study released last month by the Harvard Assessment Seminars   9
reported that men and women often approach their studies with sharply different values. The satisfaction men get from college years tends to correlate well with the grades they achieve, and they look for faculty advisers who will give them "concrete and directive suggestions." Women, by contrast, tend to put the heart before the course. Their overall academic satisfaction, the study found, is shaped "far more by personal relationships and by informal encounters and meetings with faculty and advisers."

When she was first hired by Wheaton as a consultant, Ms. Krupnick   10
expected to find no problems. "Half of the faculty members were women, and women still predominated in every class," she recalled. "I assumed that they would still be holding their own. But I was wrong."

Detailed analysis of videotapes of Wheaton classes showed that in a   11
class where they made up one-tenth of the students, male students would do a quarter of the speaking. They also tended to be more impulsive. "You ask what's the meaning of life, and four hands will shoot up, most of them male," she said.

Ms. Krupnick said that female students, by contrast, tended to want   12
time to think about a question before offering an answer and that when they did respond, they were more likely than men to "enlarge on the ideas of a previous speaker rather than to challenge his or her initial assumption."

Women at Wheaton tend to do better than their male classmates on 13
written papers, but according to Ms. Krupnick, the cost of not becoming proficient in holding an audience can be high. "In a vast number of careers," she said, "it's the ability to use language in public settings, like meetings, that leads to advancement, not the quality of work done in private."

Ms. Krupnick suggested that the goal for Wheaton—or any college, 14
for that matter—should be to promote all strengths in students. "Teachers should encourage women to initiate comments, resist interruptions and be willing to assume the risks of a public role," she said. "Likewise, men need listening skills. They must also be shown that when they give instant answers to complicated questions, mostly for the sake of social posturing, they are not getting a very good education."

Wheaton faculty members have been working with Ms. Krupnick 15
on techniques for reaching such goals.

"The most important thing is to be aware of the space in the room 16
and think about who is speaking," said Richard Pearce, a professor of English. "Then you can consciously, even physically, turn away from over-participators."

Another technique is to pause for five or ten seconds after asking a 17
question and not accept the first hand that goes up. "Americans are nudgy about silence," said Ms. Krupnick. "You have to learn to say: 'Not yet.'"

Either that, she says, or issue warning labels. 18

Vocabulary

flex (4)—to move muscles; to stretch the mind

coeducational (5)—referring to a system in which men and women attend classes together

predominated (10)—had authority or influence over

proficient (13)—skilled; highly competent

nudgy (17)—uncomfortable; restless

IN YOUR JOURNAL

According to the article you have just read, what are the ways in which men and women are treated differently in colleges? Write them down. Compare these notes with what you wrote in your journal before you read the Fiske article. In what ways, if any, have your thoughts on this subject changed?

A Closer Reading

1. What specific evidence does Fiske give to show that male and female students are treated differently?
2. How did the researchers get their information?
3. In paragraphs 7 and 8, Fiske refers to "lower order" and "higher order" questions. According to the examples given, what is the difference between these two types of questions?
4. What examples of differences in the ways men and women react and respond in the classroom are presented in the article?

Drawing Your Own Conclusions

1. Does this article offer a realistic assessment of men's and women's behaviors in class? How do your experiences confirm or contradict these examples?
2. Why do you think teachers might treat students differently?
3. In general, do you think you learn more from listening or from getting involved in the class? Explain your answer with specific examples from classes you have taken.
4. What do students gain from participating in class? Why, then, do some students rarely participate? What can be done to encourage these students to get more involved?

Thinking about Writing

1. This article begins with a question. Where in the article is the question answered? What specific information answers the question for you?

2. In paragraph 1, Fiske mentions Catherine G. Krupnick. Where in the article does he explain who Krupnick is? Where in the article does he describe her work? Do you think he should have explained her position earlier in the article? Why or why not?

3. What other names are included in this article? Where does Fiske let the readers know who those people are? What makes the reader believe that these people are authorities about college education?

4. The one-line conclusion is a response to a suggestion made earlier in the selection. Where does the suggestion occur? What does the conclusion mean?

*   *   *

Suggestions for Writing

1. Write an essay in which you describe your experiences in high school, junior high school, or elementary school in relation to the ways in which males and females were treated. Focus on your classroom and describe the seating arrangement. Who sat in the front? Who sat in the back? Who answered questions most often? Was there a teacher's favorite? Did you feel that all students were treated fairly?

2. How can people balance the need for the concrete achievement of good grades and the need to have good interpersonal relationships with faculty and advisers? Write an essay in which you make specific suggestions that will help males and females to get a good education by finding a balance in their classroom behavior. Explain how your suggestions will be effective.

3. What is the most important change that teachers need to make at your college for more of the students to be successful?

   Write an essay explaining why you chose to focus on this particular aspect of education/teaching and how it would change the college experience for everyone.

4. Considering what you have read about males and females, do you think that they should be in separate classes or separate schools at any period in their lives? If so, explain when and why. If not, explain why. Support your point of view with examples from your own experiences, your readings, or your observations of others.

5. Fiske suggests that men are more talkative in the classroom setting and that women listen more because they are not encouraged to participate in public settings as much as men are. Other researchers believe that women talk more in private settings such as at home, at parties, or on dates. Write an essay in which you compare the public and private behavior of someone you know. Explain why you think the person behaves differently in various situations.

Strategies for Revision

The following revision strategy takes place in two steps. The first is individual, and the next involves your working with a classmate.

Begin by rereading your writing with a different-colored pencil or pen in your hand. With the pencil or pen, do the following:

- Circle any words that you would like to replace or rethink.
- Circle any sentences that you think are weak or repetitive.
- Practice changing the sound of what you have written by moving parts of a sentence around so that the beginning of the sentence is now the end portion. Do this for any sentence in which you delay important information, for instance, your subject and verb.
- Put a check mark next to any sentences that you are considering moving because they would support another sentence's main point or because they are repetitive and can be combined with another sentence elsewhere.
- Put a star next to places where you would like to add some new idea that would support your point and aid in the reader's understanding.

Then share these possible changes with a classmate. Discuss whether the changes would make your writing smoother and clearer. Then reverse the process and do the same for your classmate. Using the ideas from your discussion, revise your writing. When you are satisfied with it, share it with someone who has never read your writing before. This will help you see how successful you have been.

Student writer Lisa L. Smith wrote an essay in response to suggestion 2 from the Suggestions for Writing that follow the McAuliffe selection: Paragraph 8 states, "Alike men and women have never been and never will be." Write an essay in which you agree or disagree with this statement, and support your point of view with examples from your readings, experiences, and observations.

Is the Ideal Woman a Myth?

Lisa L. Smith

The idea of "a woman's place is in the home" dates back to the 1 prehistoric era when Fred Flintstone first yelled at Wilma for not having his dinner ready. Even today, as soon as girls are born, they are taught to be sweet and dainty and to never ever disagree with a boy, conditioning girls to the role they must play as they associate with boys. Virginia Sapiro, professor of political science at the University of Wisconsin, defines gender consciousness as, "Women's beliefs that they are less powerful than men as a group and are accorded fewer resources" (14). Many girls become aware of gender stereotyping at an early age and set their aspirations accordingly. Although sexual discrimination is usually blamed on men, a closer examination may prove that conclusion to be inaccurate. Maybe women accept and even perpetuate their subservient position to men. And could the responsibility for gender discrimination be more fairly assigned to society as a whole?

In 1956, *Life* magazine did a cover story focusing on the ideal 2 woman. It stated, "The ideal woman is a pretty and popular suburban housewife who attends club or charity meetings, drives the kids to school, does the weekly grocery shopping, makes ceramics, and plans to study French" (Tindall 823). This ideal image of women is still alive today, but with high rates of divorce the ideal is unattainable. At the end of 1990, 74% of women 20 to 44 years of age were employed outside the home. Of these women, 60% were employed in low-paying clerical and retail sales jobs (Saltzman 42). Many of these women have not learned the skills necessary to qualify for higher paying jobs because they were always taught that men would take care of them.

In addition to these societal expectations, education plays a major 3 role in how a woman views herself and her ability to succeed. In 1986 a study was performed surveying women who had graduated from high school in 1980. It was found that 28% of the women with a high school education or less believed that it was best for men to be the achievers, in comparison with only 10% of women with a college education (Sapiro 13). From my own personal experience, I have found that in elementary and secondary schools, little emphasis is placed on young women to take courses, such as science and math, to qualify themselves for higher paying jobs. These subjects are more often geared toward males. If a woman does make the decision to attend college, she is usually steered into "women's jobs" like elementary education or social work. These occupations usually pay significantly less than "men's jobs" such as engineering and business, professions which often require the same level of education and training. Being channeled into a lower-paying career creates a problem when a woman is faced with divorce or death of her husband and finds herself financially responsible for her family.

To explain the economic disparity between what men and women   4
earn, feminst organizations want to blame these problems on men. Feminists believe that men don't see women as their equals and intentionally discriminate against them. Some scholars, however, see the gender problem not as intentionally discriminatory, but as conditioned. According to Virginia Sapiro, "It is perfectly possible—and very common—for individuals to believe in equality but to perceive women and men in their traditional stereotypes" (13). This idea could explain the statement made by Ross Virgin, president of the Toronto based organization, In Search of Justice: "Women have not been, in our view, discriminated against. There's no conspiracy." (Underwood 47). The key phrase in that statement is "in our view." Maybe men don't understand that they are discriminating against women because male behavior is more conditioned than malicious.

In high school today, there are always the boys' football and basket-   5
ball teams with their cheerleaders, mostly girls, standing on the sidelines cheering them on. And in high school what does almost every girl want to be? A cheerleader. As men and women graduate and enter the workforce together, it is perfectly possible that men still view women in this way—standing on the sidelines, cheering them on. In fact, in a survey of nine major companies, men in authority assumed that a woman with a family wouldn't even want a promotion due to the extra hours it would involve (Saltzman 41). Although there are men out there who do deliberately discriminate, it is important to keep in mind that there are others who are simply being protective as they have always been taught to do.

There is no easy answer to this complex issue. Dr. Anthony Layng, 6
professor of anthropology at Elmira College, suggests, "Sexual equality
will not be achieved until we face up to the fact that inequality is a
product of our own behavior and attitudes. Only then might we discard
this vestige of our tribal heritage" (91). Therefore, the solution does not
lie solely in passing laws that force men and women to be equal. It
might be more beneficial to educate both men and women on the
capabilities and aptitudes of women, then make sure we develop sufficient female role models (in areas such as medicine, law, engineering,
and business) to set the example for the young influential minds of
today.

Works Cited

Layng, Anthony. "What Keeps Women 'in Their Place'?" *U.S.A. Today* May
    1990: 91.

Saltzman, Amy. "Trouble at the Top." *U.S. News & World Report* 17 June 1991:
    41–42.

Sapiro, Virginia. "Feminism: a generation later." *The Annals of the American
    Academy of Political and Social Science* March 1991: 13–14.

Tindall, George B., and David E. Shi. *America.* 2nd ed. New York: Norton,
    1989.

Underwood, Nora, and Dan Burke. "An Emerging Male Backlash." *MacClean's*
    14 August 1989: 47.

Questions to Think About

1. What is Smith's point of view?
2. What examples does she use to show that both woman and men
   have played a role in perpetuating the myth?
3. What statistics does Smith rely on? What are the strengths and
   weaknesses of using statistics in a paper such as this? Are statistics more convincing that narrative to you? Why or why not?
4. Why doesn't Smith provide a definite answer in her conclusion?
   How does this affect you as a reader?
5. What is the best part of the essay? Why?
6. What is the weakest part of the essay? Why? How could it be
   made stronger?

MAKING CONNECTIONS

The World of Gender: *Being Men and Women*

1. Helen Fisher, the anthropologist interviewed by Kathleen McAuliffe (see page 183), believes that women are more verbal and more attuned to nonverbal cues than are men. She also states that men have superior mathematical and visual-spatial skills to those of women. Write an essay in which you use information from the Carol Tavris and Carole Wade article (see page 195) to respond to Fisher's ideas.

2. Imagine that you had to design a one-day required orientation for entering freshmen in your college that would teach students about men and women. Referring to the reading you have done in this unit, decide what topics should be included in the course. Choose two articles from this unit that should be included. In an essay, explain your choices. What do you think men and women should learn about each other in order to work together well in college?

3. Write an introduction to this unit in which you recommend to other students one piece of writing in this unit. Which piece of writing is the best? The most interesting, the most informative, the best written? Using quotations from the selection, convince your reader to choose this particular piece to read.

4. Imagine that Hoerburger (see page 206) and Barry (see page 189) met to discuss the limitations that men feel. After rereading their selections, write down their conversation, using dialogue and quotations. What conclusions do you think they might draw about male stereotyping?

5. Write an essay in which you choose one piece of writing that made you think about how women and men are stereotyped and treated based on their genders. Reread the McAuliffe article on page 183, the Tavris/Wade article on page 195, and the Fiske article on page 223 for ideas. Explain what you learned from these pieces of writing.

6. According to the articles you have read in this unit, in what ways have women and men been stereotyped and treated differently? Refer to particular articles to support your position. In what ways have your ideas about the abilities of men and women changed as a result of reading selections in this unit?

5

THE WORLD OF INTIMACY

Connecting with Another Person

Part of growing up involves finding a person that we can love and with whom we can share our lives. In some cases, this process involves many false starts and disappointments. Conflicts may occur when families want to have control over the choice of the people with whom their children will spend their futures. Other conflicts develop between individuals as they attempt to satisfy their own needs while attempting to share their lives with another person.

The first selection, "Coming of Age in Mississippi" by Anne Moody, is about a friendship between two college sophomores that progresses through cycles of intimacy. Moody describes how peer pressure at her southern college campus influences her feelings, insecurities, and behaviors.

Family pressure to follow an old tradition intrudes on the love felt by a young couple in an excerpt from Laura Esquivel's novel *Like Water for Chocolate*. This tale about a traditional Mexican family explores the problems that develop when a mother's needs conflict with the desires of her children.

Like the star-crossed lovers in the Esquivel story, many of us like to think that our choice of a partner is personal and spontaneous. Sociologist Ian Robertson questions that idea in his textbook selection, "Courtship, Marriage, and Divorce." Robertson presents evidence that courtship and marriage usually take place between very similar people who have similar backgrounds.

Anthropologist Marjorie Shostak further explores the choice of partners in her selection, "Marriage." Shostak lived for almost two years with the !Kung San people of Botswana, and during that time she interviewed members of that community, focusing primarily on the life of Nisa, a fifty-year-old woman. In this selection, Shostak describes Nisa's courtship and arranged marriage.

Next, we read Raymond Carver's "Distance," a story about a young couple and their new baby. Although these young parents chose each other and love each other very much, they are having problems fulfilling their responsibilities to a newborn child while also meeting their own needs.

Learning to deal with the problems that develop in an intimate relationship is the subject of psychologist Lori H. Gordon's article "Intimacy: The Art of Working Out Your Relationships." In it, Gordon explains the origin of many of the problems people face in their relationships, and she suggests some methods for solving those problems.

The unit ends with student writer Tracy Brooks's essay describing the findings of her interview with Kanchan Mohindra, an eighteen-year-old young woman, born in India, who came to the United States at the age of four. Brooks describes Mohindra's problems balancing her family and cultural expectations about dating and marriage with those found in the United States.

*   *   *

Think about the following questions before reading the selections in this unit:

1. What are the four most important characteristics you look for in a friend?

2. What are the four most important characteristics you look for in a lover or spouse?

3. What differences are there between your answers to questions one and two? Why?

Coming of Age in Mississippi
Anne Moody

Like Water for Chocolate
Laura Esquivel

Courtship, Marriage, and Divorce
Ian Robertson

Marriage
Marjorie Shostak

Distance
Raymond Carver

Intimacy: The Art of Working Out Your Relationships
Lori H. Gordon

Marriage Traditions in the Indian Culture
Tracy Brooks

IN YOUR JOURNAL

Write about your first date. How did you meet the person? Who took the initiative in getting to know the other? Did you enjoy being with each other? Did you see each other again?

Coming of Age in Mississippi

Anne Moody

Anne Moody worked for the NAACP (National Association for the Advancement of Colored People), CORE (the Congress of Racial Equality), and SNCC (the Student Nonviolent Coordinating Committee) in the 1950s and 1960s to fight racism in the United States. Moody's autobiography, *Coming of Age in Mississippi*, published in 1969, tells what it was like to grow up poor and black in the rural South before the civil rights movement. The following excerpt describes her life as a student at Natchez Community College and her experiences with her first boyfriend.

That second year at Natchez, I discovered that I had changed. The 1 year before almost every boy on campus had tried to make it with me, especially the basketball boys, and I had turned them down one after the other. Now I found myself wondering whether I should have been so rude to them. When I saw girls and boys sneaking kisses out under the trees, I got curious. Sometimes I wished I had a boyfriend. I was twenty years old and I had never been kissed, not even a smack on the lips. I wanted to know how it felt.

There was a new basketball player on campus named Keemp, 2 whom all the girls and boys were talking about. He was tall—six feet five—and slim. Besides being tall, he had a "cool" about him that most girls liked. So they all went around talking about how handsome he was. It was early October and we hadn't started practicing yet, so I didn't know whether he was a good player or not, but I certainly didn't think his looks were anything special. He looked just like my daddy without a mustache and I never thought Daddy was handsome. I used to see Keemp walking around on campus and wondered what was it that all the girls saw in him. Then too he made me wonder what all the women had seen in my daddy when he was young.

One Sunday after church, I was leaving chapel when Keemp walked   3
up to me and said, "So you are Anne Moody, huh?"

"Yes. Why?" I asked, and kept walking.   4

"I heard a lot of talk about you," he said, walking beside me. "Where   5
are you going now?"

"To the dorm," I answered.   6

"If you'll slow down, I'll walk you over there," he said coolly.   7

For the first time in my life I slowed down for a boy. I was a little   8
surprised at myself.

As we walked together, Keemp didn't try to force the conversation.   9
He hardly said anything and whenever he did it was like a brother to a
sister. When we got to the dorm he asked if he could walk me to dinner.
I again surprised myself by answering yes.

Because Natchez College was so small, most of the relationships be-   10
tween girls and boys were a public thing. Everybody knew everybody
else's business. The students were all shocked when I started going with
Keemp, especially the sophomore boys who had tried to make it with me
the year before. A couple of the guys who had tried hardest came up and
bluntly asked me what did I see in Keemp or what did Keemp have to offer me that they didn't. I was a little surprised at the girls' reaction. Most
of them seemed glad that I had finally decided to join the club. So much
so that they started giving me all kinds of advice about how to handle men.

When Keemp started playing basketball, I really began to like him.   11
He had the longest limbs I had ever seen. As he moved down the
basketball court, he was so light he looked like he was flying. He could
just walk up to the goal and dunk the ball with ease. Through basketball, he became the most popular boy on campus.

Keemp tried to kiss me many times but I wouldn't let him. I always   12
told him that I had a headache or something. When we traveled to play
other teams, all the other boys and their girls on the team kissed around
on the bus. Keemp, the best player on the team, sat beside me begging
me to kiss him. Everyone else on the bus knew that Keemp wasn't
getting anywhere with me, and most of the boys began to tease him.

There were a couple of girls on the team who were having spasms   13
over Keemp. One of them sat in the seat behind us and late at night she
would start clawing on the seat like a big cat. When Keemp started
answering her clawing, I went to one of my friends, seeking advice on
how to kiss. She told me that I didn't have to do anything but part my lips

to Keemp and he would do the rest. For the next two months I thought of how I would part my lips. Then one night I dreamt that Keemp and I were kissing around nude on the back seat of the bus and just as we were about to have intercourse, I woke up screaming. I was so frightened by the dream, I began to think that if I kissed Keemp it might lead to something else. The mere thought of getting sexually involved caused me all kinds of anxieties. But I had a tremendous guilt about treating Keemp the way I did when another girl would have treated him better, so I made up my mind to quit him and let that clawing girl have him.

One night in November, when we were playing Philander Smith College in Little Rock, Arkansas, I decided that this would be the night I would quit Keemp. Since the game was one of our biggest, I decided to wait and tell him after it was over. I knew we would lose if he wasn't at his best. **14**

Keemp shot forty-some points during that game. He played better than I had ever seen him play. Just about every time he raised his arms, it was two points for us. When the game was over, the rest of the boys hugged him down to the floor, then picked him up and declared him "King of Basketball." As I watched him play and then saw how everyone loved him, it suddenly dawned upon me that he was a terrific person and that I was a fool to be thinking about quitting him. **15**

When the boys let him go, he walked up to me smiling. Without saying a word, he put his arms around my shoulders and walked me to the bus. As he touched me, a warm current ran through my body. **16**

As I sat on the bus beside Keemp that night, a feeling I had never known before came over me. He held my hands, and it seemed like every hormone in my body reacted. Neither one of us said a word. As the bus was coming to a stop, Keemp leaned over and gently placed his lips on mine. They were like a magnet slowly pulling my lips apart. Once my mouth was open his tongue explored areas that had never been touched by anything but a toothbrush. I completely forgot where I was until one of the boys sitting near us started banging on the basketball and yelling. **17**

"Jesus! Y'aaaall! It finally happened! Keemp done did it!" **18**

The bus had stopped. The lights were on and everybody was looking at us. Keemp wouldn't stop. He pretended that he didn't even hear the yelling, that we weren't on a bus surrounded by spectators. I tried to pull away but I was so weak I couldn't control myself, so I just gave in to his kisses. **19**

Didn't anyone on the bus say one word or stir, not even Mrs. Evans. No one made a move to get off the bus until Keemp and I did. When **20**

Keemp finished kissing me, I saw that he had lipstick all over his mouth. My first reaction was to wipe it off real quick before anyone could see it. Keemp just smiled as I wiped it off. When I finished, he took me by the hand, pulled me up out of the seat, buried my head in his shoulder and we walked off the bus.

I was very embarrassed about the fact that my first kiss had been such a public thing. But I didn't regret the kiss at all. Once we were back on campus, Keemp and I greeted each other with a kiss every time we met.   21

We never did hide behind trees or posts to sneak kisses like the other students. When Mrs. Evans blinked the lights for the girls to come in, I'd give Keemp a smack on the lips right in front of her. Soon most of the other girls started smacking kisses on their boyfriends in front of Mrs. Evans too. Finally, one day Mrs. Evans called me in for a "conference" and accused me of leading the kissing game on campus.   22

During the first six months of our relationship I was happier than I had ever been. Keemp turned me on so much that I made the first straight-A average that had been made at Natchez in many years. Studying was a cinch and everything else seemed so easy. But that spring when the basketball season was all over and the excitement of traveling was gone and boys and girls began swarming all over each other like bees, I slowly began to drift away from the whole scene. I had gotten tired of being part of "the club." There was something about the way couples were relaxing into relationships and making them everything that bothered me. I didn't want to get all wrapped up in Keemp the way some of the other girls did with their boyfriends. My relation with him had gradually become a brother-sister thing. He could tell I was moving away from him, so he got himself a girl in the city. I wasn't even jealous and I didn't say anything. I just didn't care. I knew I would be leaving him behind next year and figured he'd have somebody else. I pretended that I didn't know he had another girl and went on being friends with him. He was the best friend I had had since Lola, and I told him everything.   23

Vocabulary

limbs (11)—arms and legs

spasms (13)—sudden violent and temporary emotion

quit him (13)—slang expression that means she is going to stop dating him

spectators (19)—observers

cinch (23)—something easy to do; a sure thing

IN YOUR JOURNAL

Write down what you remember about Moody's relationship with Keemp. Overall, do you think it was a positive or negative experience for her? Why? How does her first date compare to yours?

A Closer Reading

1. Is Moody interested in getting to know Keemp? What evidence in the story supports your answer?

2. How does Moody let Keemp know that she is an independent woman? What specific incidents in the story support this idea?

3. Why does she think about "quitting" Keemp? Why does she change her mind?

4. How does Keemp feel about Moody? What specific incidents in the story support your answer?

Drawing Your Own Conclusions

1. Even though Moody is independent, she does not take the initiative in her relationship with Keemp. Under what basic assumptions are she and Keemp working in their relationship? Do you think women should ask men out on dates?

2. How do you decide who should pay for a date? Do you feel differently about this after you have gone out with someone several times?

3. Why does Moody break up with Keemp? Do people who have dated usually remain friends? Why or why not?

4. What peer pressure does Moody feel? What peer pressure does Keemp feel? How does this pressure influence their behavior?

Thinking about Writing

1. Moody's autobiography was published in 1969. Reread the selection to find any slang expressions. Are these expressions still used today? If she were rewriting this piece today, should she include, change, or eliminate these slang expressions? Why?

2. Look at the dialogue. Notice how Moody begins a new paragraph each time a person speaks. Where does she use quotation marks? Where does she put capital letters in each quotation? How does she use other punctuation along with the quotation marks?

3. In what order does Moody tell her story? What other stories that you have read thus far in this book are ordered in a similar way?

4. What words and phrases tell us about Moody? How do we come to an understanding of her as a person? What is her personality like? What are her goals? Her beliefs?

5. Make a list of the words Moody uses to describe Keemp. Does she emphasize his appearance? His personality? His behavior? Do you feel that you have a clear picture of him? What aspect of him is still lost to you?

*   *   *

Suggestions for Writing

1. Dating patterns vary in different colleges in different parts of the country. Dating also varies according to your age and/or life experience. Describe the dating patterns you have witnessed either in your circle of friends or among other people your age or with your same experiences. In an essay, first briefly describe the people you will talk about. Then answer some of the following questions: Who usually initiates the first contact? Where do these people tend to meet? Do they go on formal or informal dates? Is the dating conducted in a relaxed atmosphere? Is it kept private or shared with others? What did you learn about other people's beliefs and behavior, as well as your own, from writing about this subject?

2. Can women and men just be friends? Write an essay in which you respond to this question, supporting your answer with your own experiences, your observations, and your readings.

3. In many colleges, athletes are treated differently from other students. They often get scholarships and have other special privileges (see Thurber, page 143). Do you think athletes should be given such special treatment in college? What do you think Moody believes about this subject? Answer these questions, sup-

porting your point of view with your personal experience, your observations, and your readings.

4. Moody's autobiography takes place during the time of the civil rights movement in the United States, in the 1960s. Conduct some research on this important time in American history. Write a report explaining what the civil rights movement was and how it affected the United States.

Strategies for Revision

As soon as you have completed the first draft of your essay, separate yourself from your writing by spending ten minutes reading and writing in your journal. Write about what you have learned about writing from the Moody selection. How does she present her ideas? How did her writing affect the writing of your essay?

This time has created a distance that can help you revise and rethink what you have written. Reread your draft, thinking about the following questions:

- What am I trying to communicate in this piece of writing?
- Who am I writing this essay for?
- Is there a clear beginning?
- Does each paragraph have a focus and a reason for existence?
- Am I choosing words that best express my ideas?
- Does one idea connect to the next?
- Is there a clear ending?

If you discover any problem areas in your draft, focus on those areas as you revise. You may decide to add new material, discard repetitive or useless material, or move sentences and even paragraphs around so they connect ideas better. You may even decide to change words, examples, or details to make your writing more effective.

Share your revised draft with a classmate.

IN YOUR JOURNAL

Write in your journal about a tradition, rite, or ceremony that you
know reasonably well and that you would like to see ended. This could
be as large as an important worldwide cultural ceremony or as small as a
tradition in your own family. Explain what it is and why you wish it
would be abolished.

Like Water for Chocolate

Laura Esquivel

Laura Esquivel is a writer who lives in Mexico. *Like Water for
Chocolate* (*Como agua para chocolate*), originally published in Spanish
in 1989, was Esquivel's first novel. She also wrote the screenplay for
the 1993 film made from her novel. The translation of Esquivel's
book, by Carol and Thomas Christensen, was published in English
in 1992. The novel, set in rural Mexico in the early part of this
century, concerns an old tradition practiced by the De la Garza family. This excerpt clearly illustrates how a tradition created to help one
family member complicates the lives of three sisters.

On Mama Elena's ranch, sausage making was a real ritual. The day   1
before, they started peeling garlic, cleaning chiles, and grinding spices.
All the women in the family had to participate: Mama Elena; her daughters, Gertrudis, Rosaura, and Tita; Nacha, the cook; and Chencha, the
maid. They gathered around the dining-room table in the afternoon,
and between the talking and the joking the time flew by until it started
to get dark. Then Mama Elena would say:

"That's it for today."   2

For a good listener, it is said, a single word will suffice, so when   3
they heard that, they all sprang into action. First they had to clear the
table; then they had to assign tasks: one collected the chickens, another drew water for breakfast from the well, a third was in charge of
wood for the stove. There would be no ironing, no embroidery, no
sewing that day. When it was all finished, they went to their bedrooms
to read, say their prayers, and go to sleep. One afternoon, before
Mama Elena told them they could leave the table, Tita, who was then

fifteen, announced in a trembling voice that Pedro Muzquiz would like to come and speak with her. . . .

After an endless silence during which Tita's soul shrank, Mama Elena asked: 4

"And why should this gentleman want to come talk to me?"   5

Tita's answer could barely be heard: 6

"I don't know."   7

Mama Elena threw her a look that seemed to Tita to contain all the years of represssion that had flowed over the family, and said: 8

"If he intends to ask for your hand, tell him not to bother. He'll be wasting his time and mine too. You know perfectly well that being the youngest daughter means you have to take care of me until the day I die."   9

With that Mama Elena got slowly to her feet, put her glasses in her apron, and said in a tone of final command: 10

"That's it for today."   11

Tita knew that discussion was not one of the forms of communication permitted in Mama Elena's household, but even so, for the first time in her life, she intended to protest her mother's ruling.   12

"But in my opinion . . ."   13

"You don't have an opinion, and that's all I want to hear about it. For generations, not a single person in my family has ever questioned this tradition, and no daughter of mine is going to be the one to start."   14

Tita lowered her head, and the realization of her fate struck her as forcibly as her tears struck the table. From then on they knew, she and the table, that they could never have even the slightest voice in the unknown forces that fated Tita to bow before her mother's absurd decision, and the table to continue to receive the bitter tears that she had first shed on the day of her birth.   15

Still Tita did not submit. Doubts and anxieties sprang to her mind. For one thing, she wanted to know who started this family tradition. It would be nice if she could let that genius know about one little flaw in this perfect plan for taking care of women in their old age. If Tita couldn't marry and have children, who would take care of her when she got old? Was there a solution in a case like that? Or are daughters who stay home and take care of their mothers not expected to survive too long after the parent's death? And what about women who marry and can't have children, who will take care of them? And besides, she'd like to know what kind of studies had established that the youngest daughter and not the eldest is best suited to care for their mother. Had the opinion of the daughter affected by the plan ever been taken into ac-   16 count? If she couldn't marry, was she at least allowed to experience love? Or not even that?

Tita knew perfectly well that all these questions would have to be   17
buried forever in the archive of questions that have no answers. In the De la Garza family, one obeyed—immediately. Ignoring Tita completely, a very angry Mama Elena left the kitchen, and for the next week she didn't speak a single word to her.

What passed for communication between them resumed when   18
Mama Elena, who was inspecting the clothes each of the women had been sewing, discovered that Tita's creation, which was the most perfect, had not been basted before it was sewed.

"Congratulations," she said, "your stitches are perfect—but you   19
didn't baste it, did you?"

"No," answered Tita, astonished that the sentence of silence had   20
been revoked.

"Then go and rip it out. Baste it and sew it again and then come and   21
show it to me. And remember that the lazy man and the stingy man end up walking their road twice."

"But that's if a person makes a mistake, and you yourself said a   22
moment ago that my sewing was . . ."

"Are you starting up with your rebelliousness again? It's enough   23
that you have the audacity to break the rules in your sewing."

"I'm sorry, Mami. I won't ever do it again."   24

With that Tita succeeded in calming Mama Elena's anger. For once   25
she had been very careful; she had called her "Mami" in the correct tone of voice. Mama Elena felt that the word *Mama* had a disrespectful sound to it, and so, from the time they were little, she had ordered her daughters to use the word *Mami* when speaking to her. The only one who resisted, the only one who said the word without the proper deference was Tita, which had earned her plenty of slaps. But how perfectly she had said it this time! Mama Elena took comfort in the hope that she had finally managed to subdue her youngest daughter.

Unfortunately her hope was short-lived, for the very next day Pedro   26
Muzquiz appeared at the house, his esteemed father at his side, to ask for Tita's hand in marriage. His arrival caused a huge uproar, as his visit was completely unexpected. Several days earlier Tita had sent Pedro a message via Nacha's brother asking him to abandon his suit. The brother swore he had delivered the message to Pedro and yet, there they were, in the house. Mama Elena received them in the living room; she was extremely polite and explained why it was impossible for Tita to marry.

"But if you really want Pedro to get married, allow me to suggest   27
my daughter Rosaura, who's just two years older than Tita. *She* is one
hundred percent available, and ready for marriage. . . ."

At that Chencha almost dropped right onto Mama Elena the tray   28
containing coffee and cookies, which she had carried into the living
room to offer don Pascual and his son. Excusing herself, she rushed
back to the kitchen, where Tita, Rosaura, and Gertrudis were waiting
for her to fill them in on every detail about what was going on in the
living room. She burst headlong into the room, and they all immediately stopped what they were doing, so as not to miss a word she said.

They were together in the kitchen making Christmas Rolls. As the name   29
implies, these rolls are usually prepared around Christmas, but today they
were being prepared in honor of Tita's birthday. She would soon be sixteen years old, and she wanted to celebrate with one of her favorite dishes.

"Isn't that something? Your ma talks about being ready for marriage like   30
she was dishing up a plate of enchiladas! And the worse thing is, they're
completely different! You can't just switch tacos and enchiladas like that!"

Chencha kept up this kind of running commentary as she told the   31
others—in her own way, of course—about the scene she had just witnessed. Tita knew Chencha sometimes exaggerated and distorted things,
so she held her aching heart in check. She would not accept what she had
just heard. Feigning calm, she continued cutting the rolls for her sisters
and Nacha to fill.

It is best to use homemade rolls. Hard rolls can easily be obtained   32
from a bakery, but they should be small; the larger ones are unsuited for
this recipe. After filling the rolls, bake for ten minutes and serve hot.
For best results, leave the rolls out overnight, wrapped in a cloth, so
that the grease from the sausage soaks into the bread.

When Tita was finishing wrapping the next day's rolls, Mama Elena   33
came into the kitchen and informed them that she had agreed to Pedro's
marriage—to Rosaura.

Hearing Chencha's story confirmed, Tita felt her body fill with a   34
wintry chill: in one sharp, quick blast she was so cold and dry her cheeks
burned and turned red, red as the apples beside her. That overpowering
chill lasted a long time, and she could find no respite, not even when
Nacha told her what she had overheard as she escorted don Pascual
Muzquiz and his son to the ranch's gate. Nacha followed them, walking
as quietly as she could in order to hear the conversation between father
and son. Don Pascual and Pedro were walking slowly, speaking in low,
controlled, angry voices.

"Why did you do that, Pedro? It will look ridiculous, your agreeing   35
to marry Rosaura. What happened to the eternal love you swore to
Tita? Aren't you going to keep that vow?"

"Of course I'll keep it. When you're told there's no way you can   36
marry the woman you love and your only hope of being near her is to
marry her sister, wouldn't you do the same?"

Nacha didn't manage to hear the answer; Pulque, the ranch dog,   37
went running by, barking at a rabbit he mistook for a cat.

"So you intend to marry without love?"   38

"No Papa, I am going to marry with a great love for Tita that will   39
never die."

Vocabulary

suffice (3)—to be enough

repression (8)—the control of emotion or other type of response

archive (17)—a place where public records or private papers are kept

audacity (23)—insolence; daring

subdue (25)—to conquer; to bring under control

esteemed (26)—honored; highly respected

enchiladas (30)—tortillas rolled with meat or beans inside and topped with a chili sauce

feigning (31)—pretending

respite (34)—a rest or temporary relief

IN YOUR JOURNAL

Write in your journal about one of the characters in this story. Tell why this character interested you. What do you see as his or her dilemma or condition? Do you think this person acted properly, considering the family situation?

A Closer Reading

1. What information does Esquivel provide that describes the character of Mama Elena? What specific words and phrases tell readers about her behavior and feelings toward herself and the other members of her family?

2. Define the tradition described in the story. Why was it initiated? Who stands to benefit from it? Can you think of any reasons in history why widowhood would be so prevalent as to warrant the development of such a tradition?

3. Why is Tita bothered by the family tradition? Why is it so rigidly enforced? Is there any way for her to get Mama Elena to reconsider? What happens to the youngest daughter after the mother dies? On what events in the story did you base your answer?

4. According to this story, during that time period what steps did couples take before they got married?

5. What does the sewing story indicate about the importance of following rules in the De la Garza family?

Drawing Your Own Conclusions

1. What kind of lives do women lead in the rural Mexico that is described here? What were their typical daily tasks?

2. What is the connection between food and love in this story?

3. Mama Elena's husband died two days after Tita was born. The story takes place near Tita's sixteenth birthday. How has Papa's death affected the mother's and daughter's lives? What characteristics do they have that support your point of view? Do any of their actions or words reveal their individual attitudes?

4. Why did Pedro agree to marry Rosaura? What other ways could he have chosen to be near the woman he loves? Why doesn't he?

5. Because Tita is in love with Pedro, she only sees the negative side of the family tradition. Without this tradition, what do you think might happen to the mothers after their husbands died?

6. Can you see any positive side to the tradition described in this story? Why do you think it developed?

Thinking about Writing

1. The story begins with a description of a recipe for making sausage. Reread the story, noticing where Esquivel inserts informa-

tion on cooking. How does she link food and cooking with the rest of the story? How does this affect you as a reader?

2. Esquivel includes not only traditional recipes but also traditional sayings that the family lives by. Reread the story, looking for expressions such as the one in paragraph 3: "For a good listener, it is said, a single word will suffice." Make a list of expressions like these. What does each seem to mean? In what ways do the characters live by these expressions?

3. In paragraph 16, the reader enters Tita's mind, and we come to know her thoughts. Reread the story, noticing if there are other examples of Esquivel's describing the inner world of a character. Some writers tell a story from the perspective of several characters, but many tell it from the perspective of one main character. How does Esquivel tell this story?

4. Tita was born at home on the kitchen table, with Nacha delivering the baby. Most of the story takes place in the kitchen. Why do you think Esquivel chose the kitchen as the central location of this story? What is the significance of the kitchen for families that you know?

*   *   *

Suggestions for Writing

1. Write an essay in which you describe a tradition, rite, or ceremony that you have been a part of or witnessed and that disturbed you. You may want to use your journal entry as notes for an essay. Describe the event in detail and then explain why it disturbed you. What changes in the event would you like to see occur? Do you think these changes are possible? Why or why not?

2. Write an essay in which you explain how to cook a dish that is special in your family or cultural history. Explain why you have chosen this dish and what it means to your heritage and to you. Explain in detail what ingredients are necessary and show, step by step, how to make it. Make sure your readers know whether this dish is made for special occasions (and what they are) or whether it is an everyday dish.

3. Write your own continuation of the story that shows what you think will happen next to Tita, Pedro, Rosaura, and Mama

Elena. Reread the excerpt carefully, so that you can base the actions of the characters on what they have said and done in the story.

4. Write a story that takes place in a particular room and in which the room itself takes on meaning (as the kitchen does in the Esquivel story).

Additional Project

Read the rest of *Like Water for Chocolate*. Write an essay in which you describe your reaction to the book. Did your feelings about any of the characters change? Were you surprised at the resolution of the conflict?

Strategies for Revision

If you have written a story, read your draft and make notes to yourself about the following questions:

- In what order do the events take place? Do they follow a chronological order?
- Is each character a separate and unique individual with her or his own voice and actions?
- Is the place where the event took place important to your story? If it is, do you describe it clearly, with enough details?

Write a revision of your first draft, keeping in mind your responses to these questions. Share your revision with a classmate; then review the questions with that person, to determine if you have been successful.

IN YOUR JOURNAL

Why do people get married? Write in your journal all the reasons why people get married even though in today's world many marriages end in divorce.

Courtship, Marriage, and Divorce

Ian Robertson

Ian Robertson's textbooks on sociology are used in hundreds of colleges. Robertson is originally from South Africa and was president of the multiracial National Union of South African Students. In that capacity, he organized several campaigns against South Africa's apartheid laws. After leaving that country, he studied at Oxford, Cambridge, and Harvard University, from which he received his doctorate. He has taught young children in England, high school students in Massachusetts, and college students at Harvard, Cambridge, the University of California at Los Angeles, and at William Paterson College in New Jersey. At present, he is a full-time writer. The following excerpt is from his 1989 book, *Society: A Brief Introduction*. In this selection, Robertson describes in detail how people meet, marry, and divorce each other.

A courtship system is essentially a marriage market. (The metaphor   1
of the "market" may seem a little unromantic, but, in fact, the participants do attempt to "sell" their assets—physical appearance, personal charms, talents and interests, and career prospects.) In the matter of mate selection, different courtship systems vary according to how much choice they permit the individual. The United States probably allows more freedom of choice than any other society. In this predominantly urban and anonymous society, young people—often with access to automobiles—have an exceptional degree of privacy in their courting. The practice of dating enables them to find out about one another, to improve their own interpersonal skills in the market, to experiment sexually if they so wish, and finally to select a marriage partner.

Who marries whom, then? Cupid's arrow, it turns out, does not   2
strike at random. Despite the cultural emphasis on love as something

mysterious and irrational, the selection of marital partners is actually fairly orderly and predictable. In general, the American mate-selection process produces **homogamy,** marriage between partners who share similar social characteristics. In general, spouses tend to be of similar age, social class, religious affiliation, and educational level, and they are also much more likely to marry within their own racial or ethnic group than outside it. The reason is not hard to find, for there is considerable parental and peer pressure for young people to restrict their social contacts to those who are "suitable"—which usually means "similar."

Of course, homogamy provides only the general framework in which 3 specific people choose their specific mates. In selecting their partners, people are influenced by psychological as well as social factors. Some researchers claim that people want partners whose personalities match their own in significant respects. In this "birds of a feather" view, conservatives may be attracted by other conservatives, or alcoholics may tend to seek out other alcoholics. But other researchers claim that people look for partners whose personality traits are different from, but complementary to, their own. In this "opposites attract" view, dominant people may look for passive mates, or those who love to eat may link up with those who love to cook. Both views are probably valid, depending on the psychological "chemistry" of the couple in question—a chemistry that may well change over the course of the relationship.

Marital Breakdown

The divorce rate in the United States is believed to be the highest in 4 the world, and statistics on the subject are often quoted as conclusive evidence of the decay of the family. This evidence indicates that about 50 percent of recent marriages will end in divorce, the average duration of these ill-fated unions being around seven years.

Divorce constitutes official social recognition that a marriage has 5 failed, and it can be a traumatic experience for all concerned. Most states now offer a "no fault" divorce on grounds of simple incompatibility, but there is still room for fierce resentment over the custody of offspring and child-support payments. Children are present in over 70 percent of the families that break up through divorce: more than a million children are involved every year. The children inevitably suffer through the divorce of their parents—particularly during the first year or two—but many people believe that it may be even more emotionally disturbing for them to remain in a home where the marriage is deeply unhappy.

Both divorcing parties may also be in for a difficult time emotionally. Divorce ruptures one's personal universe; it is no coincidence that men are much more likely to be fired from their jobs after divorce, nor that the death rate for divorced people is significantly higher than that for married people, at all age levels (Weiss, 1975; Emery et al., 1984).

The ex-wife may face severe economic problems, especially if she has 6 to raise young children. In the past, when most wives were not expected to work outside the home, courts frequently awarded alimony to divorced women; but now that women are considered capable of earning their own living, they receive alimony in only about 15 percent of divorce settlements. Courts award child custody to mothers rather than to fathers in 90 percent of cases, however, and usually require that the fathers provide child support. But many divorced women find that they have low earning power—particularly if they have spent their entire married lives as housewives and have no job skills or experience—and a majority of divorced fathers default on their child-support payments. More than half of American children in families where the father is absent live below the poverty line, and many single mothers become long-term welfare recipients.

Who gets divorced? The social characteristics of divorce-prone 7 partners have been well-established. Divorces are especially common among urban couples, among those who marry very young, among those who marry after only short or shallow acquaintance, and among those whose relatives and friends disapprove of the marriage. In general, the people who are most likely to get divorced are those who, statistically, would be considered the least likely to marry. And the greater the wife's ability to support herself, the more likely she is to leave an unhappy marriage. Partners who have been married before are more likely to become involved in subsequent divorce. Most divorces take place within the first few years of marriage—and the longer a marriage has lasted, the less likely it is to end in divorce (Carter and Glick, 1976; Goode, 1982; Fisher, 1987).

Works Cited

Carter, Hugh, and Paul C. Glick. 1976. *Marriage and Divorce: A Social and Economic Study.* Cambridge, Mass.: Harvard University Press.

Emery, Robert E., et al. 1984. "Divorce, children, and social policy," in Harold W. Stevenson and Alberta E. Siegal (eds.), *Child Development Research and Social Policy.* Chicago: Univ. of Chicago Press.

Fisher, Helen. 1987. "The four-year itch." *Natural History, 96,* pp. 22–23.
Goode, William J. 1982. *The Family.* 2nd ed. Englewood Cliffs, N.J.: Prentice-Hall.
Weiss, Robert S. 1975. *Marital Separation.* New York: Basic Books.

Vocabulary

predominantly (1)—most frequently

urban (1)—of the city

anonymous (1)—lacking individuality

irrational (2)—absurd; going against reason

complementary (3)—serving to complete each other

conclusive (4)—final; decisive

duration (4)—amount of time that something lasts

traumatic (5)—producing upsetting or painful and sometimes long-lasting emotional reaction

incompatibility (5)—inability to get along

ruptures (5)—breaks apart

IN YOUR JOURNAL

Write down at least three ideas from the Robertson article that were new or interesting to you.

A Closer Reading

1. In what ways is the courtship system a "marriage market," according to Robertson?

2. What does dating enable people to do in the United States that people may not be able to do in other parts of the world?

3. What "similar" characteristics do most people look for in their mate?

4. According to this article, what does the popular phrase "opposites attract" mean? Do you believe this to be true?

5. What are the personal characteristics that often lead to divorce?

6. What societal problems have developed because of the high divorce rate in the United States?

Drawing Your Own Conclusions

1. Judging from your own experience, are couples more likely to be successful if they are very similar, or if they complement each other?

2. What problems might people face if they marry outside their religion, race, or ethnic group? How can their family, friends, or society help them face these problems?

3. Why do divorcing women who have been solely housewives and mothers face more economic problems than women who have also worked for a living outside the home?

4. What types of problems in a couple's relationship often lead to divorce? What skills should people develop to help them deal with these problems?

Thinking about Writing

1. In paragraph 1, Robertson writes that the United States allows more freedom than any other society. What details does he provide to support his point?

2. In paragraph 2, Robertson defines the word "homogamy." What does he include in the definition? What is another example of homogamy that he does not include?

3. Robertson makes a distinction between social and psychological factors. What are examples of social factors? What are examples of psychological factors?

4. Reread the selection, looking for numbers. Where does Robertson use statistics? How do these statistics add evidence to Robertson's theories?

*　　*　　*

Suggestions for Writing

1. Why do college graduates tend to marry other college graduates? Is it important for both members of a couple to have similar levels of education? Take a position on this issue and support it with your own experiences, your observations, and your readings.

2. Why is the divorce rate in the United States the highest in the world? Before you begin, consider how our culture as a whole

differs from others around the world. In your answer, identify at least one social, psychological, and economic reason. Explain how these factors have led to a high divorce rate.

3. It is better for children to experience the divorce of their parents, or to remain in a home in which the parents do not get along? Take a position on this issue and write an essay in which you support your point of view with your own experience, your observations, and your readings.

4. Describe a movie, play, or novel in which a couple fall in love outside of traditional social lines. What happens to the couple? Are they able to resolve the differences? If so, how? If not, what keeps them from doing so? What did you learn from this story about relationships in general?

Collaborative Project

Write a one-page summary of the Robertson selection (see page 51 for suggestions about summary writing) in your own words. Share your summary with other members of the class. Discuss how you decided which were the important points and which were the less important ones. Compare your work with others. Would you change your summary now that you have seen other interpretations? If so, how?

Strategies for Revision

If you have written a persuasive essay in which you are trying to convince your reader to share your point of view, ask yourself the following questions:

- What is my point of view? Do I state it clearly in the beginning of the draft?
- For whom did I write my essay? What do my readers need to know about the topic? Did I provide this information?
- Do I provide enough evidence to support my point of view? Do I rely on more than one source or example?
- Is my evidence organized in a clear, easy-to-follow way?
- Is there a solid ending to the draft with a firm concluding statement?

Revise your essay, using your answers to these questions. Share your revision with a classmate.

IN YOUR JOURNAL

The idea of arranged marriage, in which your husband or wife is chosen for you, is still popular in many parts of the world. People who believe in arranged marriage argue that these marriages end in fewer divorces than do marriages based on love.

Before you read this selection, write down your opinion of arranged marriage. Would you want this to happen to you or not? What do you expect will happen in the following story about an arranged marriage?

Marriage

Marjorie Shostak

Marjorie Shostak teaches anthropology at Emory University in Atlanta and is an associate of the Peabody Museum of Archaeology and Ethnology at Harvard University. Her book *Nisa: The Life and Words of a !Kung Woman* (1981) is based on her two and a half years among the !Kung San of Botswana and her meeting with Nisa, a woman of this group. When they meet, Nisa is almost fifty years old, and she tells the anthropologist the story of her life. In this excerpt Nisa describes the circumstances of her marriage, which took place when she was about fifteen and just entering puberty.

Long ago, my parents traveled far, to a distant water hole. There   1
we met Old Kantla and his son Tashay, who had also come to live near the well. One day soon after we had arrived, I went with my friend Nukha to get water at the well. That's when Tashay saw me. He thought, "That woman . . . that's the young woman I'm going to marry." He called Nukha over to him and asked, "Nukha, that young woman, that beautiful young woman . . . what is her name?" Nukha told him, "Her name is Nisa." He said, "Mmm . . . that young woman . . . I'm going to tell my mother and father about her. I'm going to ask them if I can marry her."

Nukha came back and we finished filling the water containers. We   2
left and walked the long way back to our village. When Nukha saw my mother, she said, "Nisa and I were getting water and while we were there, some other people came to the well and began filling their water

containers. That's when a young man saw Nisa and said he would ask his parents to ask for her in marriage."

I didn't say anything. Because when you are a child and someone 3 wants to marry you, you don't talk. But when they first talked about it, my heart didn't agree. Later, I did agree, just a little; he was, after all, very handsome.

The next night there was a dance at our village. We were already 4 singing and dancing when Tashay and his family came. They joined us and we danced and sang into the night. I was sitting with Nukha when Tashay came over to me. He touched my hand. I said, "What? What is the matter with this person? What is he doing? This person . . . how come I was just sitting here and he came and took hold of me?" Nukha said, "That's your husband . . . your husband had taken hold of you. Is that not so?" I said, "Won't he take you? You're older. Let him marry you." But she said, "He's my uncle. I won't marry my uncle. Anyway, he, himself, wants to marry you."

Later his mother and father went to my mother and father. His 5 father said, "We came here and joined the dance, but now that the dancing is finished, I've come to speak to you, to Gau and Chuko. Give me your child, the one you both gave birth to. Give her to me and I will give her to my son. Yesterday, while he was at the well, he saw your child. When he returned, he told me that in the name of what he felt, I should today ask for her. Then I can give her to him. He said he wants to marry her."

My mother said, "Eh, but I didn't give birth to a woman. I gave birth 6 to a child. She doesn't think about marriage, she just doesn't think about the inside of a marriage hut." Then my father said, "Eh, it's true. The child I gave birth to is still a child. She doesn't think about her marriage hut. When she marries a man, she just drops him. Then she gets up, marries another, and drops him, too. She's already refused two men."

My father continued, "There is even another man, Dem, his hut 7 stands over there. He is also asking to marry her. Dem's first wife wants Nisa to sit beside her as a co-wife. She goes out and collects food for Nisa. When she comes back, she gives Nisa food to cook so Nisa can give it to her husband. But when the woman unties the ends of her kaross (woman's dress and pouch) and leaves it full of food beside Nisa, Nisa throws the food down, ruins it in the sand and kicks the kaross away. When I see that, I say that perhaps Nisa is not yet a woman."

Tashay's father answered, "I have listened to what you have said. 8 That, of course, is the way of a child; it is a child's custom to do that.

When she first marries, she stays with her husband for a while, then she refuses him. Then she goes to another. But one day, she stays with one man. That is also a child's way."

They talked about the marriage and agreed to it. I was in my aunt's   9
hut and couldn't see them, but I could hear their voices. Later, I went and joined them in my father's hut. When I got there, Tashay was looking at me. I sat down and he just kept looking at me.

When Tashay's mother saw me, she said, "Ohhh! How beautiful this   10
person is! You are certainly a young woman already. Why do they say that you don't want to get married?" Tashay said, "Yes, there she is. I want you to give me the one who just arrived."

The day of the wedding, everyone was there. All of Tashay's friends   11
were sitting around, laughing and laughing. His younger brother said, "Tashay, you're too old. Get out of the way so I can marry her. Give her to me." And his nephew said, "Uncle, you're already old. Now, let *me* marry her." They were all sitting around, talking like that. They all wanted me.

I went to my mother's hut and sat there. I was wearing lots of beads   12
and my hair was completely covered and full with ornaments.

That night there was another dance. We danced, and some people   13
fell asleep and others kept dancing. In the early morning, Tashay and his relatives went back to their camp; we went into our huts to sleep. When morning was late in the sky, they came back. They stayed around and then his parents said, "Because we are only staying a short while—tomorrow, let's start building the marriage hut."

The next day they started. There were lots of people there—Tashay's   14
mother, my mother, and my aunt worked on the hut; everyone else sat around, talking. Late in the day, the young men went and brought Tashay to the finished hut. They set him down beside it and stayed there with him, sitting around the fire.

I was still at my mother's hut. I heard them tell two of my friends to   15
go and bring me to the hut. I thought, "Oohh . . . I'll run away." When they came for me, they couldn't find me. They said, "Where did Nisa go? Did she run away? It's getting dark. Doesn't she know that things may bite and kill her?" My father said, "Go tell Nisa that if this is what she's going to do, I'll hit her and she won't run away again. What made her want to run away, anyway?"

I was already far off in the bush. They came looking for me. I heard them   16
calling, "Nisa . . . Nisa . . ." I sat down looking at the base of a tree. Then I head Nukha, "Nisa . . . Nisao . . . my friend . . . a hyena's out there . . . things will bite and kill you . . . come back . . . Nisa . . . Nisao . . ."

When Nukha finally saw me, I started to run. She ran after me, 17
chasing me and finally caught me. She called out to the others, "Hey!
Nisa's here! Everyone, come! Help me! Take Nisa, she's here!"

They came and brought me back. Then they laid me down inside the 18
hut. I cried and cried. People told me, "A man is not something that
kills you; he is someone who marries you, who becomes like your father
or your older brother. He kills animals and gives you things to eat. Even
tomorrow, while you are crying, Tashay may kill an animal. But when
he returns, he won't give you any meat; only he will eat. Beads, too. He
will get beads but he won't give them to you. Why are you so afraid of
your husband and what are you crying about?"

I listened and was quiet. Later, we went to sleep. Tashay lay down 19
beside the opening of the hut, near the fire and I lay down inside; he
thought I might try and run away again. He covered himself with a
blanket and slept.

While it was dark, I woke up. I sat up. I thought, "How am I going 20
to jump over him? How can I get out and go to my mother's hut to
sleep beside her?" I looked at him sleeping. Then came other thoughts,
other thoughts in the middle of the night, "Eh . . . this person has just
married me . . ." and I lay down again. But I kept thinking, "Why did
people give me this man in marriage? The older people say he is a good
person, yet . . ."

I lay there and didn't move. The rain came beating down. It fell 21
steadily and kept falling. Finally, I slept. Much later dawn broke.

In the morning, Tashay got up and sat by the fire. I was so fright- 22
ened I just lay there, waiting for him to leave. When he went to urinate,
I went and sat down inside my mother's hut.

That day, all his relatives came to our new hut—his mother, his 23
father, his brothers . . . everyone! They all came. They said, "Go tell
Nisa she should come and her in-laws will put the marriage oil on her.
Can you see her sitting over there? Why isn't she coming so we can put
the oil on her in her new hut?"

I refused to go. They kept calling for me until finally, my older 24
brother said, "Uhn uhn. Nisa, if you act like this, I'll hit you. Now, get
up and go over there. Sit over there so they can put the oil on you."

I still refused and just sat there. My older brother grabbed a switch 25
from a nearby tree and started coming toward me. I got up. I was afraid.
I followed him to where the others were sitting. Tashay's mother
rubbed the oil on me and my aunt rubbed it on Tashay.

Then they left and it was just Tashay and me. 26

Vocabulary

hut (6)—a little simple house built of straw, mud, or animal skins

ornaments (12)—things worn to decorate or adorn the body

hyena (16)—a wolflike animal that lives in parts of Africa and Asia and lives on carrion (flesh of dead animals)

switch (25)—a thin, flexible branch or stick used to hit someone

---

IN YOUR JOURNAL

Write a summary of the story of Nisa's marriage. Write down as many details as you can remember from Shostak's reporting of this. Look at the journal entry you wrote before reading this selection and see how successfully you predicted what the story would be about. Why did Nisa want to run away from the marriage arranged for her?

A Closer Reading

1. Where does Tashay see Nisa for the first time? What makes him think that he wants to marry her?

2. How does Tashay get permission to marry Nisa? What is the girl's role in the marriage arrangement?

3. What happens when Nisa does not want to marry Tashay?

4. In Nisa's society, when people get married do they live in the same community as the husband's family or the wife's?

5. What is the role of the man/the husband among the !Kung San?

Drawing Your Own Conclusions

1. Why does Tashay tell Nukha that he wants to marry Nisa?

2. Why do Tashay and his family come to the dance in Nisa's village?

3. Why does Nukha tell everyone where Nisa is hiding?

4. What is the role of Nisa's older brother in the family? Do you think he actually would have hit Nisa as he threatened to do?

5. Who has more power in the !Kung San society—the men or the women? What evidence in the story supports your answer?

6. "This story was told to me in the !Kung language by Nisa, an African woman of about fifty years of age, living in a remote corner of Botswana, on the northern fringe of the Kalahari desert. It was March 1971, the last month of my twenty-month field stay among the !Kung San."

   This statement comes from the introduction to Shostak's book *Nisa: The Life and Words of a !Kung Woman*. How do you think Shostak learned the !Kung language? How do you think her presence affected these people? What other aspects of Nisa's life would you expect to find in this book? What do anthropologists learn from living with cultures different from our own that could be helpful to us?

Thinking about Writing

1. Shostak's writing about Nisa is based on twenty-one taped interviews and hundreds of pages of typewritten transcripts of the tapes translated into English. Why do you think Shostak decided to tell the story from Nisa's point of view instead of writing it as a third-person narrative?

2. Shostak writes in her introduction that she arranged the stories in chronological order but that this is not the way that she was told the stories. Why do you think Shostak decided to arrange the stories in chronological order? How else can stories be arranged?

3. Shostak's study is anthropological. What do you think she focused on when she wrote about the !Kung people?

4. On what aspects of human experience do writers who are sociologists focus? You might want to reread the selections by Alvin Toffler (see page 103) or Sara Lawrence Lightfoot (see page 76). How are their selections different from this one?

5. This article and McAuliffe's selection (see page 183) refer to the !Kung San of Botswana. What similarities do you find in the themes they write about? Which do you prefer reading—the story of Nisa or the journalistic style of McAuliffe? Why?

*   *   *

Suggestions for Writing

1. Interview someone in your family and find out the story of that person's marriage. Find out about how the couple met, if they dated, if they were allowed to go out alone on dates, how they got engaged, what their actual wedding was like, and if their married life was what they expected it to be. Write the findings from your interview as a descriptive essay, a story using a form similar to Shostak's, or just a transcription of the interview.

2. If you know someone who had an experience with an arranged marriage, interview that person and find out the details. Did the couple meet before the wedding day? Did they date? Were they in love? Who decided on their marriage? Write an essay describing this arranged marriage. Reread the Esquivel story on page 244 for another perspective before you begin.

3. Write an essay in which you persuade your reader that marriages should be arranged. Support your point of view based on your observations, experiences, and readings.

4. Write an essay in which you persuade your reader that individuals should decide on their marriage partners for themselves. Support your point of view based on your observations, experiences, and readings.

5. Compare Nisa's marriage experience with another marriage experience, based on love, with which you are familiar. In your essay write about the similarities and the differences as you know them. (See page 74 for suggestions for comparing and contrasting.)

6. Write an essay in which you describe in detail a wedding that you have attended as a guest. Describe how the bride and groom were dressed and how their attendants were dressed, as well as the ceremony and where it took place. If there was a reception afterward, describe where it took place, what kind of food was served, the way people behaved, and any other aspects of the situation that you think would be interesting to your reader.

Strategies for Revision

When you have completed your first draft, reread a piece of your writing that you did at an earlier time. As you read it, examine your writing objectively as though it had been written by another writer.

What are its strong points? Where are its weak points? What do you like about your writing? What do you still want to change?

Then look at your new piece of writing. Now that you have thought about yourself as a writer, focus on the areas you looked at in your earlier piece of writing, thinking about the following questions:

- How has my writing improved? What specific changes do I observe?
- What still needs to be improved? Be as specific as possible.
- Do my ideas connect from paragraph to paragraph?
- Is it clear each time why I started a new paragraph?
- If I were advising a friend about this piece of writing, what suggestions would I make?

After you have asked yourself these questions and any others pertaining to your own writing, revise and rewrite in light of your own observations of your work. Share your revision with a classmate.

IN YOUR JOURNAL

The author of the next story describes his characters this way: "They were kids themselves, but they were crazy in love, this eighteen-year-old boy and his seventeen-year-old girl friend when they married. Not all that long afterwards they had a daughter."

After reading this description, write down what you think this story will be about.

Distance

Raymond Carver

Born in Oregon, Raymond Carver lived from 1938 to 1988. He was a writer of short stories, poems, and essays. His short story collections include *Will You Please Be Quiet, Please* (1976), *What We Talk About When We Talk About Love* (1981), *The Stories of Raymond Carver* (1985), *Cathedral* (1988), *No Heroics, Please: Uncollected Writings* (1992), and *Short Cuts: Selected Stories* (1993). His poetry collections include *This Water* (1985) and *Ultramarine* (1986). When being interviewed for *The Paris Review* (1983), Carver was asked why he never wrote a novel. He replied, "Nobody ever asked me to be a writer. But it *was* tough to stay alive and pay bills and put food on the table and at the same time to think of myself as a writer and to *learn* to write. After years of working crap jobs and raising kids and trying to write, I realized I needed to write things I could finish and be done with in a hurry. There was no way I could undertake a novel. . . ." "Distance," taken from *Fires* (1984)—a collection of Carver's stories, essays, and poems—is about the relationship of two newly married teenagers and their baby.

She's in Milan for Christmas and wants to know what it was like   1
when she was a kid. Always that on the rare occasions when he sees her.

Tell me, she says. Tell me what it was like then. She sips Strega,   2
waits, eyes him closely.

She is a cool, slim, attractive girl, a survivor from top to bottom.   3

That was a long time ago. That was twenty years ago, he says.   4
They're in his apartment on the Via Fabroni near the Cascina Gardens.

You can remember, she says. Go on, tell me.   5

What do you want to hear? he asks. What can I tell you? I could tell 6
you about something that happened when you were a baby. It involves
you, he says. But only in a minor way.

Tell me, she says. But first get us another drink, so you won't have to 7
interrupt half way through.

He comes back from the kitchen with drinks, settles into his chair, 8
begins.

They were kids themselves, but they were crazy in love, this 9
eighteen-year-old boy and his seventeen-year-old girl friend when they
married. Not all that long afterwards they had a daughter.

The baby came along in late November during a severe cold spell 10
that just happened to coincide with the peak of the waterfowl season in
that part of the country. The boy loved to hunt, you see, that's part of it.

The boy and girl, husband and wife now, father and mother, lived in 11
a three-room apartment under a dentist's office. Each night they cleaned
the upstairs office in exchange for their rent and utilities. In the summer
they were expected to maintain the lawn and the flowers, and in winter
the boy shoveled snow from the walks and spread rock salt on the
pavement. The two kids, I'm telling you, were very much in love. On
top of this they had great ambitions and they were wild dreamers. They
were always talking about the things they were going to do and the
places they were going to go.

He gets up from his chair and looks out the window for a minute 12
over the tile rooftops at the snow that falls steadily through the late
afternoon light.

Tell the story, she says. 13

The boy and girl slept in the bedroom, and the baby slept in a crib in 14
the living room. You see, the baby was about three weeks old at this
time and had only just begun to sleep through the night.

One Saturday night, after finishing his work upstairs, the boy went 15
into the dentist's private office, put his feet up on the desk, and called
Carl Sutherland, an old hunting and fishing friend of his father's.

Carl, he said when the man picked up the receiver. I'm a father. We 16
had a baby girl.

Congratulations, boy, Carl said. How is the wife? 17

She's fine, Carl. The baby's fine, too, the boy said. Everybody's fine. 18

That's good, Carl said. I'm glad to hear it. Well, you give my regards 19
to the wife. If you called about going hunting, I'll tell you something.
The geese are flying down there to beat the band. I don't think I've ever

seen so many of them and I've been going for years. I shot five today. Two this morning and three this afternoon. I'm going back in the morning and you come along if you want to.

I want to, the boy said. That's why I called.   20

You be here at five-thirty sharp then and we'll go, Carl said. Bring lots   21
of shells. We'll get some shooting in all right. I'll see you in the morning.

The boy liked Carl Sutherland. He'd been a friend of the boy's father,   22
who was dead now. After the father's death, maybe trying to replace a loss they both felt, the boy and Sutherland had started hunting together. Sutherland was a heavy-set, balding man who lived alone and was not given to casual talk. Once in a while, when they were together, the boy felt uncomfortable, wondered if he had said or done something wrong because he was not used to being around people who kept still for long periods of time. But when he did talk the older man was often opinionated, and frequently the boy didn't agree with the opinions. Yet the man had a toughness and woods-savvy about him that the boy liked and admired.

The boy hung up the telephone and went downstairs to tell the girl.   23
She watched while he laid out his things. Hunting coat, shell bag, boots, socks, hunting cap, long underwear, pump gun.

What time will you be back? the girl asked.   24

Probably around noon, he said. But maybe not until after five or six   25
o'clock. Is that too late?

It's fine, she said. We'll get along just fine. You go and have some   26
fun. You deserve it. Maybe tomorrow evening we'll dress Catherine up and go visit Sally.

Sure, that sounds like a good idea, he said. Let's plan on that.   27

Sally was the girl's sister. She was ten years older. The boy was a   28
little in love with her, just as he was a little in love with Betsy, who was another sister the girl had. He'd said to the girl, If we weren't married I could go for Sally.

What about Betsy? the girl said. I hate to admit it but I truly feel   29
she's better looking than Sally or me. What about her?

Betsy too, the boy said and laughed. But not in the same way I could   30
go for Sally. There's something about Sally you could fall for. No, I believe I'd prefer Sally over Betsy, if I had to make a choice.

But who do you really love? the girl asked. Who do you love most in   31
all the world? Who's your wife?

You're my wife, the boy said.   32

And will we always love each other? the girl asked, enormously   33
enjoying this conversation he could tell.

Always, the boy said. And we'll always be together. We're like the 34
Canada geese, he said, taking the first comparison that came to mind,
for they were often on his mind in those days. They only marry once.
They choose a mate early in life, and they stay together always. If one of
them dies or something, the other one will never remarry. It will live off
by itself somewhere, or even continue to live with the flock, but it will
stay single and alone amongst all the other geese.

That's sad, the girl said. It's sadder for it to live that way, I think, 35
alone but with all the others, than just to live off by itself somewhere.

It is sad, the boy said. But it's Nature. 36

Have you ever killed one of those marriages? she asked. You know 37
what I mean.

He nodded. He said, Two or three times I've shot a goose, then a 38
minute or two later I'd see another goose turn back from the rest and
begin to circle and call over the goose that lay on the ground.

Did you shoot it too? she asked with concern. 39

If I could, he answered. Sometimes I missed. 40

And it didn't bother you? she said. 41

Never, he said. You can't think about it when you're doing it. You 42
see, I love everything there is about geese. I love to just watch them
even when I'm not hunting them. But there are all kinds of contradictions in life. You can't think about the contradictions.

After dinner he turned up the furnace and helped her bathe the 43
baby. He marveled again at the infant who had half his features, the eyes
and mouth, and half the girl's, the chin and the nose. He powdered the
tiny body and then powdered in between the fingers and toes. He
watched the girl put the baby into its diaper and pajamas.

He emptied the bath into the shower basin and then he went up- 44
stairs. It was cold and overcast outside. His breath streamed in the air.
The grass, what there was of it, looked like canvas, stiff and gray under
the street light. Snow lay in piles beside the walk. A car went by and he
heard sand grinding under the tires. He let himself imagine what it
might be like tomorrow, geese milling in the air over his head, the gun
plunging against his shoulder.

Then he locked the door and went downstairs. 45

In bed they tried to read but both of them fell asleep, she first, 46
letting the magazine sink to the quilt. His eyes closed, but he roused
himself, checked the alarm, and turned off the lamp.

He woke to the baby's cries. The light was on out in the living 47
room. He could see the girl standing beside the crib rocking the baby in

her arms. In a minute she put the baby down, turned out the light and came back to bed.

It was two o'clock in the morning and the boy fell asleep once more.   48
The baby's cries woke him again. This time the girl continued to   49
sleep. The baby cried fitfully for a few minutes and stopped. The boy listened, then began to doze.

He opened his eyes. The living room light was burning. He sat up   50
and turned on the lamp.

I don't know what's wrong, the girl said, walking back and forth   51
with the baby. I've changed her and given her something more to eat. But she keeps crying. She won't stop crying. I'm so tired I'm afraid I might drop her.

You come back to bed, the boy said. I'll hold her for a while.   52

He got up and took the baby while the girl went to lie down.   53

Just rock her for a few minutes, the girl said from the bathroom.   54
Maybe she'll go back to sleep.

The boy sat on the sofa and held the baby. He jiggled it in his lap   55
until its eyes closed. His own eyes were near closing. He rose carefully and put the baby back in the crib.

It was fifteen minutes to four and he still had forty-five minutes that   56
he could sleep. He crawled into bed.

But a few minutes later the baby began to cry once more. This time   57
they both got up, and the boy swore.

For God's sake what's the matter with you? the girl said to him. May-   58
be she's sick or something. Maybe we shouldn't have given her the bath.

The boy picked up the baby. The baby kicked its feet and was quiet.   59
Look, the boy said, I really don't think there's anything wrong with her.

How do you know that? the girl said. Here, let me have her. I know   60
that I ought to give her something, but I don't know what I should give her.

After a few minutes had passed and the baby had not cried, the girl   61
put the baby down again. The boy and girl looked at the baby, and then they looked at each other as the baby opened its eyes and began to cry.

The girl took the baby. Baby, baby, she said with tears in her eyes.   62

Probably it's something on her stomach, the boy said.   63

The girl didn't answer. She went on rocking the baby in her arms,   64
paying no attention now to the boy.

The boy waited a minute longer then went to the kitchen and put on   65
water for coffee. He drew on his woolen underwear and buttoned up. Then he got into his clothes.

What are you doing? the girl said to him.   66

Going hunting, he said. 67

I don't think you should, she said. Maybe you could go later on in the 68
day if the baby is all right then. But I don't think you should go hunting
this morning. I don't want to be left alone with the baby crying like this.

Carl's planning on me going, the boy said. We've planned it. 69

I don't give a damn about what you and Carl have planned, she said. 70
And I don't give a damn about Carl, either. I don't even know the man.
I don't want you to go is all. I don't think you should even consider
wanting to go under the circumstances.

You've met Carl before, you know him, the boy said. What do you 71
mean you don't know him?

That's not the point and you know it, the girl said. The point is I 72
don't intend to be left alone with a sick baby.

Wait a minute, the boy said. You don't understand. 73

No, you don't understand, she said. I'm your wife. This is your 74
baby. She's sick or something. Look at her. Why is she crying? You can't
leave us to go hunting.

Don't get hysterical, he said. 75

I'm saying you can go hunting any time, she said. Something's 76
wrong with this baby and you want to leave us to go hunting.

She began to cry. She put the baby back in the crib, but the baby 77
started up again. The girl dried her eyes hastily on the sleeve of her
nightgown and picked the baby up once more.

The boy laced his boots slowly, put on his shirt, sweater, and his 78
coat. The kettle whistled on the stove in the kitchen.

You're going to have to choose, the girl said. Carl or us. I mean it, 79
you've got to choose.

What do you mean? the boy said. 80

You heard what I said, the girl answered. If you want a family you're 81
going to have to choose.

They stared at each other. Then the boy took his hunting gear and 82
went upstairs. He started the car, went around to the windows and,
making a job of it, scraped away the ice.

The temperature had dropped during the night, but the weather had 83
cleared so that the stars had come out. The stars gleamed in the sky over
his head. Driving, the boy looked out at the stars and was moved when
he considered their distance.

Carl's porchlight was on, his station wagon parked in the drive with 84
the motor idling. Carl came outside as the boy pulled to the curb. The
boy had decided.

You might want to park off the street, Carl said as the boy came up   85
the walk. I'm ready, just let me hit the lights. I feel like hell, I really do,
he went on. I thought maybe you had overslept so I just this minute
called your place. Your wife said you had left. I feel like hell.

It's okay, the boy said, trying to pick his words. He leaned his weight   86
on one leg and turned up his collar. He put his hands in his coat pockets.
She was already up, Carl. We've both been up for a while. I guess there's
something wrong with the baby. I don't know. The baby keeps crying, I
mean. The thing is, I guess I can't go this time, Carl.

You should have just stepped to the phone and called me, boy, Carl   87
said. It's okay. You know you didn't have to come over here to tell me.
What the hell, this hunting business you can take it or leave it. It's not
important. You want a cup of coffee?

I'd better get back, the boy said.   88

Well, I expect I'll go ahead then, Carl said. He looked at the boy.   89

The boy kept standing on the porch, not saying anything.   90

It's cleared up, Carl said. I don't look for much action this morning.   91
Probably you won't have missed anything anyway.

The boy nodded. I'll see you, Carl, he said.   92

So long, Carl said. Hey, don't let anybody ever tell you otherwise,   93
Carl said. You're a lucky boy and I mean that.

The boy started his car and waited. He watched Carl go through the   94
house and turn off all the lights. Then the boy put the car in gear and
pulled away from the curb.

The living room light was on, but the girl was asleep on the bed and   95
the baby was asleep beside her.

The boy took off his boots, pants and shirt. He was quiet about it.   96
In his socks and woolen underwear, he sat on the sofa and read the
morning paper.

Soon it began to turn light outside. The girl and the baby slept on.   97
After a while the boy went to the kitchen and began to fry bacon.

The girl came out in her robe a few minutes later and put her arms   98
around him without saying anything.

Hey, don't catch your robe on fire, the boy said. She was leaning   99
against him but touching the stove, too.

I'm sorry about earlier, she said. I don't know what got into me. I   100
don't know why I said those things.

It's all right, he said. Here, let me get this bacon.   101

I didn't mean to snap like that, she said. It was awful.   102

It was my fault, he said. How's Catherine?   103

She's fine now. I don't know what was the matter with her earlier. I changed her again after you left, and then she was fine. She was just fine and she went right off to sleep. I don't know what it was. Don't be mad with us. 104

The boy laughed. I'm not mad with you. Don't be silly, he said. Here, let me do something with this pan. 105

You sit down, the girl said. I'll fix this breakfast. How does a waffle sound with this bacon? 106

Sounds great, he said. I'm starved. 107

She took the bacon out of the pan and then she made waffle batter. He sat at the table, relaxed now, and watched her move around the kitchen. 108

She left to close their bedroom door. In the living room she put on a record that they both liked. 109

We don't want to wake that one up again, the girl said. 110

That's for sure, the boy said and laughed. 111

She put a plate in front of him with bacon, a fried egg, and a waffle. She put another plate on the table for herself. It's ready, she said. 112

It looks swell, he said. He spread butter and poured syrup over the waffle. But as he started to cut into the waffle, he turned the plate into his lap. 113

I don't believe it, he said, jumping up from the table. 114

The girl looked at him and then at the expression on his face. She began to laugh. 115

If you could see yourself in the mirror, she said. She kept laughing. 116

He looked down at the syrup that covered the front of his woolen underwear, at the pieces of waffle, bacon, and egg that clung to the syrup. He began to laugh. 117

I was starved, he said, shaking his head. 118

You were starved, she said, laughing. 119

He peeled off the woolen underwear and threw it at the bathroom door. Then he opened his arms and she moved into them. 120

We won't fight any more, she said. It's not worth it, is it? 121

That's right, he said. 122

We won't fight any more, she said. 123

The boy said, We won't. Then he kissed her. 124

He gets up from his chair and refills their glasses. 125

That's it, he says. End of story. I admit it's not much of one. 126

I was interested, she says. It was very interesting if you want to know. But what happened? she says. I mean later. 127

He shrugs and carries his drink over to the window. It's dark now but still snowing. 128

Things change, he says. I don't know how they do. But they do   129
without your realizing it or wanting them to.

Yes, that's true, only—but she does not finish what she started.   130

She drops the subject then. In the window's reflection he sees her   131
study her nails. Then she raises her head. Speaking brightly, she asks if
he is going to show her the city, after all.

He says, Put your boots on and let's go.   132

But he stays by the window, remembering that life. They had   133
laughed. They had leaned on each other and laughed until the tears had
come, while everything else—the cold and where he'd go in it—was
outside, for a while anyway.

Vocabulary

coincide (10)—to occur at the same time

woods-savvy (22)—slang expression for knowing a lot about the woods or the forest

contradictions (42)—situation or statements in opposition to each other

---

IN YOUR JOURNAL

Carver described two relationships in his story—one between a
father and daughter and the other between two teenage newlyweds.
Write your response to this story in your journal. How did it make you
feel? Did you care about the people in the story? What did the ending of
the story mean to you?

A Closer Reading

1. What evidence in the story can you find of how often the father
   and daughter see each other?

2. Using evidence from the story, describe the lifestyle of the teenage couple.

3. What indications in the text convince you that the teenagers are
   in love?

4. What is Carl's role in the boy's life? What is Carl's role in the story?

Drawing Your Own Conclusions

1. Why does the daughter ask her father to tell her the story? Do you think she has heard this story before? If so, why does she want to hear it again?

2. Why does the boy tell the story about killing the geese? And why does the girl ask him whether he has "killed one of those marriages"?

3. Why does the boy leave his wife alone with the crying baby? Why does he come back?

4. What happens to the young couple? In the end the father says to his daughter, "Things change." What does this response mean to you as a reader?

5. Why is the story entitled "Distance"?

Thinking about Writing

1. At what point in the story do you realize that the two people speaking are father and daughter? What other possible relationships could they have had? Why do you think Carver waits to let the reader know the relationship?

2. Carver does not describe the young couple. As you read the story, did you picture them in your mind? If so, what did they look like to you? Do you prefer stories in which there is more description?

3. In this story, Carver shifts time periods. What differences in the writing itself distinguish between the two time periods? Read the Noda selection on page 31, the Modupe story on page 20, and the Wideman story on page 68. How do these authors signal time shifts to their readers?

4. Why do you think Carver does not name the boy and girl? Does this technique distance you from them? In "The Father from China" (see page 85), Maxine Hong Kingston does not name the wife. Why might writers decide to do this in a story?

*   *   *

Suggestions for Writing

1. Write a summary of this story so that someone who has never read it will know what it is about. (See page 51 for information about writing a summary.)

2. Teenagers are not ready to become parents; they are still children themselves. Write an essay in which you take this position. Use the story to support your position and add examples and observations based on your life experience.

3. Younger parents are better than older ones. They are closer in age and therefore better able to understand their children's needs. Write an essay in which you take this position. Support your position with examples and observations from what you have read and experienced.

4. Rewrite the story so it is the girl who plans to go to the movies with her sister while the boy stays home with the crying baby. What happens when the girl comes home?

5. If you know a couple who married when they were teenagers, talk to them about their experiences. Some questions you could ask them include: What were the best parts and the worst parts about getting married at such a young age? How did the two resolve their problems? Are they still together? Would they advise another young couple to get married at that age? Then write an essay in which you describe this couple, their experience, and their advice.

Strategies for Revision

1. If you have written a summary of this story, ask yourself the questions that appear on page 52.

2. If you have written an essay or a story, reread the Carver story, paying attention to his use of detail and simple description. Then read what you have written out loud. Slowly and carefully, read only the actual words that you have written on the paper.

   As you read, make a small check every time you stop or hesitate. When you finish, go back and reread the draft, looking closely at the check marks. Ask yourself the following questions:

   - Is part of an idea missing?
   - Is a word missing? (We may not notice this until we read the writing out loud word by word.)
   - Does each idea connect with the ideas that come before and after?

- Is there a reason for each new paragraph?
- Are there sufficient details to support your point of view?
- Are there sufficient details to make each character unique and real?

Revise what you have written, keeping the answers to these questions in mind. Share your revision with another class member.

IN YOUR JOURNAL

Write in your journal about a problem that you faced with a family member, close friend, or boyfriend/girlfriend. What was the problem? How did you handle it?

Intimacy: The Art of Working Out Your Relationships

Lori H. Gordon

Lori H. Gordon, Ph.D., is a psychotherapist who works at helping couples improve their communication and teaching them how to express their feelings to resolve conflicts. This excerpt is from her article that appeared in the September/October 1993 issue of *Psychology Today*. She outlines the typical problems that couples face and makes suggestions for dealing with these problems.

Confusion. Hurt. Silence. Missed opportunity. It is one of the iro-   1
nies of modern life that many couples today are living together as complete strangers. Or worse, in great unhappiness. The data on divorce lead us to conclude that intimate relationships have been falling apart for the last 20 years or so. The truth is that couples have never learned reliably how to sustain pleasure in intimate relationships. The difference is it never mattered so much before.

Here at the close of the 20th century we have the luxury of living in   2
splendid isolation. Unlike in more "primitive" cultures, most Americans no longer live as part of a large family or community where we develop a sense of comfort and safety, a network of people to confide in, to feel at home with. This, I have come to believe, is what has drawn many people into cults—the need to feel part of a bonded community, where there is a sense of being at home emotionally as well as physically. Our culture provides for meeting all other needs, especially the need for autonomy, but not for intimacy. Within this framework, couples today must provide for each other more of the emotional needs that a larger community used to furnish.

Compounding the wide-scale deprivation of intimacy we actually   3
experience, our cultural talent for commercialization has separated out

sex from intimacy. In fact, intimacy involves both emotional and physical closeness and openness. But we wind up confusing the two and end up feeling betrayed or used when, as often happens, we fail to satisfy our need for closeness in sex.

Shifts in our general views about what makes life worth living have **4** also contributed to a new demand for intimacy. For many generations the answer lay in a productive life of work and service in which the reward of happiness would be ours, in Heaven. That belief has broken down. People want happiness here and now. And they want it most in their intimate relationships.

Here, it's clear, we are unlikely to find it easily. Couples today are **5** struggling with something new—to build relationships based on genuine feelings of equality. As a result, we are without role models for the very relationships we need. And rare were the parents who modeled intimacy for us; most were too busy struggling with survival requirements. Yet the quality of our closest relationships is often what gives life its primary meaning.

Intimacy, I have come to believe, is not just a psychological fad, a **6** rallying cry of contemporary couples. It is based on a deep biological need. Shortly after I began my career as a family therapist I was working in a residential treatment center where troubled teenage boys were sent by the courts. Through my work I began to discover what had been missing for these kids: They needed support and affection, the opportunity to express the range and intensity of their emotions. It was remarkable to discover their depth of need, their depth of pain over the lack of empathy from significant people in their lives.

It is only in the last 20 years that we recognize that infants need to **7** be held and touched. We know that they cannot grow—they literally fail to thrive—unless they experience physical and emotional closeness with another human being. What we often don't realize is that that need for connection never goes away. It goes on throughout life. And in its absence, symptoms develop—from the angry acting out of the adolescent boys I saw, to depression, addiction, and illness. In fact, researchers are just at the very beginning of understanding the relationship of widespread depression among women to problems in their marriages.

When I brought the boys together with their families, through **8** processes I had not learned about in graduate school, it transformed the therapy. There was change. For the adolescent boys, their problems were typically rooted in the often-troubled relationships between their parents. They lacked the nurturing environment they needed for healthy growth. What I realized was that to help the children I first had to help their parents. So I began to shift my focus to adults.

From my work in closely observing the interactions of hundreds of couples, I have come to recognize that most of what goes wrong in a relationship stems from hurt feelings. The disappointment couples experience is based on misunderstanding and misperception. We choose a partner hoping for a source of affection, love, and support, and, more than ever, a best friend. Finding such a partner is a wonderful and ecstatic experience—the stage of illusion in relationships, it has been called.   9

To use this conceit, there then sets in the state of disillusion. We somehow don't get all that we had hoped for. He didn't do it just right. She didn't welcome you home; she was too busy with something else; maybe she didn't even look up. But we don't have the skills to work out the disappointments that occur. The disappointments big and little then determine the future course of the relationship.   10

If first there is illusion, and then disillusion, what follows is confusion. There is a great deal of unhappiness as each partner struggles to get the relationship to be what each of them needs or wants it to be. One partner will be telling the other what to do. One may be placating—in the expectation that he or she will eventually be rewarded by the other. Each partner uses his or her own familiar personal communication style.   11

Over the disappointment, the partners erect defenses against each other. They become guarded with each other. They stop confiding in each other. They wall off parts of themselves and withdraw emotionally from the relationship, often into other activities—or other relationships. They can't talk without blaming, so they stop listening. They may be afraid that the relationship will never change but may not even know what they are afraid of. There is so much chaos that there is usually despair and depression. One partner may actually leave. Both may decide to stay with it but can't function. They live together in an emotional divorce.   12

Love is a feeling. Marriage, on the other hand, is a contract—an invisible contract. Both partners bring to it expectations about what they want and don't want, what they're willing to give and not willing to give. Most often, those are out of awareness. Most marriage partners don't even know they expected something until they realize that they're not getting it.   13

The past is very much present in all relationships. All expectations in 14 relationships are conditioned by our previous experience. It may simply be the nature of learning, but things that happen in the present are assimilated by means of what has happened in the past. This is especially true of our emotions: every time we have an experience in the present we also are experiencing it in the past. Emotional memory exists outside of time. It is obvious that two partners are conditioned by two different pasts. But inside the relationship it is less obvious. And that leads to all kinds of misunderstanding, disagreement, disappointment, and anger that things are not going exactly as expected.

The upshot is statements like "I can't understand women," "who 15 knows what a woman wants," and "you can never please a man." All of the classic complaints reflect hidden expectations that have never surfaced to the point where they could be discussed, examined, kept, or discarded.

To add insult to injury, when one partner is upset, the other often 16 compounds it unintentionally. When, for example, a woman is unhappy, men often feel they are expected to charge out and fix something. But what she really wants is for her partner to put his arms around her and hold her, to soothe her, to say simply, "I'm sorry you feel bad." It is a simple and basic longing. But instead of moving toward her, he moves away. And if when you are upset you don't get what you want from the person you are closest to, then you are not going to feel loved. Men, too, I hasten to say, have the same basic need. But they erect defenses against it for fear it will return them to a state of helplessness such as they experienced as children.

At the heart of intimacy, then, is empathy, understanding, and com- 17 passion; these are the humanizing feelings. It is bad enough that they are in short supply among distressed couples. Yet I have observed that certain careers pose substantial roadblocks to intimacy because the training involves education not in humanization but in dehumanization. At the top of the list is law. Built primarily on the adversarial process, it actively discourages understanding and compassion in favor of destroying an opponent. Careers in the military and in engineering also are dismissive of feelings and emotions. Men and women who bring what they learn from such work into a love relationship may find that it can't survive.

An understanding of intimacy has its own logic. But it runs counter 18 to conventional wisdom and most brands of psychology. They hold that to understand the nature of, and to improve, relationships, the proper place to start is the self. The thinking is that you need to understand yourself before you can confide in a partner. But I have found just the opposite to be true.

An exploration of the self is indeed absolutely essential to attaining   19 or rebuilding a sense of intimacy. Most of the disappointments that drive our actions and reactions in relationships are constructed with expectations that are not only hidden from our partners but also ourselves. From our families of origin and past relationship experiences, we acquire systems of belief that direct our behavior outside of our own awareness. It is not possible to change a relationship without bringing this belief system into our awareness.

But a man or a woman exploring their personal history experiences   20 some powerful feelings that, in the absence of a partner to talk to, may make one feel worse rather than better. So the very first step a couple must take to rebuild intimacy is to learn to express their own thoughts and feelings and carefully listen to each other. A partner who knows how to listen to you can then be on hand when you open up your past.

Exploration of the self is an activity often relegated to psychother-   21 apy; in that case a psychotherapist knows how to listen with empathy. But that is not necessarily the only way and at best is a luxury affordable only by a few. It is not only possible but desirable for couples of all economic strata to choose to confide in each other and build a relationship with a life partner rather than with a paid confidant. Both partners have an ongoing need to open up the past as well as share the present. But there are skills that have to be learned so that such interaction can be safe. Both partners need to learn how to listen without judging or giving unwanted advice. Disappointment in a partner's ability to hear is what often sends people to a psychotherapist in the first place.

All of us bring to our intimate relationships certain expectations   22 that we have of no one else. On the positive side they usually involve undivided attention—words and gestures of love and caring, loyalty, constancy, sex, companionship, agreement, encouragement, friendship, fidelity, honesty, trust, respect, and acceptance. We are all too alert to the possibility that we will instead find their exact opposites.

If we are not aware of our own expectations (and how they are   23 affected by our history), there is no hope of expressing them to a partner so that he or she has a shot at meeting them. More often than not, we engage instead in mind reading.

Mind reading is often related to a past disappointing relationship   24
experience. We tend to expect what we previously had the opportunity
to learn; we make assumptions based on our history. And when in
personal history there are people or situations that were the source of
heartache, resentment, or anxiety, then any action by a partner in the
present that is similar in some way often serves as a reminder—and
triggers an intense emotional reaction. I call this "emotional allergy." As
with other forms of prior sensitization, the result tends to be an explosive reaction—withdrawal, counterattack—and it is typically incomprehensible to a current partner.

If I had to summarize how to change the hidden expectations that   25
work to distort a relationship, I would boil it all down to a few basic
rules:

• If you expect a partner to understand what you need, then you   26
have to tell him or her. That of course means you have to figure out for
yourself what you really need.

• You cannot expect your partner to be sensitive and understand   27
exactly how you feel about something unless you're able to communicate to him or her how you feel in the first place.

• If you don't understand or like what your partner is doing, ask   28
about it and why he or she is doing it. And vice versa. Explore. Talk.
Don't assume.

Expressing your feelings about a given situation and asking for your   29
partner's honesty in return is the most significant way to discover truth
in your relationship. Instead, most communication between intimates is
nonverbal and leans heavily on mind reading. The only thing you have
to go on is your own internal information, which could easily be
skewed by any number of factors. This is also why genuine responses
are so important. Telling your partner what you think he or she wants
to hear, instead of what is really going on, complicates and postpones a
useful solution to the problem.

Confiding is much more than being able to reveal yourself to another.   30
It is knowing with absolute certainty that what you think and feel is being
heard and understood by your partner. Instead, we tend to be passive
listeners, picking up only those messages that have a direct bearing on
ourselves, rather than listening for how things are for our partner.

Listening with empathy is a learned skill. It has two crucial ingredi-   31
ents: undivided attention and feeling what your partner feels. Never
assume that you know something unless it is clearly stated by your

partner. And you need to understand fully what your partner's thoughts and feelings mean to him or her. Instead of focusing on the effects of your partner's words on you, pay attention instead to your partner's emotions, facial expression, and levels of tension. The single biggest barrier to such empathic listening is our self-interest and self-protective mechanisms. We anticipate and fill in the blanks. One of the simple truths of relationships is that often enough, all we need to do to resolve a problem is to listen to our partner—not just passively listen but truly hear what is in the mind and in the heart.

What more often happens is that, when we experience threats to our   32
self-esteem or feel stressed, we resort to styles of communication that usually lead to more of a problem than the problem itself. The styles of communication that we resort to during stress then often prevent real contact from happening. If your partner tends to be a blamer, you will distance yourself. You develop a rational style of relating, but no feelings are ever dealt with. Not only is no love experienced, but at the emotional level nothing can get resolved.

Most people tend to react to stress with one or more of four commu-   33
nication styles:

• *Placating.* The placater is ingratiating, eager to please, apologetic,   34
and a "yes" man or woman. The placater says things like "whatever you want" or "never mind about me, it's okay." It's a case of peace at any price. The price, for the placater is worthlessness. Because the placater has difficulty expressing anger and holds so many feelings inside, he or she tends toward depression and, as studies show, may be prone to illness. Placaters need to know it is okay to express anger.

• *Blaming.* The blamer is a fault-finder who criticizes relentlessly and   35
speaks in generalizations: "You never do anything right." "You're just like your mother/father." Inside, the blamer feels unworthy or unlovable, angry at the anticipation he or she will not be getting what is wanted. Given a problem, the best defense is a good offense. The blamer is unable to deal with or express pain or fear. Blamers need to be able to speak on their own behalf without indicting others in the process.

• *Computing.* The computer is super reasonable, calm and collected,   36
never admits mistakes, and expects people to conform and perform. The computer says things like, "Upset? I'm not upset. Why do you say I'm upset?" Afraid of emotion, he or she prefers facts and statistics. "I don't reveal my emotions and I'm not interested in anyone else's." Computers need someone to ask how they feel about specific things.

• *Distracting.* The distractor resorts to irrelevancies under stress, 37
avoids direct eye contact and direct answers. Quick to change the subject, he or she will say, "What problem? Let's have Sam and Bridget
over." Confronting the problem might lead to a fight, which could be
dangerous. Distractors need to know that they are safe, not helpless,
that problems can be solved and conflicts resolved.

Each style is a unique response to pain, anger, or fear, which keeps 38
us from understanding each other. Knowing that, the next time you
find yourself resorting to blame, you can conclude there is something
painful or scary bothering you and try to figure out what it is. If it's
your partner who is blaming, you can conclude he or she is possibly not
intending to be aggressive or mean but probably afraid of some development. What's needed is to find a way to make it safe to talk about the
worry; find out what is bothering him or her.

How, then, can you say what is bothering you, or express what you 39
really need, in a way that your partner can hear it, so that your message
can be understood? This is a basic step in building the relationship you
want.

Vocabulary

autonomy (2)—independence;
condition of existing without
being controlled by others

empathy (6)—an ability to share
in someone else's feelings or
emotions

nurturing (8)—nourishing or
caring for

ecstatic (9)—extremely delighted

conceit (10)—an idea, thought,
or concept

placating (11)—stopping someone from being angry by
giving in

chaos (12)—extreme confusion
or disorder

assimilated (14)—taken in by the
mind and completely understood

soothe (16)—to calm or comfort

hasten (16)—to be quick

adversarial (17)—functioning as
an enemy or opponent

confidant (21)—a close, trusted
friend

fidelity (22)—faithfulness

skewed (29)—distorted; not symmetrical

relentlessly (35)—persistently;
without stopping

IN YOUR JOURNAL

Look at the problem you wrote about in your first journal entry. Consider Gordon's suggestions and write about ways that you could have dealt with the problem in a more effective and productive way.

A Closer Reading

1. What are the differences between sex and intimacy? What happens when people confuse the two?

2. What evidence does Gordon provide to support her idea that humans of both sexes and all ages need intimacy?

3. What explanations does Gordon give of the three stages—illusion, disillusion, and confusion—that occur in many relationships?

4. What are the basic rules that Gordon suggests for successful relationships? What are the problems she describes that destroy many relationships?

Drawing Your Own Conclusions

1. Even though many people think that having an intimate relationship is natural and instinctual, Gordon suggests that some skills need to be learned. What are these skills? Why do they need to be learned?

2. How does the high divorce rate relate to the problems described in the Gordon article?

3. How do people respond to stress? What are the four "communication styles"? Why are they often destructive? Where do these styles come from? How can they be changed?

4. What problems with intimacy did you find the couple in Carver's story, "Distance" (see page 266), to be suffering from? What could that couple have done to deal with their problems in a better way, one that might have prevented them from drifting apart? What problems does the couple in the Baxter story, "Lake Stephen" (see page 212), have that they should address to maintain their intimate relationship?

Thinking about Writing

1. Gordon begins this article with a series of one-word sentences. They are not complete sentences. How did this affect you as a reader? Revise the beginning, making these words into complete sentences. Read both versions. Which do you prefer? Why?

2. In paragraph 2, notice how Gordon makes a statement and then explains it: "This, I have come to believe, is what has drawn many people into cults—the need to feel part of a bonded community, where there is a sense of being at home emotionally as well as physically." Find the other similar structures in this selection.

3. Find the quotations in the selection. Where are they located? What is their purpose?

4. Gordon makes lists of categories at several points in the selection. Find these lists. How do they affect you as a reader? This technique, often used in textbooks to highlight important material, is not usually used in expository essays. Why does she do this?

*   *   *

Suggestions for Writing

1. Write a one-page summary of this article. Reread the information on page 51 on writing a summary. Discuss your summaries with other class members. How did you decide what should be included and what should be excluded?

2. "At the heart of intimacy, then, is empathy, understanding and compassion," writes Lori H. Gordon. Write an essay in which you define these three concepts and explain the difference between them using your own experiences, observations, and readings.

3. Gordon writes that the past is very much present in all relationships. Write an essay in which you describe how a past event has caused someone to make a desicion or take an action. Reread some of the following selections for ideas: Viramontes (page 5), Modupe (page 20), Noda (page 31), Wideman (page 68), Lightfoot (page 76), Kingston (page 85), Carver (page 266). What did the person(s) learn from their actions?

4. What are the three most important skills that a person needs in order to develop and maintain a good intimate relationship with

another person? Refer to the Gordon article for ideas. In your essay, explain what these skills are and why you have chosen them. Give examples of each. Explain why each is necessary to a successful intimate relationship.

Strategies for Revision

Gordon writes, "Listening with empathy is a learned skill. It has two crucial ingredients: undivided attention and feeling what your partner feels." Practice this skill by discussing your draft with a classmate.

Listen with undivided attention while your classmate reads her or his essay. Once the person has finished reading, discuss the essay focusing on the following:

- What ideas, words, or sentences do I like?
- What ideas stood out in my mind as I listened?
- What do I want to know more about?
- What did I learn from this essay?

Next, read your own essay to your classmate, who will be giving you the same undivided attention. Discuss the same questions. Revise your essay basing your changes on your discussion. Share your revisions with the same classmate.

Tracy Brooks wrote this essay in response to suggestion 1 from the Suggestions for Writing that follow the Shostak essay: If you know someone who had an experience with an arranged marriage, interview that person and find out the details. Did the couple meet before the wedding day? Did they date? Were they in love? Who decided on their marriage? Write an essay describing this arranged marriage. Reread the Esquivel story on page 244 for another perspective.

Marriage Traditions in the Indian Culture

Tracy Brooks

Family ties have great importance in India. Indians regard marriage as more of a relationship between two families than between two persons. Young Indians generally are not allowed to have dates, and parents arrange most of the marriages. However, many young people have the right to reject an arrangement made by the parents.   1

I have had the pleasure of interviewing a young woman by the name of Kanchan Mohindra. Kanchan is a twin of 18 years who was born in India and at the age of four her parents decided to come to America. Kanchan says she finds it very hard trying to follow Indian customs living in America because growing up in an Indian household is a lot different from growing up in the average American household. For example, many Indian households include not only parents and children, but also the sons' wives and their children.   2

Kanchan feels Indians are stricter when it comes to dating or going out in general. As she stated in our interview, "Dating is not considered normal; girls who date wind up getting a bad reputation in the Indian community." Kanchan told me that neither she nor her sister are allowed to date because her father is very overprotective, but she feels it is because he doesn't trust her. One night when she went out with her friends, she got home a little late and when her father found out that boys had gone along, he forbade her from ever going out at night again. He said, "Whatever you can do at night, you can do in the day as well." Now her father hardly lets her go out in the day with her friends because he says he doesn't want anything to happen to her and he says he is doing this because he loves her.   3

She feels he should trust her to make the right decisions because he raised her that way. She said some girls disobey their parents and date people behind their backs, but she could never do that to them because she has too much respect for them and besides they give her everything she needs.

Since her senior year in high school, Kanchan's parents have been   4 trying to find suitable mates for their daughters to marry. "My parents are always bringing me pictures of well-educated men from my country who have seen my pictures and heard things about me. They would like to marry me, but they are all skinny and ugly," says Kanchan. She feels she is too young to get married and would like to have a career first. As she said, "I would like to be a doctor so I can help people; that is my goal in life. Not to just get married and have a lot of kids. Don't get me wrong, I would like that too, but just not now."

Because she is a child of an arranged marriage, I asked Kanchan   5 what her views were on arranged marriages. She told me that she strongly believes that her parents love each other very much but they had to grow to love each other after they were married, so they really had no choice but to love one another. Kanchan told me that she believes that there is such a thing as true love and she would like to find it. She would like to be the one who finds her own husband and falls in love with him for all the qualities he possesses. She wants to get to know him and love him for who he is and not only for the education that he has had. Kanchan said she is also scared to have an arranged marriage because some guys just want to get married so they can get their green card, but most Indian men have been known to stick by their wives.

Kanchan told me in average arranged marriages, pictures of differ-   6 ent potential mates are brought to the individuals and they are allowed to choose whether or not they would like to meet these people. Additional information is sent with the pictures as well, such as the name, age, family background, and educational status. Sometimes the woman may have a dowry to offer. If they both find interest in one another, a meeting between the families is arranged where they talk to one another in private as well as with the families. This is where they decide whether or not they would like to marry. Sometimes if a person keeps refusing to get married, the parents will threaten them saying, "I would like to see you get married before I die." If the parents are sickly, this scares them into marrying someone just to make their parents happy.

Also in India, they believe in child marriages. Some marriages are arranged from as early as a year of age, and when the children are maybe about fifteen years old, they must get married. If they do not, their family is shunned in the Indian community and their family loses their respect. There are also some parts of India where the people of other cities are not allowed to marry.

Respect is highly important in the Indian community. A family's reputation is most important to them. This is why when Kanchan's twin sister told her father that she wanted to be an Indian model, he told her no because most Indian models have to sleep with a lot of different people to work their way up to the top to become famous. If she did it, her whole family would be looked down upon and neither daughter would be worthy of a good man's hand in marriage.

Kanchan says she finds it hard to live this way. She cannot tell her parents her true feelings about dating and marriage, but that is why she is going to school, to better herself so she can have the life she wants and deserves.

Questions to Think About

1. What questions do you think Tracy Brooks asked Kanchan?
2. What is the most interesting information you discovered from reading this essay?
3. What information would you still like to know?
4. What is the purpose of this essay? Is Brooks trying to convince her readers to change their points of view in any way?

MAKING CONNECTIONS

The World of Intimacy: *Connecting with Another Person*

1. Write an essay in which you choose one piece of writing that made you think about intimacy and relationships in a new way. Use quotations and paraphrases to explain what you learned from the piece of writing. Explain how reading it affected you.

2. Write an essay in which you explain how culture can affect a person's attitude toward intimacy and marriage. Review the selections in this unit. Think about your own cultural background. What cultures are represented in this unit? What attitudes toward intimacy and marriage do the parents have in these cultures? What attitudes toward these do the children have? What role does the larger family play in assisting young couples and their children?

3. Write an essay in which you compare Mama Elena (see Laura Esquivel's story on page 244), the couple in Raymond Carver's story (see page 266), and Nisa's views (see Marjorie Shostak's selection on page 258) toward marriage. Before you begin to write, review each of the selections so you can better understand their points of view. What ideas do you think they would have in common? What ideas would you expect to be different?

4. Imagine that Ian Robertson and Lori H. Gordon met to write a joint article. Reread each of their selections and, using quotations and paraphrases, write an article that expresses both of their most important ideas about marriage and intimacy.

5. Write an essay in which you explain which two authors from this unit have the most in common in relation to their points of view and their ideas. Which two authors have the least in common? Support your point of view by referring to specific words and phrases from their writing.

6. Write an introduction to this unit in which you tell other students which piece of writing is the most interesting, the most informative, or the best written. Using quotations from the selection, convince a potential reader to choose this particular piece of writing to read.

6

THE
INTERDEPENDENT
WORLD

Taking Action Together

Our world is often violent and filled with cruelty, yet frequently the response of many people to this is apathy. In this unit, we will respond to this charge of apathy and examine not only the problems but also some of the ways people can work together to solve the problems and conflicts of living.

"Apathy is dead," begins the essay by Bill Clinton written just weeks after his inauguration as the president of our country. In "National Service—Now," President Clinton advocates passage of his program of national service in exchange for tuition benefits for college students. Clinton believes that if young adults get involved in making the United States a better place, they will also learn to respect themselves more and find a purpose for their lives.

David Gelman takes a less optimistic view of our world in his essay, "The Violence in Our Heads." Gelman suggests that the media promotes violence in its images and stories because it knows violence will sell even though it also knows that violence hurts. Gelman would like the media to begin to take more responsibility for the message it is sending to us.

In "Moving Toward Independence," Geeta Dardick describes her relationship with her physically disabled husband and the problems they have had to face in our largely insensitive society. Dardick and her husband take political action. Even after legislation is passed, ensuring rights for disabled people, they find they must continue their activism to make sure that our society becomes more accessible for disabled people.

Physician Abigail Zuger describes her long-term patient-doctor relationship with an HIV-positive woman. "The Long Goodbye" tells of the effect on the patient's life of taking determined action.

Although personal actions are critical, sometimes institutions have to take actions as well. In "Care and Feeding of Commuters," Perry Garfinkel describes actions taken by colleges across the country to integrate commuter students better into college activities. Although at present there are more commuter than dormitory students, until recently colleges have done little to incorporate commuters' needs into college planning.

Judith Ortiz Cofer's essay, "The Paterson Public Library," recalls both the pleasures of visiting the library and the experience of racial conflict in her urban neighborhood. The first step in change is an awareness of the pervasiveness of racism and discrimination in our society and its public institutions and of the effect of bigotry on the children of our country.

294

This unit ends with a student essay written by Natividad Baez in which she researches the national service program put forth in President Clinton's essay. Baez uses interviews and readings to broaden her understanding of this program.

*   *   *

Think about the following questions before reading the selections in unit:

1. Is there one social problem that has affected you personally? How? Why?

2. What change would you like to see in the way society responds to this problem?

3. Have you had an experience in which you worked with others to do something about a social problem? What was the result?

IN YOUR JOURNAL

Write about any experience you had serving as a volunteer. What kind of work did you do? Why did you do it? How did you feel about it later?

National Service—Now

Bill Clinton

William Jefferson Clinton began service as president of the United States in January 1993. One month later, he wrote this article, which appeared in the *New York Times* on February 28, 1993, about his plans for a program of national service for young adults. This plan is designed to provide opportunities for young people to work in community service jobs in exchange for financial aid for their college educations.

Apathy is dead. 1

Of everything I've learned in my first few weeks in the White 2 House, that's the thing that's made me the happiest. Whether or not the people I've met outside the capital support the changes I have proposed, they're all saying they're ready to rebuild our country.

But they know, as I do, that no economic plan can do it alone. A 3 plan can make vaccines available to children, but alone it will not administer the shots to all of them. It can put security guards in the schools, but alone it will not take gangs off the streets. And it can provide more aid for college, but alone it will not make the costs of college less daunting for the middle class.

That's why I believe we need national service—now. 4

If Congress acts quickly enough, just months from now more than 5 1,000 young people will start serving our country in a special summer effort. In four years, the successors to these pioneers will multiply a hundredfold. Imagine: an army of 100,000 young people restoring urban and rural communities and giving their labor in return for education and training.

National service is an idea as old as America. Time and again, our 6 people have found new ways to honor citizenship and match the needs of changing times.

Lincoln's Homestead Act rewarded those who had the courage to 7
settle the frontier with the land to raise a family. Franklin D. Roosevelt's
Social Security Act insured that Americans who work a lifetime can
grow old with dignity. Harry S Truman's G.I. Bill rewarded the service
of my father's generation, transforming youthful veterans into an army
of educated civilians that led our nation into a new era.

For my generation, the reality of national service was born 32 years 8
ago tomorrow, when President John F. Kennedy created the Peace
Corps. At its peak, the Peace Corps enrolled only 16,000 volunteers yet
it changed the way a generation of Americans look at themselves and
the world.

Today, the spirit of our people once again can meet head-on the 9
troubles of our times.

The task is as complex as our challenge is great. We must combine 10
the intensity of the post–World War II years with the idealism of the
early 1960's—and help young people afford a college education or job
training.

In 1993, we'll restore the spirit of service by asking our people to 11
serve here at home. We won't refight the wars we won, but we'll tackle
the growing domestic dangers that threaten our future.

Our new initiative will embody the same principles as the old G.I. 12
Bill. It will challenge our people to serve our country and do the work
that should—and must—be done. It will give those who serve the
honor and rewards they deserve. It will invest in the future of the quiet
heroes who invest in the future of others.

The national service legislation that I will send to Congress shortly 13
will give our people the chance to serve in two basic ways:

First, it will make it easier for young people to hold low-paying 14
public service jobs and still pay off their student loans.

Under our program, Americans will be able to borrow the money 15
they need for college and pay it back as a small percentage of their
income over time. By giving graduates the chance to repay loans on an
affordable, reasonable schedule, this "income-contingent" program will
allow our people to do the work that our communities really need.

Second, our legislation will create new opportunities for Americans 16
to serve our country for a year or two—and receive financial support for
education or training in return.

We'll offer people of different ages and educational levels different 17
ways to serve. And to focus our energies and get the most for our
money, we'll direct special attention to a few areas:

- We'll ask thousands of young people to serve in our schools—   18
some as teachers, others as youth mentors, reading specialists and math
tutors. They'll join the effort to insure that our schools offer the best
education in the world.
- We'll send people into medical clinics to help immunize the   19
nation's 2-year-olds. Some participants will be qualified to give the
shots, but thousands of others can provide essential support, contact-
ing parents and following up to make sure children get the shots
they need.
- We'll help police forces across the country through a new Police   20
Corps trained to walk beats. We'll also organize others in our communities to keep kids out of gangs and off drugs.
- We'll put still others to work controlling pollution and recycling   21
waste, to help insure that we pass on to our children a nation that is
clean and safe for years to come.

Our national service program will offer more than benefits to indi-   22
viduals. We'll help pay operating costs for community groups with
proven track records, providing the support they'll need to grow. And
we'll let entrepreneurs compete for venture capital to develop new service programs.

While the Federal Government will provide the seed money for   23
national service, we are determined that the participants—the individuals who serve and the groups that sponsor their service—will guide the
process. Spending tens of millions of tax dollars to build a massive
bureaucracy would be self-defeating; it would squash the spirit of innovation that national service demands.

By design, our national service program will not happen overnight.   24
Instead, it will grow year by year, with funding reaching $3 billion in
1997. And as I've said many times, I believe it will be the best money we
ever spend.

If Congress gives us the chance, this summer we'll create an eight-   25
week leadership training program. We'll recruit more than 1,000 young
people for special projects to meet the needs of children at risk—and to
train the first class of full-year participants.

In the first full year of our initiative, we'll launch our flexible loan   26
program and aim to put tens of thousands of people to work. By 1997,
more than 100,000 citizens could be serving our country, getting education and training benefits in return. And hundreds of thousands more
people could be doing invaluable work because college loans no longer
block the way.

But the best planning and the most ambitious design won't make   27
this vision of national service a reality. That responsibility ultimately
rests with the American people.

I am convinced that after 12 years of drifting apart instead of   28
working together we are ready to meet the challenge. From a 14-year-
old boy in North Dakota who sent us $1,000 to help pay off the
deficit, to a 92-year-old widower in Kansas who followed his example,
people are demonstrating that they want to give something back to
our nation.

National service will exercise our talents and rebuild our communi-   29
ties. It will harness the energy of our youth and attack the problems of
our time. It will bring together men and women of every age and race
and lift up our nation's spirit. And for all of us, it will rekindle the
excitement of being Americans.

Vocabulary

apathy (1)—indifference; lack of
feeling

daunting (3)—intimidating; discouraging

embody (12)—to make real; give
substance to

contingent (15)—depending on
something else

entrepreneurs (22)—persons who
begin and manage a business
undertaking

rekindle (29)—to stir up again .

IN YOUR JOURNAL

Write about your personal response to the suggested federal program for national service. What are its positive aspects? What are its
negative aspects? Would you like to be a part of it or not? Why?

A Closer Reading

1. Why does President Clinton think this is the right time for a
   national service program to be put into effect? What evidence
   does he provide to support his point of view?

2. What are the two ways in which the plan will allow people to
   serve the country? What is an "income-contingent" program?

3. What types of work does he propose that national service workers will do?

4. What are the phases or steps involved in the plan? Why does it start with only a thousand young people?

5. In trying to create a historical precedent for this plan, Clinton makes reference to past presidents of the United States. To which presidents does he refer? To what political party did they belong? How does he connect those men with his program?

Drawing Your Own Conclusions

1. Why might young people want to get involved in the national service program? What benefits will they get from it? Why might they not want to get involved?

2. Which institutions do you think would support this plan, and which would oppose it—colleges, banks, police forces, armed forces, religious institutions, and so on? Explain your answers.

3. Is there any group of students who might feel excluded by this plan? Why? What changes could be made to include these students in some way?

4. In what ways would this plan solve some of the problems faced by students who have to work while they attend college? What new problems might be created?

Thinking about Writing

1. The opening paragraph is one sentence: "Apathy is dead." How does President Clinton connect this idea with the body of his essay?

2. What is the purpose of this essay? To whom is he speaking? What information that is not in the essay would you have liked him to have included?

3. Why does Clinton use "we" in this essay?

4. What words and phrases does Clinton use to make the idea of a nation of unity, of harmony, and of national pride appealing?

5. In what parts of the essay is Clinton emphatic? Why?

6. What do readers learn about the Peace Corps from reading this essay? What are the differences and similarities between the new plan and the Peace Corps? What information does he provide about the G.I. Bill? What are the similarities and differences between the new plan and the G.I. Bill?

*   *   *

Suggestions for Writing

1. Find out more about the national service program and write a paper in which you describe it in more detail. Decide whether or not you would support such a program, and explain your decision.

2. Some people have suggested that the national service program be mandatory and that all young people should be required to serve their country for two years in some capacity. Write an essay in which you take a position on this issue. Support your point of view with your personal experiences, your observations, and your readings.

3. Imagine that volunteers from the national service program were sent to your community to work for one year. Decide on three types of work in which they would do the most good. For example, does your community need help in teaching, medicine, construction, food preparation, drug and sex counseling, or gardening? Explain how you chose these three areas and describe the types of work that volunteers could do to make your community a better place.

4. Is apathy dead? In your opinion, are the young people in your college or community interested enough in the political, social, or personal problems of others to do something about them? Do they feel helpless because of the seriousness of social problems today? Write an essay in which you discuss these questions, referring to specific events and people in your school and community.

Strategies for Revision

When you read your draft, think about the following:

- What points in your essay do you want to emphasize? What techniques did you use to accomplish this goal? Move your most important point in the essay to the beginning. Move it to the end of the draft. Which is more effective?

- Is your essay written in first person (I, we), second person (you), or third person (he, she, they)? Change it to a different person. How does this change the impact of what you have written? Which is more effective?

When you have decided on the most effective way to make your points, revise your draft and share it with a classmate.

IN YOUR JOURNAL

"Teenagers don't invent violence, they learn it." Write a response to this statement in your journal.

The Violence in Our Heads

David Gelman

David Gelman wrote this essay for the August 2, 1993, *Newsweek* magazine. Gelman confronts the increase of violence in our society and addresses the ways in which violence is connected to sports, entertainment, and news coverage. Gelman thinks that as long as advertisers and other media executives believe there is a demand in the market for violence, its prevalence will not decrease.

Teenagers don't invent violence, they learn it. To a considerable ex-   1
tent, they act out the attitudes and ethics of the adults closest to them. Thus any study of the causes of teen crime might look first at the violence grown-ups have been carrying in their heads. In the last 30 years, Americans have developed a culture of violence surpassing in its pervasiveness anything we experienced before. It shows up in our speech, in our play, more than ever in the entertainments we fashion and fancy, in business style. "There's an extraordinary degree of violence in the language, and it's the window to the actual feelings and mores of the culture," says Dr. Robert Phillips, director of forensic services for the Connecticut Department of Public Health. "You get a sense of how the social fabric is beginning to wear thin—a lot of it is directed at minorities."

Everyone seems aggressively on the defensive these days. A rampant   2
"make my day" ethic expressed at various levels of the culture may be largely to blame for both the rise in teen crime and its increasing callousness, says Deborah Prothrow-Stith, an assistant dean at the Harvard School of Public Health. Our national icons tend to be men who excel at violence, from John Wayne to Clint Eastwood. When President Clinton ordered a retaliatory airstrike on Baghdad because of an alleged plot against George Bush, his popularity rating took a leap, just as Bush's had when, as president, he ordered up the gulf war, in which an estimated 100,000 Iraqi civilians were killed by bombs and missiles.

Ironically, a quarter century of feminist consciousness-raising has 3 managed, among worthier achievements, to bring us back to a macho mystique. Meanwhile the Schwarzenegger generation is pumping iron and signaling "Don't mess with me." T-shirts are broadcasting more direct messages—and so are rap lyrics: "Beat that bitch with a bat," one of them urges. "Violence is hip right now," says Jack Levin, a professor of sociology and criminology at Northeastern University. Better than hip: it's commercial.

In her 1991 book, *Deadly Consequences*, Prothrow-Stith says that, 4 for adolescents, an attraction to violence is developmentally normal. But what accounts for adults' voyeuristic fascination with it? Are Rambo and RoboCop our surrogate avengers, as one psychologist suggests? It's not only teenagers who flock to the latest kung fu epic. It's certainly not teenagers alone who are guzzling beer and starting brawls at sports contests that are themselves turning ever more violent.

With new, improved technology, films grow more and more like 5 demolition derbies. Trailers for these movies are edited to breathtaking montages of blazing guns, exploding cars and heads, and bodies hurtling out of windows. The destruction is cartoonish, but the shattered glass and bodies look real enough to leave disturbing afterimages. On the tube, growly-voiced promos whip up viewers' lust for bone-crunching, blood-letting sports contests to come. Videos capture football's hardest hits, complete with spliced-in grunts and groans. On the field, despite a be-lated ban, players still dance the obscene little touchdown shimmy that is intended to add manly insult to injury. If that doesn't sate your appetite, you can always attend the fights, at the hockey game—and, lately, at basketball and baseball games as well. Fans seem to love them. The danger, psychiatrists say, is that the constant repetition of violence and violent imagery desensitizes us in much the way a therapist desensitizes a phobia patient: by deliberate exposure to what's scary.

Images are not reality, but they feed into the perception many people 6 have of an inescapable, "out of control" violence in the country. And it would be a mistake to think this sensory inundation doesn't have an impact on the young. By now, the media-violence relationship is one of the best-researched connections in social science, says Myriam Meidzian, author of *Boys Will Be Boys: Breaking the Link Between Masculinity and Violence*. But it is also, she adds, one of the best-kept secrets. "There's been an enormous reluctance to deal with this. Mothers will still say, 'Oh, I took the kids to see the Slasher, and they came home and had milkshakes and cookies'."

In fact, milkshakes and cookies may not be such a bad idea. The   7
impact of violent movies and TV—almost impossible to put off-limits
since the advent of VCRs—can be mitigated by a caring parent who sits
down with the children and helps put things in perspective. That, of
course, assumes a caring parent is available. "It's virtually impossible
when the parent is working 50 or 60 hours a week," says Stephen
Klineberg, a professor of sociology at Rice University, in Texas. In 1974,
for the first time, 50 percent of American children had nobody at home
when school let out at 3 o'clock. Now, it's closer to 80 percent, but
schools still kick kids out at 3. "While the family has undergone a revolution, there's been a failure of these other structures to change accordingly," says Klineberg. "It's what sociologists call a cultural lag."

The failure of schools to adapt is only one example of what social   8
analysts believe is a general failure of will, a kind of paralysis in the face
of the growing dimensions of the problem. The token gesture of the TV
networks in volunteering parental-guidance labels for certain shows
scarcely changes the picture. There are obvious dangers in imposing
more aggressive restraints and flinging the doors open wider to censorship. But meanwhile, the levels of tolerated violence in the media, in
sports and in the real world keep ratcheting upward. When do we stop
feeling helpless and start doing something? "The surgeon general's reports for years have said that violence on television is related to violence
in children," says Carol Nagy Jacklin, dean of the division of social
science and communication at the University of Southern California.
"It's so upsetting that, on the one hand, we seem to deplore this violence but, on the other, we are not stopping it in the ways that we know
it needs to be stopped."

Taken down to cases, there are more proximate causes of adolescent   9
crime in this country—guns and drugs, to name just two. But in the
longer view, they may be no more responsible than the cultural violence
of which we are the principal makers and consumers, and which we still
hesitate to bring under effective control.

Vocabulary

surpassing (1)—excelling; going
beyond the average
pervasiveness (1)—the state of
being widespread
rampant (2)—widespread

callousness (2)—insensitivity,
hardness
icons (2)—images of a venerated
or worshiped person or thing
voyeuristic (4)—exaggeratedly in-

terested in vile or scandalous things

surrogate (4)—substitute

sate (5)—to satisfy an appetite fully

inundation (6)—flood or deluge

ratcheting (8)—catching and holding to prevent backward movement

proximate (9)—near or next in time or space

IN YOUR JOURNAL

Where are you most frequently exposed to violence in your life—on television, in the street, in your home? Write about violence in your life, violent incidents you have been involved in, or incidents you have witnessed.

A Closer Reading

1. What examples of violence in entertainment media does Gelman point out? What examples of violence in sports?

2. What shifts in family life have resulted in children's increased exposure to violence?

3. Why have schools been unable to stop the spread of violence? What actions could schools take to reduce the spread of violence?

4. What role has technology played in increasing our exposure to violence?

Drawing Your Own Conclusions

1. What specific words that relate to violence do you hear on a daily basis? From what sources have these words entered our vocabulary?

2. What connection is there between music and violence? What recent news events connect music and violence?

3. What connection is there between video games and violence? Why are violent video games popular?

4. What laws could be passed that would lead to a decrease in violence in our society? Should these laws be passed? Why or why not?

5. Who benefits from the increase in violence in media—the public, the entertainment industry, the police forces, big corporations, or others? Explain your answers.

Thinking about Writing

1. What is Gelman's main idea or point of view? Where does he state it in this essay?

2. Gelman quotes from several sources. Find their names. What does Gelman tell us about these sources to prove that they are credible or knowledgeable about violence?

3. What books does Gelman mention in the article? Why does he mention these books? How do they support his point of view?

4. What numbers or statistics does Gelman provide? How do they support his point of view?

* * *

Suggestions for Writing

1. Many people are troubled by the violence in music lyrics, movies, and television. Write an essay in which you state your opinion about the violence found in one of these areas. How does being exposed to so much violence affect our relationships with each other? Are there any solutions to this?

2. What actions could you take today to prevent violence from destroying the lives of the children in your neighborhood? Write an essay in which you describe in detail three specific steps that can be taken to decrease the spread of violence in your neighborhood. Include examples of each step.

3. Recent actions have been taken to remove violent video games from the market. Even though researchers have established a link between violent entertainment and violent behavior, many people think violent video games still should be made available in the market. Take a position on this issue, supporting your point of view with your experiences, observations, and readings.

4. If there were no market for violence, it would not be so widespread. Why does violence sell? Write an essay in which you

discuss the appeal of violence and include suggestions for reducing its appeal.

Collaborative Project

Divide your class into four groups. One group should watch two hours of cartoons a day for a week. The second group should watch two hours of prime time (8 to 10 P.M.) shows a day for a week. The third group should watch two hours of made-for-television movies (9 to 11 P.M.) a day for a week. The fourth group should watch two hours of news coverage a day. Each group should make a graph on violence in the media. How many times do people or creatures (in cartoons) use violent language? How many times do they hit, punch, or attack someone? How many times are weapons used? How many people or creatures are killed, maimed, or injured?

At the end of the week, the groups should compare their results. What did you learn about television from this experience? Each person should write a paper discussing your findings and what this experience taught you about television.

Strategies for Revision

1. After you have completed your first draft, reread aloud what you have written. As you read, you may find yourself stopping and reading what came before in the text. You may not be able to follow your own line of reasoning. Each time you stop or hesitate, mark a small dot in the margin. Then return and reread the writing, concentrating on those lines in which you see dots. Make any changes that make the writing flow more smoothly or make the ideas connect more clearly. Rewrite this draft.

2. Share your rewritten draft with another member of your class. Read what you have written aloud—slowly and clearly. Stop whenever your classmate seems confused. Mark these stops with dots in the margin. When you finish reading, ask your classmate the following:

   - Tell me in your own words everything you can remember from the draft.
   - What was my draft really about? What was the main point?

- What was the best part of the writing? Why did you prefer that part?
- If you did not understand a part of the draft, what was it?
- If you had to make only one suggestion to improve this piece of writing, what would it be?

Your classmate can then share his or her rewritten draft, asking you the same questions. Based on what the two of you discuss, each of you should revise your drafts again. Share your revisions with one another.

IN YOUR JOURNAL

Write about any experience you have had with a person who has a physical or mental disability. What did you learn about yourself through knowing this person?

Moving Toward Independence

Geeta Dardick

Geeta Dardick wrote this article for the Fall 1992 edition of *Whole Earth Review,* and it was reprinted in the March/April 1993 edition of *Utne Reader.* Dardick's husband is paraplegic and uses a wheelchair for mobility. Through him, she became aware of the lack of appropriate bathrooms and of accessible public transportation and public spaces. They became political activists when they fought for the passage of the Americans with Disabilities Act (ADA) of 1990. Despite its passage, the work has just begun. Now they are fighting for implementation of its provisions in the long-term struggle for equal rights for the disabled.

In 1963 I fell in love with Sam Dardick, a man who happened to   1
have a disability. After I announced my engagement to Sam, some narrow-minded "friends" tried to convince me that I shouldn't choose a wheelchair user for a husband, but I ignored their negative comments. To me, Sam Dardick was a charming and sexy guy, and the fact that he'd had polio as a kid didn't dampen my ardor for him.

Still, during the early years of our marriage, when we lived in St.   2
Louis, Sam's wheelchair was a problem for both of us. We'd try to rent an apartment, and find that 100 percent of them had stairs. We'd go to the movies: stairs again. We'd plan to take the bus . . . more stairs. It soon became obvious that architects, builders, and designers did not take Sam's and my needs into consideration (ironic, since Sam was a graduate of Washington University's School of Architecture).

I felt extremely annoyed every time we encountered an architectural   3
barrier, but I had no way to vent my anger. There weren't any disability laws in Missouri at that time. All I could do was stuff my feelings about the lack of wheelchair access and move on with my life.

In the early 1970s, we gave up our urban lifestyle, bought land on   4
the San Juan Ridge in Nevada County, California, and became back-to-
the-land farmers. Now I worried about the simple things in life, like
keeping the woodstove burning so the cabin would be warm enough
for the whole-wheat bread to rise. Access seemed irrelevant, since we
rarely left our land.

My feelings about accessibility issues remained dormant for many   5
years; then one sunny day in the spring of 1984, like Rip Van Winkle, I
woke up. Sam and I were celebrating his birthday by lunching together
at the Posh Nosh Restaurant in Nevada City. After we paid for our
beers and pastrami-on-rye sandwiches, Sam suddenly felt an urgent call
of nature.

He wheeled his wheelchair over to the bathroom and discovered   6
that the door was two feet wide. His wheelchair measured two and one-
half feet wide. There was no way his chair was going to pass through
that door.

Sam wheeled back to our table about 20 feet from the bathroom   7
door. Without telling me what he intended to do, Sam jumped out of
his wheelchair and dropped himself onto the floor of the restaurant.
And then he started crawling rapidly toward the bathroom door.

Paraplegics like Sam can use their arms, but not their legs. Sam's   8
crawl was a two-handed movement in which he dragged himself across
the room like a caterpillar. I sat there watching him in disbelief. Here
was the man who was my lover, my husband, the father of my three
children, the president of the San Juan Ridge School Board, a guy with
graduate degrees in architecture and city planning: here he was, being
forced to crawl across the floor of the Posh Nosh Restaurant to use the
bathroom. As I watched Sam crawling, I pledged that I was going to do
something, to help make sure that neither my husband nor anyone else
would be forced to crawl to a bathroom again.

The following day I started making phone calls. I found out that   9
California already had laws requiring wheelchair accessibility. I also
found out that Sam and I could join a state-sponsored program, called
the Community Access Network (CAN), that would teach us the state's
accessibility codes and then send us back into Nevada County to enforce
them.

That summer, I trained as a CAN volunteer; from that moment on, I   10
became an access cop, with my evil eye turned on the country's innumera-
ble inaccessible structures. Rather than act alone, Sam and I networked
with persons from all disability groups and formed a broad-based local

access committee to raise community awareness of the need for accessibility and to police new construction projects.

During the next few years, Sam and I volunteered thousands of   11
hours for disability causes throughout California. We marched for access to public transportation in San Francisco, testified for accessible apartments in Sacramento, busted inaccessible city-council meetings in Nevada City, and started an Independent Living Center in Grass Valley. Every victory was celebrated with gusto, but there was always one caveat. We realized that the state of California, with its progressive legislation promoting architectural accessibility, was more advanced on disability issues than most other states. Would the fight for accessibility have to be fought over and over again in every state in the nation? Wasn't there ever going to be a national disability policy?

We didn't have long to wait. Back in 1984, then-president Ronald   12
Reagan directed the National Council on the Handicapped to prepare a special report that would present legislative recommendations for enhancing the productivity and quality of life of Americans with disabilities.

The council's report, submitted to President Reagan in 1986, was   13
entitled *Toward Independence,* and it was much more hard hitting than might have been expected. It recommended "enactment of a comprehensive law requiring equal opportunity for individuals with disabilities, with broad coverage and setting clear, consistent, and enforceable standards prohibiting discrimination on the basis of handicap." That bold recommendation was the seed that resulted in the development of legislation for the Americans with Disabilities Act (ADA), the first national civil-rights bill for people with disabilities.

Opposition to the ADA from business and transportation interests   14
forced disability leaders to wheel and deal. The right to universal health-insurance coverage was bartered away for support from some key legislators. After a great deal of behind-the-scenes negotiation, the ADA passed the House of Representatives 377–28 and the Senate 91–6, with its most important provisions still intact.

The ADA is a comprehensive piece of legislation. The regulations of   15
the ADA (which went into effect on January 26, 1991) will eventually eliminate many of the barriers faced by people with disabilities. All "public accommodations," such as restaurants, hotels, medical offices, and retail stores, will need to be built with full accessibility. (Adding accessibility to a new structure increases the total cost by 1 percent or less.) Typical accessibility features include ramps, bathrooms with

ample space for wheelchairs to turn around, and lightweight doors that are easy to open.

Businesses that decide to remodel will have to make the remodeled   16
area accessible, as well as the path of travel to the area. In existing buildings, inaccessible features must be eliminated if such changes are "readily achievable" without much difficulty or expense. An example would be placing a ramp over one or two steps leading into a store or office.

Businesses must provide auxiliary aids to enable a person with a   17
disability to use available materials and services. For example, any video presentations about products would need to be closed-captioned for the deaf, and brochures would need large print so that those with low vision could read them. Another example: providing special pens that have large, spongy, easy-to-hold grips—helpful for many people with arthritis.

The ADA also makes major changes in employment criteria. Under   18
the ADA, an employer cannot refuse to hire a qualified applicant with a disability, just because of the person's disability. An employer does not, however, have to give preference to a qualified applicant with a disability over other applicants. An employer must also make "reasonable accommodations" for a person with a disability so he or she can perform the job. This might mean putting an amplifier on a telephone, lowering a desk, or establishing a flexible work schedule. And in new or remodeled facilities, all employee areas including sales and service areas must be made fully accessible. If the accommodations would impose an "undue hardship" (be too costly), however, they will not be required.

There are many incentives written into the law to encourage busi-   19
nesses to comply with the ADA. Businesses can receive tax deductions of up to $15,000 for the removal of architectural barriers (if it costs $12,000 to replace stairs with a ramp, for example, the entire amount is tax-deductible). Businesses can receive tax credits equal to 50 percent of all costs of meeting the Americans with Disabilities Act, providing those costs are over $250 and under $10,250. If, for instance, you hired a sign-language interpreter to be present for the signing of contracts with deaf buyers, or if you made a workstation accessible for an employer who uses a wheelchair, you could deduct half of the cost.

Public services also come under the ADA umbrella. All new   20
public buildings and all new buses and rail vehicles must be accessible. By 1993, telephone companies must provide telecommunications

relay services for hearing-impaired and speech-impaired individuals, 24 hours a day.

Of course, passing a law is only a first step to full equality. Imple- 21
mentation is the second step, and it is just as important. Congress-
man Steny Hoyer put it most succinctly when he said, "Passing ADA
was incredibly historic. Now every day we must fight to make sure
that the words in the law, the words on the White House lawn, the
words in the House, and the words in the Senate become reality for
43 million Americans with disabilities and millions more around the
world who are looking to American leadership for the rights of the
disabled."

Vocabulary

ardor (1)—passion; emotional
  warmth
vent (3)—to release
dormant (5)—inactive; still

caveat (11)—a warning
comply (19)—to obey an order
succinctly (21)—clearly and
  briefly

IN YOUR JOURNAL

Write about the Americans with Disabilities Act. What is it? Why
was it passed? What changes have been made because of its passage?

A Closer Reading

1. What information does Dardick provide about her husband? In
   paragraph 8, she contrasts his abilities with his limitations. What
   examples of each does she include?

2. What is the Community Access Network? What is its purpose?
   What is an "access cop"? What specific activities did the Dardicks
   perform in their roles as access cops?

3. What was the process for passing the Americans with Disabilities
   Act? Who was opposed to its passage? Why? What incentives
   were provided for the business community?

4. What are some of the regulations of the ADA? Why is this bill
   called the first national civil rights bill for people with disabilities?

Drawing Your Own Conclusions

1. Why does Dardick want her readers to know that her husband is a college graduate, a father, and an architect?

2. What changes have you noticed in your community that make public spaces accessible to the disabled?

3. How have the lives of the disabled improved because of the ADA? In what ways has the whole society benefited because of the ADA?

4. In the Walker article on page 152, she describes life with her hearing impaired parents. What similarities and differences do you find in the feelings expressed by Dardick and Walker? How might the ADA affect the lives of Walker's parents?

Thinking about Writing

1. What dramatic fictional elements does Dardick use at the beginning of her essay to grip her readers? How effective is including her personal story in this essay?

2. This article is divided into two parts—one that tells a personal story, and the other that describes the current problem and offers a viable solution. In which part of the article do you find each part? Where does the selection shift from one to the other? How does Dardick make the transition from personal to general?

3. Notice any quotations that Dardick includes in her selection. What are the quotations? How does she let her readers know the sources of these quotations? Why did she use them?

4. What specific laws does Dardick include? How do these laws make her article more understandable to you as the reader?

5. What figures does Dardick include throughout the article? How do these support the idea that there are many disabled in the United States and that their needs are important?

* * *

Suggestions for Writing

1. In an essay, write about how the special needs of the disabled are met in your community. What changes have been made in restaurants, in public transportation, and on the sidewalks of your

streets? What changes do you think need to be made to help the disabled to live even fuller lives?

2. The disabled are the fastest-growing group in the United States. Most people, at one time or another in their lives, will be disabled in some way. Write an essay in which you discuss these statements. What changes would you like to see in society to increase tolerance toward the needs of the disabled?

3. Some colleges require students to take a course on disabilities. In an essay, explain why there is a need for such a course in college, list some of the topics you would like such a course to cover, and decide in what department it should be located. After you have written about this subject, decide whether it should be a required or an elective course and why.

4. President Clinton's national service program (see page 297) involves the use of volunteers throughout the country. Write an essay in which you describe one way in which volunteers could work with the disabled to make their lives more enjoyable and productive. Describe the service and explain why it would be helpful to a particular group of disabled people.

Collaborative Project

Working with two classmates, conduct research about the accessibility of buildings and other places on your campus. Are there ramps for wheelchairs? How wide are the doorways? Are there elevators? Is the school cafeteria accessible for wheelchair users and visually impaired and hearing impaired people? Are there any specially designated toilet facilities for wheelchair users? Are water fountains accessible to people in wheelchairs?

Are there large-print editions of college and student publications? Are there books on audiotape in the library? Is there a program to provide volunteer readers for visually impaired students?

Are there any special provisions made for hearing impaired students? Are sign language interpreters used in public meetings? Is closed-captioned television available?

Are special computer services available for the disabled?

Divide into groups to investigate the accessibility of various parts of your school. Make notes about your findings. Write a paper in which you describe what is available and what still needs to be made available.

You may decide to send your paper to the college president, the school newspaper, and/or to the student union.

Strategies for Revision

After you have finished reading your draft, reread the Dardick article, noticing how she combined facts and personal information. Reread what you have written, thinking about the following questions:

- Is there a personal story to provoke my reader's interest?
- Do I have a clearly stated point of view?
- Are there facts to support the personal information?
- Do I make it clear from what sources my facts come? Have I spelled the names correctly? Have I used only last names when referring to the sources after the first time?
- Do I use quotation marks when necessary?
- If I paraphrased, did I make it clear who was the source or originator?
- Do I have a strong, clear concluding paragraph?

IN YOUR JOURNAL

Write down the facts that you know about HIV and AIDS. How do people become infected? What can infected people do to help themselves stay otherwise healthy? What can noninfected people do to avoid becoming HIV positive?

The Long Goodbye

Abigail Zuger

Dr. Abigail Zuger is the medical director of an AIDS clinic in the Bronx, New York. Zuger wrote this essay about one of her patients who is HIV positive. Zuger adopts a personal tone as she describes her relationship with a very determined and courageous woman who at first refuses to believe that she has the HIV virus, and then turns her life around. The essay appeared on July 25, 1993, in the *New York Times Magazine.*

She is sitting in the clinic waiting room, bent over a magazine, half an 1 hour early for her appointment and looking fine. Year after year now, as the others sitting out there slowly fade into shadows, she alone has remained solid, substantial, voluptuous, the only image left on the screen.

She first came to our clinic four years ago for an H.I.V. test. It was 2 her fifth. The other tests had all been positive, but refusing to believe the unbelievable, she still felt there was the possibility of a mistake and had no patience for anyone who suggested otherwise.

"I don't trust any doctor but Dr. B.," she announced, standing in 3 the middle of my examining room and looking belligerent. She was referring to the doctor in our group who had cared for her second husband, her passport to infection, during his final days.

The temptation in these situations is always to usher the disap- 4 pointed party directly into the office of the beloved, but Dr. B.'s clinic attendance was irregular and that busy afternoon his cubicle was dark. She glowered at this news, shrugged, cracked her gum and sat. We had clearly made each other's day.

She was all show. Despite the lush classical profile inherited directly 5 from a Roman coin, despite the grating voice, the brassy hair, the stretch-denim jeans and punishing heels, despite her early departure from all forms of organized education, she proved to have the charm and savvy of an orphaned pup. By her second visit (the test was positive), she was giving me details of her love life. When Dr. B. reappeared a month later, she was unmoved. She belonged to me.

At the beginning, I didn't suspect what I was getting into. Technically speaking, in the spectrum of the H.I.V.-infected, she was, and still is, "asymptomatic." The virus, latent in her body, is causing no medical problems at all. Her immune system is still working. Technically speaking, all she would be needing from me in the clinic was a wave and a wink from time to time.   6

In fact, over the years I saw her at the clinic she was almost a full-time job. She had aches and twinges, numbness and tingling, rashes and wheezes, terrible breathlessness and a continual rippling of her sight. Her symptoms always came on at night, in the dark. I could never find anything wrong.   7

Finally I caught on. Her husband had died blind, numb and screaming, and she knew all too well what to expect for herself. "Just tell me how long," she would plead. "Just say, 'More than five years' or 'Less than five years.' Just tell me when."   8

It took a long time to convince her that if I could have told her I would have. Instead of a prognosis, she had to settle for statistics, and at this point the statistics are not very helpful in predicting futures like hers. The great majority of people in her situation have gone on to develop AIDS after a grace period that ranges from a few years to more than a dozen. A small, baffling minority have remained absolutely well, living with the virus with no apparent ill effects. AZT given at the right time seems to prolong the grace period for some people, but not for all. The chances are that other prophylactic regimens more successful than AZT will be developed in the near future. No one can predict quite when.   9

Meanwhile, they all ask us the same questions; we tell them all the same things: "Probably, but not definitely." "Nobody can predict exactly when." They nod, shrug, smile, go home to husbands and wives, to friends, to children, to empty rooms. How do they live? That answer is never in our clinic rooms, never in our charts.   10

It's not in her medical record either, which, despite the false alarms, the frantic phone calls, the emergency visits, is as bland as they come. Nothing we can measure has happened to her. Her vision is fine. No blotches or bumps have ever been located by me. Her blood tests are   11 normal. Her cholesterol's a little high. Nobody, looking into that chart, would have a clue to the H.I.V.-infected person unfolding in my clinic room over the last three years.

When we first met, she had a life composed mostly of souvenirs. Her first husband had died years earlier, leaving her with a young son. From her second husband she got her infection and the vivid nightmare of his passing. The third man in her life, and possibly worst bargain of them all, drank, used drugs and slugged her periodically as a record of his possession.

At some point after that fifth (and last) H.I.V. test, she managed to reset the balance of power. None of us can imagine how or why she found the strength to do it—and none of us ever worked up the nerve to ask her. My own theory is that she simply had to demonstrate what an outrageous error in bookkeeping somebody had made, sending her a comeuppance clearly intended for someone else.

It was quite a show. Month after month, she came into the clinic with new reports.

She got her high-school equivalency diploma. ("Do you think I could become a nurse?")

She got the guy who slugged her out of her house and life. ("I miss him but it's like, when he says he's going to be different, I don't believe him.")

She got her 12-year-old son through elementary school on the honor roll. ("Do you think I should tell him why we come to this clinic all the time?")

Slowly, she got rid of her symptoms. ("I knew you would say it was nothing, so when I looked again it wasn't there.")

And now she's gotten herself out of the South Bronx. ("I'm so scared I can't sleep.")

She borrowed money to buy a plot of land and a mobile home in North Carolina, in the community where her son's grandparents live. She's packed up her apartment and reserved a 20-foot truck. They're leaving an hour after the boy graduates from sixth grade.

Tomorrow, the clinic psychiatrist, the Legal Aid lawyer who drafted her will and I are taking her out for a goodbye lunch. This is something we don't ordinarily do. Our goodbyes are usually said at the bedside, rarely scheduled in advance over tuna. I suppose it should be a cheerful occasion—after all, how many graduations from our clinic, or from life with a slugger, or from the South Bronx, do we get to celebrate?

But what I realize now, as she looks up from her magazine in the   22
waiting room and grins at me, is that all I want is for her to stay with us
("How long, Dr. Zuger? Just tell me how long. Can't you just say,
'Probably never'? Can't you say it just for me?") until I can tell her
everything she wants to hear.

Vocabulary

voluptuous (1)—having a full,
shapely figure

belligerent (3)—warlike, fighting
and angry

glowered (4)—stared angrily

spectrum (6)—a continuous range

prognosis (9)—the prediction of
the probable chance for recovery and/or survival from a
disease

prophylactic (9)—preventive or
protective

regimens (9)—regular systems of
diet, exercise, and so on for
the maintenance or improvement of health

IN YOUR JOURNAL

What did you learn from Dr. Zuger about this patient? What steps
does she take to change her life from one full of abuse to one of
accomplishment? What can you learn from her experience?

A Closer Reading

1. Why does the patient originally go to see Dr. B.? What happens
   that makes her want to stay with Dr. Zuger? What evidence does
   the author provide that the relationship between doctor and
   patient becomes personal as well as professional?

2. Zuger states that the patient "reset the balance of power" in her
   life. What evidence does Zuger present to support this statement?

3. What does the term "asymptomatic" mean? How can the patient
   be asymptomatic if she comes to the clinic with symptoms?

4. Why can't doctors predict the course of an HIV-positive patient's life with certainty? What variations in the development of
   AIDS does Zuger present?

Drawing Your Own Conclusions

1. What is the difference between being HIV positive and having AIDS? If you are not sure, how can you find the answer?

2. Why doesn't the patient believe the doctors who tell her that she is HIV positive?

3. What changes do people need to make in their lives when they are diagnosed as being HIV positive?

4. How does the will to live affect the patient's response to finding that she has the human immunodeficiency virus? Support your answers with specific words and phrases from the essay. What do you think about the role of the will to live in dealing with an incurable disease?

Thinking about Writing

1. Why is this essay entitled "The Long Goodbye"?

2. Is the purpose of this essay to persuade, to explain, to define, to compare, or to narrate a story? What aspects of the essay support your answer?

3. What specific facts does Zuger include in this essay? What opinions does she include to support her point of view?

4. What source does the conclusion come from? Why does Zuger end the essay this way?

5. What examples of dialogue are there in the essay? How do these describe each of the patient's crises?

*   *   *

Suggestions for Writing

1. Write an essay in which you tell the story of someone you know or have read about who has a life-threatening illness. Describe the ways in which that person's life has been altered. Has society done enough to provide medical care and emotional support for the person? What changes would you like to see in the way that such people are treated in our society today?

2. What specific information do people need to know to prevent the spread of AIDS? How can colleges make sure that students

get this information? Choose one approach colleges can use and explain why it is appropriate. Support your point of view with your personal experience, your observations, and your readings.

3. What role could college-age students from the national service program (see page 297) have in informing high school and junior high school students about sexually transmitted diseases? Write an essay in which you discuss why sex education taught by young people would be advantageous. Describe the specific information they should present and the techniques they could use that would be effective with the younger students.

4. Should all high school and college students be required to take an HIV test? If they test positive, should their parents be informed? Write an essay in which you take a position on these issues. Support your point of view with your personal experiences, your observations, and your readings.

Collaborative Project

Find out as much information as you can about HIV and AIDS. Make oral reports together, sharing the information with the rest of your class. As a group, write an information paper on what you have found. You may want to submit this to your college newspaper or make it available to a local high school so that teachers may disseminate the information to their students.

Strategies for Revision

Reread your first draft with a classmate. Together, determine the strongest parts and the weakest parts of the essay. Decide together how to rework the problem areas so that they can be improved.

If you have included dialogue, reread the Zuger essay, focusing on her use of small pieces of dialogue to create a mood or feeling. Is your dialogue short and to the point? Does it have the effect that you intended?

Pay attention to the places in the essay in which you have relied on facts and the places in which you have relied on opinions to support your point of view. Have you included the sources of your facts? Are the opinions strong enough to support your point of view? Did you include enough examples?

Revise and rewrite your essay, thinking about the suggestions made during the discussion with your classmate. Share your revised essay with the same person.

IN YOUR JOURNAL

Write about the differences between the life of a commuter student who travels to your school every day and that of a student who lives on campus. What factors influence a student's decision whether or not to live on campus?

Care and Feeding of Commuters

Perry Garfinkel

This article by Perry Garfinkel, which appeared in the April 7, 1991, *New York Times,* explores the issues related to living off campus. At present more students live off campus than on campus. Colleges have had to make adjustments to make sure that these students can be an integral part of campus activities and experiences.

Michael Lucas earned a respectable 3.0 grade point average in his freshman year at Rutgers College. But he was still dissatisfied, and it had nothing to do with grades.   1

"I was apathetic toward the whole so-called college experience," said Mr. Lucas, who lives with his parents in nearby Edison, N.J. "To me it was just like 13th grade. I had no identity. I just showed up for classes and then I went home."   2

Then he discovered the college's Off-Campus Student Association. "I got involved—it was that simple," said Mr. Lucas, who is now a junior and vice president of the organization and has a 3.7 average.   3

An Emerging Force

Mr. Lucas is one of a large group of undergraduates who frequently slip through the academic cracks—"commuter" college students who do not live in institution-run residences on campus. They represent 83 percent of American higher education students, and after years of neglect are emerging as a potent group.   4

The commuter's is not the typical life style so glamorously portrayed in college brochures. Juggling a job, family, housing and transportation while bearing a full academic load, the commuter has distinctive needs   5 and concerns. Many see their college years go by in a blur of traffic, with no place on campus they can call home.

"To many, their car is not just their vehicle, it's a lounge, a cafeteria, a library," said Thomas Miller, vice president for student affairs at Canisius College in Buffalo. "They literally live their college years out alone in their car." 6

"Many institutions are operated under traditional residential models, in which their perception of the real student is someone who attends full time, lives on campus and is 18 to 22 years old," said Barbara Jacoby, director of the Office of Commuter Affairs and the National Clearinghouse for Commuter Programs at the University of Maryland, College Park. 7

"Regrettably," she added, "although adult learners and part-time students greatly outnumber traditional residential students in the United States today, many institutions continue to operate as though nontraditional students were marginal to the educational enterprise." 8

To cope with the current decline in the number of traditional-age students, many colleges have begun programs for the 10 million commuters that, Ms. Jacoby estimates, attend institutions of higher education. "If we ignore their needs, they will go away angry," she said. "That's why commuters have not been good alumni. If we give the impression that we don't care about them, why should they care about us after they graduate?" 9

Parking Lot Tours

This new enlightenment has given birth to offices, departments, programs, publications and services that make commuters feel more at home on campus. The Off-Campus Student Association at Rutgers, for example, offers campus tours with special attention to parking lots and commuting tips. The organization sponsors trips to New York and a student-awareness week that includes talks on inexpensive diversions within driving distance and workshops on auto mechanics. The group recently persuaded administrators to make earlier radio announcements of school closings during snowstorms. 10

Many colleges offer similar commuter-awareness weeks, designate sections of student lounges for commuters, give them a voice in campus policy making, devote columns in college newspapers specifically to their concerns and are establishing commuter alumni associations. But serving commuters' needs has been complicated by the fact that they are a diverse lot. "They defy definition," Mr. Miller said. "While residential 11 students form social core groups and join fraternal organizations, commuters are not coordinated. They travel alone."

Commuters include full-time students who live with their parents, 12
and fully employed adults with children. They are single mothers and retirees. They may live in their own apartments within walking distance of campus or they may drive 120 miles one way, as in the case of some students who live in Houston and attend Texas A & M University in College Station.

The National Clearinghouse for Commuters now defines them simply as "students who do not live in institution-owned housing." It 13
estimates that their numbers are growing dramatically.

Tracking commuters, however, is not easy. Prince George's Community College in Largo, Md., borrowed the aggressive marketing strate- 14
gies of retailers like L. L. Bean, said the director of college activities, Jay Boyer, "We developed a database programming system of tracking attendance at events through commuters' social security numbers," he said. "We then follow up by targeting certain age groups with direct-mail fliers promoting events we think they'd be interested in based on their attendance records."

The most popular events so far are dinner theater parties featuring 15
comedy, Mr. Boyer said. "The key thing for commuters," he explained, "is that because they're so strapped for time, the perceived value of an event has to be very high."

Of the 18,000 undergraduates at the University of California at 16
Davis, 14,000 are commuters living within a three-mile radius of campus. With rents up 8 percent and available housing down to 1 percent, the university's Student Housing Service is vital to many students' lives. It offers spring orientation workshops for students moving off campus, distributes model leases now used by 90 percent of Davis landlords and provides a rent-mediation service.

At Canisius College, a Jesuit school, 78 percent of the 2,700 under- 17
graduates are commuters, of whom 80 percent hold jobs, according to Mr. Miller. With financing from the Charles A. Dana Foundation, a national nonprofit organization that makes grants to private liberal arts institutions, the college's Office of Student Affairs developed a program that finds career-relevant work on campus for commuters.

"We turned one of their biggest distractions into a point of engage- 18
ment," Mr. Miller said.

David Schmitz, a 20-year-old Canisius biology major who com- 19
mutes 10 miles from his suburban apartment, is a Dana grant recipient

and a research assistant in immunogenetics at the State University of New York at Buffalo medical school. "This program is the cornerstone of my undergraduate experience," he said. "It's had substantial influence in preparing me for medical school. I've made valuable contacts with faculty and developed some strong friendships, too."

Another Canisius program addresses the parents of entering fresh-   20
men commuters. "Because commuting students are statistically more apt to be the first generation in their family to attend college," Mr. Miller said, "we invite parents to attend enrichment programs in which they sit in on classes to better understand the rigors of college-level work. The message is, 'Johnny may be less available to do family chores and he may be tying up the family car more frequently.'"

At Douglass College, across town from Rutgers, a section of the   21
student lounge has been set aside for older women commuters, "where they can kick off their shoes and where rock music is banned," said Gail Wittman, the commuter coordinator and dean of student staff at the college. The result of this and other Douglass programs, Ms. Wittman said, has been a "win-win situation all around."

Patricia Peters, for example, is a 48-year-old married mother of two   22
and a junior at the college. She travels 10 miles to campus from East Brunswick. Initially apprehensive about entering a milieu of younger students, she became involved in the college's Bunting Program for adult commuting students and is now one of its counselors.

"I am assigned to 11 women whom I touch base with often to   23
reassure them," Ms. Peters said. "I realize we all have the same worries coming in: 'How will I fit in?' 'How do I juggle family, school and work?'" She said her involvement had given her "a more connected feeling to the college."

At Hofstra University on Long Island, 21-year-old Nick Stanziani, a   24
senior, who commutes 20 miles from his parents' home in Elmhurst, Queens, to the college campus in Hempstead, was just elected president of the Organization of Commuter Students. Mr. Stanziani has helped organize seminars on stress management, rape prevention and the perils of drunken driving. The organization sponsors social events and pub-lishes a newsletter called "Dashboard Light."

"It's tough for us to get involved in student activities at Hofstra   25
because so many of us spend our so-called free time working or commut-ing," he said. "But at least now, we have a representative in the student government and there are things planned that consider our crazy sched-ules. We're not forgotten."

Vocabulary

alumni (9)—graduates of a school; alumna is a female graduate, alumnus a graduate of either sex, and alumni the plural form.

designate (11)—to set apart for a particular group

apprehensive (22)—fearful

IN YOUR JOURNAL

Write about your experience as a college student. Have you decided to commute or to live on campus? How did you reach that decision? Are you happy with this situation? Do you feel your school has reached out to make you feel welcome?

A Closer Reading

1. What facts mentioned in the article explain why commuter students are being treated differently than are resident students in many colleges today?
2. What types of outreach programs for commuter students have colleges instituted?
3. What variations are there in the lifestyles of commuter students? How do those variations affect their needs?
4. What is the Canisius program? Why is the college reaching out to the parents of college-age students? What results does the college expect?

Drawing Your Own Conclusions

1. What are the advantages of being a commuter college student? What are the disadvantages?
2. Why do some students return to college after a break in their education? How are their expectations different from those of students who attend college right after high school?
3. What types of student activities appeal to commuter students? Why?

4. What types of students does Garfinkel label as "nontraditional" students? How many nontraditional students are in your writing class? Are you one of them? Why?

Thinking about Writing

1. How many different colleges does Garfinkel refer to in this article? In what states are they located? How does he use them to reinforce his argument?
2. Garfinkel quotes from several sources. Identify them. What does Garfinkel tell his readers about these sources to prove that they are credible or knowledgeable about the life of commuter students?
3. What numbers or statistics does Garfinkel provide? How do they support his point of view?
4. In paragraph 18, Mr. Miller said, "We turned one of their biggest distractions into a point of engagement." Who is Mr. Miller? What is this distraction? What does he mean by a "point of engagement"?

*   *   *

Suggestions for Writing

1. Write an essay in which you compare the daily life of a commuter student with that of a resident student. After describing the everyday activities of both students, decide which type of student would find it easier to succeed at your college. Explain why.
2. Write an essay in which you explain how you learned to get along in your college. If you took an orientation course, was it helpful? Did you learn more about the college from experiencing it, from talking to other students, or from specially designed classes and programs? Explain in what ways your initiation experience was or was not effective.
3. Interview a sophomore or junior in your college. Ask that person what an incoming student needs to know to succeed at your college. Ask your interviewee to focus on three techniques that would help a student to be successful. Write about these in a

paper, explaining how they will assist an incoming student to make the transition to college life.

4. Should students work while they are in college? Take a position on this in your essay, and support your ideas with personal experiences, observations, or your readings.

Collaborative Project

As a class, imagine that you have been requested to design a Student Awareness Week for your college. Together, decide on appropriate activities and programs. What do students need to know? How can they meet people, design a good plan of study, find good teachers, and feel that they are a part of the college community? After you have made decisions about these matters, write a paper describing the plans for your Student Awareness Week.

Strategies for Revision

The following revision strategy takes place in two steps. The first is individual, and the next involves your working with a classmate.

Begin by rereading your writing with a colored pencil or pen in your hand. Do the following:

- Circle any words that you would like to replace or rethink.
- Circle any sentences that you think are weak or repetitive.
- Practice changing the sound of what you have written by turning one sentence around so that the beginning of the sentence is now the end portion.
- Put check marks next to any sentences that you are considering moving or in the places where you would like to add something else.

Then share these possible changes with a classmate. Discuss whether you agree that the changes would make your writing smoother and clearer. Then reverse the process and do the same for your classmate. Using the ideas from your discussion, revise your writing. When you are satisfied with it, share it with someone who has never read your writing before.

IN YOUR JOURNAL

Write about any early experience you had in a library. Why did you go to the library? How did you learn to find books and to take them out? Did you go to the library for pleasure, or only to fulfill school assignments?

The Paterson Public Library

Judith Ortiz Cofer

Judith Ortiz Cofer was born in Puerto Rico and now lives in Georgia. She is the author of *The Line of the Sun* (1989), several poetry collections, and a collection of personal essays and poems, *Silent Dancing: A Partial Remembrance of a Puerto Rican Childhood* (1990). Her essay "The Paterson Public Library" first appeared in the February 1992 *Witness* and was reprinted in *Daily Fare: Essays from the Multicultural Cultural Experience* (1993). It describes the conflict that developed between her desire to go to the public library and her fear of walking to it through her racially divided neighborhood.

It was a Greek temple in the ruins of an American city. To get to it I 1
had to walk through neighborhoods where not even the carcasses of rusted cars on blocks or the death traps of discarded appliances were parted with, so that the yards of the borderline poor, people who lived not in a huge building, as I did, but in their own decrepit little houses, looked like a reversed archeological site, incongruous next to the pillared palace of the Paterson Public Library.

The library must have been built during Paterson, New Jersey's, 2
boom years as the model industrial city of the North. Enough marble was used in its construction to have kept several Michelangelos busily satisfied for a lifetime. Two roaring lions, taller than a grammar school girl, greeted those brave enough to seek answers there. Another memorable detail about the façade of this most important place to me were the phrases carved deeply into the walls—perhaps the immortal words of Greek philosophers—I could not tell since I was developing astigmatism at that time and could only make out the lovely geometric designs they made.

All during the school week I both anticipated and feared the long   3
walk to the library because it took me through enemy territory. The
black girl Lorraine, who had chosen me to hate and terrorize with
threats at school, lived in one of the gloomy little houses that circled
the library like sackclothed suppliants. Lorraine would eventually carry
out her violence against me by beating me up in a confrontation
formally announced through the school grapevine so that for days I
lived with a panic that has rarely been equaled in my adult life, since
now I can get grown-ups to listen to me, and at that time disasters had
to be a fait accompli for a teacher or a parent to get involved. Why did
Lorraine hate me? For reasons neither one of us fully understood at
the time. All I remember was that our sixth-grade teacher seemed to
favor me, and her way of showing it was by having me tutor "slow"
students in spelling and grammar. Lorraine, older and bigger than
myself since she was repeating the grade, was subjected to this ritual
humiliation, which involved sitting in the hallway, obviously separated
from the class—one of us for being smart, the other for the opposite
reason. Lorraine resisted my efforts to teach her the basic rules of
spelling. She would hiss her threats at me, addressing me as *"You little
Spic."* Her hostility sent shudders through me. But baffling as it was, I
also accepted it as inevitable. She would beat me up. I told my mother
and the teacher, and they both reassured me in vague adult terms that
a girl like Lorraine would not dare get in trouble again. She had a
history of problems that made her a likely candidate for reform school.
But Lorraine and I knew that the violence she harbored had found a
target: me—the skinny Puerto Rican girl whose father was away with
the navy most of the time and whose mother did not speak English; I
was the perfect choice.

Thoughts like these occupied my mind as I walked to the library on   4
Saturday mornings. But my need for books was strong enough to
propel me down the dreary streets with their slush-covered sidewalks
and the skinny trees of winter looking like dark figures from a distance:
angry black girls waiting to attack me.

But the sight of the building was enough to reassure me that sanctu-   5
ary was within reach. Inside the glass doors was the inexhaustible treasure of books, and I made my way through the stacks like the beggar
invited to the wedding feast. I remember the musty, organic smell of the
library, so different from the air outside. It was the smell of an ancient
forest, and since the first books that I read for pleasure were fairy tales,
the aroma of transforming wood suited me as a prop.

With my pink library card I was allowed to check out two books   6
from the first floor—the children's section. I would take the full hour
my mother had given me (generously adding fifteen minutes to get
home before she sent my brother after me) to choose the books I
would take home for the week. I made my way first through the
world's fairy tales. Here I discovered that there is a Cinderella in every
culture, that she didn't necessarily have the white skin and rosy cheeks
Walt Disney had given her, and that the prince they all waited for
could appear in any color, shape, or form. The prince didn't even have
to be a man.

It was the way I absorbed fantasy in those days that gave me the   7
sense of inner freedom, a feeling of power and the ability to fly that is
the main reward of the writer. As I read those stories I became not only
the characters but their creator. I am still fascinated by the idea that fairy
tales and fables are part of humankind's collective unconscious—a familiar theory that acquires concreteness in my own writing today, when I
discover over and over that the character I create or the themes that
recur in my poems and in my fiction are my own versions of the "types"
I learned to recognize very early in my life in fairy tales.

There was also violence in these stories: villains decapitated in   8
honorable battle, goblins and witches pursued, beaten, and burned at
the stake by heroes with magic weapons possessing the supernatural
strength granted to the self-righteous in folklore. I understood those
black-and-white duels between evil and justice. But Lorraine's blind
hatred of my person and my knee-liquifying fear of her were not so
clear to me at that time. It would be many years before I learned about
the politics of race, before I internalized the awful reality of the struggle for territory that underscored the lives of blacks and Puerto Ricans
in Paterson during my childhood. Each job given to a light-skinned
Hispanic was one less job for a black man; every apartment leased to a
Puerto Rican family was one less place available to them. Worst of all,
though the Puerto Rican children had to master a new language in the
schools and were often subjected to the scorn and impatience of teachers burdened with too many students making too many demands in a
classroom, the blacks were obviously the ones singled out for "special"
treatment. In other words, whenever possible they were assigned to
special education classes in order to relieve the teacher's workload,
mainly because their black English dialect sounded "ungrammatical"
and "illiterate" to our white Seton Hall University and City College–
educated instructors. I have on occasion become angry at being treated

like I'm mentally deficient by persons who make that prejudgment upon hearing an unfamiliar accent. I can only imagine what it must have been like for children like Lorraine, whose skin color alone put her in a pigeonhole she felt she had to fight her way out of every day of her life.

I was one of the lucky ones; as an insatiable reader I quickly   9
became more than adept at the use of the English language. My life as a navy brat, moving with my family from Paterson to Puerto Rico every few months as my father's tours of duty demanded, taught me to depend on knowledge as my main source of security. What I learned from books borrowed from the Greek temple among the ruins of the city, I carried with me as the lightest of carry-on luggage. My teachers in both countries treated me well in general. The easiest way to become a teacher's pet, or *la favorita,* is to ask the teacher for books to read—and I was always looking for reading material, even my mother's romantic novels by Corin Tellado and her *Buenhogar* (Spanish *Good Housekeeping* magazine) were not safe from my insatiable word hunger.

Since the days when I was stalked by Lorraine, libraries have   10
always been an adventure for me. Fear of an ambush is no longer the reason why I feel my pulse quicken a little when I approach a library building, when I enter the stacks and inhale the familiar smell of old leather and paper. It may be the memory of the danger that heightens my senses, but it is really the expectation that I felt then and that I still feel now about books. I gained confidence in my intelligence by reading books. They contained most of the information I needed to survive in two languages and in two worlds. When adults were too busy to answer my endless questions, I could always look it up; when I felt unbearably lonely, as I often did during those early gypsy years traveling with my family, I read to escape, and also to connect: you can come back to a book as you cannot always to a person or place you miss. I read and reread favorite books until the characters seemed like relatives or friends I could see when I wanted or needed to see them.

I still feel that way about books. They represent my spiritual life. A   11
library is my sanctuary, and I am always at home in one. It is not surprising that in recalling my first library, the Paterson Public Library, I have always described it as a temple.

Lorraine carried out her threat. One day after school, as several of   12
our classmates, Puerto Rican and black, circled us to watch, Lorraine

grabbed a handful of my long hair and forced me to my knees. Then she slapped my face hard enough that the sound echoed off the brick walls of the school building and ran off while I screamed at the sight of blood on my white knee socks and felt the throbbing on my scalp where I would have a bald spot advertising my shame for weeks to come.

No one intervened. To this crowd, it was one of many such violent   13
scenes taking place among the adults and the children of people fighting over a rapidly shrinking territory. It happens in the jungle and it happens in the city. But another course of action other than "fight or flight" is open to those of us lucky enough to discover it and that is channeling one's anger and energy into the development of a mental life. It requires something like obsessiveness for a young person growing up in an environment where physical labor and physical endurance are the marks of a survivor—as is the case with minority peoples living in large cities. But many of us do manage to discover books. In my case, it may have been what anthropologists call a cultural adaptation. Being physically small, non–English speaking, and always the new kid on the block, I was forced to look for an alternate mode to survival in Paterson. Reading books empowered me.

Even now, a visit to the library recharges the batteries in my brain.   14
Looking through the card catalog reassures me that there is no subject I cannot investigate, no world I cannot explore. Everything that is, is mine for the asking. Because I can read about it.

Vocabulary

carcasses (1)—dead bodies, usually of animals

suppliants (3)—persons who humbly request or pray for something

fait accompli (3)—French expression for an event so inevitable that opposition is useless

collective unconscious (7)—the thoughts, feelings, and desires of which we are not aware but that are shared by all people

decapitated (8)—beheaded

insatiable (9)—unable to be satisfied; constantly wanting more

IN YOUR JOURNAL

Why does the girl continue to go to the library despite her fear of being hurt on the way there? What does she find in the library that she cannot find anywhere else in her life?

A Closer Reading

1. What evidence does Cofer provide that the architectural style of the library is "incongruous" in her urban neighborhood?

2. What relationship does Cofer have with Lorraine in school that affects their relationship outside of school?

3. What role does fantasy play in Cofer's life? How does the library feed into her fantasy?

4. How does the fact that English is not Cofer's first language affect the relationships as she describes them in this essay?

Drawing Your Own Conclusions

1. Why is it important to Cofer that Cinderella occurs in every culture? Why does it matter that she does not necessarily have white skin and rosy cheeks, or that the prince can appear in any color, shape, or form, or even sex? How does she learn this from books?

2. How are African-American students treated in Cofer's classes? How are children for whom English is not their first language treated? Why do these two groups of children sometimes become enemies instead of friends?

3. What role do books play in Cofer's life? What role have they played in your life? What book have you read that changed you in a significant way? Tell your class about it and why it affected you.

4. Reread the Modupe essay on page 20 and compare the relationship he describes between the African Americans and the Italian Americans with the one between the Puerto Ricans and the African Americans that Cofer describes in this essay. What causes dissension between the groups?

Thinking about Writing

1. Read the essay, focusing on the specific words and phrases that evoke the senses of sound, smell, sight, taste, and touch.

2. Reread the essay, noticing Cofer's use of words that describe colors. Make a list of these colors. How are they used in the essay?

3. Notice the words that Cofer uses to describe her neighborhood, and the words she uses to describe the library. How do these words make each place unique? What contrasts can you find?

4. Reread the first and the last paragraphs in this essay. What theme connects the two? What idea is expressed in the two paragraphs?

*   *   *

Suggestions for Writing

1. Write an essay describing a public building in your neighborhood in great detail—a school, library, church, hospital, police station, and so on. How does the architecture of the building complement its function?

2. Write an essay in which you compare your college library with the library that Cofer describes in her essay. Look at the building itself, the ways books are stacked, the kinds of library cards, the availability of computers and CD-ROMs. What items can be borrowed—books, films, CDs, and so on? What similarities and differences between the libraries do you find? How do you feel when you walk into your college library? How does this compare to Cofer's feelings about the Paterson Public Library?

3. Write an essay in which you discuss why people who seem to have similar goals, similar living conditions, and even similar family backgrounds often become antagonists instead of allies. How does the expression "United they stand, divided they fall" relate to this situation?

4. Visit the public library in your community. Look closely at the facilities—the building itself, the tables, chairs, bathrooms. Notice the people who use the library and those who work in it. Write an essay describing the library and explaining the role it plays in the community.

Strategies for Revision

Read your draft with a classmate, asking the following questions:

- Why did you decide to answer this question? What about it did you find interesting?
- What part of the essay was easiest for you to write? Why?
- What part was hardest? Why?
- What is the main idea of the essay? If it is stated directly, where is it stated? If it is implied, what evidence supports the idea?
- What do you want your reader to remember about your essay?
- What does your reader feel is the strongest part of the essay?
- What part of the essay needs reworking? Why?

Think about your partner's comments as you revise your essay. Share your revision with that person.

Natividad Baez wrote an essay in response to suggestion 1 from the Suggestions for Writing that follow the Clinton essay: Find out more about the national service program and write a paper in which you describe it in more detail. Decide whether or not you would support such a program, and explain your decision.

National Service for College Students

Natividad Baez

Students suffer from high tuition and interest they need to pay on 1
student loans. President Bill Clinton is worried about these high costs
jeopardizing students' already unstable education. Presently, the students who take out loans have to pay them back within six months after
they graduate or leave college although students who continue their
education as graduate students can get a deferment. Clinton, however,
wants to "change the way Americans pay for college" (Friedman, 1).
His plan would require students to work as volunteers for the country
for their education. Thus, in January 1993, President Clinton introduced a plan called "national service" to make changes in the college
student loan system and to enable students to get experience working
with others. Some congress members were against it because of the
cost. Banks also opposed it because they wouldn't be able to collect
interest from student loans.

National Service is a program that consists of college students work- 2
ing for the country for one or two years as tutors in inner-city schools,
as health care aides, as police cadets, as antipollution workers, as apartment cleaners, or as community workers (Clinton, 15). Each student
will receive $5,000 for his or her tuition. This program will give incom-
ing undergraduate and graduate students experience in their field. Moreover, society will gain since the students will be serving their country.
The students will also gain since they will be able to care for other
people and will learn from their working experience too. National Service, therefore, is a great idea.

This plan is in effect in 1994; so in the summer of 1993, Clinton 3
went to universities to speak to students about the program. Some of
the public and private academies are disappointed with this plan because there are already a lot of students who have dropped out of school
because of economic problems and they are scared that a lot of students

will not finish their education without the school's financial aid (Scott, A27). I think it won't happen that way because a lot of students cannot pay for the increases in tuition and are forced to take loans that are devastating. There are two kinds of loans now; those that they have to pay when they are in school, and the other that they have to pay when they finish their education. Students are suffering because of the interest on loans. For example, a friend of mine is a dentist, and she has been paying back a college loan for four years after her graduation. She still has not reached the end of the payments; and the interest continues to increase. Like her, there are millions of students in similar situations.

Worried about the students' problems, the Clinton administration   4 passed its new plan to Congress. Some Congress members did not approve of the plan since it was too expensive, but they finally accepted it on September 8, 1993. The legislation agreed to pay 20,000 volunteers in its first years. This is only a small percentage of all students who will be working as volunteers in the end. When the students complete their work, they will receive stipends. The total program will not be in effect up to 1997.

Clinton's plan is to provide $2 billion to clear the deficit in the Pell   5 Grant program and prevent reduction in the grants for 1993–1994. This plan will create a national direct-lending system for student loans within the next four years. This plan will be good for the nation's economic recovery because students will be working for the country while getting money. Also students who need money can have the option of taking out loans. With this plan, they can work as volunteers and get stipends or take out loans. It is better because they will be able to choose how to pay for their education.

President Clinton will change the student loan program by allowing   6 the student "to borrow money directly from the Government" (Friedman, 1) instead of from the bank. At the present, the U.S. Treasury makes $13.6 billion in federally insured student loans. President Clinton's plan will affect the banking industry since they would not earn so much money in interest from the students. Through lobbying, banks tried to stop direct lending because they did not want to lose millions of dollars in subsidies. However, their measures failed. The Department of Education states that by 1996 direct lending will be instituted at 60% of all eligible schools. Eventually, the people who work in the banks may become consultants to universities and colleges.

There are plenty of professionals (doctors, lawyers) who took out   7 loans for their graduate and undergraduate education. Now they won't pay back the loans, so they are in default. This plan will reduce these defaults which cost the government a lot of money.

The plan varies throughout the states. Some students work for less 8 or more periods of time and their college stipend is different (Saltzman, 65). Mrs. Marie Leonard, Director of Financial Aid in my college, said that this plan is a great idea since the students will be able to work in a field that they enjoy. Moreover, they can have a sense of responsibility. Right now some students have grants and do not have a sense of responsibility. Also, she wants President Clinton to have career counseling available for students as part of the pre-commitment. In that way, students can be working with the plan up to the time they graduate instead of waiting to graduate and being told to start working.

This is a good plan because it is going to help society, especially 9 communities that don't have hospitals, schools, or enough community members to work. Some similar agencies, such as the Peace Corps and Teach America, have sent students throughout the world to help others that are in bad condition. So far, students have worked successfully. Through this new plan students will also get education and training in their careers. Practice is more valuable than just reading books since one learns a lot by helping others.

Works Cited

Clinton, Bill. "National Service—Now." *The New York Times,* February 28, 1993:15.

Friedman, Thomas L. "Clinton's Proposed Services Program to Aid Students." *The New York Times,* May 1, 1993:1.

Saltzman, Amy. "National Service—Now." *U.S. News and World Report* April 12, 1993: 64–67.

Scott, Jaschick. "Clinton's National Services Plan Disappoints Students and College." *The Chronicle of Higher Education* May 12, 1993: A27, A32–34.

Questions to Think About

1. What information did Baez provide about Clinton's national service program that his essay (see page 297) did not provide?

2. What is Baez's point of view about the program? What specific words and phrases support your answer?

3. Has reading Baez's essay changed your feelings about the national service program? If so, how? Why?

MAKING CONNECTIONS

The Interdependent World: *Taking Action Together*

1. Choose a social dilemma for which you would like to find creative alternatives—poverty, racism, sexism; discrimination against the seriously ill, mentally or physically disabled and the like. Then reread some of the selections in this unit. Describe the dilemma on which your essay will focus and propose viable alternatives that you feel offer creative solutions to the problems.

2. Imagine that Gelman (see page 304) and Cofer (see page 333) met to discuss the problems of violence in our society today. After rereading their selections, write down their conversation, using dialogue and quotations. What conclusions do you think they might come to about ways to decrease the amount of violence to which people are exposed every day?

3. Imagine that Dardick (see page 311) and Zuger (see page 319) met to discuss the problems people face as political activists for such causes as AIDS and the ADA. After rereading their selections, write down their conclusions, using dialogue and quotations. What conclusions do you think they might come to about whether people benefit most from resistance or passive acceptance?

4. What role could college students have in making needed social changes? Referring to some of the selections you read in this unit, write an esssay in which you explore the roles that might be played by college students who are active and involved in making societal changes.

5. Write an essay in which you choose from this unit one piece of writing that caused an emotional reaction—it may have angered you, made you sad, or made you happy. Explain the effect of this piece of writing and tell why it had this effect.

6. Write an introduction to this unit in which you tell other students which piece of writing is the most interesting, the most informative, or the best written. Using quotations from the selection, convince a potential reader to choose this particular piece of writing to read.

7

THE WORLD OF NATURE

Connecting with the Wilderness

As our country becomes more developed and the needs of civilization impinge on the needs of the wild, we must reassess our values and make decisions about the world we live in and the world we want to leave for our children. In this unit, we examine the conflict that arises in thinking about wilderness for our use as opposed to wilderness for its own sake. To do this, we focus on the interrelationships of animals, places, and people.

Nature writer Annie Dillard opens this unit with her essay, "Living Like Weasels," in which she describes an encounter with a weasel in the wild and its effect on her. Dillard is forced to think about herself, her decisions, and her future. She ends up convinced that one should go after one's desire, whatever the consequences.

Ken Chowder questions our relationship to wilderness by referring to a debate that took place between naturalist John Muir and politician James D. Phelan almost one hundred years ago. One man wanted to preserve the wild for its own sake, and the other wanted to use the wild to fulfill human needs. Chowder examines the ways in which this conflict continues today.

Ted Williams, naturalist and fisherman, presents a placid view of the wilderness from a lovely brook in Massachusetts. In "Rivertops," Williams describes nature in its most idyllic sense, and fishing as an ideal sport.

Bill McKibben turns idealism on its side in "The End of Nature," as he presents the controversial notion that nature exists for itself and not for humans. He questions our ethic of consumption and waste, and the overdevelopment and overuse of our natural resources.

In "She Got Herself Shot," Hope Burwell describes her harmonious farm life and her relationship with nature and its animals. This harmony is interrupted by the hunting season. Over time, Burwell has grown to have little empathy for hunters who threaten her and other landowners and their pets.

Another perspective on a relationship with animals is presented in Reynolds Price's story, "A New Stretch of Woods." Price tells about a boy who comes to terms with changes in his life at a critical moment through his interactions with a series of animals.

Cynthia Mazzotti, a student writer, examines the dynamics of the relationship of predator and prey. She looks at the changes in the populations of wolf and moose on Isle Royale over time, acquiring a respect for nature's ability to maintain its balance.

*   *   *

Think about the following questions before reading the selections in this unit:

1. What do you know about the wilderness in our country? How did you learn about it?

2. What is the biggest problem that exists today in relation to the wilderness?

3. What changes would you like to see in our relationship to nature and the wilderness? Why?

Living Like Weasels

Annie Dillard

Born in Pittsburgh, Annie Dillard is a poet, novelist, and writer
of nonfiction who lives in Connecticut and in Cape Cod, Massachusetts. She is the author of many articles and ten books, including *Holy
the Firm* (1977) and *An American Childhood* (1987). In 1975, *Pil-
grim at Tinker Creek,* a narrative about nature, won the Pulitzer
Prize. The following essay is from *Teaching a Stone to Talk,* published
in 1982. From a chance encounter with a weasel, Dillard learns
something about herself and about the nature of life.

A weasel is wild. Who knows what he thinks? He sleeps in his   1
underground den, his tail draped over his nose. Sometimes he lives in
his den for two days without leaving. Outside, he stalks rabbits, mice,
muskrats, and birds, killing more bodies than he can eat warm, and
often dragging the carcasses home. Obedient to instinct, he bites his
prey at the neck, either splitting the jugular vein at the throat or crunching the brain at the base of the skull, and he does not let go. One
naturalist refused to kill a weasel who was socketed into his hand deeply
as a rattlesnake. The man could in no way pry the tiny weasel off, and he
had to walk half a mile to water, the weasel dangling from his palm, and
soak him off like a stubborn label.

And once, says Ernest Thompson Seton—once, a man shot an eagle   2
out of the sky. He examined the eagle and found the dry skull of a
weasel fixed by the jaws to his throat. The supposition is that the eagle
had pounced on the weasel and the weasel swiveled and bit as instinct
taught him, tooth to neck, and nearly won. I would like to have seen
that eagle from the air a few weeks or months before he was shot: was
the whole weasel still attached to his feathered throat, a fur pendant? Or

did the eagle eat what he could reach, gutting the living weasel with his talons before his breast, bending his beak, cleaning the beautiful airborne bones?

I have been reading about weasels because I saw one last week. I   3
startled a weasel who startled me, and we exchanged a long glance.

Twenty minutes from my house, through the woods by the quarry   4
and across the highway, is Hollins Pond, a remarkable piece of shallowness, where I like to go at sunset and sit on a tree trunk. Hollins Pond is also called Murray's Pond; it covers two acres of bottomland near Tinker Creek with six inches of water and six thousand lily pads. In winter, brown-and-white steers stand in the middle of it, merely dampening their hooves; from the distant shore they look like miracle itself, complete with miracle's nonchalance. Now, in summer, the steers are gone. The water lilies have blossomed and spread to a green horizontal plane that is terra firma to plodding blackbirds, and tremulous ceiling to black leeches, crayfish, and carp.

This is, mind you, suburbia. It is a five-minute walk in three direc-   5
tions to rows of houses, though none is visible here. There's a 55 mph highway at one end of the pond, and a nesting pair of wood ducks at the other. Under every bush is a muskrat hole or a beer can. The far end is an alternating series of fields and woods, fields and woods, threaded everywhere with motorcycle tracks—in whose bare clay wild turtles lay eggs.

So. I had crossed the highway, stepped over two low barbed-wire   6
fences, and traced the motorcycle path in all gratitude through the wild rose and poison ivy of the pond's shoreline up into high grassy fields. Then I cut down through the woods to the mossy fallen tree where I sit. This tree is excellent. It makes a dry, upholstered bench at the upper, marshy end of the pond, a plush jetty raised from the thorny shore between a shallow blue body of water and a deep blue body of sky.

The sun had just set. I was relaxed on the tree trunk, ensconced in   7
the lap of lichen, watching the lily pads at my feet tremble and part dreamily over the thrusting path of a carp. A yellow bird appeared to my right and flew behind me. It caught my eye; I swiveled around—and the next instant, inexplicably, I was looking down at a weasel, who was looking up at me.

Weasel! I'd never seen one wild before. He was ten inches long, thin   8
as a curve, a muscled ribbon, brown as fruitwood, soft-furred, alert. His

face was fierce, small and pointed as a lizard's; he would have made a good arrowhead. There was just a dot of chin, maybe two brown hairs' worth, and then the pure white fur began that spread down his underside. He had two black eyes I didn't see, any more than you see a window.

The weasel was stunned into stillness as he was emerging from beneath an enormous shaggy wild rose bush four feet away. I was stunned into stillness twisted backward on the tree trunk. Our eyes locked, and someone threw away the key.   9

Our look was as if two lovers, or deadly enemies, met unexpectedly on an overgrown path when each had been thinking of something else: a clearing blow to the gut. It was also a bright blow to the brain, or a sudden beating of brains, with all the charge and intimate grate of rubbed balloons. It emptied our lungs. It felled the forest, moved the fields, and drained the pond; the world dismantled and tumbled into that black hole of eyes. If you and I looked at each other that way, our skulls would split and drop to our shoulders. But we don't. We keep our skulls. So.   10

He disappeared. This was only last week, and already I don't remember what shattered the enchantment. I think I blinked, I think I retrieved my brain from the weasel's brain, and tried to memorize what I was seeing, and the weasel felt the yank of separation, the careening splashdown into real life and the urgent current of instinct. He vanished under the wild rose. I waited motionless, my mind suddenly full of data and my spirit with pleadings, but he didn't return.   11

Please do not tell me about "approach-avoidance conflicts." I tell you I've been in that weasel's brain for sixty seconds, and he was in mine. Brains are private places, muttering through unique and secret tapes—but the weasel and I both plugged into another tape simultaneously, for a sweet and shocking time. Can I help it if it was a blank?   12

What goes on in his brain the rest of the time? What does a weasel think about? He won't say. His journal is tracks in clay, a spray of feathers, mouse blood and bone: uncollected, unconnected, loose-leaf, and blown.   13

I would like to learn, or remember, how to live. I come to Hollins Pond not so much to learn how to live as, frankly, to forget about it. That is, I don't think I can learn from a wild animal how to live in particular—shall I suck warm blood, hold my tail high, walk with my footprints precisely over the prints of my hands?—but I might learn   14 something of mindlessness, something of the purity of living in the physical senses and the dignity of living without bias or motive. The weasel lives in necessity and we live in choice, hating necessity and dying at the last ignobly in its talons. I would like to live as I should, as the weasel lives as he should. And I suspect that for me the way is like the weasel's: open to time and death painlessly, noticing everything, remembering nothing, choosing the given with a fierce and pointed will.

I missed my chance. I should have gone for the throat. I should have   15
lunged for that streak of white under the weasel's chin and held on, held on through mud and into the wild rose, held on for a dearer life. We could live under the wild rose wild as weasels, mute and uncomprehending. I could very calmly go wild. I could live two days in the den, curled, leaning on mouse fur, sniffing bird bones, blinking, licking, breathing musk, my hair tangled in the roots of grasses. Down is a good place to go, where the mind is single. Down is out, out of your ever-loving mind and back to your careless senses. I remember muteness as a prolonged and giddy fast, where every moment is a feast of utterance received. Time and events are merely poured, unremarked, and ingested directly, like blood pulsed into my gut through a jugular vein. Could two live that way? Could two live under the wild rose, and explore by the pond, so that the smooth mind of each is as everywhere present to the other, and as received and as unchallenged, as falling snow?

We could, you know. We can live any way we want. People take   16
vows of poverty, chastity, and obedience—even of silence—by choice. The thing is to stalk your calling in a certain skilled and supple way, to locate the most tender and live spot and plug into that pulse. This is yielding, not fighting. A weasel doesn't "attack" anything; a weasel lives as he's meant to, yielding at every moment to the perfect freedom of single necessity.

I think it would be well, and proper, and obedient, and pure, to   17
grasp your one necessity and not let it go, to dangle from it limp wherever it takes you. Then even death, where you're going no matter how you live, cannot you part. Seize it and let it seize you up aloft even, till your eyes burn out and drop; let your musky flesh fall off in shreds, and let your very bones unhinge and scatter, loosened over fields, over fields and woods, lightly, thoughtless, from any height at all, from as high as eagles.

Vocabulary

supposition (2)—something supposed, an idea

nonchalance (4)—casual indifference

terra firma (4)—Latin expression for firm earth or ground

tremulous (4)—trembling, quivering

lichen (7)—mossy plant that clings to rocks and trees

careening (11)—lurching from side to side while moving rapidly

ignobly (14)—without nobility; basely

IN YOUR JOURNAL

Write down what you learned about weasels from reading this essay. What do the animals look like? How do they live?

A Closer Reading

1. In what part of the United States does Dillard meet the weasel? Is it in an urban, suburban, or rural area? What does Dillard's description tell you about the habitat of weasels?

2. Why is Dillard sitting on the fallen tree at Hollins Pond at the time she sees the weasel?

3. What specific comparisons does Dillard make between human life and weasel life? Reread the essay, looking for the specific words and phrases Dillard uses.

4. What lessons does Dillard think she can learn from the weasel?

Drawing Your Own Conclusions

1. What does the anecdote Dillard tells in paragraph 2 reveal about the character of the weasel? What does it reveal about the eagle?

2. What do you think Dillard feels about the weasel—fear, awe, respect, love, hate, anger? Explain your answer by referring to specific words and phrases in her essay.

3. Although Dillard does not mention hunting as a human activity in this essay, she mentions the hunting that eagles and weasels do for survival. What do you think are the differences between the way the weasels and eagles hunt and the way human hunters hunt?

4. What does Dillard mean in paragraph 17 when she writes, "I think it would be well, and proper, and obedient, and pure, to grasp your one necessity and not let it go, to dangle from it limp wherever it takes you"?

Thinking about Writing

1. What is Dillard's main point? Does she ever state it explicitly in the essay? If so, where? If not, how do you as a reader know what it is?

2. Dillard establishes her feelings about nature by using words that are descriptive of the senses. Find words that describe sight, sound, smell, taste, and touch. How does her choice of these words enable Dillard to present her feelings about nature?

3. What is the tone of the essay? What is Dillard's relationship to nature? Support your answers with specific words and phrases from the essay.

4. The concluding paragraph is different in tone and content from the rest of the essay. Reread it, thinking about Dillard's purpose for ending this way. What does this paragraph mean? How does it connect with the rest of the essay? How does she connect this with the character of the weasel? How does this connect with the title of the essay?

*   *   *

Suggestions for Writing

1. Write about any encounter you have had with an animal in the wild. Where did the encounter occur? What was the animal's reaction to your presence? How did you respond? Dillard writes that she goes to Hollins Pond "not so much to learn how to live as, frankly, to forget about it." Did you learn something similar from your encounter?

2. Is there any reason why wild animals should be removed from the wild? Think about zoos, keeping animals in captivity to save them from extinction, circus animals, and scientific research using animals. Focus your essay on one or two of these areas. Write an essay taking a position on this issue. Support your point of view with personal experiences, observations, and evidence from your reading.

3. Describe a book or movie in which there was a depiction of an animal of which you approved or did not approve. After briefly outlining the incident, explain why you felt the depiction was or was not appropriate.

4. Write an essay from the point of view of a different species. Imagine that you are a different animal. How do you see the world? What do you think of humans? How do you communicate with other members of your species? What would you like humans to learn from your species?

Strategies for Revision

As soon as you have completed the first draft of your essay, put it aside. Separate yourself from your writing by spending ten minutes reading and writing in your journal.

Think about your draft by asking yourself the following questions, which you should answer in your journal:

- What is the most important idea that I am trying to communicate in this piece of writing? (Write this idea in your journal.)
- Do I reveal my feelings about animals? (Reread Dillard as a model for writing about animals.)
- Is there a clear beginning?
- Does each paragraph have a focus and a reason for existence?
- Am I choosing words and phrases that best express my ideas? (Copy your favorite phrase or sentence from this essay into your journal.)
- Does one idea connect to the next?
- What specific ideas make this draft interesting to read?
- Is there a clear ending?

If you discover any problem areas as you read and think about these questions, focus on those areas as you prepare to revise. Remember that revision involves rethinking. Sometimes this means that a writer adds new material, discards repetitive or useless material, or moves sentences and even paragraphs around so they connect ideas better. Sometimes writers change words or even examples and details to make them more specific and meaningful.

When you have decided on the best way to make your writing sharp and clear, begin to revise. Share your revision with another member of your class.

IN YOUR JOURNAL

What do you expect this essay to be about? Write down what you know about wilderness problems that face the United States today.

Can We Afford the Wilderness?

Ken Chowder

Ken Chowder, the historian/environmental activist, has written a novel, *Jadis*, and a screenplay, *The Wilderness Idea*. This article, which appeared in the June/July 1990 issue of *Modern Maturity* magazine, describes a debate that has existed for close to one hundred years in the United States—the debate between the needs of an ever-expanding civilization and the protection of the wilderness and the early conflicts between John Muir and James D. Phelan about the future of the wilderness.

John Muir (1838–1914) was a naturalist and writer whose efforts aided in the 1890 passage of the Yosemite National Park Bill, which established Yosemite and Sequoia National Parks. Muir also persuaded President Theodore Roosevelt to set aside 148,000,000 acres of forest reserves. A redwood forest in California near San Francisco is named John Muir Woods National Monument in honor of his efforts for the conservation and preservation of wilderness.

James D. Phelan was the reform mayor of San Francisco in 1901. In the name of the public good, Phelan proposed damming the Hetch Hetchy Valley to provide water for San Francisco. This met with Muir's opposition, because the Hetch Hetchy Valley was located in Yosemite National Park.

The present flourishing triumphant growth of the wealthy wicked, the Phelans . . . and their hirelings, will not thrive forever . . . . We may lose this particular fight, but truth and right must prevail at last.

—John Muir

He [John Muir] is a poetical gentleman. I am sure he would sacrifice his own family for the sake of beauty. He considers human life very cheap.

—James D. Phelan

They were both good men. John Muir, a self-described "poetico-   1
trampo-geologist-bot," was the first great American advocate for wilderness, the first president of the Sierra Club, a nationally popular writer
and naturalist. James D. Phelan, the reform mayor of San Francisco,
was the fiery opponent of monopolies, a champion of the public good.
They were good men—and they were vitriolic enemies.

In fact, the dispute between Muir and Phelan still rages today, in   2
only slightly altered form. There are still two conflicting answers to the
question What is wilderness for?

The particular argument between Muir and Phelan concerned a   3
remote mountain valley more than 150 miles from San Francisco with
the odd name of Hetch Hetchy. San Francisco, a city on the end of a dry
peninsula, was in chronic need of fresh water; in 1901 Mayor Phelan
proposed damming the valley to create a reservoir for San Francisco. At
the time, only a few hundred people had ever seen Hetch Hetchy—but
it was, not so coincidentally, in Yosemite National Park.

John Muir had spent many years in Yosemite, climbing its moun-   4
tains, exploring its most remote corners, and Hetch Hetchy was one of
his favorite places on Earth. It is "one of Nature's rarest and most
precious mountain temples," he wrote. "Dam Hetch Hetchy! As well
dam for water-tanks the people's cathedrals and churches, for no holier
temple has ever been consecrated by the heart of man."

Muir and the Sierra Club raised enough of a protest to have Phelan's   5
proposal turned down. Undaunted, Phelan tried again in 1903, again in
1905, again in 1907. To his way of thinking, a dam in Hetch Hetchy
would provide drinking water and electricity, and, crucially, free San
Francisco from the monopoly of the Spring Valley Water Company.
The idea that preserving *scenery* was more important than saving his city
from economic injustice infuriated Phelan. "John Muir loves the Sierras
and roams at large, and is hypersensitive on the subject of the invasion
of *his* territory," Phelan wrote. "The 400,000 people of San Francisco
are suffering from bad water and ask Mr. Muir to cease his quibbling."

Subduing the Wild

Actually it was far from quibbling. The debate over Hetch Hetchy   6
concerned the very definition of conservation. At the time conservation
was still very new. For the first European settlers the wild continent had
been a wolfish, godless enemy to be subdued; the mark of Satan, the
Puritans thought, was on all things wild. As naturalist Aldo Leopold

put it, "A stump was our symbol of progress." But as wilderness slowly became both less dangerous and less infinitely vast, it began to seem more valuable, more attractive.

By 1901 the new conservation movement was already a house divided. The "utilitarian" school of conservation believed in "wise use" of the land: husbanding the resources of wilderness to provide the greatest benefit to the greatest number of people. The "preservationist" school believed that wilderness should be left exactly as is, untouched, like a cathedral of God. Which should have priority, the needs of man or those of wilderness itself? The debate began early and it persists to this day. 7

The first national debate over the use of wilderness in U.S. history, the Hetch Hetchy struggle lasted 12 years. To most people the conflict seemed one between two Goods: water and light for San Francisco versus saving the beauty of the wild mountain valley. But both sides saw it as simple Right vs. Wrong, and the invective flowed. Muir wrote of "James Phelan, Satan and company." He described the dam's proponents as "mischief-makers and robbers," as "temple destroyers, devotees of ravaging commercialism." Dam supporter William Kent wrote of Muir that he was "a man entirely without social sense. With him, it is me and God and the rock where God put it, and that is the end of the story." San Francisco's city engineer called the preservationists "short-haired women and long-haired men"; the pro-dam *San Francisco Chronicle* called them "hoggish and mushy esthetes." Muir said of his critics: "They all show forth the proud sort of confidence that comes of a good sound irrefragable ignorance." 8

The 1906 earthquake, causing a fire that destroyed much of San Francisco, seemed to underline the city's need for water; and in 1908 a city referendum resulted in a 7–1 margin in favor of a dam. But in the nation at large Muir and the Sierra Club, using articles, pamphlets and broadsides, successfully whipped up public opinion in favor of preserving the valley. Letters began to pour into Congress by the thousand; most major newspapers published editorials condemning the dam. "The people are now aroused. Tidings from far and near show that almost every good man and woman is with us," Muir wrote in 1913. "Therefore be of good cheer, watch, and pray and fight!" 9

On December 6, 1913, after 12 years of fighting, the Hetch Hetchy question came to a final vote. The U.S. Senate passed the bill authorizing the dam with a 43–25 vote. *The New York Times* wrote, "The American people have been whipped in the Hetch Hetchy fight." 10

"I'll be relieved when it's settled, for it's killing me," Muir had   11
written. In fact, he did become sick not long after the bill's passage, and
died of pneumonia in December 1914.

But John Muir had his revenge. The Hetch Hetchy defeat did won-   12
ders for his cause. The grassroots nature of the anti-dam protest wid-
ened preservationist support tremendously; a vague general approval of
wilderness hardened into a movement capable of sustained political
action. "The conscience of the whole country," as Muir put it, was
"aroused from sleep."

The Hetch Hetchy decision was the beginning, not the end. Curi-   13
ously, many of the great wilderness struggles since Hetch Hetchy have
had the same general outline: The argument is often about a dam
proposed for a site in a national park or protected area. "In the view of
conservationists, there is something special about dams," wrote author
John McPhee, "something . . . metaphysically sinister." David Brower,
longtime head of the Sierra Club, put it succinctly: "I hate all dams,
large and small. If you are against a dam, you are for a river."

In 1913, the time of the Hetch Hetchy decision, only a handful of   14
conservation organizations existed; 40 years later the number was over
300. And in 1954 they all mobilized for war.

This time the dam was proposed for Echo Park—part of the Dino-   15
saur National Monument on the Colorado–Utah border. Again the
integrity of the National Park system was at stake. Again the dam's
opponents, led by David Brower of the Sierra Club, took their case
directly to the public. The wilderness advocates saturated the press with
anti-dam advertisements, produced a cautionary film (*Two Yosemites*)
and a book (*This Is Dinosaur*). The public-relations campaign was massive and the public response unparalleled—mail to members of Congress ran 80–1 against the dam.

This time the preservationists won. After five years of public pres-   16
sure, the project's backers caved in. Ironically, it was the well-honed
political skills of the environmentalists—in theory the group *without*
political clout—that carried the day. A member of the House Committee on Interior and Insular Affairs said the proponents of the dam had
"neither the money nor the organization to cope with the resources and
mailing lists" of the preservationists.

The Dinosaur debate had many familiar elements. Congressmen   17
constantly expressed ambivalence, citing the difficulty of choosing between two Goods. The wild canyon was undoubtedly a good thing; but

so were water, light and food for the desolate Southwest. Similarly, preservationists were reluctant to denigrate dams in general, or dismiss the whole of progress. What had come to the surface again was a characteristically American duality. Paired contradictions—such as Beauty and Utility, or Religion and Science—can often occupy twin places of honor in the American pantheon. One pair that has much affected wilderness in the 20th century is the will to master the wild yoked to the desire to worship it: progress and preservation. As author and environmentalist Wallace Stegner wrote, "No other nation on Earth so swiftly wasted its birthright; no other, in time, made such an effort to save what was left."

After Dinosaur, preservationists began to press for an umbrella bill   18
that would create a national system of wilderness protection. The Wilderness Act had a rough passage, with Congress spending eight years debating and revising the measure. The final enactment was largely the result of one man's tireless devotion: Howard Zahniser of the Wilderness Society plugged the initial idea, wrote the original draft, saw the bill through no fewer than 66 rewrites, spoke to all 18 hearings—only to die four months before his beloved brainchild became law.

The Wilderness Act of 1964 did not, of course, close the book on   19
struggles between utilitarians and preservationists. During the 1960s dams were proposed for two sites in the Grand Canyon itself. The Central Arizona Project had the support of the President, but in a result that would have been almost unimaginable in 1913, environmentalists, led by David Brower, defeated the dams and preserved the canyon. Today, the broad concept of wilderness has achieved a certain sanctity; wilderness, in its dotage, has become hallowed. "For it can be a means," Wallace Stegner wrote, "of reassuring ourselves of our sanity as creatures, a part of the geography of hope."

Still, there are at any given time numerous firestorms over wilder-   20
ness raging in this country. Some of the hottest of the moment: The Bush Administration, despite the huge Exxon *Valdez* oil spill, still hopes to open the Arctic National Wildlife Refuge in Alaska to oil development; the U.S. Forest Service is under fire for logging 450 million board feet of timber annually from Alaska's Tongass National Forest; and environmentalists in the Pacific Northwest are pushing hard to save old-growth National Forests and protect the imperiled spotted owl.

The battle sites change, but the basic problem remains the same: "the   21
very old problem," as Roderick Nash wrote in *Wilderness and the American
Mind*, "of whether parks, reserves and wildernesses are for man . . . or for
nature." In conservation, as in everything else, some things never change.
But what *has* changed, in the 77 years since the Hetch Hetchy decision, is
the face of the land itself. So much less wild land remains that the reasons
for developing it need to be that much stronger before they begin to make
sense. In short, we need wilderness more because there is less of it.

As the next century gallops closer, a second change in the ongoing   22
Man vs. Nature argument grows increasingly clear: One of the species
that has become endangered by the rush of progress is humankind itself.
The accidental but terrifying byproducts of modernity—such as nuclear
waste and acid rain—have made preservation, in the end, perhaps the
most utilitarian stance of all. So the old duality of Nature and Civilization is, in some sense, no longer a duality; the two have become an
environmental version of the Odd Couple—their fortunes curiously but
inextricably linked, from now on.

History, of course, is the playground of irony. It is certainly true that   23
the steady growth of the preservationist cause is John Muir's revenge for
the Hetch Hetchy defeat; but I've recently discovered that Muir's revenge has a second, more private side.

Exploring the grounds of Villa Montalvo—James D. Phelan's lovely   24
Saratoga, California, estate—I found a bust of John Muir, of all people,
in a central place. So the craggy visage of John Muir himself now lords
it over James Phelan's garden, gazing out from atop the steps. Meanwhile, the former utilitarian mayor no doubt turns ceaselessly, furiously,
and uselessly in his grave.

For Further Reading

The American Conservation Movement: John Muir and His Legacy, Stephen Fox
    (University of Wisconsin, 1986).
Wilderness and the American Mind, Roderick Nash (Yale University Press, 1982).
Encounters with the Archdruid, John McPhee (Farrar, Straus & Giroux, 1971).
"The Wilderness Letter," Wallace Stegner in *The Sound of Mountain Water*
    (Doubleday, 1969).
The Wilderness Idea, a 58-minute film by Lawrence Hott and Diane Garey
    (1989). For information write Direct Cinema, Ltd., P.O. Box 69799, Los
    Angeles, CA 90069, or telephone 213-396-4774.

Vocabulary

vitriolic (1)—sharp and bitter

undaunted (5)—not discouraged; intrepid

quibbling (5)—evading the main point by focusing on a petty detail

invective (8)—curses, insults, or other forms of verbal abuse

irrefragable (8)—indisputable

broadsides (9)—term from the seventeenth century for a type of newspaper with a political message printed on both sides of a large sheet of paper, sometimes with advertisements

metaphysically (13)—based on ideas beyond the material; abstractly

well-honed (16)—well-sharpened

denigrate (17)—to deny the worth of something

dotage (19)—the state of decline due to old age

irony (23)—the difference between what is expected and the actual result

---

IN YOUR JOURNAL

Choose three pieces of new information that you learned from reading this essay. Write about them and explain why you will remember them.

A Closer Reading

1. Who was John Muir? Who was John D. Phelan? Why were they enemies? How were their differences resolved? To what irony concerning these two men does Chowder refer at the end of the essay?

2. What is the Sierra Club? What is Muir's connection to the Sierra Club?

3. What was the Wilderness Act of 1964? Is it still in effect? Does it still provide protection? Why or why not?

4. What changes have occurred at the end of the twentieth century that have altered the issues involved in the People vs. Nature dispute?

Drawing Your Own Conclusions

1. What is a dam? Why do some preservationists believe in the statement "If you are against a dam, you are for a river"?

2. What are the 1990 environmental disasters to which Chowder refers in his essay? What are some environmental problems that are important today? How have they been responded to by the environmental groups? By the government? By politicians? By the media? By the general people? How should they be handled?

3. In what way is calling preservationists "short-haired women and long-haired men" meant to be insulting? What other articles have you read in this book about the dangers of stereotypes and the limited thinking they reflect?

4. What national parks are mentioned in this article? What is the difference between a national park and a local park in terms of who takes care of it, how its resources are used, and who makes decisions about its future? What are some other national parks in the United States? What was John Muir's role in the national park system?

Thinking about Writing

1. In paragraph 1, Chowder refers to John Muir as a self-described "poetico-trampo-geologist-bot." What interests were most important to Muir, according to his description?

2. The subtitle of this article is "Battle Still Rages." What words and phrases in the article relate to battle and to war imagery?

3. Has does Chowder set up Muir and Phelan as opponents? How does he describe each?

4. This is an essay about oppositions. Make a list of the paired contradictions referred to in this article. For example:

right	wrong
preservationist	utilitarian
progress	preservation

5. What dates does Chowder refer to in the article? How does he connect those dates with historical occurrences? How do the occurrences connect with the debate over nature vs. civilization?

6. Notice the number of quotations that Chowder uses throughout. How does he inform his readers about the sources of his quotations?

*   *   *

Suggestions for Writing

1. Write an essay in which you describe an experience you had in the wilderness, in a place away from civilization, where you were surrounded by trees, the sky, and the earth. Where were you? How did you feel? Use vivid language to portray the sights, sounds, and smells around you so that your readers will be able to picture the place you describe.

2. Write an essay in which you explain how you would make a decision between two public goods such as those described in the Chowder article—whether to build a dam to bring water to a city, or whether to create a public park site to maintain the wilderness for generations to come. What factors would you consider in making such a decision today? On whose opinions would you rely to help you make your decision? Decide what decision you would make and why.

3. Write an essay in which you describe a serious problem the government will have in making decisions about wilderness areas. After identifying the problem, explain why you think it is critical, and describe the steps that should be taken to resolve the problem.

4. Choose one pair from the list of contradictions you developed in answer to question 4 above. Write an essay in which you define the two words, and explain in what ways they refer to opposite concepts or ideas.

5. Who should make decisions about what parts of the wilderness should be saved and what parts can be sold to developers— politicians, voters, environmentalists, loggers, construction workers, or any other group you can think of? Decide which of these groups should make the decisions and explain why, based on your experiences, observations, and readings.

Strategies for Revision

The strategy for revision that follows involves your working in a group of four students. Begin by making enough copies of your draft to share with the three other members of your group. The other members should do the same.

Before you begin to discuss the writing, each of you should decide on three questions about your writing that you would like to have a reader consider. Tell the group your questions before you begin to read your writing aloud. Members should write the three questions on the top of the reader's paper and use those questions as a guide to the paper.

Then, each writer should take a turn reading what she or he has written. As the members of the group discuss the writing, they should keep in mind that they are trying to help each writer make a piece of writing more effective and clear.

After a reading is finished and the group has had enough time to think about the writing, discuss the writer's three questions. Each member may also want to ask the following:

- What one piece of information did you remember from my writing?
- What was my overall point of view?
- Was there any part of the writing that was confusing?

When each member has had a chance to read a draft and discuss it, each student should rewrite and revise, taking into consideration the group's responses. Share your revisions with one another.

IN YOUR JOURNAL

Have you ever found a secret place that you did not want to share with anyone? Yet there is a part of you that wants people to know that you have found something special, private, all your own. The essay, written by a trout fisherman, describes the place where he likes to fish, a brook that is part of a larger river. He does not want to share it, but he wants to share its beauty with his words.

Write about a secret special place where you go by yourself.

Rivertops

Ted Williams

Born in Massachusetts, Ted Williams is a writer who specializes in wildlife and the environment. He is a contributing editor to *Audubon* magazine and *Gray's Sporting Journal*. In 1985 he published *The Reservation,* and in 1986 he published a nonfiction book, *Don't Blame the Indians.* "Rivertops," which appeared in *On Nature: Essays on Nature, Landscape and Natural History* (1986), describes a special trout stream whose true name Williams refuses to reveal.

Having one's rivers is important, like having family or a country. 1
With rivers, though, you get to choose. I prefer mine rippling with wild brook trout, which is to say clean and secluded, and because my time and place coincide with an irruption of my species, this means my rivers also must be small. Headwater streams really, the tops of systems known even in Boston's Back Bay.

An hour west of Worcester, Massachusetts, is the rivertop I love 2
best. Hyla Brook, I call it, for that is not its name. Here under bald eagles and turkey vultures, in woods demanding good boots, lunch, the better part of a day and, sometimes, a compass, it's hard to remember you're not in Maine. In the general watershed are dozens of other brooks, some bigger than Hyla, some smaller, none quite so lovely. All are as safe from human defilement as is possible for running water to be, not because people enjoy their beauty or revel in the rich communities of plants and animals that flourish in and around them or spend time

near them or in any way treasure them for what they are. Only because
Boston drinks them. . . .

Better to tell what rivertop trouting is like, to encourage it, if not ac-   3
tually on Hyla Brook, at least on other forgotten Eastern rivertops that you
can find yourself. I used to think that more native-brook-trout fishermen
would mean fewer native brook trout. Now I think that the reverse is true,
that more native-brook-trout fishermen mean more wild water preserved.

I first saw Hyla on a green topo map while ensconced in my easy chair   4
beside a black-cherry fire. Having established that the brook was *not* on
the state stocking list, a prerequisite for even casual consideration, I
looked more closely at the map. Lots of unbroken green all around; I got
interested. Gradient looked good; I got *very* interested. There were riffles
and pools, and meadows where gaudy, stream-bred brook trout could sip
mayflies and lounge in icy, air-charged current that tumbled down from
hemlock-shaded ledges. I rushed there the next morning.

At this point I should note that finding healthy wild trout popula-   5
tions is like finding flying squirrels. You'll tap twenty or maybe a hundred
hollow trees before a coal-eyed head appears. But troutlust is only one
reason to find and keep rivertops. Rivertops are magnetized wires drawing and concentrating all the best things forests have. One may be equally
infatuated with wildflowers or woodland butterflies or berries or wood-
peckers or herons or deer or mink or beaver or drumming grouse or
visions of silver spilling over moss. . . . Come to think of it, to me each of
these good things is all of them and more, and if I didn't hang around
rivertops because of trout, it would be because of something else.

No day on a rivertop is ever better than your first. That magic   6
morning on Hyla Brook ten Mays ago I had found one of the few spots
in Massachusetts where you can hike hard for thirty minutes and be
deeper into the woods than when you started—a secret, timeless place
fragrant with skunk cabbage, leaf mulch and wet earth, where wood
frogs quacked and redfin pickerel streaked from swampy shallows,
where newts lay suspended in backwaters and sashayed into muck,
where spring azures skipped among unfurling ferns and fields of water-
cress waved gently in clear current over clean gravel. In and out of the
brook, clumps of marsh marigolds were in brilliant yellow bloom and,
as far back as I could see, the banks were carpeted with pale yellow trout
lilies. A pair of wood ducks burst from an ancient beaver flowage and
went squealing downriver. Trout were too much to hope for.

Here and there, in the deeper pockets, I flipped out a puffy dry fly   7
on a two-pound tippet, but nothing rose to it save fallfish—"chubs,"

trouters call them, spitting the word. Fallfish grunt like pigs. The bigger they are the louder they grunt. Once, in Maine, I ate one, and it tasted like wet Kleenex. But something about Hyla Brook made me look hard at fallfish, and I saw them for the first time not as "trash fish" to be squeezed and bush-tossed, but as a part that belonged. Really, they are quite beautiful, very streamlined, silver in their youth, bronze and pewter in maturity. Thoreau, who fished for them passionately, called them "chivin" and basically found them to be "cupreous dolphin."

Not expecting trout, I naturally found them, suddenly and in aston- 8
ishing abundance. They were rising to little blue mayflies in the deep, quick water at the head of the first meadow exactly as I had imagined the night before. I pushed through thick alders, wiping spiderwebs from my face and grimacing as ice water rose to my waist. Finally, feeling like Sylvester tossed into the birdcage and told to help himself, I was in position. The fly drifted about six inches before it disappeared in a lusty boil. It is difficult for brook-trout anglers to admit, but the brutal truth is that these noble fish not only are nonselective in their feeding behavior, but reckless, suicidal even. One can "match the hatch" if one chooses or one can toss out a Japanese machine-tied Bumble Boogie. Nine times out of ten the results will be the same—instant slurp.

That first trout from Hyla Brook was the third biggest I have ever 9
taken there—eleven inches. (I won't say I set *no* premium on bigness.) She ran the line around a beaver cutting, and I reached down and tickled her smooth flanks, lifting her toward the surface so slowly she never struggled until she was on the bank. She was perfectly proportioned, deep-bodied, with a smallish head indicative of good feed and fast growth. The markings on her green back resembled old worm trails on the inside of elm bark, and her chestnut sides were flecked with scarlet, each fleck ringed with blue. Her belly was orange, pectoral, ventral and anal fins crimson and trimmed with ivory. I fished on for two miles, catching wild brook trout all the way—little fish of big country—and at dusk a great horned owl floated out of the woods and settled on a drowned cedar under a crescent moon.

There have been scores of other important days on Hyla Brook: The 10
time I got there late and couldn't tear myself away and got lost in the drizzly dark, plowing till 2:00 A.M. through grape and jewelweed with only the cold, green light of fireflies all around, feeling like Bottom in *Midsummer Night's Dream*. The time I almost stepped on a deer. The time last year I sat on a sandbar, cleaning trout in the bright moonlight and listening to Eastern coyotes howling and moving on the hill in back of me.

I want more people on rivertops, but it does not follow that I want   11
more of them on mine. Rivertops are very personal things, like axes and
shotguns, and I have shared mine only with a seven-year-old named
Beth and a ten-year-old named Scott. Rivertops are not to be tattled on.
To quote my friend John Voelker, who quit the state's supreme court in
order to chase brook trout and write about them, . . . "[Wild] trout,
unlike men, will not—indeed cannot—live except where beauty dwells,
so that any man who would catch a trout finds himself inevitably surrounded by beauty: he can't help himself." That's what I've been trying
to say.

Vocabulary

irruption (1)—an abrupt increase in population

defilement (2)—pollution; dirty-
ing

revel (2)—to delight in

topo map (4)—a topographic
map; it shows the surface
features of an area

gradient (4)—the degree of
slope of

riffles (4)—shallow areas in a
stream or pond

sashayed (6)—walked casually

cupreous (7)—copper-colored

IN YOUR JOURNAL

What does Williams want his reader to know about his rivertop? Is
there anything in his description that makes you want to find it and visit
there? Imagine yourself at the rivertop on a sunny afternoon. What will
you see, hear, smell, feel?

A Closer Reading

1. Why does Williams refuse to give the proper name of his
   rivertop?

2. What in this essay indicates that Williams goes to his rivertop for
   more than the wild trout?

3. What does Williams mean by this simile: "feeling like Sylvester
   tossed into the birdcage and told to help himself"?

4. How does Williams feel about the trout? Support your answer with evidence from his essay.

5. What analogy (a comparison in which the writer explains something unfamiliar by comparing it with something familiar) does Williams make between rivers, family, and one's country?

Drawing Your Own Conclusions

1. What is Williams's attitude toward other people? How does he feel about the "irruption" of the human species? Is he an elitist or a realist? Support your answers with words and phrases from his essay.

2. Williams refuses to fish in state-stocked trout streams, preferring to fish in native streams. What does Williams mean in paragraph 3 when he writes that he no longer thinks that "more native-brook-trout fishermen would mean fewer native brook trout," but that in fact, he now thinks "that more native-brook-trout fishermen mean more wild water preserved"?

3. Why does the author refer to the trout in paragraph 9 as "she"? In the last paragraph, Williams quotes from Voelker in a reference to "man." Do you think Williams wrote this essay for a male or a mixed male and female audience? Explain your answer, referring back to the essay.

4. In paragraph 1 Williams writes, "Having one's rivers is important, like having family or a country." How does this attitude compare to Dillard's attitude (see page 349) toward the location she describes?

Thinking about Writing

1. What are some of the descriptive words that Williams uses to picture his eleven-inch trout?

2. Reread the essay, locating Williams's use of references to color to describe the fish, other creatures, and his rivertop.

3. Compare Williams's essay with Dillard's essay about the weasel (see page 349). In what structural ways are these essays similar? How does each of these writers use descriptive language?

4. Williams uses metaphors and similes to compare his experience to other experiences that his readers may have had. What examples of metaphors and similies can you locate? How do these help you to see Williams's rivertop? What mood does Williams create through his use of these figures of speech?

*   *   *

Suggestions for Writing

1. Write a descriptive essay about a place that is meaningful to you but whose location you do not want revealed. Reread Williams's essay for ideas about description and organization. You may expand your journal entry, or you may want to start over.

2. Write an essay in which you describe a sport that you have played and enjoyed. Tell your reader about the sensations of being involved in the sport. Describe the looks of the game from the inside, the fears, the excitement. Use your words to bring it alive for your reader.

3. Write an essay in which you compare your experiences fishing with those of Williams. Write to an audience of avid fishermen like him. Add as much detail as possible so your readers will know your feelings about fishing.

4. A step-by-step *process essay* is a type of writing that teaches readers how to do something for themselves, such as how to install a telephone answering machine, or helps them to understand a process, such as the way electricity works. The writing is arranged in chronological order, so readers can follow from one step to the next. The writer uses words such as *first, second, next,* and *then* to connect ideas together. The steps should be sequential and clear so readers will be able to do something themselves or to understand a concept or process after reading the essay.

   Write a step-by-step process essay in which you teach a person who has never gone fishing how to fish. You should specify what type of fishing you are going to do (river, stream, ocean, in a boat, or on foot). Tell your reader what equipment is needed and, in easy-to-follow steps, what the novice will need to know to enjoy a day's fishing.

5. Write a step-by-step process essay in which you teach someone how to go hiking in the deep woods. Remember to include a list of items to bring along. Try to make your steps simple and clear so that a novice could have an enjoyable time on his or her first trip into the deep woods.

Strategies for Revision

After you have completed the first draft of your essay, put it away for at least one entire day. When you read it again, you will have created some distance so that you can look at your own work more objectively. Read the Williams selection again, focusing on his use of description. Then read your draft aloud to yourself, focusing on the following questions:

- Do the descriptions include any metaphors and similes? Are the comparisons original and unusual? Do the descriptions help my reader "see" them as well?
- Do the descriptive words evoke a variety of senses—sight, sound, smell, taste, and touch—as Williams does in his description of the trout?
- If the draft described step by step how to do something, are the steps in order? Can a reader follow them? Would someone be able to do what the essay describes just by using this piece of writing as a guide? If not, how could it be clearer?
- Are there parts of the draft that do not connect well? After time away from your draft, it may become clear that the transitions do not hold varying information together well.
- Are some of the word choices not appropriate? Through the choice of words and phrases, what attitude do you present in relation to nature and to your subject? Should any words and phrases be rethought and changed?
- Are there ideas to be added and some to be deleted?

After thinking about these things, rewrite your draft, making revisions. Share your revised essay with a classmate.

IN YOUR JOURNAL

Write down all the problems we face today because of human interaction with the environment. Is the earth so damaged that the possibility of a genetically engineered world is in our near future? Answer this question, taking into account some of the problems you just listed.

The End of Nature

Bill McKibben

Bill McKibben, journalist and environmentalist, lives in the Adirondack Mountains of New York State. He has written hundreds of articles for the *New Yorker* magazine demonstrating humankind's effect on the processes of nature. McKibben has also written about nature for the *New York Review of Books* and the *New York Times*. This excerpt is from his first book, published in 1989, *The End of Nature*.

Several years ago, Jim Stolz shouldered a pack at the Mexican border and hiked eight or nine hundred miles north to the Idaho mountains for a meeting of a small environmental group. 1

This, he told me as we sat by a stream three months later, was not all that unusual for him. Some years earlier, he had walked the Appalachian Trail, Georgia to Maine. "I spent the next two years going coast to coast. I took the northern route—I spent a couple of months on snowshoes through Wisconsin and Minnesota." He'd never seen the Pacific till he got there on his own two feet. After that, he walked the Continental Divide trail. And then he began to lay out a new trek—the Grand West Trail, he calls it. It runs north and south between the Pacific Crest and the Continental Divide trails, traversing the Grand Canyon and the lava plains, climbing over the Sawtooths. All it lacks is people. "I spent one nine-and-a-half-day stretch this trip when I didn't see anyone," Stolz said. "I see someone else maybe every fourth day." 2

In the course of his long walks he had twelve times come across grizzly bears, the continent's grandest mammals, now nearly gone from the lower forty-eight. "The last one, he stood on his hind legs, clicked 3 his jaws, woofed three times. I was too close to him, and he was just letting me know. Another one circled me about forty feet away and wouldn't look me in the eye. When you get that close, you realize you're part of the food chain. When we go into grizzly country, we're going into *their* home. We're the intruders. We're used to being top dog. But in griz country we're part of the food chain."

That seemed a quietly radical idea to me—the idea that we don't necessarily belong at the top in every way. It seemed to me, thinking about it later, that it might be a good way to describe a philosophy that is the opposite of the defiant, consumptive course we've traditionally followed. What would it mean to our ways of life, our demographics, our economics, our output of carbon dioxide and methane if we began to truly and viscerally think of ourselves as just one species among many? 4

The logic of our present thinking—that we should increase in numbers and, especially, in material wealth and ease—leads inexorably in the direction of the managed world. It is, as a few rebels have maintained, a rut, a system of beliefs in which we are trapped. When Thoreau declared that the mass of men lead lives of quiet desperation, it was to this rut that he referred. He went to live at Walden Pond to prove how little man needed to survive—$61.99¾ for eight months, including the cost of his house. 5

But most of us have lived in that rut without rebelling. A few, often under Thoreau's influence, may have chucked their sophomore year to live in a tent by some wild lake, but even most of them returned to normal society. Thoreau's explanation—that we think there's no choice—may help explain this fact. But the terrible truth is that most of us rather like the rut. We like acquiring more things; the aphorists notwithstanding, they make us happy. We like the easy life. I was skimming through an old copy of the *New Yorker* not long ago and came across an advertisement, from what in 1949 was still the Esso Company, that summed up our century to this point. "The better you live," it shouted, "the more oil you use." And we live well. The world, as most of us in the West experience it in the late twentieth century, is a reasonably sweet place. That is why there aren't more hippies camped by the lake. We like to camp, but for the weekend. 6

The only trouble is that this system of beliefs, this pleasant rut, seems not to be making *the planet* happy. The atmosphere and the forests are less satisfied than we are. In fact, they are changing, dying. And those changes affect us, body and soul. The end of nature sours all 7 my material pleasures. The prospect of living in a genetically engineered world sickens me. And yet it is toward such a world that our belief in endless material advancement hurries us.

As long as that desire drives us, there is no way to set limits. We   8
won't develop genetic engineering to eradicate disease and not use it to manufacture perfectly efficient chickens; there is nothing in the logic of our ingrained beliefs that would lead us to draw those lines. Direct our beliefs into a new stream, and that stream will soon be a torrent just like the present one: if we use fusion energy instead of coal, we will still plow ahead at our basic business, accumulation, with all its implications for the natural world. If there is one notion that virtualy every successful politician on earth—socialist or fascist or capitalist—agrees on, it is that "economic growth" is good, necessary, the proper end of organized human activity. But where does economic growth end? It ends—or, at least, it runs straight through—the genetically engineered dead world that the optimists envision. That is, provided we can surmount our present environmental troubles.

Those troubles, though, just might give us the chance to change the   9
way we think. What if they gave us a practical—as opposed to a moral or an aesthetic—reason to climb out of our rut and find a new one that leads in some different direction? A reason based on atmospheric chemistry, not Eastern spirituality. That is why Stolz's phrase caught my ear, his notion that we might be no more important than anything else. If a new idea—a *humble* idea, in contrast to the conventional defiant attitude—is going to rise out of the wreckage we have made of the world, this is the gut feeling, the impulse, it will come from.

The idea that the rest of creation might count for as much as we do   10
is spectacularly foreign, even to most environmentalists. The ecological movement has always had its greatest success in convincing people that we are threatened by some looming problem—or, if we are not threatened directly, then some creature that we find appealing, such as the seal or the whale or the songbird. The tropical rain forests must be saved because they contain millions of species of plants that may have medical uses—that was the single most common argument against tropical deforestation until it was replaced by the greenhouse effect. Even the American wilderness movement, in some ways a radical crusade, has argued for wilderness largely as places for man—places big enough for backpackers to lose themselves in and for stressed city dwellers to find themselves.

But what if we began to believe in the rain forest *for its own sake?*   11
This attitude has very slowly begun to spread in recent years, both in
America and abroad, as the effects of man's domination have become
clearer. Some few people have begun to talk of two views of the
world—the traditional, man-centered—anthropocentric—view and the
biocentric vision of people as a part of the world, just like bears.

Many of those who take the biocentric view are, of course, oddballs,   12
the sort who would walk two thousand miles instead of flying. (Prophets, false or true, are inevitably oddballs. There's not much need for
prophets who are in synch with their society.) And theirs is, admittedly,
a radical idea, almost an unrealistic idea. It strikes at the root of our
identities. But we live at a radical, unrealistic moment. We live at the
end of nature, the moment when the essential character of the world
we've known since we stopped swinging from our tails is suddenly
changing. I'm not intrinsically attracted to radical ideas anymore. I have
a house, and a bank account, and I'd like my life, all other things being
equal, to continue in its current course. But all other things are not
equal—we live at an odd moment in human history when the most
basic elements of our lives are changing. I love the trees outside my
window; they are a part of my life. I don't want to see them shrivel in
the heat, nor sprout in perfect cloned rows. The damage we have done
to the planet, and the damage we seem set to do in a genetically engineered business-as-usual future, make me wonder if there isn't some
other way. If there isn't a humbler alternative—one that would let us
hew closer to what remains of nature, and give it room to recover, if it
can. An alternative that would involve changing not only the way we act
but also the way we think. . . .

The small but rapidly growing American environmental group   13
Earth First! provides one of the purest examples of putting the rest of
creation ahead of exclusively human concerns.

A decade ago Dave Foreman was wearing a suit and tie and working   14
in Washington as chief lobbyist for the Wilderness Society. His thinking, though, was evolving in the same direction as Abbey's. "The whole
time I'd been in Washington I'd been radical philosophically—I believed in wilderness for its own sake. But for a long time I'd believed the
best way to get more wilderness was to be reasonable, to take Republi-
can politicians to lunch." The Sagebrush Rebellion—the protests in the
late 1970s by Western miners, ranchers, and timber barons led by men
like James Watt who claimed that the small gains of environmentalists
were too much—convinced him otherwise. "It made me realize we

were fighting for crumbs under the table. I guess I came to the conclusion that the industrial empire was a cancer on the earth and that saving
some dinky recreational areas was not enough. That we had to offer a
fundamental challenge to Western civilization."

Earth First!—the group Foreman formed with a few friends when   15
he left Washington and the Wilderness Society—is one of a few fledg-
·ling attempts to translate the philosphical radicalism of a Muir or an
Abbey into action. Its motto is "No compromise in defense of Mother
Earth," and its symbol is the monkey wrench. The group has grown
quickly in the West, partly because of this tough image. Its journal, for
instance, includes tips for sabotage, or "ecodefense," helpful hints that
go well beyond Hayduke's level of expertise. When disabling heavy
machinery, for instance, sugar is completely passé. Rock-polishing grit,
mixed in a ratio of four parts motor oil to one part silicon carbide,
works much better. Or perhaps the government has put a dirt airstrip in
a wilderness area near you: if you go out at night and liberally salt the
runway, chances are deer, elk, and moose will soon come along and paw
it up, leaving large holes.

Such "ecotage" has worked in some places and backfired in others,   16
often making life more difficult for conventional environmentalists.
(Foreman was arrested late in the spring of 1989 on charges that he had
conspired to cut down power lines. An FBI informant had apparently
infiltrated Earth First! and Foreman charged that the government was
attempting to destroy the group.) Indisputably, Earth First!'s confronta-
tional tactics have earned the group far more publicity than it could
have gotten any other way.

But all the attention paid to the sabotage has usually overshadowed   17
the group's message, which is at least as radical as its methods. It wants
a different world, where roads are torn out to create vast new wildernesses, where most development ceases, and where much of man's imprint on the earth is slowly erased. Earth First! and the few other groups
like it have a purpose, and that purpose is defense of the wild, the
natural, the nonhuman.

The first time I heard Foreman speak, it was in a Sacramento,   18
California, church basement. He began by ripping off his button-down
shirt to reveal a black T-shirt with the raised monkey wrench embla-
zoned on it. He told of his days in Washington: "From my Wilderness
Society experience, I began to wonder, Why preserve a wilderness area?
Because it's a nice place to go and relax? Because you can make pretty
books of pictures of it? To protect a watershed? No. You protect a river

because it's a river. For its own sake. Because it has a right to exist by itself. The grizzly bear in Yellowstone Park has as much right to her life as any one of us has to our life," Foreman told the crowd. "Each of you is an animal and you should be proud of it."

"There are fundamental problems of philosophy at the root of all of this," insists Foreman. Most environmental groups discuss the need to "balance continued economic growth" with the "protection for future generations of our natural heritage." Foreman says, "I have really thought about it and tried to look for good news, for signs that reform will work. And I have come to the belief that the flaw is fundamental, unreformable. We can have big wildernesses, and we can reintroduce extirpated species, but unless the fact that there are way too many people on the earth is dealt with, unless the idea that the world is a resource for us to use is dealt with, unless humans can find their way home again, then the problems will continue." 19

Foreman and others have a name for this idea of people "finding their way home"—"deep ecology." In contrast to conventional, or "shallow," ecology, which basically accepts the anthropocentric worldview of the industrial state and merely wants to reform it—to turn mankind into better stewards—deep ecologists, in Foreman's words, "ask harder questions, such as: Where are we from? What is our relationship to the rest of the world? Are we really at the apex of evolution?" Their answers, not sand in the gas tanks of bulldozers, constitute "the fundamental challenge to Western civilization." 20

And, because we are all products and beneficiaries of that civilization, such ideas are a horrible challenge, even to those who think of themselves as environmentalists. When the *Nation* magazine printed an article outlining some of the tenets of deep ecology, it drew many angry letters. Deep ecology takes "the side of nature over culture," complained an "ecofeminist" named Ynestra King in a long missive, and in so doing it overlooks "the structures of entrenched economic and political power within society." Foreman "and his macho crowd . . . represent nothing more than the Daniel Boone mentality in ecological drag," she said. But to her the real problem is that Earth First! and deep ecology represent a "deep insensitivity to human suffering." 21

And in a profound way she is right. It is an intensely disturbing idea that man should not be the master of all, that other suffering might be just as important. And that individual suffering—animal or human—might be less important than the suffering of species, ecosystems, the planet. It is disturbing in a way that an idea like, say, Marxism is not. It is 22 not all that radical to talk about who is going to own the factories, at least compared with the question of whether there are going to *be* factories.

Vocabulary

trek (2)—a difficult trip

consumptive (4)—consuming; wasteful

viscerally (4)—instinctively or emotionally, but not intellectually

inexorably (5)—unchangably; inevitably

aphorists (6)—tellers of short statements of truth

eradicate (8)—to wipe out

extirpate (19)—completely destroyed

apex (20)—the highest point; the top

tenets (21)—principles or beliefs

missive (21)—a letter

IN YOUR JOURNAL

What ideas stand out in your mind from reading the McKibben selection? What did you learn from this? What questions do you have?

A Closer Reading

1. How do encounters with grizzly bears connect with the idea that humans are just one species among many?

2. What is a genetically engineered world? What examples of this does McKibben provide? What other examples of this exist today?

3. Who is Dave Foreman? What is Earth First!? What is "eco-defense" and "ecotage"? Why does this group think it must take drastic measures?

4. What is the difference between an "anthropocentric" view of the world and a "biocentric" view of the world? Which view does McKibben have? Which does Dave Foreman have? Which one did John Muir (see Chowder selection on page 357) have? Use words and phrases from the selections to support your answers.

Drawing Your Own Conclusions

1. Are human beings superior to other animals? Why or why not?

2. How does the human need to have material things connect with the problems McKibben mentions?

3. What is the difference between the idea that the wilderness should be preserved for the good of humankind and the ideas promoted by Earth First!? Why is the monkey wrench an appropriate symbol for this group?

4. Define the ambivalence that McKibben feels about his own life and his feelings about nature. Why does he seem to feel this way? Do you feel the same way or differently? Explain.

5. "It is not all that radical to talk about who is going to own the factories, at least compared with the question of whether there are going to *be* factories," writes McKibben. What does he mean by this statement? How does this sum up the main point of the selection?

6. What similarities do you find between Williams's feelings about nature and McKibben's (see page 374)? How do each of these writers feel about the "irruption" of the human species? Explain your answer by referring to words and phrases from the two essays.

Thinking about Writing

1. What is McKibben's point of view? Where is it stated in the selection? In what way is it different from those expressed by John Muir and other preservationists quoted in the Chowder article on page 357?

2. What does the title "The End of Nature" mean in relation to the entire essay?

3. Identify the people to whom McKibben refers in this essay. Why are they important to his argument? In what ways do they support or oppose his point of view? Be specific.

4. Find any places in the article where McKibben uses description. Find places where he contrasts and compares. Find places where he analyzes. Find places where he argues a position. Which of these approaches to presenting information do you find most

frequently in this selection? What does that tell you about his purpose in writing this piece?

*   *   *

Suggestions for Writing

1. Many environmentalists state, "We have not inherited the earth from our fathers and mothers; we are borrowing it from our children." Write an essay in which you take this point of view. Suggest ways in which we can make the world a better place for our children.

2. Write an essay in which you explain what McKibben means by the idea that humans should have a humbler attitude toward nature and that we should show it more respect. What does he mean by the phrase "nature for nature's sake"? How do these concepts fit with your own feelings about nature, humans, and the environment?

3. Should trees be cut down to preserve the jobs of loggers in the United States, even if cutting down these trees endangers the survival of a species of bird or animal or alters the climate of our planet and therefore affects our lives? Write an essay in which you state and support your position on this issue.

4. Recently the bark of a protected species of tree was discovered to hold a potential cure for one type of cancer. Environmentalists and medical researchers clashed over whether or not some of the trees should be cut down and used for medical research on this potential cure. Who do you think is right—the environmentalists or the medical researchers? How did you reach this decision? Write an essay explaining your position and your reasons for it.

Strategies for Revision

This revision activity will involve working with a classmate who has never before seen your writing and whose writing you have never seen. You will be getting feedback on your writing from a new person who is unfamiliar with your strengths and weaknesses, and giving it to an unknown writer as well.

Before you meet to discuss what you have written, on a separate piece of paper complete the following statements (your partner should do the same):

- The draft is about . . .
- The reason I chose this topic was . . .
- If a reader gets only one new thought from this piece of writing, I would like it to be . . .
- It helps me the most when a reader . . .
- I had the most problems with . . . and I would like you to read that part more closely.

Give the answers to these statements and your draft to your partner. After he or she has read your writing and your answers, discuss your writing together. Your partner may have questions about your writing that will be helpful to you as you revise. After you have talked about your writing and you feel you are ready to begin to revise, change roles and discuss the other person's writing, using the same technique.

Revise what you have written, and share your revision with your partner.

IN YOUR JOURNAL

Write about an experience in which you found yourself in physical danger because you stood up to defend someone or some issue. What was the situation? Why did you take your position? How did you feel?

She Got Herself Shot

Hope Burwell

Hope Burwell, who lives in Iowa, is a farmer, a teacher, and a writer. In this essay, which appeared in the September/October 1992 issue of *Ms.* magazine, Burwell writes about her experiences on her farm during deer hunting season. Despite her No Hunting signs, hunters still roam her property every season. Burwell explores the personalities of these recreational hunters as well as her own feelings toward their trespassing and their sport.

It's autumn in Iowa. Already a winter's ability to steal one's breath   1
threatens as we wade through the predawn blue completing chores. Now, livestock and wood furnace fed, I sit, stocking feet propped on the picture windowsill, a cup of coffee in my left hand and binoculars in my right. Against a backdrop of scarlet sumac, orange maples, golden hickories, and burnt umber oaks, 17 white-tailed deer graze our hayfield. They blow warm breath against the frost coverlet muting emerald alfalfa, and when the ice has melted, pull water-drenched protein into their mouths.

It's difficult to describe the pleasure we derive sitting here, sharing   2
our morning coffee in silent reverence for this land and the wildlife who share it. Moments like these make bearable the hours stacking hay in the blazing sun, or stretching fence among mosquitoes; make bearable the months on end chained to livestock who must be fed twice a day. So we sit, enjoying one of the perks of rural life, and luxuriate in the pleasure.

The old doe, the one with the scars on her left flank, is here again,   3
this year's twins just out ahead where she can keep an eye on them. Several of the younger does, some of them her daughters, fan out, maintaining the same formation: fawns out front, mothers behind, ever

watchful. And far behind them all, visible near the does only in this rutting season, the buck stands, blending against low oak boughs. "Nine points this year," Sandy whispers beside me, and two does look up, turn their heads warily in our direction, hesitate, sink slowly back to grazing.

Suddenly, all the sleek brown necks jerk. Before their heads are   4
completely raised, the whole herd is moving, flowing like a muddy river over alfalfa. We hear the shots, late and distorted. By the time the *pop pop pop pop* reaches our ears the deer are sailing over a second fence line and heedlessly across the highway.

"Damn it," I snarl as my feet hit the floor. "Did they get the buck?"   5

"No." Anger clenches Sandy's teeth. "He went onto the road last."   6

And the slow simmer of blood roiling in my ears marks another deer   7
hunting season.

It begins sometime in August: a steady trickle of pickup trucks,   8
Broncos, and station wagons crunching down our quarter-mile gravel lane. Out of them step men, usually alone, usually strangers, who want to know if they can speak with the man of the house. "There isn't a man in this house," we say if we are feeling polite. "No," we say when we're cranky, hot, tired. They shuffle, grin, talk about the weather, and finally get around to it.

"Umm, ma'am, would you mind if I hunt your place this fall?"   9

"Yes," we say, "we'd mind."   10

They always look surprised. Often they look affronted, like boys did   11
back in high school when they believed that because they'd screwed up the courage to ask for a date we were obligated to go. The rare ones smile, shrug their shoulders, and say, "O.K., just thought I'd ask." More often, they argue: how badly the deer herd needs thinning, how cruel it is to let them die of starvation.

In response I am beginning to ask why I never see starving deer, just   12
healthy ones feasting on our crops, crossing our roads, decorating our landscape. I am beginning to ask if they realize that an autumn loss of body weight is a purely endogenous cycle. I am beginning to ask which is more cruel: apparently starving deer or wounded ones?

One fall we built a gate at the end of the lane. We posted a big   13
orange NO HUNTING sign in the center. They had to get out of the car, open the gate, get back in the car and drive through, get out of the car, and close the gate to keep the cattle from getting out while they drove down the lane to knock on our door and ask if they could do what the sign said they couldn't. Still they came.

It's our land, in the sense that we work it, keep up the fences, pay the   14
taxes—and we choose to see it used for other purposes. We walk it,
marking our seasons by the transformations under our feet. We spend
long autumn hours bent over collecting sticky green butternuts, ashen
rock-hard hickories, black walnuts like chunks of charcoal, so that we
can feast on fresh nuts and fall mushrooms, the last of the garden's
broccoli, all braised in fresh butter. We collect wild apples, with snow-
white flesh that turns cinnamon-brown in the sauce kettle on rainy
afternoons. We step quietly listening for turkeys, watching the blue
herons taking rest after raising their brood.

And we watch the deer, as voyeurs peeping in on their life cycles. In   15
late October, a raw patch of naked tree stands out against bark black
with autumn rain. Go close enough and you can smell the musk, acrid
natural incense left by bucks marking out their mating arena. Autumn
after autumn they choose and mark the same squares of land.

The adult does breed first. We can tell from the picture window   16
when the timber is drawing them. For the first time since fawning in
late May they leave their young unattended, creep off to the starkly
naked timber. Two weeks later the female fawns follow. And all of this
necessary activity occurs in the peak of hunting season.

On our autumn walks we are also confronted by the presence of   17
strangers. One can step over or crawl under barbed wire fences, but
cutting lets us know they were there, so they do it. We find discarded
liquor bottles, the entrails of poached deer bright red against the snow,
and bodies of decapitated bucks abandoned because all that was wanted
was the head, the rack. We find fox and coon and squirrels shot for the
thrill, and abandoned. We find deer stands, vinyl-padded metal chairs,
bolted to the trees we nurture; spikes driven into their sides.

Last month a fellow customer at the feed mill leaned against the   18
doorjamb, blocking my passage, and said, "You'd better start wearing
some orange out there when you're cuttin' wood. Heard ya 'bout got
yourself shot last weekend."

Got myself shot? That's an interesting grammatical construction.   19
Two years ago a jury in Maine acquitted a man who had shot a woman
130 feet from her house. It was deer season. She was wearing white
mittens. The jury thought it reasonable that a man with a gun had
mistaken a woman with a laundry basket for a white-tailed deer. She got
herself shot.

Yesterday my basset and I were snuffling through the timber, pick-   20
ing up the tangs of autumn. An irregular glint of light pierced my eyes

and I dropped instantly to the ground. Beside me Grace "boofed," a gutteral, lip-blowing sound of fear. Then the man's eyes and mine fastened, experienced the same instant recognition of human iris. I eased to standing at the same pace that his gun barrel slipped toward the ground.

Before I could recover my voice, he snarled, "Jesus, you could get   21 killed, lady. What're you doin' here? Don'tchya know there's a season on?"

Finally, Grace barked, raised her hackles, ran for the gutted buck I   22 hadn't yet picked out of the forest floor.

He followed her with his gun barrel. "You'd better call off that dog,"   23 he said, "or I'll shoot her."

And so it started, the conversation I've had more times than I can   24 count. Alone in the woods, unarmed, facing a man, or two, or three, with loaded guns and often bellies loaded with liquor. "On whose property do you believe yourself to be hunting?"

They hesitate, they shuffle, they look anywhere but into my eyes.   25 They offer a name out of a plat book, hoping it isn't my own. I explain more or less angrily where fence lines lie and ask them, firmly, to leave. Now.

This man was waiting for buddies to help him drag the gutted deer   26 the mile or more he was from anyone else's fence line. This man may have heard the news from Maine. After I had called the dog off and his buck was safe, he cocked the butt of his shotgun on his pelvic bone, aimed the barrel directly over my left shoulder and said, "You know, lady, you got no orange on. I could shoot you right here and they'd call it a huntin' accident."

We wear blaze orange stocking hats now, in the woods, or even   27 when we're moving from barn to pump house doing chores. We wear blaze orange, and we wait for the season of rut to end.

Vocabulary

reverence (2)—deep respect or awe

rutting season (3)—the period of sexual excitement or "heat" in animals when mating occurs

heedlessly (4)—carelessly

affronted (11)—offended; insulted

endogenous (12)—developing or originating from within

entrails (17)—internal organs

acquitted (19)—judged to be not guilty

plat book (25)—a book describing land and building lots and divisions in an area

IN YOUR JOURNAL

Compare your response to Burwell's response. What differences and similarities do you find? Would you respond differently if the same situation happened today? Do you think Burwell would? Why?

A Closer Reading

1. According to the essay, what position has Burwell taken? When did she take a stand? What specifically propelled her into action? In what way is she in danger because of her position? Why is she not frightened by the hunters?

2. What feeling does Burwell have for her land and the animals on it? Cite specific words and phrases that support your answer.

3. How does she feel about the hunters? Cite specific words and phrases that support your answer.

4. How does the fact that Burwell is a woman affect the hunters?

5. In paragraph 20, why does Burwell drop to the ground? What is the hunter's reaction to this?

6. What evidence does Burwell provide to suggest that the courts are lenient with hunters? Why does she start wearing "blaze orange stocking hats" during hunting season?

Drawing Your Own Conclusions

1. Why is Burwell opposed to hunting? What does Burwell decide about the hunters' attitude when she finds "bodies of decapitated bucks abandoned because all that was wanted was the head, the rack"?

2. What bothers Burwell about the phrase "got yourself shot," which the man at the feed mill says to her in paragraph 18?

3. Is the hunter in paragraph 26 threatening Burwell? Is she in danger at that moment?

4. Why do the hunters described in this article continue to hunt Burwell's land even though it is well marked? Why is there so much antagonism between Burwell and them?

5. In his essay on page 367, Williams describes fishing as an activity in harmony with nature. How does this compare with Burwell's point of view about hunting?

Thinking about Writing

1. What is the purpose of this essay—to persuade, to describe, to compare, to analyze, to tell a story? Explain your answer by referring to specific parts of the essay.

2. What is Burwell's main point? Does she ever state it explicitly in the essay? If so, where? If not, how do you know what it is?

3. Burwell establishes her feelings about the land by using words that are descriptive of the senses. Find words that describe sight, sound, smell, taste, and touch. How do these words help Burwell present a unique picture of her land?

* * *

Suggestions for Writing

1. If you have ever had an experience in which you visited or lived on a farm, write about that in your essay. What activities do farmers do every day? What relationship do they have with the land? The weather? The animals? Describe the farm, the animals, the crops, and people who worked the land. How did you feel about farming based on your experience?

2. Describe a book, movie, or television program in which hunting figures prominently. What point of view did the creator of the piece have about hunting? How did you know this? How was your point of view influenced by the book, movie, or television program?

3. Is there a connection between hunting and violent behavior (see Gelman essay on page 304)? In an essay, discuss your views on hunting. Think about the reasons why some people hunt and the reasons why other people are opposed to this activity. Think about the violence in our society today. Decide if there is any connection between the two, and explain your answer.

4. Many farm and rural families have concerns about hunters who hunt on private land. Adults, children, and dogs have been shot

because they were not dressed in bright orange. Write an essay in which you describe the actions each group should take to ensure the safety of all.

Strategies for Revision

Make a copy of your draft for another person in your class. The other student should do the same. Each of you will have a turn being interviewer and interviewee discussing the writing you are preparing to revise. The interviewer will read your draft aloud. Then, he or she will ask you the following questions and write down each of your answers:

- What is the main point of the draft? What are you really trying to say?
- If you had to leave out one line or one part, what would it be? Why do you think you could delete it?
- If you had to add something to one part of the draft, where would you add it and what would you add? What makes you think that that part of your draft needs more development?
- What part(s) of your draft do you like best?
- What part(s) would you like to rewrite completely?
- Does your draft as a whole present the ideas you wanted to present? How and where could you have written it clearer?

When each of you has finished interviewing the other, give the draft and the written interview to your partner. Read your own interview and revise your draft, keeping in mind your answers. Share your revisions with one another.

IN YOUR JOURNAL

Write about a time when you took a walk by yourself to a place you had never been before. What happened? What will you always remember about that experience?

A New Stretch of Woods

Reynolds Price

Reynolds Price was born in North Carolina, where he has spent much of his life as writer of stories, novels, essays, and plays. His novel *Kate Vaiden* won the National Book Critics Circle Award in 1987. His memoir of his childhood and family, *Clear Pictures,* was published in 1989. *A Whole New Life: An Illness and a Healing* (1994), Price's most recent book, describes his battle with cancer. "A New Stretch of Woods" was first published in *The Leader* in August 1989 and was reprinted in the *Chicago Tribune Magazine* in December 1989 and in *The Sound of Writing* in 1991. It is a story about a boy and an event that shows him how the mind can feel and sense things the eyes cannot see.

My mother was down for her afternoon nap, so I was taking my 1 second aimless walk of the winter day. We lived way out in the country, then. Three sides of our house were flanked by woods—deep stands of pine, oak, poplar, and hickory that you could walk beelines in for hours and meet nobody, no human being. But the ground teemed with foxes, raccoons, possums, squirrels, snakes, occasional skittish but kingly deer, and frogs, salamanders, and minnows in the narrow creek, not to speak of the birds, who'd learned to trust me as if I could also fly and worry, which were their main gifts.

I was sure I'd formed an intricate union with each and all, even the 2 snakes. I'd managed to touch one live wild bird. I'd handled three nonpoisonous snakes. But even when they hid, I could sit by their haunts and talk my sorrows out by the minute; and childhood sorrow is bitterer than most, being bare of hope. As often as not, my mournful words would charm them. They'd edge into sight, then cock their heads and fevered eyes and wait till I finished. Often they'd stay on for a long last moment, in silence that I could read as their answer, before disappearing. They generally managed to vanish like fog. Since I never scared them, they at least never ran.

But the strangest time began with the dog. My Boston bull terrier 3
had died that fall; and with Mother pregnant, Father had told me to wait till the baby was settled in. As a man, I can see his practical wisdom—Mother didn't need one more job now, a messy pup; and once a rival child arrived, I'd need a tangible private possession to share the trials of learning that I was no longer the fulcrum of household love. We had two housefuls of neighbors on the road and they had dogs, but the dog that found me that afternoon was not one of theirs.

It was an odd pale shade of gray with solid gray eyes that seemed to 4
lack pupils, as if it saw without using light. Those traits today would make me think of a weimaraner, but that dog then was half the size. It was also sleek as a grayhound or whippet; and though it never actually spoke, of the animals I was to meet that day, the dog came nearest and triggered the others. Those eyes alone plainly yearned to say what it knew so well but could not deliver.

And I know it was real, an actual thing with hair and bone, weight 5
and heat. When it broke in on me at the Indian Round, I thought at once that it meant me well. I stopped to stroke it, then hefted it onto my lap for a moment. It bore those attentions with quiet ease; but it gave me none of the wild affection small dogs mostly give, the desperate kisses that put all human lovers to shame. So I set it back on the ground and watched. (I call the dog *it* since, that day, I never thought to look for its sex. For years I told myself it was male—it came at a time when female friends mean little to a boy—but now I feel the need for precision.)

The Indian Round was a secret name I'd given to a natural cleared 6
ring in the woods where, for whatever reason, no trees or weeds grew. At once I felt that the Indians made it or found it countless ages before me. In any case I knew on sight that it had sacred power. I'd given very little close attention to God, but I knew when the ground gave off a force no human could name or overcome. And through the years we'd lived nearby, I brought any fine or mystic object I found back here and set it in the midst: a big white rock, three real arrowheads, and the skull of what I guessed was a wolf, with a crest of bone to which the mighty jaw and throat muscles had once been attached.

What I made, and was making, was more a museum than an altar or 7
temple. I never prayed here or enacted rites. I recognized a fact. This spot on Earth was clearly magic; it gave off invisible force like a god and therefore deserved my childish tributes of care and beauty. The only private

thing I did was sometimes to strip and lie on my back, staring at the hole of distant blue sky and telling myself all others were dead now, the whole world empty of all but me and the beasts I knew were watching me from secret lairs in reach of my voice and the smells of my body. I'd only begun to love my body late that summer, when I turned ten. So I already knew how dangerous my own loving hands could be, even then when I'd touched no body but mine and, rarely, the public parts of my parents.

But that first day, when I set the dog down, I suddenly knew that it came as a guide. And next it walked to the far north edge of the Indian Round, where the woods began again, thicker still. At every few steps, it would look back toward me and give a hook of its avid head, calling me on. Then it entered the thicket.

In my mind, from then on, I called it Scout and thought of it as male. And I followed him close as the woods would let me, the briars and vines, the stinging limbs against my eyes. Scout stayed in sight, just glimpses and sounds, till we came to the stream. At first I thought it was my old creek, the one I explored in all kinds of weather, wading and probing under rocks with sticks or lying on the bank and going silent to watch its surface and deeps for long minutes, as one by one the ghostly transparent crawfish or toads the size of your little fingernail offered their private acts to my eyes, their brute and merciful transactions, grander and surer to last than ours.

But I quickly understood I was elsewhere. This was not the same creek I'd known before, no part I had seen. It was twice as wide and way too deep to see into. With a running start I just might jump it, but how would I get a running start in such dense undergrowth? And was that Scout's intention for me?

He was gone anyhow. I stood entirely still to listen. Even in winter no live stretch of woods is thoroughly silent. If nothing else, the drying hearts of the trees themselves will groan and crack. But now I was sunk in a well of stillness that was not only new to me but scary, though my favorite virtue was bravery. The trees and bushes were normal species, the water was wet and cold to the touch; only the air between us had changed. I doubt I'd heard of a vacuum, but I knew I was in peculiar space and that, all around me, the air was thinning in a quiet rush to leave me entirely unimpeded, more naked than ever, though I wore my leather jacket and aviator's cap.

Scout never returned. But in the new thin air around me, in my bald fear, his message sounded plainer than words: *Cross this water.* I retreated the few available steps, turned my fear into reckless strength, and tried the leap—which I made, and to spare. I landed an easy yard

past the water on ground I could feel was new to my feet. And before I
was firmly upright on my pins, I called myself brave.

Then came the bird, a perfectly normal golden eagle. The strange-   13
ness dawned only two days later when I learned that golden eagles were
unheard of in the coastal plain where we lived. It stood on a pine limb,
four yards above me, and kept its head in rigid profile like something
Egyptian but fixed on me, the way nothing can but meat-eating birds
with the talons and beaks to do their will. For the better part of two or
three minutes, it never so much as shut an eye.

I tried to freeze my body in respect, but after a while I needed to prove   14
it was still alive, the ferocious bird. So I bent right over and touched the
ground, just to make a move—I didn't plan to pick up a rock to throw.

Before I was back upright, it raised off its limb on wings the size of a   15
black four-door new roadster.

If I'd been thinking clear and fast, I might have feared it was aimed   16
at me and covered my eyes. But it went skyward so straight and fast,
with so much perfect power to burn, that I know I actually laughed a
high note and followed with some such word as "Lord!"—I hadn't yet
got to the harsher cries. Only when it had also vanished did I understand the words it left me, silent as the dog: *Stay still right here.*

I stayed till the sun was nearly gone and an evening chill was taking   17
my feet. I hadn't interpreted the eagle strictly. A few minutes after it
disappeared, I went to sit on a bent tree trunk near the stream and
waited there but facing the woods, the strange territory, not the way
back home. Something had let me know, all along, that I wasn't lost,
that home lay behind me the way I'd come. All I had to do was leap that
stream a second time, while I still had daylight, and wind my old trail
back up beneath me like a thread I'd laid behind me or crumbs.

The only question was, What would come next? And would it come   18
before night fell and Father got home and started calling my name to
the dark and scaring Mother, tender as she was these last weeks? For all
I knew, Scout might come back and guide me in or onward to some
whole other new life, elsewhere than here. I turned that last thought
over awhile and knew I would go, wherever he led, whoever wound up
with a broken heart if I too vanished and no trace of me was found on
Earth, no thread of my clothes. Most honest men will own to similar
vengeful thoughts in late childhood.

Then the black snake streamed on out of the woods, crossed the   19
narrow bank six feet beyond me, poured itself down the slope, swam
most of the stream in a straight line across, then sank a few inches short

of land and never surfaced, nowhere I could see. Like the eagle, it had all the normal traits of its kind. Only it was thick as a plump young python; and where I lived then, all snakes are deep asleep in winter and would no more enter an ice-cold stream than a raging fire.

But when I'd thought my way through that, I got the final news of 20 the day. It stuck up mean in the quick of my mind like the snake itself, that strong and rank: *The baby your mother wants to make is a boy. It would be your brother, but it will not live.*

The news itself didn't hurt at first, but I wanted to stay for amplifica- 21 tion. Had I caused the promise? Was it good or bad? Would I be blessed or punished next? Did it mean I must act thus or so, from here on? And I did linger there on the tree till I knew I had only five more minutes of light, then freezing dark with its own business that I couldn't yet face. I thought if anything, good or evil, was using me, it could follow me home and tell me there. I thought I'd say at least a short prayer for strength to make the leap again and bravery to see me back through the woods. But I found my mind would simply not pray; all I heard was the last news again: *It will not live.*

So I leaped and made it, though with no ground to spare. And each 22 hedged step of the backward way was hard and cowardly. I somehow still couldn't pray for help, for me or for my brother, who had been so lively this afternoon when Mother told me to press her belly and feel his foot. Worse, I couldn't even pray for her—that whether he came out well or dead, she be spared pain, not to mention bloody death. She was three fourths of all I'd known or loved, and she'd earned every calorie of all my heat.

But my arms and legs worked on as before; and by the time it was 23 actual night, my hands alone could guess I was almost home by the touch of familiar trees, especially pines, with the scaly bark I knew as well as my favorite skin. The last few yards took what seemed years, but the hands were right. At last home was there, bright before me in its own safe clearing.

Inside, in Mother and Father's room, my mother's face was hid in 24 their pillows. She was fully dressed but the tan wool skirt she'd worn all day was dark with blood, and I could count the wrenching cries that tore her heart. Around us three, the air had the hot iron smell of blood. It was so much my strongest sight till then that I can call it up whole this minute and be there again. I wanted of course to flee to the woods and learn a way to reverse the spell my trip had cast. But bravery showed me my kind-eyed father standing beside her; hands at his sides, unable to help. When he saw my face, he said, "She lost your brother, son."

I saw his words had calmed her cries, for the moment at least, which 　25
was all it took to brace myself for the sight of the eyes she turned on me
next, her mouth like a razor wound in her face. I told her the only thing
I knew. "I will be him too. You can love us more than ever."

　　Father shook his head and touched his lips for silence. 　26

　　But slowly my mother rigged a smile and pressed it toward me 　27
before her head sank back to sleep.

Vocabulary

flanked (1)—placed at the side of

tangible (3)—real; able to be
touched

fulcrum (3)—the important
point of influence

traits (4)—characteristics

hefted (5)—lifted

lairs (7)—animal dens

avid (8)—eager

vengeful (18)—desiring to inflict
an injury to right a perceived
wrong

amplification (21)—the addition
of details

hedged (22)—careful; trying to
avoid problems

rigged (27)—put together for a
particular purpose

IN YOUR JOURNAL

What do you think will linger in your mind about this story and
about the boy? Why did that part of the story affect you?

A Closer Reading

1. Who are the human characters in the story? What do we learn
   about each of their characters and personalities?

2. Who are the animal characters in the story? What do we learn
   about each of their characters and personalities? What does each
   of them do that is strange, considering their normal behavior and
   the time of year in the story?

3. What is the Indian Round? Why is it important to the boy?
   What happens there that begins the boy's adventure?

4. Why do the adults let the boy go off by himself for the day?
   What suggests that the boy has gone off by himself before?

Drawing Your Own Conclusions

1. What is the setting for the story? In what ways is the setting similar to some children's fairy tales?

2. Why does the boy blame himself for what happened to the baby?

3. Compare the interactions the boy has with the dog, the eagle, and the snake with Dillard's interaction with the weasel (see page 349). What similarities do you find? What differences? What lesson does each learn from the animals?

4. Many writers use animals to symbolize human qualities and characteristics; for example, a cat may be associated with mystery and sometimes with jealousy. What qualities and characteristics are symbolized by the three animals in this story?

Thinking about Writing

1. Where in the story does Price reveal that he is writing this story as an adult? How does he indicate a shift in the time periods in his story? How does this show how memory works?

2. Reread the story, focusing on the questions that the boy asks. Does Price answer those questions in the story? How do they direct the reader's thoughts?

3. How do the first lines and the last lines of the story connect? In what way do these tie the story together effectively?

4. Reread the story, focusing on descriptions. How does Price describe the boy? The mother? The father? The woods? The dog? The eagle? The snake? What does this tell you about Price's main concern in telling this story?

5. What specific words and phrases does Price use to show memory? To show loss, grief, and fear?

*   *   *

Suggestions for Writing

1. Do you think that all children need to have some experience in the wilderness—whether by living in rural areas or by going away to camp? Write an essay in which you explain your feelings about the above question using examples from your own experience, your observations, and your readings.

2. Observe a human being with a domesticated animal (a dog out for a walk with its owner, a cat in someone's lap, and so on). Write an essay in which you describe your observations in as much detail as possible. What seems to be the relationship between the two beings? How are needs communicated between the species? Try to be as objective as possible, describing only what you see.

3. Should children have pets when they are growing up? Write an essay in which you take a position on this issue. Explain your position by telling of your own experiences or the experiences of others, or by referring to your readings.

4. Write a story in which a child has an unusual encounter with an animal. Describe the setting, the animal, and the encounter in great detail. Reread the Price story and the Dillard essay (on page 349) for ideas about how to describe animals and settings. End your story by showing that the child learned something from the experience.

Strategies for Revision

The following revision strategy involves your working with a partner. Read each other's drafts. Then, writing down the answers on a separate sheet of paper, ask your partner the following questions about your writing:

- Is the animal I have described particular and unique?
- Is the reason I have chosen to write about this animal obvious? If not, how can I make this clearer?
- Where in the essay have I used comparison, description, narration, and argument? Is there enough of a balance?
- What is the point of my essay? Is it clear?

Your partner can then ask you the same questions about his or her writing.

Using the answers to these questions, each of you can revise what you have already written. Keep in mind that any writing can be improved. In addition, each writer has to make a personal decision about when a piece of writing is complete. As each of you makes changes, share your drafts. Discuss with each other the changes that you make.

Cynthia Mazzotti wrote this essay in response to suggestion 2 from the Suggestions for Writing that follow the McKibben selection: Write an essay in which you explain what McKibben means by the idea that humans should have a humbler attitude toward nature and that we should show it more respect. What does he mean by the phrase "nature for nature's sake"? How do these concepts fit with your own feelings about nature, humans, and the environment?

Isle Royale's Predator/Prey Relationship

Cynthia Mazzotti

The relationship between predators and prey is a critical link in the 1 stability of the ecosystem, or the habitat and environmental conditions in which a particular species lives.

A predator is any species of animal that obtains its food primarily by 2 killing and consuming animals of a different species, called the prey species. Predators will feed on whatever prey species is in their area, and they will not limit themselves to only one species of prey.

Prey, usually game animals such as deer, elk, rabbits, and the like, is 3 any animal that is hunted and killed for food. A large prey species is the staple of a large predator's diet, but smaller prey may make a light snack for a larger predator. If predators did not control the number of individuals in a prey species, the prey species could suffer from overpopulation, starvation, and decimation.

Every action has an opposite reaction, and this is true among wild- 4 life populations. All species of animal experience population increases. Sometimes several factors, one being the extermination of wolves in the lower forty-eight states, will contribute to the dramatic increase of another population, such as elk in Yellowstone or moose on Isle Royale.

Man interferes with the normal balance between predators and prey 5 by hunting moose and other game animals for sport or for food, and by poisoning and trapping wolves who, by nature, prey on those same species. This interference does not occur at Isle Royale, where the laws of nature alone determine the number of animals that are compatible with the food supply. The relationship between predator and prey without the influence of man is clearly demonstrated by wolves and moose on Isle Royale National Park.

It is suspected that moose first arrived on Michigan's Isle Royale at 6 the beginning of this century. In the 1940's, the island was declared a national park and fell under the jurisdiction of the National Park Service. Activities such as mining, logging, and hunting were prohibited. Because humans would not interfere with wildlife numbers by hunting moose or by destroying wolves, biologists were provided with the opportunity to study a complete ecosystem with its predators and prey intact.

Shortly after the park was established, biologists began to study the   7
herds of moose. It was determined that the moose were periodically building up their population beyond the point where the food resources could sufficiently nourish them.

When food becomes scarce for any species of animal, competition   8
among individuals increases as do restlessness and aggression. Tolerance of one animal for another of its same species decreases and social bonds weaken.

Physiological and emotional stress also occur due to changes in the   9
endocrine system. Chemicals are released into the body of an animal, which cause it to believe that it is threatened. A constant state of fear engulfs the creature, but there is no way to alleviate the fear; there is no danger to flee from. This weakened condition opens up the animal's immune system to the invasion of disease brought about by parasites.

Arthritis is another symptom of physiological stress. A disabled   10
animal will have trouble foraging and may become undernourished. Disease, starvation, and declining health are all symptoms of a species experiencing overpopulation.

After the population peaked, moose numbers dropped dramatically   11
due to malnutrition and stress related disease. During such periods of decline, the vegetation of the isolated island recovered. Fewer moose were eating fewer plants, and the flora began to flourish again. By the time the vegetation had reasserted itself, the moose numbers had increased again. More vegetation led to more moose, and the cycle began to repeat.

During the late forties, rumors began circulating among biologists   12
that wolves from Ontario had crossed the ice-covered Lake Superior. A breeding pair and various lone wolves were thought to have arrived and established a population of about eleven gray wolves in 1955. In addition to the abundant supply of moose, wolves had the opportunity to choose from several smaller types of prey. Rabbits and especially beavers were sampled by the predators during the summer months.

At first the wolves could not reproduce quickly enough to bring the   13 moose herds into balance with the ecosystem. By 1970, the moose on Isle Royale numbered 1200 while the wolves numbered only twenty. From 1970 to 1971 the moose experienced a decrease to about 900 animals. Wolf predation was responsible for some fatalities, but most moose died from the previously mentioned ailments. 14

In 1973 the moose began to recover. A thousand moose were counted that year, and the population continued to rise throughout the next year. The wolf numbers also grew to twenty-three in 1973 and swelled to an amazing forty-four in 1974. 15

The periodic cycle began, and the number of moose plummeted to 500 by 1977. Predation by wolves was responsible for a relatively small amount of moose fatalities compared to the horrible numbers that the general population of Anglo-America imagines. In addition to the moose numbers' falling, the wolf population declined to thirty-five. 16

Just as the moose had crashed from 1200 to 500 in seven years, it was time for the wolves to crash in number. Five packs totaling some fifty wolves were counted in the park in 1980. The moose numbered between 500 and 600, and could not support that many wolves. Because the sick had died and the malnourished had fallen prey to wolves, the moose population was again becoming healthy. Vegetation was returning, providing all moose with a healthy food source. Healthy moose, in turn, have more and healthier offspring than malnourished moose. 17

This flourishing of healthy moose meant that wolves would have to work harder to find sick individuals. Wolves must chase between eleven and thirteen moose just to take down one. The lame, the old and young, and the undernourished were the easiest to catch, which is why wolves pursued these individuals. This abundance of healthy moose made hunting difficult as wolf numbers reflected. 18

By 1982 there were fourteen wolves and 700 moose on Isle Royale. The shortage of wolves allowed moose to bring their population to 1062 in 1984. The wolves also began to increase as their chances of catching prey increased with the moose population's growth. 19

In 1984, all twenty-two wolves in the park were able to catch prey without having to fight each other for it. 20

When a mild winter and abundant vegetation allow more moose to survive than usual, the wolf population will grow accordingly. Likewise, moose populations in the following years will decline somewhat. The wolves will then go through their own decline in numbers until the 21 moose population recovers. This cycle lasts about twenty-four years on the isolated island. The prey animals decline first, followed by the predator species eight to ten years later. Other predator-prey research, particularly the lynx-hare relationship in Alaska, supports the findings of the Isle Royale study.

Only in rare and unusual circumstances would the numbers of either 22 population rise or drop sharply. Wolves kept the moose population in check; likewise, the moose kept the wolves from increasing their numbers beyond the point that their food supply could sustain them. Predators will not hunt their prey species into extinction; that would be suicide for predators. Predators and prey establish a balance between themselves that fluctuates naturally and does not need man's intervening.

Source

R. D. Lawrence. *In Praise of Wolves.* (New York: Henry Holt and Company) 1986.

Questions to Think About

1. What is Mazzotti's main idea? How does this correspond with the idea that humans should have a humbler attitude toward nature and that we should show more respect for nature? Would you have liked Mazzotti to have made this connection clearer? If so, where in the essay should she have done so?

2. Where does Mazzotti define the terms "predator" and "prey"? Are these definitions clear?

3. What information does she provide to illustrate the relationship between these two types of animals?

4. Where in the essay does Mazzotti use factual information? What is the purpose of including these facts?

5. What information does Mazzotti include in the conclusion that ties together the ideas from the rest of the essay? Is the conclusion effective?

MAKING CONNECTIONS

The World of Nature: *Connecting with the Wilderness*

1. For almost a hundred years, people in the United States have debated about which should have priority—the needs of human beings or the needs of the natural world. They have felt and still do feel caught between nature and civilization. Reread some of the selections in this unit (especially the Chowder essay on page 357), thinking about these issues. Write an essay in which you describe the dilemma of today's overdeveloped world, and describe some of the creative ways in which you would like to see it handled.

2. Price, Dillard (see page 349), and Williams (see page 367) go to private, secret places in nature. What reason does each give for going into nature alone? Are their reasons convincing? In what ways are their reasons similar? In what ways are they different? Whose reason makes the most sense to you? Why? Compare their descriptions of those places. Which of their places would you like most to visit? Why?

3. McKibben writes, "That seemed a quietly radical idea to me— the idea that we [human beings] don't necessarily belong at the top in every way." Imagine that Chowder (see page 357), Williams (see page 367), and McKibben (see page 374) met to discuss this issue. After rereading their selections, write down their conversation, using dialogue and quotations. What would they decide about this issue?

4. Focus on one of the issues about which you have read in this unit. Write an essay in which you identify the issue that grabbed you and about which you would like to do something. Explain why this issue is important to you. Refer to the specific article from which you got your information. What needs to be done to solve this problem?

5. How have your feelings about nature and the environment changed because of your reading the selections in this unit? Write an essay in which you choose one piece of writing from this unit that changed your thinking in some way. Explain the effect this piece of writing had on you. Why did it have this effect?

6. Write an introduction to this unit in which you tell other students which piece of writing is the most interesting, the most informative, or the best written. Using quotations from the selection, convince a potential reader to choose this particular piece of writing to read.

8

THE WORLD OF OUR PAST

Learning from Myths and Rites

$\mathbf{M}$yth is one of the oldest forms of stories. Myths may have emerged from our human desire to understand the world. Through myths, we learn about the origins of life, cultural customs, natural phenomena, traditional rites, and even superstitions. In this unit, we look at the function of myth; next, we examine some myths themselves and then look at ritual practices and superstitions from many countries that reveal the universality of myth.

The first selection is an interview between journalist Bill Moyers and mythologist Joseph Campbell. The two men discuss the functions of myth in the past and in our contemporary world.

The three myths that follow present African, Native American, and Asian traditional myths about nature. The first is a poem from the Dinka, a people of the Sudan, about the cycles of the sun, moon, and stars. Then, an excerpt by Black Elk explains the significance of the circle for the Dakota Sioux. Third is a Chinese myth about the moon and about saving the world from disaster.

Leslie Marmon Silko's "The Man to Send Rain Clouds" describes the Laguna Pueblo ritual in response to a death in the family. Family and neighbors join in the burial ceremony to return their grandfather to the land and provide him with the power to bring rain that will ensure good crops.

"Flower Myths: Narcissus, Hyacinth, Adonis" by Edith Hamilton portrays the nature myth that connects growth and life to death. Hamilton describes the Greek mythological origin stories for three well-known wildflowers.

The next selection reveals the personal power of connecting with our origins through early rites and traditions. Chester Higgins, Jr., in his essay, "A Father's Rite," describes a trip that he and his son take to Africa to find their beginnings and to perform a rite that connects the two generations of men with their ancestors.

Maintaining connections between the generations is also the theme of "Superstitious Minds," by Letty Cottin Pogrebin. Pogrebin writes about how family superstitions have enabled her to maintain a connection with her mother, who died when the writer was a teenager. Further, she sees a generational connection as her son shares some of these old superstitions as well.

Finally, student writer Rachele Deveras tells about an incident in which the truth behind a superstition seemed to be verified in her life.

* * *

Think about the following questions before reading the selections in this unit:

1. How did you first learn about myths?
2. How did learning about myths affect you?
3. What myth has had personal meaning in your life? Why?

IN YOUR JOURNAL

In the following interview, Bill Moyers refers to myths in this way: "Myths are stories of our search through the ages for truth, for meaning, for significance. We all need to tell our story and to understand our story. . . . We need for life to signify, to touch the eternal, to understand the mysterious, to find out who we are." Write about what myths you remember from your childhood. How important are myths to you? Why?

Myths in Our Lives: An Interview with Joseph Campbell

Bill Moyers

Born in Texas, Bill Moyers is a journalist, writer, and producer of many television programs. After working for President Lyndon B. Johnson during the 1950s and 1960s, Moyers left government service and went to work as an editor for *Newsday*. In 1970 he took a thirteen-thousand-mile journey across the United States and then wrote *Listening to America: A Traveler Rediscovers America* (1971). This brought him to television, as the host first of the Public Broadcasting Service's *This Week* and then of *Bill Moyers' Journal*, which he has hosted for the past twenty years. His series *The Power of Myth* featured Moyers interviewing Joseph Campbell (1904–1987), a scholar and authority on myths. The following excerpt is from the book made from these interviews, *The Power of Myth* (1988) by Joseph Campbell with Bill Moyers. Moyers has since published *Bill Moyers' World of Ideas* (1989) and *Healing and the Mind* (1993).

Moyers: I came to understand from reading your books—*The Masks of   1 God* or *The Hero with a Thousand Faces,* for example—that what human beings have in common is revealed in myths. Myths are stories of our search through the ages for truth, for meaning, for significance. We all need to tell our story and to understand our story. We all need to understand death and to cope with death, and we all need help in our passages from birth to life and then to death. We need for life to signify, to touch the eternal, to understand the mysterious, to find out who we are.

Campbell: People say that what we're all seeking is a meaning for   2
life. I don't think that's what we're really seeking. I think that what
we're seeking is an experience of being alive, so that our life experiences
on the purely physical plane will have resonances within our innermost
being and reality, so that we actually feel the rapture of being alive.
That's what it's all finally about, and that's what these clues help us to
find within ourselves.

Moyers: Myths are clues?   3

Campbell: Myths are clues to the spiritual potentialities of the hu-   4
man life.

Moyers: What we're capable of knowing and experiencing within?   5

Campbell: Yes.   6

Moyers: You changed the definition of a myth from the *search* for   7
meaning to the *experience* of meaning.

Campbell: Experience of *life.* The mind has to do with meaning.   8
What's the meaning of a flower? There's a Zen story about a sermon of
the Buddha in which he simply lifted a flower. There was only one man
who gave him a sign with his eyes that he understood what was said.
Now the Buddha himself is called "the one thus come." There's no
meaning. What's the meaning of the universe? What's the meaning of a
flea? It's just there. That's it. And your own meaning is that you're
there. We're so engaged in doing things to achieve purposes of outer
value that we forget that the inner value, the rapture that is associated
with being alive, is what it's all about.

Moyers: How do you get that experience?   9

Campbell: Read myths. They teach you that you can turn inward,   10
and you begin to get the message of the symbols. Read other people's
myths, not those of your own religion, because you tend to interpret
your own religion in terms of facts—but if you read the other ones, you
begin to get the message. Myth helps you to put your mind in touch
with this experience of being alive. It tells you what the experience is.

Moyers: Do you remember the first time you discovered myth? The   11
first time the story came alive in you?

Campbell: I was brought up as a Roman Catholic. Now one of the   12
great advantages of being brought up a Roman Catholic is that you're
taught to take myth seriously and to let it operate on your life and to
live in terms of these mythic motifs. I was brought up in terms of the
seasonal relationships to the cycle of Christ's coming into the world,
teaching in the world, dying, resurrecting, and returning to heaven. The
ceremonies all through the year keep you in mind of the eternal core of

all that changes in time. Sin is simply getting out of touch with that harmony.

And then I fell in love with American Indians because Buffalo Bill   13
used to come to Madison Square Garden every year with his marvelous Wild West Show. So I began to read American Indian myths, and it wasn't long before I found the same motifs in the American Indian stories that I was being taught by the nuns at school.

Moyers: Creation—   14

Campbell:—creation, death and resurrection, ascension to heaven,   15
virgin births—I didn't know what it was, but I recognized the vocabulary. One after another.

Moyers: What appealed to you about the Indian stories?   16

Campbell: In those days there was still American Indian lore in the   17
air. Indians were still around. Even now, when I deal with myths from all parts of the world, I find the American Indian tales and narratives to be very rich, very well developed.

And then my parents had a place out in the woods where the Dela-   18
ware Indians had lived, and the Iroquois had come down and fought them. There was a big ledge where we could dig for Indian arrowheads and things like that. And the very animals that play the role in the Indian stories were there in the woods around me. It was a grand introduction to this material.

Moyers: Did these stories begin to collide with your Catholic faith?   19

Campbell: No, there was no collision. The collision with my reli-   20
gion came much later in relation to scientific studies and things of that kind. Later I became interested in Hinduism, and there were the same stories again. And in my graduate work I was dealing with the Arthurian medieval material, and there were the same stories again. So you can't tell me that they're not the same stories. I've been with them all my life.

Moyers: They come from every culture but with timeless themes?   21

Campbell: The themes are timeless, and the inflection is to the culture.   22

[Moyers refers to Campbell's as yet uncompleted work of a four-   23
volume anthology that divides world mythology into four periods: *The Way of the Animal Powers, The Way of the Seeded Earth, The Way of the Celestial Lights,* and *The Way of Man.*]

Moyers: But in modern times we have moved beyond the animal   24
powers, beyond nature and the seeded earth, and the stars no longer interest us except as exotic curiosities and the terrain of space travel. Where are we now in our mythology for the way of man?

Campbell: We can't have a mythology for a long, long time to come. 25
Things are changing too fast to become mythologized.

Moyers: How do we live without myths, then? 26

Campbell: The individual has to find an aspect of myth that relates to 27
his own life. Myth basically serves four functions. The first is the mystical
function—that is the one I've been speaking about, realizing what a
wonder the universe is, and what a wonder you are, and experiencing awe
before this mystery. Myth opens the world to the dimension of mystery,
to the realization of the mystery that underlies all forms. If you lose that,
you don't have a mythology. If mystery is manifest through all things, the
universe becomes, as it were, a holy picture. You are always addressing
the transcendent mystery through the conditions of your actual world.

The second is a cosmological dimension, the dimension with which 28
science is concerned—showing you what the shape of the universe is,
but showing it in such a way that the mystery again comes through.
Today we tend to think that scientists have all the answers. But the great
ones tell us, "No, we haven't got all the answers. We're telling you how
it works—but what is it?" You strike a match, what's fire? You can tell
me about oxidation, but that doesn't tell me a thing.

The third function is the sociological one—supporting and validat- 29
ing a certain social order. And here's where the myths vary enormously
from place to place. You can have a whole mythology for polygamy, a
whole mythology for monogamy. Either one's okay. It depends on
where you are. It is the sociological function of myth that has taken over
in our world—and it is out of date.

Moyers: What do you mean? 30

Campbell: Ethical laws. The laws of life as it should be in the good 31
society. All of Yahweh's pages and pages and pages of what kind of
clothes to wear, how to behave to each other, and so forth, in the first
millennium B.C.

But there is a fourth function of myth, and this is the one I think 32
everyone must try today to relate to—and that is the pedagogical function, of how to live a human lifetime under any circumstances. Myths
can teach you that.

Meyers: So the old story, so long known and transmitted through the 33
generations, isn't functioning, and we have not yet learned a new one?

Campbell: The story that we have in the West, so far as it is based on 34
the Bible, is based on a view of the universe that belongs to the first
millennium B.C. It does not accord with our concept either of the
universe or of the dignity of man. It belongs entirely somewhere else.

We have today to learn to get back into accord with the wisdom of   35
nature and realize again our brotherhood with the animals and with the
water and the sea. To say that the divinity informs all things is condemned as pantheism, but pan*theism* is a misleading word. It suggests
that a personal god is supposed to inhabit the world, but that is not the
idea at all. The idea is transtheological. It is of an undefinable, inconceivable mystery, thought of as a power, that is the source and end and
supporting ground of all life and being.

Moyers: Don't you think modern Americans have rejected the an-   36
cient idea of nature as divinity because it would have kept us from
achieving dominance over nature? How can you cut down trees and
uproot the land and turn the rivers into real estate without killing God?

Campbell: Yes, but that's not simply a characteristic of modern   37
Americans, that is the biblical condemnation of nature which they inher-
ited from their own religion and brought with them, mainly from
England. God is separate from nature, and nature is condemned of
God. It's right there in Genesis: We are to be the masters of the world.

But if you will think of ourselves as coming out of the earth, rather   38
than having been thrown in here from somewhere else, you see that we
are the earth, we are the consciousness of the earth. These are the eyes of
the earth. And this is the voice of the earth.

Moyers: Scientists are beginning to talk quite openly about the Gaia   39
principle.

Campbell: There you are, the whole planet as an organism.   40

Moyers: Mother Earth. Will new myths come from this image?   41

Campbell: Well, something might. You can't predict what a myth is   42
going to be any more than you can predict what you're going to dream
tonight. Myths and dreams come from the same place. They come from
realizations of some kind that have then to find expression in symbolic
form. And the only myth that is going to be worth thinking about in
the immediate future is one that is talking about the planet, not the city,
not these people, but the planet, and everybody on it. That's my main
thought for what the future myth is going to be.

And what it will have to deal with will be exactly what all myths have   43
dealt with—the maturation of the individual, from dependency through
adulthood, through maturity, and then to the exit; and then how to relate
to this society and how to relate this society to the world of nature and the
cosmos. That's what the myths have all talked about, and what this one's
got to talk about. But the society that it's got to talk about is the society of
the planet. And until that gets going, you don't have anything.

Vocabulary

resonances (2)—ideas that reflect or correspond with other ideas

rapture (2)—great joy or happiness

motifs (12)—main themes or subjects

lore (17)—learning known by a particular people, often in the form of folktales

inflection (22)—a quality or change of tone or pitch

terrain (24)—area; territory

manifest (27)—clear; plain

transcendent (27)—beyond the limits of possible experience

validating (29)—confirming; showing to be legitimate

pedagogical (32)—relating to teaching

condemnation (37)—strong disapproval

IN YOUR JOURNAL

Write as much as you can remember from this interview about the nature of myths. What new ideas do you have now that you did not have when you began this reading? What did you notice about the kinds of questions Moyers asked Campbell? Did you consider it to be an effective interview? Is there anything you would have asked Campbell that Moyers did not ask?

A Closer Reading

1. According to Campbell, what is the reason to read myths?
2. What are some of the themes that Campbell found in Roman Catholicism and in myths worldwide?
3. What are the four functions of myth?
4. What is the Gaia principle?
5. What does Campbell predict will be the myth of the future?

Drawing Your Own Conclusions

1. Why does Campbell tell the Zen story of the flower? How does it relate to his ideas?
2. Why does Campbell suggest that we read other people's myths, not the myths of our own culture or religion?

3. What is the purpose of the first function of myth?

4. Why does the third function of myth enable a myth to change from society to society?

5. When Campbell died at the age of eighty-three, he was still writing and still learning. If you had to chose one subject today that you would like to continue to learn about and write about for the rest of your life, what would it be, and why would you choose that subject?

6. Cofer (see page 333) mentions fairy tales as a part of "humankind's collective unconscious." How does this idea connect to myths? What else do myths and fairy tales have in common?

7. Moyers and Campbell talk about our relationship with wilderness in paragraphs 36–42. How do their ideas compare to Chowder's (see page 357) and McKibben's (see page 374)?

Thinking about Writing

1. An interview is made up of questions and answers. Reread this interview. What do you notice about Moyers's questions? Do you think they were planned in advance? Why or why not? Which questions seem to receive the most interesting answers?

2. In a small group, reread this interview aloud. You should listen and take notes about what is happening in this interview. Some areas to concentrate on are: What is the difference between an interview and a conversation? How do Moyers's questions control the direction of the interview? What else have you learned from other interviews you have read or heard? How do you decide if someone is a good interviewer or not?

3. What is Moyers's point of view as an interviewer? How might it change if he were as much an authority on myths as Campbell?

4. What would you do to prepare to interview someone?

* * *

Suggestions for Writing

1. Campbell states in paragraph 35, "We have today to learn to get back into accord with the wisdom of nature and realize again our brotherhood with the animals and with the water and the sea." Write an essay agreeing or disagreeing with this point of view. Re-

read the writing of McKibben (see page 374) and Dillard (see page 349) to get support for your arguments. You may also support your point of view with your own experiences and other readings.

2. Interview a professor in your college who is a scholar in a particular field that is of interest to you. Before you meet, write out some of the questions you would like to ask, referring to the Campbell and Moyers interview for ideas. Write out your interview using "Myths in Our Lives" as a model.

3. Campbell once wrote, "Whether dream or myth, in these adventures there is an atmosphere of irresistible fascination about the figure that appears suddenly as a guide, marking a new period, a new stage, in the biography." Write an essay explaining this statement, using as an example the experiences of the boy in the Price story on page 391 or one of the *Star Wars* movies. What happens to the main characters in these stories? What do they learn about themselves through their guide(s)?

4. Write an essay describing a movie that is set in the present day and contains the mythological elements described by Campbell.

5. The composer and lyricist Barry Keating said, "Comic books are the way we accept mythology today. We need this stuff." Write an essay in which you agree or disagree with this statement. Support your point of view with examples from your readings and your knowledge of comic book heroes.

Strategies for Revision

This revision strategy involves your working with a partner. Choose a partner who is familiar with your writing.

Make a copy of your writing and give it to your classmate. Write out the questions below and give them to each other:

- What does this writer think about myths? Where is that stated?
- What personal experience does the writer include in this essay? How is this integrated with the main theme of the essay?
- What connections does the writer make between this essay and other writing or reading done earlier this semester?
- Is the draft interesting to read? What makes you want to read from paragraph to paragraph? How could these connections be made stronger?

- If the writing is an interview, is it clear who the interviewee is and why the person is important to the writer? Are the opinions and ideas of the interviewee stated in clear and accessible language?

Read the drafts to one another. Then each should answer the questions about the other's writing. As you are writing your answers, you may want to reread your classmate's writing.

When both of you have completed your answers to the questions, exchange what you have written. Discuss any answers that are confusing. Then both of you can begin your revision, using the answers you have received and your discussion. When you have finished your revisions, share them with each other.

IN YOUR JOURNAL

Throughout time, people in all parts of the world have regarded the heavens—the sun, the moon, the stars—in a spiritual way. You will read a poem by a people of the Sudan, an excerpt from the biography of a Native American, and an old Chinese myth retold in English. What do you think they will concentrate on?

What are your feelings toward the sun, moon, or stars? Write the first thoughts that come into your mind. Write for at least three minutes without stopping.

Three Nature Myths

The Dinka

Black Elk

Ping Ruan

The Dinka are one of three tribes in the Southern Sudan in Africa, along with the Nuer and the Shilluk. They have a complex society whose laws include the concept of divine kingship. As part of their customs, the Dinka bury alive a dying chief to avoid the involuntary death that is the fate of ordinary humans and animals. The Dinka's view of human's relation to the natural cycles of the universe is clearly described in the following song taken from *The Tree Where Man Was Born: The African Experience* (1972), transcribed by Peter Matthiessen.

Black Elk (Hehaka Sapa), an Oglala Sioux, was born in 1863 in "the Moon of the Popping Trees" (December). When he was thirteen years old, he witnessed the death of many of his people at the Battle of Little Big Horn, and he saw the massacre at Wounded Knee in 1890. Before Black Elk's own death in 1950, he related the history and traditions of his people to the epic poet John G. Neihardt. "The Configuration of the Circle" is excerpted from his account, *Black Elk Speaks: Being the Life and Story of a Holy Man of the Oglala Sioux* (1932).

Ping Ruan was born in mainland China and came to the United States at the age of fourteen. Ruan majored in education with an emphasis in early childhood. She has an interest in world myths and folktales. She wrote this adaptation of an old Chinese myth when she was a student in Hunter College in New York City.

Old Dinka Song

In the time when Dendid created all things,   1
He created the sun,
And the sun is born, and dies, and comes again.
He created the moon,
And the moon is born, and dies, and comes again;   5
He created the stars,
And the stars are born, and die, and come again;
He created man,
And man is born, and dies, and does not come again.

The Configuration of the Circle
by Black Elk

You have noticed that everything an Indian does is in a circle, and 1
that is because the Power of the World always works in circles, and
everything tries to be round. In the old days when we were a strong
and happy people, all our power came to us from the sacred hoop of
the nation and so long as the hoop was unbroken the people flourished. The flowering tree was the living center of the hoop, and the
circle of the four quarters nourished it. The east gave peace and light,
the south gave warmth, the west gave rain, and the north with its
cold and mighty wind gave strength and endurance. This knowledge
came to us from the outer world with our religion. Everything the
Power of the World does is done in a circle. The Sky is round and I
have heard that the earth is round like a ball and so are all the stars.
The Wind, in its greatest power, whirls. Birds make their nests in
circles, for theirs is the same religion as ours. The sun comes forth
and goes down again in a circle. The moon does the same, and both
are round.

Even the seasons form a great circle in their changing, and always 2
come back again to where they were. The life of a man is a circle from
childhood to childhood and so it is in everything where power moves.
Our tipis were round like the nests of birds and these were always set in

a circle, the nation's hoop, a nest of many nests where the Great Spirit meant for us to hatch our children.

Moon Lady

retold by Ping Ruan

According to Chinese legend, during the ancient time, China had ten suns which were burning the earth. There were also wild fowl and fierce beasts who tried to dominate and destroy the universe. In that time, there was a hero called Hou who was very strong and very brave. He was also a great archer and with his arrows he destroyed nine of the suns and all the wild creatures. He saved the universe and the people had a happy life.   3

After that, Hou became the emperor. But soon, he became cruel and ruthless. He robbed people's properties without caring. He wished to live like this forever. He obtained the immortal medicine from the great old lady from the West. He planned to continue his emperorship forever. However, his beautiful wife called Chiang-O knew her husband was a mean and wild creature. She knew if he swallowed the immortal medicine and became immortal, then the people would suffer more. Therefore, Chiang-O tried to save the universe and stole the immortal medicine behind her husband's back.   4

She swallowed the elixir and floated up to the moon. There she became immortal, but led a lonely life in the wild and cold moon palace. The only companion she had was a jade rabbit.   5

This is the story of how the Moon Lady flew to the moon. Even today, the Chinese think that they can see the shadow of the rabbit and Moon Lady when they look at the moon.   6

Vocabulary

hoop (1)—a circular ring that holds something together

tipis (2)—also spelled tepees; cone-shaped tents made of animal skins

fowl (3)—birds used for food

elixir (5)—a substance guaranteed to make whoever drinks it live forever

IN YOUR JOURNAL

Write your impression of these three myths. What are their similarities? What are their differences? How did they make you feel? What can we in our modern technological world learn from these pieces?

A Closer Reading

1. What is the connecting theme of these three pieces of writing?
2. Compare the descriptions of the sun, moon, and stars in the three selections.
3. How did human experiences with nature affect the themes and discoveries of the three selections?
4. What is the significance of the circle in each of the selections?

Drawing Your Own Conclusions

1. What is the main idea of each of the selections?
2. Why does it make sense to look at these three pieces of writing together?
3. Do you think the people of these cultures believe that humans are the center of, or the most important creatures in, the universe? What in your reading supports your answer? Compare the points of view in these selections with the one presented by McKibben (see page 374) in relation to this issue.
4. When people grow up hearing songs like the "Old Dinka Song" and myths like "Moon Lady," or sitting around a circle talking about the elements of sun, moon, and stars, how might these experiences influence their thinking and feeling about the natural world?
5. What are your first memories of the sun, moon, and stars? How do you think you first learned about them? What songs or myths about these elements do you remember from your childhood? What does your answer tell you about how your culture regards them?

Thinking about Writing

1. The Dinka tell a story about the origin of human suffering: In the beginning, God lived in the sky so close to the earth that the first woman and man had to be careful not to hit when they lifted their tools and spears. At that time, God gave each of them one grain of millet every day. One day the woman took more than her share and was using a longer pestle to grind it when she hit the sky. The sky and God moved out of human reach. Ever since, humans have had to work for their food and have known pain and death because God is now so far away that he cannot hear their suffering.

   What does this story tell you about the way the Dinka view life? What does it tell about the way the Dinka view God? How do the Dinka view women?

2. Poems and songs often contain many repetitions. Why do you think this is so? How do the repetitions affect you as a reader?

3. What does Black Elk mean by this metaphoric description in paragraph 2: "The nation's hoop, a nest of many nests where the Great Spirit meant for us to hatch our children"?

4. In which voice (first person, second person, or third person) is each of these selections written? How does that affect you as a reader?

*   *   *

Suggestions for Writing

1. Black Elk says, "The life of a man is a circle from childhood to childhood and so it is in everything where power moves." Write an essay in which you explain this point of view, and support it with your readings, observations, and experiences.

2. Write an essay in which you explain the meaning of the "Old Dinka Song" and how it applies to someone living in the modern world at the turn of the twenty-first century.

3. Write an essay in which you explain the lesson or moral of "Moon Lady." What can we learn from this myth that is relevant for our lives today?

4. Do you think advanced technological societies such as ours have anything to learn from less technologically advanced peoples?

Take a position in an essay on this issue, and support your point of view with examples from your observations, readings, and experiences.

5. Write a short story in which nature—the sun, moon, stars, animals, and humans—all function together. As you write, keep in mind that your audience will be your classmates.

Strategies for Revision

Work in a group of three or four students. Each writer should read her or his draft aloud to the group. As soon as the writer has finished reading the draft, the other members of the group should write answers to the following questions:

- How does the writer make connections between ideas from the past and our lives in the present? If these connections are not clear, what changes would improve this part of the writing?
- What words and phrases does the writer use to describe nature? Does the writer choose exciting and sparkling words that bring the writing alive? What particular expression do you recall from the reading?
- When the writer relates events, are they in a logical order that you can follow and understand?

After you have finished reading each essay and writing the answers to the questions, discuss the essay with the writer. Think about the strong points of the essay, and suggest one way in which the essay can be improved.

Each writer should revise his or her essay and share the revision with the same group.

IN YOUR JOURNAL

This story is about a traditional culture and its burial rituals. If you have experienced the death of a relative or a neighbor or friend, think about how you and the people around you responded to that death. If you have never had this experience, write about the way people you have read about or seen in movies or television respond to death. What differences have you observed in the way people from other cultures or religions than your own react to death?

The Man to Send Rain Clouds

Leslie Marmon Silko

Born in Albuquerque, New Mexico, Leslie Marmon Silko is a member of the Laguna Pueblo people. She has taught writing at the Navajo Community College in Many Farms, Arizona. She has written several books, *Ceremony* (1977), *Storyteller* (1989), *Almanac of the Dead* (1991), *Yellow Woman* (1993), and *Sacred Water* (1993), as well as many short stories, essays, and poems. Silko received an award from the National Endowment for the Arts in 1974 and was given a MacArthur Fellowship in 1981. Her primary area of interest has been her people, the Laguna Pueblo of New Mexico. "The Man to Send Rain Clouds," a story about the death of a grandfather, is from an anthology of contemporary stories by American Indians entitled *The Man to Send Rain Clouds* (1974). Silko writes about her people's attitude toward death in a recent essay:

> You see that after a thing is dead, it dries up. It might take weeks or years, but eventually if you touch the thing, it crumbles under your fingers. It goes back to dust. . . . Human remains are not so different. They should rest with the bones and rinds where they all may benefit living creatures—small rodents and insects—until their return is completed. The remains of things—animals and plants, the clay and the stones—were treated with respect. Because for the ancient people all these things had spirit and being.

One

They found him under a big cottonwood tree. His Levi jacket and   1
pants were faded light-blue so that he had been easy to find. The big
cottonwood tree stood apart from a small grove of winterbare cotton-
woods which grew in the wide, sandy arroyo. He had been dead for a
day or more, and the sheep had wandered and scattered up and down
the arroyo. Leon and his brother-in-law, Ken, gathered the sheep and
left them in the pen at the sheep camp before they returned to the
cottonwood tree. Leon waited under the tree while Ken drove the truck
through the deep sand to the edge of the arroyo. He squinted up at the
sun and unzipped his jacket—it sure was hot for this time of year. But
high and northwest the blue mountains were still deep in snow. Ken
came sliding down the low, crumbling bank about fifty yards down, and
he was bringing the red blanket.

Before they wrapped the old man, Leon took a piece of string   2
out of his pocket and tied a small gray feather in the old man's long
white hair. Ken gave him the paint. Across the brown wrinkled
forehead he drew a streak of white and along the high cheekbones he
drew a strip of blue paint. He paused and watched Ken throw
pinches of corn meal and pollen into the wind that fluttered the
small gray feather. Then Leon painted with yellow under the old
man's broad nose, and finally, when he had painted green across the
chin, he smiled.

"Send us rain clouds, Grandfather." They laid the bundle in the back   3
of the pickup and covered it with a heavy tarp before they started back
to the pueblo.

They turned off the highway onto the sandy pueblo road. Not long   4
after they passed the store and post office they saw Father Paul's car
coming toward them. When he recognized their faces he slowed his car
and waved for them to stop. The young priest rolled down the car
window.

"Did you find old Teofilo?" he asked loudly.   5

Leon stopped the truck. "Good morning, Father. We were just out   6
to the sheep camp. Everything is O.K. now."

"Thank God for that. Teofilo is a very old man. You really shouldn't   7
allow him to stay at the sheep camp alone."

"No, he won't do that any more now."   8

"Well, I'm glad you understand. I hope I'll be seeing you at Mass   9
this week—we missed you last Sunday. See if you can get old Teofilo to

come with you." The priest smiled and waved at them as they drove away.

Two

Louise and Teresa were waiting. The table was set for lunch, and the   10
coffee was boiling on the black iron stove. Leon looked at Louise and
then at Teresa.

"We found him under a cottonwood tree in the big arroyo near   11
sheep camp. I guess he sat down to rest in the shade and never got up
again." Leon walked toward the old man's bed. The red plaid shawl had
been shaken and spread carefully over the bed, and a new brown flannel
shirt and pair of stiff new Levis were arranged neatly beside the pillow.
Louise held the screen door open while Leon and Ken carried in the red
blanket. He looked small and shriveled, and after they dressed him in
the new shirt and pants he seemed more shrunken.

It was noontime now because the church bells rang the Angelus.   12
They ate the beans with hot bread, and nobody said anything until after
Teresa poured the coffee.

Ken stood up and put on his jacket. "I'll see about the grave-   13
diggers. Only the top layer of soil is frozen. I think it can be ready
before dark."

Leon nodded his head and finished his coffee. After Ken had been   14
gone for a while, the neighbors and clanspeople came quietly to em-
brace Teofilo's family and to leave food on the table because the grave-
diggers would come to eat when they were finished.

Three

The sky in the west was full of pale-yellow light. Louise stood   15
outside with her hands in the pockets of Leon's green army jacket that
was too big for her. The funeral was over, and the old men had taken
their candles and medicine bags and were gone. She waited until the
body was laid into the pickup before she said anything to Leon. She
touched his arm, and he noticed that her hands were still dusty from the
corn meal that she had sprinkled around the old man. When she spoke,
Leon could not hear her.

"What did you say? I didn't hear you."   16
"I said that I had been thinking about something."   17
"About what?"   18

"About the priest sprinkling holy water for Grandpa. So he won't be 19
thirsty."

Leon stared at the new moccasins that Teofilo had made for the 20
ceremonial dances in the summer. They were nearly hidden by the red
blanket. It was getting colder, and the wind pushed gray dust down the
narrow pueblo road. The sun was approaching the long mesa where it
disappeared during the winter. Louise stood there shivering and watching his face. Then he zipped up his jacket and opened the truck door.
"I'll see if he's there."

Four

Ken stopped the pickup at the church, and Leon got out; and then 21
Ken drove down the hill to the graveyard where people were waiting.
Leon knocked at the old carved door with its symbols of the Lamb.
While he waited he looked up at the twin bells from the king of Spain
with the last sunlight pouring around them in their tower.

The priest opened the door and smiled when he saw who it was. 22
"Come in! What brings you here this evening?"

The priest walked toward the kitchen, and Leon stood with his cap 23
in his hand, playing with the earflaps and examining the living room—
the brown sofa, the green armchair, and the brass lamp that hung down
from the ceiling by links of chain. The priest dragged a chair out of the
kitchen and offered it to Leon.

"No thank you, Father. I only came to ask you if you would bring 24
your holy water to the graveyard."

The priest turned away from Leon and looked out the window at 25
the patio full of shadows and the dining-room windows of the nuns'
cloister across the patio. The curtains were heavy, and the light from
within faintly penetrated; it was impossible to see the nuns inside eating
supper. "Why didn't you tell me he was dead? I could have brought the
Last Rites anyway."

Leon smiled. "It wasn't necessary, Father." 26

The priest stared down at his scuffed brown loafers and the worn 27
hem of his cassock. "For a Christian burial it was necessary."

His voice was distant, and Leon thought that his blue eyes looked tired. 28

"It's O.K., Father, we just want him to have plenty of water." 29

The priest sank down in the green chair and picked up a glossy 30
missionary magazine. He turned the colored pages full of lepers and
pagans without looking at them.

"You know I can't do that, Leon. There should have been the Last 31
Rites and a funeral Mass at the very least."

Leon put on his green cap and pulled the flaps down over his ears. 32
"It's getting late, Father. I've got to go."

When Leon opened the door Father Paul stood up and said, "Wait." 33
He left the room and came back wearing a long brown overcoat. He
followed Leon out the door and across the dim churchyard to the adobe
steps in front of the church. They both stooped to fit through the low
adobe entrance. And when they started down the hill to the graveyard
only half of the sun was visible above the mesa.

The priest approached the grave slowly, wondering how they had 34
managed to dig into the frozen ground; and then he remembered that
this was New Mexico, and saw the pile of cold loose sand beside the
hole. The people stood close to each other with little clouds of steam
puffing from their faces. The priest looked at them and saw a pile of
jackets, gloves, and scarves in the yellow, dry tumbleweeds that grew in
the graveyard. He looked at the red blanket, not sure that Teofilo was so
small, wondering if it wasn't some perverse Indian trick—something
they did in March to ensure a good harvest—wondering if maybe old
Teofilo was actually at sheep camp corraling the sheep for the night. But
there he was, facing into a cold dry wind and squinting at the last
sunlight, ready to bury a red wool blanket while the faces of the parishio-
ners were in shadow with the last warmth of the sun on their backs.

His fingers were stiff, and it took him a long time to twist the lid off 35
the holy water. Drops of water fell on the red blanket and soaked into
dark icy spots. He sprinkled the grave and the water disappeared almost
before it touched the dim, cold sand; it reminded him of something—
he tried to remember what it was, because he thought if he could
remember he might understand this. He sprinkled more water; he
shook the container until it was empty, and the water fell through the
light from sundown like August rain that fell while the sun was still
shining, almost evaporating before it touched the wilted squash flowers.

The wind pulled at the priest's brown Franciscan robe and swirled 36
away the corn meal and pollen that had been sprinkled on the blanket.
They lowered the bundle into the ground, and they didn't bother to
untie the stiff pieces of new rope that were tied around the ends of the
blanket. The sun was gone, and over on the highway the eastbound lane
was full of headlights. The priest walked away slowly. Leon watched
him climb the hill, and when he had disappeared within the tall, thick
walls, Leon turned to look up at the high blue mountains in the deep

snow that reflected a faint red light from the west. He felt good because it was finished, and he was happy about the sprinkling of the holy water; now the old man could send them big thunderclouds for sure.

Vocabulary

arroyo (1)—a hollow where a stream has dried up

pueblo (3)—a Native American communal village in southwestern United States

shriveled (11)—wrinkled and shrunk

mesa (20)—a small high plateau with steep sides

cassock (27)—a long black outer garment worn by Roman Catholic and Anglican clergymen

adobe (33)—sun-dried brick made of clay

IN YOUR JOURNAL

What did you learn about the response to death in the Laguna Pueblo community that Silko describes? In what ways was it similar to your own experience, and in what ways was it different? What do you think will remain in your memory about this story? Why?

A Closer Reading

1. How do the family members prepare their grandfather for his burial? How is this different from the ritual for death in the Roman Catholic non–Native American community? In other cultures?

2. How does Silko describe the actions of the neighbors and clanspeople at the time of this death? How is this similar to the way your family and neighbors behave when there is a death?

3. How does the young priest seem to feel when Leon arrives at his home? How does the priest feel when he first hears that Teofilo is dead?

4. Are Leon and Father Paul able to communicate and understand each other? What evidence did you use from the story to decide on your answer?

5. What might the colors of face paint—blue, yellow, green, and white—signify?

Drawing Your Own Conclusions

1. What do you think the cornmeal and pollen may be thought to bring the old man in the after life?

2. How do the Native Americans combine Christianity with their traditional beliefs?

3. Why do you think the men decide not to tell Father Paul about Teofilo's death at first?

4. Why does Father Paul finally decide to come to the gravesite and sprinkle the holy water?

5. Silko writes that after Father Paul has sprinkled the holy water, Leon "felt good because it was finished." Do you think the priest felt good about what he had done? What in the story gave you the evidence for your answer?

6. What evidence do you find in the story that Father Paul and Leon do or do not trust each other?

Thinking about Writing

1. Silko divides the story into four sections. Why does she divide the story at those places?

2. Give examples of the descriptive words that Silko uses to tell about the place and people. How do these words help you to see the American Southwest and the Native American in a new way?

3. Give examples of words that describe the emotional state of the people at Teofilo's death. What does this tell you about the people's attitude toward death? How is it similar to or different from your culture's attitude toward death?

4. A death occurs in Pearl Rowe's story on page 61 and in Reynold Price's story on page 391. What is similar and what is different in the attitudes of Rowe, Price, and Silko toward death?

*   *   *

Suggestions for Writing

1. Some Native Americans continue to try to hold on to their traditions despite pressure around them to change. Should they give up these traditional ways and learn the new culture and ways of the country? Write an essay in which you take a position on this issue, and support it using your experiences, observations, and readings.

2. Schools encourage students to be more alike instead of encouraging differences that could be valuable to all students. Schools should teach more courses about the various cultural myths and rites held dear by different cultural communities. They could teach about traditional rituals for birth, marriage, various holidays, and death, as well as common myths. Write an essay in which you agree or disagree with this position, and support it using examples from your experiences, observations, and readings.

3. Write an essay in which you describe a death in your family. What do people actually do—with the body, during a religious or memorial service, at the gravesite or crematory site? In your essay, move from the personal to the abstract as you try to analyze how the rituals indicates the society's feelings about death.

4. Write an essay in which you describe a conflict relating to religion, traditional behavior, or cultural beliefs that has created a problem in your family or community. Explain the conflict, the problems it has caused, and the way it has been resolved.

Strategies for Revision

In this revision activity you will be working with a partner. Photocopy your draft to give to your classmate and then cut it into individual paragraphs. Have your partner do the same, and exchange cut paragraphs. Each of you should then think about the following:

- What is the purpose of each paragraph? What does it make me think or feel about this subject?
- Are there clear and sufficient details in each paragraph?
- Do all the sentences belong together in each paragraph?
- Does the writer seem to be writing the same ideas in several different paragraphs? If so, should a paragraph be discarded?
- If it is a story, are the characters developed? What is the best order

in which to tell the story? Is there a clear and satisfying end to the story?

Without looking at the original draft, each of you should next make pencil marks where you think changes would be appropriate, and then put the paragraphs in the order that makes the most sense. After marking any paragraphs that are repetitious and could be discarded, tape the draft together so it reads most clearly and effectively. You can then exchange drafts again, explaining to each other your decisions about ordering the drafts. You may want to compare the original order of the draft with the suggested revised order.

When you feel satisfied about the best way to improve what you have written, write your revision. Share your revision with the same classmate.

IN YOUR JOURNAL

Write down the story of a myth you enjoy telling and hearing. Explain why you like to think of it.

Flower Myths: Narcissus, Hyacinth, Adonis

Edith Hamilton

Edith Hamilton (1868–1963) published *Mythology,* a collection of myths of the Western world, in 1942. Never out of print, Hamilton's book provides a clear, readable introduction to Greek, Roman, and Norse mythology. Hamilton was headmistress of the Bryn Mawr School in Baltimore, Maryland. Upon her retirement, she began to write about a subject she knew and loved. In this excerpt from her book, Hamilton describes myths connected with flowers. These are stories of young men who died in the prime of life. Upon their deaths, and often from their blood, spring beautiful wildflowers.

The first story about the creation of the narcissus is told only in an early Homeric Hymn of the seventh or eighth century, the second I have taken from Ovid. There is an immense difference between the two poets, who are separated from each other not only by six or seven hundred years, but also by the fundamental difference between the Greek and the Roman. The Hymn is written objectively, simply, without a touch of affectation. The poet is thinking of his subject. Ovid is as always thinking of his audience. But he tells this story well. The bit about the ghost trying to look at itself in the river of death is a subtle touch which is quite characteristic of him and quite unlike any Greek writer. Euripides gives the best account of the festival of Hyacinthus; Apollodorus and Ovid both tell his story. Whenever there is any vividness in my narrative it may be ascribed securely to Ovid. Apollodorus never deviates into anything like that. Adonis I have taken from two third-century poets, Theocritus and Bion. The tale is typical of the Alexandrian poets, tender, a little soft, but always in exquisite taste.

In Greece there are the most lovely wild flowers. They would be   1
beautiful anywhere, but Greece is not a rich and fertile country of wide meadows and fruitful fields where flowers seem at home. It is a land of

rocky ways and stony hills and rugged mountains, and in such places the exquisite vivid bloom of the wild flowers,

> A profusion of delight,
> Gay, bewilderingly bright,

comes as a startling surprise. Bleak heights are carpeted in radiant colors; every crack and crevice of a frowning crag blossoms. The contrast of this laughing, luxuriant beauty with the clear-cut, austere grandeur all around arrests the attention sharply. Elsewhere wild flowers may be little noticed—but never in Greece.

That was as true in the days of old as it is now. In the faraway ages 2 when the tales of Greek mythology were taking shape men found the brilliant blossoms of the Greek spring a wonder and a delight. Those people separated from us by thousands of years, and almost completely unknown to us, felt as we do before that miracle of loveliness, each flower so delicate, yet all together covering the land like a rainbow mantle flung over the hills. The first storytellers in Greece told story after story about them, how they had been created and why they were so beautiful.

It was the most natural thing possible to connect them with the 3 gods. All things in heaven and earth were mysteriously linked with the divine powers, but beautiful things most of all. Often an especially exquisite flower was held to be the direct creation of a god for his own purpose. That was true of the narcissus, which was not like ours of that name, but a lovely bloom of glowing purple and silver. Zeus called it into being to help his brother, the lord of the dark underworld, when he wanted to carry away the maiden he had fallen in love with, Demeter's daughter, Persephone. She was gathering flowers with her companions in the vale of Enna, in a meadow of soft grass and roses and crocus and lovely violets and iris and hyacinths. Suddenly she caught sight of something quite new to her, a bloom more beautiful by far than any she had ever seen, a strange glory of a flower, a marvel to all, immortal gods and mortal men. A hundred blossoms grew up from the roots, and the fragrance was very sweet. The broad sky above and the whole earth laughed to see it, and the salt wave of the sea.

Only Persephone among the maidens had spied it. The rest were at 4 the other end of the meadow. She stole toward it, half fearful at being alone, but unable to resist the desire to fill her basket with it, exactly as Zeus had supposed she would feel. Wondering she stretched out her hands to take the lovely plaything, but before she touched it a chasm opened in the earth and out of it coal-black horses sprang, drawing a chariot and driven by one who had a look of dark splendor, majestic and beautiful and terrible. He caught her to him and held her close. The next moment she was being borne away from the radiance of earth in springtime to the world of the dead by the king who rules it.

This was not the only story about the narcissus. There was another, as magical, but quite different. The hero of it was a beautiful lad, whose name was Narcissus. His beauty was so great, all the girls who saw him longed to be his, but he would have none of them. He would pass the loveliest carelessly by, no matter how much she tried to make him look at her. Heartbroken maidens were nothing to him. Even the sad case of the fairest of the nymphs, Echo, did not move him. She was a favorite of Artemis, the goddess of woods and wild creatures, but she came under the displeasure of a still mightier goddess, Hera herself, who was at her usual occupation of trying to discover what Zeus was about. She suspected that he was in love with one of the nymphs and she went to look them over to try to discover which. However, she was immediately diverted from her investigation by Echo's gay chatter. As she listened amused, the others silently stole away and Hera could come to no conclusion as to where Zeus's wandering fancy had alighted. With her usual injustice she turned against Echo. That nymph became another unhappy girl whom Hera punished. The goddess condemned her never to use her tongue again except to repeat what was said to her. "You will always have the last word," Hera said, "but no power to speak first."

This was very hard, but hardest of all when Echo, too, with all the other lovelorn maidens, loved Narcissus. She could follow him, but she could not speak to him. How then could she make a youth who never looked at a girl pay attention to her? One day, however, it seemed her chance had come. He was calling to his companions, "Is anyone here?" and she called back in rapture, "Here—Here." She was still hidden by the trees so that he did not see her, and he shouted, "Come!"—just what she longed to say to him. She answered joyfully, "Come!" and stepped forth from the woods with her arms outstretched. But he turned away in angry disgust. "Not so," he said; "I will die before I give you power over me." All she could say was, humbly, entreatingly, "I give you power over me," but he was gone. She hid her blushes and her shame in a lonely cave, and never could be comforted. Still she lives in places like that, and they say she has so wasted away with longing that only her voice now is left to her.

So Narcissus went on his cruel way, a scorner of love. But at last one   7
of those he wounded prayed a prayer and it was answered by the gods:
"May he who loves not others love himself." The great goddess Nemesis, which means righteous anger, undertook to bring this about. As
Narcissus bent over a clear pool for a drink and saw there his own
reflection, on the moment he fell in love with it. "Now I know," he
cried, "what others have suffered from me, for I burn with love of my
own self—and yet how can I reach that loveliness I see mirrored in the
water? But I cannot leave it. Only death can set me free." And so it
happened. He pined away, leaning perpetually over the pool, fixed in
one long gaze. Echo was near him, but she could do nothing; only
when, dying, he called to his image, "Farewell—farewell," she could
repeat the words as a last good-by to him.

They say that when his spirit crossed the river that encircles the   8
world of the dead, it leaned over the boat to catch a final glimpse of
itself in the water.

The nymphs he had scorned were kind to him in death and sought   9
his body to give it burial, but they could not find it. Where it had lain
there was blooming a new and lovely flower, and they called it by his
name, Narcissus.

Another flower that came into being through the death of a beautiful   10
youth was the hyacinth, again not like the flower we call by that name,
but lily-shaped and of a deep purple, or, some say, a splendid crimson.
That was a tragic death, and each year it was commemorated by

> The festival of Hyacinthus
> That lasts throughout the tranquil night.
> In a contest with Apollo
> He was slain.
> Discus throwing they competed,
> And the god's swift cast
> Sped beyond the goal he aimed at

and struck Hyacinthus full in the forehead a terrible wound. He had been
Apollo's dearest companion. There was no rivalry between them when
they tried which could throw the discus farthest; they were only playing a
game. The god was horror-struck to see the blood gush forth and the lad,
deathly pale, fall to the ground. He turned as pale himself as he caught
him up in his arms and tried to staunch the wound. But it was too late.
While he held him the boy's head fell back as a flower does when its stem

is broken. He was dead and Apollo kneeling beside him wept for him, dying so young, so beautiful. He had killed him, although through no fault of his, and he cried, "Oh, if I could give my life for yours, or die with you." Even as he spoke, the bloodstained grass turned green again and there bloomed forth the wondrous flower that was to make the lad's name known forever. Apollo himself inscribed the petals—some say with Hyacinth's initial, and others with the two letters of the Greek word that means "Alas"; either way, a memorial of the god's great sorrow.

There is a story, too, that Zephyr, the West Wind, not Apollo, was 11 the direct cause of the death, that he also loved this fairest of youths and in his jealous anger at seeing the god preferred to him he blew upon the discus and made it strike Hyacinth.

Such charming tales of lovely young people who, dying in the spring- 12 time of life, were fittingly changed into spring flowers, have probably a dark background. They give a hint of black deeds that were done in the far-distant past. Long before there were any stories told in Greece or any poems sung which have come down to us, perhaps even before there were storytellers and poets, it might happen, if the fields around a village were not fruitful, if the corn did not spring up as it should, that one of the villagers would be killed and his—or her—blood sprinkled over the barren land. There was no idea as yet of the radiant gods of Olympus who would have loathed the hateful sacrifice. Mankind had only a dim feeling that as their own life depended utterly on seedtime and harvest, there must be a deep connection between themselves and the earth and that their blood, which was nourished by the corn, could in turn nourish it at need. What more natural then, if a beautiful boy had thus been killed, than to think when later the ground bloomed with narcissus or hyacinths that the flowers were his very self, changed and yet living again? So they would tell each other it had happened, a lovely miracle which made the cruel death seem less cruel. Then as the ages passed and people no longer believed that the earth needed blood to be fruitful, all that was cruel in the story would be dropped and in the end forgotten. No one would remember that terrible things had once been done. Hyacinthus, they would say, died not slaughtered by his kinsfolk to get food for them, but only because of a sorrowful mistake.

Of these deaths and flowery resurrections the most famous was that 13 of Adonis. Every year the Greek girls mourned for him and every year they rejoiced when his flower, the blood-red anemone, the windflower, was seen blooming again. Aphrodite loved him; the Goddess of Love, who pierces with her shafts the hearts of gods and men alike, was fated herself to suffer that same piercing pain.

She saw him when he was born and even then loved him and   14
decided he should be hers. She carried him to Persephone to take charge of him for her, but Persephone loved him too and would not give him back to Aphrodite, not even when the goddess went down to the underworld to get him. Neither goddess would yield, and finally Zeus himself had to judge between them. He decided that Adonis should spend half the year with each, the autumn and winter with the Queen of the Dead; the spring and summer with the Goddess of Love and Beauty.

All the time he was with Aphrodite she sought only to please him.   15
He was keen for the chase, and often she would leave her swan-drawn car, in which she was used to glide at her ease through the air, and follow him along rough woodland ways dressed like a huntress. But one sad day she happened not to be with him and he tracked down a mighty boar. With his hunting dogs he brought the beast to bay. He hurled his spear at it, but he only wounded it, and before he could spring away, the boar mad with pain rushed at him and gored him with its great tusks. Aphrodite in her winged car high over the earth heard her lover's groan and flew to him. He was softly breathing his life away, the dark blood flowing down his skin of snow and his eyes growing heavy and dim. She kissed him, but Adonis knew not that she kissed him as he died. Cruel as his wound was, the wound in her heart was deeper. She spoke to him, although she knew he could not hear her:—

> "You die, O thrice desired,
> And my desire has flown like a dream.
> Gone with you is the girdle of my beauty,
> But I myself must live who am a goddess
> And may not follow you.
> Kiss me yet once again, the last, long kiss,
> Until I draw your soul within my lips
> And drink down all your love."

> The mountains all were calling and the oak trees answering,
> Oh, woe, woe for Adonis. He is dead.
> And Echo cried in answer, Oh, woe, woe for Adonis.
> And all the Loves wept for him and all the Muses too.

But down in the black underworld Adonis could not hear them, nor   16
see the crimson flower that sprang up where each drop of his blood had
stained the earth.

Vocabulary

crag (1)—a steep rugged rock
that sticks out beyond others
austere (1)—severe; stern
chasm (4)—a crack in the earth's
surface; an abyss
scorner (7)—person who ex-

presses contempt for someone or something
crimson (10)—bright red
staunch (10)—to stop the flow
of blood

IN YOUR JOURNAL

Write the part of the flower myth that you will remember most from
this selection. Explain why you liked it.

A Closer Reading

1. What differences are there in the two stories of Narcissus? Which
   is more familiar to you?

2. What differences are there in the two stories of Hyacinth? Which
   is more familiar to you?

3. What characteristics do the goddesses have in these myths? What
   characteristics do the gods have? How do their lives affect the
   human lives in the myths?

4. From what source does Hamilton think the flower myths
   emerged? What other explanation could there be for the deaths
   of young people?

Drawing Your Own Conclusions

1. In *Mythology and You: Classical Mythology and Its Relevance to
   Today's World* (1984), authors Donna Rosenberg and Sorelle
   Baker write that "the Greek myths supplied humankind with a
   gallery of models, both positive and negative." What models

were evident in the flower myths? Which were positive and which negative? Cite specific aspects of the selection to support your answer.

2. Myths began as stories told orally. What effect do you think this had on the nature of early myths? What other selections in this book deal with oral culture? Why is memory so important in oral culture?

3. No one knows when the Greek myths were first told in their present form. The first written record of Greece is the *Iliad* by Homer. Hamilton writes that through the Greek myths

> mankind became the center of the universe, the most important thing in it. This was a revolution in thought. Human beings had counted for little heretofore. In Greece, man first realized what mankind was. The Greeks made their gods in their own image. That had not entered the mind of man before. Until then, gods had no semblance of reality. In Egypt, a towering colossus, immobile, beyond the power of the imagination to endow with movement, as fixed in the stone as the tremendous temple columns, a representation of the human shape deliberately made unhuman. Or a rigid figure, a woman with a cat's head . . . Or a monstrous mysterious sphinx, aloof from all that lives. In Mesopotamia, bas-reliefs of bestial shapes unlike any beast ever known, men with birds' heads and lions with bulls' heads and both with eagles' wings. (*Mythology*, pp. 7–8)

How might the fact that the Greeks' gods were anthropomorphic, or like human beings, have contributed to people identifying with their stories?

4. Hamilton states that the Greeks were the first to place humans in the center of the universe in their myths. Reread the McKibben selection on page 374 and the Moyers interview on page 409. Do you think we should continue to think of humankind as the center of the universe?

Thinking about Writing

1. What is the function of the introductory passage that Hamilton includes?

2. Why do you think Hamilton includes poetry? What is the effect of the poetry on you as a reader? Which of the poetry selections do you prefer? Why?

3. Notice how Hamilton connects one story to the next. In paragraph 10, Hamilton presents a theory about the creation of the flower myths. She follows this with one more myth. Reread the last paragraphs, moving paragraph 10 to the very end. Which ending do you prefer and why?

4. Hamilton refers to "man" and "mankind." How does her word choice affect you as a reader? Is this selection, although written by a woman, an example of sexist writing? How could she have rewritten certain passages to include both sexes without changing the total meaning of what she wrote?

*   *   *

Suggestions for Writing

1. According to Joseph Campbell, myth serves four functions (see Bill Moyers's interview with Campbell on page 409). The first is the mystical function, and it is concerned with the mystical or religious nature of the universe. The second is cosmological, and it deals with the makeup of the universe—the "What is fire?" type of question. The third is sociological, supporting and validating a certain social order. The fourth is pedagogical, teaching a person how to live a life. Write an essay focusing on one of the flower myths. Retell the story of the myth in your own words, and explain which of these four functions it serves. Explain how you made your choice.

2. In *Mythology and You: Classical Mythology and Its Relevance to Today's World*, Rosenberg and Baker write, "Blood, gore, and personal tragedy . . . still sell newspapers and glue listeners to their television sets. Now, as then, violence and personal tragedy are an integral part of human life." Write an essay in which you use examples from your personal experiences, observations, or readings to illustrate that this statement still holds true in our present world. Reread the Gelman essay (see page 304) on violence for ideas.

3. Myths teach us about human nature and usually present a moral or ethical point of view. Should myths be taught in schools? Should schools teach moral and ethical values, or should this be left to the parents? Take a position and write an essay, supporting your position with your experiences, observations, and readings.

Strategies for Revision

Before you begin to revise your draft, write in your journal five discoveries that you have made about your writing so far this semester. Of what have these discoveries made you aware as you write and as you revise what you have written?

Then, to revise your writing, share it with a group of three other students, who, in turn, will share their writing with you. Take turns reading your drafts aloud to one another. Do not write or read anything else while someone else is reading. Listen carefully, and try to concentrate totally on the meaning of the writing. When it is your time to read, do so slowly and carefully.

After each person reads, allow several minutes for everyone in the group to write the following:

- His or her interpretation of what the draft is about
- The main points and the ideas that stood out in the reading of the draft
- Three specific questions about the writing

When each person has finished reading and each has finished writing response notes, give the notes to the writer. As a writer, you should read the notes from the three respondents. If you do not understand anything in the notes, ask questions while you are still in your group. Then each writer will make revisions, considering the questions and suggested changes.

When you have completed your revision, make copies of it for each member of your group.

IN YOUR JOURNAL

Write about a trip you took that taught you something about your
cultural heritage. What details do you remember about that trip? Where
did you go? With whom did you travel? What were your reasons for
going?

A Father's Rite

Chester Higgins, Jr.

Chester Higgins, Jr., is a staff photographer for the *New York
Times*. He traveled through the world photographing people of African descent for his book, *Feeling the Spirit: The Family of Africa*
(1994). This essay, which appeared in "About Men" in the *New York
Times Magazine* of December 27, 1992, describes a trip to Africa
made by Higgins and his son. There, the two men perform a ritual
developed out of their knowledge of African myths and history in an
attempt to bring them closer to each other and to their African
heritage.

I took my son to Africa this year. For three weeks my 20-year-old   1
son and I explored the past and present of our people in Egypt and
Ethiopia. I wanted him to see what I regard as the land of his heritage; I
wanted him to experience the ecstasy I felt on my first visit to Africa
when I was in my 20's.

I had envisioned a kind of rite of passage for my son; what tran-   2
spired between us became a turning point—in our relationship, for me
as his father and I hope for him as well.

Being a father seems to require skills never taught to me. Through-   3
out my son's 20 years and my daughter's 22 years, I have often felt as if I
were in a boat slipping along the water in a dark night without a lamp
or a lighthouse to guide me. I felt like an impostor. I was reared by my
stepfather, a distant man, and at 19 I sought out my biological father,
whom I had never known. Those experiences made me determined to
take the role of a father seriously.

When my son was 9 years old and my daughter was 11, their mother   4
and I divorced, and it nearly sank the already adrift boat. With divorce

often comes anger, a welter of conflicting feelings and much pain for everybody. New York State court-restricted visitations for a father can reduce his relationship with his children to that of an uncle. Having been deprived of my own father, I was determined to maintain as much contact with my children as the law would allow.

For my 15th trip to Africa, in July, to photograph the reinterment of   5
His Majesty Haile Selassie on what would have been his 100th birthday, I decided to ask my son, Damani, to come along as my assistant. Damani, who has dreadlocked his hair, shares my love of His Majesty and of reggae, the music of the Rastafarians who worship Selassie. I added to our itinerary a stopover in Egypt so that my son could also see the pyramids, temples and tombs of our ancestors.

Haile Selassie's reinterment was postponed by the new Ethiopian   6
regime about two weeks before we were to arrive. Though deeply disappointed, neither Damani nor I considered canceling our trip, nor did the thousands of Rastafarians who annually gather for Selassie's birthday. While we were in Ethiopia, my son in his dreadlocks blended into the population; his enthusiasm for this venerable African country warmed my heart. On a four-day trip to visit the ancient sacred city of Lalibala, where, in the 12th century, churches were hewn out of the surrounding mountains, I had a dream. In my dream, I saw two men, one older and one younger, facing one another against a background of temples and pyramids. The father was speaking as he anointed the head of his son.

I became enamored of the possibility of enacting a ceremony with   .7
my son in Africa. For the next six days I privately wondered what words to use in such a ceremony. Gradually the words came to me. By the time we arrived in Cairo, I was ready. I told my son that there was a ceremony I wanted to perform with him in the tombs at Luxor, Egypt. His eyes shone with anticipation. But I wondered if he would still be receptive after my next statement. In the dream I remembered that the son was anointed, as it were, with a dry substance. I took this to mean that powder rather than oil was used. But what powder? I ruled out ground herbs and flowers, and finally settled on sand. Sand represents the Sahara, and sand also contains the remains of the ancient people of Pharaonic Egypt. That made metaphysical sense to me, but in the real world, young adults or almost anybody for that matter, are disinclined to have sand poured on their hair.

"I will need sand to anoint your head," I told my son.   8
"Sand?" he asked, hesitantly. "How much?"   9

"Just a little; you can put some in a film canister," I said hastily. We　10
both knew a 35-millimeter film canister wouldn't hold much sand.
"Take the canister and find sand you feel special about and I'll use that."

Once he was in control of the amount of sand and where it would　11
come from, he decided to take some from the desert in the shadow of
the pyramids in Cairo. Days later, when we reached Luxor, he collected
more from around the remains of the Temple of Karnak—one of the
largest, oldest stone temples in the world.

The next afternoon we sailed across the Nile to Thebes and to the　12
Valley of the Kings, a basin formed by towering mountains. From the
heavenly perch of the ancient Egyptian gods, the valley resembles a
huge bowl to which there is one narrow entrance, flanked by more tall
peaks. The tombs of the Pharaohs are hewn into the lower part of the
mountains that form the basin. Inside each tomb, 12-foot-square pas-
sageways lead down several thousand feet into the solid rock. The
scene that greets modern-day visitors to these sacred chambers is astonishing: Ornately painted walls reveal images of animals, people and
scenes that were part of the real and imaginary lives of Pharaonic
Egyptians. It was here, inside one of the tombs of an 18th Dynasty
Pharoah, that I chose to perform the ceremony revealed to me in my
dream in Ethiopia.

In front of an enormous wall painting of Osiris, the god of resurrec-　13
tion, my son and I faced each other. I poured the sand he had collected
into the palm of my left hand, and with my right, I anointed the top of
his head with this sand. Looking into his eyes, I said:

"I, your father, anoint the crown of your head with the soil of　14
Africa. This piece of earth is a symbol of the lives of your ancestors. It is
a bonding of their lives to yours. Like your father, you, too, are African.
We are Africans not because we were born in Africa, but because Africa
was born in us. Look around you and behold us in our greatness.
Greatness is an African possibility; you can make it yours. Just as the
great ones before you have, by their deeds, placed their names on
history, so can you by your deeds place your name on tomorrow . . . So
here, in the company of those great ones who have waited patiently for
your visit—you are loved, you are encouraged. Our faces shine toward
yours. Go forward, may you live long, may you prosper and have
health."

We hugged each other, enjoying the specialness of the moment.　15
Leaving him alone inside the tomb to meditate, I walked back toward
the light and waited for him outside on the valley floor.

Here in the land of our ancient fathers, in the tomb of one of the   16
great fathers of the ancient Egyptian empire, my perception of what it
means to be a father was unalterably expanded and enhanced.

Vocabulary

welter (4)—confusion or turmoil
reinterment (5)—reburial
anointed (6)—applied with oil
    or other substance in a cere-
    mony or rite

hewn (12)—made or shaped by
    cutting or chopping

IN YOUR JOURNAL

Reread your first journal entry. Consider how that trip affected you
and write about the effect of that trip on you today as you reflect back
on your experiences. In what ways do you now see the trip differently
from the way you originally saw it?

A Closer Reading

1. In what ways does the experience described in this essay meet
   the qualifications of the first function of myth mentioned by
   Joseph Campbell (see page 412)? Does this experience meet the
   qualifications of any of the other functions of myth (see page
   412)?

2. What in Higgins's essay tells the reader that the relationship
   between the father and son has been difficult? What in the essay
   tells the reader that by the end of the trip the two men feel
   respect for each other and that Higgins has begun to see Damani
   as a man and not a boy?

3. What interests and beliefs do the father and son have in common?

4. What traditions or characteristics of Ethiopia are mentioned?
   Where is reggae music known outside the Rastafarian world?

5. What specific geographic, natural, and human-made sites are
   mentioned? In what parts of Africa do the two men travel?

Drawing Your Own Conclusions

1. Why do you think Higgins wants to take this trip with Damani? What does this trip teach Higgins about being a father? What does it teach Damani about being a son?

2. Have you ever had a dream that affected your behavior? What function do dreams have for you? Do you know anyone for whom dreams have a greater significance? Describe the function of dreams in that person's life as well as in your own.

3. What other religious ceremonies or ethnic traditions involve pouring (or putting) a substance on someone and saying particular words at the same time? Why do you think this is a common tradition among many different peoples in the world? What is the significance of the sand used in the Higgins's rite?

4. Joseph Campbell wrote about the importance of a guide in mythical adventures—those that mark a new period in someone's life. Who is the guide in this essay? In what way do you think this will mark a new period in the relationship between the father and son?

Thinking about Writing

1. Where in the essay does Higgins tell the readers about his personal background? What specific information does he include? How does knowing about his background affect you as a reader?

2. Where in the essay does Higgins use dialogue? What does this dialogue tell the reader about the relationship between Higgins and Damani?

3. How many different tenses does Higgins use in paragraph 2? Which verb refers to the future? What other tenses are used to help the reader understand the different time periods in this paragraph? Why does Higgins shift to different tenses?

4. What does the last paragraph mean to you? What in the article has influenced your understanding of this paragraph?

*   *   *

Suggestions for Writing

1. Write an essay in which you describe a traditional rite or cere-mony that you witnessed or in which you participated. What kind of impact did it have on you? Describe the incident in detail, and explain the significance of the experience for you.

2. Imagine that you win a trip to any place in the world in which you can learn something about your own heritage or back-ground. Write an essay in which you explain where you will go and what you think you can learn from this experience.

3. Write an essay in which you describe a dream and the effect it had on your life. Include details of the dream, and explain why you felt the dream had significance for you.

4. Recently, much has been written about the African custom of female circumcision. Many women have taken a position against this custom. Others feel strongly that we must accept the cultural norms of various societies. Does learning about different cultures and customs mean that the learners must sanction all the custom-ary practices of a culture? Take a position on this issue, support-ing your point of view with your personal experiences, your observations, and your readings.

Strategies for Revision

Before you begin actually to reread or revise your writing about this selection, write your answers to the following questions in your journal:

- What did I learn about writing from the Higgins article?
- What techniques does he use to integrate personal experience and general information?
- How does he use dialogue? Reread the dialogue in the essay, focusing on its form and function.
- How does he use description? Reread the descriptions, thinking about how Higgins helped you to see his experience.

Reread your draft, thinking about the same questions in relation to your own work:

- How do I use what I learned about writing from Higgins in the draft?

- How do I integrate personal experience and general information?
- How and where do I use dialogue? Look at its form and function in your draft. Use dialogue when it shows something about the person speaking that cannot be described in words.
- How and where do I use description? Do my words create a unique picture for my readers?

IN YOUR JOURNAL

"I am a very rational person. I tend to trust reason more than feeling. But I also happen to be superstitious—in my fashion." Write in your journal a response to the first lines from Pogrebin's essay. Note any superstitions you have and their origins.

Superstitious Minds

Letty Cottin Pogrebin

Letty Cottin Pogrebin is one of the founding editors of *Ms.* magazine. She has written many books, most recently *Deborah, Golda & Me: Being Female & Jewish in America* (1991), *Among Friends* (1987) and *Family Politics* (1983), and *Growing Up Free: Raising Your Kids in the 80's* (1980). "Superstitious Minds" first appeared in the February 1988 issue of *Ms.* magazine. Myths were used to explain puzzling events and phenomena such as events in the heavens. Superstitions developed similarly. As humans tried to understand the strange experiences and fates that befell them, they developed beliefs that they thought would keep them and their loved ones safe and in good health. Pogrebin's essay describes how superstitions are passed down through generations in her family.

I am a very rational person. I tend to trust reason more than feeling. But I also happen to be superstitious—in my fashion. Black cats and rabbits' feet hold no power for me. My superstitions are my mother's superstitions, the amulets and incantations she learned from *her* mother and taught me. 1

I don't mean to suggest that I grew up in an occult atmosphere. On the contrary, my mother desperately wanted me to rise above her immigrant ways and become an educated American. She tried to hide her superstitions, but I came to know them all: Slap a girl's cheeks when she first gets her period. Never take a picture of a pregnant woman. Knock wood when speaking about your good fortune. When ready to conceive, eat the ends of bread if you want to have a boy. Don't leave a bride alone on her wedding day. 2

When I was growing up, my mother often would tiptoe in after I   3
seemed to be asleep and kiss my forehead three times, making odd
noises that sounded like a cross between sucking and spitting. One
night I opened my eyes and demanded an explanation. Embarrassed,
she told me she was exorcising the "Evil Eye"—in case I had attracted
its attention that day by being especially wonderful. She believed her
kisses could suck out any envy or ill will that those less fortunate may
have directed at her child.

By the time I was in my teens, I was almost on speaking terms with   4
the Evil Eye, a jealous spirit that kept track of those who had "too
much" happiness and zapped them with sickness and misery to even the
score. To guard against this mischief, my mother practiced rituals of
interference, evasion, deference, and above all, avoidance of situations
where the Evil Eye might feel at home.

This is why I wasn't allowed to attend funerals. This is also why my   5
mother hated to mend my clothes while I was wearing them. The only
garment one should properly get sewn *into* is a shroud. To ensure that
the Evil Eye did not confuse my pinafore with a burial outfit, my
mother insisted that I chew a thread while she sewed, thus proving
myself very much alive. Outwitting the Evil Eye also accounted for her
closing the window shades above my bed whenever there was a full
moon. The moon should only shine on cemeteries, you see; the living
need protection from the spirits.

Because we were dealing with a deadly force, I also wasn't supposed   6
to say any words associated with mortality. This was hard for a 12-year-
old who punctuated every anecdote with the verb "to die," as in "You'll
die when you hear this!" or "If I don't get home by ten, I'm dead." I
managed to avoid using such expressions in the presence of my mother
until the day my parents brought home a painting I hated and we were
arguing about whether it should be displayed on our walls. Unthinking,
I pressed my point with a melodramatic idiom: "That picture will hang
over my dead body!" Without a word, my mother grabbed a knife and
slashed the canvas to shreds.

I understand all this now. My mother emigrated in 1907 from a   7
small Hungarian village. The oldest of seven children, she had to go
out to work before she finished the eighth grade. Experience taught
her that life was unpredictable and often incomprehensible. Just as an
athlete keeps wearing the same T-shirt in every game to prolong a
winning streak, my mother's superstitions gave her a means of imposing order on a chaotic system. Her desire to control the fates

sprung from the same helplessness that makes the San Francisco 49ers' defensive more superstitious than its offensive team. Psychologists speculate this is because the defense has less control; they don't have the ball.

Women like my mother never had the ball. She died when I was 15,   8
leaving me with deep regrets for what she might have been—and a growing understanding of who she was. *Superstitious* is one of the things she was. I wish I had a million sharp recollections of her, but when you don't expect someone to die, you don't store up enough memories. Ironically, her mystical practices are among the clearest impressions she left behind. In honor of this matrilineal heritage—and to symbolize my mother's effort to control her life as I in my way try to find order in mine—I knock on wood and I do not let the moon shine on those I love. My children laugh at me, but they understand that these tiny rituals have helped keep my mother alive in my mind.

A year ago, I woke in the night and realized that my son's window   9
blinds had been removed for repair. Smiling at my own compulsion, I got a bed sheet to tack up against the moonlight and I opened his bedroom door. What I saw brought tears to my eyes. There, hopelessly askew, was a blanket my son, then 18, had taped to his window like a curtain.

My mother never lived to know David, but he knew she would not   10
want the moon to shine upon him as he slept.

Vocabulary

amulets (1)—things worn on the body as a protection against evil or injury

incantations (1)—the chanting of magical words or sounds to cast a spell

occult (2)—mysterious and secret; part of the mystical arts like magic, alchemy, and witchcraft

conceive (2)—to become pregnant

deference (4)—yielding of opinion, judgments, or wishes out of respect for another

shroud (5)—cloth used to wrap a corpse

matrilineal heritage (8)—heritage through the mother's side of the family

IN YOUR JOURNAL

According to the article you have just read, why is the author superstitious? What are some of the superstitions she mentions in her article? Do you agree with the author's point of view that people can be rational and superstitious at the same time?

A Closer Reading

1. What are some of the specific superstitions the author mentions? What do these superstitions have in common? What do these superstitions suggest that people fear?

2. How does Pogrebin's mother teach her superstitions to her daughter? How does Pogrebin teach them to her son?

3. Why does Pogrebin's mother slash the painting? Why is she afraid of words that are associated with death?

4. According to Pogrebin, what is the reason that her mother was superstitious? Does this reason apply in today's world?

Drawing Your Own Conclusions

1. What is Pogrebin's attitude about superstitious people in general? What evidence do you have from her essay? Why does her son put the blanket over his window?

2. What evidence do you have that people are still superstitious today? Do people from different cultural backgrounds have different superstitions?

3. What superstitions did you learn about as a child? How do they affect your life today? Have you ever made a decision based on superstitions?

4. Are you more affected by the superstitions you learned or by the myths you read in early life? Explain your answer.

5. Do you believe in any superstitions? If so, how did you come to believe in them? Would you like your children to believe in them too? What would you do to influence their beliefs?

Thinking about Writing

1. Pogrebin wrote this essay in the first person. Change the first paragraph to third person (for instance, Letty Cottin Pogrebin is a very rational person. She tends to trust . . .). Read the original paragraph and your altered paragraph. How does this alter the tone of the writing? Which do you prefer? Which is more academic? Which is more convincing? Why?

2. In paragraph 1, Pogrebin gives two examples of superstitions. What are they? What are her feelings about them? What is she trying to suggest to her readers about her personal superstitions?

3. What is the main idea of this essay? Where is it stated? How did you know it was the main idea of the essay?

4. In paragraph 7, Pogrebin includes information about her mother's background. How does this information support the main idea of her essay?

*   *   *

Suggestions for Writing

1. Interview a classmate (or family member) in order to discover the person's superstitions. Your first step will be to develop questions for the interview. Try to find where the superstitions came from and what the person does because of those superstitions. Write the person's responses to your questions. Show your notes to the person and discuss them before writing an essay describing the person's superstitions, their origins, and the ways they have affected the person's behavior.

2. Write an essay in which you compare the superstitions that you have heard in your family with those that Pogrebin was taught. Speculate on why there may be similarities or differences. (See page 74 for suggestions for comparing and contrasting.)

3. Should superstitions hold any power in someone's life? In your essay, take a stand on this issue. Support your point of view with examples from your experiences or observations.

4. Meet with a small group in your class or with your friends to discuss superstitions. Ask each person to tell about two superstitions and how they have influenced the person's life. How does the person cope with them? What steps are taken to keep evil in check, and so on? If someone in the group does not have any superstitions, find out if the person grew up in a superstitious family. Then write an essay describing your findings and analyzing the reasons for the ways that superstitions influenced your group.

5. Write an essay in which you examine the connection between superstitions and myths. Are some superstitions based on cultural myths?

Strategies for Revision

The following revision strategy involves working with a partner. You will be sharing a draft of your writing on superstitions, so you should make a copy of it for your partner to read and write on. Your partner should do the same. Read each other's writing slowly and carefully. Ask each other the following questions:

- What do you think I am trying to say?
- What did you like best about my writing?
- Did any part of it make you stop and read it again in order to understand what I meant?
- When I wrote about specific superstitions, did I choose good examples? Was there enough detail for you to understand?
- Without looking at the writing again, what part of it do you remember the best?
- What questions do you still have about this piece of writing?

After you have discussed each of your drafts, revise and share your second drafts with the same partner.

Rachele Deveras wrote this essay in response to Writing Suggestion 3 following the Pogrebin article: Should superstitions hold any power in someone's life? In your essay, take a stand on this issue. Support your point of view with examples from your experiences or observations.

The Two Mosquito Bites

Rachele Deveras

A little over a month ago while on vacation in my homeland, the Philippines, I learned a very important lesson from two painful mosquito bites on my right leg. It had been fourteen years since I last set foot there. I was only six when I left in 1978 to live with my family in the U.S.A. Due to the many years of living in the U.S.A. and total ignorance of my homeland, I felt like a foreigner visiting for the first time. Right before my departure from Kennedy Airport, my ancient grandmother ominously warned me of the behavior of the native mosquitos around visitors like me. She said, "Ooh! You had better believe me, Miss Know-it-all . . . there is an old saying that says the longer you stay away from the motherland, the sweeter your blood grows to the mosquitos; and since you haven't been back for so many years, the mosquitos will think you're a piece of candy!" 1

Not believing because she was old and a notoriously superstitious woman, I replied, "Grandmaaaaa, that's just an old wives' tale . . . cornballs! . . . just like your ineffective herbal grass medicine." 2

Angered, she lashed back saying, "Ooh! You'll see . . . You'll see . . . Ha, Ha, Ha, Ha . . . Hee . . . Hee." 3

Well, less than a week after my arrival in Manila, I was already carpeted by a blanket of mosquito bites, even in strange and unmentionable places. There wasn't a day that passed during which I would not get at least five more new bites. Although I came fully armed with defensive artillery such as mosquito nets, noxious insecticide, thick impenetrable clothing and a gallon of "OFF" lotion; they all proved useless. It even got so bad that I would violently refuse to take a bath or go to the bathroom, because it would mean exposing my veins to those invisible beasts. 4

Late one night in my cousin's home in Manila, I was so overwhelmed by the pain of the bites and the uselessness of my calamine lotion, that I was determined to kill at least one mosquito. Frenzied and crazed with torment, I turned on the light in my cousin's room and I sat on my bed with claw-like hands ready to backhandedly catch a live 5 mosquito and begin to unmercifully pluck its limbs off. Unfortunately, the mosquitos were too fast and I was completely out of my mind. Finally, I started to cry in sheer agony. I sobbed, ". . . die, you demonic creatures . . . die . . . die!"

Hoping to find some comfort, I woke up my cousin who was   6
sleeping peacefully in the bed next to mine. In the midst of dreaming, and annoyed that I interrupted her, she said yawning, "Rache, there is nothing you can do. Go back to sleep and STOP scratching those bites! That's why they hurt so much!" With a few tosses and turns, she returned to her restful slumber. Enviously watching her sleep, I prayed that a slow and succulent mosquito would land on her face, thus giving me a justified reason to slap her.

I was still waiting to strike an unlucky mosquito, when I noticed   7
something very strange and funny. The mosquito would lightly dance around my cousin's forehead and quickly fly away, never lingering long enough to bite and suck her blood. It appeared as if they simply refused to bite. Amazed, I ran to all the household members' rooms and watched them sleep soundlessly as the same phenomenon occurred again and again. I cautiously lifted the maid's blanket to expose her feet to the mosquitoes. In the light coming from the street, I saw that the mosquitos would land on her toes then, very quickly, as if repulsed, they would fly away from her feet. They never lingered long enough to bite.

On the same night in the dimly-lit kitchen, I curiously pulled up the   8
right leg of my thick jogging pants to see what would happen. Less than a minute passed before two mosquitos clung to my leg, giving me two big, juicy bites. It appeared as if those two demons were attracted to this sweet and exotic, foreign blood; blood that belonged to me. From those two annoying bites, I came to realize and accept my grandma's silly tale. From then on, I always tried to keep an open mind about those strange old wives' tales because they do have some truth to them.

Questions to Think About

1. What is Rachele Deveras's tone in this essay?
2. What specific descriptive details does she include that make the places she is describing come alive to you?
3. What specific words and phrases does she use to let you know what she thinks about superstitions?
4. Does the dialogue add anything to this essay?

MAKING CONNECTIONS

The World of the Past: *Learning from Myths and Rites*

1. What is the connection between myths (see Moyers, page 409, Nature Myths, page 418, and Flower Myths, page 433), rites (see Higgins, page 433 and Silko, page 424), and superstitions (see Pogrebin, page 450)? Write an essay in which you explain why these three topics are included in a unit on the world of the past. Use quotations and paraphrases from specific pieces included in this unit to support your main idea.

2. Imagine that Higgins, Silko, and Pogrebin met to discuss the importance of ritual in our society today. After rereading each of these selections, write a dialogue that reflects each of their points of view. Use quotes and paraphrases from their selections in addition to your own interpretations of their ideas.

3. Reread the selections in this unit focusing on how culture affects values and beliefs in the world. What are some of the similarities in the values and beliefs expressed by at least two of the many cultures represented in this unit? What are some of the differences? In conclusion, compare your own culture to those that you have described, and explain what you have learned about your culture from reading in this unit about other cultures.

4. In an essay, show how one or more recent movies have a mythic story line. Explain which of Joseph Campbell's four functions of myth they fulfill and in what ways they do so.

5. Write an essay in which you choose one piece of writing from this unit that caused an emotional reaction—it may have angered you, made you sad, or made you happy. Explain the effect of this piece of writing and tell why it had this effect.

6. Write an introduction to this unit in which you tell other students which piece of writing is the most interesting, the most informative, or the best written. Using quotations from the selection, convince a potential reader to choose this particular piece of writing to read.

9

THE WORLD OF SCIENCE

Understanding and Exploring

Science helps us know the world and understand how it functions. We take for granted the results that come from scientific discoveries and constantly expect new and better products. When diseases are identified, we look to science to cure us of them and find ways to prevent them from occurring again. Yet most people, unless they are directly involved in science, rarely think about what makes scientific thought and work different from other ways of studying natural phenomena. In this unit, we look at the scientist and science, at what science has provided, and how we come to know what we know.

"Take This Fish and Look at It" by Samuel H. Scudder tells about a student who, in learning to be a keen and careful observer, finds out what it means to be a scientist. Scudder learns the importance of detail in forming a broad understanding of a complex subject.

Adam Frank describes the process of finding a question and turning it into a workable research project. "A Dialogue of Questions" illustrates that one of the most important skills for scientists is the ability to formulate questions. Without effective questions, there can be no answers.

Pat Murphy interviews a physician, Margarita Loinaz, to discuss the types of problems faced every day by a doctor in a clinic. In "The Problem Solvers," Murphy asks Loinaz to explain in what ways her medical education and her actual experience have assisted her in making complex decisions regarding her patients' health and treatment.

In "The Geologist as Private Eye," Raymond C. Murray examines the role of the forensic geologist in pinpointing locations and in finding the answers that help to solve crimes. Murray asserts that the fictional character Sherlock Holmes would have been impressed by the new analytic techniques available to geologists because of increasingly sophisticated technology.

The invention of new technology and products interests science writer Ira Flatow. In "The First Video Game: If You Build It, They Will Come," Flatow tells us about the little-known inventor of the video game. He also provides evidence that this very invention could have lowered the national debt if only its inventor had gotten a patent.

Diane Beran, a student writer, explains in "Max" how a trip to the veterinarian changed her life and helped her find her future career.

*   *   *

Think about the following questions before reading the selections in this unit:

1. What was your best experience learning about science? Why does that experience stand out in your mind?

2. What field of science do you want to know more about? Why?

3. How will you find out about that field of science?

IN YOUR JOURNAL

What is the difference between how you might look at something in everyday life and how a scientist might look at it? What does the title suggest that the selection will be about? Write down your reflections.

Take This Fish and Look at It

Samuel H. Scudder

Samuel H. Scudder (1837–1911) was educated at Williams College and Harvard University. He became an entomologist (a person who studies insects) and was well known for his studies of butterflies and Orthoptera, an order of insects that includes the grasshopper and cricket. Scudder wrote the following selection about an incident that occurred when he was studying with Louis Agassiz, a famous professor of natural history at Harvard University. The incident affected how Scudder felt about the study of science for the rest of his life.

It was more than fifteen years ago that I entered the laboratory of   1
Professor Agassiz, and told him I had enrolled my name in the Scientific School as a student of natural history. He asked me a few questions about my object in coming, my antecedents generally, the mode in which I afterwards proposed to use the knowledge I might acquire, and, finally, whether I wished to study any special branch. To the latter I replied that, while I wished to be well grounded in all departments of zoology, I purposed to devote myself specially to insects.

"When do you wish to begin?" he asked.   2

"Now," I replied.   3

This seemed to please him, and with an energetic "Very well!" he   4
reached from a shelf a huge jar of specimens in yellow alcohol. "Take this fish," he said, "and look at it; we call it a haemulon; by and by I will ask you what you have seen."

With that he left me, but in a moment returned with explicit instruc-   5
tions as to the care of the object entrusted to me.

"No man is fit to be a naturalist," said he, "who does not know how   6
to take care of specimens."

I was to keep the fish before me in a tin tray, and occasionally 7 moisten the surface with alcohol from the jar, always taking care to replace the stopper tightly. Those were not the days of ground-glass stoppers and elegantly shaped exhibition jars; all the old students will recall the huge neckless glass bottles with their leaky, wax-besmeared corks, half eaten by insects, and begrimed with cellar dust. Entomology was a cleaner science than ichthyology, but the example of the Professor, who had unhesitatingly plunged to the bottom of the jar to produce the fish, was infectious; and though this alcohol had a "very ancient and fishlike smell," I really dared not show any aversion within these sacred precincts, and treated the alcohol as though it were pure water. Still I was conscious of a passing feeling of disappointment, for gazing at a fish did not commend itself to an ardent entomologist. My friends at home, too, were annoyed when they discovered that no amount of eau-de-cologne would drown the perfume which haunted me like a shadow.

In ten minutes I had seen all that could be seen in that fish, and 8 started in search of the Professor—who had, however, left the Museum; and when I returned, after lingering over some of the odd animals stored in the upper apartment, my specimen was dry all over. I dashed the fluid over the fish as if to resuscitate the beast from a fainting fit, and looked with anxiety for a return of the normal sloppy appearance. This little excitement over, nothing was to be done but to return to a steadfast gaze at my mute companion. Half an hour passed—an hour— another hour; the fish began to look loathsome. I turned it over and around; looked it in the face—ghastly; from behind, beneath, above, sideways, at a three-quarters' view—just as ghastly. I was in despair; at an early hour I concluded that lunch was necessary; so, with infinite relief, the fish was carefully replaced in the jar, and for an hour I was free.

On my return, I learned that Professor Agassiz had been at the 9 Museum, but had gone, and would not return for several hours. My fellow-students were too busy to be disturbed by continued conversation. Slowly I drew forth that hideous fish, and with a feeling of desperation again looked at it. I might not use a magnifying-glass; instruments of all kinds were interdicted. My two hands, my two eyes, and the fish: it seemed a most limited field. I pushed my finger down its throat to feel how sharp the teeth were. I began to count the scales in the different rows, until I was convinced that was nonsense. At last a happy thought struck me—I would draw the fish; and now with surprise I began to discover new features in the creature. Just then the Professor returned.

"That is right," said he; "a pencil is one of the best of eyes. I am glad   10
to notice, too, that you kept your specimen wet, and your bottle
corked."

With these encouraging words, he added: 11

"Well, what is it like?"   12

He listened attentively to my brief rehearsal of the structure of parts   13
whose names were still unknown to me: the fringed gill-arches and
movable operculum; the pores of the head, fleshy lips and lidless eyes;
the lateral line, the spinous fins and forked tail; the compressed and
arched body. When I finished, he waited as if expecting more, and then,
with an air of disappointment:

"You have not looked very carefully; why," he continued more ear-   14
nestly, "you haven't even seen one of the most conspicuous features of
the animal, which is plainly before your eyes as the fish itself; look
again, look again!" and he left me to my misery.

I was piqued; I was mortified. Still more of that wretched fish! But   15
now I set myself to the task with a will and discovered one new thing
after another, until I saw how just the Professor's criticism had been.
The afternoon passed quickly; and when, towards its close, the Professor inquired:

"Do you see it yet?"   16

"No," I replied, "I am certain I do not, but I see how little I saw   17
before."

"That is next best," said he, earnestly, "but I won't hear you now;   18
put away your fish and go home; perhaps you will be ready with a
better answer in the morning. I will examine you before you look at the
fish."

This was disconcerting. Not only must I think of my fish all night,   19
studying, without the object before me, what this unknown but most
visible feature might be; but also, without reviewing my discoveries, I
must give an exact account of them the next day. I had a bad memory;
so I walked home by Charles River in a distracted state, with my two
perplexities.

The cordial greeting from the Professor the next morning was reas-   20
suring; here was a man who seemed to be quite as anxious as I that I
should see for myself what he saw.

"Do you perhaps mean," I asked, "that the fish has symmetrical sides   21
with paired organs?"

His thoroughly pleased "Of course! of course!" repaid the wakeful   22
hours of the previous night. After he had discoursed most happily and

enthusiastically—as he always did—upon the importance of this point, I ventured to ask what I should do next.

"Oh, look at your fish!" he said, and left me again to my own   23 devices. In a little more than an hour he returned, and heard my new catalogue.

"That is good, that is good!" he repeated; "but that is not all; go   24 on"; and so for three long days he placed that fish before my eyes, forbidding me to look at anything else, or to use any artificial aid. "Look, look, look," was his repeated injunction.

This was the best entomological lesson I ever had—a lesson whose   25 influence was extended to the details of every subsequent study; a legacy the Professor had left to me, as he has left it to so many others, of inestimable value, which we could not buy, with which we cannot part.

A year afterward, some of us were amusing ourselves with chalking   26 outlandish beasts on the Museum blackboard. We drew prancing star-fishes; frogs in mortal combat, hydra-headed worms; stately crawfishes, standing on their tails, bearing aloft umbrellas; and grotesque fishes with gaping mouths and staring eyes. The Professor came in shortly after, and was as amused as any at our experiments. He looked at the fishes.

"Haemulons, every one of them," he said; "Mr. ——— drew them."   27

True; and to this day, if I attempt a fish, I can draw nothing but   28 haemulons.

The fourth day, a second fish of the same group was placed beside   29 the first, and I was bidden to point out the resemblances and differences between the two; another and another followed, until the entire family lay before me, and a whole legion of jars covered the table and surrounding shelves; the odor had become a pleasant perfume; and even now, the sight of an old, six-inch, worm-eaten cork brings fragrant memories.

The whole group of haemulons was thus brought in review; and,   30 whether engaged upon the dissection of the internal organs, the preparation and examination of the bony framework, or the description of the various parts, Agassiz's training in the method of observing facts and their orderly arrangement was ever accompanied by the urgent exhortation not to be content with them.

"Facts are stupid things," he would say, "until brought into connec-   31 tion with some general law."

At the end of eight months, it was almost with reluctance that I left   32 these friends and turned to insects; but what I had gained by this outside experience has been of greater value than years of later investigation in my favorite groups.

Vocabulary

antecedents (1)—the preceding events or causes

zoology (1)—a science that deals with animals

ichthyology (7)—the branch of zoology that studies fishes— their structure, classification, and life histories

ardent (7)—enthusiastic

entomologist (7)—a person who studies insects

resuscitate (8)—to bring back to life

loathsome (8)—repulsive

interdicted (9)—forbidden; prohibited

operculum (13)—the bony cover that protects the gills of fishes

piqued (15)—feeling resentful because of ruffled pride

perplexities (19)—confusions

exhortation (30)—warning; advice

IN YOUR JOURNAL

Pretend you are studying under Professor Agassiz, and write down as many details as you can remember from this article. What do you think is Scudder's most important point? Do you think Scudder would agree with you? Do you think Agassiz could find other details? Go back and check, writing down any you missed. What did you learn about detailed observation from doing this exercise?

A Closer Reading

1. What is the first event that occurs when Scudder meets Agassiz? What do the two men learn about each other from this experience?

2. What specific responsibility does Agassiz refer to when he tells Scudder that a man is not fit to be a naturalist unless he knows how to take care of specimens? Why is this so important to Agassiz?

3. What change of attitude occurs in Scudder in paragraph 14? What happens because of this change in attitude?

4. Why does Scudder believe that the incident with the fish was the best "entomological" lesson he ever had?

Drawing Your Own Conclusions

1. What characteristics does Agassiz have that make him a "good" teacher?

2. Should teachers challenge students to go beyond themselves? From your perspective, how can teachers help students grow?

3. What does Scudder learn from drawing the fish? What does he learn from thinking about the fish?

4. Agassiz tells his students, "Facts are stupid things until brought into connection with some general law." What examples from your own experience illustrate what this statement means?

5. What does Scudder learn that will help him throughout his life, even if he changes careers?

Thinking about Writing

1. Reread the first and last paragraphs of this essay. In what ways do these paragraphs correspond in theme? In time?

2. Why is the title appropriate for the essay?

3. Reread the dialogue, the words actually spoken, in the essay. What can you learn about the relationship of the student and teacher just from reading the dialogue?

4. What descriptive words and phrases does Scudder use that convince you that he is now a good observer of detail? Was it always true of him? Does it appear that this is something he learned from Agassiz? Look at the passages that describe what takes place in the lab.

5. Compare Scudder's description of his fish with Williams's (see page 367). What differences and similarities do you find? What do you learn about the two writers from their descriptions?

*   *   *

Suggestions for Writing

1. Write an essay in which you describe a scientific experiment or experience in which you participated at any level of your education. Explain the steps that were involved, what you wanted to find out, what you did find out, any mistakes that were made, and what you learned about yourself from your experience.

2. Closely observe a flower, a piece of fruit, a plant, or an animal. Use your abilities to see and record details. Think about what Scudder did as he observed his fish. While you are looking at your object, write about it in detail. Make a drawing, however rough, of your object. Then write out your research findings, including any descriptive details that are unusual or insightful. At the end of your essay, tell your reader what you learned from this experience.

3. Write an essay in which you describe an experience with a teacher that at first you found difficult but that led you to learn something about the subject and something about yourself. Make sure to use dialogue in your essay, and include descriptive details so that your readers will get a full picture of your experience.

4. Some students refuse to dissect animals in science classes. They believe that as much can be learned using computer-assisted study as by actually dissecting and observing an animal that has been killed for research. Take a position on this issue. In your essay, explain your point of view, using personal experiences, observations, and readings for support.

Strategies for Revision

Observe yourself as a writer, and write in your journal about your own process for writing this draft. Think about the following questions and write about them in your journal:

- How did I decide on a topic?
- How did I come up with ideas and information to include in the essay?
- Why did I organize my ideas in this order?
- What do I do now when I write that has changed since I began using this book?

- What steps do I usually take to revise what I have written?
- What steps do I take to edit my writing?

After you have completed your journal entry, carefully look at your draft and think about the following questions:

- What have I learned from the Scudder article about ordering ideas? How did I order my ideas? Is my order effective or not?
- What did I learn from Scudder about descriptive details? How did I use descriptive details? Are my details clear and strong?
- What did I learn from Scudder about using a personal experience to illustrate a general idea? How effective is my use of personal experience and general statements?
- What value does Scudder give to patience and to reworking something until it is perfect? How can this help me improve my work?

Revise your draft until you are satisfied with your writing, and share your revision with a classmate.

IN YOUR JOURNAL

Make a list of questions you think scientists might ask themselves as they struggle to understand the world. For example, a scientist might say, "What is this I am looking at? What kind of structure does it have? Where is it found?" Think of more questions, keeping in mind the many fields of science and the way people study them. Consider how these scientists might go about finding the answers to their questions.

A Dialogue of Questions

Adam Frank

Adam Frank is an astrophysicist who is interested in the way that forming one set of questions leads scientists to certain answers that then lead them to new questions. Advancement in science and technology is built on this inevitable progression. Frank's article on this subject appeared in the Summer 1993 issue of the journal *Exploring*. In it, Frank tries to show how discovering tough questions in scientific study is stimulating and challenging and leads to greater understanding.

For most people, finding a problem means finding trouble. For scientists, finding a problem is the beginning of understanding. The trick is finding the right problem. Learning to be a good scientist means learning to find the special problems that go along with important questions, the questions that need to be asked, the questions that can be answered. The rest, as a wizened old theorist once told me, is technique—all vacuum tubes and algebra.   1

How do scientists create problems? The answer, as we will see by looking at a few examples, is both mundane and profound.   2

One Brick at a Time: Adding to the Big Picture

Scan the table of contents of any scientific journal and you will probably surmise that scientists spend a great deal of time working on tiny problems. The papers in most journals appear to focus on the arcane and even trivial details of obscure matters. The narrow focus of these questions, however, belies their importance. By choosing small   3 problems individually, scientists collectively work out the broad patterns of the most all-encompassing theories.

When a scientist chooses a research interest, the first thing that happens is that he or she learns "the Story." The Story is basically the consensus of opinion in the community of researchers in that field. It's the present state of those scientists' attempts to create an all-encompassing theory for their discipline.   4

A scientist learns the Story by talking to people already involved in an area and by reading what are considered seminal papers in the professional literature. The Story provides an overview of what the community thinks it knows, what it thinks is important, and what problems it thinks need to be solved.   5

Along with the Story, each discipline has its Problems-with-a-capital-P—one or two big questions that are like the Holy Grail for that particular community. In biochemistry, for example, finding the structure of life's building blocks used to be the big Problem—until James Watson and Francis Crick unraveled the mystery of DNA. In modern high-energy physics, finding a subatomic particle called the top quark currently constitutes the big Problem. The existence of this elusive (and perhaps imaginary) particle would confirm some of physicists' most crucial theories about the structure of matter.   6

Problems like these are so big and so involved that it usually takes an army of scientists working for years to find the answers. Over the years, a lot of people add small pieces to the puzzle. The solution to the Problem builds on the work of scientists who have gone before.   7

Science, by its nature, operates by consensus and usually moves slowly. Most scientists create smaller problems within the community's framework, where the edges of the big Problem are being tested and chipped away.   8

One day, a few years back, when I was an astrophysics graduate student studying in the Netherlands, my thesis advisor took me to a smoky old bar in the town of Gouda. There he introduced me to the wonders of Dutch beer and gave me my first shot at a medium-sized problem in astrophysics. We were studying planetary nebulae—big clouds of gases that surround dying stars. These gas clouds are blown off the stars in powerful stellar winds—at least, that was the Story.   9

The Problem that went with this particular Story was figuring out how and why these winds are blown off the star. My advisor's approach was to use the shapes of planetary nebulae as a key to understanding their history and the history of the central star.   10

According to the Story, the stellar winds that generate planetary 11 nebulae should stream out into empty space. If that were true, then the outer edges of these planetary nebulae would look fuzzy as the gas expanded into a vacuum. My advisor had, however, noticed a curious pattern. Many planetary nebulae have sharp, not fuzzy, edges. My advisor thought this was an important pattern. He thought that the origin of the sharp edges of planetary nebulae might be a question worth asking. Since I was building a computer program to simulate the stellar winds, he also knew it was a question we could ask.

After experimenting with my computer program, I found I could 12 reproduce the sharp edges found in planetary nebulae. Instead of letting the stellar wind expand into empty space, I let it expand into another wind, one that the star had blown off in an earlier phase of its evolution. Where the two winds collided, my program produced that distinctive sharp edge.

In the end, we found that we could match the patterns seen in real 13 planetary nebulae quite well, and at the same time perform a kind of stellar wind paleontology. By seeing the sharp edges in planetary nebulae as the fossil imprints of old stellar winds, we could tell something about the history of the wind and of the star.

This observation didn't fundamentally change the way astronomers 14 understood stellar evolution or planetary nebulae. It did, however, give me great pleasure. In a maze of data, we had found a small corner of order. When we asked the right question and looked the right way, one small pattern emerged. Out of the pattern, the right question, and the tools we had just built (the computer program), we could build a small tale to add to the big Story.

Allowing for the Unexpected

I was led to the problem of sharp-edged planetary nebulae by the 15 benign guiding hand of my thesis advisor. Problems are not always so easy to find. Sometimes, crucial problems emerge from the worst clouds of frustration, appearing when things just don't go the way you expect them to. In these cases, the willingness of an individual researcher to turn away from expectations and confront confusion may allow a new and important problem to be defined and then solved.

In 1966, Arno Penzias and Robert Wilson, two Bell Laborabory 16 researchers, had a problem. They had designed a big, horn-shaped antenna to pick up microwave radiation from communications satellites.

But along with the microwaves from satellites, the antenna picked up an annoying little hiss that the researchers couldn't fix. No matter where they pointed the antenna, they found the hiss. It seemed to fill the sky with a perfectly uniform background of noise.

Since nothing in the sky could be that uniform, Penzias and Wilson   17
reasoned that the hiss must be coming from the electronics in the antenna. They rebuilt the circuitry, but the hiss was still there. Then they thought that the hiss must be coming from the antenna itself. They checked and rechecked all the components in the antenna, and even went so far as to evict the pigions who had nested there and scrub the bird droppings from the antenna's walls. For more than a year, they tried to get rid of the hiss, but to no avail. The noise would not go away.

Penzias and Wilson thought their problem was about electrical   18
engineering, but when they asked electrical engineering questions they only found confusion and a mysterious hiss. But they didn't give up. Instead, they stopped asking what was going on with their antenna and started asking what was going on out in the universe. What could create a steady hiss that appeared to be coming from everywhere at once?

When they finally changed the question, they found the answer. By   19
digging around, they found a paper published twenty years earlier that had predicted a steady hiss of microwave background radiation. The paper was known to only a small group of astronomers. By finding this paper and talking with these astronomers, Penzias and Wilson realized that the noise in the antenna was real. It was literally the echo of the moment of creation, fossilized radiation from the Big Bang, the primordial fireball that launched the universe.

Turning away from what you think is your goal is difficult. The   20
expectations that scientists bring to their research are so powerful that data that don't fit are often simply ignored. Mathematician and philosopher of science Alfred North Whitehead once said, "Everything of importance has already been seen by somebody who didn't notice it." Other researchers at Bell Labs had known about the hiss that plagued Penzias and Wilson, but they thought it was of no importance.

Penzias and Wilson were certainly fortunate in their discovery of   21
what is now called Cosmic Microwave Background Radiation. But they were not lucky; they were creative. They tried everything to make their problem fit what they thought was happening. When that failed, they turned away from the door they had been trying to open for over a year—and found a different door.

They came to their problem, their real problem, through the back   22
door. By turning away from their expectations, Penzias and Wilson
turned their frustration into a Nobel Prize. In the process, they also
launched the modern science and Story of cosmology.

Creating a Better Problem; Asking a Better Question

Sometimes a new and important problem is created by sheer force of   23
will, rather than serendipity. When the moment is ripe, a particular mix
of arrogance and vision will enable someone to turn the Story on its
head and precipitate a scientific revolution.

In the late 1800s, the great Victorian scientist Lord Kelvin proudly   24
announced that physics was over. All the important problems had been
solved. Nothing new could be expected. All that remained was getting
more accurate measurements of a few numbers and cleaning up one or
two small, unresolved details. One of those little details concerned the
speed of light.

Electromagnetic waves (of which visible light is but one form) had   25
been discovered about twenty years before Kelvin's pronouncement.
Everyone knew that waves had to travel through something: water
waves traveled through water and sound waves traveled through air. So
the Story in the late 1800s said that all space was filled with a mysterious substance called "ether," through which light waves traveled. At the
time, one of the big Problems in the Story of physics was the determination of the speed of light through the ether.

There had been a fair amount of effort to detect the ether. Sound   26
waves travel faster when the wind is blowing than when the air is still.
(That's because the speed of the sound wave equals the speed of sound
plus the speed of the wind.) Scientists reasoned that light traveling
through the ether would act the same way. People tried to use the
earth's motion through the ether to measure changes in the speed of
light, but, much to everyone's amazement, the earth's motion through
the ether didn't seem to matter. All the experiments showed that the
speed of light was constant. This bothered some people, but most
thought that the apparent constancy of the speed of light would eventually get worked into the Story.

Then came Einstein. The young patent clerk from Bern didn't solve   27
the problem of the ether. He didn't explain why the speed of light was
constant, either. In fact, he ignored both questions. He played a kind of
trick on physics by deciding there was a better question.

"What would happen," he asked, "if the speed of light were con- 28
stant? What would the world be like then?"

To Einstein, the constancy of the speed of light wasn't a problem. 29
It was an assumption. He used that assumption for building a new set
of questions, a whole new problem. Einstein told people to forget
about the ether and just make light a special kind of wave that needs
no medium through which to travel. That was, and still is, a weird
idea, but so what? Just because something is weird doesn't mean it
can't work.

From the constancy of the speed of light, Einstein built the Theory 30
of Relativity. That Einstein was willing to ask new questions showed his
arrogance. The fact that they were the right questions shows his genius.

Learning to Love the Questions

There is a special kind of courage in Einstein's audacity. Yet what is 31
worthy in his story did not depend on his special talents. By reinventing
the world around his own questions, Einstein played out a deeply
human drama, one that every child must star in. The world is a mess—a
mess of sounds, colors, shapes, tastes, and touches. We feel compassion
for newborn infants because they are thrown into a world that must be
astonishing to their senses, a world that is buzzing with the unfamiliar
and the unexpected. Somehow, in growing up, each of us learns to
transform the buzz into something familiar, something that has sense
and structure.

That is no small task. In our maturity, we tend to forget that the 32
world and its buzz was ever so astonishing. But science cannot forget.
Each time science tries to tell one of its Stories it must make the world
unfamiliar again. Then the unexpected can stand forward. Science invents order through the willingness to recognize and question the astonishing chaos that lies at the heart of the world.

Vocabulary

wizened (1)—shriveled and wrinkled

mundane (2)—everyday; ordinary

surmise (3)—to guess without
proof

arcane (3)—secret, or known
only by a few

belies (3)—gives a false impression

seminal (5)—original; a first in
development

paleontology (13)—the branch of geology that examines fossils to understand prehistoric forms of life

primordial (19)—existing at the beginning of time

cosmology (22)—the branch of philosophy and science that studies the universe as a whole and its form as a physical system

serendipity (23)—accident or by chance. This term comes from the tale *The Three Princes of Serendip* (Ceylon, 1754) by Horace Walpole, in which the heroes have the ability to make fortunate discoveries by accident.

audacity (31)—courage; daring

IN YOUR JOURNAL

Write about a problem or question that you had about the way things are, and tell how you found the answer. What did you learn from your experience?

A Closer Reading

1. Frank asks this question: "How do scientists create problems?" What answers does he provide for his readers?

2. What is the Story? What are the Problems in a particular discipline?

3. What question did Albert Einstein ask that changed our understanding of the way the world operates?

4. What connections does Frank make between the method scientists use and the way a newborn baby learns about the world? What evidence have you seen to support his point of view?

Drawing Your Own Conclusions

1. What role does working with others play in Frank's descriptions of scientists at work? Support your answer by referring to specific examples in the article.

2. What is the difference between an assumption and an expectation? What examples of each can you find in the Frank selection?

3. According to Frank, why do scientists usually focus on "arcane and even trivial details"? What examples of this does he provide? How does Frank's description of what scientists do relate to Scudder's description of his experience with the fish (see page 463)?

4. How would Cole (see page 135) respond to the fact that Frank did not refer to any women scientists in this article? What scientific questions do you think might interest women more than men?

Thinking about Writing

1. Frank defines several words and phrases in the article. What are they? Reread the article to verify your answers. In which cases does Frank define a new word or phrase by telling a story, and in which cases does he use a simple definition?

2. Which scientists does Frank refer to in this article? How much information does he give his readers about each of them?

3. What steps does Frank outline in the first part of the essay to explain how scientists go about their research? What words and phrases connect one idea to the next in this part of the article?

4. What specific sciences (for instance, biochemistry) does Frank mention in the article? Does he provide enough information to teach a reader unfamiliar with that field something about it? If not, what type of information would you have liked him to include?

*   *   *

Suggestions for Writing

1. Write an essay in which you describe a problem that you solved because of your knowledge in a scientific area. Explain what the problem was, the steps you took to find the answer, any errors you made, and the frustrations you felt. When and how did you find the answer? What did you learn about the problem and about yourself in the process of trying to find an answer?

2. Many believe that people learn more by working together than by working alone. Explain your position on this subject by referring to any experience you had in which you worked with a group to solve a problem. Or describe a scientific process that involved group work (you may want to reread the Frank article for ideas). Include the problem the group worked on, the steps they took to solve it, and how by working together they were or were not able to make discoveries that they would not have made working alone.

3. Should all students, regardless of their majors, be required to take courses in science? If so, which course or courses? Why? Write an essay in which you take a position on this issue. Support your point of view with your personal experiences, observations, and readings.

4. Some people feel that it is important to invest money in studying the stars and space exploration because this will eventually provide us with a new way of living and dealing with our problems on earth. Others think that with all the problems on earth, we should not be wasting money on exploring space. Take a position on this issue. Support your point of view with your own experiences, your observations, and your readings.

Strategies for Revision

Reread your draft with a partner, asking each other the following questions constructed from Frank's description of the process for doing research:

- What is the issue that interests you? How do you reduce a big problem into a small question that you can answer? Is your question focused enough so that you can answer it in one essay?
- What have others written about your area of interest? How do you include the ideas and opinion of others in your writing? Do you make clear where you have found your information?
- What do others have to say about your area of interest? Do you conduct interviews, or do you ask others how they feel? How do you incorporate this information into your essay? How do you let your readers know that ideas come from others?
- What do others think about your ideas and the way you have expressed them? Have you shared your essay with classmates to

find out if it is clear and expressive, and if it answers the question you have tried to address?

After rereading and discussing your draft with others, focusing on these questions, think about the best way to make your draft more effectively communicate your ideas. Rewrite your draft, making any changes you think necessary, and share it with your classmates.

IN YOUR JOURNAL

Write about a problem that you have faced and solved. What was the problem? How did you decide what steps to take to solve it?

The Problem Solvers: Interview with Margarita Loinaz, M.D.

Pat Murphy

Pat Murphy interviewed Margarita Loinaz, a doctor in a clinic for homeless and low-income people, as part of her series on the methods that people use to solve work problems. The series appeared in the Summer 1993 edition of the journal *Exploring,* and included interviews with an auto mechanic, a physician, an exhibit builder, and an artist.

Pat Murphy's interview with Margarita Loinaz reveals Loinaz's expertise in problem solving, as she responds to the myriad of situations that occur in the clinic.

Margarita Loinaz is a doctor at San Francisco's Tom Wadell clinic for 1 *homeless and low-income people. She works in both the drop-in clinic, where people come with immediate problems, and in the primary care clinic, where she sees patients on an ongoing basis. She also visits a number of homeless shelters providing backup for nurse practitioners, and provides medical service at San Francisco's Day Laborers' program. Her patients include people from many ethnic backgrounds and she sees a variety of medical problems.*

Pat Murphy: Suppose a patient comes to you with a complaint—like a 2 *skin rash or a headache. How do you go about figuring out what's wrong?*

Margarita Loinaz: Before I can answer that, maybe I could try and 3 give you a sense of what goes into making a doctor. Because the minute I start getting information from the patient, I'm tacking it on to this whole other fund of knowledge.

You start by studying basic sciences—chemistry, biochemistry, biol- 4 ogy. Then you move on to anatomy and physiology; you start by describing the norm—how does a healthy body work? From that, you move on to pathology and the various diseases. What are the symptoms? How does the person feel? What's the epidemiological setting?

The epidemiological setting? What does that mean?   5

Epidemiology refers to the study of diseases or "epidemics" in par-   6
ticular populations. What ethnic groups have what kinds of diseases; in
what parts of the world are certain diseases more prevalent.

Of course. I've run across that because I travel. If you come back to the States   7
with some disease you picked up in Nepal, you have to make sure that the doctors
know where you've been. Otherwise they won't know what to look for.

Yes. That's really important because the symptoms for some weird   8
parasite from the Himalayas and the symptoms for giardia, which is
common in the States, could be similar. If you're not looking for a weird
one, you may not catch it for a long time.

Let's get back to what happens when someone first walks into your office   9
with a medical problem. What do you do?

First you take a history. You find out what's the chief complaint. It   10
may be a cough—that's so common. And you want to know: Is it a dry
cough or a productive cough? How long has the patient had the cough?
Is there fever? Weight loss? Any other things going on? Nausea, headache, so on.

Once you know the chief complaint, you start seeing what else is   11
associated with it—this is the history of the present illness. Then you
move on to past medical history. That's going to influence things, too.
If it's somebody who has asthma or who has risks for tuberculosis or
cancer, the cough takes on a whole other dimension. And then you ask
if they are taking any medicines—sometimes medicine can give you a
cough. You ask about allergies to medicines.

You get this information and you associate it to your past experience   12
and knowledge and you make a differential diagnosis. That sounds
simple, but asking the right questions and doing a good assessment is a
skill that develops with experience. That's why some old docs are just
incredible. They hear a history and they know the problem's going to be
this or this. Your clinical judgment develops over time. Sometimes, just
by looking at a patient, you know when you can't afford to waste time
and when maybe you can take your time.

It almost sounds like pattern recognition . . . like, you have the history,   13
and you have your past experience, and you make associations, and then you
see where this problem fits into what you've seen before.

That's exactly it. It is pattern recognition. And as you work and   14
acquire more experience, the more patterns you recognize and the
subtleties of those patterns increase. Yeah! I guess you probably
could pretty much reduce things to that. Even when you just get a

kind of instinctive feel about somebody that's walking into the clinic and you look at them and you say, "OK, let's take care of this one first."

You've seen this before. You recognize it.   15
You get a feel for it. Exactly. You recognize it.   16
So you take the patient's history. Then what?   17
Then you move on to the physical exam. When you're training, you   18
do a complete physical from one end to the other. But in the real world, when you're out there practicing, your exam is geared to the chief complaint. If you're dealing primarily with cough and shortness of breath, you're going to be concentrating mostly on the lung exam and maybe on the heart exam. Your exam is guided by what you think may be going on.

For example, if you have a young, healthy person with a cough,   19
you're not necessarily going to worry about their heart. But an elderly person with a history of heart disease could develop a cough from heart failure, which causes fluid to build up in the lungs.

After you take the history and do your physical exam, you order the   20
tests you want. You could get an electrocardiogram if you need to check the heart, or X-rays if you're worried about pneumonia or fluid in the lungs. And when you get the results back you make a decision. Sometimes—a lot of times—we're not a hundred percent sure.

That's interesting. Other problem solvers that we talked with mentioned   21
the role of the mistake in the process. When you're working on a car, for
instance, you try to fix it and maybe it still doesn't work. But in our society, we
tend to think of doctors as people who aren't supposed to make mistakes.

Medicine is by no means an exact science. Give the same set of   22
information to three different doctors and they'll give you three different treatments. If you're dealing with bronchitis, say, one doctor may let the person go away without antibiotics, another might give them this kind of antibiotic, and a third might say, "I would never give them that! I would use this." There's room for different approaches.

So basically, it's a judgment call.   23
Many times I'm very conscious that I'm making a judgment call and   24
I try and cover for the worst. When you know you're not certain, then you cover for the thing you think is going to kill the person. But you still may not have a definite diagnosis.

When you say a diagnosis you mean you know exactly . . .   25
It means you are certain. You know what is really going on. Is this   26
definitely pneumonia or is this just a bronchitis, for example.

You get to the point where you think, "Well I'm pretty sure it's this," and   27
then you decide how to treat it. When you're figuring out the treatment,
what sorts of things do you take into account? Do you take into account age or
ethnic background or living situation?

Absolutely. Let's take bronchitis. There's a viral bronchitis that you   28
can't do anything about. You just treat the symptoms. But let's say the
person is elderly, or a smoker, or they have asthma, or cardiac disease
and heart failure. In those people, I'm going to be a lot more aggressive
and err on the side of over-treating. Because if I'm wrong and it's not a
virus, if it's a bad bacteria, they can develop much worse consequences if
I miss it, so I would probably use antibiotics.

It's a very multi-dimensional approach to problem solving, where   29
you are taking a lot of things into account. I think that's why the
training takes a long time.

What other factors affect what treatment you might prescribe?   30

You have to make sure the person is going to comply with the   31
treatment. If you have somebody who doesn't have a place to live and
they have an infection in their leg and you tell them to lie down and put
their leg up—it's ridiculous. So I ask all the time, "Do you have a place
to live? Is my treatment going to be something you can follow?"

Or suppose you have a patient from Asia. Many people in those   32
communities look at Western medicine as being really "strong." They feel
that their herbs are much milder; our stuff is too concentrated. So if you
tell them to take one pill twice a day they'll take it maybe once a day. Or
once every other day. They're adjusting it to what they think is the proper
concentration for them. So you have to make sure they understand how
important it is for them to follow through with the treatment.

Do you ever get stumped? If you can't figure out the answer to a problem,   33
what do you do?

Well, different things. You can just keep testing until you run out of   34
tests that are reasonable to do. And sometimes you just watch. They
always talk about the "tincture of time" letting time sort things out.
And it's true. Often, people improve without any treatment. It's also
important to know your limits. You should know when to get other
specialists involved in the case.

Obviously you've got a patient and you're dealing with a person. But at   35
the same time, you're dealing with a problem and you can get intrigued by
the problem. Is that something that you've observed—that you get intrigued
by the problem?

And you forget about the person?   36

Maybe forgetting about the person is too strong, but it seems like you must   37
be shifting back and forth between two viewpoints all the time.

It's true. Especially when you get somebody with an unusual prob-   38
lem. It's very exciting. I think a lot of us love that part of medicine that
is like being a detective and figuring out the answer. I've caught myself
at times searching in my head and reeling with ideas because it's an
interesting situation that I've just read about or something. At the same
time, you have to come back to your relationship to the person and
support them and be compassionate and caring.

I think that the best doctors are the ones that are really intrigued.   39
Physicians need to have a real curiosity. Because it's the curiosity that
drives you to keep going, to keep looking when you don't have a ready
answer.

Vocabulary

pathology (4)—the branch of medicine that deals with the nature of disease, the structure and functional changes caused by the disease

parasite (8)—an organism that lives on or in an organism of another species (the host), often causing harm to the host

err (28)—to be wrong

IN YOUR JOURNAL

What did you find out about the role of a physician that you did not know before?

A Closer Reading

1. What information does Loinaz reveal about the subjects that need to be learned by someone becoming a physician? Why are these subjects important for a doctor to know in order to diagnose people?

2. What steps does Loinaz take to diagnose a patient who comes into her office? How does she decide whether to take additional tests or just to rely on her own judgment?

3. What does Loinaz does when she is not sure of a diagnosis?

4. What is pattern recognition? How does it fit in with what Loinaz does when she diagnoses people?

Drawing Your Own Conclusions

1. What can you tell about Margarita Loinaz's personality from the interview?

2. What do you think intrigues Loinaz about medicine?

3. What evidence is provided in the interview that Loinaz is a problem solver? That all doctors are problem solvers?

4. Why is medicine not an exact science? Are the sciences described in the Scudder essay (see page 463) and the Frank article (see page 471) exact sciences? Why or why not?

5. What similarities do you find between Loinaz's and Margaret Lawrence's (see Lightfoot article on page 76) attitudes toward being a doctor? What differences?

Thinking about Writing

1. What is the purpose of the first paragraph? What context does it set for you as a reader? What conclusions do you reach immediately; what can you surmise about Loinaz before you read the interview?

2. What questions does Murphy ask that are the most effective? How does each of these reveal an important aspect of Loinaz's character?

3. What questions are weakest? Why? What is missing?

4. What questions would you have asked Loinaz that Murphy did not? Why?

*   *   *

Suggestions for Writing

1. Write an essay in which you describe the types of problems that you have to solve as a student, for example: registration, choice of major and courses, themes for papers, places to study, study-

ing alone or in groups. Choose the problems on which you would like to focus. Describe the problems, how they affect you, and what you have done to solve them.

2. Many urban and rural areas of the United States do not have sufficient doctors and medical personnel to take care of their population. In addition, work in these areas pays little and is often difficult. Should all doctors and dentists be required to do community service for two years in a poor or remote part of the United States? Should their community service reduce the medical school loans that doctors and dentists owe upon graduating? In an essay, take a position on these issues. Support your point of view with your experiences, observations, and readings.

3. Should the federal government provide national health care for all people in the United States, even if it means that the defense budget may have to be cut? Take a position on this issue, supporting your point of view with your personal experiences, your observations, and your readings.

4. Read your college catalogue, looking for information about required courses. Write an essay in which you describe the numbers and types of science and math courses required in your college. Are these courses required for all majors? If not, explain the differences in requirements.

Collaborative Project

Form groups of three to five students. Each group should interview a scientist (biologist, chemist, physician, nurse, laboratory technician, and so on) in your college or community. Find out how that person chose his or her career. Some questions to ask include the following:

- What education is necessary to be accredited in the field?
- What courses are useful in understanding the everyday activities of the discipline?
- What kinds of problems does the person encounter frequently?
- How does the person go about solving the problems?
- Has the person ever encountered any professional problems that he or she was not able to resolve? If so, what did the person do to handle the situation?

- Does the person ever work with others to solve on-the-job problems? If so, when? How do they make decisions?

As a group, write three more questions of your own. (Reread the Murphy interview for ideas.) One or two students should do the actual interviewing (one asking questions and one writing down the answers, or taping them if the interviewee agrees). One student should transcribe or write out the interview. You should all discuss what was learned from the interview and each group should write a paper that will be shared with the whole class about the person, the job, the education, and the opportunities in that field today.

Strategies for Revision

Share your drafts in a small group (three to five students) in your class. Each student should read your draft and, on a separate piece of paper, should tell you:

- Where in the draft is the problem stated? Is the problem narrow enough to answer in one essay but broad enough to be interesting?
- How is the problem broken down into parts that can be handled in separate paragraphs? Does the reader know in each case which part of the problem you are describing?
- What is the strongest part of the draft?
- What are the best words and phrases in the draft? Why?
- What are the weakest points in the draft? Why?

As a group, read the notes aloud. Discuss each piece of writing. Decide on two specific recommendations for improvement for each draft. Then, when each piece of writing has been discussed, each person should write a revision to be shared with the other group members.

IN YOUR JOURNAL

Geologists have studied about the earth in order to know about rocks, minerals, fossils, soils, and so on. Use your imagination and write about how this knowledge could be used to help solve crimes.

The Geologist as Private Eye

Raymond C. Murray

Born in Massachusetts, Raymond C. Murray now resides in Montana, where he is the Dean of the Graduate School at the University of Montana. Prior to this, Murray was chairman of the geology department at Rutgers University. Murray's book *Forensic Geology* (1975) was one of the first on this subject. He has written several articles for *Natural History* magazine, including "The Geologist as Private Eye," in which Clark describes the field of forensic geology. The forensic geologist searches for clues hidden in earth, rocks, and minerals that can provide evidence in criminal investigations and trials.

All geologists are detectives. Most use their knowledge about the earth to trace the movement of global plates, uncover the origin of ancient rocks, or locate hidden deposits of metals and fossil fuels. The microscopic clues present in fossil debris provide the material for determining the path of evolution. The evidence for the history of the moon has come from the study of rocks brought back by the astronauts. A small but increasing number of earth scientists, however, are applying their talents and tools not only to science and technology but also to one of the most important societal goals—justice. Forensic geology is the name given to that branch of earth sciences that uses rocks, minerals, fossils, soils, and related materials and ideas to provide evidence in criminal investigations and trials. 1

The modern criminologist employs fingerprints, tool marks, paint, glass, hair and fibers, firearms identification, and other physical evidence. In general this type of evidence assists an investigation either by providing clues that lead to a suspect or by subsequently assisting in convicting the guilty or exonerating the innocent. 2

The use of geology in crime detection began, as did many of the   3
other kinds of physical evidence, with Sherlock Holmes. Sir Arthur
Conan Doyle, who wrote the Holmes series between 1887 and 1893,
had his fictional detective suggest many of the methods that were later
developed and applied by professional scientists in real cases. Dr. Watson, like all the latter-day Holmes fans, knew that the great detective
could "tell at a glance from which part of London the various splashes
of soil on his trousers had been picked up." In 1893 Hans Gross, an
Austrian professor of criminology, published the *Handbook for Examining Magistrates*. This volume was to have a profound effect on the
development and use of science in criminal investigation. Although no
actual cases involving forensic geology had appeared at the time of
publication, Gross made the prophetic statement, "Dirt on shoes can
often tell us more about where the wearer of those shoes had last been
than toilsome inquiries." With the idea appearing in print, in both
fiction and the professor's *Handbook,* it was not long before minerals,
rocks, and fossils in the hands of a geologist would become clues and
evidence in an actual criminal case.

In October, 1904, Georg Popp, a chemist, microscopist, and earth   4
scientist in Frankfurt, Germany, was asked to examine the evidence in a
murder case in which a seamstress named Eva Disch had been strangled
in a bean field with her own scarf. A filthy handkerchief had been left at
the scene of the crime and the nasal mucus on the handkerchief contained bits of coal, particles of snuff, and most interesting of all, grains
of minerals, particularly hornblende. A prime suspect was known to
work both in a coal-burning gasworks and at a local gravel pit. Popp
found coal and mineral grains, including hornblende, under the suspect's fingernails. It was also determined that the suspect used snuff.
Examination of soil removed from the suspect's trousers revealed that
minerals in a lower layer in contact with the cloth matched those of a
soil sample taken from the place where the victim's body had been
found. Encrusted on this lower layer, a second soil type was found.
Examination of the minerals in the upper layer revealed a mineralogy
and size of particle, particularly crushed mica grains, that Popp determined were comparable with soil samples collected along the path that
led from the murder scene to the suspect's home. From these data it was
concluded that the suspect picked up the lower soil layer at the scene of
the crime and that this lower and thus earlier material was covered by
splashes of mica-rich mud from the path on his return home. When
confronted with the soil evidence the suspect admitted the crime, and

the Frankfurt newspapers of the day carried such headlines as, "The Microscope as Detective."

It is impossible to determine from the distance of three-quarters of a 5 century how a contemporary forensic geologist or a jury would evaluate the geologic evidence amassed by Popp. Nevertheless, one fact is evident. Minerals had been used in an actual case, fulfilling Gross's prophecy and providing a real-life example worthy of Holmes. Popp worked on many other criminal cases and made substantial contributions to forensic science. He probably should be considered the founder of forensic geology.

In 1906 Conan Doyle became involved in an actual criminal case 6 during which he applied some of the methods of his fictional creation, Holmes. An English solicitor was accused and convicted of killing and mutilating horses and cows. After serving three years in prison he was released but not given a pardon despite some evidence that he was actually innocent of the crimes. Doyle observed that the soil on the shoes worn by the convicted man on the day of the crime was black mud and not the yellow, sandy clay found in the field where the animals had been killed. This observation, combined with other evidence, ultimately led to a full pardon and contributed to the creation of a court of appeals in England.

Today rocks, minerals, and other natural and synthetic materials are 7 studied in connection with the thousands of criminal cases tried each year. The Federal Bureau of Investigation laboratory in Washington, D.C., one of the first forensic laboratories in the United States to have geologists study soils and related material as physical evidence, is a world-wide leader in forensic geology. Several other major laboratories, such as that of the New Jersey State Police; the Virginia Bureau of Forensic Sciences; the famous Center for Forensic Sciences in Toronto, Canada; and the Home Office, Central Research Establishment, at Aldermaston, England, employ geologists. They have made many contributions to the science of forensic geology and thus to justice. Regretfully, there are also many public and private laboratories where lack of trained scientists and equipment or simply the investigators' ignorance of the value of earth materials as evidence had led to the overlooking or misuse of important geologic clues.

Physical evidence, unlike human evidence, cannot subvert the crimi- 8 nal justice system through a combination of memory, emotion, or outright lying. But the integrity and competence of the scientific expert in a criminal case must be equal to the challenge. Physical evidence is divided into two general types, individual items and class items. Fingerprints, some tool marks, and spent ammunition are said to be individual items, meaning they have only one possible source. But most physical evidence—for example, blood, paint, glass, and hair—is grouped under the heading of class items and could come from a variety of sources. The value of a class item in general depends on how common that item is. Forty-three percent of the population has type O blood, whereas only 3 percent of the population has type AB. Type AB blood would thus be a more valuable bit of evidence than type O. Similarly, the paint from a 1932 Rolls Royce would be more valuable as evidence than that from a 1970 Ford.

Although geologic materials can seldom be considered as truly indi-   9
vidual items, there are exceptions. One such was a vandalism case in which a concrete block was broken into fragments that were thrown through a number of store windows from a moving car. In that instance it was possible to piece together the fragments found in the stores and those remaining in the car to reconstruct the original block. Not only did the pieces fit together but individual mineral grains lined up across the pieces and all the fragments were shown to be of the same kind of concrete.

In most examples, geologic material is class evidence, but its value   10
lies in the fact that the different kinds and combinations of rocks, minerals, fossils, and related materials are almost limitless. The evidential potential of geologic materials is therefore greater than that of almost all the other kinds of physical evidence of the class type.

There are more than 2,200 different minerals, many of which are   11
not common. Almost all of these minerals exist in a wide range of compositions, with the result that there is an almost unlimited number of recognizable kinds of minerals. More than a million different kinds of fossils have been identified. Most fossiliferous rocks have populations of fossils that commonly reflect the environment or deposition in which the rock was formed. These groups of fossils provide a very large number of possible combinations.

Almost all rocks—igneous, sedimentary, and metamorphic—are   12
composed of minerals. In any given igneous or metamorphic rock, the kinds and amounts of minerals, their size and texture, represent a wide range of variations. The possible combinations of minerals, the sizes and shapes of minerals, and the kinds and amounts of cement between the grains in sedimentary rocks offer an almost unending diversity. The weathering processes that break up rocks and produce soil add new

dimensions to the possible variations. Also, in most urban areas the soils contain particles contributed by man, which further increase the complexity and diversity.

Anyone who has seen the Grand Canyon, noticed the variety of pebbles in a stream bed, or simply observed the color differences in the soils of his own background can appreciate the variety and rapid changes that exist in natural earth materials. 13

In a case of a rape in an eastern United States city, the victim reported that the crime took place in a vacant lot, which was underlain by the beach sands of an ancient glacial lake. The suspect had sand in the cuffs of his trousers. Study of the sand from the cuffs and samples collected at the crime scene showed that the two sands were comparable. Both contained the same minerals and rock grains in the same amounts. Thus it was established with a high degree of probability that the two samples could have come from a common source. One of the rock types was fragments of anthracite coal. These fragments were very common but were not natural to the area. Coal fragments are widely found in the soils of our older cities. In this case, however, there was too much coal in the sand. Further investigation revealed that sixty years before the crime the site had been the location of a coal pile for a laundry. Although the minerals involved in this case might have been duplicated in other places, the presence of the coal became a crucial factor in greatly increasing the probability of a common source. This geologic evidence, when combined with other evidence and testimony by the victim, led to the conviction of the suspect. 14

Many man-made and commercially manufactured mineral products such as face powder, cleaning powder, abrasives, masonry, and wallboard become the study material for the forensic geologist. Hundreds of criminals have been brought to justice because of the minerals found on their burglary tools or clothing. 15

Most interesting is the insulation material used in safes and strong boxes. When fire-resistant safes are broken into by drilling, blowing, cutting, or prying, the fire insulating material that fills the space between the outer and inner metal walls is disrupted. It commonly clings to the tools and clothing of the safe breaker. There is a classic case in which a man was arrested and brought to the police station on a routine minor charge. An observant detective, noticing that the suspect appeared to have a severe case of dandruff, examined his hair. The substance found was, not dandruff, but diatoms, the microscopic fossils that make up the diatomaceous earth used to insulate some safes. On 16 further examination it was learned that the diatoms in the suspect's hair were of the same species as those present in the insulation of a safe that had been blown the previous day. The suspect was accordingly charged with the burglary.

Geologic maps can often be used in crime investigation to outline the areas where rocks and minerals associated with crimes or suspects could have originated. The owner of some valuable gems found chips of common rock instead of precious stones when she opened the cargo box that had been sent by air. Study of the chips indicated that they came from a foreign country that was a stopover point on the air route. Examination of the geologic map for that area indicated the probable source of the rock chips. This evidence cleared the air-freight handlers at the final destination and led to the apprehension of those responsible for the substitution. 17

Even topographic maps, which record contour lines and indicate the elevation of land, have made their contribution. An informer reported that an illegal still was located somewhere between two towns in southern New Jersey in an area of swamps and higher gravel ridges and that the water well at the site of the still reputedly had a water level twenty feet below the ground. Since the groundwater table and the swamps were on approximately the same level, to find the still it was necessary to find a place on a ridge twenty feet above the local swamp level. A study of the topographic maps of the area showed there was only one place on one ridge where the elevation met that requirement. A church occupied that location. A warrant was obtained and the still was found in the church cellar. 18

Geology can thus be seen to have made many contributions to crime detection and justice. These contributions will undoubtedly increase and become even more significant as imaginative criminal investigators realize the value of geologic material as evidence and make use of competent forensic geologists. 19

Vocabulary

exonerating (2)—declaring someone to be innocent of charges
subvert (8)—undermine or overthrow something already established

apprehension (17)—arrest
contour lines (18)—lines on a map that connect places that are the same height above sea level

IN YOUR JOURNAL

What did you learn from reading this article about how the science of geology can be applied to criminology?

A Closer Reading

1. What is the origin of the use of geology in crime detection?
2. Who is Georg Popp, and what was his role in this field?
3. Who was Arthur Conan Doyle, and how did his fiction influence real life?
4. What is the difference between "individual" items and "class" items? What examples of each can you find in the article?
5. Why is the finding of certain blood types more valuable as evidence than the finding of others? What other types of evidence are particularly valuable in identifying a criminal?

Drawing Your Own Conclusions

1. Paragraph 8 contains the following statement: "Physical evidence, unlike human evidence, cannot subvert the criminal justice system through a combination of memory, emotion, or outright lying." What does this mean? Can you think of any way that physical evidence can be falsified?
2. According to this article, how is soil produced? What human-made particles would you expect to find in city soil that you would not find in soil in a rural area?
3. What are some examples of the ways in which forensic geology has helped to solve crimes?
4. What similarities are there in the way that forensic geologists solve problems, the way scientists do in ichthyology or entomology (see Scudder, page 463), and the way physicians such as Loinaz do (see Murphy, page 481)? What differences do you find?

Thinking about Writing

1. Murray breaks down larger categories (for example, physical evidence such as rocks) into smaller categories or classifications. What examples of this can you find in the selection?

2. Reread paragraphs 1 and 19. How are they tied together? What is the purpose of the conclusion?

3. In paragraph 7, what is the main idea? What are the supporting details? Why is this paragraph important?

4. How does the author combine information about real cases with more theoretical information?

*   *   *

Suggestions for Writing

1. Write a one-page summary of this article. See page 51 for ideas about writing summaries. Reread the Murray article, deciding on the most important ideas and examples to use in your summary. Remember to use quotation marks if you use Murray's exact words.

2. Write an essay in which you describe some possible applications of the computer in criminology and especially in the field of forensic geology. How can this advanced technology help detectives and criminologists to solve their cases? Think about recent cases you have read about in the news in which such technology was used.

3. Write a newspaper article with the headline "GEORG POPP POPS OPEN ANOTHER CASE—The Disch Bean Field Story." Use this article and your imagination to tell the story of the Disch murder case.

4. Write a short story entitled "The Cracking of the SafeCracking Caper." Use your imagination and this article to tell the story of the safecracker, the crime, and police apprehension of the felon.

Strategies for Revision

As you prepare to revise a draft of your writing, think about Murray's use of detail and examples to illustrate his ideas. Keep that in mind as you look at your own work. In your journal, answer the following questions about your draft.

- How did you decide what to write about?
- How did you narrow down your ideas?
- Did you use any type of outline? (Many scientists use outlines to help them write and organize material.)
- What details do you include in your draft? Do you break down larger ideas into smaller categories or classifications?
- What examples do you include? Are they precise and well chosen?
- How did you decide what should come first in the essay?
- How did you know when to end the essay?
- When you revise, what will you concentrate on improving?

When you have answered the questions to your satisfaction, reread your essay, thinking about what you wrote in in your journal. Mark any problem areas, and concentrate on improving these as you revise. Share your revised essay with a classmate.

IN YOUR JOURNAL

Write about the first time you played a video game. What did you like or not like about the video game?

The First Video Game: If You Build It They Will Come

Ira Flatow

Ira Flatow is the host of National Public Radio's weekly science talk show, *Talk of the Nation: Science Friday.* For six years, he was the host of the public television program *Newton's Apple,* from which he developed a book by the same name. He has written many articles on science subjects, as well as a book entitled *Rainbows, Curve Balls & Other Wonders of the Natural World Explained* (1988).

The following chapter on the invention of video games comes from Ira Flatow's 1993 book, *They All Laughed . . . From Light Bulbs to Lasers: The Fascinating Stories Behind the Great Inventions That Have Changed Our Lives.* Flatow describes the book as:

> an attempt to demythologize the world of invention and discovery, to prove that truth *is* stranger than fiction. . . . Each story is a tale about people. Yes, the table of contents lists a host of inventions and discoveries. But at the heart of each one of these objects is the story of the people behind the inventions and ideas, people who have certainly earned the title of inventor but who above all are mostly inquisitive souls who share one thing in common: They refuse to take no for an answer.

The world's playing fields have served as more than the sites of great 1
sporting events. Some of the most memorable milestones in the history of this century have occurred in sports arenas when sporting events were absent. On the road to the atom bomb, scientists built the world's first nuclear reactor at a football stadium at the University of Chicago, under the stands at Stagg Field. It went on line December 2, 1942.

Every student of history knows this story. But how many are aware 2
of the historic event that occurred at another playing field, this one located at one of the country's leading nuclear labs? Unlike the stands at

Stagg Field, this site witnessed a historic event that has gone virtually unnoticed. No plaque commemorating the event has ever been put up; no encyclopedia has included the place—or the event—in its hallowed text.

Yet every day at noon dozens of lunchbreak athletes gather to play   3
basketball on a court that served as the site of an important leap forward in modern technology, an event that would influence our lives for decades to come. When asked between dribbles if they know of the historic nature of the playing site, most athletes try to name a historic game. Was it Harvard vs. Yale? Could it be the Celtics vs. the Lakers? No. No famous athletic competition occurred beneath these hoops more than thirty years ago. Few if any can correctly answer, "This is where the world's first video game was played in 1958."

Decades before Pac-Man swallowed his first dot, eons before Space   4
Invaders were blasted from video screens, and generations before the Mario Brothers opened shop, the world's first video game was quietly born. Without fanfare, without hype—even without a marketing plan—the video game slipped quietly into existence as a last-minute entry in the history of the quiet little Long Island town of Upton.

These days video games are introduced with multimillion dollar   5
promotions: tie-ins to Saturday morning cartoons and free offers on overly sweet kids' cereals. (Of course, you finance this schlock by agreeing to pay the exorbitant prices for glorified designer chips of sand.)

But back in the good old innocent days of the 1950s, when the most   6
exciting addition to TV twin-leads was a rotary antenna, America existed, even thrived, without video games. No Nintendo. No Ninja Turtles.

All that changed one day in 1958 when physicist Willy Higin-   7
botham, from Brookhaven National Laboratory in Upton, got bored with what he was doing and invented the world's first video game.

Remember that name Higinbotham, because years from now   8
Higinbotham will become as famous as the other legendary names in sports. What Naismith was to basketball and Doubleday to baseball (rightly so or not), Higinbotham will be to video games. (I'm doing everything I can, Willy, to get you that recognition you deserve!)

Higinbotham was no newcomer to invention. Willy, as all his   9
friends call him, was a very serious scientist. (A physicist on the Manhattan Project, he observed the explosion of the first atomic bomb.) The whole affair started innocently enough. Each year in the late fifties, Brookhaven Lab would hold an open house. In the post-*Sputnik* era, America was in the grip of an intense nuclear bomb mania. The govern-

ment had printed up booklets describing how to survive a nuclear attack in your own hand-built fallout shelter. Being a government nuclear research facility devoted to the peaceful use of atomic energy, Brookhaven Lab decided it could best stem the nuclear hysteria of the day by inviting the public into the labs to see that its employees didn't actually glow in the dark.

Parents and kids filed by the traditional radiation detectors, compli-   10
cated electronic circuits, and newly hatched brine shrimp (always good to have an animal on display). Rather boring black and white pictures showed peaceful research under way at the lab. Not much happening among the cardboard and wood stand-up displays. How many times can you watch a shrimp wriggle under a light bulb?

Willy, who headed the lab's instrumentation division, was as bored   11
as the tourists. And in 1958, Willy couldn't stand it anymore. Stretching his full five-foot, four-inch frame, Willy decided he'd concoct something more interesting. Something to bring people in on Saturday. Something that moved.

Putting his Cornell training and his MIT electronics background to   12
work, Willy hit upon the idea of building an exhibit around that new and wonderful mesmerizer of the public, television. Only this time Higinbotham didn't need the whole TV set, just the part that people watched: the tube. In fact, he didn't even need to use a real TV picture tube, but the TV's ancestor: a cathode-ray tube from a laboratory instrument called an oscilloscope.* Dusting off an instruction manual packed with the lab's small analog computer, Willy found directions for hooking the scope to the computer and making a bouncing ball appear on the screen. Would it be possible to control the action of the ball at will? Willy thought so. Scrounging around the lab for assorted resistors, capacitors, and potentiometers, Willy wired the first crude video game out of spare parts.

"We looked around and found that we had a few pieces we could use   13
together and make a game," recalled Willy years later, "which would

---

* As a test instrument, the oscilloscope is a way to view complicated TV signals or simple AC house current. If you were a keen observer of science fiction on TV in the 1950s and 1960s, you've seen an oscilloscope in the background of a laboratory. It has lots of squiggly sign waves running across its screen; it signifies laboratory "reality." *The Outer Limits* highlighted an oscilloscope in its opening scene.

have a ball bouncing back and forth, sort of like a tennis game viewed from the side."

Two hours of scratching a design on paper and two weeks of wiring   14
and debugging, and the game was complete. The tennis game was
displayed on a tiny, five-inch screen. It involved two players, each having a box with a button and a knob. If you pushed the button, you hit
the ball to the opponent's court. The knob controlled how high the ball
was hit.

"You could actually hit the ball into the net," recalled Dave Potter,   15
Willy's associate, "see it bounce into the net and see it bounce onto the
floor back to you. So it was a very cleverly designed game Willy came up
with."

Set up on a table in the gym right under the basketball hoop on the   16
far wall, the tennis game was practically lost among the other electronic
gadgets on display. But when the doors to the gym were opened, the
public had no trouble finding the video game. Willy and Dave could
hardly believe their eyes.

"Willy's tennis game was a hit," remembered an astonished Potter,   17
"there were long lines. People wanted to play."

Willy was shocked. What was so attractive about a dot bouncing   18
around an oscilloscope screen?

"It never occurred to me that I was doing anything very exciting.   19
The long line of people I thought was not because this was so great but
because all the rest of the things were so dull."

For the following year's (1959) open house, Willy improved the   20
game. The picture tube was enlarged to ten or fifteen inches and a novel
feature was added: Visitors could play tennis on the moon with very
low gravity or on Jupiter with very intense gravity. Again the game was
a great success; hundreds stood in line to play.

Most fathers of such a success might have immediately set out to   21
cash in on their invention. But not Willy. Despite the game's popularity,
Willy never made a nickel off his invention. He never saw any commercial value in it. The idea seemed too obvious. Anybody with simple
equipment bought at Radio Shack could make the game. So Willy never
patented the idea.

Years later, Willy told me, "My kids complained about this and I   22
kept saying: Kids, no matter what, even if I patented it, I wouldn't have
made any money." Because he worked at a government institution,
Uncle Sam would have owned the patent and Willy might have col-

lected a ten-dollar royalty. And anybody wanting to market a video game would have had to pay the U.S. Treasury royalties.*

"I never realized it until many years later," Willy said in 1983,   23
"when the first dumb games came out about 1970–71, that these [video games] would be as popular as they have turned out to have been."

About that time, 1971, video games were beginning to make their   24
first commercial appearances. Pong, a video arcade game marketed by Atari, Inc., was becoming the hit of the bar scene. In Pong, a ball was hit back and forth over a net by two players. (Looking amazingly like Willy's tennis game, Pong would become known as granddaddy of video games.) Odyssey, the first home video game, was also being released by Magnavox.

According to Higinbotham, the patent for the first video game was   25
applied for by Sanders Associates in 1964. It was purchased by Magnavox, who realized there was real money to be made here. Of course where there's money, there are lawyers. Armed with the patent, Magnavox's lawyers set out to sue all other video game competitors. It was just a matter of time before the legal mess found its way to Willy's door.

"About 1976," wrote Willy in an article for the quarterly *Alumni*   26
Review of William College in 1984, "a patent lawyer for a competitor found someone who had played the game at Brookhaven and tracked me down. By good luck, we had made some drawings of the system. Thus began an on and off relationship with patent attorneys."

Lawyers have been interviewing Willy ever since. Over the last fif-   27
teen years, they've cross-examined him, had him sign affidavits, telephoned him to confirm or deny rumors. In 1981 one of Magnavox's competitors (Willy's memory is a bit foggy on this) figured it had enough ammunition to break the patent. A trial was scheduled for June 1982 in Chicago. At the last moment the case was settled out of court. Magnavox made the competitor an offer it couldn't refuse. The competitors figured they'd better settle.

Disappointed, Higinbotham lost his chance to put his story before   28
the public. "We didn't get our day in court," he wrote. But the legal battle was a learning experience. After watching the enormous legal fees change hands, Willy learned how silly he had been for not patenting his

*Can you imagine the dent video game royalties would have made in the national debt if every Nintendo, NEC, and Atari sale put a few cents into the federal coffers?

video game. A holder of twenty patents, Willy realized that holding one more couldn't hurt.

"At my deposition, one of the lawyers said that he was very sorry to   29
see the end of an enterprise that had paid him well for five years. It was then obvious that I should have applied for a patent." Willy finally did testify in court in San Francisco in 1985 in a case pitting Activision against Magnavox.

Willy is getting his share of public (vs. legal) recognition now. Too   30
much, he says. His video-pioneering role came to light in 1982 in an article written in *Creative Computing* magazine. That, and a story I did for National Public Radio's *All Things Considered* in 1983, have brought him instant fame.

"I get letters from friends I haven't seen in thirty years who say 'Hey,   31
Willy! I didn't know you did that!' or 'I remember [when it happened.]' So that's kind of nice. But it's not the only thing of any means that I've done in my life."

Wouldn't it be ironic, I suggested to Willy in an interview, if fifty   32
years from now when historians write about the history of Brookhaven National Laboratory, they overlook all the famous high-tech radiation work that has gone on there and point to the spot on the gym floor where the video game stood?

"Nobel Prize winners are going to be awfully disappointed if that   33
happens," he said jokingly.

If Willy is the father of the first video game—and no one else is   34
staking that claim—it's because, like Bell with his telephone, Willy was properly prepared, in the Pasteurian sense of the word, to invent it.*

In January 1941 Willy joined the staff of the MIT Radiation Labora-   35
tory. He was assigned to help develop radar, specifically the cathode-ray tube displays. "I worked on circuits to display the radar data on cathode-ray tubes. I authored several patents for the government." His picture tube did not differ substantially from the problems involved in the tennis game display.

Before going to Los Alamos, New Mexico, in December 1943 to work   36
on development of the A-bomb, Higinbotham worked on advanced radar displays for the high-flying B-28. To perfect this radar, Willy invented and obtained patents for special kinds of amplifiers like those that later showed up in the analog computer that he used in the tennis game.

---

*Louis Pasteur, when asked what role luck plays in discovery, said: "Chance favors the prepared mind."

So it was not by accident that Higinbotham envisioned how the   37
tennis game would work. Just the opposite. Willy had spent the last
twenty years preparing his mind to make the leap. He had invented key
elements of it years before. Key pieces of his invention had been coming
together for over two decades. The puzzle assembled itself in Willy's
mind in 1958. To Willy, inventing the video game was like reinventing
the wheel: "It was a natural progression for me."

No plaque has been erected in the Brookhaven gym where the first   38
video game was played. You won't find the game stored in the attic of
the Smithsonian; Willy dismantled the gadgetry after the exhibit ran for
two years.

If Willy has his way, he hopes he's remembered for more than the   39
video game. What leaves the sharpest image in Willy's mind is the day
he witnessed the detonation of that first atomic bomb at Los Alamos.
As designer of the timing device for the bomb, Willy watched the
explosion from his vantage point twenty-four miles from ground zero.
Since that blast Willy has devoted his energies to making sure another
one never goes off. As senior scientist at Brookhaven, Willy spent years
amassing the world's biggest library devoted to nuclear safeguards. He
has spent the last forty-plus years working on arms control. It's his arms
control achievements that Willy hopes to be remembered for at
Brookhaven.

Vocabulary

hallowed (2)—honored; highly
   respected
concoct (11)—to devise; to invent
novel (20)—new and unusual
affidavits (27)—written statements made on oath before a
   person in authority

deposition (29)—the testimony
   of a witness
dismantled (38)—took apart
detonation (39)—the explosion
   of a bomb
amassing (39)—collecting together

IN YOUR JOURNAL

What facts did you learn about the beginnings of video games in this essay?

A Closer Reading

1. What video games does Flatow mention in this article? How many of these have you heard of? Played? What, if any, aspects of these games do you find interesting?

2. What are the "glorified designer chips of sand" Flatow is referring to in paragraph 5?

3. Who is Willy Higinbotham? Why is he important to this story? Why does he prefer not to be remembered only for video games?

4. What is a patent? Why does an inventor need a patent in order to make money from an invention? Why didn't Higinbotham make any money from video games?

Drawing Your Own Conclusions

1. Do you agree with Flatow that the video game is an important invention? Why or why not?

2. What differences have you seen in the development of video games over the past five years? What do you predict will happen to video games in the near future?

3. In what way would Higinbotham like to be remembered in relation to the invention of nuclear power? How do you think he feels about the use of nuclear power as a weapon? What evidence is there in the article that supports your point of view?

4. Louis Pasteur is quoted in Flatow's notes as saying, "Chance favors the prepared mind." What does this mean? What qualities make the prepared mind for a physician, according to Loinaz (see Murphy interview on page 481)? For a forensic geologist (see Murray article on page 489)? For a research scientist in general (see Frank article on page 471)?

Thinking about Writing

1. How does the anecdote contained in the first two paragraphs relate to the body of the essay? Why does Flatow include this? How does he connect paragrpah 2 to paragraph 3?

2. What tone or feeling does Flatow have in this piece of writing? Support your answer by referring to specific ideas from the article.

3. What does the title of Flatow's book tell you about his attitude toward the invention of video games?

4. In what part of the essay does Flatow tell his readers about Higinbotham's personal history? Where else could it have occurred in the writing? Move it in your mind and reread. In which part of the essay do you prefer it? Why?

*   *   *

Suggestions for Writing

1. Write an essay about a person who is like the inventors Flatow describes in his book: "They refuse to take no for an answer." Describe the person. How has this personality trait affected the decisions the person has made? Explain whether it is generally a positive or negative personality trait.

2. Write an essay in which you describe a recent invention that has changed your life in a positive way. Describe the invention and tell how you use it in your life. What changes have you made in your life because of the existence of this invention?

3. Write an essay in which you describe a recent invention that has changed your life in a negative way. Describe the invention, and tell how it has created problems in your life. What impact has this invention had on other people around you? If you could have prevented its invention, would you? Why or why not?

4. Choose three inventions that have changed the world in the last twenty-five years. Identify the inventions, explain why you have chosen them, and describe the impact thay have had on the world as you know it.

Strategies for Revision

Working with a partner, share the draft of the essay you have just written. Together, discuss the following questions:

- How does Flatow make his material seem important? How do you do this in your draft?
- How does Flatow combine personal and general information? How do you do this in your essay?
- How does Flatow begin his essay? What do you think about this beginning? What makes your beginning work or not work?
- What details or examples does Flatow use to support his main points? What supporting details or examples do you use? Are they effective?
- Where is Flatow's writing particularly clear and easy to follow? Where is your writing particularly clear and easy to follow?
- Is there any place where Flatow's writing is not clear? Is there any place where your writing is not clear? How can these trouble spots be improved?
- Is there any place where Flatow's ideas do not clearly connect? Is there any place where your ideas do not clearly connect? How can the connections be improved?
- What makes Flatow's ending work or not work? What makes your ending work or not work? What improvements can be made?

After you have discussed all the writing, think about how you can improve what you have written. Write your revision and share that with the same partner.

Diane Beran wrote an essay in response to suggestion 1 from the Suggestions for Writing that follow the Scudder selection: Write an essay in which you describe a scientific experiment or experience in which you participated at any level of your education. Explain the steps that were involved, what you wanted to find out, what you did find out, any mistakes that were made, and what you learned about yourself from your experience.

Max

Diane Beran

I was first suspicious of something being wrong with my cat when   1
he had more frequent than normal trips to the litter box, and prolonged squatting and straining when urinating. Baffled by his peculiar mannerisms, I finally passed it off as my overactive imagination.

Throughout the day, I observed Max walking around aimlessly   2
through the house, as if he was searching for a place to urinate. Puzzled by this uncharacteristic behavior, I decided to call the veterinarian, who asked me to bring him in immediately.

As I prepared to leave for the veterinarian's office, Max began throw-   3
ing up a yellowish, chalky mucus-like substance, which I later learned was his own urine. He also began to get very sluggish, his eyes were glossy and his pupils became fixed and dilated. Not realizing what these symptoms meant, I quickly loaded Max into the car and off to the animal hospital we rushed. I would later learn that Max was slipping into a coma.

As we arrived at the vet's, we were immediately met at the door by   4
Dr. Greenburg, who began to examine Max. After addressing the full gamut of symptoms, Dr. Greenburg diagnosed him as having F.U.S., Feline Urologic Syndrome. F.U.S. is a very serious disease that can be fatal to a cat left untreated. It is a clinical condition that occurs as a result of cystitis and/or urethritis (inflammation of the urethra). It is characterized by the frequent passing of bloody urine, or partial to complete obstruction of the urinary tract. Max was obstructed with struvite crystals that are formed in the bladder and caused by high concentration of the mineral magnesium, alkaline P.H. and a high ash content in the food he was eating on a daily basis.

The struvite crystals are sand-like, and can form stones in the blad-   5 der if they are not passed. When they become too large to pass, they can completely obstruct the flow of urine. F.U.S. occurs with equal frequency in both sexes of cats, however, since the anatomy of the male yields a much higher degree of danger, obstruction is much more serious in male cats.

Since Max is a male, I asked Dr. Greenburg to elaborate in detail the exact diagnosis of his anatomy.   6

"The urethra is a tube coming from the bladder and narrows as it enters the penis, therefore, Max experienced a blockage somewhere in his penis. Because of that narrowness, it's hard if not impossible to pass these crystals that were in his bladder," said Dr. Greenburg.   7

Seeing my obvious concern and love for this helpless animal, Dr. Greenburg asked if I wanted to assist her in the treatment of my cat. Without hesitation I began to assist the doctor in the preparation stages of Max's surgery.   8

He was given a shot of a drug called Ketamine, which is used to tranquilize, so he could have the blockage surgically removed.   9

As the doctor took inventory on the surgical apparatuses she turned to me and with a calming voice said,   10

"I want you to apply this ointment to Max's eyeballs because when cats are tranquilized, their eyes do not make moisture."   11

She handed me a half empty tube that closely resembled a half emptied tube of toothpaste. After a slight hesitation, I squeezed the clear, cool, oozing ointment on the tip of my index finger. Max's eyeball was smooth and marble-like, as my own eyes began to water from just the thought of touching my own eye sockets.   12

The doctor asked me to hold back his prepuce or foreskin that surrounded his penis. By holding it back it forces his penis to extend and become erect for further examination.   13

We first tried a procedure called a urethral massage, which is rolling the penis back and forth between the thumb and index finger. By doing this, the struvite crystals may loosen and exit on their own.   14

With no success, she began to do a procedure called cystocentesis, which is running a needle through the belly into the bladder, while removing the urine from beyond the blocked area. This would prevent Max from slipping deeper into a coma that could be caused by the urine backing up into his system.   15

The long, shimmering, 12 inch needle began to disappear into Max's stomach as I cringed at the sight imagining the needle exiting out his other side.   16

Not knowing the extent of his blockage, we tried a second measure   17
called Urethral Catherization. We inserted a grayish, four inch tube,
that was as wide as a cotton swab, through the penis and into the
bladder. This instrument would widen the urethra to help pass the
crystals. Then we would do a urethral flushing.

Attaching a saline filled syringe to the end of the catheter, the doctor   18
began to quickly inject and withdraw the solution, in and out of the
bladder in a plunging motion. In most situations this procedure will
help loosen and eject the stones. Max was so densely clogged, that each
procedure produced the same result—no breakup in the clogged area.
As the doctor applied more pressure, a mixture of saline and blood mass
squirted everywhere.

I'd always imagined that I would become fainthearted at the grue-   19
some sight such as this, but my love for animals prevailed as blood,
urine and saline shot all over my face and hair. All I cared about was the
physical well-being of this helpless animal.

The last step was surgery. I only stayed for the preparation,   20
and then left the doctor alone to save the life of my cat. She gave
him another shot to keep him sedated for the duration of the surgery
and started an I.V. to prevent dehydration. She then shaved his poste-
rior, as I was leaving the room to wait for the final results from
surgery.

As I sat in the waiting room, my eyes wandered across the walls,   21
looking at the numerous posters and various illustrations of information about proper animal care. Sounds of cats and dogs chaotically
yelping filled the air as time seemed to slow down to a standstill. The
entire atmosphere seemed to put what had just happened into a much
clearer focus. I realized that although this job is not clean or glamorous,
it takes a lot of patience, understanding and love for animals, to be able
to perform a life and death task.

That's when it hit me. An unmistakable yet questionable feeling of   22
self-worth and pride overcame me. That's when I understood what
destiny lies ahead of me. My career questions had been answered on
that operating table—I was destined to become a veterinarian.

Nearly 40 minutes had passed when Dr. Greenburg came out of   23
the office and told me that Max would be fine. She performed an
operation called Urethostomy—which means to cut a new opening
into the urethra. By totally removing the penis, she stretched and
stiched back the urethra, making it wider. This would also prevent
blockage from reoccuring.

I thanked the doctor for saving my cat. And I thanked my cat for 24 helping me to make up my mind.

Little did I know that the near death of my cat would create the 25 birth of my future.

Questions to Think About

1. What examples from Beran's essay support Scudder's idea of the importance of observation in science? In writing?

2. List the steps that Beran describes in dealing with her cat's illness.

3. What specific descriptive words and phrases does Beran use to portray the experience? Choose those that you think are the most effective in the essay. Explain your choices.

4. What did you learn about veterinary medicine from this essay?

5. What is the effect of the last four paragraphs of this essay?

MAKING CONNECTIONS

The World of Science: *Understanding and Exploring*

1. Pat Murphy's interview with Margarita Loinaz (see page 481) deals with problem solving. Reread the other selections in this unit, thinking about how the various science professionals solve problems. Write an essay in which you describe the problem solving techniques of at least three scientists. What did you learn that will help you become a better problem solver?

2. Colleges nationwide are concerned about the small numbers of students who major in sciences. Write an essay explaining how what you have you learned from reading the various selections in this unit has made you curious about, interested in, and/or convinced that knowing more about science will enhance your understanding of the world in general. Refer to specific selections to support your point of view.

3. Write an essay in which you explain what you think nonscientists can learn from the scientific method about problem solving in everyday life. How can this method help us to reason better and become better thinkers?

4. What is the role of curiosity in science? Choose several of the selections from this unit and write an essay explaining the role curiosity has played in the experiences these scientists have described. Refer to specific selections to support your point of view.

5. Imagine that Samuel Scudder (see page 463) and Adam Frank (see page 471) met to discuss the way that scientific knowledge has changed their understanding of the world. After reading their selections, write down their conversation using dialogue and quotations. Do you think they will decide that scientific knowledge has made the world a better place? Support your point of view with references to their writing.

6. Choose the piece of writing from this unit from which you learned the most. In an essay, tell what you learned and why this selection influenced you more than the others did.

7. Write an essay in which you choose one piece of writing from this unit that caused an emotional reaction—it may have angered you, made you sad, or made you happy. Explain the effect of this piece of writing, and tell why it had this effect.

10

THE WORLD IN REFLECTION

Examining Complex Issues

In this final unit of the book, we do not focus on a single topic, as we have in the other units, but instead—informed by our earlier readings, discussions, and writing—we reflect on some of the complex and difficult problems that exist in our world today. We examine such issues as freedom versus responsibility, tolerance versus intolerance, separation versus unity, and authority versus obedience. These issues affect the way we live and interact with the various worlds that we all share.

We begin with "The Recoloring of Campus Life," an essay by Shelby Steele. In it, Steele explores the efforts made by some black students to separate themselves from white students on many college campuses. He looks at the origins of the movement for separatism and differentism that is pervasive in our world today.

In "Abortion, Right or Wrong?" Rachel Richardson Smith writes about the complexities of the abortion issue. She presents both sides of the issue and her reasons for agreeing with each of them.

Journalist and educator Jonathan Kozol describes the life of a homeless family in a welfare hotel in New York City. "The Homeless and Their Children" paints a bleak picture of a young illiterate mother struggling to make a life for her children in a hostile environment.

In the next selection, Martin Lee and Norman Solomon present evidence that much of the way we know and judge the world is influenced by the media. In "Women's Rights and Media's Wrongs," the two authors discuss the absence of women from positions of authority in media and criticize media's coverage of violent crimes. They condemn media's coverage of rape and speculate about the effect of focusing attention only on the "attractive" rape cases.

An interview between psychologist Edward Krupat and professor of social ethics Herbert Kelman, "On Authority and Obedience," questions how we make decisions about personal responsibility and about the need to defy authority and to disobey. They present several complex situations to explore the conflicts involved in making such decisions.

Chimpanzee researcher Jane Goodall visits animal research laboratories in this country and is appalled by the treatment of the chimpanzees in their care. "A Plea for the Chimps" calls out for humane treatment of these animals now being used for medical research.

In her essay, "Pursuit of a Goal," student writer Georgeanne Snyder reflects on a difficult decision she made at a turning point in her life.

*   *   *

Think about the following questions before reading the selections in this unit:

1. What are the three most serious problems affecting our society today?

2. In what ways have these situations become better or worse over the last five years?

3. What steps should we take to begin to resolve these problems? How can going to college put you in a better position to do something about them?

IN YOUR JOURNAL

This essay begins with this statement: "I have long believed that trouble between the races is seldom what it appears to be." Write about what this statement means to you.

The Recoloring of Campus Life

Shelby Steele

Shelby Steele is a writer who often deals with societal problems. His book The Content of Our Character: A New Vision of Race in America *(1990) won the National Book Critics Circle award. In "The Recoloring of Campus Life," which originally appeared in the February 1989 issue of* Harper's Magazine, *Steele discusses the conflicts that have emerged in the last thirty years since the civil rights movement, as blacks and whites live, learn, worship, and work together in the United States today.*

I have long believed that trouble between the races is seldom what it appears to be. It was not hard to see after my first talks with students that racial tension on campus is a problem that misrepresents itself. It has the same look, the archetypal pattern, of America's timeless racial conflict—white racism and black protest. And I think part of our concern over it comes from the fact that it has the feel of a relapse, illness gone and come again. But if we are seeing the same symptoms, I don't believe we are dealing with the same illness. For one thing, I think racial tension on campus is the result more of racial equality than inequality. 1

How to live with racial difference has been America's profound social problem. For the first 100 years or so following emancipation it was controlled by a legally sanctioned inequality that acted as a buffer between the races. No longer is this the case. On campuses today, as throughout society, blacks enjoy equality under the law—a profound social advancement. No student may be kept out of a class or a dormitory or an extracurricular activity because of his or her race. But there is a paradox here: On a campus where members of all races are gathered, mixed together in the classroom as well as socially, differences are more exposed than ever. And 2 this is where the trouble starts. For members of each race—young adults coming into their own, often away from home for the first time—bring to this site of freedom, exploration, and now, today, equality, very deep fears and anxieties, inchoate feelings of racial shame, anger, and guilt. These feelings could lie dormant in the home, in familiar neighborhoods, in simpler days of childhood. But the college campus, with its structures of interaction and adult-level competition—the big exam, the dorm, the "mixer"—is another matter. I think campus racism is born of the rub between racial difference and a setting, the campus itself, devoted to interaction and equality. On our campuses, such concentrated micro-societies, all that remains unresolved between blacks and whites, all the old wounds and shames that have never been addressed, present themselves for attention—and present our youth with pressures they cannot always handle.

I have mentioned one paradox: racial fears and anxieties among   3
blacks and whites bubbling up in an era of racial equality under the law, in settings that are among the freest and fairest in society. And there is another, related paradox, stemming from the notion of—and practice of—affirmative action. Under the provisions of the Equal Employment Opportunity Act of 1972, all state governments and institutions (including universities) were forced to initiate plans to increase the proportion of minority and women employees—in the case of universities, of students too. Affirmative action plans that establish racial quotas were ruled unconstitutional more than ten years ago in *University of California Regents v. Bakke.* But quotas are only the most controversial aspect of affirmative action; the principle of affirmative action is reflected in various university programs aimed at redressing and overcoming past patterns of discrimination. Of course, to be conscious of patterns of discrimination—the fact, say, that public schools in the black inner cities are more crowded and employ fewer top-notch teachers than white suburban public schools, and that this is a factor in student performance—is only reasonable. However, in doing this we also call attention quite obviously to difference: in the case of blacks and whites, racial difference. What has emerged on campus in recent years—as a result of the new equality and affirmative action, in a sense, as a result of progress—is a *politics of difference,* a troubling, volatile politics in which each group justifies itself, its sense of worth and its pursuit of power, through difference alone.

In this context, racial, ethnic, and gender differences become forms of   4
sovereignty, campuses become balkanized, and each group fights with whatever means are available. No doubt there are many factors that have contributed to the rise of racial tension on campus: What has been the

role of fraternities, which have returned to campus with their inclusions and exclusions? What role has the heightened notion of college as some first step to personal, financial success played in increasing competition, and thus tension? Mostly what I sense, though, is that in interactive settings, while fighting the fights of "difference," old ghosts are stirred, and haunt again. Black and white Americans simply have the power to make each other feel shame and guilt. In the "real" world, we may be able to deny these feelings, keep them at bay. But these feelings are likely to surface on college campuses, where young people are groping for identity and power, and where difference is made to matter so greatly. In a way, racial tension on campus in the Eighties might have been inevitable.

Vocabulary

archetypal (1)—like the original model from which it was patterned

paradox (2)—a situation with characteristics that seem to be contradictory

inchoate (2)—just begun; not yet completely formed

redressing (3)—compensating for a wrong

volatile (3)—unstable; explosive

sovereignty (4)—supreme and independent political rule

balkanized (4)—broken up into small hostile political units; from the breakup of the Balkan peninsula (including Yugoslavia, Greece, Bulgaria, Albania, Romania, and part of Turkey) after World War I

IN YOUR JOURNAL

Write about any experiences you have had with racism in your school or community. If you have not had personal experiences with racism, write down your view of the racial situation in the United States today and how it affects you.

A Closer Reading

1. What connection does Steele establish between racial equality and racial tension on college campuses?

2. What legislation has come into existence in the last twenty years that has affected the makeup of the student body on college campuses?

3. What occurs in the lives of young people during their college years that is different from other periods in their lives? What do young people, especially those who live in college dorms, experience for the first time in their lives?

4. What factors does Steele mention as existing on college campuses that may contribute to the rise of racial tension?

Drawing Your Own Conclusions

1. What is the "politics of difference" to which Steele refers in paragraph 3? What examples of this have you seen on your campus?

2. What does Steele mean when he says that "campuses become balkanized," that groups divide up into factions and fight for power and recognition? What recent events have occurred that illustrate that this is happening on college campuses?

3. What special interest groups exist on your campus? In what ways do these groups have a positive influence on students? In what ways do they have a negative influence? Do you belong to any of these groups? Why?

4. Steele finds that there are certain conflicting effects of affirmative action and equal opportunity laws. How do these laws compare to the Americans with Disabilities Act described by Dardick on page 311? What problems might develop because of the ADA that are similar to what is happening in relation to race?

Thinking about Writing

1. What is Steele's main idea? Where is it stated in the essay?

2. Steele mentions three paradoxes in this essay. What are they? Why are they paradoxes? How do these paradoxes support Steele's main idea?

3. Steele refers to two pieces of legislation. What words and phrases does he use to describe these pieces of legislation? Would you have liked more information about them? How can you get that information?

4. What does the title of this article mean? What other meaning could this title have?

*   *   *

Suggestions for Writing

1. It has recently been reported in the news that in many colleges, black students often choose to live, study, and socialize separately from white students. In an essay, explain why this situation has developed. What should the colleges do about this situation? How can colleges integrate activities and situations in which all students participate?

2. People approach the issues of gender, race, ethnicity, and class from two basic perspectives. One is difference—people should be recognized and celebrated for their differences. The other is sameness—all people should be treated the same; humans have more commonalities than differences. In an essay, explain which approach you prefer and why. Use examples from your own life and those around you to support your point of view.

3. Should colleges be permitted to exclude people because of their sex and race? A recent court case involved a woman who fought to be admitted to an all-men's school. Take a position on this issue. Support your point of view with your experiences, your observations, and your readings.

4. "Racial, ethnic, and gender differences become forms of sovereignty, campuses become balkanized, and each group fights with whatever means are available." Write an essay in which you explain what this statement means. Cite examples of how this "politics of difference" has caused problems in colleges. What do you believe will be the results of these problems?

Strategies for Revision

Look at Steele's essay as you work with a partner on your draft. Take notes about any suggestions that are made on your draft. Use the following questions to direct your writing discussion:

- Notice how Steele introduces the problem he addresses in his issue. How do I introduce the problem I am addressing?
- Notice how Steele includes and uses historical information to support his main idea. Do I use any historical information? If not, would historical information make my draft stronger?
- Notice how Steele presents contradictions and paradoxes. Does my draft include any contradictions or paradoxes? Do I present both sides of the issue clearly?

- Choose the strongest sentence, paragraph, and concept in the Steele article. Why is this the strongest? What part of my draft is the strongest? Why?
- Notice how carefully Steele has chosen his words. What words, sentences, or paragraphs need to be rethought and reworked for the next draft?

Read through the notes you have written during your discussion. Decide what changes you would like to make to revise your essay. After you write the next draft, share it with the same partner.

IN YOUR JOURNAL

Why is abortion such a difficult issue to resolve in the United States today? Write about your feelings on the subject.

Abortion, Right or Wrong?

Rachel Richardson Smith

Rachel Richardson Smith was a student of theology when she wrote this essay; it appeared in *Newsweek* magazine on March 25, 1985. Richardson Smith begins by stating, "I cannot bring myself to say I am in favor of abortion. . . . I cannot bring myself to say I am against choice." In this essay, she explores the complexities of the abortion issue and the sadness that surrounds the debate. Richardson Smith writes a piece of argumentation, yet she recognizes both sides of the issue. She compares the arguments and formulates her own response to this controversial issue.

I cannot bring myself to say I am in favor of abortion. I don't want   1
anyone to have one. I want people to use contraceptives and for those
contraceptives to be foolproof. I want people to be responsible for their
actions; mature in their decisions. I want children to be loved, wanted,
well cared for.

I cannot bring myself to say I am against choice. I want women who   2
are young, poor, single or all three to be able to direct the course of their
lives. I want women who have had all the children they want or can
afford or their bodies can withstand to be able to decide their future. I
want women who are in bad marriages or destructive relationships to
avoid being trapped by pregnancy.

So in these days when thousands rally in opposition to legalized   3
abortion, when facilities providing abortions are bombed, when the
president speaks glowingly of the growing momentum behind the
anti-abortion movement, I find myself increasingly alienated from the
pro-life groups.

At the same time, I am overwhelmed with mail from pro-choice   4
groups. They, too, are mobilizing their forces, growing articulate in

support of their cause, and they want my support. I am not sure I can give it.

I find myself in the awkward position of being both anti-abortion and pro-choice. Neither group seems to be completely right—or wrong. It is not that I think abortion is wrong for me but acceptable for someone else. The question is far more complex than that.

Part of my problem is that what I think and how I feel about this issue are two entirely different matters. I know that unwanted children are often neglected, even abandoned. I know that many of those seeking abortions are children themselves. I know that making abortion illegal will not stop all women from having them.

Absolutes: I also know from experience the crisis an unplanned pregnancy can cause. Yet I have felt the joy of giving birth, the delight that comes from feeling a baby's skin against my own. I know how hard it is to parent a child and how deeply satisfying it can be. My children sometimes provoke me and cause me endless frustration, but I can still look at them with tenderness and wonder at the miracle of it all. The lessons of my own experience produce conflicting emotions. Theory collides with reality.

It concerns me that both groups present themselves in absolutes. They are committed and they want me to commit. They do not recognize the gray area where I seem to be languishing. Each group has the right answer—the only answer.

Yet I am uncomfortable in either camp. I have nothing in common with the pro-lifers. I am horrified by their scare tactics, their pictures of well-formed fetuses tossed in a metal pan, their cruel slogans. I cannot condone their flagrant misuse of Scripture and unforgiving spirit. There is a meanness about their position that causes them to pass judgment on the lives of women in a way I could never do.

The pro-life groups, with their fundamentalist religious attitudes, have a fear and an abhorrence of sex, especially premarital sex. In their view abortion only compounds the sexual sin. What I find incomprehensible is that even as they are opposed to abortion they are also opposed to alternative solutions. They are squeamish about sex education in the schools. They don't want teens to have contraceptives without parental consent. They offer little aid or sympathy to unwed mothers. They are the vigilant guardians of a narrow morality.

I wonder how abortion got to be the greatest of all sins? What about poverty, ignorance, hunger, weaponry?

The only thing the anti-abortion groups seem to have right is that abortion is indeed the taking of human life. I simply cannot escape this one glaring fact. Call it what you will—fertilized egg, embryo, fetus. What we have here is human life. If it were just a mass of tissue there would be no debate. So I agree that abortion ends a life. But the anti-abortionists are wrong to call it murder. 12

The sad truth is that homicide is not always against the law. Our society does not categorically recognize the sanctity of human life. There are a number of legal and apparently socially acceptable ways to take human life. "Justifiable" homicide includes the death penalty, war, killing in self-defense. It seems to me that as a society we need to come to grips with our own ambiguity concerning the value of human life. If we are to value and protect unborn life so stringently, why do we not also value and protect life already born? 13

Mistakes: Why can't we see abortion for the human tragedy it is? No woman plans for her life to turn out that way. Even the most effective contraceptives are no guarantee against pregnancy. Loneliness, ignorance, immaturity can lead to decisions (or lack of decisions) that may result in untimely pregnancy. People make mistakes. 14

What many people seem to misunderstand is that no woman wants to have an abortion. Circumstances demand it; women do it. No woman reacts to abortion with joy. Relief, yes. But also ambivalence, grief, despair, guilt. 15

The pro-choice groups do not seem to acknowledge that abortion is not a perfect answer. What goes unsaid is that when a woman has an abortion she loses more than an unwanted pregnancy. Often she loses her self-respect. No woman can forget a pregnancy no matter how it ends. 16

Why can we not view abortion as one of those anguished decisions in which human beings struggle to do the best they can in trying circumstances? Why is abortion viewed so coldly and factually on the one hand and so judgmentally on the other? Why is it not akin to the same painful experience families must sometimes make to allow a loved one to die? 17

I wonder how we can begin to change the context in which we think about abortion. How can we begin to think about it redemptively? What is it in the trauma of loss of life—be it loved or unloved, born or unborn—from which we can learn? There is much I have yet to resolve. Even as I refuse to pass judgment on other women's lives, I weep for the children who might have been. I suspect I am not alone. 18

Vocabulary

momentum (3)—the strength or force

mobilizing (4)—bringing into readiness for active service for a cause

languishing (8)—being weak; pining

abhorrence (10)—hatred or repugnance

vigilant (10)—watchful; alert to a danger

sanctity (13)—holiness

stringently (13)—severely; rigidly

anguished (17)—worried; distressed

akin (17)—similar; related

IN YOUR JOURNAL

What aspects of Richarson Smith's essay impressed you the most? Why? What did you learn from reading this essay?

A Closer Reading

1. What reasons does Richardson Smith provide to explain why she is "in the awkward position of being both anti-abortion and pro-choice"?

2. What does Richardson Smith mean when she writes: "Theory collides with reality"? What examples does she give to explain this statement?

3. What positions have pro-life groups taken against alternatives to abortion? Why is Richardson Smith fearful that the results of taking these positions will lead to more abortions?

4. What types of "justifiable" homicide exist in our society?

Drawing Your Own Conclusions

1. Richardson Smith writes: "Part of my problem is that what I think and how I feel about this issue are two entirely different matters." What does this mean for her in relation to abortion? What conflicts do you have in which what you "think" and what you "feel" are at odds?

2. How have Richardson Smith's personal experiences affected her position on this issue? Is it possible to depersonalize and remove oneself from individual experiences? Should a writer try to do this? Why or why not?

3. What is an absolute? In what ways does each side present itself as an absolute, according to Richardson Smith? Why does this make it difficult to understand another point of view?

4. What is an ambiguity? What ambiguities does Richardson Smith focus on in this essay? What other ambiguities pose problems in our society? What other ambiguities have been discussed in other selections in this book?

Thinking about Writing

1. What effect do the first two paragraphs have on you as a reader? Do you prefer essays in which a writer takes a definite point of view? Why or why not?

2. Reread paragraph 6, focusing on the topic sentence. What support does Richardson Smith provide for the topic sentence? Look at other paragraphs in the essay. Identify the topic sentence. Find the supporting details. Are they sufficient? Are they convincing?

3. In what parts of the essay does Richardson Smith use different rhetorical techniques? Where does she compare? describe? narrate? persuade? analyze? What is the overall purpose of this essay? What elements of the essay helped you make your decision?

4. Although Richardson Smith states that abortion is an issue fraught with ambiguities, she does state some absolutes to support her own conflicts. For example, she writes: "No woman wants to have an abortion." What other absolute statements can you find? How do they support Richardson Smith's purpose in writing this essay?

*   *   *

Suggestions for Writing

1. Choose an issue in which the way you think and the way you feel are at odds. Write an essay in which you state the issue. Identify the various positions that surround the issue. Explain the con-

flicts that arise in choosing one side over another. Convince your readers that the issue is complex and difficult to resolve.

2. Write an essay in which you describe a difficult decision that you had to make to resolve a conflict in your life. Explain the situation, the conflict, and your decision. What did you learn about yourself from going through this process?

3. Should sex education be taught in school? Would teaching about sex reduce the number of abortions in this country? Take a position on this issue. Support your point of view with your experiences, your observations, and your readings.

4. Richardson Smith writes: "I wonder how abortion got to be the greatest of all sins? What about poverty, ignorance, hunger, weaponry?" Of the problems she identified, which do you think is most destructive to our society? Write an essay in which you explain your choice, and describe the societal problems that result from this problem. What steps should be taken to resolve the problem?

5. Many of the essays you write in college require you to take a position on a controversial issue. This is not always easy to do, because controversial issues are often ambiguous in nature. Write an essay in which you choose one controversial issue that you have written about, but about which you had difficulty deciding how you felt. What was the issue? Why was it difficult to take a position? What position did you take? How did you decide? If you were rewriting the essay, what position would you take now, and why?

Strategies for Revision

Richardson Smith wrote an argumentation piece, yet she recognized both sides of the issue. Learning to do this is an important aspect of learning to write effective persuasive essays.

When you have completed the first draft of your writing, reread the Richardson Smith essay, thinking about what you can learn about formulating an argument from her writing. Look at her essay and yours as you ask yourself the following questions:

- How does Richardson Smith let her readers know that her issue is complex? How do I do this?
- How does Richardson Smith tell her readers about her own conflicts? How do I present my conflicts?

- Where, how, and why does Richardson Smith include her personal experiences and beliefs? How do I include these? Are they effective? If not, what changes would make them more effective?
- What questions does Richardson Smith ask? Does she answer them? How do I use questions in my draft?
- How does Richardson Smith conclude her essay? Why is it a fitting conclusion? How do I conclude my draft? How can I make it even more effective?

Revise your draft, thinking about these questions. Share your revision with your classmates.

IN YOUR JOURNAL

The author of the next section begins with this observation: "The Martinique Hotel . . . is one of the largest hotels for homeless people in New York City. . . . nearly four hundred homeless families, including some twelve hundred children, were lodged in the hotel."

Write about why the problem of homelessness continues in our society.

The Homeless and Their Children

Jonathan Kozol

Jonathan Kozol has taught at Yale University, the University of Massachusetts at Amherst, and at South Boston High School. He has written about social problems, often focusing on their relation to education. Some of his books include *Death at an Early Age,* which won the National Book Award in 1967, *Free Schools* (1972), *The Night is Dark* (1975), *On Being a Teacher* (1981), *Savage Inequalities: Children in America's Schools* (1991), and *Blueprint for a Democratic Education* (1992). "The Homeless and Their Children," which first appeared in *The New Yorker* magazine, is excerpted from *Rachel and Her Children* (1988). Kozol describes the extreme hardships of a homeless family and their life in a welfare hotel in New York City.

The Martinique Hotel, at Sixth Avenue and Thirty-second Street, is   1
one of the largest hotels for homeless people in New York City. When I visited it, in December of 1985, nearly four hundred homeless families, including some twelve hundred children, were lodged in the hotel, by arrangement with the city's Human Resources Administration. One of the residents I spoke to at some length was an energetic, intelligent woman I'll call Kim. During one of our conversations, she mentioned a woman on the seventh floor who had seemingly begun to find her situation intolerable. Kim described this woman as "a broken stick," and offered to arrange for us to meet.

The woman—I will call her Laura, but her name, certain other   2
names, and certain details have been changed—is so fragile that I find it hard to start a conversation when we are introduced, a few nights later.

Before I begin, she asks if I will read her a letter from the hospital. The oldest of her four children, a seven-year-old boy named Matthew, has been sick for several weeks. He was tested for lead poisoning in November, and the letter she hands me, from Roosevelt Hospital, says that the child has a dangerous lead level. She is told to bring him back for treatment. She received the letter some weeks ago. It has been buried in a pile of other documents that she cannot read.

Although Laura cannot read, she knows enough about the dangers   3
of lead to grasp the darker implications of this information. The crumbling plaster in the Martinique Hotel is covered with sweet-tasting paint, and children eat or chew chips of the paint as it flakes off the walls. Some of the paint contains lead. Children with lead poisoning may suffer loss of coordination or undergo convulsions. The consequences of lead poisoning may be temporary or long-lasting. They may appear at once or not for several years. This final point is what instills so much uneasiness; even months of observation cannot calm a parent's fear.

Lead poisoning, then, is Laura's first concern, but she has other   4
problems. The bathroom plumbing has overflowed and left a pool of sewage on the floor. A radiator valve is broken, and every now and then releases a spray of scalding steam at the eye level of a child. A crib provided by the hotel appears to be unstable. A screw that holds two of its sides together is missing. When I test the crib with my hand, it starts to sway. There are four beds in the room, and they are dangerous, too. They have metal frames with unprotected corners, and the mattresses do not fit the frames; at one corner or another, metal is exposed. If a child has the energy or the playfulness to jump or turn a somersault or wrestle with a friend, and if he falls and strikes his head against the metal corner, the consequences can be serious. The week before, a child on the fourteenth floor fell in just this way, cut his forehead, and required stitches. Most of these matters have been brought to the attention of the hotel management; in Laura's case, complaints have brought no visible results.

All of this would be enough to make life difficult for an illiterate   5
young woman in New York, but Laura has one other urgent matter on her hands. It appears that she has failed to answer a request for information from her welfare office, and, for reasons that she doesn't understand, she did not receive her benefits this week. The timing is bad; it's a weekend. The city operates a crisis center in the Martinique, where residents can go for food and other help, but today the crisis center is

not open, so there's nobody around to tide her over with emergency supplies. Laura's children have been eating cheese and bread and peanut butter for two days. "Those on welfare," the Community Service Society of New York said in a report published in 1984, may be suddenly removed from welfare rolls "for reasons unrelated to their actual need," or even to eligibility standards. Welfare workers in New York City call this practice "churning." Laura and her children are being churned.

The room is lighted by fluorescent tubes in a ceiling fixture. They cast a stark light on four walls of greenish paint smeared over with sludge draining from someone's plumbing on the floor above. In the room are two boys with dark and hollowed eyes and an infant girl. A third boy is outside and joins us later. The children have the washed-out look of the children Walker Evans photographed for *Let Us Now Praise Famous Men*. Besides the four beds and the crib, the room contains two chairs, a refrigerator, and a television set, which doesn't work. A metal hanger serves as an antenna, but there is no picture on the screen. Instead, there is a storm of falling flakes and unclear lines. I wonder why Laura keeps it on. There are no table lamps to soften the fluorescent glare, no books, no decorations. Laura tells me that her father is of Panamanian birth but that she went to school in New York City. Spanish is her first language. I don't speak Spanish well. We talk in English.

"I cannot read," Laura says. "I buy the New York *Post* to read the pictures. In the grocery, I know what to buy because I see the pictures."

What of no-name products—generic brands, whose labels have no pictures but which could save her a great deal of money?

"If there are no pictures, I don't buy it," she says. "I want to buy pancakes, I ask the lady, 'Where's the pancakes?' So they tell me."

She points to the boys and says, "He's two. He's five. Matthew's seven. My daughter is four months. She has this rash." She shows me ugly skin eruptions on the baby's neck and jaw. "The carpets, they was filthy from the stuff, the leaks that come down on the wall. All my kids have rashes, but the worst she has it. There was pus all over. Somewhere here I have a letter from the nurse." She shuffles around but cannot find the letter. "She got something underneath the skin. Something that bites. The only way you can get rid of it is with a cream."

She finds the letter. The little girl has scabies.

Laura continues, "I have been living here two years. Before I came here, I was in a house we had to leave. There was rats. Big ones, they crawl on us. The rats, they come at night. They come into our house, run over my son's legs. The windows were broken. It was winter. Snow, it used to come inside. My mother lived with us before. Now she's staying at my grandma's house. My grandma's dying in the bed. She's sixty-five. My mother comes here once a week to do the groceries. Tomorrow she comes. Then she goes back to help my grandma.

"I know my name, and I can write my name, my children's names.   13 To read, I cannot do it. Medicines, I don't know the instructions. I was living here when I was pregnant with Corinne. No, I didn't see no doctor. I was hungry. What I ate was rice and beans, potato chips and soda. Up to now this week we don't have food. People ask me, 'Can you help? Do you got this? Do you got that? I don't like to tell them no. If I have something, I give it. This week, I don't got. I can read baby books—like that, a little bit. If I could read, I would read newspapers. I would like to know what's going on. Matthew, he tells me I am stupid. 'You can't read.' You know, because he wants to read. He don't understand what something is. I tell him 'I don't know it. I don't understand.' People laugh. You feel embarrassed. On the street. Or in the store." She weeps. "There's nothing here."

Laura sweeps one hand in a wide arc, but I can't tell whether she   14 means the gesture to take in the room or something more. Then she makes her meaning clear: "Everything I had, they put it on the sidewalk when I was evicted. I don't know if that's the law. Things like that— what is the law, what isn't? I can't read it, so I didn't understand. I lost everything I had. I sign papers. Somebody could come and take my children. They could come. 'Sign this. Sign that.' I don't know what it says. Adoption papers—I don't know. This here paper that I got I couldn't understand."

She hands me another letter. This one is from the management of   15 the hotel: "This notice is to inform you that your rent is due today. I would appreciate your cooperation in seeing to it that you go to your center today." Another form that she hands me asks her to fill out the names and the ages of her children.

"Papers, documents—people give it to me. I don't know it: I don't   16 understand." She pauses, and then says, "I'm a Catholic. Yes—I go two weeks ago to church. This lady say they have these little books that learn me how to spell. You see the letters. Put them together. I would like to read. I go to St. Francis' Church. Go inside and kneel—I pray. I don't talk to the priest. I done so many things—you know, bad things. I buy a bottle of wine. A bottle of beer. That costs a dollar. I don't want to say to God. I get a hundred and seventy-three dollars restaurant allowance. With that money I buy clothes. Food stamps, I get two hundred dollars.

That's for groceries. Subway tokens I take out ten dollars. Washing machine, I do downstairs. Twenty-five dollars to dry and wash. Five dollars to buy soap. Thirty dollars twice a month."

Another woman at the Martinique calculates her laundry costs at my request, and they come out to nearly the same figure. These may be the standard rates for a midtown site. The difficulty of getting out and travelling to find lower prices, whether for laundromats or for groceries, cannot be overstated. Families at the Martinique are trapped in a commercial district. 17

I ask Laura who stays with the children when she does her chores. 18

"My mother keeps the children when I do the wash," she replies. "If she can't, I ask somebody on the floor. 'Give me three dollars. I watch your kids.' For free? Nothing. Everything for money. Everybody's poor." 19

Extending a hand, she says, "This is the radiator. Something's wrong." She shows me where the steam sprays out. I test it with my hand. "Sometimes it stops. The children get too close. Then it starts— like that! Leak is coming from upstairs down." I see the dark muck on the wall. "The window is broke. Lights broke." She points to the fluorescent tubes. They flicker on and off. "I ask them, 'Please, why don't you give me ordinary lights?' They don't do nothing. So it been two weeks. I go downstairs. They say they coming up. They never come. So I complain again. Mr. Tuccelli—Salvatore Tuccelli, the manager of the Martinique—said to come here to his office. Desks and decorations and a lot of pictures. It's above the lobby. So the manager was there. Mr. Tuccelli sat back in his chair. He had a gun. He had it here under his waist. You know, under his belt. I said, 'Don't show it to me if you isn't going to use it.' I can't tell what kind of gun it was. He had it in his waist. 'You are showing me the gun so I will be afraid.' If he was only going to show it, I would not be scared. If he's going to use it, I get scared. 20

"So he says, 'You people bring us trouble.' I said, 'Why you give my son lead poison and you didn't care? My child is lead-poisoned.' He said, 'I don't want to hear of this again.' What I answer him is this: 'Listen. People like you live in nice apartments. You got a home. You got TV. You got a family. You got children in a school that learn them. They don't got lead poison.' 21

"I don't know the reason for the guards. They let the junkies into the hotel. When my mother comes, I have to sign. If it's a family living good, they make it hard. If it's the drug dealers, they come in. Why they 22 let the junkies in but keep away your mother? The guards, you see them taking women in the corner. You go down twelve-thirty in the night, they're in the corner with the girls. This is true. I seen it."

She continues, "How I know about the lead is this: Matthew sits there and reaches his fingers in the plaster and he put it in his mouth. So I ask him, 'Was you eating it?' He says, 'Don't hit me. Yes, I was.' So then I took him to the clinic and they took the blood. I don't know if something happen to him later on. I don't know if it affects him. When he's older . . ."   23

I ask Laura why she goes to church.   24

"I figure: Go to church. Pray to God. Ask Him to help. I go on my   25
knees. I ask Him from my heart, 'Jesus Christ, come help me, please. Why do you leave me here?' When I'm lying down at night, I ask, 'Why people got to live like this?' On the street, the people stare at you when you go out of the hotel. People look. They think, I wonder how they live in there. Sometimes I walk out this door. Garbage all over in the stairs. When it's hot, a lot of bugs around the trash. Sometimes there are fires in the trash. I got no fire escape. You have to get out through the hall. I got no sprinkler. Smoke detector doesn't work. When I cook and food is burning, it don't ring. If I smoke, it starts to ring. I look up. I say, 'Why you don't work? When I need you, you don't work. I'm gonna knock you down.' I did!" She laughs.

There is a sprinkler system in the corridor. In 1987, the hotel manage-   26
ment informed residents that the fire-alarm system was "inoperable."

I ask Laura if the older children are enrolled in school. Nodding at   27
Michael, her middle son, she says, "This one doesn't go to school. He's five. I need to call tomorrow. Get a quarter. Then you get some papers. Then you got to sign those papers. Then he can start school.

"For this room I pay fifteen hundred dollars for two weeks. I don't   28
pay. The welfare pays. I got to go and get it." The room, although it is undivided, was originally a two-room suite and is being rented at the two-room rate. "They send me this. I'm suppose to sign. I don't know what it is. Lots of things you suppose to sign. I sign it but I don't know what it is."

While we are talking, Matthew comes in and sits beside his mother.   29
He lowers his eyes when I shake his hand.

Laura goes on, "Looking for a house, I go to do it." She explains   30
that she's required to give evidence that she is searching for a place to live. "I can't read, so I can't use the paper. I get dressed. I put my makeup on. If I go like this, they look afraid. They say, 'They going to

destroy the house!' You got to dress the children and look nice. Owners don't want homeless. Don't want welfare. Don't want kids. What I think? If they pay one thousand and five hundred dollars every two weeks, why not pay five hundred dollars for a good apartment?"

She hands me another paper. "Can you tell me what is this?"   31

It's a second letter from the hospital, telling her to bring her son for   32 treatment.

She says, "Every day, my son this week, last week was vomiting.   33 Every time he eat his food, he throw it right back out. I got to take him to the clinic.

"Christmas, they don't got. For my daughter I ask a Cabbage Patch.   34 For my boys I ask for toys. I got them stockings." She throws me four cotton stockings tacked to the wall with nothing in them. "They say, 'Mommy, there's no toys.' I say not to worry. 'You are going to get something.' But they don't. They don't get nothing. I could not afford. No, this isn't my TV. Somebody lended it to me. Christmas tree I can't afford. Christmas I don't spend it happy. I am thinking of the kids. What we do on Christmas is we spend it laying on the bed. If I go outside, I feel a little better. When I'm here, I see those walls, the bed, and I feel sad. If I had my own apartment, maybe there would be another room. Somewhere to walk. Walk back and forth."

I ask here, "How do you relax?"   35

"If I want to rest, relax, I turn out the light and lie down on the   36 bed," she says. "When I met his father, I was seventeen." She says she knew him before she was homeless, when she lived in Brooklyn with her mother. He was working at a pizza parlor near her mother's home. "One night, he bought me liquor. I had never tasted. So he took me to this hallway. Then my mother say that what I did is wrong. So I say that I already did it. So you have to live with what you did. I had the baby. No. I did not want to have abortion. The baby's father I still see. When he has a job, he brings me food. In the summer, he worked in a flower store. He would bring me flowers. Now he don't have any job. So don't bring me flowers."

She sweeps her hand in a broad arc and says again, "Nothing here. I   37 feel embarrassed for the room. Flowers, things like that, you don't got. Pretty things you don't got. Nothing like that. No."

In the window is a spindly geranium plant. It has no flowers, but   38 some of the leaves are green. Before I go, we stand beside the window. Blowing snow hits the panes and blurs the dirt.

"Some of the rooms high up, they got a view," Laura says. "You see   39
the Empire State."

I've noticed this—seen the building from a window. It towers high   40
above the Martinique.

"I talk to this plant. I tell him, 'Grow! Give me one flower!' He   41
don't do it." Then, in an afterthought, "No pets. No. You don't got.
Animals. They don't allow."

It occurs to me that this is one of the few places I have been except a   42
hospital or a reform school where there are hundreds of children and
virtually no pets. A few people keep cats illegally.

"I wish I had a dog," Laura says. "Brown dog. Something to hug."   43

Vocabulary

intolerable (1)—unbearable
convulsions (3)—violent involuntary spasms of the muscles

illiterate (5)—unable to read and
 write

IN YOUR JOURNAL

Briefly, tell the story of Laura and her family in your own words.
Then write about what you think should be done to ensure that Laura's
children have a chance for a happy future. What should the community's responsibility be for the homeless?

A Closer Reading

1. How does Laura's illiteracy affect her life? Use specific examples
   from the text to explain your answer.

2. Why does Laura only buy the more expensive brand-name
   foods?

3. Using the information in the text, tell how much it costs the city
   to keep families like Laura's in hotels.

4. What is "churning"? What does "churning" mean to Laura and
   her children?

Drawing Your Own Conclusions

1. Why do you think so many of the families in welfare hotels consist of single women and children? Where are the men? Re-read the Wideman story on page 68 and the Baker essay on page 39. What responsibilities did the mothers of those young men have?

2. What are some of the reasons that life in the Martinique Hotel is so dangerous for the twelve hundred children who live there?

3. Some people are critical of journalists who interview or photograph people in need or in life-threatening circumstances. They think journalists should take an active role in helping people and not just record what they observe. Others feel that by exposing a life-threatening situation they are creating an awareness that could lead to change. What is your opinion?

4. How does the mother in Pearl Rowe's story (see page 61) cope with her inability to write in English? How does the mother in Kingston's story (see page 85) cope with the loss of her children, her language and her country? In what ways are these women's lives different from and in what ways are they similar to Laura's life?

5. How does Laura's situation correspond to Alvin Toffler's description of the family (see page 103)?

Thinking about Writing

1. What do you think Kozol wants his readers to learn from reading his article? Use the text to support your answer.

2. What do you think Kozol's feelings are for Laura and her family? Use the text to support your answer.

3. Most writers have a specific audience of readers in mind. For whom do you think Kozol was writing this article? On what evidence do you base your answer?

4. Is the purpose of this article to compare, to analyze, to persuade, to describe, to narrate, or a combination of these? Explain the reason for your choice.

*   *   *

Suggestions for Writing

1. Laura and her children have become victims in our society. Some people believe that the only way a victim's life can change is for the victim herself to change, to begin to see that she has power. Write the next five years of Laura's life as she begins to take control of her own life. What should she do first, next, and thereafter?

2. Rewrite this article as a letter to the managers of the Martinique Hotel asking them to make some changes in the hotel.

3. Homelessness and poverty are the biggest problems that American cities face today. What is the responsibility of the cities for their homeless populations? Review your journal entry, and write an essay in which you make concrete suggestions for solutions to this major problem.

4. We have all seen people asking for money on the streets of our cities. Write an essay in which you describe how you make a decision about whether or not to give help. Be specific and use your own experiences to make this essay more informative.

5. Choose one of the characters from any of the selections you have read so far in this book to meet with Laura and to help her change her life. Write an essay in which you explain how you made your choice, describe the two characters' first meeting, and then explain how this character will be able to help Laura.

Strategies for Revision

Kozol's article is the outcome of a series of interviews. We can learn many things from interviews, including information about our own and our classmates' writing. Interview a student who has never seen your writing before. Each of you should make a copy of a draft of your writing. Before you read each other's drafts, discuss these questions:

- How did you decide which question you were going to answer?
- How did you get started writing this piece?
- Did you use an outline, or do you have another technique that you use to organize your thoughts before you begin to write?

- Did you have one main idea that you wanted to convey in your writing?
- Did you learn anything new as you started to write?
- What do you want me to know about this piece before I read it?

(You may add other questions of your own.)

After this discussion, read each other's writing. Now that you know what each of you hoped to accomplish in the writing and have read the pieces, you should be able to talk about them more knowledgeably—discussing strong points and weak areas. Make specific suggestions for improvement.

After your discussion, each of you should revise your writing. Share the revision with one another.

IN YOUR JOURNAL

"A study of the front pages of ten major newspapers found that only about one-quarter—27 percent of the bylines were women's. . . . On network television the picture was similar; researchers found that on the nightly news, 22.2 percent of the stories of CBS were reported by women, 14.4 percent on NBC and 10.5 percent on ABC." What is the role of women in media?

Women's Rights and Media's Wrongs

Martin Lee and Norman Solomon

Martin Lee, investigative journalist and media critic, is the co-founder of FAIR (Fairness and Accuracy in Reporting) and publisher of FAIR's journal *Extra!*. He is also the author of *Acid Dreams: The CIA, LSD and the Sixties Rebellion.* Lee's articles have been published in *Rolling Stone, Newsday, Village Voice, The Nation,* and *San Francisco Chronicle,* among others. He is also a frequent radio commentator and has been interviewed on all the major networks.

Norman Solomon is coauthor of *Killing Our Own: The Disaster of America's Experience with Atomic Radiation.* His news analyses and articles have been published in the *Los Angeles Times, Boston Globe, Chicago Tribune,* and *Baltimore Sun,* among others. He has been a guest on numerous TV and radio programs, including *Crossfire* and *All Things Considered.*

Their book explores the way mass media shapes our news, our perceptions, and our world. The following article discusses the role women play in the media and the way media has treated them.

The printed pages we read, and the broadcasts we tune in, are said to mirror society. But mass media also continue to *shape* our society—reinforcing certain attitudes and actions while discouraging others. If television, for instance, were not capable of fundamentally affecting people's behavior, then corporations would not be spending billions of dollars every month for commercials. If what appears in print had little impact on day-to-day lives, advertisers would not be so heavily invested in newspaper and magazine ads.

For many women, media messages reflect the kind of attitudes that rudely confront them on a daily basis. For people who are black, Latino, Native American or of Asian ancestry, the largely white world of U.S. mass media resonates with many of the prejudices that they repeatedly encounter in a white-dominated country. And for those whose sexual orientation draws them to people of the same gender, the main news media commonly leave them out or put them down. 2

Media that habitually stereotype, debase and overlook the humanity of some of us are not doing a good job of serving any of us. Rather than isolating and pigeonholing the wide diversity of people in the United States, shouldn't the mass media illuminate commonalities and differences, aiming to increase genuine understanding? Instead of recycling the dregs of past prejudicial views, media could help us all to take fresh looks at antiquated preconceptions. 3

All this may sound like nothing more than common sense. But despite all the progress that's been made in recent decades, common nonsense still finds its way into American mass media portrayals of issues surrounding gender and race. 4

Picture this scene at the 1987 Pan Am games: U.S. basketball player Jennifer Gillom dribbles the ball up the court as millions of people across the United States watch on TV. Then they hear CBS commentator Billy Packer say, "Doesn't Gillom remind you of a lady who someday is going to have a nice large family and is going to be a great cook? Doesn't she look like that? She's got just a real pleasant face." 5

Or consider what happened on NBC Television at the 1984 Democratic National Convention, as Geraldine Ferraro—the first woman nominated for national office by a major party—looked out from the podium while the convention hall erupted with cheers from the delegates. On the air, Tom Brokaw provided this narration: "Geraldine Ferraro . . . The first woman to be nominated for Vice President . . . Size six!" 6

When the *Washington Post*'s venerated columnist David Broder wrote that the National Organization for Women was "strident and showboating," *USA Today* founder Al Neuharth liked the comment so much that he quoted it in his own column. Only ten days earlier, another Neuharth commentary had called for the return of the "sky girls" he preferred to look at. "Many of the young, attractive, enthusiastic female flight attendants—then called stewardesses—have been replaced by aging women who are tired of their jobs or by flighty young 7 men who have trouble balancing a cup of coffee," Neuharth complained. He yearned for the days when a flight attendant was "a nurse; unmarried; under age 25; not over 5 feet 4 inches tall; weight less than 115 pounds." This conveyed something of the mentality of the man who invented and ran *USA Today* for its first half-dozen years. His unabashed sexism so appalled many staffers at the newspaper that 175 (out of 426 in the newsroom) quickly signed a letter declaring they were "offended, outraged and embarrassed" by the founding father's column.

Between the lines and between the transmitters is an invisible shrug 8 about the status of women in America. We are told that it's improving— but usually without reference to how bad the situation remains. The mass media, ill-equipped to play a constructive role, are key contributors to the problems facing women. That's not surprising, since news media companies are bastions of male supremacy themselves.

In 1989 men held 94 percent of the top management positions in 9 the U.S. news media. As for reporters, men had the highest profiles. A study of the front pages of ten major newspapers found that only about one-quarter—27 percent—of the bylines were women's. (*USA Today* ranked best at 41 percent; in contrast 16 percent of the *New York Times'* front-page bylines belonged to women.) On network television the picture was similar; researchers found that on the nightly news, 22.2 percent of the stories on CBS were reported by women, 14.4 percent on NBC, and 10.5 percent on ABC. . . .

Women's voices are also scarce in news coverage. Surveys of ten 10 leading newspapers found that 11 percent of people quoted on the front page were female. (For the *New York Times* the figure was five percent.) Betty Friedan called the absence of women on front pages "a symbolic annihilation of women. I don't think it's a systematic attempt to do that by editors, but I do think it is clearly related to the style and content decisions of what makes news, and those are still being defined by men." Said Junior Bridge, a researcher for the surveys: "Is the news that appears on the front page really the news we want? We raise men in this country to believe that things in our daily lives are irrelevant, and things women do are irrelevant." . . .

In 1974, Ann Simonton was the model who appeared on the cover 11 of the *Sports Illustrated* annual swimsuit issue. But, she now says, that type of media emphasis dehumanizes women, encouraging violence against them. In an interview, Simonton described the process this way:

"The media indoctrinates the masses to view women as consumable products. Women, now viewed as 'things,' are much easier to violate and to harm because they aren't seen as human beings." She offered the following equation: *Woman = product = consumption = what one purchases has no will of its own.*

Perhaps the situation in the USA is not much different than in 12 France, where the government Women's Rights Minister, Michele Andre, said: "If a man beats a dog on the street, someone will complain to the animal protection society. But if a man beats his wife in the street, no one moves." In the United States, a country which has no high governmental post for women's rights, the city of Chicago had three times as many shelters for animals as for battered women in 1989; the animal shelters had a total budget several times higher too.

The *Time* magazine cover story "Women Face the '90s" include poll 13 results showing that 88 percent of American women rated rape as an issue "very important" to them. Yet nowhere else in the six-page spread did *Time* so much as mention rape—or any other form of violence against women. While the women of America are justifiably concerned, the media of America paper over the issue.

A brutal assault is apt to be written off as the product of a sick mind, 14 unconnected to the cultural attitudes that go unchallenged and routinely fueled by the dominant media of the country. But, as former Brooklyn district attorney Elizabeth Holtzman says, "Rape is only superficially a sexual act. It is foremost an act of violence, degradation and control . . . Sexual violence against women exists because attitudes dehumanizing women exist." And, she adds, "Society should stop identifying sex with violence and with denigration of women, and that includes the images on television and in the other media."

According to the FBI's national statistics, a forcible rape gets reported to police once every six minutes, and one woman in ten will be raped during her lifetime—an extreme underestimate. Studies calculate that up to one-third of females in the United States will be raped during their lifetimes. Whatever the data, media usually report the figures fatalistically—as if rape were a natural occurrence.

News reporting of rape is selective. "Think of all the women," suggests poet and essayist Katha Pollitt, "who have not entered the folklore of crime because their beatings and/or rapes and/or murders lacked the appropriate ingredients for full-dress media treatment—which include, alas, being white, young, middle-class and, as the tabloids love to say, 'attractive.' " These kinds of imbalances in coverage are magnified when sensationalized stories stress rape as a black-on-white crime. In fact, most rape is *intra*racial.

Also obscured is the reality that—whatever the race of the assailant— 17 rape is almost entirely a male-on-female crime. After the highly-publicized and extremely brutal gang rape of a young woman jogging in New York's Central Park in 1989, such points were rarely discussed in mass media. That was certainly the case when six men and no women appeared on ABC's *This Week with David Brinkley* to discuss the Central Park rape—just another instance of how male voices dominate the media, defining what the "issues" are, and are not.

When a woman publicly charged that Senator Brock Adams—a 18 longtime friend of her family—had sexually assaulted her, *U.S. News and World Report* began its account this way: "The senator is not the first politician accused of hanky-panky." A press that uses "hanky-panky" as a synonym for sexual assault is part of the nation's milieu that tacitly accepts rape.

More than half of the rapes in the United States are perpetrated by 19 men who are not strangers to the women they attack—but you wouldn't know that from our mass media. When rape happens between people who know each other, news coverage is usually skimpy or nonexistent, says Robin Warshaw, author of the landmark book *I Never Called It Rape*. When people don't see "acquaintance rapes" or "date rapes" reported in the media, the implication is that such rapes don't happen, or that there's nothing much wrong with them when they do. And the reporting "still really focuses on what women should do, what limits they should do in order to be safe. There is very little examination of men and why they do it. The focus is on making the woman responsible for being raped."

Until the news media start reporting rape for what is—a viciously 20 violent crime—society will fail to treat it that way. And until the media start defining the prevalence of rape in the U.S. as a crisis, the dominant public messages about rape will imply acceptance.

Vocabulary

dregs (3)—the worthless parts

antiquated (3)—obsolete; old-fashioned

strident (7)—harsh-sounding; shrill

bastions (8)—fortified places

scarce (10)—not common and not plentiful

annihilation (10)—total destruction

apt (14)—likely

denigration (14)—the denial of someone's importance; belittling

fatalistically (15)—inevitably, predeterminedly

intraracial (16)—between members of the same race

perpetrated (19)—committed; was responsible

IN YOUR JOURNAL

What information were you surprised to find out in the Lee and Solomon article? How will reading this article make you a more critical reader of the daily newspaper and observer of television news? What will you be looking out for?

A Closer Reading

1. What makes the comments quoted from Billy Packer, Tom Browkaw, David Broder, and Al Neuharth sexist? Who are each of these men, and how do their actions support the main idea of this article?

2. What does Betty Friedan's calling the absence of women on front pages of newspapers "a symbolic annhilation of women" mean? Who is Betty Friedan, and why is her opinion on this issue used as evidence to support the main point of view in this article?

3. In what way has Ann Simonton reversed her opinion about the *Sports Illustrated* annual swimsuit issue since her appearance in the magazine in 1974?

4. What is the problem with the group on *This Week With David Brinkley* that discussed a gang rape of a woman in a city park?

5. According to this article, what are the problems in the way rape is reported in the media?

Drawing Your Own Conclusions

1. How can the media alter our perceptions of the importance or triviality, seriousness or silliness, danger or ease of a situation? Think about past news events and how they were presented in

the media. How did the presentation affect your response to these events?

2. What should be the responsibility of media to the general public? Why is it impossible to present information without any bias? What steps should the various media take to reduce bias?

3. Why is the term "hanky-panky" an offensive term for sexual assault? What is the connotation of this expression?

4. How does a woman's being "attractive" affect the public's perception of the seriousness of a woman's rape or assault? How does her being white, young, or middle class affect the perception? Why? What has been the role of the media in creating these attitudes? What specific steps can be taken by the media to change these attitudes?

5. What issues do these authors focus on as important to women? Do you think these issues are presented fairly in newspapers, magazines, and on television news?

6. What similarities do you find between the information presented in this article and in the Gelman article on violence on page 304? Reread both articles, looking for similar themes and ideas. Which article do you prefer? Why?

Thinking about Writing

1. What is the main point of this article? Where is it stated?

2. What types of evidence do the writers use to support their ideas? Which of these pieces of evidence is the strongest? Why? Which is the weakest? Why?

3. How do the writers use a variety of rhetorical devices to present information? Where in the article do they compare? use dialogue? narrate a story? explain terms? analyze information? argue a point? Which of these is the overall purpose of this article? On what did you base your answer?

4. What is the tone of this article—serious, humorous, angry, and so on? On what did you base your answer?

*   *   *

Suggestions for Writing

1. Thinking about your classroom discussion, write an essay explaining what you think the media's role should be in presenting information to the general public. What steps should be taken to guard against bias? What steps should be taken to ensure fair and accurate presentation of news that is of interest to both men and women?

2. Is the news that appears on the front page of a major daily newspaper or news magazine the news that you want to read? Look at the front page of a major daily newspaper every day for one week. Write an essay in which you describe what is front page news and why or why not it is the news you want to read. What bias is expressed in the choice of the important front page articles? What kinds of articles are chosen as newsworthy? Which are delegated to the middle pages? What have you learned from this experience about how news is presented to the general public?

3. "The media indoctrinates the masses to view women as consumable products. Women, now viewed as 'things,' are much easier to violate and to harm because they aren't seen as human beings." Do you agree or disagree with this statement? Write an essay in which you present your point of view, supporting it with your personal experiences, your observations, and your readings.

4. Much criticism has been addressed to those who blame the victims for their situations. By suggesting that the way women dress and act is a justification for rape, the media perpetuates this idea. Write an essay in which you discuss the issues raised in this statement. What steps can be taken in presenting information about rape and assault that could change this perception?

Collaborative Project

Divide your class into five groups. One group should read the three major news magazines of that week. The second group should choose and read one major daily newspaper each day for a week. The third group should read a tabloid newspaper each day for one week. The fourth group should watch two hours of television news coverage a day for one week. The fifth group should listen to two hours of radio programs that present current events.

Each group should keep a graph of the news that is presented in the media. How many times are violent actions in which women are victims reported on the front pages or in the first minutes of television news? How many other stories feature women? What is the role of the women—are they women of power, decision makers, women of ideas, caretakers, or victims? What pictures are shown of women in the media that week? Are the women clothed in ordinary clothing or are they in bathing suits, evening gowns, or other semi-clothed states?

At the end of the week, the class should compare their results. What did you learn about the role of media from this experience? Each of you should write a paper discussing your findings and what you learned from this experience.

Strategies for Revision

Lee and Solomon presented and analyzed much complex information about a serious subject. Learning to do this is an important aspect of learning to write effective persuasive essays.

When you have completed the first draft of your writing, reread their article, thinking about what you can learn from their writing about presenting a complex subject. Look at their essay and yours as you ask yourself the following questions:

- How do Lee and Solomon convince their readers that their issue is complex? How do I do this?
- How do they include supporting evidence? Where do they use statistics? quotations? anecdotes? Which of these techniques do I use? Where should I add other types of evidence to make my draft stronger?
- How do Lee and Solomon conclude their essay? Why is it a fitting conclusion? How do I conclude my draft? How can I make it even more effective?

Revise your draft, thinking about these questions. Share your revision with your classmates.

IN YOUR JOURNAL

There are many types of authority in our lives: various people, the government, and our laws tell us what to do. We obey the authorities most of the time. However, almost everyone has questioned authority at one time or another.

Write about authority and how you feel about it. When do you question authority and when do you just accept it?

On Authority and Obedience: An Interview with Herbert Kelman

Edward Krupat

Edward Krupat teaches psychology at Boston College. He has written *People in Cities: The Urban Environment and Its Effects* (1985) and a textbook, *Readings and Conversations in Social Psychology: Psychology Is Social* (1975), which includes chapters detailing research as well as eight conversations with well-known psychologists. The following selection is excerpted from an interview with Herbert Kelman, a professor of social ethics at Harvard University, about the psychology of conformity. Kelman is the author, with Lee Hamilton, of *Crimes of Obedience: Toward a Social Psychology of Authority and Responsibility* (1989).

Kelman: When a holdup man comes to you with a gun saying, "Turn over your money," and you do, one might say you're obeying, but I think that would be an imprecise use of the term. You are complying with his coercive demands because it just would not be smart to do otherwise, but you are not obeying.

The term "obedience to law," for example, implies that you have an obligation to obey, and an obligation to follow. You're not just going along because you've decided it's wiser to do so; you're doing it because the other has the right to make certain demands and you have the obligation to meet them. By contrast, the more standard kind of conformity or influence situation is one in which we are dealing with preferential choices.

Even in the holdup situation I described, people comply because   3
they *prefer* to do it in the sense that, while they have every right to
refuse, it's in their best interest not to refuse. Now, what makes an
authority situation different is that it is one in which a nonchoice element predominates. And, therefore, the kind of challenge it takes to say
"No" is in many ways a more fundamental challenge. You are really
challenging the basic way in which the other has presented herself or
himself. She has said she is an authority and you say, "No, you're not an
authority; you don't have the right to tell me to do that." In other cases,
I agree, there are also challenges involved, but they are more specific.
When you challenge the way a person has presented himself, it requires
a complete redefinition of the situation.

Krupat: Now that I think of it, my sixth-grade teacher never did say   4
to me "How dare you nonconform!" She always said, "How dare you
disobey!" But then, where does obedience begin; why do individuals
accept a person's legitimacy in the first place? Is there something inherent in the relationship between a parent and a child, a citizen and the
government, which makes them obey, makes them feel they have *no*
choice? Is this a type of "blind" conformity?

Kelman: My answer to that has to be a bit long and complicated. To   5
begin with, I want to distinguish between authority and legitimacy, on
the one hand, and unquestioning obedience to authority, on the other. I
happen to believe in the importance and necessity of authority in any
kind of social system, but I do not believe in *unquestioned* authority. So I
do not want to identify acceptance of authority with this kind of blind
or unquestioning obedience. This may be one way of reacting to authority, and we have evidence that it is a fairly common way, but it is not
necessarily the *only* way.

A major reason why authority exists in social systems is that it would   6
be difficult to run a system without it. Take the political system, for
example. In order to administer complex institutions effectively, to allo-
cate resources and adjudicate competing interests equitably, and to manage international relations dependably, the government must be able to
assume that its demands—within certain specified limits—will be met,
even if they do not correspond with the short-term preferences of every
citizen. This, in turn, implies that the authorities must be trusted—
which is really, to a large extent, what is meant by *legitimate* authority. If
the system is to operate smoothly, a certain degree of credit or trust
must be extended to people in responsible positions. . . . But, that trust
has to be earned, and so does the continuation of that trust. Once

people have been put in positions of authority, they have to act within certain constraints in order to maintain the trust of system members. *Legitimacy* implies the use of power within specified limits, rather than in arbitrary fashion. If leaders abuse their authority, if they go beyond the limits of what they are allowed to do by virtue of their position, they must be held accountable. And this clearly calls for a readiness, among system members, to question authority—to challenge policies and demands that exceed the bounds of legitimacy.

Krupat: Yet, as you've said, the evidence is that for a great many 7 individuals authority goes unquestioned. Where and how does the individual come to both respect, and also potentially to question, authority?

Kelman: From the point of view of the individual, this is something 8 that has to be learned. Acceptance of authority itself presupposes a fairly advanced stage of moral development, which recognizes the need for certain kinds of rules and mechanisms in the society that make it possible to balance the interests of individuals in various segments of the society, and to coordinate complex social processes so that everyone's rights will be protected and needs will be met. But questioning of authority calls for a *higher* stage of moral development, which recognizes that—even though there is a need for such rules and mechanisms, which imply delegating authority to certain people and the obligation of individuals to obey laws and meet authoritative demands even when they are not personally convenient—these rules and mechanisms cannot be justified as ends in themselves. They have to be justified by reference to certain higher principles, which means essentially that the person also has an obligation to evaluate and question authority.

Now, disobedience of laws or authoritative demands is something 9 that, in my view, ought not to be undertaken lightly; it ought not to be done simply because you find a particular law inconvenient or uncongenial to your own interests. But, under special circumstances, when you feel that a higher principle demands it, the right to disobey—in fact, the *duty* to disobey—is in my opinion a very crucial one. . . .

Krupat: It's not very difficult for me to infer that you believe that we 10 could do with some more healthy independence when it comes to accepting influence in general. As a final matter, to what do you think the person's ability to question authority is related, and how can we bring about more of it?

Kelman: To me, the degree to which people are able to question 11 authority depends on their sense of personal efficacy, on their feeling of personal power and control.

Vocabulary

imprecise (1)—vague, indefinite
coercive (1)—intended to force
   someone to do something
preferential (2)—giving priority
   or advantage

inherent (4)—basic; essential
uncongenial (9)—unfriendly
efficacy (11)—effectiveness

IN YOUR JOURNAL

In this interview Kelman explains the need for authority as well as the need to question authority. Write as many ideas as you can remember from what you have just read. What in this selection did you think about for the first time?

A Closer Reading

1. Why is the holdup man incident mentioned by Kelman *not* a good example of "obeying"? What term does Krupat use instead of "obeying"?
2. Read the paragraph in which the term "nonchoice element" appears. What does Kelman mean by this term?
3. Why does Kelman think that societies need "authority"?
4. What does "legitimacy" mean to Kelman?
5. When does Kelman think that individuals have a "*duty* to disobey"? What examples does he provide of reasons why individuals should disobey?

Drawing Your Own Conclusions

1. How do we show our "obedience to law" in our everyday lives? What are examples of laws that most of us follow without questioning? Why do you think we do not question these laws?
2. How and where do children learn to accept authority figures? Be specific in your answer.
3. Why do you think Kelman refers to the questioning of authority in paragraph 8 as a "*higher* stage of moral development"?

4. Under what circumstances might Kelman consider committing a crime to be an appropriate response to unreasonable authority?

5. In what ways is the little boy's taking of the money under the cup in John Edgar Wideman's story (see page 68) different from the circumstances described in this essay?

6. How do you think Krupat and Kelman would explain the tenants in the hotel (see Kozol, page 530) defying the management's authority?

Thinking about Writing

1. In paragraphs 5 and 6, Kelman attempts to distinguish between unquestioned authority and legitimate authority. What examples does he use? Are they clear and are there a sufficient number for you to understand the distinction?

2. What in this interview suggests to you that either Krupat or Kelman used notes when this conversation took place? When you have conducted interviews, did you have some of your questions prepared? Why would someone do this before beginning an interview?

3. Is Kelman's purpose to persuade people to question authority, to explain and illustrate his ideas, to tell a story, to teach a process, or to compare and contrast different points of view? Use examples from the interview to support your answer.

4. Compare Bill Moyers's question (see page 409), Pat Murphy's questions (see page 481), and those of Krupat. What did you learn about the interviewing process from reading these interviews?

*   *   *

Suggestions for Writing

1. Write an essay in which you define "legitimate authority," and use examples from your existence and readings to illustrate this concept.

2. If you have ever been in a courtroom, write an essay describing the procedures you witnessed there. What did the room look like? How did the judge act? How did the judge act? How did

the lawyers behave? How were the witnesses treated? How did any of them question authority? If you have never been in a courtroom, you might want to visit night court or observe a trial in your city. Take notes as you observe, and then write your essay.

3. Every social system has a need for authority, but this should not be *unquestioned* authority. In order for a system to work well, there must be people who are willing to take the risk of questioning existing rules and laws. Write an essay agreeing or disagreeing with this view. Support your point of view with examples from your observations of the world around you, your experiences, and your readings.

4. Imagine that your area has been chosen to be the largest site in the country for burial of toxic waste. Write an essay in which you outline what you could do to question the authority that has made this decision. When, if ever, do you think it would be appropriate to commit a crime in dealing with this issue?

Strategies for Revision

In a group with three other students, write the word "REVISION" at the top of a piece of paper, and together list your ideas about what is important to you as you write a revision or make suggestions to another student.

List at least ten considerations that you think about when you look at your own or someone else's writing. How do you make suggestions for change? How do you know when a piece of writing is complete? What is the most difficult part of revision for you? What works best when revising individually, with a partner, or in a small group?

When you have developed your ideas to everyone's satisfaction, each student should read a draft of writing pertaining to this selection to the group. Everyone should make enough copies to share with the group. Members can make suggestions for improvement based on the considerations the group has listed. At the end of the discussion, each of you can then revise your writing and share it with the others again.

IN YOUR JOURNAL

According to the author of the next selection, "the chimpanzee is more like us, genetically, than any other animal." Because of this similarity, the chimpanzee is frequently used in medical research. The question remains as to how we should treat this captive animal as we inflict upon it a variety of diseases and often pain. Before you read this selection, write about what you think of our using animals in medical research.

Write the first thoughts that come into your mind on this topic. Write for at least three minutes without stopping.

A Plea for the Chimps

Jane Goodall

Born in London, England, Jane Goodall has lived for many years at the Gombe Stream Research Center in Tanzania, East Africa. She is well known for her work with chimpanzees and has written extensively about her relationship with these animals. Her books include *Primate Behavior* (1965), *My Friends, the Wild Chimpanzees* (1967), *My Life with Chimpanzees* (1988), and *Through a Window: My Thirty Years with the Chimpanzees of Gombe* (1990). She published several books with Hugo Van Lawick, including *In the Shadow of Man* (1971) and *Grub: The Bush Baby* (1972). "A Plea for the Chimps" appeared in the *New York Times Magazine* of May 17, 1987. It describes the living conditions of research chimps and suggests ways that these conditions could be improved.

The chimpanzee is more like us, genetically, than any other animal.   1
It is because of similarities in physiology, in biochemistry, in the immune system, that medical science makes use of the living bodies of chimpanzees in its search for cures and vaccines for a variety of human diseases.

There are also behavioral, psychological and emotional similarities   2
between chimpanzees and humans, resemblances so striking that they raise a serious ethical question: are we justified in using an animal so close to us—an animal, moreover, that is highly endangered in its African forest home—as a human substitute in medical experimentation?

In the long run, we can hope that scientists will find ways of exploring human physiology and disease, and of testing cures and vaccines, that do not depend on the use of living animals of any sort. A number of steps in this direction already have been taken, prompted in large part by a growing public awareness of the suffering that is being inflicted on millions of animals. More and more people are beginning to realize that nonhuman animals—even rats and guinea pigs—are not just unfeeling machines but are capable of enjoying their lives, and of feeling fear, pain and despair. 3

But until alternatives have been found, medical science will continue to use animals in the battle against human disease and suffering. And some of those animals will continue to be chimpanzees. 4

Because they share with us 99 percent of their genetic material, chimpanzees can be infected with some human diseases that do not infect other animals. They are currently being used in research on the nature of hepatitis non-A non-B, for example, and they continue to play a major role in the development of vaccines against hepatitis B. 5

Many biomedical laboratories are looking to the chimpanzee to help them in the race to find a vaccine against acquired immune deficiency syndrome. Chimpanzees are not good models for AIDS research; although the AIDS virus stays alive and replicates within the chimpanzee's bloodstream, no chimp has yet come down with the disease itself. Nevertheless, many of the scientists involved argue that only by using chimpanzees can potential vaccines be safely tested. 6

Given the scientists' professed need for animals in research, let us turn aside from the sensitive ethical issue of whether chimpanzees *should* be used in medical research, and consider a more immediate issue: how are we treating the chimpanzees that are actually being used? 7

Just after Christmas I watched, with shock, anger and anguish, a videotape—made by an animal-rights group during a raid—revealing the conditions in a large biomedical research laboratory, under contract to the National Institutes of Health, in which various primates, including chimpanzees, are maintained. In late March, I was given permission to visit the facility. 8

It was a visit I shall never forget. Room after room was lined with small, bare cages, stacked one above the other, in which monkeys circled round and round and chimpanzees sat huddled, far gone in depression and despair. 9

Young chimpanzees, 3 or 4 years old, were crammed, two together, into tiny cages measuring 22 inches by 22 inches and only 24 inches 10 high. They could hardly turn around. Not yet part of any experiment, they had been confined in these cages for more than three months.

The chimps had each other for comfort, but they would not remain   11
together for long. Once they are infected, probably with hepatitis, they will be separated and placed in another cage. And there they will remain, living in conditions of severe sensory deprivation, for the next several years. During that time, they will become insane.

A juvenile female rocked from side to side, sealed off from the   12
outside world behind the glass doors of her metal isolation chamber. She was in semidarkness. All she could hear was the incessant roar of air rushing through vents into her prison.

In order to demonstrate the "good" relationship the lab's caretaker   13
had with this chimpanzee, one of the scientists told him to lift her from the cage. The caretaker opened the door. She sat, unmoving. He reached in. She did not greet him—nor did he greet her. As if drugged, she allowed him to take her out. She sat motionless in his arms. He did not speak to her, she did not look at him. He touched her lips briefly. She did not respond. He returned her to her cage. She sat again on the bars of the floor. The door closed.

I shall be haunted forever by her eyes, and by the eyes of the other   14
infant chimpanzees I saw that day. Have you ever looked into the eyes of a person who, stressed beyond endurance, has given up, succumbed utterly to the crippling helplessness of despair? I once saw a little African boy, whose whole family had been killed during the fighting in Burundi. He too looked out at the world, unseeing, from dull, blank eyes.

Though this particular laboratory may be one of the worst, from   15
what I have learned, most of the other biomedical animal-research facilities are not much better. Yet only when one has some understanding of the true nature of the chimpanzee can the cruelty of these captive conditions be fully understood.

Chimpanzees are very social by nature. Bonds between individuals,   16
particularly between family members and close friends, can be affectionate, supportive, and can endure throughout their lives. The accidental separation of two friendly individuals may cause them intense distress. Indeed, the death of a mother may be such a psychological blow to her child that even if the child is 5 years old and no longer dependent on its mother's milk, it may pine away and die.

It is impossible to overemphasize the importance of friendly physi-   17
cal contact for the well-being of the chimpanzee. Again and again one

can watch a frightened or tense individual relax if she is patted, kissed or embraced reassuringly by a companion. Social grooming, which provides hours of close contact, is undoubtedly the single most important social activity.

Chimpanzees in their natural habitat are active for much of the day. They travel extensively within their territory, which can be as large as 50 square kilometers for a community of about 50 individuals. If they hear other chimpanzees calling as they move through the forest, or anticipate arriving at a good food source, they typically break into excited charging displays, racing along the ground, hurling sticks and rocks and shaking the vegetation. Youngsters, particularly, are full of energy, and spend long hours playing with one another or by themselves leaping through the branches and gamboling along the ground. Adults sometimes join these games. Bunches of fruit, twigs and rocks may be used as toys.   18

Chimpanzees enjoy comfort. They construct sleeping platforms each night, using a multitude of leafy twigs to make their beds soft. Often, too, they make little "pillows" on which to rest during a midday siesta.   19

Chimps are highly intelligent. They display cognitive abilities that were, until recently, thought to be unique to humans. They are capable of cross-model transfer or information—that is, they can identify by touch an object they previously have only seen, and vice versa. They are capable of reasoned thought, generalization, abstraction and symbolic representation. They have some concept of self. They have excellent memories and can, to some extent, plan for the future. They show a capacity for intentional communication that depends, in part, on their ability to understand the motives of the individuals with whom they are communicating.   20

Chimpanzees are capable of empathy and altruistic behavior. They show emotions that are undoubtedly similar, if not identical, to human emotions—joy, pleasure, contentment, anxiety, fear and rage. They even have a sense of humor.   21

The chimpanzee child and the human child are alike in many ways: in their capacity for endless romping and fun; their curiosity; their ability to learn by observation, imitation and practice; and, above all, in their need for reassurance and love. When young chimpanzees are brought up in a human home and treated like human children, they learn to eat at a table, to help themselves to snacks from the refrigerator, to sort and put away cutlery, to brush their teeth, to play with dolls, to   22 switch on the television and select a program that interests them and watch it.

Young chimpanzees can easily learn over 200 signs of the American 23
language of the deaf and use these signs to communicate meaningfully with humans and with one another. One youngster, in the laboratory of Dr. Roger S. Fouts, a psychologist at Central Washington University, has picked up 68 signs from four older signing chimpanzee companions, with no human teaching. The chimp uses the signs in communication with other chimpanzees and with humans.

The chimpanzee facilities in most biomedical research laboratories 24
allow for the expression of almost none of these activities and behaviors. They provide little—if anything—more than the warmth, food and water, and veterinary care required to sustain life. The psychological and emotional needs of these creatures are rarely catered to, and often not even acknowledged.

In most labs the chimpanzees are housed individually, one chimp to 25
a cage, unless they are part of a breeding program. The standard size of each cage is about 25 feet square and about 6 feet high. In one facility, a cage described in the catalogue as "large," designed for a chimpanzee of up to 25 kilograms (55 pounds), measures 2 feet 6 inches by 3 feet 8 inches, with a height of 5 feet 4 inches. Federal requirements for cage size are dependent on body size; infant chimpanzees, who are the most active, are often imprisoned in the smallest cages.

In most labs, the chimpanzees cannot even lie with their arms and 26
legs outstretched. They are not let out to exercise. There is seldom anything for them to do other than eat, and then only when food is brought. The caretakers are usually too busy to pay much attention to individual chimpanzees. The cages are bleak and sterile, with bars above, bars below, bars in every side. There is no comfort in them, no bedding. The chimps, infected with human diseases, will often feel sick and miserable.

What of the human beings who administer these facilities—the care- 27
takers, the veterinarians and scientists who work at them? If they are decent, compassionate people, how can they condone, or even tolerate, the kind of conditions I have described?

They are, I believe, victims of a system that was set up long before 28
the cognitive abilities and emotional needs of chimpanzees were understood. Newly employed staff members, equipped with a normal measure of compassion, may well be sickened by what they see. And, in fact,

many of them do quit their jobs, unable to endure the suffering they see inflicted on the animals yet feeling powerless to help.

But others stay on and gradually come to accept the cruelty, believ-   29
ing (or forcing themselves to believe) that it is an inevitable part of the struggle to reduce human suffering. Some become hard and callous in the process, in Shakespeare's words, "all pity choked with custom of fell deeds."

A handful of compassionate and dedicated caretakers and veterinari-   30
ans are fighting to improve the lot of the animals in their care. Vets are often in a particularly difficult position, for if they stand firm and try to uphold high standards of humane care, they will not always be welcome in the lab.

Many of the scientists believe that a bleak, sterile and restricting   31
environment is necessary for their research. The cages must be small, the scientists maintain, because otherwise it is too difficult to treat the chimpanzees—to inject them, to draw their blood or to anesthetize them. Moreover, they are less likely to hurt themselves in small cages.

The cages must also be barren, with no bedding or toys, say the   32
scientists. This way, the chimpanzees are less likely to pick up diseases or parasites. Also if things are lying about, the cages are harder to clean.

And the chimpanzees must be kept in isolation, the scientists be-   33
lieve, to avoid the risk of cross-infection, particularly in hepatitis research.

Finally, of course, bigger cages, social groups and elaborate furnish-   34
ings require more space, more caretakers—and more money. Perhaps, then, if we are to believe these researchers, it is not possible to improve conditions for chimpanzees imprisoned in biomedical research laboratories.

I believe not only that it *is* possible, but that improvements are   35
absolutely necessary. If we do not do something to help these creatures, we make a mockery of the whole concept of justice.

Perhaps the most important way we can improve the quality of life   36
for the laboratory chimps is to increase the number of carefully trained caretakers. These people should be selected for their understanding of animal behavior and their compassion and respect for, and dedication to, their charges. Each caretaker, having established a relationship of trust with the chimpanzees in his care, should be allowed to spend time with the animals over and above that required for cleaning the cages and providing the animals with food and water.

It has been shown that a chimpanzee who has a good relationship 37
with his caretaker will cooperate calmly during experimential procedures, rather than react with fear or anger. At the Dutch Primate Research Center at Rijswijk, for example, some chimpanzees have been
trained to leave their group cage on command and move into small,
single cages for treatment. At the Stanford Primate Center in California,
a number of chimpanzees were taught to extend their arms for the
drawing of blood. In return they were give a food reward.

Much can be done to alleviate the pain and stress felt by younger 38
chimpanzees during experimental procedures. A youngster, for example, can be treated when in the presence of a trusted human friend.
Experiments have shown that young chimps react with high levels of
distress if subjected to mild electric shocks when alone, but show almost
no fear or pain when held by a sympathetic caretaker.

What about cage size? Here we should emulate the animal-protection 39
regulations that already exist in Switzerland. These laws stipulate that a
cage must be, at minimum, about 20 meters square and 3 meters high for
pairs of chimpanzees.

The chimpanzees should never be housed alone unless this is an 40
essential part of the experimental procedure. For chimps in solitary
confinement, particularly youngsters, three to four hours of friendly
interaction with a caretaker should be mandatory. A chimp taking part
in hepatitis research, in which the risk of cross-infection is, I am told,
great, can be provided with a companion of a compatible species if it
doesn't infringe on existing regulations—a rhesus monkey, for example,
which cannot catch or pass on the disease.

For healthy chimpanzees there should be little risk of infection from 41
bedding and toys. Stress and depression, however, can have deleterious
effects on their health. It is known that clinically depressed humans are
more prone to a variety of physiological disorders, and heightened
stress can interfere with immune function. Given the chimpanzee's similarities to humans, it is not surprising that the chimp in a typical laboratory, alone in his bleak cage, is an easy prey to infections and parasites.

Thus, the chimpanzees also should be provided with a rich and 42
stimulating environment. Climbing apparatus should be obligatory.
There should be many objects for them to play with or otherwise
manipulate. A variety of simple devices designed to alleviate boredom
could be produced quite cheaply. Unexpected food items will elicit great
pleasure. If a few simple buttons in each cage were connected to a
computer terminal, it would be possible for the chimpanzees to feel they

at least have some control over their world—if one button produced a grape when pressed, another a drink, or another a video picture. (The Canadian Council on Animal Care recommends the provision of television for primates in solitary confinement, or other means of enriching their environment.)

Without doubt, it will be considerably more costly to maintain   43 chimpanzees in the manner I have outlined. Should we begrudge them the extra dollars? We take from them their freedom, their health and often their lives. Surely, the least we can do is try to provide them with some of the things that could make their imprisonment more bearable.

There are hopeful signs. I was immensely grateful to officials of the   44 National Institutes of Health for allowing me to visit the primate facility, enabling me to see the conditions there and judge them for myself. And I was even more grateful for the fact that they gave me a great deal of time for serious discussions of the problem. Doors were opened and a dialogue begun. All who were present at the meetings agreed that, in light of present knowledge, it is indeed necessary to give chimpanzees a better deal in the labs. . . .

I have had the privilege of working among wild, free chimpanzees   45 for more than 26 years. I have gained a deep understanding of chimpanzee nature. Chimpanzees have given me so much in my life. The least I can do is to speak out for the hundreds of chimpanzees who, right now, sit hunched, miserable and without hope, staring out with dead eyes from their metal prisons. They cannot speak for themselves.

Vocabulary

replicates (6)—reproduces

professed (7)—openly declared

sensory (11)—connected with the sense impressions

incessant (12)—constant; unceasing

succumbed (14)—given yp

altruistic (21)—unselfishly concerned for others

condone (27)—to treat as if something is harmless

mockery (35)—a ridiculing imitation

alleviate (38)—to relieve; to reduce

deleterious (41)—injurious; destructive

begrudge (43)—to give unwillingly

IN YOUR JOURNAL

How do you feel about these chimps now that you have read this article? Have your attitudes changed in any way? Imagine your pet in the same situation. What new feelings emerge with this idea? Write down your various thoughts.

A Closer Reading

1. What evidence does Goodall use to argue that changes should be made in the treatment of research chimpanzees? According to her article, what are some of the changes that could be made to improve the quality of life of the research chimp?

2. What do you find out about Goodall from reading this article that makes her qualified to write about the chimps?

3. What specific examples does Goodall cite of poor treatment of the research chimps? What facilities did she visit, and what does she report about these visits?

4. What specific suggestions does Goodall make for improving the chimps' quality of life?

5. What suggestions does Goodall make in relation to caretakers? What qualities should be sought in hiring and training caretakers?

Drawing Your Own Conclusions

1. Did Goodall write this article to persuade researchers not to use chimps for research? If not, what is the purpose of the article? Use the article for evidence to support your answer.

2. Why is isolation so destructive to chimps? What similarities between chimps and humans does Goodall cite with regard to isolation?

3. What are some of the similarities between a human child and a chimpanzee child? How could this knowledge be used to create better environments for young chimps?

4. In paragraph 41 Goodall writes:

It is known that clinically depressed humans are more prone to a variety of physiological disorders, and heightened stress can interfere with immune function. Given the chimpanzee's similarities to humans, it is not surprising that the chimp in a typical laboratory, alone in his bleak cage, is an easy prey to infections and parasites.

What does this suggest to you about the accuracy of the findings in such research?

5. Describe the research environment that Goodall would find acceptable. Use the article to gather your data.

6. How do you think Kelman (see page 550) would interpret the situation described in this article in which Goodall makes a "legal" attempt to help research chimps? How might he interpret the actions of those who illegally break into research labs and free the animals?

Thinking about Writing

1. Goodall begins this piece with these words: "The chimpanzee is more like us, genetically, than any other animal." What effect did this statement have on you as a reader? Why does Goodall begin the essay this way?

2. At first, Goodall discusses the ethical question of using animals in research, and then she moves to discussion of the specific treatment of research chimps. Using the article, point out where the change takes place. Why do you think she begins with the ethical question? Why do you think she does not continue with this line of reasoning?

3. Goodall makes suggestions for improvements. Where are these suggestions found in the article? Why do you think she places the suggestions at this point?

4. What makes Goodall's conclusion different from the rest of the article? Is it an effective conclusion?

5. What specific words and phrases in this article tell you that Goodall is writing about an issue that is of great importance to her? In what ways do you see that her emotional involvement adds to the persuasive tone of this article?

*   *   *

Suggestions for Writing

As a class or in small groups, discuss the following questions in order to help you write a persuasive essay:

- What makes an essay persuasive?
- Should the writer be an authority on the issue?
- Should the writer use facts?
- Should the writer include quotes from other sources?
- Should the writer rely on personal experience?
- Should the writer remain detached and objective?
- Should the writer be emotional and subjective?
- Which persuasive essays that you have read in this book did you prefer? What about them worked for you?

Apply some of the ideas and techniques of persuasive writing that you have discussed in writing some of the following essays. You may prefer to choose an essay involving descriptive writing for one of the last two suggestions.

1. Since chimpanzees are so similar to humans genetically, are scientists justified in using these animals in medical research and experimentation? Write an essay in which you take a position, supporting it with your observations and readings. It would be helpful to go to the library and read about this issue before you begin to write.

2. Should research laboratories invest additional money in improving the conditions of the research animals? Write an essay in which you take a position, supporting it with your observations and readings. It would be helpful to go to the library and read about this issue before you begin to write.

3. Many people accept the use of animals in medical research but do not believe animals should be blinded or put through pain to test cosmetics and household products. Write an essay in which you agree or disagree with this position, supporting it with your observations and readings.

4. Recently people concerned about animal rights broke into research laboratories and removed the animals from these facilities. Write an essay in which you agree or disagree with this

action. In order to understand this issue better, you may need to review articles from the newspapers and news magazines in your library.

5. Visit the animal lab facility in your college. Write an essay describing the conditions that you encountered. Evaluate those conditions based on what you understand of Goodall's criteria for ideal lab conditions.

6. Visit a local zoo. Write an essay describing the conditions that you observed. Evaluate those conditions based on what you understand of Goodall's criteria for an ideal animal environment.

Strategies for Revision

Before you begin the revision process, in a group of four students, write down what you believe are the five most important criteria for an essay. Then add three other qualities that you look for when you read a persuasive essay.

Use your list as an evaluation tool when you read one another's essays. Write the list on a blank piece of paper each time you read an essay. Read each draft in your group, looking to see if it fulfills your criteria. Write next to the first item on your list the strengths and weaknesses of draft 1 with regard to this item. Then do the same with the next item. Continue until you have finished the list. Then do the same with draft 2 until you have finished all the drafts in your group. You will get back your draft and the three responses from group members. Read them carefully.

Ask the other group members any questions you may have about their comments on your draft. Then, considering their suggestions, revise. Share your revision with the group. Keep the list and use it when you review other drafts of your writing.

Georganne Snyder wrote the following essay in response to suggestion 2 from the Suggestions for Writing that follow the Richardson
Smith selection: Write an essay in which you describe a difficult decision that you had to make to resolve a conflict in your life. Explain the
situation, the conflict, and your decision. What did you learn about
yourself from going through this process?

Pursuit of a Goal

Georganne Snyder

Often people reach a point in their lives when they want to make   1
changes. This represents a turning point, and it causes people to evaluate
themselves and set goals. Recently, I chose to pursue my college degree
and a future career instead of having a family, because now I have a job
which offers few opportunities for financial gain, or advancement. I am
limited to a position which is unrewarding and unchallenging. Presently,
the roles available to me are that of housewife, mother and employee in
unskilled and low paying jobs. I want and deserve more from my life.
Therefore after much consideration, I choose to pursue my college degree, because it will provide me with better job opportunities, increased
earning potential, a personal accomplishment and the freedom to pursue
future goals.

I realize that by deciding not to have children I am sacrificing many   2
pleasant experiences unique to families such as the first step, kindergar-
ten, graduation and so on. However, children create hindrances to
personal or professional advancement. As a step parent, I know that
children create both blessings and responsibilities. In making this decision, I considered the possibility of having a child while going to
school, but this would not allow me to devote myself fully to one or the
other. Consequently, if I had a child my goal for a degree or a career
would become secondary, because this child would need, and should
receive much of my time. Since I do not wish to make a half-hearted
attempt at either pursuit, I had to make this difficult choice.

By choosing to pursue my college degree, I access more challenging   3
jobs and enjoy the experience of learning many new things. I want a
degree in secondary education, English, and Spanish because I hope to
teach adolescents to construct papers effectively, appreciate literature,

and to communicate using good English and Spanish. By choosing to teach, I value the added benefit of working with children every day, and in many ways influencing their lives like a parent. For example, when I was a child I had an English teacher, Mr. Clara, who I believed understood some of the most wonderful aspects of life. As he taught me the literature of William Shakespeare, Edgar Allen Poe, Emily Dickinson, Robert Frost, Robert Browning, and many other authors of poetry and prose, and taught me to write fairly well, he created for me a new appreciation for education and a different way of looking at life. Also, Mr. Clara believed in his students. He took the time to talk to each of them, understand them and help them cope with becoming adults. Moreover, he was a model of good character, values, and success.

As I look back to Mr. Clara and other teachers who have given me so   4
much, I want to have the same kinds of good influences, and enjoy inspiring students to believe in themselves.

Facing the challenge of college and a new career, and giving up   5
motherhood at age 31 with my biological clock ticking loudly is frightening, but many women confront the same difficult decision. According to Anita Gates of *Working Woman,* the tough times of unemployment and the recession have caused many women to make career and lifestyle changes, ". . . especially if there's something . . . they've always wanted to do" (Gates 57). Also, Helen Lucas of the New York executive search firm Tama Lucas, Ltd., says "Clients who are interested in . . . careers are far more serious about making a change than they used to be, . . . They ask tougher questions . . . [and] want to be sure they find new situations that will enhance their lives and their sense of security" (Gates 58).

Certainly a college degree will qualify me for a better job. Peter D.   6
Syverson, the director of information services at the Council of Graduate Schools says, "there is some defensive credentialing going on. If you are worried about keeping the job you've got, or if you're concerned about getting a new [better] job . . . you may earn a degree" (Gates 59). Now, I work as a sales person at a local lumber yard making only $16,000.00 a year; and if I am lucky, I get a raise of $500.00 a year. My schedule is terrible! I work several nights a week, twelve hour days, every weekend, all year long. Even though I have been the sales transaction leader in the company for three years (meaning I make the most number of sales every month), I never get any positive feedback from the boss or my customers for my service. I am expected to remain on

top and give my customers excellent and prompt service with a smile. As well, my boss is a narrow-minded man who refers to me as a "good girl," but promotes only males within his company because he fails to recognize the potential of his female employees.

As a college graduate, I will have more earning potential, and I will enjoy better job opportunities. Granted teachers are not highly paid, but many people appreciate them. Also, they can observe their students making progress and enjoy this accomplishment; they make more than $16,000.00 a year; they work week days and enjoy summers off; and especially if they do not have children of their own they can pursue future goals such as higher education and other job opportunities during their time off.   7

I am not pursuing a career in education blindly. I recognize that with a teaching job come many responsibilities; such as lesson plans which effectively reach students with varying learning styles and abilities, tests to prepare, papers to grade, discipline problems to resolve and so on. However, I welcome the challenge, and I enjoy studying new things. Through my college education, I am experiencing a personal accomplishment little by little. To be clearer, with each step taken, each test, each paper written, each project and each semester successfully completed I move closer to attaining one of my personal goals, an accomplishment, my college degree. Although many people have degrees, this remains one of my personal goals. I want and deserve to earn it.   8

Since I am already 31 and a year away from earning my degree, I know that I may not get to enjoy both motherhood and a career. This does make me feel sad, but through working on my bachelor's degree, and doing quite well in college I have realized that I can handle the responsibility of education, and I am confident that I will succeed in my goal to become a teacher. Furthermore, through my experience in college I have identified my educational strengths and interests, and have set goals for future educational pursuits and possible alternative employment.   9

I chose to pursue my college degree because it will establish better job opportunities with better pay, and because I need to fulfill my goals. Often when people die, they are remembered for what they accomplished, or what they contributed to society. So far, my challenge of a degree, and a career has enriched my life. Consequently, I want to leave a positive imprint on other people.   10

Work Cited

Gates, Anita, "A Guide to Changing Careers in the 90's," *Working Woman*, April 1992: 57–63.

Questions to Think About

1. What was Georganne Snyder's conflict? How does she show her readers both sides of her problem?

2. Where does she explain her decision? Where else could she have placed this in the essay? Try moving her decision somewhere else in the essay. Which placement do you prefer? Why?

3. What reasons did Snyder give for making the decision she made?

4. Where does Snyder use quotations? What is the purpose of including them?

5. What information does Snyder include to support her statement that she is not pursuing a career in education blindly? Does she convince you?

6. What is the purpose of her conclusion? In what ways is it effective?

7. What do you think Snyder learned about herself from writing this essay?

MAKING CONNECTIONS

The World in Reflection: *Examining Complex Issues*

1. Write a dialogue that Jonathan Kozol (see page 530) and Herbert Kelman and Edward Krupat (see page 550) might have about authority in its role of maintaining the status quo (keeping things they way they are) in our society. What suggestions do you think they would make about how individuals should or should not confront authority in order to make changes in their lives?

2. Why has our society evolved into one of difference and separation—of men and women, blacks and whites, rich and poor, educated and uneducated, pro-life and pro-choice, and so on? In an essay, explain the development of these differences and what it means for our society today. Should members of society try to work together? What steps can be taken through education, religion, mass media, and so on to make this possible? Refer to some of the selections you have read or some of the writing you have done in this unit to support your point of view.

3. Imagine that Shelby Steele (see page 517) and Martin Lee and Norman Solomon (see page 541) met to discuss the role that media has played in our perceptions of race. After rereading their selections, write a dialogue that reflects their points of view. Use quotes and paraphrases from their selections in addition to your own interpretations of their ideas.

4. Why do many of us feel ambivalent about our relationships to other people? We need others to enrich our lives, yet we are also aware that our relationships bring responsibilities and problems. Write an essay in which you explore this issue. You may want to paraphrase or directly quote from some of the selections you have read or some of the writing you have done in this unit.

5. Write an essay in which you choose one piece of writing that made you reflect on a complex issue in a new way. Explain what you learned from the piece of writing and how it affected you.

6. What do you think one can learn from exploring complex and difficult issues through reading, discussion, and writing? Why is

it important to think about issues that do not have easy solutions? Write an essay in which you discuss these questions, and explain what you have learned about yourself through exploring such issues.

7. Write an essay in which you choose one piece of writing from this unit that caused an emotional reaction—it may have angered you, made you sad, or made you happy. Explain the effect of this piece of writing, and tell why it had this effect.

Acknowledgments

Baker, James N., "Coming Out Now." From *Newsweek,* Summer/Fall 1990 aand © 1990, Newsweek, Inc. All rights reserved. Reprinted by permission.

Barry, John Byrne, "Daddytrack." Excerpted with permission from *Mothering,* Volume #51. Subscriptions available from Mothering, PO Box 1690, Santa Fe, NM 87504. All rights reserved.

Baxter, Charles, "Lake Stephen" is reprinted from *A Relative Stranger,* Stories by Charles Baxter, by permission of the author and W.W. Norton & Company, Inc. Copyright © 1990 by Charles Baxter.

Burwell, Hope, "Ecofeminism: She Got Herself Shot." From *Ms.* magazine, Sep/Oct 1992. Reprinted by permission of Ms. Magazine, © 1992.

Campbell, Joseph and Bill Moyers, "Myths in Our Lives." From *The Power of Myth* by Joseph Campbell & Bill Moyers. Copyright © 1988 by Apostrophe S Productions, Inc. and Bill Moyers and Alfred Van der Marck Editions, Inc. for itself and the estate of Joseph Campbell. Used by permission of Doubleday, a division of Bantam Doubleday Dell Publishing Group, Inc.

Carver, Raymond, "Distance." From *Fires* by Raymond Carver, copyright © 1983. Reprinted by permission of Capra Press.

Chowder, Ken, "Can We Afford the Wilderness?" From *Modern Maturity* magazine, June–July 1990. Reprinted by permission of the author.

Clinton, Bill, "National Service—Now." As appeared in the *New York Times,* February 28, 1993.

Cofer, Judith Ortiz, "The Paterson Public Library." From *The Latin Deli* by Judith Ortiz Cofer. Copyright © 1993 by Judith Ortiz Cofer. Published by the University of Georgia Press. Reprinted by permission.

Cole, K. C., "Women and Physics." From the *New York Times,* December 3, 1981. Copyright © 1981 by The New York Times Company. Reprinted by permission.

Craig, Grace J. From *Human Development.* Reprinted by permission of Prentice-Hall, Inc.

Dardick, Geeta, "Moving Toward Independence." From *Whole Earth Review,* Fall 1992; subscriptions to WER are $20 a year (4 issues) from PO Box 38, Sausalito, CA 94966, (415) 332-1716. Copyright © 1992 Geeta Dardick. Reprinted by permission of the author.

Dillard, Annie, "Living Like Weasels." From *Teaching a Stone to Talk* by Annie Dillard. Copyright © 1982 by Annie Dillard. Reprinted by permission of HarperCollins Publishers, Inc.

Esquivel, Laura. From *Like Water for Chocolate* by Laura Esquivel. Copyright Translation © 1992 by Doubleday, a div. of Bantam, Doubleday, Dell Publishing Group Inc. Used by permission of Doubleday, a division of Bantam Doubleday Dell Publishing Group, Inc.

Fiske, Edward B., "Gender Issues in the College Classroom." From the *New York Times,* 1990. Copyright © 1990 by The New York Times Company. Reprinted by permission.

Flatow, Ira, "The First Video Game: If You Build It They Will Come." From *They All Laughed* . . . by Ira Flatow. Copyright © 1992 by Ira Flatow. Reprinted by permission of HarperCollins Publishers, Inc.

Frank, Adam, "A Dialogue of Questions." Reprinted from *Exploring,* (vol. 17, no. 2, Summer 1993) with permission of The Exploratorium. 3601 Lyon Street, SF, CA 94123.

Garfinkel, Perry, "Care and Feeding of Commuters." From the *New York Times,* April 7, 1991. Copyright © 1991 by The New York Times Company. Reprinted by permission.

Gelman, David, "The Violence in Our Heads." From *Newsweek,* August 2, 1993 and © 1993, Newsweek, Inc. All rights reserved. Reprinted by permission.

Goleman, Dan, Paul Kaufman and Michael Ray, "Intelligence: A Revolutionary View." From *The Creative Spirit* by Dan Goleman, Paul Kaufman and Michael Ray. Copyright © 1992 by Alvin H. Perlmutter, Inc. Used by permission of Dutton Signet a division of Penguin Books USA Inc.

Goodall, Jane, "A Plea for the Chimps." From the *New York Times Magazine,* May 17, 1987. Copyright © 1987 by The New York Times Company. Reprinted by permission.

Gordon, Ph.D., Lori H., "Intimacy: The Art of Working Out Your Relationships." Reprinted from *Psychology Today* magazine, September/October 1993. Copyright © 1993 (Sussex Publishers, Inc.)

Hamilton, Edith, "Flower-Myths: Narcissus, Hyacinth, Adonis." From *Mythology* by Edith Hamilton. Copyright 1942 by Edith Hamilton; © renewed 1969 by Dorian Fielding Reid aand Doris Fielding Reid. By permission of Little, Brown and Company.

Higgins, Jr., Chester, "A Father's Rite." From the *New York Times,* December 27, 1992. Copyright © 1992 by The New York Times Company. Reprinted by permission.

Hoerburger, Rob, "Gotta Dance!" From the *New York Times,* July 18, 1993. Copyright © 1993 by The New York Times Company. Reprinted by permission.

Kingston, Maxine Hong, "The Father from China." From *China Men* by Maxine Hong Kingston. Copyright © 1980 by Maxine Hong Kingston. Reprinted by permission of Alfred A. Knopf, Inc.

Kozol, Jonathan, "The Homeless and Their Children." From *Rachel and Her Children* by Jonathan Kozol. Copyright © 1988 by Jonathan Kozol. Reprinted by permission of Crown Publishers, Inc.

Krupat, Edward, "On Authority and Obedience: An Interview with Herbert Kelman." Excerpt from *Psychology Is Social* by Edward Krupat, © 1975 by Scott, Foresman and Company. Reprinted by permission of Herbert C. Kelman.

Lee, Martin A. and Norman Solomon, "Women's Rights and Media's Wrongs." From *Unreliable Sources: A Guide to Detecting Bias in News Media* by Martin A. Lee and Norman Solomon. Copyright © 1990 by Martin A. Lee and Norman Solomon. Published by arrangement with Carol Publishing Group. A Lyle Stuart Book.

Lightfoot, Sarah Lawrence, "Beginnings." From *Balm in Gilead* (pp. 1–19). © 1988 by Sarah Lawrence Lightfoot. Reprinted by permission of Addison-Wesley Publishing Company, Inc.

Loinaz, M.D., Margarita and Pat Murphy, "The Problem Solvers." Reprinted.from *Exploring* (vol. 17, no. 2, Summer 1993) with permission of The Exploratorium, 3601 Lyon Street, SF, CA 94123.

Malcolm X. From *The Autobiography of Malcolm X* by Malcolm X, with the assistance of Alex Haley. Copyright © 1964 by Alex Haley and Malcolm X and copyright © 1965 by Alex Haley and Betty Shabazz. Reprinted by permission of Random House, Inc.

McAuliffe, Kathleen, "A Primitive Prescription for Equality." Copyright, August 8, 1988, *U.S. News & World Report.* Reprinted by permission.

McKibben, William. From *The End of Nature* by William McKibben. Copyright © 1989 by William McKibben. Reprinted by permission of Random House, Inc.

Modupe, D. S., "First Born." Copyright © 1993 by D. S. Modupe. Reprinted by permission.

Moody, Anne. From *Coming of Age in Mississippi* by Anne Moody. Copyright © 1968 by Anne Moody. Used by permission of Doubleday, a division of Bantam Doubleday Dell Publishing Group, Inc.

Murray, Raymond C., "The Geologist as Private Eye." Reprinted with permission from *Natural History,* February 1975. Copyright © 1975 the American Museum of Natural History.

Neihardt, John G., "The Configuration of the Circle." Reprinted from *Black Elk Speaks,* by John G. Neihardt, by permission of the University of Nebraska Press. Copyright 1932, 1959, 1972, by John G. Neihardt. Copyright © 1961 by the John G. Neihardt Trust.

Noda, Kesaya E., "Growing Up Asian in America." From *Making Waves* by Asian Women United. Copyright © 1989 by Asian Women United. Reprinted by permission of Beacon Press.

Pogrebin, Letty Cottin, "Superstitious Minds." Reprinted from *Superstitious Minds* by Letty Cottin Pogrebin, published in *Ms.* magazine, February 1988. Copyright © 1988 by Letty Cottin Pogrebin. Reprinted by permission of the author.

Price, Reynolds, "A New Stretch of Woods." Reprinted with the permission of Atheneum Publishers, an imprint of Macmillan Publishing Company from *The Collected Stories* by Reynolds Price. Copyright © 1993, 1992, 1991, 1990, 1989, 1987, 1986, 1982, 1970, 1969, 1968, 1967, 1965, 1964, 1963, 1962, 1961, 1959, 1958, 1954 by Reynolds Price.

Robertson, Ian, "Courtship, Marriage and Divorce." From *Society: A Brief Introduction* by Ian Robertson, Worth Publishers, New York, 1989.

Rowe, Pearl, "Cookies at Midnight." Originally appeared in the *Los Angeles Times,* 1980.

Shone, Mark, "The Diary of a First-Year Teacher." From the *New York Times,* August 1, 1993. Copyright © 1993 by The New York Times Company. Reprinted by permission.

Shostak, Marjorie, "Marriage." Excerpt from *Nisa* by Marjorie Shostak, Harvard University Press. Copyright © 1981 by Marjorie Shostak. Reprinted by permission.

Silko, Leslie Marmon, "The Man to Send Rain Clouds." Copyright © Leslie Marmon Silko, reprinted with the permission of Wylie, Aitken & Stone, Inc.

Smith, Rachel Richardson, "Abortion, Right or Wrong?" by Rachel Richardson Smith, as appeared in *Newsweek,* March 25, 1985. Copyright © 1985 by Rachel Richardson Smith. Reprinted by permission of the author.

Steele, Shelby, "The Recoloring of Campus Life." Copyright © 1989 by *Harper's* magazine. All rights reserved. Reprinted from the February issue by special permission.

Stone, Elizabeth, "Myths of Blame: The Family Scapegoat." From *Black Sheep and Kissing Cousins* by Elizabeth Stone. Copyright © 1988 by Elizabeth Stone. Reprinted by permission of Times Books, a division of Random House, Inc.

Tavris, Carol and Carole Wade, "Sex Differences, Real and Imagined." Excerpt from *The Longest War: Sex Differences in Perspective,* Second Edition by Carol Tavris and Carole Wade, copyright © by Harcourt Brace & Company, reprinted by permission of the publisher.

Thurber, James, "University Days." Copr. © 1933, 1961 James Thurber. From *My Life and Hard Times* published by Harper & Row.

Toffler, Alvin, "Families of the Future." From *The Third Wave* by Alvin Toffler. Copyright © 1980 by Alvin Toffler. Used by permission of Bantam Books, a division of Bantam Doubleday Dell Publishing Group, Inc.

Trask, Willard R., "Old Dinka Song." Reprinted with permission of Macmillan Publishing Company from *The Unwritten Song,* Vol. 1, edited, with translations, by Willard R. Trask. Copyright © 1966 by Willard R. Trask.

Viramontes, Helena María, ""Nopalitos: The Making of Fiction." Reprinted from *Breaking Boundaries: Latina Writing and Critical Readings*, Asuncion Horno-Delgado, Eliana Ortega, Nina M. Scott, and Nancy Saporta Sternbach, eds. (Amherst: The University of Massachusetts Press, 1989), copyright © 1989 by The University of Massachusetts Press.

Walker, Lou Ann, "Outsider in a Silent World." From the *New York Times Magazine,* August 31, 1986. Copyright © 1986 by The New York Times Company. Reprinted by permission of The New York Times Company and Liz Darhansoff Agency.

Wideman, John Edgar, "Across the Wide Missouri." From *Damballah* by John Edgar Wideman. Copyright © 1988 by John Edgar Wideman. Reprinted by permission of Vintage Books, a Division of Random House, Inc.

Williams, Ted, "Rivertops." From *On Nature,* edited by Daniel Halpern, Antaeus/North Point Press. Copyright © 1986 Ted Williams. Reprinted by permission of the author.

Zadrzynska, Ewa, "A Bracelet, an Odd Earring, Cracked Teacups." From the *New York Times,* June 8, 1988. Copyright © 1988 by The New York Times Company. Reprinted by permission.

Zuger, Abigail, "The Long Goodbye." From the *New York Times,* July 25, 1993. Copyright © 1993 by The New York Times Company. Reprinted by permission.

Picture Credits   Page 1: © Jean-Claude Lejeune, Stock, Boston, Inc. **Page 57:** *Family Generations,* Comstock Inc./Phil Mezey. **Page 115:** *Medical Student, Harvard Medical School,* © Jerry Berndt, Stock, Boston, Inc. **Page 179:** *Father and Son at Home,* © Dorothy Littel, Stock, Boston, Inc. **Page 233:** *Moscow: Bride and Groom at Tomb of Unknown Soldier,* © Jim Harrison, Stock, Boston, Inc. **Page 293:** *Boston Youth, City Year,* © Bill O'Connell 1994. **Page 345:** *Red Fox,* Ewing Galloway, Inc. **Page 405:** *Eskimo Shaman,* © Arthur Tress, Photo Researchers. **Page 459:** © Jeff Dunn, Stock, Boston, Inc. **Page 513:** *Homeless, Old, and Out of Touch,* David M. Grossman Photography.

INDEX

Instructor's Manual to Accompany

A WRITER'S WORLDS

Explorations through Reading

Second Edition

TRUDY SMOKE

Instructor's Manual to Accompany

A WRITER'S WORLDS

Explorations through Reading

Second Edition

Trudy Smoke

St. Martin's Press
New York

Manufactured in the United States of America.

9 8 7 6 5
f e d c b a

For information, write:
St. Martin's Press, Inc.
175 Fifth Avenue
New York, New York 10010

ISBN: 0-312-09566-X

PREFACE

A Writer's Worlds is designed for students in developmental writing and reading classes. Depending on the institution, it may also be appropriate for some freshman composition classes. All students bring to the classroom the strengths of their experiences, intelligence, and curiosity about the world. By reading about and discussing provocative and timely issues, they can discover ways to express their strengths in writing. The topics presented in this book are intended to build on your students' inherent knowledge and curiosity. They are meant to stimulate thinking and talking and to reinforce the link between reading and writing.

This Instructor's Manual offers suggestions to help you use A Writer's Worlds, Second Edition more effectively. It is also meant to introduce the new features of the book to instructors. The newly expanded student introduction now provides a user-friendly guide to writing that your students can use over and over again throughout the course. There are now vocabulary lists following every selection. You may decide to use these lists in vocabulary-building exercises you devise or simply encourage students to pay attention to the use of language.

In the Instructor's Manual you will also find some attention paid to the photographs appearing at the beginning of each thematic unit. These discussion questions and writing assignments ask students to recognize the visual text and the details of the various images.

Some parts of the text apparatus, such as exercises like the pre- and post-reading journal suggestions and the revision strategies included with each selection, may be new to instructors. Therefore included below are some tips on how to generate these activities in the classroom.

Having students write in their journals before they read a selection encourages them to explore their ideas. After reading, thinking about, and sometimes discussing the selection, students write in their journals again. By comparing the two entries, they learn about the influence that reading can have on their thinking and learning processes. They observe through their own responses the power that reading can have to inform, inspire, or persuade. The journals also provide students with a place to explore in writing some of the conflicts they are feeling as they begin college. Journals can help students who have difficulty getting started writing. The journals can also be used as a source of ideas for other writing.

Many instructors collect their students' journals from time to time and write short responses to the content and ideas expressed by the students. This sets up an informal dialogue that may enhance the writing process. Instructors can use the journals to respond to students, to suggest further readings, and to ask the students questions.

Some instructors choose to keep their own journals and write while their students are writing. It is helpful for beginning writers to see their instructors as writers too, struggling to find the right word or the best way to express an idea.

Another special feature of the book is the revision section at the end of each chapter. Although there are general suggestions for revision in the beginning of the book, each chapter has a particular revision strategy that focuses on some aspect of the selection they have just read. After they complete a first draft, students can work alone, with a partner, or with a group to discuss and prepare to revise what they have written. Talking about writing and learning to negotiate meaning helps writers to take their own work and the work of the other students in the class more seriously.

The suggestions in this Instructor's Manual will help your students learn to use their observational skills, do primary and secondary research, interview, and work collaboratively or alone. These suggestions are intended to help your students think and write about real issues and ideas. Some of the suggestions may be helpful for those instructors who are linking writing classes with discipline-specific courses. Linking classes can help students and teachers break down the barriers of isolation that often exist in individual academic disciplines. Students see the collaborative process in action when their teachers work together on course work and responses to their writing.

Many colleges are using writing portfolios as part of their assessment process. The portfolios enable students to decide on the best pieces of their semester's work. Each student keeps a portfolio typically containing four or five pieces of writing, all except for one with a final draft and several earlier drafts; one written in class; and a cover letter describing the student's reasons for choosing the particular selections. Some teachers require students to include one piece of writing that was done as part of a group as well as writing done individually. A Writer's Worlds, Second Edition includes writing activities for students working alone or in groups. The various Collaborative Projects that appear with many of the selections invite students to work together to solve a problem or do research. Following the Gelman selection on page 309, for instance, is a project requiring students to work together doing primary research about violence in the media. Another very effective group project follows the Dardick selection on page 317. Students work together to assess the accessibility of the college campus for the disabled. These group projects lead students to new understandings and good portfolio writing pieces. Many teachers also ask their students to write short essays reflecting on what they learned from the group writing experience and to attach these short pieces to their larger paper.

The book also presents a wide range of writing assignments so that rhetorically based teachers can require their students to include, for example, a narrative, descriptive, comparison/contrast, and/or persuasion essay in their portfolios.

Many teachers recommend that students include one piece in their portfolios from the writing done in relation to "The World of Self." This unit includes selections such as the Viramontes and the Noda essays, which illustrate how the act of writing itself

iv

creates meaning in one's life. Keeping portfolios is a good way for students to assess their own progress and for you to know how well they are doing in your writing classes. The portfolios can be discussed in your writing conferences with students. If you link your classes, portfolios can be shared with and graded by teachers in both disciplines. Instructors teaching the same level writing courses may want to meet as a group to read and assess portfolios.

CONTENTS

1. THE WORLD OF SELF—Developing an Identity

> When people care about what they write and see connections to their own lives, they both learn and write better.
>
> James Moffett, <u>Teaching the Universe of Discourse</u>

Photograph, p. 1

The first picture shows a young woman looking into the distance with her clasped hands resting against her face. She seems to be thinking about something. Our lives are spent thinking about ourselves, our relationships with others, our intellectual interests, and about our place in this world.

WRITING SUGGESTIONS:

1. Use your imagination and write a story of the young woman in the photograph. What happened to her that day? What is she thinking about? How does she feel about having her photograph taken? Who is taking the picture?

2. Write an essay in which you describe the difficulties of being a young adult in today's society. What problems are young people faced with that are different from those faced by young people in the past? What problems are the same? How does one know the right actions to take?

3. Write an essay in which you describe the photograph and then convince a reader that this photograph is a good (poor) choice to illustrate a unit on self. How does this photograph relate to self?

Helena María Viramontes, "NOPALITOS": THE MAKING OF FICTION, p. 5

Before reading Viramontes's essay, students should write in their journals about important family events. One of the goals of this book is to help students find ways to use their personal experiences to discover general truths in order to validate and build on their own knowledge. Family stories are a good base to progress from the personal to the general. Students can learn this by sharing their stories and finding common-alities, and by discussing and writing about Viramontes's experiences.

The second journal entry helps students to focus, to describe, and to reflect on what they have learned from focusing on a personal family event. Working in small groups, students can share their family stories and their reflections.

The questions in <u>Drawing Your Own Conclusions</u> can be discussed as a class or in small interest groups. The class can be divided into four groups—focusing on sexism in our society (question 1), oppression and liberation (question 2), alienation and belonging (question 3), and self-identity (question 4). Students can develop their own questions and present their ideas to the class. Encourage them to create their own essay questions about their discussion topics.

The Suggestions for Writing topics allow students to explore the personal (question 1), to interview someone (question 2), to do library research (question 3), and to do additional reading and writing on that reading (question 4). Varying the writing assignments provides students with experience in the types of activities they will be required to do in many other college courses.

Ewa Zadrzynska, A BRACELET, AN ODD EARRING, CRACKED TEACUPS, p.14

Zadrzynska's essay is about how particular items, tastes, smells, etc., provoke memories of the author's past life, before she arrived in the United States. Much of our identity is made up of early childhood memories, and when we make great changes in our lives, small details or items can bring back these early memories and feelings. In the first journal entry students focus on details and items that have brought back memories in order to identify with Zadrzynska's experience. In the second entry, while making their own lists students focus on their own lives and the importance of details.

In Drawing Your Own Conclusions students begin to connect the personal with the wider world. In question 1, they examine what it means to belong to a place. Ask them what they need to do to feel that they belong to their college community. Which students seem to feel most comfortable in the college? What characteristics do they have? Which parts of the school are most homey? Most unfriendly? Where is it easiest to meet people? What steps should new students take to feel that they belong?

In question 4, students can explore the ideas of reconstruction and interpretation. When we tell about ourselves, where do we begin? What do we include? What do we leave out? What do we want people to think about us? How do we interpret an experience? How else can the same experience be interpreted by another?

In both the Viramontes essay and the Zadrzynska essay, students are encouraged to identify names used by the authors. Discuss why the author selected these particular names. Students should be aware that literary and cultural allusions give authority to writing. They should make note of some of the names in the essays and read about them in the library biography section as part of developing their frames of reference.

Danjuma Sinue Modupe, FIRST BORN, p. 20

Our names represent us and become part of our self-identity. Many of us have different names at different points in our lives. We have names of endearment and names that include family and professional titles. Some people, as the author Modupe did, decide to change their names in midlife as part of developing their self-identity. Some women change their last names when they marry. In focusing on names, students can think about their own identities and how these have developed throughout their lives.

In Thinking About Writing, question 1 refers to the time switches in the story.

Modupe uses names to connect his time changes. He begins the story as an adult reflecting on an event that occurred early in his marriage when he forgot his wife's name. Then, after explaining that he has recently changed his own name, he moves back to an even earlier event and signals this to his readers, by referring to "a name I haven't heard in over forty years rings in my ears. . . ." The story shifts to the time when the author was a young boy newly moved to Harlem from the South. Modupe jumps to Harlem in the present with the phrase, "a place I return to frequently now," and then returns to his childhood.

Even within the story, Modupe shifts time. In paragraph 2, he uses the past perfect tense to show present reflections on the way he felt in the past: "The scene reminded me then of how Grandma Allie had insisted . . ." In paragraph 3, students should notice the use of "that" to point out time perspective in the following sentence: "Missy and I were both seven years old that early summer." Then, in paragraph 52, Modupe signals a return to the present and reminds his readers that they are reading and he is writing in the present: "I put down my pencil, . . ."

Students are usually told to present a story in chronological order, although we are aware that many writers explore time shifts to present new perspectives and interpretations of events. Students can become aware of some of the techniques for showing multiple time perspectives through a close examination of Modupe's writing.

Suggestions for Writing 2, 3, and 4 ask students to write a story. Although it is suggested that these stories be based on reality, some students may prefer to write a fictional narrative. In all cases, students should explore methods for shifting time perspectives from the present to the past. They may refer to Modupe's story for ideas about how to show various time shifts. In addition, because many students will write in the narrative form, this is a good opportunity to discuss criteria for judging a story, introducing terms such as "plot," "character," "dialogue," etc.

Kesaya E. Noda, GROWING UP ASIAN IN AMERICA, p. 31

Part of self-identity includes one's identity with a place, a community, and a country. In recent years, people have started to hyphenate their origins, as in "African-American" and "Asian-American." Why do we rarely hear the term "European-American"? Do your students refer to themselves as hyphenated Americans? Discuss the reasons for using or not using these hyphenated descriptions of family origins.

Question 2 in Drawing Your Own Conclusions asks why Japanese-Americans agreed to go to detention camps. Noda states that they went without resistance. She saw them as silent victims. However, Noda explains that they became silent victims as proof of their loyalty to America. She also states that when they went to the camps, they were afraid for their lives. In paragraph 17, Noda states that the money of Japanese-Americans "had been frozen in banks; that there was a five-mile travel limit; that when the early evening curfew came and they were inside their houses, some of them watched helplessly as people they knew went into their barns to steal their belongings. The police were patrolling the road, interested only in violators of the curfew. There was no help for them in the face of thievery. . . ."

In Thinking About Writing, question 3 asks about Noda's description of her experience in California. As part of this analysis, ask your students to explain the reaction Noda has to her uncle's anger in paragraph 15. Why isn't she devastated by his anger? According to Noda, how did Japanese-Americans transform California from a barren land to fertile farmland?

To reinforce the concept that self-identity is connected to a place, you may want your students to read the Zadrzynska essay on page 14 and the Higgins essay on page 443. Both essays explore the idea of returning to one's country of origin in memory or in person to better understand oneself.

Each of the essay ideas in Suggestions for Writing can be transformed into a definition essay to give students the experience of doing this type of writing. It is important to point out that the definition is usually only part of the essay that is then supported by appropriate examples.

James N. Baker, COMING OUT NOW, p. 39

The pre-reading journal writing for this selection is meant to be private, to illustrate that although most writing is done to communicate, some of it is done for personal reasons, to understand ourselves better. Some students may choose to keep separate private journals to explore intimate ideas and experiences. You should encourage this while making it clear that you would like them to keep a journal that is for dialogue with you and perhaps with other class members.

Teachers sometimes discover misunderstandings and prejudices when they deal with a subject as sensitive as homosexuality. The college or other community resource may provide information about hetero- , bi- , and homosexuality, AIDS, sexually transmitted diseases, or other issues that students may have questions about but for which you do not have answers. If you are not comfortable discussing these issues, inform students about the resources available to them.

The topics in Suggestions for Writing call for analysis of complicated issues using a variety of rhetorical modes. All the questions require students to observe, describe, explain, and take a position and support it. Ask students the following questions: What does "explain" mean in an essay? What does "explore" mean? What does "describe" mean? What does "analyze" mean? What does "take a position" mean? Looking at the selections you have already read or the writing you have done, what examples can you find of these types of writing? Share these with your class.

If your students have shown a serious interest in the media and in homosexuality, the Collaborative Project topic for this selection is an excellent way for them to gain experience working together to find out more about a subject. Through working

4

collaboratively, students can learn to divide up responsibilities, write questions, conduct interviews, make charts, and present group findings in writing or orally.

Grace J. Craig, EARLY ADULTHOOD: ROLES AND ISSUES, p. 46

This textbook selection was chosen to expose students to the types of reading that will be required of them throughout college. Moreover, the topic of early adulthood is of practical interest to most college students. The pre-reading journal entry focuses on decisions that students have made in their recent lives. In the post-reading journal entry, students look at their decisions from the perspective of time and the way that time changes our response to some events in our lives. You could also ask students to write about a decision they made before the age of 13 and then ask them to write about how they would handle the same situation today.

The questions in Thinking About Writing are intended to help students understand textbook material and learn how to obtain information from it. Question 1 focuses on the main idea, which is stated at the end of paragraph 1: ". . . there are some commonalities in the developmental processes of adulthood." Question 3 focuses on the categories that are referred to in the selection. Craig is presenting the findings of the researcher Roger Gould. Gould divided his findings into six-year stages in a person's life. Students need to learn how to break down large blocks of information into smaller segments that are easier to comprehend. Question 4 focuses on the ways in which research is presented, paraphrased, and indicated in a formal paper. To examine the presentation of this research material further, ask your students how the author deals with the generalizations presented in the selection. How many people did Gould interview? How many were men? Women? Did he interview them over time? If the answers are not in Craig's text, how can students find the answers?

A valuable exercise from Suggestions for Writing would be for the class as a whole or in small groups of four or five students to write a summary of the article. Writing summaries is an important skill for students to have in many college classes and many students enter college with little knowledge about how to do this.

Yvette Montalvo, THE TRUNK, p. 54

This essay was chosen for the first unit because it is a good example of a developmental writer at the beginning of the semester. Although she relies heavily on the Zadrzynska essay as a model, Montalvo uses her imagination to create a trunk filled with her own past. She has a sense of humor and playfulness as she describes her grandmother smoking cigars, and the rusty old blow dryer. The items she chooses and the explanations for each choice show that she cares for her family and her boyfriend. Students enjoy reading this essay because they identify with the writer and enjoy discussing ways to improve the writing.

2. THE WORLD OF THE FAMILY—Making the First Connections

The stories people tell have a way of taking care of them. If stories come to you, care for them. And learn to give them away where they are needed. Sometimes a person needs a story more than food to stay alive. That is why we put these stories in each other's memory. This is how people care for themselves.

Barry Lopez, <u>Crow and Weasel</u>

<u>Photograph, p. 57</u>

The photograph opening this unit shows several generations of a big family. The youngest member of the family sits at the feet of the oldest members of the family. There are smiles on the faces of most of the family group. They are physically close to each other, their postures indicating their connection.

WRITING SUGGESTIONS:

1. Use your imagination and write the story of this day in this family's life. Why are they all together? Are they celebrating a special event? Where have people come from to be in this family gathering? Who is taking the picture? How do they feel about each other?

2. Write an essay describing the members of this family and their relationships. Think about the way they are standing. Think about the expressions on their faces. Think about the way they are dressed.

3. Write an essay in which you define the extended family. Use the family in this photograph to illustrate what the various generations can learn from each other.

Pearl Rowe, <u>COOKIES AT MIDNIGHT</u>, p. 61

Most students have an emotional response to this story, which originally appeared in <u>The Los Angeles Times</u> in 1980. Discuss with your class the ways in which the story is contemporary and the ways in which it is dated. In what ways is the story culture bound? What aspects of the theme are universal?

Instructors can explore how the structure of the story influences the response by discussing some of the following questions with the class: From whose point of view is this story told? How does this affect the reader's response? How would the story change if there were a different narrator? If the author acknowledged that she was an adult looking back at this incident, as Modupe does on page 20, how might the story change?

For question 2 in <u>Thinking About Writing</u>, the students rewrite part of the story in the third person. Does this depersonalize the story? Does using the third person affect the sense of immediacy? How does extensive use of dialogue affect the reader?

You can also instruct students to change parts of the story from dialogue to reported speech, i.e., My mother said that special people live forever and she said that I was special. How does this change the feeling of the story? When do writers use reported speech? How does it affect the reader?

In the Suggestions for Writing, students have the opportunity in assignments 1 and 2 to write a story, in assignment 3 to make comparisons with other readings they have done and analyze what insights they have gained, in assignment 4 to write a position paper persuading a reader about their point of view, and in assignment 5 to write a letter persuading a reader and describing a project. Encourage your students to try different modes of writing. If students work in groups revising their first drafts, you can group them by the question they answered and they can discuss the elements that make for a good analysis, persuasion essay, etc.

John Edgar Wideman, ACROSS THE WIDE MISSOURI, p. 68

Wideman's story tells about a complex relationship between a parent and child. In Drawing Your Own Conclusions, question 2 asks about the boy's motive for taking the money. Students may develop some interesting insights as to why the boy does this. Does he feel that he is owed something from his distant father? Does he feel somehow cheated when he looks at the wealth and beauty of the restaurant? Question 5 explores the reason for the title. The metaphor "Across the Wide Missouri" aptly describes the wide divide between the father and son, the river with its two banks side by side flowing with the same water (or blood) but still separate. Some students may know the song and have associations with it. These associations would be interesting to explore as well as the power that song has to evoke memory.

Wideman's story takes place in two time frames with one narrator at different points in his life. In Thinking About Writing, question 4 focuses the students' attention on differences in the narration when the narrator is an adult and when a child. Students will get a better understanding of this story if they understand its structure. Question 5 points to the stream-of-consciousness technique that Wideman employs. Students may benefit from discussing how this form reflects the way many people remember incidents in their lives. They may try writing about an event in this manner or they may read something else written in this style.

You can also assign " 'Nopalitos': The Making of Fiction" by Helena María Viramontes on page 5 or "Distance" by Raymond Carver on page 266. These stories also describe complex parent/child relationships. Viramontes expresses the benefit of writing about such relationships to understand them better. Your students can compare and contrast the way the various writers express a similar theme.

Because many of the Suggestions for Writing encourage students to write a comparison/contrast essay, this is a good opportunity to discuss this form of writing.

You can take one of the topics, such as the differences between the lifestyles of the time when students' parents were college age and the students own lifestyles. You can decide on categories such as technology, music, politics, fashion, etc. and make lists together. Then as a group write one paragraph illustrating comparison and contrast, using one of the categories you have worked on together.

Sara Lawrence Lightfoot, BEGINNINGS, p. 76

As students enter college, they often start to perceive their families differently. This selection can help them to focus on some of these perceptions. Lightfoot writes about the conflicts she felt about her mother's going to work and, even worse, her mother's apparent enjoyment of her job. This perception of work as a choice and not a necessity will be peculiar for those students who think of women as having to, not wanting to work. Your class should discuss some of their assumptions about the role of the father and mother in the family.

Instructors can assign primary research that can be written about in a later class. Divide the class into groups that watch television at varying times—prime time, early afternoon (soap opera time), morning news, evening news, or eleven o'clock news. Each student takes notes on the commercials shown during these programs, focusing on: the products being advertised at particular times; the people who are in the commercials (if a family is shown, which members of the family are shown and what are they doing); the ethnic or cultural composition of the people; the overall message of the commercial. Students should present their findings to the class. The group should analyze what the commercials indicate about society's attitudes toward family and if the attitudes differ at particular times of day and why.

In Drawing Your Own Conclusions, students should think about the changing relationship of Lightfoot and her mother. They should understand that writing this biography revealed to Lightfoot her mother's strengths and her survival mechanisms for coping with racism and sexism.

Maxine Hong Kingston, THE FATHER FROM CHINA, p. 85

Students are usually fascinated by this story. They are surprised that the marriage described by Kingston has survived a 15-year separation. In their journals they can speculate about what keeps this couple together and what might happen to an American couple separated for the same length of time. You can discuss the differences between the two cultures, encouraging students to avoid stereotyping either culture. What cultural occurrences are revealed in the Kingston story? How are the students' own cultural backgrounds reflected in their ideas about this subject? Discuss what a stereotype is. Ask students who benefits from stereotyping people. What assumptions do the students' responses reflect?

What does this story tell the reader about the relationship between the couple? What values do they express in their behavior toward each other? What do they learn about the United States? What values does one learn from living in the United States? Do people's values change? If so, when and why? If not, explain.

The Collaborative Project can also be instructive for students to learn about their own backgrounds and the backgrounds of others in their community. Students may choose to find out about the history of their own families and then other families who came from the same country. Students who have been in an area for generations can sometimes find fascinating documents in local libraries. Some classes choose to focus on an area other than a specific immigrant group. They may want to look at job or educational opportunities, relations between men and women, child rearing, crime rates, etc. Working collaboratively enables students to learn about listening and talking to others, dividing up responsibilities, negotiating, and compromising. These are skills that are often neglected in the college curriculum and are frequently called for in the workplace.

Elizabeth Stone, MYTHS OF BLAME: THE FAMILY SCAPEGOAT, p. 94

As students focus on the family and on family stories in this unit, they may find it interesting to reflect on the roles that various members play in the family. This selection uses a family story to illustrate how these roles are assigned and how they affect the lives of members of a particular family. Stone tries to show how "any one family story derives its meaning not only from daily family life but from the family's entire jigsaw puzzle of stories."

In A Closer Reading question 2, the "covert agenda" and "unconscious conspiracy" of the story about the water validate the role that Blanche has been assigned as the "bad" child and victimize Peter, "the golden boy." The family members are probably unaware of the way the story has fed into family mythology. In response to question 3, Dr. Ferreira states that family myths are shared beliefs that "go unchallenged by everyone involved in spite of the reality distortions. . . ." Such myths serve to protect the family from falling apart or into chaos. These myths can be analyzed and understood with assistance from outside the family. Peter is able to analyze his story with the help of Elizabeth Stone and to realize why this family story came to be maintained.

Stone persuades her readers about her understanding of the function of family myths by defining what she means by this term, providing the Mott story, analyzing it, and then explaining why this example corroborates her notion of the function of the family myth. Examining the structure of the selection may help students understand how to include a story within an expository or persuasive essay.

The Suggestions for Writing are intended to enable students to focus on families other than their own and so develop their analytical and interpretive abilities without having to reveal personal problems. Students should try to combine narrative and exposition as they construct their essays.

Students who are interested in psychology and in the role of family may also read "Early Adulthood: Roles and Issues" on page 46.

Alvin Toffler, FAMILIES OF THE FUTURE, p. 103

Toffler questions whether the nuclear family is the ideal model for society anymore. He uses the rhetorical mode of division and classification to explain his "First, Second, and Third Wave" theory. This selection encourages your students to view the family not as an abstract ideal, but as a vibrant changing force in our world.

Toffler describes a world in which there will be a wide variety of family structures. He thinks people will "trace personalized or 'customized' trajectories during the course of their lives." You should discuss what is meant by these terms. Your students should describe family groupings they have experienced and observed and discuss how these compare to Toffler's descriptions. In what ways is the family structure of today different from the family structure of the time when the students' parents were growing up? If students do not know, they can interview their parents and if possible their grandparents to develop a time perspective for societal change.

Toffler states that the family system is becoming de-massified. He claims this is also happening in the production and information systems in our society. One example that is familiar to students is the way in which computers have given individuals communication abilities (i.e., e-mail, desktop publishing, and production and dissemination of information) that were possible only for corporate or institutional groups even a decade ago. What effect have computers had on family life? On the dissemination of information?

Sharon Cassell, TEARING DOWN WALLS TO BUILD BRIDGES, p. 111

Cassell is describing her father and the changes in her relationship with him over the years. Her father has been a difficult man to get to know. She explains that his overwork and stern nature created difficulties for them. In paragraph 5, she introduces the notion of a bridge: "I still felt a gap between us that I wanted to close, but I felt that I had no bridge with which to do so." Later in the essay, Cassell describes simply and well the moment when her father tells her that he loves her. At the end of the essay, when they both find out that her mother is doing well, the reader knows they have torn down the walls between them and built a bridge to each other. As she writes in her last sentence, "Both of us were laughing as we walked into Mom's room; the wall was down: the bricks had been used to complete the bridge." Do your students think she needs the final sentence or has it already been implied?

3. THE WORLD OF LEARNING—Finding One's Purpose

> As a teacher, she believed she had to trust each student's experience, although as a person or a critic she might not agree with it. To trust means not just to tolerate a variety of viewpoints, acting as an impartial referee, assuring equal time to all. It means to try to <u>connect</u>, to enter into each student's perspective.
>
> Mary Field Belenky, Blythe McVicker Clinchy, Nancy Rule Goldberger, Jill Mattuck Tarule, <u>Women's Ways of Knowing: The Development of Self, Voice, and Mind</u>

Photograph, p. 115

The photograph for this unit shows a young man in the foreground holding some papers. In the background, another man is writing on the blackboard. The young man is looking down and seems to be thinking about something. The other man appears to be the teacher who seems focused on getting his message on the board.

WRITING SUGGESTIONS:

1. Use your imagination and write the story of the day on which this photograph was taken. What is the young man in the foreground thinking about? What is he holding in his hand? What papers is he holding? What do they mean to him? What is his relationship to his teacher?

2. Look at this photograph as if it was a metaphor for the classroom. Write an essay in which you explain who is responsible for most of the movement and activity in the classroom—the teacher or the student. How can students begin to take more responsibility for their own learning?   How can the classroom be restructured so that this is possible? Describe the ideal classroom in which you feel you are most comfortable learning.

3. Write an essay in which you describe how the photographer captured motion and stillness in this picture. Look at the elements of the picture. Which parts are softer? Which are more defined? What actions are the individuals in the photograph performing? Who is the focus of the photograph? Is this photograph art? Explain your answer.

<u>Daniel Goleman, Paul Kaufman, and Michael Ray, INTELLIGENCE: A REVOLUTIONARY VIEW, p. 119</u>

Goleman, et al. present Harvard psychologist Howard Gardner's theory of multiple intelligences. Students usually find this theory interesting and enjoy discussing the limitations of the IQ or intelligence testing they experienced in schools. As part of the discussion, you can ask students what other types of intelligences are not covered in this theory. What activities indicate a person's ability in these areas? Who are the notables in these areas? How could the abilities be tested?

Students also can make lists of well-known people whose abilities fit the descriptions, but whose names are not included in the article. Divide the class into special-interest groups—women, African-Americans, Asian-Americans, etc. Students should share their lists with each other. Identify the names of the people included in the lists both in the article and in the classroom. Students will continue to build their frames of reference as they work on activities such as this one.

In working on the questions in <u>A Closer Reading</u>, it can be useful to break the class into seven groups, each one focusing on a particular ability. Each group should present its ideas to the entire class. Class participation enables each group to add to its ideas and share them with each other.

The first question in <u>Thinking About Writing</u> is about categories. As suggested in question 4, students can read "Early Adulthood: Roles and Issues" on page 46 and "Families of the Future" on page 103 to see how other authors developed categories and described their characteristics. In analyzing these selections, students need to become aware of how writers use a combination of different rhetorical modes in their presentation of ideas.

Students who are particularly interested in this topic may want to work on the <u>Collaborative Project</u>. In addition, you might be able to get copies of old intelligence tests from your college testing and measurement or psychology department. You could discuss the types of questions and answer possibilities with your students.

Malcolm X, LEARNING WORDS, p. 129

Many students are interested in reading about Malcolm X. Some may want to read his autobiography in its entirety. An article in the Spring 1994 issue of the <u>Journal of Basic Writing</u>, "<u>The Autobiography of Malcolm X</u> as a Basic Writing Text" by Geoffrey Sirc, illustrates how he used the book as a key text in his basic writing class at the University of Minnesota's General College. Sirc writes that Malcolm X's book is an "inspiring educational memoir of an outsider who becomes an insider [of sorts], it allows the center/margin question to be a central reflection in class." Sirc explains how he used this text to create powerful writing in his computer-networked writing class. You can contact Sirc directly for more information or obtain a copy of the journal by sending $5.00 and requesting the particular issue. Write to: The City University of New York, Journal of Basic Writing, Office of Academic Affairs, Instructional Resource Center, 535 East 80th Street, New York, New York 10021.

Discuss with your students in what context they learned to use the dictionary. Who taught them? How often do they use it each week? What time in their lives did they use the dictionary the most? Do they carry a dictionary to school? If one of your students is particularly adept with the dictionary, that student may present her/his techniques for using the dictionary to the class. Some questions you can discuss with the class: How could the dictionary be made more user friendly? How has the computer replaced the dictionary in some students' lives? When do students use the computer spell-check and/or thesaurus? When do they use the dictionary? What is the benefit of each?

In discussing question 2 in Drawing Your Own Conclusions, students should differentiate between what they learn about Malcolm X from reading this selection and what they have learned about him from other media. What is fact? What is opinion? What is myth? For what purposes would one consult different sources for information about Malcolm X: the autobiography, Spike Lee's film, the encyclopedia, and newspaper articles written during his lifetime?

K. C. Cole, WOMEN AND PHYSICS, p. 135

Students may find it interesting to discuss why fewer women enter physics than enter the other sciences. Some questions to discuss: What is studied in physics classes? Is this of equal interest to the men and women in your class? Does your college attempt to interest women in studying physics or other sciences? What methods have been used in your college to let incoming students know about the availability of physics courses? Have you met any of the physics or science faculty in your college?

Doing primary research prepares students for future college courses. A project might entail a group of interested students visiting the physics department, a physics class, and the college bookstore in your college. Is the department welcoming to visiting students? Is there a booklet or handout describing courses? Are introductory courses conducted as large lecture courses? Are they taught by graduate students? Are there women faculty members in the department? Are there many women students in the classes? Are any of the textbooks written by women? What financial aid or scholarships are available for students who are interested in studying physics? Is the atmosphere that you found, as Cole writes, "unfriendly to women"? Discuss the findings with the class and make suggestions for change if the group feels change is appropriate. The class may want to send a letter with its findings and suggestions to the college newspaper.

The first question in Drawing Your Own Conclusions does not make the distinction that the toys given to boys relate to future professions that differ from person to person, while the toys given to girls relate to family responsibilities (as well as to potential future careers) that could be considered the responsibility of both sexes. Class discussions could consider: In what situations is chemistry used in everyday life? In what situations is math used in everyday life? In what situations is logic used in everyday life? Are any of these disciplines used more by men or women in everyday life? Explain your answers. What role should men have in child care? What role should women have in child care? What role should men have in home maintenance and cooking? Women? Explain your answers.

In the Strategies for Revision for this selection, students work together in small groups. They need to make extra copies of their first drafts to give to the students in their group. If possible, students should move into various areas of the classroom to allow them to read aloud. This activity gives students a chance to read out loud in a revision group, to listen to each other, to respond by focusing on particular questions related to the writing, and to explain the decisions made while writing. Each person should collect the comments made by classmates and be able to ask questions of those students as part of the revision process. Some students enjoy this activity so much that they request that all their first drafts be responded to in this manner.

James Thurber, UNIVERSITY DAYS, p. 143

Many students enjoy this story because they identify with Thurber as he tries to negotiate his way around a largely uninviting college. Most have also had a similar experience to the one Thurber has with his botany professor—an inability to understand a professor, to do the work, or to communicate with the teacher. Focusing on the inability of the professor to communicate may take the burden from the student who often feels frustrated and inadequate. Some questions to consider: Did Thurber communicate clearly about his vision problem to the professor? Why do you think Thurber took botany even though he had vision problems? What science courses are appropriate for someone who cannot see through a microscope or telescope? What role could the other students in the class have had in helping Thurber?

In question 2 of A Closer Reading, students reflect on the way the economics professor assists the student on an athletic scholarship. Your students can discuss the role of colleges and sports with the following questions: Should colleges give scholarships to academically poor students who are good athletes? If they do, what requirements should those students have to fulfill? What is the college's role in helping them to fulfill their requirements? In what ways are college athletes stereotyped by the media? What special privileges do college athletes receive in college? in the media? in our society? What changes, if any, should be made?

The Strategies for Revision requires students to rewrite their drafts, trying to make them humorous. This is a difficult task and you can make it easier by asking a student to volunteer to share his or her draft. If possible, put it on the computer network or make copies for the class. First, everyone should read the draft. Then, as a group, work together to decide on how to make the piece more humorous. In this way you model the revising process and discuss the elements of humor and how to present them in writing.

Lou Ann Walker, OUTSIDER IN A SILENT WORLD, p. 152
Walker's selection forces students to question what language means. It also introduces

students to a world that many of them have never experienced or thought about before—the world of the hearing handicapped. Although this selection is long, it is easy to read. To make it more challenging, instructors may want students to focus on Walker's tone as well as on the actual story she tells. Linguist George Yule selection asked his students to try to communicate the following sentence without words: "My uncle thinks he is invisible." You can instruct your students to try to sign this or another such complex sentence to experience communicating without words.

In Drawing Your Own Conclusions students should think about Walker's family responsibilities. They may realize that these responsibilities have contributed to the contradictions about which she writes. She cares about and wants to be able to help her parents; on the other hand, she wants to be independent of the responsibility of always having to care for someone else. In this context, you may direct your students to think about the responsibilities they have for their parents, brothers, sisters, or children, and how these responsibilities have affected them and their career choices for the future.

Some rentable films that deal with related themes include: "Children of a Lesser God," which is about the conflict of speech vs. signing for the hearing handicapped, and "Crazy Moon," which is the story of romance of an alienated teen and a feisty, independent deaf girl.

Mark Shone, THE DIARY OF A FIRST-YEAR TEACHER, p. 165

The pre- and post-reading journals suggest that students keep daily journals for one week. The journals are intended to help students reflect on school and begin the discipline of daily writing. Some students respond well to this assignment and begin keeping journals for themselves. Looking at the Shone diary helps them to see that personal writing does not have to focus on the triumphs and failures in life. Rather it can be a daily or at least a frequent chronicle of events, including frustrations and pleasant moments. Some teachers require students to hand in their week's journals and just check them off.

Question 5 in Thinking About Writing is about the philosophy and overview of teaching that Shone presents in his diary. The incident on March 23 with Alonzo shows Shone to be analytical, trying to understand his student's frustration. On March 31, Shone tries to be authoritative but noncritical. He wants to encourage his students' participation, but sometimes his need for authority and control ends up discouraging or upsetting his students, as in the event with Ruth on May 25th. He presents material to his class combining visual (wall charts), Alonzo's diorama, oral (his presentations, class discussions, brainstorming), and writing. He seems to value freedom within limits. He decides on the topics for the class (he may have an imposed syllabus). Shone never mentions collaborating with other teachers in his school, and so appears to work alone. He is frequently frustrated by the meaningless interruptions of the authorities of the school. Shone seems logical, orderly, and rational, a 19th-century man in some ways.

Students can discuss what it means to be a role model for someone. Who are the role models in their lives? Who are the academic role models? Who helped them with their class work? What is an academic stance? What academic stance have they adopted to help them succeed in college?

Sheila Renee Shallenberger, RETURNING TO COLLEGE, p. 174

Shallenberger made the decision to come back to college as an adult. It was not easy for her, especially because she found that she had to take courses, such as writing, in which she was not interested. Shallenberger describes the frustrations of learning to write in a simple and honest style. Her last sentence, "While writing does seem a talent for some, I am still striving to achieve personal satisfaction" is realistic and suggests that she has set goals for herself. Students may find her experiences inspiring and true for them as well.

4. THE WORLD OF GENDER—Being Men and Women

> If we had a keen vision and feeling of all ordinary human life, it would be like hearing the grass grow and the squirrel's heart beat, and we should die of that roar which lies on the other side of silence.
>
> George Eliot, <u>Middlemarch</u>

<u>Photograph, p. 179</u>

In this photograph we see a young father holding his child. He is looking directly at the child's face. The child is holding something and looking at the object. The child seems happy and playful. The father seems tender and caring.

WRITING SUGGESTIONS:

1. Use your imagination and write the story of the moment when the photograph was taken. How does the father feel about his child? How does he feel about being a father? What is he doing with his child? Who is taking the photograph?

2. In an essay describe the ideal parent-child relationship. Explain how the relationship needs to change during the different ages of the child. What should the relationship be like during the first two years? from two to five? from five to fifteen? from fifteen to adulthood? Why should these changes take place?

<u>Kathleen McAuliffe, A PRIMITIVE PRESCRIPTION FOR EQUALITY, p. 183</u>

In the pre- and post-reading journal suggestions, students are asked to think about what equality between men and women means. They are asked to make a distinction between equality and "a more equitable division of power." You can discuss the difference in these two terms by discussing such questions as: Should men and women be required to meet the same physical requirements for a job? Should men and women both get personal leave for childbirth? Should job and school applications require that people identify themselves as male or female? Should insurance companies charge lower rates based on whether the person is a male or female?

In <u>A Closer Reading</u>, students look at the McAuliffe article to identify ways in which she made and supported her point of view. In question 1, students should discuss what it means to be "economically autonomous." In a hunter-gatherer society, how is economic worth decided? What benefit derives from being a man or woman in such a society? Why might older people be the most valued in such a society?

In question 2, McAuliffe presents the idea that divorce may be the sign that our society is moving from a male-dominated culture to a more egalitarian society. She suggests that when both partners work, earn money, and own property jointly, divorce becomes more common. In this explanation, divorce is more related to economic than emotional issues. Students may find it interesting to look at divorce and contemporary society from this point of view.

Students will benefit from rereading this selection to find and then evaluate the effectiveness of the supporting details used by McAuliffe to support Fisher's assertion that our lifestyles are more closely related to those of the hunting-gathering communities than to the agriculture-based communities.

The selection uses comparison and contrast to argue the position that "this 'backward' trend toward the hunter-gatherer way of life is a step forward, toward equality between the sexes." You can instruct your students to focus on the comparisons and contrasts made between the two types of communities. Or you may want to focus on the comparisons made between the two sexes.

John Byrne Barry, DADDYTRACK, p. 189

Many students are interested in parenting and the roles that men and women play in their children's lives. This article focuses on the importance of having two involved parents. Child care becomes a responsibility and enjoyment for both mother and father. Students who are taking psychology courses may make the connection between what they are reading in psychological theory and the underlying idea of this article. Many theorists believe that inequality between men and women comes from women functioning as sole caretakers of young children. Students can discuss how having two equally involved parents might affect a child. Is it necessarily a positive experience for the child and for the parents?

In Drawing Your Own Conclusions, students will find it interesting to discuss question 1. Once students have discussed the stereotypes about men who stay home with their children and women who go to work when they have small children, you can encourage a discussion about why these attitudes prevail. Why should women have a greater responsibility for younger children? Why are women thought to be more caring and gentle? Why are men thought to be more aggressive and ruthless? Is that because of nature or nurture? What might men learn about themselves by taking care of children? What might women learn about men by giving men the opportunity to care for children?

Question 3 is about practicality. What jobs allow for flexibility in work schedules and responsibilities? How can parents who want to stay home with their children make changes in the job situation? In what ways can flexible hours and responsibilities be beneficial in corporate and other work situations?

Strategies for Revision suggests that students practice collaboration by working together with a partner. Students should choose their own partners and focus on the questions listed in the strategy. They should not be correcting or marking each other's drafts, but should be discussing and making suggestions for change. You may want to model this type of revising strategy with a student in the class.

18

In the pre- and post-journal entries, students wrote about personal characteristics and decided if the characteristics were sex-related. Next, you could discuss whether, in general, these characteristics are privileged by one sex or not, and why. In what ways is it beneficial for a woman to be curious? for a man? In what ways is it beneficial for a man to be caring? for a woman? In what ways is it beneficial for a woman to be independent? for a man? Is what ways is it beneficial for a man to be dependable? for a woman? Continue with the other characteristics listed in the pre-reading In Your Journal and those listed by students in your class.

Students can make a list of the dualisms presented in the Tavris/Wade chart: taller/shorter; live longer/live shorter time; active/passive; etc. Discuss which of the dualisms is more valued by society and why. Why do we look at the work in terms of opposites?

In question 1, the ideas of "equal" and "different" are introduced. Many of the legal decisions about men and women have centered around these two concepts. Should women be allowed to serve in combat positions in the armed forces? Yes, if they are equal to men. Perhaps no, if they are different although equal. Should women be restricted from certain jobs? Perhaps yes, if they are different. Should schools be allowed to prohibit admission to their schools on the basis of sex? Perhaps yes, if men and women are different. Ask students to think of other legal issues that relate to equality and difference.

In the Strategies for Revision,, students are working together on what sexist language is and how it can be avoided. You may want to make this part of the larger group discussion and present the following suggestions for avoiding sexist references:

1. Avoid words using "man" or "ess" endings and use "chairperson" instead of "chairman," "mechanic" instead of "repairman," "flight attendant" instead of "stewardess," "people" instead of "mankind."
2. Be careful about sexist categorizing of professions. All teachers are not men. All nurses are not women. All secretaries are not women. All police officers are not policemen. All lawyers are not men. All doctors are not men.
3. Describing a heterosexual married couple, write "man and woman" or "husband and wife," not "man and wife."
4. When using pronouns, when possible use the plural "they," "them," or "their" rather than the singular to avoid the awkward "he/she," "her or his," " her or him."
5. Do not use stereotypes or slang expressions such as "cute babe" or "hunky guy" unless they are in quotes and clearly identified as slang expressions or part of dialogue.

Bob Hoerburger, GOTTA DANCE!, p. 206

This essay explores a stereotype about men and dancing. Hoerburger states that

19

dancing requires the same discipline that any athletic activity involves. Discuss with your class the discipline involved in being an athlete. What similarities in lifestyles are there between dancers and athletes? What kind of strength is needed to dance? (You might want to show your class a clip from "West Side Story" or another musical in which male dancing is featured.) Is dance a form of athletics?

In question 2 in A Closer Reading, the notion of taboo is introduced. Discuss what a taboo is with your class. What taboos do students know about? How do we learn about what is taboo? Do all taboos relate to sex in some way? Why are these taboos important to our society? In what college course would students expect to study about taboos? Why?

Discuss with your class how this essay relates to gender and gender expectations. Does the author reveal a bias against homosexuals? What do people in general expect of male athletes in our society? of male dancers? What do people in general expect of female athletes in our society? of female dancers? Why? What does this tell you about our society?

Charles Baxter, LAKE STEPHEN, p. 212

The gender stereotype presented in this story is that women are willing to change their personalitiesto persuade men to marry them. What evidence is in the Baxter story that supports this stereotype? Why is this stereotype true or not true today? Do women in your college feel that part of the college experience should involve finding a potential mate? According to the Baxter story, is the man willing to change his personality to please his girlfriend? What evidence of this do you find in the story?

At the turn of the century, men and women often have equal educational and professional status. In what ways are the relations between men and women affected by the equalization in educational and professional status? In what ways has marriage been affected by these changes? Do people marry earlier? Do people decide not to marry at all? Do marriages last longer? What professional characteristics are important in deciding to marry?

As part of discussing the story, ask your class what they think about this couple. Will they have a successful marriage? Are they both in love? In what ways does this story support the stereotype that men do not want to commit to a relationship? Does the underlying theme of this story seem real or contrived? Support your answers with evidence from the story.

Edward B. Fiske, GENDER ISSUES IN THE COLLEGE CLASSROOM, p. 223

College students are usually interested in this essay about the exploration of power and advantage in the college classroom. In doing the pre- and post-reading journal activities, some students have not noticed differences in the ways that students are treated. After reading the selection, they observe their own classrooms more closely and sometimes find evidence that corroborates what they have read. Students think back to their earlier educational experiences and remember incidents that relate to Fiske's findings. This selection provokes lively discussions.

In question 3 in A Closer Reading, "lower order" questions usually relate to facts and ideas gained by reading. "Higher order" questions usually involve opinions, analysis, and interpretations. Students should discuss the differences between these two and what the difference means in taking notes from lectures and reading, and in responding in class.

According to a study on women's knowing (Women's Ways of Knowing: The Development of Self, Voice, and Mind by Belenky, Clinchy, Goldberger, and Tarule, 1986, Basic Books, Inc.) many women begin to know the world through authorities. They absorb information from teachers, books, and other authorities but have difficulty forming their own knowledge from these sources. One of the goals of college might be to assist women and men students in making the transition from this type of learning to "constructed knowledge." In constructed knowledge, a student combines information gained from authorities with the experiences and ideas of the self and constructs new knowledge. How can students make sure that their teachers assist them in becoming constructors of knowledge? What steps do students need to take to make this transition for themselves? What resources in the college can help students make this transition? How can journals be useful in this process? How can study groups?

Lisa L. Smith, IS THE IDEAL WOMAN A MYTH?, p. 229

Smith believes that gender stereotyping in which women are discriminated against is caused by women as much as by men. She sees it as a societal problem. Smith uses generalizations to support her point of view. Her first example is about Wilma and Fred Flintstone, not prehistoric people, but recent constructions developed for late 20th-century television and movies. Students can read the McAuliffe selection on page 183 to reflect on the hunter-gatherers and roles of men and women.

In paragraph 5, Smith states that in high school, girls want to be cheerleaders not athletes. This notion should be explored in light of women and athletics today. Smith then presents a reason for not giving women promotions. She states that nine major companies assume that women with families do not want promotions because of the extra hours they would involve. She does not explore the reality of this assertion. Do higher-level jobs necessarily mean more hours? Do women with families necessarily want jobs with shorter hours? Are women totally responsible for home and childcare?

Is Smith stereotyping men and women in her essay? How could she explore the complexities of her subject in more depth? Is Smith blaming the victim for the victimization? How else might Smith's examples be interpreted?

5. THE WORLD OF INTIMACY—Connecting with Another Person

> We do not write in order to be understood; we write in order to understand.
>
> C. Day Lewis, <u>The Poetic Image</u>

<u>Photograph, p. 233</u>

The photograph shows a young bride and groom. The groom is carrying the bride through a rainy street. The bride holds flowers and has thrown a coat over her wedding dress. The couple smiles toward the camera.

WRITING SUGGESTIONS:

1. Use your imagination and write a story describing the moment the photograph was taken. How does the couple feel? How long have they known each other? Who is taking the photograph?

2. Write a description of the photograph, adding as many details as possible so your reader can see the picture through your eyes. Write about the relationship of the bride and groom as shown in this photograph.

3. Write the story of the day the couple met. What were their first words to each other? Did they like each other at first? Did they think they would fall in love? How did each of them feel about marriage?

<u>Anne Moody, COMING OF AGE IN MISSISSIPPI, p. 237</u>

In this excerpt from her autobiography, Moody describes her experiences with her first boyfriend. Students benefit from setting a story in a context. Moody is writing about her experiences in the 1960s while attending Natchez Community College, an all-black community college. Moody began to be a political force in her years at Natchez during which time she worked with other students to improve food and other services at the college. When she transferred to a four-year college, she became active in the civil rights movement. In this story, Moody establishes her personality as an independent woman who has had no sexual experience. She controls the relationship with her boyfriend, Keemp, and decides to break up with him because she feels, "I didn't want to get all wrapped up in Keemp the way some of the other girls did with their boyfriends." They remained friends after their romantic relationship ended.

The questions in <u>Drawing Your Own Conclusions</u> discuss Moody's attitude toward her relationship with Keemp. Your students may find it interesting to compare Moody's attitude toward her boyfriend with that of the woman in Baxter's short story, "Lake Stephen" on page 212. What differences and similarities are there in the two women? Which woman is more independent? What steps does each woman take to get what she wants? What differences and similarities are there in the two men in the

22

stories? Support your answers with examples from the stories.

Your students may want to read Moody's autobiography <u>Coming of Age in Mississippi</u> in its entirety. The book not only tells the story of a remarkable woman, but it also describes the place and time period of the civil rights movement in the United States. If your students are interested in this period, you can show commercial films such as "Mississippi Burning," "The Autobiography of Miss Jane Pittman," or any of the documentary films on this time available from public television or film libraries.

<u>Laura Esquivel, LIKE WATER FOR CHOCOLATE, p. 244</u>

Entering college students are often dealing with the problems involved in becoming independent of their parents and yet maintaining a close relationship with them. So they are usually fascinated by Esquivel's tale of a classic generational conflict between a selfish mother and a daughter who is in love. In addition to looking at the surface tensions between family members in this story, it is interesting to explore the historical context of the drama. The story takes place in the early 1900s after the fall of President Porfirio Díaz in 1910 and the murder of President Francisco Madero in 1913. Soon after, when Victoriano Huerta became president, many others began trying to gain control of Mexico, including Pancho Villa. The countryside was attacked by "bandits" bearing arms. So at this time, widows of some wealth such as Mama Elena probably did fear for their safety and the safety of their possessions.

Widows also depended on the care and protection of their family members. However, at the same time that old family values were important, a new independence of leadership and values filled the country. Many young people felt that it was their time to rebel against the old traditions. Set in this context, the story of the De la Garza family takes on a deeper meaning.

The activities in the <u>Strategies for Revision</u> relate to story writing. If your students wrote essays that were not narrative, you can tell them to revise their first drafts using one of the <u>Strategies for Revision</u> from an earlier selection.

<u>Ian Robertson, COURTSHIP, MARRIAGE, AND DIVORCE, p. 252</u>

In this excerpt from a popular textbook, Robertson begins by describing the courtship system as a marriage market. He states that participants try to sell their assets in order to find a mate. Discuss with your class what men and women do to make their "assets" more appealing. What attributes are important in a potential mate? Do people act differently on a date than after marriage? Is appearance more important to men or women? What aspects of appearance are most important? What personal charms make someone a candidate for marriage? How do career prospects influence some- one's potential as a mate? Should both individuals have the same level of education?

Robertson writes that there is "considerable parental and peer pressure for young people to restrict their social contacts to those who are "suitable"—which usually means "similar." What experiences have students had with parental pressure in relation to dating and marriage? What peer pressure have they experienced? Which means more to them? What should the parents' role be in relation to their children's choice of mates? What should the role of peers be in relation to their friends' choice of mates?

Robertson writes in paragraph 5 that after divorce "men are more likely to be fired from their jobs." Ask your students why this happens. Do they think women are equally likely to be fired from their jobs? Why or why not? In paragraph 6 he writes, "the ex-wife may face severe economic problems, especially if she has to raise young children. . . . many divorced women find that they have low earning power —particularly if they have spent their entire married lives as housewives and have no job skiils or experience—and a majority of divorced fathers default on their child-support payments." What do these statements tell the reader that Robertson assumes about the relationship between the husband and wife? Who does he assume is working? Who does he assume cares for the children? Are Robertson's assumptions valid in today's society? What changes need to be made to deal with the problems he describes?

Read the McAuliffe selection on page 183 to get a different perspective on divorce.

Marjorie Shostak, MARRIAGE, p. 258

Shostak's selection, although a simple narration of the circumstances surrounding an arranged marriage of a young !Kung woman, can be used to discuss the complex issue of making personal decisions while still adhering to family or cultural values.

Instructors can ask students some of the following questions: Did Nisa really want to refuse Tashay? Could Nisa have refused to marry in her society? Should people have the right to break with the traditions of their family and culture to pursue their own desires? If so, when? If not, why not? Your students can read "Like Water for Chocolate" by Esquivel on page 244 and discuss these same issues in relation to that selection.

Nisa: The Life and Words of a !Kung Woman (1981) is used in many anthropology courses in colleges to illustrate the work of an anthropologist and life among the !Kung San of Botswana. Your students may be interested in reading the entire text. If some students who want to know what happens following Nisa's marriage, a small group can read that part of the book and present their findings to the rest of the class.

In the revision section, students reflect on their writing process. Instructors can return earlier papers (if students do not keep their own papers throughout the semester) and meet with individual students to talk about the progress noted by the instructor. Students may also benefit from talking to a partner who has shared much of their work throughout the semester.

Raymond Carver, DISTANCE, p. 266

Students may be interested to know that Carver was himself a teenage parent. He and his first wife divorced, and he blamed the failure of his marriage on the stresses of early parenthood and the exhaustion that went along with having to work at arduous jobs to support his family.

Carver has published this story in several different versions. Instructors may decide to share some of Carver's earlier versions with the class, so students can see that even published work can be considered work in progress. Writers are rarely totally satisfied with what they have written and if given the opportunity will make changes until they have reached the final deadline. If students are interested in examining exactly what changes Carver made in this story, they can read some of its other versions in your college library.

Instructors can ask students to write about why Carver is such a popular writer with college students. This helps them to reflect on what they have read. They may want to think about the topics he writes about and the accessibility of his style. Some students may want to read other of his stories or his poetry. These students can report to the class about what they have read and can make suggestions of further reading for their classmates. You can show the film "Short Cuts," which is based on a group of Carver's short stories, to your class and discuss how effective film is for presenting Carver's ideas about relationships.

The revision strategy for this chapter is designed as a personal response to one's writing. After they have revised, students should share these revisions with students they have worked with before. This helps students to value their writing and the relationships they have created with other students in the class.

Lori H. Gordon, INTIMACY: THE ART OF WORKING OUT YOUR RELATIONSHIPS, p. 278

Psychotherapist Lori H. Gordon presents techniques to help couples communicate better. Recent articles about abusive relationships suggest that couples need to learn how to deal with anger and resentment. Gordon writes that "our culture provides for...the need for autonomy, but not for intimacy." She suggests that couples need to learn to work together to provide for each other "the emotional needs that a larger community used to furnish." This article pairs well with the Toffler selection on family on page 103. It also will be of interest to students who are taking psychology courses.

Gordon writes that "couples today are struggling with something new—to build relationships based on genuine feelings of equality." This aspect of the article pairs well with the McAuliffe article, which also explores issues related to equality in relationships on page 183.

Students can look at the basic rules Gordon sets out "to summarize how to change the hidden expectations that work to distort a relationship." Are these rules applicable for relationships with family members, friends, and colleagues at work? Which types of relationships may not benefit from your being sensitive and communicating about how you feel? In which is it better not to ask about why the other person is doing something? Is it always good to talk? to explore? Are there times when you can assume?

Tracy Brooks, MARRIAGE TRADITIONS IN THE INDIAN CULTURE, p. 289

Brooks decided to interview a classmate about marriage traditions after she read the Shostak selection describing Nisa's arranged marriage. She decided to interview a person from a unfamiliar culture. Brooks attempted to write exactly what she had been told by her informant, Kanchan Mohindra. She tried to be honest and careful in presenting exactly what Mohindra had told her. Brooks was not judgmental and she tried not to present her own opinions about the traditions that Mohindra explained to her.

6. THE INTERDEPENDENT WORLD—Taking Action Together

> Let me plunge straight in and argue that every utterance, every text, embodies, enacts, or realizes a social act, a movement toward an other.
>> Geoffrey Summerfield, "Not in Utopia:Reflections on Journal Writing"

Photograph, p. 293

This photograph shows a community action group building a house as part of a project to build housing for the needy. The three men are working together. The expressions on their faces show that they are intent on their work. Groups such as this one are composed of volunteers who give up their time to work on projects that benefit their community.

WRITING SUGGESTIONS:

1. Use your imagination and write the story of the day on which this photograph was taken. Who are the men? What kind of work do they do during the week? Have they worked together before? What are they doing? Why have they decided to volunteer their time to help others?

2. Write an essay describing the building of something or the creating of a project on which you have worked. Explain the steps that you took to fulfill your project. Write the various steps in order. How long did it take to complete the project? Was the result satisfying to you?

3. Write an essay in which you describe the photograph and then convince a reader that this photograph is a good (poor) choice to illustrate a unit on the interdependent world. How does this photograph relate to the theme of the unit?

Bill Clinton, NATIONAL SERVICE—NOW, p. 297

Clinton's plan for national service may directly affect college students, so they may be motivated to read this article. According to his plan, students involved in national service would be asked to give two years in service to the United States in exchange for tuition help for college or job training. Clinton states that in the past bills have been passed that honored citizens and matched the needs of their times. He cites Lincoln's Homestead Act, Franklin D. Roosevelt's Social Security Act, Harry S. Truman's G.I. Bill, and John F. Kennedy's creation of the Peace Corps as examples of these bills. He asserts that his national service program will meet the needs of our times head-on.

Clinton's presentation of his ideas is optimistic and idealistic. His paragraphs are short and punchy. He does not examine problems that may make create problems for national service. Nor does he explain where the money to finance this program will come from. But he inspires his readers to believe in the project.

Discuss the idea of volunteering for two years of national service with your students. Do your students already volunteer in the school or in their community? Would they be willing to volunteer for two years if they thought it would help pay for tuition? Should national service be mandatory for all young people under the age of 21? Do your students think that college tuitions are too high? Do they feel that financial aid is adequate? If the national service program took the place of other financial aid programs, would they support national service?

David Gelman, THE VIOLENCE IN OUR HEADS, p. 304

Gelman writes that violence is marketable and that the appetite for violence has increased in recent years. He cites violence in films, on television, in sports, and in music. The desire for violence was not created by teenagers although it has begun to affect their lives in very personal ways. Teenagers' lives are threatened by violence in the schools and in the streets. The only way that violence will be decreased is to decrease the amount of violence portrayed in the media. Young people in college can have an effect on television programming and film production if they take a stand against violence in the media.

In the pre-reading journal suggestion, students write about the statement, "Teenagers don't invent violence, they learn it." Discuss this statement before they read the Gelman article. In what ways do young people learn violence in our society? How does the constant bombardment of violent images affect their lives? After reading the Gelman article, in the post-journal writing suggestions, students write about where they are most frequently exposed to violence. After they write this, discuss their findings with the class.

In question 5 of Drawing Your Own Conclusions, students should think about who makes money from violence. Who gains power from violence in our society? Who lives off violence? What can be done on a personal level to decrease the power of violence in one's life?

In the Collaborative Project, students become researchers examining media. The project suggests various media for students to look at and catalogue. Your class may think of forms of media other than the ones mentioned in the book. Students learn about the research process, they learn to work together, and they learn about the subject they are investigating when they do primary research such as described in this project.

Geeta Dardick, MOVING TOWARD INDEPENDENCE, p. 311

Dardick's selection is eye-opening to some students who are unfamiliar with or insensitive to the needs of wheelchair users. Dardick writes about the abilities that her disabled husband possesses and the difficulties he has had to face in gaining accessibility to buildings and even to bathrooms. Her essay concretely illustrates the power of activism to make change in society.

Dardick and her husband learned about their state's accessibility codes and then traveled around their county making sure the laws were enforced. They used their phone to network with other groups, did volunteer work for disability causes, marched for access, testified in court cases, wrote letters and articles about their experiences, and did behind-the-scenes work to help get the 1991 Americans with Disabilities Act (ADA) passed. Their job had just begun because then they had to work on making sure that the regulations of the law were implemented.

In A Closer Reading question 1, students need to understand that although Dardick's husband is paraplegic and can only use his arms, he is her lover, husband, father of three children, and a recipient of an undergraduate degree in architecture and several graduate degrees, as well as president of her community school board. He is a man who enjoys a full life despite his physical limitations.

Question 2 about the state-sponsored Community Access Network (CAN) is described so students will realize that community groups exist that can enable them to do important and meaningful work for the causes to which they are committed. Question 4 deals with the complications of getting a nationwide bill passed and the compromises that have to be made in order to do this. Dardick mentions that "the right to universal health-insurance coverage was bartered away for support from some key legislators." Today we are dealing with that issue. Your students might find it interesting to read the Congressional Record about the passage of the ADA and find out who forced the dropping of the universal health coverage.

Reading this article may help your students to realize the power individuals have to make change in our society. Entering college students often feel helpless and overwhelmed by college, and finding ways to express their personal interests can sometimes help them overcome these feelings.

Abigail Zuger, THE LONG GOODBYE, p. 319

Zuger tells a story of courage and transformation about a woman who has tested positive for the human immune deficiency virus, HIV. Students reading this essay will probably come away with admiration for the woman who has made it. She has left her abusive life, is asymptomatic, is a caring mother, and is on her way to a new life in a safer community where her son can grow up with his grandparents. This essay presents a different picture from the one usually associated with HIV. It is important to realize that people do not only die from this disease, but they also have to learn to live with it and make their lives as meaningful as possible while they are alive.

Question 1 in Drawing Your Own Conclusions asks an important question for students in today's society. Many people test positive for HIV and remain asymptomatic for long periods of time. The Federal Centers for Disease Control's definition for AIDS is based on the number of T4 helper cells. These cells measure immune-system strength. The normal level is about 1,000 per cubic millimeter of blood. Anyone whose number has fallen below 200 per cubic millimeter is classified as having AIDS.

In the early stage, which may last more than ten years, when the T4 cell count is around 1,000, the HIV virus is in the bloodstream but people may not have any symptoms or may have a sickness similar to mononucleosis or swollen lymph nodes.

The middle stage, which may last five or more years, occurs when the T4 cell count reaches 500. At this stage, people still may not have any symptoms although many people begin treatment with AZT, DDI, or other anti-viral drugs.

The late stage of the disease, when it is officially AIDS and the T4 count has fallen to 200 or below, lasts about two years or less. Some people still have no symptoms, but they are at great risk. Bacteria, viruses, fungi, and parasites can take advantage of their weakened immune system. They sometimes are given antibiotic treatment. People at this stage may suffer weight loss, fevers, diarrhea, and infections of the skin and mouth. As the immune system starts to collapse even further, other serious opportunistic diseases may attack the nervous system, brain, liver, bones, and skin. Some people get pneumonia and blindness. At this point the illness is gravely serious.

In the Strategies for Revision for the writing done in association with the Zuger article, students are attempting to combine dialogue and anecdotal material with factual material. As they prepare to review their drafts, you may want to examine the Zuger essay and analyze where in the text she uses anecdotal material and where she uses facts. You can also review the Elizabeth Stone selection on page 94 and the Lori H. Gordon selection on page 278 to examine how each of these writers combine anecdotal and factual information in their essays.

Perry Garfinkel, CARE AND FEEDING OF COMMUTERS, p. 326

The subject of Garfinkel's article is the commuter college student. Since 83% of today's college students are commuters who are often juggling family, job, and school responsibilities, many students in your classes may identify with the problems faced by commuter students. Garfinkel describes the situations of students of many ages and backgrounds, making the article appealing to returning adult students and newly entering students.

When students answer question 2 in A Closer Reading, they can explore the special programs and incentives your college provides. If they are dissatisfied with the offerings, they can discuss how to become activists for commuter students.

In Drawing Your Own Conclusions, question 4 asks about "nontraditional" students. You can discuss with your class what is meant by this term. Who is the traditional college student? What classifies someone as nontraditional? What special programs and course changes should colleges implement to meet the needs of nontraditional students?

Question 1 in Thinking About Writing asks about the sources for Garfinkel's information. Using sources from different locations makes his article more credible for readers in various parts of the country. Students need to realize that by relying primarily on one source, they are weakening their argument or point of view.

Judith Ortiz Cofer, THE PATERSON PUBLIC LIBRARY, p. 333

Cofer writes this essay about what helped her to be a survivor in a tough New Jersey neighborhood. Cofer describes herself as a Navy brat whose father was away much of the time and whose work moved the family back and forth from New Jersey to Puerto Rico. She learned English as her second language and was not always treated well by her teachers. But she found refuge in the Paterson Public Library, to Cofer "a Greek temple in the ruins of an American city." Many students from urban areas have had to find a place of refuge; for some it is a library, for others a school, a church, or a community center.

The second focus of this essay is on racism, the kind of racism that occurs between minority groups who are both competing for the slim resources provided in poor urban communities. The animosity between the Puerto Ricans and the African-Americans in Paterson puts Cofer in a situation in which she becomes a victim of the anger and resentment of one girl in her school. At that time she feels her own fear and rage, but in retrospect Cofer understands the elements that led to the enmity.

The questions in the exercises are divided into two themes—those that relate to the library and how students can obtain knowledge and power through reading, and those that deal with the problems of urban life—the racism, the violence, the poverty. You may want to discuss both issues or focus on the area in which your students seem to have the most interest. Students who want to read more about the role of media in violence can read the Gelman essay on page 304.

Natividad Baez, NATIONAL SERVICE FOR COLLEGE STUDENTS, p. 341

Baez became interested in the national service plan and wanted to find out more about it. She did research that involved using the library and reading journalistic articles about the plan and conducting interviews in her college with the financial aid director. She found out information that describes the national service plan. Baez supports the plan and feels it will enable students to get experience in working with others while building up funds to help pay their tuition expenses. Students may find this essay interesting to read in conjunction with the Clinton essay on page 297.

7. THE WORLD OF NATURE—Connecting with the Wilderness

> Tonight I walk. I am watching the sky. I think of the people who came before me and how they knew the placement of stars in the sky, watched the moving sun long and hard enough to witness how a certain angle of light touched a stone only once a year. Without written records, they knew the gods of every night, the small fine details of the world around them and of immensity above them.
>
> Linda Hogan, "Walking"

Photograph, p. 345

The photograph shows a fox standing in the woods on a snowy day. The fox stands still, ears alert, and looks toward the photographer. The air is crisp and the tree branch is bare.

WRITING SUGGESTIONS:

1. Imagine that you are alone walking through the woods on a cold, snowy day. Suddenly you encounter this fox. Write an essay in which you explore the following questions: What do you notice about the fox? Do you make eye contact? What is the fox's reaction to you? What do you think the fox feels? What do you feel?

2. Write an essay in which you describe a quiet moment in nature. Think about a time when you were able to look around you to reflect on the trees, sky, flowers, and animals. How did you feel? What did you notice? What did you realize about yourself?

3. Write an essay in which you describe the fox in the photograph in detail. Tell your reader why you think the fox should (not) be protected as a species.

Annie Dillard, LIVING LIKE WEASELS, p. 349

Dillard is a difficult writer for many students, but she is worth the effort. She combines a keen observer's eye with a poet's mind. Reading Dillard provides students with an experience of entering the mind of a clear thinker with a profound respect for language and for life.

This essay about Dillard's encounter with a wild weasel provides many metaphors that can be discussed in class. In paragraphs 1 and 2, Dillard describes the tenacity of the weasel and the eagle. The weasel grasps its prey and holds on till death overtakes it. The eagle in paragraph 2 eats away at the animal that is attached to its own throat. What human endeavors compare to these two types of tenacity? Have your students ever known a person who holds onto a dream, an idea, or another person with as much determination as the weasel? Have they ever known a person who destroys the thing that is destroying him or her as well? When is tenacity a virtue? When is it time to let go?

Dillard writes that "weasel lives in necessity and we live in choice." What does this mean? What examples can your students think of for each of these concepts?

In paragraph 16, when Dillard writes about living in the den of the weasel, does she mean this literally or figuratively? What is a literal meaning? What is a figurative meaning? What feeling would Dillard like to have in her life that she thinks the weasel has in its life? In paragraph 17, Dillard writes that "a weasel lives as he's meant to, yielding at every moment to the perfect freedom of single necessity." How does a human know when he or she is living as one was meant to? What examples can your students think of a person in this situation?

Ken Chowder, CAN WE AFFORD THE WILDERNESS?, p. 357

Chowder has written an essay of dualisms. He attempts to present both sides of the debate on the issue of whether to preserve the wilderness or to develop it for the benefit of people. Students can read this essay and count the number of times Chowder mentions Muir as contrasted with the number of times he mentions Phelan. They can copy out and count the number of occurrences of words that relate to preservation and those that relate to the development of nature. Do the numbers suggest that Chowder favors one side or the other? What else in the text positions Chowder on either side of this debate?

Your class can discuss whether the debate has to be an either/or debate. What compromises can be worked out to balance progress and preservation? Why is preserving the environment important? What are the problems of acid rain and nuclear waste mentioned in the article? What is their origin? Why is progress important? How do the problems of unemployment relate to the issues presented in this article? How does the need for goods to export relate to the issues presented in this article? Does preservation always mean that progress has to be halted?

Many students have difficulty understanding the meaning of irony and how it is used in literature. The last two paragraphs of this selection provide a concrete example of irony. Review these paragraphs with your students explaining why it is ironic that Muir's bust is present at Phelan's estate. Students can look for other examples of irony in selections they have already read in this book.

Ted Williams, RIVERTOPS, p. 367

Instructors should stress that although Williams refuses to reveal the location of his secret place, he has shared its beauty with words. A writer can use words to share an event, a place, or an experience with her readers. This is one of the functions of writing.

Question 1 in <u>Drawing Your Own Conclusions</u> asks whether Williams is an elitist or a realist? Ask your students what these terms mean. Who in public life is an elitist? What did this person say or do that makes him or her an elitist? Who is a realist? What did this person say or do that qualifies him or her as a realist? Can a person be an elitist and realist at the same time? Students should explain their answers by referring to specific people.

You can ask students to discuss how Williams would respond to the issue of preservation vs. progress presented in the Chowder selection on page 357? Students should support their opinions with specific statements from Williams's essay.

This chapter discusses the process essay. After the students discuss their criteria for writing a successful process essay, they can evaluate in what ways Williams's "Rivertops" meets some of the characteristics of a process essay. Students may read the Malcolm X selection on page 129 or the Dardick selection on page 311 and evaluate how well these essays met the students' criteria for process writing.

<u>Bill McKibben, THE END OF NATURE, p. 374</u>

McKibben takes a radical position in his essay about nature. In general, writers who are concerned about the environment present their ideas in the context that preserving the environment is good or necessary for human survival. McKibben does not examine the issue from this point of view. He contrasts the anthropocentric view that humans are the center of the universe with the biocentric, life-centered view that holds that all living things are equally important. McKibben presents his own ambivalence to the radical theory in that he finds progress and acquisition to be personally appealing but globally destructive. Students may find it provocative to explore McKibben's ambivalence and the concept of ambivalence itself. McKibben's selection contrasts well with Chowder's more moderate point of view in his selection on page 357.

Question 5 in <u>Drawing Your Own Conclusions</u> asks about the meaning of the quotation, "It is not all that radical to talk about who is going to own the factories, at least compared with the question of whether there are going to <u>be</u> factories." Here McKibben is contrasting the emphasis of Marxist theory on the economic domination of large corporations with the radical ecological view that factories are instruments of progress and are not necessary. In the preceding paragraph, McKibben has led into the economic factor of radical or deep ecology when he refers to a letter from ecofeminist Ynestra King who states that deep ecology does not acknowledge humanity and its suffering. It does not examine power structures, but instead reverts to "macho" violent actions to attain its ends. King is concerned that when McKibben says there may not be factories, conceptually he is suggesting the loss of jobs and financial security for hundreds of thousands of workers. McKibben is presenting a philosophy of radicalism that involves the transformation of the society as we know

34

it. He is theoretical, anti-anthropocentric, and is, therefore, not addressing the consequences of the transformation as it pertains to people.

Hope Burwell, SHE GOT HERSELF SHOT, p. 384

Burwell's essay is very powerful for most readers. Without specifically stating it, she takes the point of view that hunters are dangerous and careless. As a farmer, she feels threatened by their actions. She also presents examples of an incident in which the law supported the rights of a hunter against the rights of a victim. Students enjoy reading this and debating the rights of hunters vs. the rights of property owners. Should all people who live in wilderness areas have to wear orange during hunting season? Should hunters be fined or penalized if they do not respect No Hunting and Do Not Trespass signs on private property. Does the deer population benefit from being thinned out by hunting?

In paragraph 20, Burwell writes about making eye contact with a hunter. In the McKibben article on page 374 in paragraph 3, he tells the story of someone who cannot make eye contact with a grizzly bear. In the Dillard essay, on page 349 in paragraphs 9–11, she describes making eye contact with a weasel. Your students can read these descriptions and compare the three experiences in relation to content, style, and vocabulary. What differences are there in the experiences? What similarities are there? Which is the most frightening? the most dangerous? the loveliest? the most surprising? Your students should explain their answers referring to the specific texts.

Question 2 in Thinking About Writing asks about Burwell's main point. She never specifically states that hunting should be better regulated or that it is dangerous for nonhunters. She implies these points through her examples and her narrative. Teachers can use this essay to illustrate the use of implication to present a point of view. Read the Dillard essay on page 348, the Chowder selection on page 357, the Williams essay on page 367, and/or the McKibben selection essay on page 374. What is the main idea in each of these pieces? Where are the main ideas stated? Are the main ideas in any of these essays implied rather than directly stated? Students should support their answers with evidence from the selections.

Reynolds Price, A NEW STRETCH OF WOODS, p. 391

This story is easy to read and many students enjoy it because it tells the story of a boy discovering his own courage and strength. The references to nature and to the mythical encounters with animals make it a lovely story to read and discuss with your class.

In Drawing Your Own Conclusions question 1, students may state that the setting in the deep forest is similar to that of many fairytales. Ask them to name the fairytales and explain their similarities to the Price story. Why is a setting deep in the woods evoca-tive of mysterious things to come? It might be an enjoyable class project to

35

rewrite a familiar fairytale and set it in an urban environment. What changes would you have to make? In what ways does this rewriting change the overall message of the tale?

In question 3, Dillard learns the importance of finding what is important or necessary to one and then pursuing it to its fullest, not letting go no matter how difficult the task may become. Students may have different interpretations about the lessons the animals teach. Some students have said that the dog teaches fearlessness, to take a risk and go ahead even when the path seems dangerous. The eagle teaches patience, to wait and observe what is around you before moving ahead. The snake teaches acceptance, that there are eventualities in life that cannot be changed and problems that cannot be solved. Your students may have other ideas.

Cynthia Mazzotti, ISLE ROYALE'S PREDATOR/PREY RELATIONSHIP, p. 399

This student-written essay presents definitions of the terms "predator" in paragraph 2 and "prey" in paragraph 1. In a definition essay, as in this case, the terms are usually defined near the beginning of the essay. Mazzotti describes factually and in detail a long term relationship between moose and wolves. The description supports her main idea presented in the last sentence in the essay: "Predators and prey establish a balance between themselves that fluctuates naturally and does not need man's intervening."

In describing the predator/prey relationship, Mazzotti takes a biocentric view (see McKibben, page 374) that life systems will work out their own balances when humans do not interfere. The essay also responds to some of the issues raised in the Burwell essay on page 384 about what happens to an over-populated species. Perhaps the deer would also find their own balance whether or not the hunting season occurred.

8. THE WORLD OF OUR PAST—Learning from Myths and Rites

> The story depends upon every one of us to come into being. It needs us all, needs our remembering, understanding, and creating what we have heard together to keep on coming into being. The story of a people. Of us, peoples. Story, history, literature (or religion, philosophy, natural science, ethics)—all in one.
>
> Trinh T. Minh-ha, <u>Woman, Native, Other</u>

Photograph, p. 405

The image in the photograph is timeless and mysterious. A person clad in a hooded garment holds a large disc or drum. The person's mouth is open; the eyes are closed. There is straw-like grass in the foreground and stalk-like plants on either side of the person. A cloudless sky fills half the picture.

WRITING SUGGESTIONS:

1. Using your imagination, write the life story of this person, ending it with the moment framed in the picture.

2. Imagine that you are driving across the United States. On a strange road, you have run out of gas and have decided to walk to find a gas station. You encounter this person not far from the road. Write an essay in which you explain how you communicate your problem to this person and what happens to both of you.

3. Write an essay in which you describe the photograph in detail and explain whether this photograph is an appropriate choice to illustrate a unit on myth.

Bill Moyers, MYTHS IN OUR LIVES: AN INTERVIEW WITH JOSEPH CAMPBELL, p. 409

This selection is very popular with students because they are often familiar with myths. They are interested in Campbell's assertion of the commonalities in mythical themes of different cultures and religions. Campbell states, "The themes are timeless, and the inflection is to the culture." Campbell mentions creation, death, resurrection, ascension to heaven, and virgin births as common mythical themes.

Many students take courses on mythology in college and some colleges are linking writing courses with courses in the classics department on mythology. However, most students have not thought about the function of myth in society and they find that perspective on myths to be engaging and thought provoking.

In question 3 in <u>A Closer Reading</u>, students identify Campbell's four functions of myth—the mystical, the dimension of the mystery of life itself; the cosmological, the dimension of the universe and of scientific mysteries; the sociological, supporting and validating a particular social order; and the pedagogical, teaching one how to live and what to value. Students can work in small groups to make a list of the functions and the meaning of these functions. Students may need to use their dictionaries to understand some of Campbell's terms. The groups can discuss their personal understandings of the four functions of myth and then share these with the whole class.

Question 4 asks about the Gaia principle, the principle that the whole planet is one organism and that everything we do affects everything on the planet. Students can also read the McKibben selection on page 374 and discuss whether biocentrism, life-centered thinking, is the same as or is related to the Gaia principle.

The Moyers and Campbell interviews are available on video tape. Some colleges own them, or they can be rented from video stores or specialty rental companies. Students will gain an additional perspective from seeing the discussion of the nature of myth.

The Dinka, Black Elk, and Ping Ruan, THREE NATURE MYTHS, p. 418

In language, we are more likely to remember recurring patterns-for example, "of the people, by the people, for the people" from the Gettysburg Address—because of their powerful effect on the right brain. For this reason, much persuasive writing, and especially speeches, contains recurrences, as do poetry and other writings with a strong emotional content.

Gabriele Lusser Rico, Writing the Natural Way

Some students may feel uncomfortable reading poetry, but many enjoy memorizing lyrics of their favorite songs. They are drawn to the repetitions and rhythms of the words and sounds. To assist students in identifying similar repetitions in words and sounds in the pieces in this selection, instructors may want to read "Old Dinka Song," "The Configuration of the Circle," and "Moon Lady" aloud. Instruct your students to listen for recurrences in these pieces. They should think about how the recurrences of words and sounds affect their responses to these selections. Students can also share song lyrics that use recurrences with the class. This discussion may help them in answering question 2 in Thinking About Writing.

After reading "Old Dinka Song," "The Configuration of the Circle," and "Moon Lady," students can discuss what similarities and differences are revealed about the three cultures' attitudes toward nature. Do they find the themes of creation, death, resurrection, ascension to heaven, and virgin births in any of them? Do they serve any of what Campbell identifies as the functions of myth—the mystical, the dimension of the mystery of life itself; the cosmological, the dimension of the universe and of scientific mysteries; the sociological, supporting and validating a particular social order; and the pedagogical, teaching one how to live and what to value? Students should support their answers with evidence from the selections. As students read selections with different viewpoints, they are developing a frame of reference that they can draw upon when they discuss and write. In addition, they are developing an academic approach to learning—reading source material, talking and thinking about what they have read, and writing to explore and express what they know.

In question 1 in Thinking About Writing, students read and discuss another Dinka myth. They should be able to identify this as a creation myth and discuss its similarities to other creation stories with which they are familiar.

Leslie Marmon Silko, THE MAN TO SEND RAIN CLOUDS, p. 424

The pre- and post-journal writing for this story asks students to write about death. Experiencing the death of a loved one is usually sad and sometimes shocking. Writing about this may be cathartic, but instructors should be aware that it can also be painful for some students. You may choose to respond personally to these journal entries.

To relate this story to the overall theme of mythology, you can ask your students whether Silko deals with the common themes of mythology—creation, death, resurrection, ascension to heaven, and virgin births. Which of the four functions of myth described by Campbell does this story fulfill? What specific details in the story supports your answer?

You can remind your students that within the context of a narrative, Silko tells step by step the process that begins with the finding of Teofilo's body and concludes with his burial. Using Silko's story as a guide, students can write about the burial process of the Laguna Pueblo people.

You can explain to students that writers choose their words and images carefully. From the first sentence, when Teofilo is found under the cottonwood tree, to the last sentence, in which Leon reflects on the idea that the old man can send them thunderclouds because his grave was sprinkled with holy water, this story is filled with nature images. Students can focus on these images and then analyze the importance of nature to the Laguna Pueblo Indians.

Students can compare how the Dinka of the Sudan, the Oglala Sioux of the United States, the Laguna Pueblo, and the ancient Chinese people regard nature and the role it plays in each of their cultures.

Edith Hamilton, FLOWER MYTHS: NARCISSUS, HYACINTH, ADONIS, p. 433

Students have usually been exposed to myths from childhood in books, films, and television programs. Many of them will remember reading the Hamilton book. They may also have read other stories about narcissus, hyacinth, and Adonis. Before they read the Hamilton stories, the class can discuss the myths with which they are most familiar. When they hear the word "echo," the term "narcissus" complex or that someone suffers from "narcissism," or the idea that a person is someone's "nemesis," do they know the origins of these words and ideas?

After reading the Hamilton stories, students can discuss the characteristics of the human men and women in these stories. How do men act with women? How do women act with men? How do the gods use the desires of humans to reach their goals? Are humans' fates determined by the gods? Do humans in these stories seem to have free will?

Many students feel comfortable writing stories, but find making the transition to more academic writing difficult. Students may benefit from the experience of shifting from narrative to reflective thinking. Question 1 in Suggestions for Writing allows students to do just that. Reading and writing about myths may help students to make this transition. Writers can use specific details found in their narratives to lead to general concepts that explain, define, and persuade. When students discuss other myths, they can practice using specific details of the stories to write general concepts.

Before beginning to review their drafts, students are asked in the Strategies for Revision to "write in your journal five discoveries that you have made about your writing so far this semester." You may want to discuss these discoveries with the whole class or collect them and respond personally. Some teachers talk to students about their writing discoveries when they confer with them about writing assignments.

Chester Higgins, Jr., A FATHER'S RITE, p. 443

Higgins' essay is about a rite of passage for a father and for a son. The relationship between the two has been strained because of divorce and the pressures of modern life. Higgins decides to take his son on a trip to visit Africa so that together, they can affirm their heritage and their bond to each other.

While in Ethiopia, the elder Higgins has a dream in which he anoints his son and performs a rite with him. The two men discuss the dream and decide on the terms of the rite. The father will pour sand from Cairo and from Luxor over his son's head as the father speaks special words of honor and love. The rite is performed in Thebes in the Valley of the Kings in the tomb of one of the Pharaohs standing in front of a wall painting of Osiris, the god of resurrection. Your students may discuss how the rite and the location of it relate to myth and to cultural studies.

This essay is appealing to students because of its descriptions of Africa, African culture, and the relationship of the two men. Question 5 in Thinking About Writing refers to the last paragraph of the essay which ends "my perception of what it means to be a father was unalterably expanded and enhanced." Students can discuss what it means to be a father, a son, a mother, a daughter. What events in their lives have unalterably expanded and enhanced their parent-child relationships?

Letty Cottin Pogrebin, SUPERSTITIOUS MINDS, p. 450

This essay provides a rich basis for discussion about superstitions, family values, and beliefs. Students from all cultures have opinions about the value of superstitions. Many instructors have their students interview each other, asking questions about the role that superstitions play in each other's lives. Students who initially state that they do not have any superstitious beliefs at all sometimes like to debate their feelings with other students who believe strongly. They often end up surprised at how much they have in common. Some students become interested in finding the origin of particular superstitions and beliefs.

Instructors can also use this essay to explore the issue of family traditions—what we keep and what we reject and how we make those decisions. Pogrebin retains the family superstitions; other people keep family values or maintain particular rites. You may want to discuss whether passing these superstitions on to another generation, as Pogrebin claims to have done, wisely preserves a memory or heedlessly instills fears and worries.

Instructors may want to continue this discussion about how we decide what to keep and what to reject as we mature to include issues such as: moral values, political affiliations, family dialects or languages, traditional family celebrations, foods, etc. You may want to give writing assignments about these topics or encourage students to write about them in their journals.

In the revision activity, students are developing a dialogue with a partner. This dialogue provides the experience of talking to learn. They take responsibility for reading and carefully considering each other's writing.

Rachele Deveras, THE TWO MOSQUITO BITES, p. 456

This student essay was published in Lotus, a college student magazine dedicated to the Asian-American perspective. In the essay, Deveras describes a family belief that she calls "an old wives's tale" that states that the longer people stay away from their native land, the more the mosquitoes will bite them when they do return home. Deveras's experience confirms the belief. She returns to the Philippines after more than a ten-year absence and is bitten unmercifully by mosquitoes while the other members of her family are not bitten at all.

Discuss with your students the following questions: What are "old wives's tales"? Are they similar to superstitions? On what basis are these tales created? How are they passed from generation to generation? What old wives's tales do your students know? Is the term "old wives's tale" offensive?

9. THE WORLD OF SCIENCE—Understanding and Exploring

> When people articulate connections between new information and what they already know, they learn and understand that new information better.
>
> Jerome Bruner, The Development of Writing Abilities

Photograph, p. 459

In the photograph for this unit, we see a scientist in her lab working with material in a petri dish. She is looking toward a beaker and seems focused on her work.

WRITING SUGGESTIONS:

1. Create an imaginary experiment in which the scientist in this photograph is involved. Describe the experiment. What does she hope to find? What work has she done so far? What is she looking at in the beaker? What is in the petri dish in her hand?

2. Use your imagination and write the biography of this scientist. Who is she? How did she become interested in science? What does she want from her career? What type of work is she engaged in?

3. Write an essay in which you describe an experience that you had in a laboratory setting. What were you doing? What did you learn?

Samuel H. Scudder, TAKE THIS FISH AND LOOK AT IT, p. 463

This is a wonderful essay that students enjoy reading and discussing. It also teaches the valuable lesson that observation is one of the paths to learning. Scudder begins his lessons with the famed professor Agassiz when he is told to "Take this fish and look at it." Days later he realizes how much one can learn from looking closely and intensely at something. Students can discuss what Scudder learns from his observations besides the attributes of the fish.

In question 2 in A Closer Reading, students reflect on why a person is not fit to be a naturalist until she or he is able to take care of specimens. This can be expanded into a discussion about what students need to be responsible for to be successful writers. How can they "take care" of their writing? What aspects of writing should they have gone over before handing in their work? What do you expect of your students? What do they expect of you?

Students often have difficulty becoming independent learners in their first semesters in college. They depend on their teachers for information and direction. Part of making the transition from student to scholar is to become independent, to learn to find resources, to set up personal goals, and to create opportunities to see them through. This takes time and practice. Agassiz sets up a situation in which his student becomes an independent learner in a controlled situation. You can do this with writing assignments as well. Encourage students to create their own writing assignments or to expand on the ones in this book. Read their drafts in parts, but encourage them to share their drafts with other students in the class or with tutors in your writing center. In their journals, they can write about what they are learning about themselves. If they have to write one page each day about what they are learning, then, as Scudder does, they may begin to see new aspects of themselves and their abilities. Students need to learn to take responsibility for their own work and learning.

For question 2 in Suggestions for Writing, each student can bring in something for another student to observe and write about. Students can bring in a flower, a piece of fruit, a coin, or any other small object for another student to observe closely and write about. Some teachers ask the students to read what they have written aloud and ask the other students in the class to guess what they have written about.

Adam Frank, A DIALOGUE OF QUESTIONS, p. 471

Frank presents four basic concepts that help describe the scientific process—the Story, the Problems, the question, and the tale. Once a scientist has chosen a research interest, he or she must find out the Story or the present theory, "the consensus of opinion in the community of researchers in that field." Scientists find this out by reading and talking to people in the field. In reading the Story, the scientist finds out about the Problems in that particular area of interest. These are the major questions that are consuming the researchers in the field. Next, the researcher develops a problem that is of interest. Sometimes the question is suggested by the readings or by talks with other members in the field. The question is usually small and only peripherally related to the Problems. Sometimes the question needs to be turned around and re-examined itself. The scientist does research on the question and if successful, she or he finds an answer to the small question. Then the scientist writes that answer in the form of the tale that gets added to the Story and science changes little by little.

This process is analogous to research in any field, science, literature, or life itself. We find out as much as possible about the Story, the Problems, develop our own questions, solve them as best as we can, and add our tale to the larger Story. Discuss this concept with your class. Ask them to illustrate their learning process using this paradigm. Students are often intimidated by the enormity of learning a new discipline, but by seeing the steps involved and probing into the process of developing new knowledge, they may feel less intimidated.

In Drawing Your Own Conclusions, question 1, Frank explodes the myth that scientific pursuits are necessarily lonely and isolated. He presents the concept of a scientific community of researchers working together. Two of the scientific breakthroughs Frank presents involved two scientists working together—Watson and

Crick,and Penzias and Wilson. It would be informative for your students to find out how many Nobel Prizes have been given to pairs of scientists. The pair of acknowledged scientists itself is only a small part of the community of people working on particular questions.

Question 3 pertains to the fact that scientists usually focus on "arcane and even trivial details." In addition to this being true for science, it is appropriate for students to explore this idea in relation to writing and choosing essay or research topics. Students often think they can explore a huge topic and have difficulty in breaking down their subject into smaller, more researchable parts. Getting experience doing this will prepare them for the writing required in other courses and will improve the writing they produce for their English classes as well.

Pat Murphy, THE PROBLEM SOLVERS: INTERVIEW WITH MARGARITA LOINAZ, M.D., p. 481

Because many students are interested in knowing more about medicine, they enjoy this article. Loinaz tells her interviewer the courses one should study in order to become a medical doctor, but she also intimates that beyond the courses there are abilities that are learned over time through the experience of working with people.

As part of discussing experience, she explains the steps she takes to diagnose her patients. Your students may notice some similarities to the four concepts outlined by Frank in his article on page 471—the Story, the Problems, questions, and the tale. Loinaz asks her patients for their Story, their health history; then she asks them about their major health problems; next, she focuses on the problem or specific question that brought them to see her; and she provides a diagnosis and course of treatment for them that becomes the tale of their illness and gets added to their overall Story.

Loinaz stresses the importance of pattern recognition in medicine. She says, "as you work and acquire more experience, the number of patterns you recognize and the subtleties of those patterns increase." Similarly, as students become more experienced writers, they see patterns in essay prompts and become familiar with the rhetorical modes that help them respond to the essay questions. This takes time and needs guidance and experience, as does the study of medicine.

As teachers, we are also aware of pluralities of perspectives and responses. Loinaz states that three different doctors can have three different responses to the same symptoms. In writing, each student has a unique response to a question based on his or her own life experiences and background. And as Loinaz has observed in medicine, each writing student also has a slightly different approach to problem solving.

Where Loinaz stresses the importance of knowing one's limits, we stress the importance of knowing one's resources to be able to expand one's limits. But we all agree on the importance of curiosity.

<u>Raymond C. Murray, THE GEOLOGIST AS PRIVATE EYE, p. 489</u>

Students often study geology as undergraduates. So this essay is good preparation for some of the terms and concepts that will be covered in geology classes. Because Murray wrote this essay for the science-oriented, but general, audience of <u>Natural History</u> magazine, he does include definitions and explanations of his field of interest.

The pre-reading journal entry asks students to write about how geology can help in solving crime and some students find it difficult to do this, but instructors should encourage this creative endeavor. It is good practice for students to use their ingenuity to come up with ideas before they do the actual reading. Using writing as part of their discovery and exploration process helps them become clearer thinkers and better writers.

This is a good essay for showing students how to use examples to make a point. Murray effectively presents a wide variety of illustrations to demonstrate the connection between geology and crime detection.

Instructors should suggest that each student in the class read one Sherlock Holmes story and then write about it. Students can share their essays with the class. The public television Sherlock Holmes series is excellent, and since each episode is only an hour long, you might want to show one of them to your class. Your students can read the particular story before seeing the film and can write an essay comparing the story with the film presentation.

<u>Ira Flatow, THE FIRST VIDEO GAME: IF YOU BUILD IT THEY WILL COME, p. 498</u>

The experiences of students who have played video games at arcades or on personal computers will add an interesting dimension to the class discussion about this article. These students can become authorities on the subject of video games, and their knowledge can help other students get a better understanding of why we should find out about the person who created these games. After discussing video games in general, the class usually enjoys reading about the little-known man who created the first video game. Flatow writes with a light, humorous tone. Discuss tone with your students. What words and phrases in this piece make it seem light? What make it humorous? Reread the Murray selection on page 489. What words and phrases tell a reader the writer's tone? Why is tone important in understanding the meaning of a piece of reading?

How do the steps that led to the creation of the first video game correspond to the four concepts set out for scientific research in the Frank article on page 471? What big problem is Higinbotham interested in that is of real benefit to our world?

In question 2 in <u>Drawing Your Own Conclusion</u>, students reflect on differences in the development of video games over the past five years. Some students may have had experience with CD-ROM multimedia games and with virtual reality games. They will be good sources for this discussion. You can also discuss the computer and the ways that it figures in students' lives. Do students have access to computers in your college? For what purposes do they use them? When did they learn to use the computer? How often do they use computers for word processing? to play games? for spread sheets? for college courses?

If your students are interested in technology, an interesting project would be for each interested student to choose an invention, find out who invented it, when, what the first models were like, and what changes have been made in the device and why. The group of students who work on this project can write papers about their findings and make reports to the larger class.

Diane Beran, MAX, p. 508

Beran's essay is a good example of a descriptive, detailed student essay. It is also illustrates well the process or step-by-step essay. Beran is a marvelous observer and chronicler of the events that occurred during her cat's near fatal illness. Her style is journalistic in fact, almost clinical, from paragraph 4 until the last four paragraphs of the essay. During this middle portion, Beran omits personal and emotional responses to the events she is describing. At the end of the essay, she tells her reader the impact of this event on her. This personal ending reveals that she has decided to become a veterinarian because of this experience. Students who have their own animals find this essay fascinating because of the description and the positive outcome. Some squeamish students have found the detailed descriptions of the medical procedures upsetting to read.

10. THE WORLD IN REFLECTION—Examining Complex Issues

> Knowledge . . . necessitates the curious presence of subjects confronted with the
> world. It requires their transforming action on reality. It demands a constant
> searching. . . . .In the learning process the only person who really <u>learns</u> is s/he
> who. . . re-invents that learning.
>
> Paolo Freire, <u>Education for Critical Consciousness</u>

Photograph, p. 513

A woman walks through a city street carrying a heavy shopping bag and a newspaper
under her arms. She is wearing a coat, a hat and sneakers, and is leaning on a cane.
She looks down toward the sidewalk. A man clad in a fur hat and an overcoat crosses
the street, his back to the woman.

WRITING SUGGESTIONS:

1. Use your imagination and write the story of the woman in the picture as if you
   were a journalist interviewing her. Think about where and when she was born,
   her name, her early life, her family, and what happened to her on the day the
   picture was taken.

2. Write a story with the same information as in #1 except write it from the first
   person as if you were that woman telling about your life to the students in your
   class.

3. Almost every day in the United States, we see someone in need. We make
   decisions to help or not help that person. Write an essay in which you explain
   how you decide when to help or not help.

Shelby Steele, THE RECOLORING OF CAMPUS LIFE, p. 517

Steele's essay deals with the important and complex issue of racial tension that exists
on many college campuses. He examines this issue from the point of view of equality
and difference. He thinks that in a situation in which all people are treated as equals,
"differences are more exposed than ever." These differences can create problems.
Ask your students if they are aware of racial tensions on your campus. Are people
treated as equals in all areas of the college? What changes would improve the racial
climate in your college?

Question 2 in Thinking About Writing focuses on paradoxes. One way to help
students understand what is meant by the term "paradox" is to present and discuss
paradoxical situations. Steele presents three of them in his essay. The first paradox
is the over-riding one that racial conflicts occur in colleges where racial equality,
freedom for all, is mandated by law. The other paradoxes relate to this one. The

second is that affirmative action quotas have led colleges to develop programs to redress the problems created by the poor academic preparation provided in inadequately funded schools in minority neighborhoods. So in a paradoxical way, affirmative action can be said to maintain the poor quality of public education.

Students who do not benefit from affirmative action may feel that they are forced to compete for the same funds with those students who do, thereby creating another distancing factor. So the third paradox is that attempting to bring together all students may have led to the rise in popularity of separatist groups such as fraternities and sororities and segregated African-American dormitories.

Keeping in mind that colleges are micro-societies that reflect the climate of the country as a whole, it is sad, but not surprising, that racial conflicts occur. Do your students think that affirmative action policies should be continued? Should race and sex be part of the considerations in hiring new faculty members? in admitting new students?

Steele's article focuses on issues that relate to race. Read the Fiske article on page 223 that looks at issues related to sexism in college. How do the issues of sexism and racism interact? Also Steele's essay examines issues of college life as they relate to students living in college dormitories. Read the Garfinkel article on page 326 to get ideas about the issues that relate to commuter students in colleges. How do the racial tensions Steele discusses affect commuter students? What differences would you expect to find in the problems for dormitory and commuter students?

Rachel Richardson Smith, ABORTION, RIGHT OR WRONG?, p. 523

This essay is contained in this unit on complex issues because the author does not present a simple answer to whether abortion is right or wrong. In her essay, Smith explains why she cannot side with either the pro-choice or the pro-life constituencies. She refers to the decision to have an abortion as one of "those anguished decisions in which human beings struggle to do the best they can in trying circumstances."

In paragraph 1, Smith wishes that contraceptives were used and were foolproof. She also writes that people should be responsible for their actions and mature in their decisions. She wants children to be loved, wanted, and valued. What words or phrases suggest that she does not believe these situations to be true?

In paragraph 2, she does not use the word "abortion," but she does say that women who are "young, poor, single or all three" should be able to direct the course of their own lives. What about older, richer, married women? Is Smith suggesting that abortion should not be available for them too? What words or phrases suggest that Smith does not think the situations she describes in this paragraph are true?

Question 4 in Drawing Your Own Conclusions focuses on ambiguity, the concept that something is capable of being understood in more ways than one. As students take more courses in college, they will encounter ambiguous situations and have to make difficult decisions. This essay illustrates the concept of ambiguity very well. Smith refers to the ambiguities relating to the concept of "the sanctity of human life." When should life be venerated and when not? Smith presents the following examples of legal and socially acceptable ways to take a human life—the death penalty, war, killing in self-defense. Can your students think of any other examples? Is the "merciful death" or suicide of painfully ill, terminal patients legally and socially acceptable?

Students can read the Robertson selection on "Courtship, Marriage, and Divorce" on page 252 and the Gordon selection on "Intimacy" on page 278. What ambiguities are presented in these selections?

Jonathan Kozol, THE HOMELESS AND THEIR CHILDREN, p. 530

The Kozol selection is included in this unit because it is about homelessness, one of the most critical problems that face our society today. In a political situation in which monetary cutbacks must be made to balance the budget and to lessen the national debt, many people feel that social programs that assist the homeless, the poor, and the unemployed need to be better regulated and, perhaps, eliminated. Discuss what your students think about these issues. Should there be a limit to the number of years a person can be on welfare? the amount of time a person can reside in a homeless shelter or hotel? the amount of money paid to parents when a new child is born? Why or why not? How should laws relating to these issues be enforced?

Kozol's writing is easy to read from the standpoint of vocabulary and syntactical structure, but from the standpoint of content, the detailed descriptions of the homeless family living in the welfare hotel make the selection vivid and brutal. Your students will want to discuss the story of Laura and her children. What can society do for Laura's children? for Laura?

Students often feel more comfortable writing in the descriptive or narrative mode. It is important for them to practice techniques in which they use narrative or descriptive writing to create the supporting details for other rhetorical modes. Students can use this selection to practice using a description or narrative as the basis for writing a persuasive essay. Students can work as a group to write general statements that are supported by the details of Laura and her children's lives.

The revision strategy asks students to interview a student who has never seen their writing before. For some students, this will be difficult. If you have written an essay for this chapter, you can model this interview by asking a student in the class to interview you. It is useful for young writers to find out more about how their instructors write, about the decision making process that you go through as you put your ideas on paper. After you have modeled the interview, the students can work together. They should share their revisions with their new partners, and some of them will also want to share their writing with the students they have been working with throughout the semester.

Martin Lee and Norman Solomon, WOMEN'S RIGHTS AND MEDIA'S WRONGS, p. 541

This article discusses the power of the media to influence the public. As the authors write in paragraph 1, mass media mirror society, "but mass media also continue to shape our society—reinforcing certain attitudes and actions while discouraging others." Students can reflect on the bias or prejudice revealed through mass media by observing the way that the various media present an event. With your class, choose one newsworthy event that is of current interest. Look at the way the event is presented on different television programs—on commercial and public channels. Read the way the event is presented in different newspapers, news magazines, in editorials, and in journalistic coverage. What aspects of the event are presented first? What words and phrases are used to describe the event? What biases or prejudices are revealed?

Students should also look at the sentence structure in paragraph 1. The sentence, "If television, for instance, were not capable of fundamentally affecting people's behavior, . . ." means that television is capable of affecting human behavior. "If what appears in print had little impact on day-to-day lives, . . ." means that television has a great impact on lives. Discuss the way to construct sentences such as these with your class.

In paragraph 3, when Lee and Solomon write that media should illuminate commonalities and differences aiming to increase genuine understanding, what is their underlying assumption? How does this assumption correspond to the ideas in the Steele article on page 517?

Ask your students in what ways the information about USA Today contained in paragraphs 7 and 9 is contradictory. What does this contradiction mean to them as readers?

In question 4 in A Closer Reading, students read paragraph 17 in which the authors state that six men and no women appeared on a television program discussing a rape case. Why is this ironic? What other instances of irony do your students find in this article?

Edward Krupat, ON AUTHORITY AND OBEDIENCE: AN INTERVIEW WITH HERBERT KELMAN, p. 550

Before students write in their journals, the class can discuss what authority means and who the authority figures are in their lives, i.e., parents, teachers, religious leaders, police, etc. If your students have difficulty writing the second journal entry before they have discussed the selection in class, they can write their post-reading journal response at home after the class has talked about the reading.

In Drawing Your Own Conclusions, question 4 asks students to think about the circumstances under which it might be appropriate to commit a crime rather than be subject to unreasonable authority. Instructors can direct the students to think about whether committing the crime described is appropriate in any of the following circumstances:

A friend is a conscientious objector who refuses to list his name with the draft board when he turns eighteen years old even though he knows this is a crime.

A fellow college student tells you that she is an illegal alien who falsified her application information even though she knows she committed a crime. She can be arrested and deported to her country if you reveal her secret to anyone in authority.

A friend asks you for advice about whether he should try to save several hundred dollars by falsifying information on his income tax forms. If he is caught, he can be arrested.

A student can get a scholarship if she does not list her family's correct income. If she gets caught, she can be accused of a crime and made to pay the money back. Is there any circumstance under which you would suggest that she not tell the truth?

Then ask your students to each write one such dilemma for which they feel there is not an easy answer. The class can discuss and/or write about some of these.

Jane Goodall, A PLEA FOR THE CHIMPS, p. 556

Some students have difficulty deciding on their position about whether chimpanzees should be used in research. Writing about their ideas before reading the Goodall article and then comparing that entry with their response after reading the article helps them find out first hand how persuasive writing can influence a reader.

Students make decisions about animals every day of their lives. You can discuss with the class how they decide whether to eat meat, to drink milk from animals that have been treated with growth hormones, to buy products from companies that use animals to test products, to wear fur coats, etc. If your class shows interest, you can have a class debate, and then students may want to write on some of these topics.

Thinking about some of the issues raised in the Krupat article on page 550 about whether it is ever appropriate to commit a crime rather than be subject to unreasonable authority, your class can discuss whether they would consider freeing research animals even though it involves committing a crime.

From a structural point of view, instructors can focus on the persuasive elements of this essay. Students should examine the number and type of supporting details used by Goodall. Students should think about the following questions: Which supporting details did the students find most effective? Did they feel her descriptions or analogies were too extreme? If so, when? What did this essay teach them about persuasive writing?

<u>Georganne Snyder, PURSUIT OF A GOAL, p. 568</u>

Snyder's essay may appeal to some of your students who have had to make difficult decisions in their lives in order to achieve meaningful goals. Snyder has decided to return to college to get her degree and to give up having a family. She made this decision because she feels limited in her life and in her present job. She wants a future with a career and believes that studying to be a teacher can give her that future. She will be able to work with children and be a powerful influence in their lives. Snyder is a step-parent and realizes that she is giving up much by not having her own children, but she has thought her decision through carefully. This essay is a good one because students usually have strong responses to it, agreeing or disagreeing with Snyder's decision. Students write well-thought-out essays in response to a question about whether they agree with her decision or not.

St. Martin's